ALL TIME TOP 1000 ALBUMS

Colin Larkin

Virgin

First published in Great Britain in 1998 by
VIRGIN BOOKS
an imprint of Virgin Publishing Ltd
Thames Wharf Studios, Rainville Road
Hammersmith, London W6 9HT

A catalogue record for this book is available from
the British Library

ISBN 0 7535 0258 5

Conceived, written, edited and produced by Colin Larkin
for MUZE UK Ltd
to whom all editorial enquiries should be sent
Iron Bridge House,
3 Bridge Approach,
Chalk Farm,
London NW1 8BD

Editor In Chief: Colin Larkin
Production Editor: Susan Pipe
Editorial and Research Assistant: Nic Oliver
Copy Editor: Sarah Lavelle
Design and Typesetting: Roger Kohn
Design Assistant: Aku Young
Special thanks to: Trev Huxley, Tony Laudico,
Paul Zullo, Marc Miller, Gary Geller, Ric Hollander, Stephen
Parker and all the Klugettes at Muze Inc.,
and to Rob Shreeve of Virgin Publishing.
Thanks to: Crappolino Jacket Studio
Printed and bound in Great Britain by
Butler & Tanner Ltd, Frome and London

CONTENTS

Dedicated to my Tin Lids
who like a lot of the music in this book

INTRODUCTION

The long-promised second edition of *All Time Top 1000 Albums* is in your hand. The first edition provoked the sort of response I expected - things like 'oh come off it', 'don't be stupid, how could that get in', 'rubbish, that must be a fiddle'. One reviewer writing in the late *Vox* magazine said very possibly the most offensive thing anyone could say about me. This little salted peanut strongly implied that 'I don't like music', probably because the original *All Time Top 1000* was not his choice. The other bizarre assumption is that nothing in the list could have appealed to him. I would love to know what branch of popular music did appeal. This particular Percy, like a number of others, forgot to study the original foreword. Once again, let me state:

This ultimate list of the *ALL TIME TOP 1000 ALBUMS* has been assembled by me and for the most part written by me. However, this is *not* my list of favoured albums. Many of my favourites are included, and there are some I would love to see a lot higher. By the same token there is a bit of inexplicable dross that continues to get in, and as much as I would like to dispense with it or them, I cannot alter the democratic process of the public's vote.

This book has been compiled in the most sophisticated way over a period of five years. All the polls that have appeared in the past three years since the last edition have been monitored and used in compiling this list. Additionally, we sent out our own polling forms to musicians, journalists, writers, fans and, most of all, the general public. Our youngest voter was nine years old and our oldest was 62. We had a very strong input from the USA, and that vote is reflected in many albums that would not have normally appeared, finding their way in. Some number 1 albums in the USA failed to chart in the UK, and vice versa.

I estimate that close to 200,000 votes have been factored into this chart. And yes, I know, there are millions of other people who could have voted and changed the shape of the book. This is still the only book that has attempted to set it down in print, even though I know (and hope) that when we come to do the third edition in a couple of years or so, things will have dramatically changed.

In the past three years, for example, Bruce Springsteen has continued to slide out of people's minds. Elton John albums seem to have polarized and poor old Cliff Richard has disappeared. Celine Dion clearly does not appeal to our voters and Status Quo failed to register even one vote. The president of the Quo fan club is immediately going to protest that we did not consult him/her, but then neither did we consult the Bob Dylan fan club, and look how well he did.

The two most significant things in watching this poll change and grow over the past years is that it does reflect the tastes of today. What is particularly rewarding is that my belief that popular music should have no barriers is in some way proven. Next to Frank Zappa we can have Ella Fitzgerald, next to Nine Inch Nails next to Eric Dolphy next to the Kingston Trio next to Moby Grape.

I have no doubt (by the way, where were No Doubt?) that many of the high-charting new entries will have dropped considerably next time around. The popularity of the most recent albums by the Verve, Manic Street Preachers and Pulp has kicked into play their back catalogue. I know that they would not have enjoyed a look-in previously. Similarly, albums by Placebo, Cast, Ocean Colour Scene and Kula Shaker are very much albums of the moment (or at least when polling was taking place) and may well drop. Paul Weller has *Stanley Road* and *Heavy Soul*, but not a carrot for *Wild Wood*. This inconsistency is what makes this project so rewarding, when the Top 100 has some screwballs next to the dinosaurs next to the current flavours.

Big questions I can ask: where will Alanis Morissette be (look how badly Sheryl Crow did this time)? Is it cast in stone that Pink Floyd, Dylan and Bowie are the favourites for absolutely all time? Oasis, Blur, Pulp, Nirvana, R.E.M.: do we call them dad rockers next time? And where, may I ask, will be the renegade albums that have fed off critical acclaim? The truly brilliant *Forever Changes*, which I can remember buying in 1967, is still around. I speak to many much younger fans who share my views. Why has *Trout Mask Replica* continued to grow in popularity? Neither of these albums were commercial successes in their day so why do they stand out from the pack 30 years later?

Other miracles such as Nick Drake, Tim Buckley and, to a lesser degree, John Martyn and Richard Thompson, all appear in great strength. Similarly, Rap and Reggae are more than standing their ground, as the older these genres become, so their classic albums become separated from the pack - so much so that this must elicit curiosity from your regular rock fan. This is very healthy for music, and just might open up people's narrow ears to something to which they would not normally have listened.

Among the many letters I received as a result of the last edition was a fairly angry letter criticizing my choice (again, the author did not read the foreword).

I had great pleasure in writing back and putting him in place about one or two things. Above all, use your own ears. Don't assume that something is great because the cognoscenti say so. More importantly, don't dismiss something because an influential reviewer didn't like it. One example would be David Crosby's first solo album, *If I Could Only Remember My Name*. Yes, I know it's easy to dismiss CSN and some of their ipsy dipsy stuff, but give this album a listen. I can reveal that it is my favourite album of all time, and has been so for many years. Three of my highly respected music writer colleagues also agree. Give it a listen and make up your own mind, but above all, don't dismiss it because it's cool to do so.

I thought I had a similar problem with many of the albums in this book, but listening to them, sometimes for the first time, was quite a challenge. Sitting with my four typing fingers poised in front of my Apple Mac gave me a huge responsibility, and yet I discovered at least 50 albums in this book for the first time.

So, no appearances for Sir Cliff Richard, Status Quo or the Hollies. Cliff has had over 130 hits in the UK singles chart, yet has never made a truly great album, other than a Greatest Hits compilation. Artists such as the Move would not have made an appearance were it not for the strong cult following they command in the USA. The significant contribution from the USA this time has altered the chart considerably. Artists such as Janet Jackson, They Might Be Giants, Maze and some of the Rap artists would not have had a whiff if it had been left to the UK voters. Similarly, Oasis, the Verve, Blur and Manic Street Preachers had a massive input from the UK, but little from the USA.

It has been fascinating to watch the pattern that formed as the votes came in over the past three years. *Pet Sounds* took the lead for a few months and then *Revolver* gained momentum over the past year and held the lead continuously. Like it or not, the stranglehold the Fab Four have on the chart is no fluke. Time and time again a Beatles album was number one on the voting form. Maybe they are such a part of popular culture that the voter feels obliged to vote for at least one Beatles album. Why then did Elvis Presley slide down the listings in such spectacular fashion?

The new artists have really made a serious impression in people's minds, and I suspect that certain new albums will have already peaked. As yet they still do not have time on their side. *OK Computer* and *Be Here Now*, enjoy very high positions. Will they still be as high in three years' time? The Verve and Placebo are in strong positions; will they have been forgotten? And where will the dinosaurs be; will the public start listening to *Saint Dominics Preview* instead of *Astral Weeks*, will a few *Pet Sounds* lovers defect to *Sunflower*? And where will my beloved Moby Grape be?

As I said before, this really is the *All Time Top 1000 Albums*, until next time.

Colin Larkin, July 1998

ACKNOWLEDGEMENTS

One thousand albums might not seem that many, but just you try and sort them into batches and lay them on the floor. Then you discover how many still have to be listened to and reviewed.

Thanks in the first instance to the record company press offices who responded to my requests. The ones who ignored us really are a great disappointment. Unusually, a major record company comes out on top (usually it's the indies). Thanks to Barbara Charone, Denise Burrup and Andrea Gibbs at WEA; Lee Ellen Newman at East West; Mark Istead at Mute; Pat Naylor at Rykodisk; Murray Chalmers and his team at Parlophone; Narrinder and Anita at RCA; Richard Dawes at A&M; Garry Cotter at Grapevine; Darren Anderson at Columbia. As always, Tones Sansom and Vanessa Cotton at Creation, Julia Honeywell at Ace, Dorothy Howe at Castle and the truly capable Alan Robinson, who used to be at Demon but will soon return, when other record companies know he is back on the market.

Other record companies who responded to our pleas were Shane O'Neill at Universal; Sarah at Arista; Mercury Records; Island Records; Mike Gott and Andy Gray at BGO; See For Miles Records and Charleen at Polydor.

Those who pitched in from the outside with help on entries are thanked profusely; Oor Alex Ogg, the extraordinarily underrated Roy Sheridan, Johnny Rogan, Dawn Petite Powerhouse Eden, Mike Nevins and David Gritten. From the inside, my colleagues Sarah Lavelle and Nic Oliver took a pile of their favourites and lavished them with praise. Some bits from the old edition may remain, and they were supplied by Brian Hogg, John Martland, Neil Slaven, Harry Hawke, Spencer Leigh, Phil Wilding, Simon Jones, Bruce Crowther and Linton Chiswick.

Additional covers were loaned to me from Sarah Lavelle, Nic Oliver, Alex Ogg, Mark Simpson, Roy Sheridan, Marc Miller, Mike Nevins, Slipped Disc and Dan Larkin.

At the very last minute Jim Allen, Mike Nevins, Ric Hollander, Stephen Parker and Marc Miller helped locate the final piece of text and covers.

I did plan to list the voters, but that soon got completely out of hand. Please forgive me for not carrying out my promise but we needed an extra 24 pages to do it. Those that I can thank, however, are neatly sandwiched between the very first voting form received for this edition, and the very last. The first was from Chris Charlesworth of Omnibus Press and the last was from Rob Shreeve of Virgin Publishing: now that's a bit spooky, don't you think? Thank you everybody else; this book is not possible without you all, including: John Aizlewood, Jim Allen, Itamar Alves, Craig Baguley, Barry Ballard, Ken Barnes, Julie Bauer, Dave Bedford, Tony Beesley, David Belcher, David Bellm, Esmerdis Berelian, Brian Bertie, Jim Bishop, Johnny Black, Stewart Brinnen, Stuart Brooks, Chris Bugbee, J. Burgoyne, Kevin Burns, George Caldwell, Chris Charlesworth, Jon Clelford, Tam Cohen, Peter Cowley, Stewart Cruickshank, Dave De Rubio, Fred Dellar, Peter Doggett, Ian Dowson, Paul Du Noyer, Mark Ellen, Casey Fahy, Nancy Figler, Tim Footman, Joe Francis, Deborah Freedman, Frank Garcia, Owen Gerboth, Pat Gilbert, David Good, Jo Grant, George L. Guttler, Jim Harrison, Terry Heard, Michael Hingston, Brian Hogg, Eric Holland, Barney Hoskyns, M. Howard, Joseph Hughes, Patrick Humphries, Andy Hunt, Jim Irvin, Phil Jackson, Jonathan Jago, Todd Jennings, Cindy Jimenez, Brian Johnson, Peter Kelly, Kimberly Kerstler, Andrew King, Roger Kohn, Dan Larkin, Tom Larkin, David Lashmar, Sarah Lavelle, Scott Lehr, Robin Lilley, Tony Littman, Chris Loader, Lisa Lobb, David Love, Darryn McAtee, Jim McDonald, Ian McGrath, Vivian Manning, James Marsh, Robert Mason, Peyton Mays, Max Merry, Marc Miller, Jon Monnick, Stephen Morgan, M. Alexander Morse, John Mulvey, Lorne Murdoch, Dennis Musgrave, Paul Nauman, Michael Nevins, Paul Norman, Robert Nussbaum, Salsri Nyah, Alex Ogg, Nic Oliver, Kimberly Osorio, Rick Parks, Tom Parsons, Mark Paytress, Steve Phillips, John Poole, Jeff Portnoy, Cathy Ramey-Johnson, Steve Redmond, Paul Rees, Jonathan Rice, N.J. Richards, James Robert, Alan Robinson, David Roberts, Johnny Rogan, Liam Sawyer, David Schnider, Jon Scott, Jamie Sellers, Shaque, Roy Sheridan, Adam Silver, James Sleigh, Irving Smith, Steve Smith, Colin Souter, David Steed, David Stockley, Paul Summers, Sam Sutherland, Adam Sweeting, Peter Togneri, Gary Trevartha, Martin Turley, Alex Varon, Robbie Vincent, Terry Vinyard, Ruth Wagner, Tom Warrington, K. Watkins, Chris Welch, Darren Willis, Cheryl Zoeller, Bill Zurat.

Thank you for the continued help of my Carlin Music colleagues, especially Terry Heard, Lisa Lobb and Nikki Tighe, always a smile, hardly a moan. No thanks whatsoever to the dreadful tea boy Paul Kinane. At Virgin Publishing, from their palatial new offices, thanks to everybody involved, especially the suave and demure Roz Scott and her problematical, but ultimately loveable, boss, Rob Shreeve. Thanks to the Quite Great Emma Morris, Emily Williams and the magnificent Pete Bassett. To Paul Toal of Audio T, the helpful supplier of my new hi-fi system, which enabled me to listen to everything. To Norman Michael, who, in addition to being arguably the world's greatest handyman, supplied me with chocolate doughnuts every day that he worked here, and experienced listening to lots of different kinds of music. To Jane Burton, who lays a splendid floor, and Mike Whitaker who does a nice line in kitchens. Last minute thanks to Slipped Disc in Chelmsford, Essex. Their manager Carl Newsum loaned us most of the missing record sleeves for us to scan; support your local record shop, especially this one. To Graham, the village postman, who brings my CDs safely to the door. To Mike Kaye, our superb software developer. To Chris Braham, who after a quarter of a century knows that nostalgia is not just about looking back. To Roger Kohn, the designer of this book, who never once lost his rag, and to the parrot of my dreams, the lovely Aku. To my brilliant MUZE UK staff, Susan Pipe, Nic Oliver and Sarah Lavelle, who I believe could have won the World Cup.

To Johnny Rogan, who showed enthusiasm throughout this project; it was great talking to someone who shares a similar fascination for chart positions. To Mark Cohen, always to be credited. To Diana who knows there is more to monogamy than just having one partner. Over at MUZE Inc. in New York, the reorganization is nearing completion and perfume is in the air. They have not only been a great support but they have taken a keen interest in the progress of this book. Both Marc 'Boris' Millar and the cooly coiffeured Paul Zullo have given me great impetus. Other invaluable help, suggestions and abuse came from Tony Laudico, Trev's wife Cathy, Mike Nevins, Silvia Kessel, Steve 'Numbers' Figard, Chris Bugbee, Cathy Ramey-Johnson, Amanda Denhoff, Ric Hollander, Stephen Parker and my cherubic room-mate Gary Geller. To Trev Huxley, the gentle giant at the end of the road; always there, always cool, always able to laugh. Finally to John, Paul, George and Ringo; putting this book together reaffirms how important they have been in my life.

Colin Larkin, July 1998

1 **REVOLVER** (5) ▲
THE BEATLES

M usic critics have always preferred *Revolver* to its famous successor, while fans were at first a little wary of the brilliantly bizarre 'Tomorrow Never Knows', the eastern promise of 'Love You To' or the goodtime brass of 'Got To Get You Into My Life'. Years of repeated listening unfolds quiet gems such as Harrison's exceptional 'I Want To Tell You' and Lennon's wondrously hazy 'I'm Only Sleeping', or as he sings 'I'm only seeping'. McCartney was also on a creative roll with the unabashed and brave romanticism of 'Here There And Everywhere' and the classical sadness of 'Eleanor Rigby'. Subtly original and beautifully recorded. A shamelessly perfect record.

● TRACKS: *Taxman; Eleanor Rigby; I'm Only Sleeping; Love You To; Here, There And Everywhere; Yellow Submarine; She Said She Said; Good Day Sunshine; And Your Bird Can Sing; For No One; Dr. Robert; I Want To Tell You; Got To Get You Into My Life; Tomorrow Never Knows.*

● FIRST RELEASED 1966
● UK PEAK CHART POSITION: 1
● USA PEAK CHART POSITION: 1

2 SGT. PEPPER'S LONELY HEARTS CLUB BAND (1) ▼ THE BEATLES

The Beatles reached for the sky, and they got it. This one album revolutionized, altered and reinvented the boundaries of 20th century popular music, style and graphic art. Thirty years on, this four-track recording is still a masterpiece. Equal credit is now justifiably placed with the elegant George Martin. He was the chemist who made their crazy ideas work. He shaped their glorious songs and fantasmagorical lyrics with melody and harmony, pushing recording technique into unknown waters. Much of late 60s pop was fashioned out of this one record; a mass of third rate orange-coated-treacle-airship-jasmine-mushroomheaded-dreamweavers followed. Nothing came near it, and together with *Revolver*, nothing ever will.

● TRACKS: *Sgt. Pepper's Lonely Hearts Club Band; With A Little Help From My Friends; Lucy In The Sky With Diamonds; Getting Better; Fixing A Hole; She's Leaving Home; Being For The Benefit Of Mr. Kite; Within You Without You; When I'm Sixty-Four; Lovely Rita; Good Morning Good Morning; Sgt. Pepper's Lonely Hearts Club Band (Reprise); A Day In The Life.*

● FIRST RELEASED 1967
● UK PEAK CHART POSITION: 1
● USA PEAK CHART POSITION: 1

③ THE BEATLES (WHITE ALBUM)
(15) ▲ THE BEATLES

The BEATLES

W hile it was mooted that this could have been edited to make a great single album instead of a double, we did at least get the efforts of four different, yet troubled, individuals. The Beatles demonstrated that they could be way above our heads with items such as 'Revolution No. 9', and downright kitsch with 'Martha My Dear' and 'Good Night'. Lennon excelled with 'Happiness Is A Warm Gun' and McCartney tore his throat with 'Birthday'. Above all, and for the first time on record, they showed that they could really play, as displayed by 'Helter Skelter' and 'Back In The USSR', even though they enlisted Eric Clapton for support on 'While My Guitar Gently Weeps'.

● TRACKS: *Back In The USSR; Dear Prudence; Glass Onion; Ob La Di, Ob La Da; Wild Honey Pie; The Continuing Story Of Bungalow Bill; While My Guitar Gently Weeps; Happiness Is A Warm Gun; Martha My Dear; I'm So Tired; Blackbird; Piggies; Rocky Raccoon; Don't Pass Me By; Why Don't We Do It In The Road?; I Will; Julia; Birthday; Yer Blues; Mother Nature's Son; Everybody's Got Something To Hide Except Me And My Monkey; Sexy Sadie; Helter Skelter; Long, Long, Long; Revolution 1; Honey Pie; Savoy Truffle; Cry Baby Cry; Revolution 9; Good Night.*

● FIRST RELEASED 1968
● UK PEAK CHART POSITION: 1
● USA PEAK CHART POSITION: 1

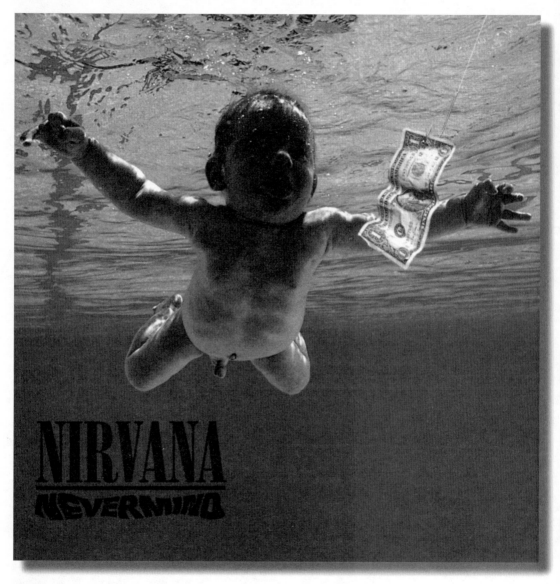

Historically, America's north-west coast has produced edgy, rebellious music, of which grunge was one manifestation. An offspring of punk, speed metal and the 'slacker' lifestyle, it found an apotheosis in Nirvana, who combined such elements with a faultless grasp of hooklines. On *Nevermind*, group leader Kurt Cobain unleashed frustrated alienation, his ravaged rasp and bone-crunching guitar soaring through a tight, intensive sound, courtesy of former hardcore producer Butch Vig. Cobain's solipsism proved tragically prophetic and his suicide elevated him to cultural icon status. This should not obscure the singer's empathy for the mechanics of classic rock, reworked and infused with new life on this emphatic statement.

● TRACKS: *Smells Like Teen Spirit; In Bloom; Come As You Are; Breed; Lithium; Polly; Territorial Pissings; Drain You; Lounge Act; Stay Away; On A Plain; Something In The Way; Endless Nameless.*

● FIRST RELEASED 1991
● UK PEAK CHART POSITION: 33
● USA PEAK CHART POSITION: 1

5 ABBEY ROAD (58) ▲
THE BEATLES

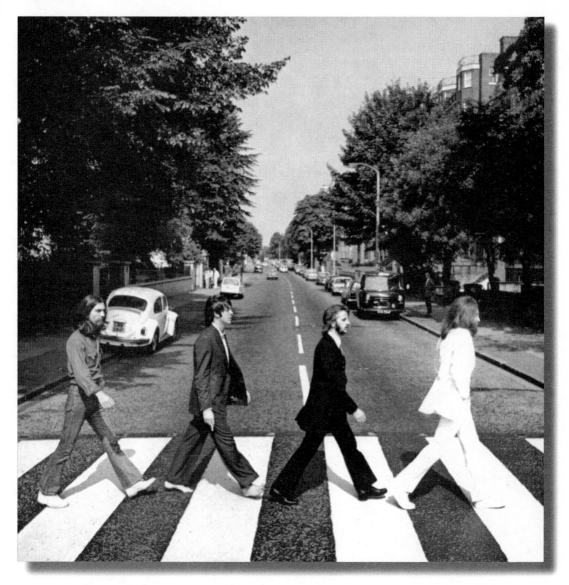

The product of the Beatles' last recording session, *Abbey Road* transcends the internecine strife gripping its participants. Individuality triumphs on side one, as each group member pursues specific callings, be it classic rock 'n' roll, Lear-like nonsense verse, riff-laden *cris de coeur* or simple, sumptuous pop. Wait for the sudden silence after 'I Want You'. Side two is a collective offering, where partworks and fragments are fused together to perfection to construct a breathtaking suite. Characters are cast and melodies envelop until the final experience is of a seamless whole, a proclamation of the ultimate joy of pop itself. And in the end, the love you make . . .

● TRACKS: *Come Together; Something; Maxwell's Silver Hammer; Oh! Darling; Octopus's Garden; I Want You (She's So Heavy); Here Comes The Sun; Because; You Never Give Me Your Money; Sun King; Mean Mr. Mustard; Polythene Pam; She Came In Through The Bathroom Window; Golden Slumbers; Carry That Weight; The End; Her Majesty.*

● FIRST RELEASED 1969
● UK PEAK CHART POSITION: 1
● USA PEAK CHART POSITION: 1

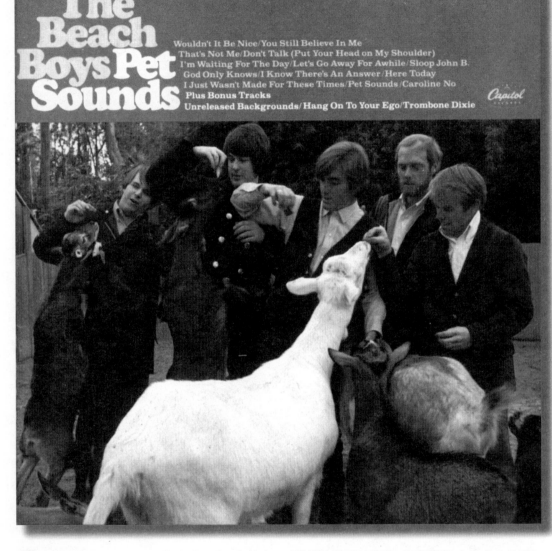

The Beach Boys, and more specifically, their acknowledged leader Brian Wilson, worked too hard to try to make this the greatest pop record of all time. At the time of recording Brian was experiencing a creative growth from which he never recovered. The intense beauty of this record grows with age and Brian Wilson should not feel any failure or underachievement in the face of the four mop-tops from Liverpool. They had George Martin; Brian had only himself, some rival siblings and a cousin to deal with. The orchestral arrangements remain magnificently lush but never sickly, yet how could this masterpiece have been given such a pedestrian cover?

● TRACKS: *Wouldn't It Be Nice; You Still Believe In Me; That's Not Me; Don't Talk (Put Your Head On My Shoulder); I'm Waiting For The Day; Let's Go Away For Awhile; Sloop John B; God Only Knows; I Know There's An Answer; Here Today; I Just Wasn't Made For These Times; Pet Sounds; Caroline, No.*

● FIRST RELEASED 1966
● UK PEAK CHART POSITION: 2
● USA PEAK CHART POSITION: 10

7 **AUTOMATIC FOR THE PEOPLE**
(27) ▲ **R.E.M.**

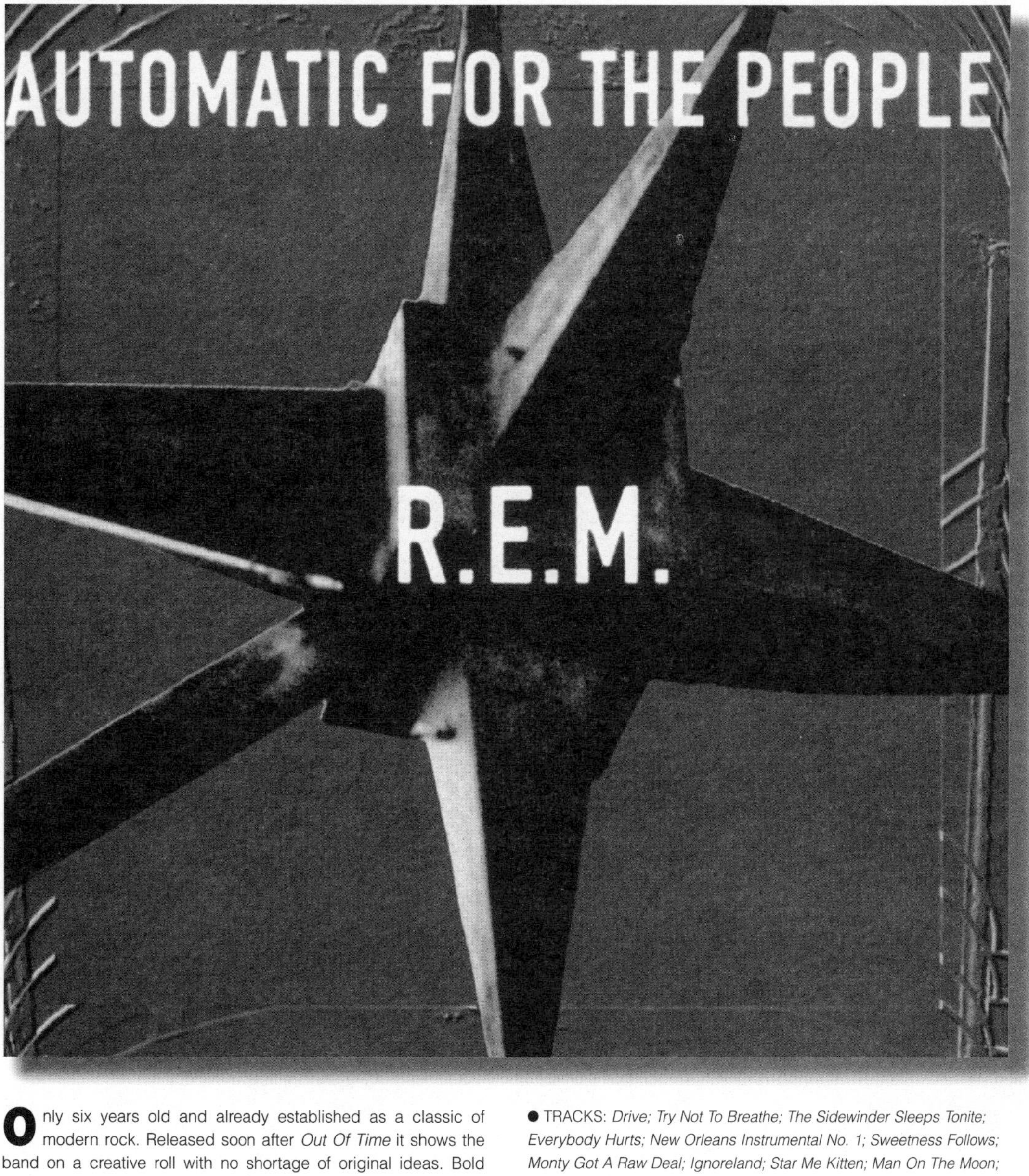

Only six years old and already established as a classic of modern rock. Released soon after *Out Of Time* it shows the band on a creative roll with no shortage of original ideas. Bold songs such as 'Drive' and 'Everybody Hurts' demonstrated that the band were not reluctant to experiment, while the Karl Denver opening on 'The Sidewinder Sleeps Tonite' and Stipe's magnificent hair-lip Elvis on 'Man On The Moon' were as good as anything they have recorded. Even with the departure of Bill Berry R.E.M. are still very much alive, but it would be asking a lot to expect any future album to match this.

● TRACKS: *Drive; Try Not To Breathe; The Sidewinder Sleeps Tonite; Everybody Hurts; New Orleans Instrumental No. 1; Sweetness Follows; Monty Got A Raw Deal; Ignoreland; Star Me Kitten; Man On The Moon; Nightswimming; Find The River.*

● FIRST RELEASED 1992
● UK PEAK CHART POSITION: 1
● USA PEAK CHART POSITION: 2

8 THE DARK SIDE OF THE MOON
(5) ▼ PINK FLOYD

An album that is destined always to be sold to and recommended by lovers of 'grown up rock' music. Now over 25 years old, it still sets standards of recording excellence for today's digitally minded customers. Dave Gilmore's piercing guitar solo on 'Money' will still make you shiver, Clare Torry's wailing vocal on 'The Great Gig In The Sky' is remarkable and Roger Waters' lyrics remain relevant in the 90s. Once the album coveted by cosy 70s couples as an essential purchase for their new home. It is now recognized by succeeding generations as a monster of a record, and one that is ok to own up to liking.

● TRACKS: *Speak To Me; Breathe; On The Run; Time; The Great Gig In The Sky; Money; Us And Them; Any Colour You Like; Brain Damage; Eclipse.*

● FIRST RELEASED 1973
● UK PEAK CHART POSITION: 2
● USA PEAK CHART POSITION: 1

9 (WHAT'S THE STORY) MORNING GLORY ? (-) ▲ OASIS

The second album from the most written-about pop band since the Beatles was an assured collection. There were enough brilliant hooks and choruses to make it instantly sound like a great record. 'Roll With It' is a prime example, being an automatically familiar and accessible pop song. Liam was happy to have the mighty 'Wonderwall', complete with *Sgt. Pepper*-style cellos and singalong chorus, but Noel gave him a run for his money with the epic 'Don't Look Back In Anger', borrowing on this occasion from Pachelbel's 'Canon & Gigue'. Despite accusations that they were taking their 'influences' a step too far, this was undeniably a gigantic album.

● TRACKS: *Hello; Roll With It; Wonderwall; Don't Look Back In Anger; Hey Now!; Some Might Say; Cast No Shadow; She's Electric; Morning Glory; Champagne Supernova.*

● FIRST RELEASED 1995
● UK PEAK CHART POSITION: 1
● USA PEAK CHART POSITION: 4

10 THE BENDS (-) ▲
RADIOHEAD

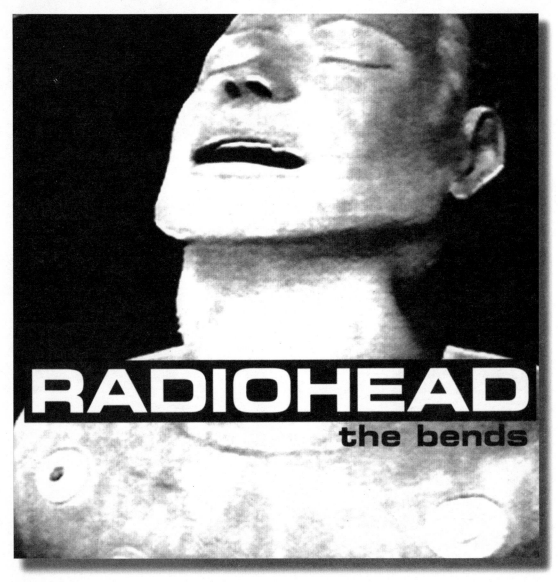

On only their second outing Oxford's Radiohead fulfilled their huge potential, fashioning an album whose relentlessly downbeat tone was offset by an ability to formulate consistently winning melodies. The title track and 'Just' throw some customary rock poses, but for the most part the band displayed a far more expansive approach. Thom Yorke emerged from the woodwork with a new-found vocal confidence, revealing a striking falsetto on two of the album's strongest tracks, 'Fake Plastic Trees' and 'High & Dry'. The last three songs build inexorably to the stunning emotional climax of 'Street Spirit (Fade Out)' with a control and poise that showcased the band's new maturity.

● TRACKS: *Planet Telex; The Bends; Fake Plastic Trees; High & Dry; Bones; (Nice Dream); My Iron Lung; Just (You Do It To Yourself); Bullet Proof .. I Wish I Was; Black Star; Sulk; Street Spirit (Fade Out)*.

● FIRST RELEASED 1995
● UK PEAK CHART POSITION: 6
● USA PEAK CHART POSITION: 88

11 THE RISE AND FALL OF ZIGGY STARDUST AND THE SPIDERS FROM MARS (19) ▲

DAVID BOWIE

David Bowie's penchant for reinvention has allowed the singer to follow a fascinating career. The blend of rock star persona and alien creature defining *Ziggy Stardust* was probably his finest creation. Buoyed by the support of guitarist Mick Ronson, Bowie produced some of his finest songs, from the raucous 'Suffragette City' to the prophetic 'Rock'n'Roll Suicide' - the singer would famously declare Ziggy dead during a live concert. Androgyny and science fiction combined with the artist's love of theatre to bring a visual nature to an album that remains central to Bowie's wide-ranging catalogue.

● TRACKS: *Five Years; Soul Love; Moonage Daydream; Starman; It Ain't Easy; Lady Stardust; Star; Hang On To Yourself; Ziggy Stardust; Suffragette City; Rock'N' Roll Suicide.*

● FIRST RELEASED 1972
● UK PEAK CHART POSITION: 5
● USA PEAK CHART POSITION: 75

12 ELECTRIC LADYLAND (72) ▲
THE JIMI HENDRIX EXPERIENCE

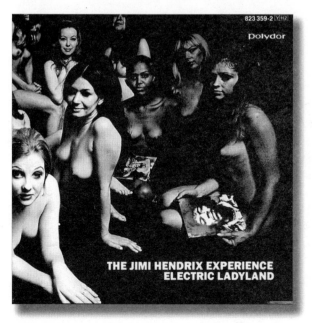

The last official Experience band contained contributions from both Traffic and Jefferson Airplane members, and presented an unrivalled collection of songs, including a brilliant rendition of Dylan's 'All Along The Watchtower', an interpretation that Dylan was later to adopt live. 'Crosstown Traffic', 'Gypsy Eyes', and 'Burning Of The Midnight Lamp', as well as the posthumous number 1, 'Voodoo Child (Slight Return)' This and the brilliant improvisation (with Winwood, Jack Casady etc) showed an incredible clarity in Hendrix's musical thinking. His vision had already moved beyond the musical confines of the trio. A rich and still somehow contemporary record.

● TRACKS: *...And The Gods Made Love; Have You Ever Been (To Electric Ladyland); Crosstown Traffic; Voodoo Chile; Little Miss Strange; Long Hot Summer Night; Come On (Let The Good Times Roll); Gypsy Eyes; Burning Of The Midnight Lamp; Rainy Day, Dream Away; 1983 (A Merman I Should Turn To Be); Moon, Turn The Tides ... Gently Gently Away; Still Raining, Still Dreaming; House Burning Down; All Along The Watchtower; Voodoo Chile (Slight Return).*

● FIRST RELEASED 1968
● UK PEAK CHART POSITION: 6
● USA PEAK CHART POSITION: 1

13 NEVER MIND THE BOLLOCKS HERE'S THE SEX PISTOLS (12) ▼ SEX PISTOLS

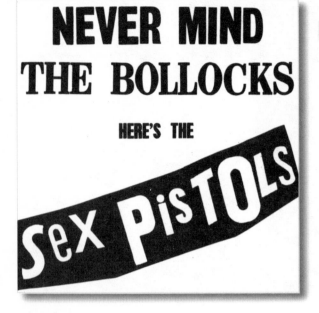

In the same way that *Sgt Pepper..* and *Revolver* are cast in stone at the top of the pop/rock genre, so this milestone stands above any other punk record of its kind. Seen by some snobs at the time as musical illiterates, the Pistols legend continues as strong as ever. The music was in such stark contrast to what we had previously been enjoying that a backlash was inevitable. This will stay as a classic because it will not date. The power of tracks such as 'Pretty Vacant' or 'No Feelings' is as strong as in 1977. This pivotal record has not mellowed with age, thankfully.

● TRACKS: *Holidays In The Sun; Bodies; Liar; No Feelings; God Save The Queen; Problems; Seventeen; Anarchy In The UK; Submission; Pretty Vacant; New York; EMI.*

● FIRST RELEASED 1977
● UK PEAK CHART POSITION: 1
● USA PEAK CHART POSITION: 106

14 THE STONE ROSES (47) ▲
STONE ROSES

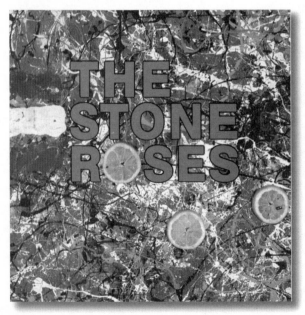

Manchester's most likely to, who escaped independent status after a lengthy court battle, signed to Geffen and then promptly disappeared for five years. They came back, and then went pop. Quite simply, their debut album is a superlative record. A Byrds-like listlessness caused listeners to swoon in wonder and slip quietly beneath the surface. 'Waterfall' and 'She Bangs The Drums' were sublime and quietly brilliant, 'I Wanna Be Adored' teased with its epic intro, and, of course, created incredible and impossible pressure for that all-important second album. A classic album, already seen as one of the finest records of the past 30 years.

● TRACKS: *I Wanna Be Adored; She Bangs The Drums; Waterfall; Don't Stop; Bye Bye Badman; Elizabeth My Dear; (Song For My) Sugar Spun Sister; Made Of Stone; Shoot You Down; This Is The One; I Am The Resurrection.*

● FIRST RELEASED 1989
● UK PEAK CHART POSITION: 19
● USA PEAK CHART POSITION: 86

15 ASTRAL WEEKS (7) ▼
VAN MORRISON

Quoted, recommended and worshipped by the critics for nearly 30 years, this underground masterpiece has now become part of the establishment. It cries to be listened to without interruption, which may explain why it failed to reach either the UK or US charts. It wanders and weaves, repeating themes and lyrics as if one song, yet we never tire of 'gardens wet with rain', 'champagne eyes' or the wonder of how Morrison can make a place like Ladbroke Grove seem so hauntingly evocative. The record is also a great educator in opening your eyes beyond pop, to soul and jazz, and although Morrison continues to return to its themes again and again, this is his core.

● TRACKS: *Astral Weeks; Beside You; Sweet Thing; Cyprus Avenue; Young Lovers Do; Madame George; Ballerina; Slim Slow Slider.*

● FIRST RELEASED 1968
● UK PEAK CHART POSITION: did not chart
● USA PEAK CHART POSITION: did not chart

16 HUNKY DORY (34) ▲
DAVID BOWIE

David Bowie's most eclectic album acknowledged 60s mentors and prepared the artist for subsequent musical directions. Andy Warhol, Bob Dylan and the Velvet Underground were illiberally canonized, and a veneer of menace bubbled beneath the surface of several sweet pop songs, especially 'Life On Mars'. Is it Lennon or Lenin that is on sale again? The subject matter embraced transexuality, Nietzsche and science fiction. Guitarist Mick Ronson proved a sympathetic foil amid a support cast that understood Bowie's chameleon-like qualities and reacted accordingly. The singer's eclectic interests have never been captured so confidently, even though he sings 'didn't know what I was looking for' in 'Changes'.

● TRACKS: *Changes; Oh! You Pretty Thing; Eight Line Poem; Life On Mars?; Kooks; Quicksand; Fill Your Heart (Biff); Andy Warhol; Song For Bob Dylan; Queen Bitch; The Bewlay Brothers.*

● FIRST RELEASED 1971
● UK PEAK CHART POSITION: 3
● USA PEAK CHART POSITION: 93

17 BLONDE ON BLONDE (4) ▼
BOB DYLAN

A year after *Highway 61 Revisited* Dylan repeated the act with further epitaphs of creative malarkey and intrigue. We were spoilt with a double album, longer than anything we had previously heard, yet still destined to endure. The punishing touring and high profile drove Dylan to be creative beyond belief as he scribbled these gems in his hotel rooms. Surrounding himself with the likes of Al Kooper, Robbie Robertson, Charlie McCoy and Kenny Buttrey, these seasoned musicians gave this album a relaxed confidence, quite unlike the youthful energy of *Highway 61 Revisited*. More than thirty years later this album still rewards and surprises. A gigantic record.

● TRACKS: *Rainy Day Woman Nos 12 & 35; Pledging My Time; Visions Of Johanna; One Of Us Must Know (Sooner Or Later); I Want You; Stuck Inside Of Mobile With The Memphis Blues Again; Leopard-Skin Pill-Box Hat; Just Like A Woman; Most Likely You Go Your Way (And I'll Go Mine); Temporary Like Achilles; Absolutely Sweet Marie; Fourth Time Around; Obviously Five Believers; Sad-Eyed Lady Of The Lowlands.*

● FIRST RELEASED 1966
● UK PEAK CHART POSITION: 3
● USA PEAK CHART POSITION: 9

18 THE JOSHUA TREE (48) ▲
U2

A fter their arresting appearance at *Live Aid*, U2 album sales went berserk across the globe, and the world waited impatiently for their next release. *The Joshua Tree* arrived, and fans were not disappointed. There are few weaknesses, musical or lyrical, in this album. The pure power of the music and patent honesty of the lyrics steer the band clear of whimsy and self-indulgence. The anguish and questioning is shot through with faith as they chant and stomp and batter their way through instant classics such as 'Still Haven't Found What I'm Looking For', 'Where The Streets Have No Name' and 'With Or Without You', leaving the listener bruised but elated.

● TRACKS: *Where The Streets Have No Name; I Still Haven't Found What I'm Looking For; With Or Without You; Bullet The Blue Sky; Running To Stand Still; Red Hill Mining Town; In God's Country; Trip Through Your Wires; One Tree Hill; Exit; Mothers Of The Disappeared.*

● FIRST RELEASED 1987
● UK PEAK CHART POSITION: 1
● USA PEAK CHART POSITION: 1

19 RUMOURS (17) ▼
FLEETWOOD MAC

The reviewers tell us what to buy, but the public actually part with the cash. Surely 26 million people cannot be wrong, as Peter Green's creation became the prime example of AOR in the 70s. The inner strife and turmoil of the band is credited as having helped to make this many-headed beast into such a success. Christine sparred with John and Stevie scrapped with Lindsay. Mick Fleetwood held the emotional mess together with confident steadiness as demonstrated in his drumming throughout the record. Nicks' fiery vocals on 'Go Your Own Way' complemented McVie's beautifully understated 'You Make Loving Fun'. The people have chosen, but don't ignore their catalogue.

● TRACKS: *Second Hand News; Dreams; Never Going Back Again; Don't Stop; Go Your Own Way; Songbird; The Chain; You Make Loving Fun; I Don't Want To Know; Oh Daddy; Gold Dust Woman.*

● FIRST RELEASED 1977
● UK PEAK CHART POSITION: 1
● USA PEAK CHART POSITION: 1

20 RUBBER SOUL (10) ▼
THE BEATLES

The album that put the Beatles into the hearts and minds of middle-class, quality Sunday newspaper readers. The working-class lads won over a new audience with a mature collection of songs that belied their age. As the art and literary worlds moved away from polo-necked bohemian jazz, the Beatles wooed them with simple melodies and clever lyrics. This album also demonstrated that the Beatles were not without their own demons as unparalleled success took its toll - witness Lennon's illicit affair in 'Norwegian Wood', Paul's profound 'I'm Looking Through You' and Harrison's continuing growth with the thoughtful 'Think For Yourself'. Lennon owned the jewel, however, with the prophetic 'In My Life'.

● TRACKS: *Drive My Car; Norwegian Wood (This Bird Has Flown); You Won't See Me; Nowhere Man; Think For Yourself; The Word; Michelle; What Goes On; Girl; I'm Looking Through You; In My Life; Wait; If I Needed Someone; Run For Your Life.*

● FIRST RELEASED 1965
● UK PEAK CHART POSITION: 1
● USA PEAK CHART POSITION: 1

21 OK COMPUTER (–) ▲
RADIOHEAD

Having seemingly peaked with 1995's *The Bends*, Radiohead emerged two years later with a spiky and 'difficult' collection of songs far removed from the epic rock of the previous album. Eschewing the easy option of grafting stadium choruses onto every track, *OK Computer* is an album of distorted guitars and eerie atmospherics, welded together by Thom Yorke's acutely modern lyrics. The album's first single, 'Paranoid Android', perfectly encapsulated the band's new agenda: a stunning tri-part song whose aura of restlessness is captured by its thrilling musical adventure. With this album, Radiohead dragged rock music kicking and screaming into the late 90s.

● TRACKS: *Airbag; Paranoid Android; Subterranean Homesick Alien; Exit Music (For A Film); Let Down; Karma Police; Fitter Happier; Electioneering; Climbing Up The Walls; No Surprises; Lucky; The Tourist.*

● FIRST RELEASED 1997
● UK PEAK CHART POSITION: 1
● USA PEAK CHART POSITION: 21

22 VELVET UNDERGROUND & NICO (20) ▼
THE VELVET UNDERGROUND

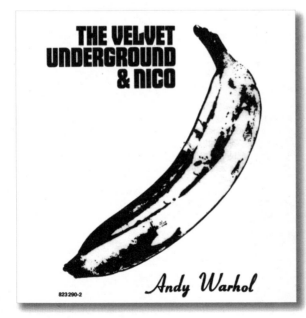

This dark, decadent and steamy album failed to sell when it was first released in deference to what was happening on the hippie-laden east coast of America. Andy Warhol's pets unconsciously produced one of the most influential rock albums of all time. Openly addressing drugs, sex and everything that was subculture, this album still smells bad. Lou Reed's brilliantly uncompromising lyrics, together with the band's sloppy sexuality, continue to influence. 'Venus In Furs', 'Heroin', 'Black Angel's Death Song' and the magnificent 'I'm Waiting For The Man', it is all here in 45 minutes of untouchable debauchery. Beautifully bent, like the banana on the cover.

● TRACKS: *Sunday Morning; I'm Waiting For The Man; Femme Fatale; Venus In Furs; Run, Run, Run; All Tomorrow's Parties; Heroin; There She Goes Again; I'll Be Your Mirror; Black Angel's Death Song; European Son (To Delmore Schwartz).*

● FIRST RELEASED 1967
● UK PEAK CHART POSITION: did not chart
● USA PEAK CHART POSITION: 171

23 THE QUEEN IS DEAD (62) ▲
THE SMITHS

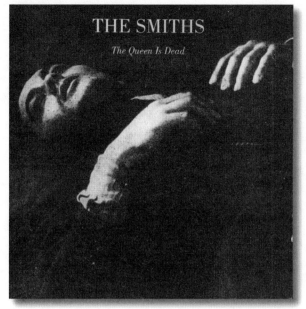

Arguably the Smiths' masterpiece album, *The Queen Is Dead* shows a group expanding horizons without sacrificing their unique sound. Vocalist Morrissey retains his self-centred romanticism, but articulates his anguish through a succession of engaging melodies, most notably 'The Boy With The Thorn In His Side'. The singer's flippant persona surfaces on 'Frankly, Mr. Shankly' and 'Vicar In A Tutu', while Johnny Marr's multi-layered guitarwork is best heard on the abrasive title track. This album shows a group aware of its strengths, but unafraid to build and expand upon them.

● TRACKS: *The Queen Is Dead; Frankly, Mr. Shankly; I Know It's Over; Never Had No One Ever; Cemetery Gates; Big Mouth Strikes Again; The Boy With The Thorn In His Side; Vicar In A Tutu; There Is A Light That Never Goes Out; Some Girls Are Bigger Than Others.*

● FIRST RELEASED 1986
● UK PEAK CHART POSITION: 2
● USA PEAK CHART POSITION: 70

24 BLOOD ON THE TRACKS (98) ▲
BOB DYLAN

No word other than 'masterpiece' can describe this album. Where Dylan had once obscured personal feelings in simile and metaphor, here he articulates disintegrating relationships with a painful, almost harrowing, honesty. There are fleeting moments of optimism, but overall the atmosphere is one of loss and the quest to come to terms with it. Lyrically, Dylan takes the specific to declare the universal, no more so than on 'If You See Her, Say Hello', one of the saddest love songs in rock's entire canon. The set, however, is far from maudlin. Its regrets, while intense, are passing and a sense of survival in spite of trauma permeates each selection. Few albums, even in Dylan's catalogue, come close to matching it.

● TRACKS: *Tangled Up In Blue; Simple Twist Of Fate; You're A Big Girl Now; Idiot Wind; You're Gonna Make Me Lonesome When You Go; Meet Me In The Morning; Lily, Rosemary And The Jack Of Hearts; If You See Her, Say Hello; Shelter From The Storm; Buckets Of Rain.*

● FIRST RELEASED 1975
● UK PEAK CHART POSITION: 4
● USA PEAK CHART POSITION: 1

25 DEFINITELY MAYBE (–) ▲
OASIS

Even though they did not go supernova until 1995's *What's The Story (Morning Glory)*, Oasis never bettered the sheer swagger and panache of their debut. The rousing statement of intent on the opening track, 'Rock 'n' Roll Star', presaged a collection of songs that brilliantly reclaimed rock music for the 90s, with both a sneer and a nod of respect to their spiritual predecessors the Beatles. An indication of the impact this album made on release was the way a whole generation seemed instantly to connect with the sentiments of 'Live Forever', and the group did not hesitate to seize the opportunity it gave them to reach for the stars.

● TRACKS: *Rock 'n' Roll Star; Shakermaker; Live Forever; Up In The Sky; Columbia; Sad Song; Supersonic; Bring It On Down; Cigarettes & Alcohol; Digsy's Dinner; Slide Away; Married With Children.*

● FIRST RELEASED 1994
● UK PEAK CHART POSITION: 1
● USA PEAK CHART POSITION: 58

26 HIGHWAY 61 REVISITED (2) ▼
BOB DYLAN

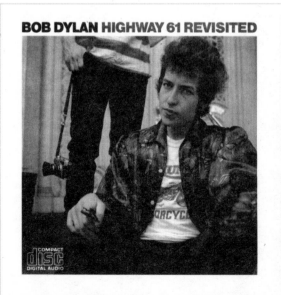

Dylan's first fully fledged electric album engendered considerable controversy. Folk purists had already waved goodbye to him, but rock had become the métier through which the singer could now best express his vision. Session organist Al Kooper and blues guitarist Michael Bloomfield were among those providing free-spirited accompaniment to a collection of songs that redefined pop music. Wrapped in a raw, driving sound, Dylan's poems - part beat, part symbolist, part concrete - ensured that contemporaries could no longer rely on traditional forms, an influence immediately apparent on recordings by the Beatles and the Rolling Stones. There are lyrics of a generation still to be found on this album.

● TRACKS: *Like A Rolling Stone; Tombstone Blues; It Takes A Lot To Laugh, It Takes A Train To Cry; From A Buick Six; Ballad Of A Thin Man; Queen Jane Approximately; Highway 61 Revisited; Just Like Tom Thumb's Blues; Desolation Row.*

● FIRST RELEASED 1965
● UK PEAK CHART POSITION: 4
● USA PEAK CHART POSITION: 3

27 EXILE ON MAIN STREET (114) ▲
THE ROLLING STONES

The Stones entered the 70s as 'the world's greatest rock 'n' roll band', an epithet confirmed by this album. Where its predecessor, *Sticky Fingers*, boasted a clear production, this rampaging double set offered a thick, muddy mix that adds an air of mystery to the proceedings. Up-tempo material, laden with riffs ('All Down The Line', 'Happy', 'Soul Survivor'), contrasts with loose, unhinged performances drawn from the rich textures of delta blues. Hedonism and bacchanalia ooze from every pore, emphasizing an air of degeneracy encapsulating the Rolling Stones' appeal. This expansive and important album is now rightly regarded as one the pinnacles of their formidable career.

● TRACKS: *Rocks Off; Rip This Joint; Hip Shake; Casino Boogie; Tumbling Dice; Sweet Virginia; Torn And Frayed; Black Angel; Loving Cup; Happy; Turd On The Run; Ventilator Blues; Just Wanna See His Face; Let It Loose; All Down The Line; Stop Breaking Down; Shine A Light; Soul Survivor.*

● FIRST RELEASED 1972
● UK PEAK CHART POSITION: 1
● USA PEAK CHART POSITION: 1

28 ACHTUNG BABY (162) ▲
U2

From their Trabant period, this is U2 at their most powerful and eloquent. This was also prior to the overblown concert stages that ignore the music. The production (Daniel Lanois, Steve Lillywhite and Brian Eno) is raw and uncompromising. On the opening track 'Zoo Station', the VU meters are driven mercilessly into the red by Larry Mullen's percussive attack. The words are equally potent, creating the lyrical equivalent of a Hieronymous Bosch painting - a tangled steel web of tortured love and urban nightmare. *Achtung Baby* spawned numerous hit singles, including 'Even Better Than The Real Thing', 'One', 'The Fly', 'Mysterious Ways' and 'Who's Gonna Ride Your Wild Horses'.

● TRACKS: *Zoo Station; Even Better Than The Real Thing; One; Until The End Of The World; Who's Gonna Ride Your Wild Horses; So Cruel; The Fly; Mysterious Ways; Tryin' To Throw Your Arms Around The World; Ultra Violet (Light My Way); Acrobat; Love Is Blindness.*

● FIRST RELEASED 1991
● UK PEAK CHART POSITION: 2
● USA PEAK CHART POSITION: 1

29 LONDON CALLING (54) ▲
THE CLASH

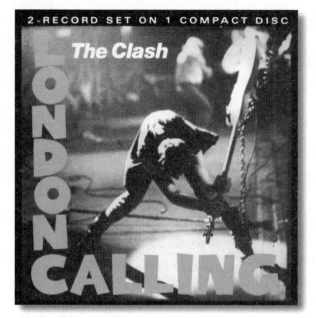

If punk rejected pop history, *London Calling* reclaimed it, albeit with a knowing perspective. The scope of this double set is breaktaking, encompassing reggae, rockabilly and the group's own furious mettle. Where such a combination might have proved over-ambitious, the Clash accomplish it with swaggering panache. Guy Stevens, who produced the group's first demos, returns to the helm to provide a confident, cohesive sound equal to the set's brilliant array of material. Boldly assertive and superbly focused, *London Calling* contains many of the quartet's finest songs and is, by extension, virtually faultless.

● TRACKS: *London Calling; Brand New Cadillac; Jimmy Jazz; Hateful; Rudie Can't Fail; Spanish Bombs; The Right Profile; Lost In The Supermarket; Clampdown; The Guns Of Brixton; Wrong 'Em Boyo; Death Or Glory; Koka Kola; The Card Cheat; Lover's Rock; Four Horsemen; I'm Not Down; Revolution Rock; Train In Vain.*

● FIRST RELEASED 1979
● UK PEAK CHART POSITION: 9
● USA PEAK CHART POSITION: 27

30 PARKLIFE (–) ▲
BLUR

Just as the Kinks' Ray Davies distilled 'Englishness' on *Something Else* in 1967, so two of Davies's greatest admirers took it a step further in 1994. Damon Albarn and Graham Coxon wrote a 'chirpy cheeky chappie' concept album without any deliberate concept. True, the pseudo-Cockney narratives frequently seemed contrived, but overall the set gelled perfectly. From the cynical 'Girls & Boys', through the punk sensibilities of 'Bank Holiday', to the sadness of 'This Is A Low', *Parklife* was a stunning album of high-quality, undeniably English pop. The title track quickly became a ubiquitous (and many would argue, highly irritating) anthem, but with this album Blur firmly established themselves as a major talent.

● TRACKS: *Girls & Boys; Tracy Jacks; End Of A Century; Parklife; Bank Holiday; Badhead; The Debt Collector; Far Out; To The End; London Loves; Trouble In The Message Centre; Clover Over Dover; Magic America; Jubilee; This Is A Low; Lot 105.*

● FIRST RELEASED 1994
● UK PEAK CHART POSITION: 1
● USA PEAK CHART POSITION: did not chart

31 WISH YOU WERE HERE (127) ▲
PINK FLOYD

Pink Floyd reaped considerable commercial acclaim with *Dark Side Of The Moon*, but it was on *Wish You Were Here* that the quartet reached an artistic maturity. The album revolves around 'Shine On You Crazy Diamond', a lengthy suite devoted to founder-member Syd Barrett, whose fragile ego snapped at the earliest whiff of success. This in mind, the group addresses music business exploitation in 'Welcome To The Machine', particularly pithy given their new-found status. A quiet determination marks this set. Roger Waters contributes some of his most openly heartfelt lyrics, while guitarist Dave Gilmour proved both economical and incisive. Free of the self-indulgence marking later work, Pink Floyd emerge as thoughtful technocrats, amalgamating and contextualizing new possibilities, rather than being swamped by them.

● TRACKS: *Shine On You Crazy Diamond (Parts 1-5); Welcome To The Machine; Have A Cigar; Wish You Were Here; Shine On You Crazy Diamond (Parts 6-9).*

● FIRST RELEASED 1975
● UK PEAK CHART POSITION: 1
● USA PEAK CHART POSITION: 1

32 WHAT'S GOING ON (9) ▼
MARVIN GAYE

Prior to this monumental release, albums recorded for Tamla/Motown were largely adjuncts to successful singles, rather than independent projects. Despite pressure to conform, Gaye was determined not only to break with tradition but also to comment on social topics. Through a seamless suite of songs the singer addressed issues including ecology, poverty and the Vietnam War, yet polemics did not deflect his artistic strengths, and 'Inner City Blues' and 'Mercy Mercy Me' boast hypnotic melodies and vocals. Gaye's sinewy voice retained its distinctive qualities and his vision was rewarded with both critical and commercial success. In turn the course of black music was irrevocably changed. The best soul album in the world, ever.

● TRACKS: *What's Going On; What's Happening Brother; Flyin' High (In The Friendly Sky); Save The Children; God Is Love; Mercy Mercy Me (The Ecology); Right On; Wholy Holy; Inner City Blues (Make Me Wanna Holler).*

● FIRST RELEASED 1971
● UK PEAK CHART POSITION: did not chart
● USA PEAK CHART POSITION: 6

33 THE FAT OF THE LAND (–) ▲
PRODIGY

Dismissed by *real* dance fans as cartoon purveyors of techno-rock, mix-maestro Liam, Keith *et al.* conquered the world with this long-anticipated album. A merciless, seering blast of punk, hip-hop and dance beats, it did not so much demand your attention as hold you at gunpoint. Never ones to admit to selling out the dance crowd, the Prodigy followed two number 1 singles ('Firestarter' and 'Breathe') with the wilfully uncommercial 'Smack My Bitch Up', complete with a highly controversial video. They also fuelled the old school revival with the masterful rapping of Kool Keith on 'Diesel Power', and, incongruously, enlisted Kula Shaker's Crispian Mills and Republica's Saffron for vocals on 'Narayan' and 'Fuel My Fire', respectively.

● TRACKS: *Smack My Bitch Up; Breathe; Diesel Power; Funky Shit; Serial Thrilla; Mindfields; Narayan; Firestarter; Climbatize; Fuel My Fire.*

● FIRST RELEASED 1997
● UK PEAK POSITION: 1
● USA PEAK POSITION: 1

34 DUMMY (–) ▲
PORTISHEAD

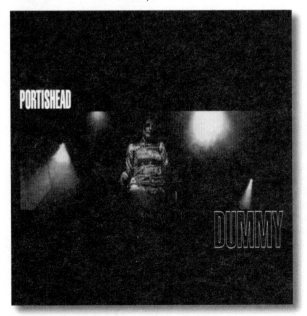

Portishead emerged from Bristol's thriving trip-hop scene with little fanfare, but produced an understated, remarkable album that was eventually lavished with critical praise and awards. Beth Gibbons' moody vocals made her the obvious focus: turning from haunting, otherworldly angel to snarling witch within a moment, the Portishead sound was completely original. Much of the credit was also due to the programming of Geoff Barrow, which combined hip-hop scratching with science-fiction samples and dense orchestration. Not an immediately accessible record, it has, nevertheless, become a classic 'dinner-party favourite' - arguably a waste of such an unsettling and cinematic album.

● TRACKS: *Mysterons; Sour Times; Strangers; It Could Be Sweet; Wandering Star; Numb; Roads; Pedestal; Biscuit; Glory Box.*

● FIRST RELEASED 1994
● UK PEAK CHART POSITION: 2
● USA PEAK CHART POSITION: 79

35 JAGGED LITTLE PILL (–) ▲
ALANIS MORISSETTE

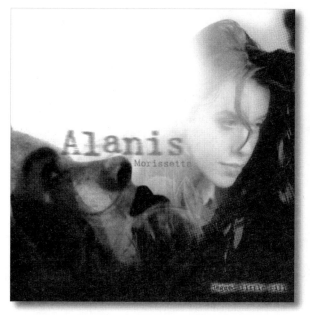

One wonders how on earth can she follow this remarkable debut. Morissette defined the independent rock chick genre started, but not completed, by Suzanne Vega and Sheryl Crow. They like men, but they don't need 'em. Most major record companies have now been signing up Morissette soundalikes for the past two years, but the popularity of this album is inflated because it caught the mood at the right time. There is no doubt that 'Ironic' and 'Hand In My Pocket' are great songs, but radio almost killed them off. Morissette is ballsy and this is a very fine rock album, but time will tell whether its current popularity will endure.

● TRACKS: *All I Really Want; You Oughta Know; Perfect; Hand In My Pocket; Right Through You; Forgiven; You Learn; Head Over Feet; Mary Jane; Ironic; Not The Doctor; Wake Up.*

● FIRST RELEASED 1995
● UK PEAK CHART POSITION: 1
● USA PEAK CHART POSITION: 1

36 BE HERE NOW (–) ▲
OASIS

Riding into the Top 100 on the coat-tails of its superior predecessors, *Be Here Now* represented more of the same in a year when Oasis could do no wrong. The fact that their third Beatles-derived album showed negligible musical progression did not dent its sales, nor affect the initially warm critical reception. Tailor-made for stadium audience singalongs, even the better tracks - 'Stand By Me', 'It's Gettin' Better (Man!!)', 'D'You Know What I Mean?' and the title track - struggled in comparison with the band's earlier work. The popular backlash was quick in coming, and whether even their most staunch fans will rate *Be Here Now* as highly in five years' time remains extremely doubtful.

● TRACKS: *D'You Know What I Mean?; My Big Mouth; Magic Pie; Stand By Me; I Hope, I Think, I Know; The Girl In The Dirty Shirt; Fade In-Out; Don't Go Away; Be Here Now; All Around The World; It's Gettin' Better (Man!!); All Around The World (Reprise).*

● FIRST RELEASED 1997
● UK PEAK POSITION: 1
● USA PEAK POSITION: 2

Primal Scream's understanding of rock's varied vistas is encapsulated on this release. At its core are a series of dance-oriented tracks that broach several musical barriers. Samples, tape loops, dub and plangent chords gel together over various grooves, at times uplifting, at others ambient. Mixmasters Terry Farley and Andy Weatherall add different perspectives to individual tracks, with gospel choirs, pumping brass and spaceward basslines bubbling around several selections. Former Rolling Stones producer Jimmy Miller generated the spirit of *Beggars Banquet* for the rousing 'Movin' On Up', while elsewhere the group imply acknowledgement to talismen the Beach Boys and Big Star. *Screamadelica* is the ultimate confluence of rock and rave cultures.

● TRACKS: *Movin' On Up; Slip Inside This House; Don't Fight It, Feel It; Higher Than The Sun; Inner Flight; Come Together; Loaded; Damaged; I'm Comin' Down; Higher Than The Sun (A Dub Symphony In Two Parts); Shine Like Stars.*

● FIRST RELEASED 1991
● UK PEAK CHART POSITION: 8
● USA PEAK CHART POSITION: did not chart

38 ## GRACELAND (93) ▲
PAUL SIMON

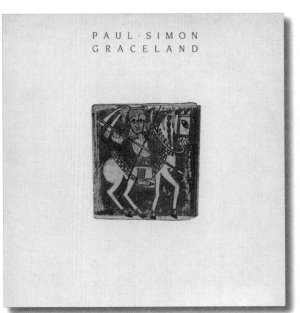

Through the mist of subsequent pale imitations, it is difficult now to recall the enormous impact of this trans-cultural album. The mould-breaking blend of rock and African rhythms is exemplified by 'Homeless', an exquisitely melancholic evocation of African beauty and desolation. The stirring harmonies of Ladysmith Black Mambazo illuminate 'Homeless' and 'Diamonds On The Soles Of Her Shoes'. The element of humour in the latter is echoed in 'You Can Call Me Al', a hit single. The lyrics are finely crafted and the result is a structure of impeccable proportions. There are angels in the architecture.

● TRACKS: *The Boy In The Bubble; Graceland; I Know What I Know; Gumboots; Diamonds On the Soles Of Her Shoes; You Can Call Me Al; Under African Skies; Homeless; Crazy Love Vol. 2; All Around The World Or The Myth Of Fingerprints.*

● FIRST RELEASED 1986
● UK PEAK CHART POSITION: 1
● USA PEAK CHART POSITION: 3

39 LED ZEPPELIN IV (38) ▼
LED ZEPPELIN

Its unscripted sleeve design suggested anonymity, but nothing was left to question over this album's content. Led Zeppelin were never so strident as on 'Rock 'n' Roll' and 'Black Dog', two selections of undiluted urgency. Blues standard 'When The Levee Breaks' is recast as a piece of unremitting power, particularly through John Bonham's expansive drumming, and the group's love of folk forms surfaces on the graceful 'Battle Of Evermore', complete with cameo from Fairport Convention's Sandy Denny. 'Stairway To Heaven' has, of course, become the album's best-known track, but the anthem-like stature it has since assumed should not obscure its groundbreaking companion selections. *Led Zeppelin IV* left much of heavy metal, and indeed rock itself, trailing in its wake.

● TRACKS: *Black Dog; Rock 'n' Roll; The Battle Of Evermore; Stairway To Heaven; Misty Mountain Hop; Four Sticks; Going To California; When The Levee Breaks.*

● FIRST RELEASED 1971
● UK PEAK CHART POSITION: 1
● USA PEAK CHART POSITION: 2

40 FOREVER CHANGES (32) ▼
LOVE

The continuing deep affection for this gem is no fluke. Its universal appeal to rock critics earns its position even though total sales have yet to exceed a million. The enigmatic Arthur Lee created the perfect hippie album, with joyous acoustic melody, strings and occasional biting guitars. The paradox was for Lee to sing a line such as 'oh the snot has caked against my pants, it has turned to crystal' and for it to sound absolutely right and sincere. The equally arresting 'Alone Again Or' features the line 'I could be in love with almost everyone', yet somehow avoids sounding like a hippie cliché. For anybody not familiar with this record, it is unconditionally recommended as one of the greatest ever made.

● TRACKS: *Alone Again Or; A House Is Not A Motel; Andmoreagain; The Daily Planet; Old Man; The Red Telephone; Maybe The People Would Be The Times Or Between Clark And Hilldale; Live And Let Live; The Good Humor Man He Sees Everything Like This; Bummer In The Summer; You Set The Scene.*

● FIRST RELEASED 1967
● UK PEAK CHART POSITION: 24
● USA PEAK CHART POSITION: 154

41 EVERYTHING MUST GO (–) ▲
MANIC STREET PREACHERS

The cathartic album title perfectly reflected not only its contents but the band itself: following the traumatic breakdown and disappearance of Richey Edwards, the other Manics were left to pick up the pieces - it was an extraordinary and unexpected recovery. Perhaps most striking was their new sober image - the make-up, military garb and much of the bravado were gone - and their characteristic disaffection seemed more pertinent and controlled. Despite losing a member, the band had discovered a new voice, delivering a collection of powerful and socially aware songs. Poignantly, Edwards' lyrics graced songs including 'Kevin Carter' and 'Small Black Flowers . . . ', all delivered in James Dean Bradfield's emotional tones.

● TRACKS: *Elvis Impersonator: Blackpool Pier; Design For Life; Kevin Carter; Enola/Alone; Everything Must Go; Small Black Flowers That Grow In The Sky; Girl Who Wanted To Be God; Removables; Australia; Interiors (Song For Willem De Kooning); Further Away; No Surface All Feeling.*

● FIRST RELEASED 1996
● UK PEAK POSITION: 2
● USA PEAK POSITION: did not chart

42 DIFFERENT CLASS (–) ▲
PULP

Jarvis Cocker's lyrical masterpiece propelled Pulp into the major league of British pop music. In 12 breathtakingly melodic pop songs, Cocker expressed his fascination for modern Britain and its social and sexual mores, exposing the banalities of life through lyrics that flow as easily as conversation. The album's centrepiece, 'I Spy', features a malevolent, breathy Jarvis in a moment of high melodrama, spitting out the classic 'take your *Year In Provence* and shove it up your ass'. Elsewhere, there are delights in the pure pop of 'Common People' and 'Disco 2000', the touchingly simple 'Something Changed', and the wrenching pathos of 'Live Bed Show' ('something beautiful left town and she never even knew its name').

● TRACKS: *Mis-Shapes; Pencil Skirt; Common People; I Spy; Disco 2000; Live Bed Show; Something Changed; Sorted For E's & Wizz; F.E.E.L.I.N.G.C.A.L.L.E.D.L.O.V.E; Underwear; Monday Morning; Bar Italia.*

● FIRST RELEASED 1995
● UK PEAK CHART POSITION: 1
● USA PEAK CHART POSITION: did not chart

43 BLUE LINES (–) ▲
MASSIVE ATTACK

One of the 90s' early classics and a landmark album in dance music, Bristol's Massive Attack invented the 'trip-hop' genre, an ambient form of hip-hop. Born from the ashes of pioneering sound system unit the Wild Bunch, the core trio of Daddy-G, Mushroom and 3-D were joined on *Blue Lines* by soul diva Shara Nelson, reggae singer Horace Andy and a young Tricky. Together they fashioned a strikingly modern urban soundtrack that added an emotional intensity to the sparseness and studied cool of hip-hop, with Nelson's impassioned vocals on 'Unfinished Sympathy' helping to create one of the songs that defined the 90s.

● TRACKS: *Safe From Harm; One Love; Blue Lines; Be Thankful For What You've Got; Five Man Army; Unfinished Sympathy; Daydreaming; Lately; Hymn Of The Big Wheel.*

● FIRST RELEASED 1991
● UK PEAK CHART POSITION: 13
● USA PEAK CHART POSITION: did not chart

44 LET IT BLEED (8) ▼
THE ROLLING STONES

The last Rolling Stones album to feature the presence of the band's creator, Brian Jones, was a brilliant culmination of all their musical influences over the previous monumental decade. The power of the opening track, 'Gimme Shelter', will haunt many of us forever with the memory of the Altamont murder, Jagger's top hat and scarf and the death of the 60s. The repeated line, 'It's just a shot away', complements the repetition of the naïvely profound lyric of the album's last track: 'you can't always get what you want'. The filling in-between, like the layered cake on the cover, is equally delectable.

● TRACKS: *Gimme Shelter; Love In Vain; Country Honk; Live With Me; Let It Bleed; Midnight Rambler; You Got The Silver; Monkey Man; You Can't Always Get What You Want.*

● FIRST RELEASED 1969
● UK PEAK CHART POSITION: 1
● USA PEAK CHART POSITION: 3

45 URBAN HYMNS (–) ▲
THE VERVE

At the time of writing the greatest musical comeback of the decade, the Verve's *Urban Hymns* was a triumph of belief over adversity. Richard Ashcroft and Nick McCabe finally managed to focus their wayward talents into a coherent whole, creating a sweeping modern psychedelic masterpiece in the process. 'Bitter Sweet Symphony' and 'The Drugs Don't Work' also broke the band in the singles chart, with the former's creepingly insistent string motif becoming one of the most recognisable sounds on UK radio in 1997. If some of Ashcroft's subsequent grandiose claims for his band grated, there was no denying that his belief in his band had been spectacularly vindicated.

● TRACKS: *Bitter Sweet Symphony; Sonnet; The Rolling People; The Drugs Don't Work; Catching The Butterfly; Neon Wilderness; Space And Time; Weeping Willow; Lucky Man; One Day; This Time; Velvet Morning; Come On.*

● FIRST RELEASED 1997
● UK PEAK CHART POSITION: 1
● USA PEAK CHART POSITION: 23

46 THE WALL (176) ▲
PINK FLOYD

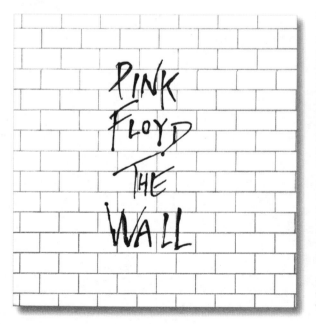

There are hidden depths to this remarkable album which fans and critics have at times dismissed. It is not the concept of tearing down the wall, of opposition to the educational system or even Roger Waters becoming intolerable for the others to work with. It is a double album that contains some outstanding songs. For example, 'Nobody Home' highlights the frustration of Waters' rock star lot, but for all the luxury we can sense his appalling frustration at finding nobody home and of sitting in his hotel room with 'thirteen channels of shit on the TV, to choose from'. Similarly, the epic 'Comfortably Numb': 'the child is gone, the dream is gone, and I have become comfortably numb'.

● TRACKS: *In The Flesh; Thin Ice; Happiest Days Of Our Lives; Another Brick In The Wall (Part 2); Mother; Goodbye Blue Sky; Empty Spaces; Young Lust; One Of My Turns; Don't Leave Me Now; Another Brick In The Wall (Part 3); Goodbye Cruel World; Hey You; Is There Anybody Out There?; Nobody Home; Comfortably Numb; Show Must Go On; Run Like Hell; Waiting For The Worms; Stop; The Trial; Outside The Wall.*

● FIRST RELEASED 1980
● UK PEAK CHART POSITION: 3
● USA PEAK CHART POSITION: 1

47 SIGN 'O' THE TIMES (84) ▲
PRINCE

A gleefully adventurous double album from Prince. Considered in some quarters as a little too ambitious at the time, it has come to be regarded as probably his greatest album. Drawing on nearly every influence with which he had previously toyed in his career, here he wove them together and created a palette rich with colour, style and life: the title track, a snapshot of modern life and its slow erosion; 'Starfish And Coffee', a precise and neat piece of storytelling; 'U Got The Look', all swagger and poise, Prince verbally jousting with Sheena Easton. Magnificent, and one album he has yet to equal.

● TRACKS: *Sign 'O' The Times; Play In The Sunshine; Housequake; The Ballad Of Dorothy Parker; It; Starfish And Coffee; Slow Love; Hot Thing; Forever In My Life; U Got The Look; If I Was Your Girlfriend; Strange Relationship; I Could Never Take The Place Of Your Man; The Cross; It's Gonna Be A Beautiful Night; Adore.*

● FIRST RELEASED 1987
● UK PEAK CHART POSITION: 4
● USA PEAK CHART POSITION: 6

48 KIND OF BLUE (28) ▼
MILES DAVIS

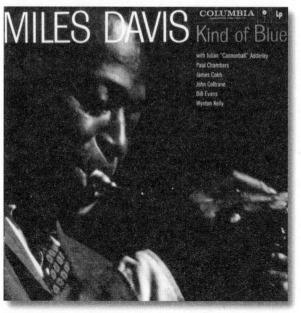

A dvocates from the many corners of jazz will argue their points, some with bigoted passion and self righteousness - a trait that has been known to follow some jazz buffs. When you find jazzers, rock and popular music followers actually unanimously united over one record, then you know something must be right. This album contains only five tracks, with musicians Julian Adderley (alto), John Coltrane (tenor), Bill Evans (piano), Paul Chambers (bass), James Cobb (drums) and Miles on trumpet. It is played with absolute cool perfection, not a drop of sweat or cigarette ash. There can be no debate, this is the greatest jazz album in the world ever; so what, just accept it.

● TRACKS: *So What; Freddie Freeloader; Blue In Green; Al Blues; Flamenco Sketches.*

● FIRST RELEASED 1960
● UK PEAK CHART POSITION: did not chart
● USA PEAK CHART POSITION: did not chart

49 THE BAND (35) ▼
THE BAND

Initially renowned as Bob Dylan's backing group, the Band emerged from the singer's shadow to proclaim a distinctive talent. Drawing upon a musical canon embracing soul, country, folk and rock 'n' roll, the quintet created a unique sound that was quintessentially American. Its rustic qualities were enhanced by principle songwriter Robbie Robertson who created vistas suggestive of a pre-industrial age, and as such, captured the restlessness of the late 60s without the need for explicit manifestos. Expressive singing, sublime melodies and telepathic musicianship instils *The Band* with quality, but its adult themes and perspectives ensure an absolute timelessness. An all-time critics' favourite.

● TRACKS: *Across The Great Divide; Rag Mama Rag; The Night They Drove Old Dixie Down; When You Awake; Up On Cripple Creek; Whispering Pines; Jemima Surrender; Rockin' Chair; Look Out Cleveland; Jawbone; The Unfaithful Servant; King Harvest (Has Surely Come)*.

● FIRST RELEASED 1969
● UK PEAK CHART POSITION: 25
● USA PEAK CHART POSITION: 9

50 PHYSICAL GRAFFITI (258) ▲
LED ZEPPELIN

One of the strongest hard rock albums ever, over 20 years later it is still much imitated and sampled, and, quite rightly, stands as the major contemporary reference point in rock music. The heavily stylized 'Kashmir', allegedly the starting point for a war of words between Plant and David Coverdale, after a very similar refrain appeared in Whitesnake's 'In The Heat Of The Night'. The blissful 'Bron-Y-Aur', which followed their limo through New York during *The Song Remains The Same*, 'Custard Pie', with its legendary intro, and the innovative 'In The Light', all combined to create a truly credible musical landmark.

● TRACKS: *Custard Pie; The Rover; In My Time Of Dying; Houses Of The Holy; Trampled Under Foot; Kashmir; In The Light; Bron-Y-Aur; Down By The Seaside; Ten Years Gone; Night Flight; The Wanton Song; Boogie With Stu; Black Country Woman; Sick Again*.

● FIRST RELEASED 1975
● UK PEAK CHART POSITION: 1
● USA PEAK CHART POSITION: 1

51 · OUT OF TIME (13) ▼
R.E.M.

R.E.M. are the most successful band of recent years, their stream of acclaimed albums illustrates the importance of R.E.M. as America's greatest post-Springsteen export. Michael Stipe's thinking person's lyrics are almost buried by the band's Byrdslike arrangements of the notable 'Radio Song' and 'Shiny Happy People'. There are those that have criticized R.E.M. for stepping out of a parochial indie scene, but their impact in the 90s was as welcome as the Sex Pistols were in the 70s. Their catalogue is destined to endure as critics reluctantly accept their considerable importance in the history of rock. They will continue to make albums as good as this.

● TRACKS: Radio Song; Losing My Religion; Low; Near Wild Heaven; Endgame; Shiny Happy People; Belong; Half A World Away; Texarkana; Country Feedback; Me In Honey.

● FIRST RELEASED 1991
● UK PEAK CHART POSITION: 1
● USA PEAK CHART POSITION: 1

52 · BRIDGE OVER TROUBLED WATER (97) ▲
SIMON AND GARFUNKEL

The measured beauty of its opening title track set the tone for this album's quiet authority. International acclaim immediately ensued and the duo's passage from folk act to popular singers was confirmed through a series of highly commercial, Simon-penned compositions. Alternately reflective, then bubbling, the collection revealed a growing maturity and, in 'El Condor Pasa', the first flowering of his infatuation with world music styles. Art Garfunkel's angelic tenor was never so perfect; when combined with Simon's lower register it created a seamless resonance, redolent of the Everly Brothers. It is no surprise that this album features a rendition of the latter's 'Bye Bye Love'.

● TRACKS: Bridge Over Troubled Water; El Condor Pasa; Cecilia; Keep The Customer Satisfied; So Long, Frank Lloyd Wright; The Boxer; Baby Driver; The Only Living Boy In New York; Why Don't You Write Me; Bye Bye Love; Song For The Asking.

● FIRST RELEASED 1970
● UK PEAK CHART POSITION: 1
● USA PEAK CHART POSITION: 1

53 · BLUE (89) ▲
JONI MITCHELL

Joni Mitchell's fourth album maintained the confessional style of its predecessors, but her biographical epistles were here infused with greater maturity. Although her lyrics remained personal, Mitchell drew upon their described scenarios to express a greater context. Stephen Stills and James Taylor added sympathetic accompaniment, but the album's musical textures were defined by the singer's use of guitar, piano and dulcimer. Mitchell's vocals showed a new depth and range absent from earlier work, emphasizing Blue's important place in her maturation as an artist. She never returned to folk after this release, she spied a bigger world for her lyrics and eclectic ideas of song.

● TRACKS: All I Want; My Old Man; Little Green; Carey; Blue; California; This Flight Tonight; River; A Case Of You; The Last Time I Saw Richard.

● FIRST RELEASED 1971
● UK PEAK CHART POSITION: 3
● USA PEAK CHART POSITION: 15

54 ODELAY (−) ▲
BECK

His debut *Mellow Gold* had been overshadowed by the huge success of the slacker anthem 'Loser', but on this 1996 major label follow-up, Beck Hansen corralled his wildly imaginative talent into a stunning collection of tracks that has made the skinny white *wunderkind* one of contemporary music's most important artists. *Odelay* is a potent mix of the new and the old, sampling from the deep wells of hip-hop, electronica, funk, blues and folk to create a multi-layered postmodern masterpiece. The album's surreal air, however, does not detract from the accessibility of songs such as 'Jack-Ass' and 'The New Pollution'.

● TRACKS: *Devils Haircut; Hotwax; Lord Only Knows; The New Pollution; Derelict; Novacane; Jack-Ass; Where It's At; Minus; Sissyneck; Readymade; High 5 (Rock The Catskills); Ramshackle.*

● FIRST RELEASED 1996
● UK PEAK CHART POSITION: 18
● USA PEAK CHART POSITION:

55 K (−) ▲
KULA SHAKER

Crispin Mills' mother (actress Hayley) must have fed her baby son a balanced diet of Jimi Hendrix, Beatles and late 60s rock. All these styles are beautifully honed on this stunning debut album. Creamy guitars, crybaby wah-wahs, and chiming sitars are all-pervading. Even the record-cover collage of famous 'K's (Ken Dodd and Lord Kitchener among them) reflects the band's mish-mash of influences. The mystical Eastern themes of 'Govinda' and 'Tattva' sit alongside unapologetically retro rockers such as 'Grateful When You're Dead/Jerry Was There' and 'Hey Dude', merely serving to reinforce the atmosphere: you can almost picture the cheesecloth and smell the patchouli from here.

● TRACKS: *Hey Dude; Knight On The Town; Temple Of Everlasting Light; Govinda; Smart Dogs; Magic Theatre; Into The Deep; Sleeping Jiva; Tattva; Grateful When You're Dead/Jerry Was There; 303; Start All Over; Hollow Man.*

● FIRST RELEASED 1996
● UK PEAK CHART POSITION: 1
● USA PEAK CHART POSITION: did not chart

56 THE HOLY BIBLE (−) ▲
MANIC STREET PREACHERS

The tragic and unresolved disappearance of Richey Edwards looms larger than life every time this album is played. Just as they were being hailed as the potential 'next big thing', the band was thrown into disarray, and as a result, this credible album was somewhat overlooked while the world searched for Richey. Now that the dust has settled and people have accepted his likely demise, this album can at last be appreciated. Even though the spoken introduction 'Of Walking Abortion' is spookily prophetic, the understated quality of all the songs puts this album much closer to the gigantic *Everything Must Go* than its success would indicate.

● TRACKS: *Yes; Ifwhiteamericatoldthetruthforonedayitsworld wouldfallapart; Of Walking Abortion; She Is Suffering; Archives Of Pain; Revol; 4st 7lb; Mausoleum; Faster; This Is Yesterday; Die In The Summertime; The Intense Humming Of Evil; P.C.P.*

● FIRST RELEASED 1994
● UK PEAK CHART POSITION: 6
● USA PEAK CHART POSITION: did not chart

57 BLUR (-) ▲
BLUR

Wisely escaping the Blur versus Oasis media hype, Damon Albarn and his band disappeared to Iceland to work on material for this, their fifth album. The result initially disappointed both critics and public, but subsequent investigation has deemed it a great piece of work. The coy sexiness of 'Beetlebum' and the tremendous, all-out thrash of 'Song 2' were light years away from the pub-chant of 'Parklife', and they and other tracks ('Country Sad Ballad Man') hinted at a new lo-fi influence, inspired by bands such as Pavement. *Blur* gave the band a magnificent chance to experiment and to cast off their chirpy image; in doing so, they reinforced their musical credibility while retaining their sense of humour.

● TRACKS: *Beetlebum; Song 2; Country Sad Ballad Man; M.O.R.; On Your Own; Theme From Retro; You're So Great; Death Of A Party; Chinese Bombs; I'm Just A Killer For Your Love; Look Inside America; Strange News From Another Star; Movin' On; Essex Dogs.*

● FIRST RELEASED 1997
● UK PEAK CHART POSITION: 1
● USA PEAK CHART POSITION: 61

58 THRILLER (14) ▼
MICHAEL JACKSON

The finest example of perfect disco pop, and a record that should be prescribed to musical snobs and manic depressives. The album is a true ambassador of what pop music can be. Jackson whoops and dances through a suite of unforgettable melodies that should be danced to with a smile on your face. While many of us will lapse into comedian Lenny Henry's 'Aston Villa' lyric to replace 'thriller', we are all touched by this quite magnificent record. Each track offers at least one musical hook, whether it is the beauty of 'Human Nature' (who can resist the 'dada dada da da da da') or the 'whoo whoo' of 'Billie Jean'. It's all too good.

● TRACKS: *Wanna Be Startin' Somethin'; Baby Be Mine; The Girl Is Mine; Thriller; Beat It; Billie Jean; Human Nature; PYT (Pretty Young Thing); The Lady In My Life.*

● FIRST RELEASED 1982
● UK PEAK CHART POSITION: 1
● USA PEAK CHART POSITION: 1

59 HOUNDS OF LOVE (385) ▲
KATE BUSH

Kate Bush

Hounds Of Love

Though not the most prolific of album artists, Bush's works make up in impact what they lack in frequency. Her style and material has always been unique, eccentric even, but *Hounds Of Love* is probably the strongest mix of controlled musical experimentation and lyrical expression. It deals with big issues - childhood fantasy and trauma, conflict, sexuality - but rarely lapses into pretension. The intense arrangements are perfectly matched to the subjects: 'Running Up That Hill' climactically erotic, 'Cloudbusting' broodingly triumphant, 'The Big Sky' just… big. And it's all her own work.

● TRACKS: *Running Up That Hill (A Deal With God); Hounds Of Love; The Big Sky; Mother Stands For Comfort; Cloudbusting; And Dream Of Sheep; Under Ice; Waking The Witch; Watching You Without Me; Jig Of Life; Hello Earth; The Morning Fog.*

● FIRST RELEASED 1985
● UK PEAK CHART POSITION: 1
● USA PEAK CHART POSITION: 30

60 MOSELEY SHOALS (–) ▲
OCEAN COLOUR SCENE

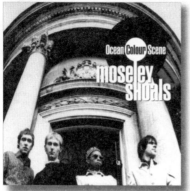

Riding on a crest of late 60s retro rock, this band have received a disproportionate dollop of criticism since their considerable success with this, their second album. Revealing influences ranging from 10CC and the Idle Race ('The Day We Caught The Train') to the Love Affair and Beatles ('The Circle'), the derivative nature of this record is nevertheless highly palatable. Even a Randy Newman soundalike rears up in 'Lining Your Pockets' and Eric Clapton's *Disraeli Gears* wah-wah guitar can also be found liberally sprinkled throughout ('The Riverboat Song', 'Policeman & Pirates'). A necessary album for anyone with a magpie complex.

● TRACKS: *The Riverboat Song; The Day We Caught The Train; The Circle; Lining Your Pockets; Fleeting Mind; 40 Past Midnight; One For The Road; It's My Shadow; Policemen & Pirates; The Downstream; You've Got It Bad; Get Away.*

● FIRST RELEASED 1996
● UK PEAK CHART POSITION: 1
● USA PEAK CHART POSITION: did not chart

61 TROUT MASK REPLICA (153) ▲
CAPTAIN BEEFHEART AND THE MAGIC BAND

Head and shoulders above every other album of its kind, this Frank Zappa-produced extravaganza remains a classic of lyrical malarkey. Accompanied by his finest ever Magic Band, the Captain entered the recording studio (actually a rented house) with a few ideas for songs. What came out is still to this day, quite astonishing. Ornette Coleman wildness and guitars thrashing in tune but deliberately off key. At times, it was alleged, Beefheart was singing in another studio. Beefheart's retirement from the music world to take up painting is a great loss. This record is living proof of his bizarre genius. A difficult but outstanding record. Fast n' bulbous, got me?
● TRACKS: *Frownland; The Dust Blows Forward 'N The Dust Blows Back; Dachau Blues; Ella Guru; Hair Pie: Bake 1; Moonlight On Vermont; Pachuco Cadaver; Bill's Corpse; Sweet Sweet Bulbs; Neon Meate Dream Of A Octafish; China Pig; My Human Gets Me Blues; Dali's Car; Hair Pie: Bake 2; Pena; Well; When Big Joan Sets Up; Fallin' Ditch; Sugar 'N Spikes; Ant Man Bee; Orange Claw Hammer; Wild Life; She's Too Much For My Mirror; Hobo Chang Ba; The Blimp; Steal Softly Thru Snow; Old Fart At Play; Veteran's Day Poppy.*
● FIRST RELEASED 1969
● UK PEAK CHART POSITION: 21   ● USA PEAK CHART POSITION: did not chart

62 DOG MAN STAR (–) ▲
SUEDE

Although guitarist/songwriter Bernard Butler quit midway through the making of this, Suede's second album, he co-wrote all the songs with singer Brett Anderson, and he remains a strong presence. *Dog Man Star*, which debuted on the UK album charts at its number 3 peak, was not nearly as successful as the group's first album, *Suede*, but it boasts more continuity and, many would argue, more depth. The David Bowie influence, so prominent on *Suede*, is, if anything, more obvious, particularly on 'Heroine', with its pained analogies between women and drugs and 'The Wild Ones', which exudes the kind of hopeless romanticism not heard since Bowie's 'Heroes'.

● TRACKS: *Introducing The Band; We Are The Pigs; Heroine; The Wild Ones; Daddy's Speeding; The Power; New Generation; This Hollywood Life; The 2 Of Us; Black Or Blue; The Asphalt World; Still Life.*

● FIRST RELEASED 1994
● UK PEAK CHART POSITION: 3
● USA PEAK CHART POSITION: did not chart

63 BORN TO RUN (16) ▼
BRUCE SPRINGSTEEN

Springsteen's standing as 'the future of rock 'n' roll' has taken a battering in recent years and his elevation and greatness is questioned as he becomes 'the past'. This much-hyped album, however, is the one that stands. The title track still makes hairs stand on end, with the images conveyed in the lyrics having an enduring power. Saxophones came back into fashion thanks to the blistering Clarence Clemons, as did forgotten 50s images of cars and drive-ins. Springsteen, meanwhile, exhumed his youth and reminded us of ours with honest tales of growing up in post-Eisenhower America.

● TRACKS: *Thunder Road; Tenth Avenue Freeze-out; Night; Backstreets; Born To Run; She's The One; Meeting Across The River; Jungleland.*

● FIRST RELEASED 1975
● UK PEAK CHART POSITION: 17
● USA PEAK CHART POSITION: 3

64 MUSIC FOR THE JILTED GENERATION (–) ▲
PRODIGY

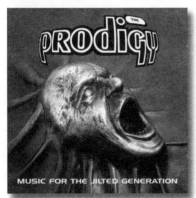

The band who stand to give the much maligned English county of Essex a 'good' reputation, Prodigy succeed where Ian Drury and Brian Poole And The Tremeloes failed, i.e., achieving worldwide acceptance and success. Braintree worked where Billericay and Dagenham failed. Their aggressive, original and extraordinarily exciting style of dance music has created a thousand imitators. Although this record has since been overshadowed by the international success of *The Fat Of The Land*, it is still a vital record for students of 90s techno/dance. Prodigy lead their pack by a mile.

● TRACKS: *Intro; Break & Enter; Their Law; Full Throttle; Voodoo People; Speedway; The Heat (The Energy); Poison; No Good (Start The Dance); One Love: The Narcotic Suite; 3 Kilos; Skylines; Claustrophobic Sting.*

● FIRST RELEASED 1994
● UK PEAK CHART POSITION: 1
● USA PEAK CHART POSITION: did not chart

65 SONGS IN THE KEY OF LIFE (45) ▼
STEVIE WONDER

An ambitious double vinyl set (plus a further freebie EP) that represented the culmination of Wonder's second golden period which started with *Music Of My Mind*. Now firmly established as a musical genius Wonder gave us longer and stronger songs. Although the hits such as 'Sir Duke', 'Another Star' and 'I Wish' are more often remembered, it is the overall incredibly high standard of all the songs that makes this such an outstanding achievement. Featuring beautiful gems such as 'Joy Inside My Tears', the brassy and funky 'Black Man', and the cloying but unforgettable 'Isn't She Lovely'. Coolio took his cover of 'Pastime Paradise' into the charts in 1996.

● TRACKS: *Love's In Need Of Love Today; Have A Talk With God; Village Ghetto Land; Confusion; Sir Duke; I Wish; Knocks Me Off My Feet; Pastimes Paradise; Summer Soft; Ordinary Pain; Isn't She Lovely; Joy Inside My Tears; Black Man; Ngiculela - Es Una Historia - I Am Singing; If It's Magic; As; Another Star.*

● FIRST RELEASED 1976
● UK PEAK CHART POSITION: 2
● USA PEAK CHART POSITION: 1

66 STANLEY ROAD (–) ▲
PAUL WELLER

Named after a street in Weller's home-town of Woking in Surrey, this album was greeted with universal approval by critics and fans. The brilliant Peter Blake collage throughout the package portrays much greater nostalgia than is contained in the lyrics. The family snapshots and the Green Line bus picture serve only to fool the listener. The title track is clearly about the terraced houses that have now given way to 90s starter apartments, but the more personal content of tracks such as 'You Do Something To Me' is where Weller truly bares his soul. It would strongly appear that before recording this album, Weller listened to many Traffic albums.

● TRACKS: *The Changingman; Porcelain Gods; I Walk On Gilded Splinters; You Do Something To Me; Woodcutters Son; Time Passes; Stanley Road; Broken Stones; Out Of The Sinking; Pink On White Walls; Whirlpools End; Wings Of Speed.*

● FIRST RELEASED 1995
● UK PEAK CHART POSITION: 1
● USA PEAK CHART POSITION: did not chart

67 THE DOORS (63) ▼
THE DOORS

The Doors were the antithesis of windblown Californian pop. Dark, brooding and alienated, every element of the quartet's métier was unveiled on their debut album. In Jim Morrison they possessed one of rock's authoritative voices, while the group's dense instrumental prowess reflected his lyrical mystery. Highly literate, they wedded Oedipean tragedy to counter-culture nihilism and, in 'Light My Fire', expressed erotic images prevously unheard in pop. Howlin' Wolf, Brecht and Weill are acknowledged as musical reference points, a conflict between the physical and cerebral that gives *The Doors* its undiluted tension.

● TRACKS: *Break On Through; Soul Kitchen; The Crystal Ship; Twentieth Century Fox; Alabama Song; Light My Fire; Back Door Man; I Looked At You; End Of The Night; Take It As It Comes; The End.*

● FiRST RELEASED 1967
● UK PEAK CHART POSITION: 43
● USA PEAK CHART POSITION: 2

68 CLOSER (266) ▲
JOY DIVISION

·CLOSER·

The news of singer Ian Curtis's suicide still hung in the air when this album was released. Given the deep introspective nature of Joy Division's music, his death invested *Closer* with an even greater pessimism. Yet there is a fragile beauty in its content and if Curtis's voice seems more distant, it complements the sparse textures created by mesmerizing synthesizer lines and occasional, highly effective, piano. Slow, hypnotic tempos increase the sense of brooding mystery and if the few faster songs provide musical relief, their lyrics prove equally tortured. Eerie, yet compulsive, *Closer* confirmed Joy Division's pre-eminent place in rock's pantheon.

● TRACKS: *Atrocity Exhibition; Isolation; Passover; Colony; A Means To An End; Heart And Soul; Twenty Four Hours; The Eternal; Decades.*

● FIRST RELEASED 1980
● UK PEAK CHART POSITION: 6
● USA PEAK CHART POSITION: did not chart

69 TRANSFORMER (95) ▲
LOU REED

Having quit the Velvet Underground, a disillusioned Lou Reed came to Britain to rethink his musical career. A low-key solo debut was followed by this highly successful release, which combined the artist's narrative compositions with the lure of contemporaneous fashions, glam-rock and androgyny. Long-time fan David Bowie co-produced the set, which emphasized the commercial nature of Reed's work without sacrificing his individuality or authenticity. Members of Andy Warhol's entourage were described graphically in 'Walk On The Wild Side' which broke taboos on lyrical content when issued as a single. Its Top 10 place ensured Reed's long-awaited commercial appreciation.

● TRACKS: *Vicious; Andy's Chest; Perfect Day; Hangin' Around; Walk On The Wild Side; Make Up; Satellite Of Love; Wagon Wheel; New York Telephone Conversation; I'm So Free; Goodnight Ladies.*

● FIRST RELEASED 1972
● UK PEAK CHART POSITION: 13
● USA PEAK CHART POSITION: 29

70 ARE YOU EXPERIENCED (39) ▼
THE JIMI HENDRIX EXPERIENCE

By 1967 Jimi Hendrix was already fêted as a genius by audience and contemporary musicians alike. His innovative, evolving guitar prowess was captured to perfection on this, his album debut. At times audacious, at others lyrical, Hendrix brought new perspectives to every style he chose to play, be it blues, pop or psychedelia. *Are You Experienced* contains a wide range of material, on which Noel Redding (bass) and Mitch Mitchell (drums) provide the ideal springboard for the guitarist's flights. Each format offered avenues for experiment, none more so than the vibrant 'Red House', on which the standard 12-bar blues is teased and twisted to new heights. Hendrix is clearly enraptured by a new-found artistic freedom, a joy that pervades this entire album. The 1997 MCA reissue with extra tracks is highly recommended.

● TRACKS: *Foxy Lady; Manic Depression; Red House; Can You See Me; Love Or Confusion; I Don't Live Today; May This Be Love; Fire; 3rd Stone From The Sun; Remember; Are You Experienced?.*

● FIRST RELEASED 1967
● UK PEAK CHART POSITION: 2   ● USA PEAK CHART POSITION: 5

71 MELLON COLLIE AND THE INFINITE SADNESS (-) ▲
SMASHING PUMPKINS

A double album was always risky business in the days of vinyl; some of those pompous 70s efforts contained only four tracks. A double album in the CD age, with so much recordable time available (and expected) is potentially suicidal. Billy Corgan had no such concerns when he formulated the lyrics to over two dozen songs. Part 1, 'Dawn To Dusk', and Part 2, 'Twilight To Starlight', contain few potato peelings, and the project was deemed an unmitigated success. Despite the heavy nature of much of the music, the Pumpkins refused to resort to formulaic riffs, and the occasional use of exquisite strings was an inspired decision.
● TRACKS: *Mellon Collie And The Infinite Sadness; Tonight, Tonight; Jellybelly; Zero; Here Is No Why; Bullet With Butterfly Wings; To Forgive; An Ode To No One; Love; Cupid de Locke; Galapogos; Muzzle; Porcelina Of The Vast Oceans; Take Me Down; Where The Boys Fear To Tread; Bodies; Thirty-Three; In The Arms Of Sleep; 1979; Tales Of A Scorched Earth; Thru The Eyes Of Ruby; Stumbleine; X.Y.U.; We Only Come Out At Night; Beautiful; Lily (My One And Only); By Starlight; Farewell And Goodnight.*
● FIRST RELEASED 1995   ● UK PEAK CHART POSITION: 4
● USA PEAK CHART POSITION: 1

72 WOODFACE (167) ▲
CROWDED HOUSE

The third and best album from the finest rock band Australia has yet produced. A good second would have been Split Enz, but they split up to become errr . . . Crowded House. The Finn brothers have been writing songs for many years and it is encouraging to see that their lyrics are as sharp, fresh and perceptive as ever. The opener 'Chocolate Cake' starts with 'not everyone in New York would pay to see Andrew Lloyd Webber, may his trousers fall down as he bows to the Queen and the crown'. Nothing lapses, no standards are dropped. No worries. This one will be around as long as the Beatles.

● TRACKS: Chocolate Cake; It's Only Natural; Fall At Your Feet; Tall Trees; Weather With You; Whispers And Moans; Four Seasons In One Day; There Goes God; Fame Is; All I Ask; As Sure As I Am; Italian Plastic; She Goes On; How Will You Go.

● FIRST RELEASED 1991
● UK PEAK CHART POSITION: 6
● USA PEAK CHART POSITION: 83

73 AFTER THE GOLDRUSH (106) ▲
NEIL YOUNG

Young's first solo release since joining Crosby, Stills And Nash, After The Goldrush confirmed the singer's talent in the full glare of the public eye. His most eclectic set to date encompassed the delicate wistfulness of 'I Believe In You' and 'Only Love Can Break Your Heart', as well as the electric anger of 'Southern Man', a raging tour de force that captured the special tension generated between Young and backing group Crazy Horse. Stills and Nils Lofgren also provided support on an album consolidating a talent while extending its range. The transformation of Don Gibson's 'Oh Lonesome Me' from canter to ballad confirmed an original musical vision, but the album's continued strength is due to Young's own remarkable compositions.

● TRACKS: Tell Me Why; After The Goldrush; Only Love Can Break Your Heart; Southern Man; Till The Morning Comes; Oh Lonesome Me; Don't Let It Bring You Down; Birds; When You Dance I Can Really Love; I Believe In You; Cripple Creek Ferry.

● FIRST RELEASED 1970
● UK PEAK CHART POSITION: 7   ● USA PEAK CHART POSITION: 8

74 THE CLASH (214) ▲
THE CLASH

The definitive punk statement, this album's power and authority have not diminished. It assails a variety of subjects; unemployment, imperialism and rebellion, deriding or lauding according to political stance. Joe Strummer's barking vocals expressed the anger of a disenfranchised generation, guitarist Mick Jones punctuating his ire with near telepathic precision. Almost every track is essential and in tackling Junior Murvin's 'Police And Thieves', the Clash show an empathy for reggae rarely heard in white rock. 'London's Burning' still manages to evoke 70s complacency in Britain, and is still relevant today.

● TRACKS: Janie Jones; Remote Control; I'm So Bored With The USA; White Riot; Hate And War; What's My Name; Deny; London's Burning; Career Opportunities; Cheat; Protex Blue; Police And Thieves; 48 Hours; Garageland.

● FIRST RELEASED 1977
● UK PEAK CHART POSITION: 12
● USA PEAK CHART POSITION: 126

75 THE NOTORIOUS BYRD BROTHERS (133) ▲
THE BYRDS

Building on the maturity of their previous effort *Younger Than Yesterday*, the Byrds delivered a suite of songs that naturally flow into one another with uncanny ease. It is one of the few vinyl releases where both sides would always be played, and 30 years later it begs to be heard uninterrupted, as played individually, the songs lose their power. This was an artistic triumph and a commercial disappointment, as the memory of Crosby faded only to be replaced (allegedly) by a horse on the album sleeve. The Byrds moved on to their country phase and numerous line-ups but they were never to sound so perfect again. The expanded CD reissue is magnificent.

● TRACKS: *Artificial Energy; Goin' Back; Natural Harmony; Draft Morning; Wasn't Born To Follow; Get To You; Change Is Now; Old John Robertson; Tribal Gathering; Dolphins' Smile; Space Odyssey.*

● FIRST RELEASED 1968
● UK PEAK CHART POSITION: 12
● USA PEAK CHART POSITION: 47

76 TUBULAR BELLS (220) ▲
MIKE OLDFIELD

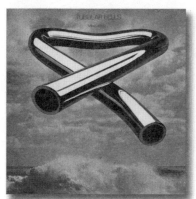

Still a firm favourite of the class of 1973, which was given a huge lease of life in 1993 with the dreaded sequel/new version. The aphorism of 'the original is always the best' can be applied here, as Virgin Records V2001 set Richard Branson down a very lucrative road. There is no denying that it is an excellent piece of instrumental music. The inspired choice of using Viv Stanshall as the orchestra master gives the album greater strength. Studying the credits we are reminded that Edgar Broughton's brother Steve plays drums. Oldfield, meanwhile, plays every instrument he can put his hands on.

● TRACKS: *Tubular Bells Part I; Tubular Bells Part II.*

● FIRST RELEASED 1973
● UK PEAK CHART POSITION: 1
● USA PEAK CHART POSITION: 3

77 BAT OUT OF HELL (90) ▲
MEAT LOAF

Pomp and circumstance of the grandest order for the multi-platinum Meat Loaf and his songwriting mentor, Jim Steinman. The grandiose intro to the title track was indication enough of the tone of the album, with songs stretching out over what at times seemed like musical infinity. Steinman set his songs in evocative wastelands populated by full orchestras and small-town weirdos, 'Paradise By The Dashboard Light' an entire two-handed play in itself, and 'Two Out Of Three Ain't Bad', an overblown symphony of regret and unrequited love. Between them, they pretty much provided the balance of the album. A huge success, only to be repeated by its follow-up in 1993.

● TRACKS: *Bat Out Of Hell; You Took The Words Right Out Of My Mouth; Heaven Can Wait; All Revved Up With No Place To Go; Two Out Of Three Ain't Bad; Paradise By The Dashboard Light, For Cryin' Out Loud.*

● FIRST RELEASED 1977
● UK PEAK CHART POSITION: 9
● USA PEAK CHART POSITION: 14

78 LEFTISM (–) ▲
LEFTFIELD

With *Leftism*, Leftfield made the crossover of techno into the pop mainstream two years before the likes of the Chemical Brothers. Embarking on a series of high-profile collaborations, they introduced to the charts a musical manifesto that had been popular in the clubs for years - including ambient ('Song Of Life'), pure techno, ragga, African tribal chants ('Afro-Left') and the all-important remix. The pumping, snarling 'Open Up', featuring John Lydon, predated the Prodigy in its blend of punk and dance, and 'Original', with Curve's Toni Halliday, ironically inspired a multitude of imitators. Most of these tracks have become ubiquitous through mainstream television and film, and it is easy to forget that, before Leftfield, techno music had only rarely stepped outside clubland.

● TRACKS: *Release The Pressure; Afro-Left; Melt; Song Of Life; Original; Black Flute; Space Shanty; Inspection (Check One); Storm 3000; Open Up; 21st Century Poem.*

● FIRST RELEASED 1995
● UK PEAK POSITION: 3
● USA PEAK POSITION: did not chart

79 PURPLE RAIN (44) ▼
PRINCE AND THE REVOLUTION

A soundtrack to a movie so appalling that it is infinitely wiser to let the record stand on its own merits. While Prince cavorted in purple kitchen foil and rode his Harley in high heels, the real star of the film, the music, was doing all the talking. A knit of funk and rock, a heavily stylized Hendrix guitar lick here and there, and a wilfully danceable backbeat all made for a huge commercial smash, and the first real international introduction for many people to a star-in-waiting. 'Darling Nikki' accidentally set the PMRC ball rolling, but the heady lilt of the title track and the crushing 'When Doves Cry' can pardon him that.

● TRACKS: *Let's Go Crazy; Take Me With U; The Beautiful Ones; Computer Blue; Darling Nikki; When Doves Cry; I Would Die 4 U; Baby I'm A Star; Purple Rain.*

● FIRST RELEASED 1984
● UK PEAK CHART POSITION: 7
● USA PEAK CHART POSITION: 1

80 LEGEND (29) ▼
BOB MARLEY

Although reggae is still perceived as a minor specialist genre, when it hits the button right, the music captures the hearts of the masses. Marley is a giant similar to Elvis Presley: both continue to sell vast numbers of records long after their deaths, and both are clear leaders of their respective genres. This album is the most perfect selection of hits. The running order is unbeatable, each track is made for the next. There is a superb four-CD box set available for serious collectors, but for those who want to put on a CD at any time of the day this will always hit the spot.

● TRACKS: *Is This Love; Jamming; No Woman No Cry; Stir It Up; Get Up And Stand Up; Satisfy My Soul; I Shot The Sheriff; One Love; People Get Ready; Buffalo Soldier; Exodus; Redemption Song; Could You Be Loved; Want More.*

● FIRST RELEASED 1984
● UK PEAK CHART POSITION: 1
● USA PEAK CHART POSITION: 54

81 A NORTHERN SOUL (–) ▲
THE VERVE

Although a fine album in its own right, the popularity of *A Northern Soul* probably owes much to the huge success of *Urban Hymns* in 1997/8. A collection of swirling, grand epics and expansive landscapes, it is more sprawling, and, many fans would argue, more inspired than its tighter, commercial successor. Richard Ashcroft's lyrics are undoubtedly less oblique than on the group's debut, *A Storm In Heaven*. The album's highlight is 'History', with its fluid guitar and crafted strings. A worthy, if rambling, record, it is significant both musically and as an indication of the group's imminent dissolution, prior to their triumphant return two years later.

● TRACKS: *New Decade; This Is Music; On Your Own; So It Goes; Northern Soul; Brainstorm; Interlude; Drive You Home; History; No Knock On My Door; Life's An Ocean; Stormy Clouds; Reprise.*

● FIRST RELEASED 1995
● UK PEAK POSITION: 13
● USA PEAK POSITION: did not chart

82 GRACE (–) ▲
JEFF BUCKLEY

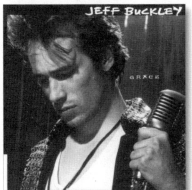

Buckley's tragic death means there will now never be an official follow-up to this astonishing album, which has already gained classic status four years on from its release. On *Grace* Buckley played up to his heartbroken troubadour image, but managed to avoid cliché by virtue of the seductive power of his multi-octave voice and a remarkably assured grasp of song structure. The album's three cover versions ('Lilac Wine', 'Hallelujah' and 'Corpus Christi Carol') showcase Buckley's ability to make a song his own, but they pale beside the inventiveness of his own material. On the title track and 'So Real', his music achieved a perfection that was staggering for a debut album.

● TRACKS: *Mojo Pin; Grace; Last Goodbye; Lilac Wine; So Real; Hallelujah; Lover, You Should've Come Over; Corpus Christi Carol; Eternal Life; Dream Brother.*

● FIRST RELEASED 1994
● UK PEAK CHART POSITION: did not chart
● USA PEAK CHART POSITION: 149

83 TEN (124) ▲
PEARL JAM

Formed from the ashes of Seattle's Band-Most-Likely-To, Mother Love Bone, who quietly fell to pieces after the untimely overdose of vocalist Andrew Wood, Stone Gossard and Jeff Ament unearthed vocalist Eddie Vedder and rescued him from a job as an all-night petrol pump attendant. The result was a most curious multi-platinum album that, like its predecessor's attempts, drew on 70s rock as a major influence. Vedder's lyrical insights were as beguiling as they were obtuse; however, they captured a disenchanted nation's imagination and success came running.

● TRACKS: *Once; Even Flow; Alive; Why Go; Black; Jeremy; Oceans; Porch; Garden; Deep; Release; Master; Slave.*

● FIRST RELEASED 1992
● UK PEAK CHART POSITION: 18
● USA PEAK CHART POSITION: 2

84 IN UTERO (83) ▼
NIRVANA

F ollowing his final act of self-destruction, Cobain will probably assume Morrison-like status, which is a little out of balance since the band have only three proper albums under their belt compared with the Doors' output. Taken as a rock band, they were the phenomenon of the 90s, both important and successful. Their penchant for romanticizing death is being followed with Pied Piper regularity. Their ability to shock was far better than any of the new wave followers. It was only the troubled Cobain who could write songs such as 'Rape Me' (an anti-rape song!) and 'Heart-Shaped Box' with real conviction.

● TRACKS: *Serve The Servants; Scentless Apprentice; Heart-Shaped Box; Rape Me; Frances Farmer Will Have Her Revenge On Seattle; Dumb; Very Ape; Milk It; Pennyroyal Tea; Radio Friendly Unit Shifter; Tourette's; All Apologies; Gallons Of Rubbing Alcohol Flow Through The Strip.*

● FIRST RELEASED 1993
● UK PEAK CHART POSITION: 1
● USA PEAK CHART POSITION: 1

85 DEBUT (539) ▲
BJÖRK

O ne of the most pleasingly quizzical and quite unexpected first albums. Although Björk's animated meanderings with the Sugarcubes hinted at a deeply singular approach to songwriting, the depth and inventiveness employed on *Debut* went far beyond what had been imagined or expected. Bringing new meaning to the word unorthodox, the record offered gems such as 'There's More To Life Than This', recorded live in the toilet of a club, replete with slamming doors. Meanwhile, the fragility of the human condition was expounded on in reflections on love and sex, each point wonderfully adorned by the rise and fall of her yearning vocal. A true delight.

● TRACKS: *Human Behaviour; Crying; Venus As A Boy; There's More To Life Than This; Like Someone In Love; Big Time Sensuality; One Day; Aeroplane; Come To Me; Violently Happy; The Anchor Song; Play Dead.*

● FIRST RELEASED 1993
● UK PEAK CHART POSITION: 3
● USA PEAK CHART POSITION: 61

86 DIG YOUR OWN HOLE (–) ▲
CHEMICAL BROTHERS

P roclaimed as the future of rock music, the Chemical Brothers broke out of clubland and into the mainstream with this album of electronica *extraordinaire*. Already kings of the funky breakbeat, infectious hook and imaginative sample, on *Dig Your Own Hole* Tom Rowlands and Ed Simons refined the formula to near-perfection. The Schoolly D-inspired 'Block Rockin' Beats' kicks off the whole in bold fashion; Oasis's Noel Gallagher does a star turn on the hypnotic 'Setting Sun'; the lovely 'Where Do I Begin?', featuring Beth Orton, brings down the mood; and the stunning 'Private Psychedelic Reel', layered with sitars and drum loops, ends the breathtaking journey. This album defied anyone not to get up and dance.

● TRACKS: *Block Rockin' Beats; Dig Your Own Hole; Elektrobank; Piku; Setting Sun; It Doesn't Matter; Don't Stop The Rock; Get Up On It Like This; Lost In The K-Hole; Where Do I Begin?; Private Psychedelic Reel.*

● FIRST RELEASED 1997
● UK PEAK POSITION: 1 ● USA PEAK CHART POSITION: 14

87 A NIGHT AT THE OPERA (164) ▲
QUEEN

The album that gave the world the inimitable 'Bohemian Rhapsody', and its pioneering video, is still a record that possesses every aspect of a true and timeless classic. Queen's sheer inventiveness, collective contribution and the original verve and displays of ingenuity that they brought to this album were immense, with the dramatic and quite theatrical strut of 'Death On Two Legs (Dedicated To...)', the graceful 'Love Of My Life', and the ritz and panache of 'I'm In Love With My Car'. Without measure, equal, or boundaries. Every home should have one. The finest Queen album without a shadow of doubt.

● TRACKS: *Death On Two Legs (Dedicated To...); Lazing On A Sunday Afternoon; You're My Best Friend; I'm In Love With My Car; Sweet Lady; Seaside Rendezvous; Good Company; '39; The Prophet's Song; Love Of My Life; Bohemian Rhapsody; God Save The Queen.*

● FIRST RELEASED 1975
● UK PEAK CHART POSITION: 1
● USA PEAK CHART POSITION: 4

88 HORSES (805) ▲
PATTI SMITH

Poet/playwright Patti Smith embraced rock as a critic and performer during New York punk's formative era. These different elements gelled to startling effect on *Horses*, which attacked preconceptions and declared innovation to great effect. Her untutored voice provides raw realism while a refusal to compromise took music into uncharted territory. Smith's splicing together of her own 'Horses' to the standard 'Land Of 1000 Dances' simultaneously declared pop history and its future. John Cale's production inevitably suggests comparisons with the Velvet Underground, but despite a sense of shared commitment, Smith's music is powerful and exciting on its own terms. Few debut albums are as intense or as fully formed.

● TRACKS: *Gloria (In Excelsis Deo); Redondo Beach; Birdland; Free Money; Kimberly; Break It Up; Land: Horses - Land Of A 1000 Dances - La Mer; Elegie.*

● FIRST RELEASED 1975
● UK PEAK CHART POSITION: did not chart
● USA PEAK CHART POSITION: 47

89 BROTHERS IN ARMS (68) ▼
DIRE STRAITS

The album most critics hate to love. Mark Knopfler's multi-million seller was the success story of the 80s in the same way that *Dark Side Of The Moon* was in the 70s. Those who doubt its greatness argue that it was not a patch on the debut album, *Love Over Gold*, or *Making Movies* a few years later. The public clearly disagreed and it continues be a steady seller. The dangerously overrated and overplayed 'Money For Nothing' and 'Walk Of Life' were perfect songs for 80s mainstream formatted rock radio. Yet it was the undeniable beauty of Knopfler's playing on tracks such as 'Brothers In Arms' that give some credence to its phenomenal success.

● TRACKS: *So Far Away; Money For Nothing; Walk Of Life; Your Latest Trick; Why Worry?; Ride Across The River; The Man's Too Strong; One World; Brothers In Arms.*

● FIRST RELEASED 1985
● UK PEAK CHART POSITION: 1
● USA PEAK CHART POSITION: 1

90 DOOLITTLE (511) ▲
PIXIES

The album that brought the Pixies commercial acclaim did so without self-sacrifice. Hammered chords, twisting melodies and obtuse lyrics still abound, pulled together and given new purpose by Gil Norton's incisive production. Black Francis and Kim Deal share the vocal spoils, imbuing the content with contrasting textures. The raw anger of 'Debaser' is offset by the aurally sweet 'Monkey Gone To Heaven', while elsewhere, dynamite tunes confirm a collective love of pop. Where later releases showed increasing schizophrenia, *Doolittle* fully captures the Pixies' unified zeal.

● TRACKS: *Debaser; Tame; Wave Of Mutilation; I Bleed; Here Comes Your Man; Dead; Monkey Gone To Heaven; Mr. Grieves; Crackity Jones; La La Love You; No. 13 Baby; There Goes My Gun; Hey; Silver; Gouge Away.*

● FIRST RELEASED 1989
● UK PEAK CHART POSITION: 8
● USA PEAK CHART POSITION: 98

91 BRINGING IT ALL BACK HOME (150) ▲
BOB DYLAN

Howls of rage greeted Dylan as he presented the world with folk rock - he was roundly booed at both the Newport Folk Festival and the Royal Albert Hall. Yet here is one of those moments of cross-influence that changed the course of popular music. *Bringing It All Back Home* gave His Bobness an audience on a plate; it was a massive breakthrough. An album of two different sides, acoustic (his past) and electric (his future), the music - covered a thousandfold - has among it 'Maggie's Farm', 'Subterranean Home Sick Blues', 'Mr. Tambourine Man', 'Love Minus Zero', and the cosmopolitan political speak of 'It's Alright, Ma.' You can debate the 'is it folk or is it rock' argument for ever. It is irrelevant, it is merely Dylan at one of his many peaks.

● TRACKS: *Subterranean Homesick Blues; She Belongs To Me; Maggie's Farm; Love Minus Zero - No Limit; Outlaw Blues; On The Road Again; Bob Dylan's 115th Dream; Mr. Tambourine Man; Gates Of Eden; It's Alright Ma (I'm Only Bleeding); It's All Over Now, Baby Blue.*

● FIRST RELEASED 1965
● UK PEAK CHART POSITION: 1　● USA PEAK CHART POSITION: 6

92 HARVEST (115) ▲
NEIL YOUNG

Only after the release of *Harvest Moon* in 1993 did the Young aficionados reluctantly admit that this was a superlative album in deference to the depressing *Tonight's The Night* and symbolic *On The Beach*. Young knew he had a winner when he recorded it, and revisited it 20 years later. Using the Stray Gators as his foils and even recording two tracks in Barking Town Hall, Essex, Young sounds wonderfully old before his time. Introspective and pleading, he has to remind listeners in 'Old Man' that he is 'twenty-four and there's so much more'; well over 24 more glorious albums, 29 to be precise.

● TRACKS: *Out On The Weekend; Harvest; A Man Needs A Maid; Heart Of Gold; Are You Ready For The Country?; Old Man; There's A World; Alabama; The Needle And The Damage Done; Words (Between The Lines Of Age).*

● FIRST RELEASED 1972
● UK PEAK CHART POSITION: 1
● USA PEAK CHART POSITION: 1

93 NEW ADVENTURES IN HI-FI (–) ▲
R.E.M.

The deeper you dig in a goldmine, the better the quality of the gold. This is R.E.M.'s secret gem, an album of rich songs that has been overlooked by the record-buying public at large. Low-key production, gentle themes and Michael Stipe's crystal-clear vocals grace great compositions such as 'E-Bow The Letter', 'Electrolite', 'So Fast, So Numb' and the simple but glorious 'Be Mine'. Like so much of the band's work, there was virtually nothing to fault, even if, equally, there was nothing that was truly innovative. The latter, irrelevant concern has arguably prejudiced critics against this album, which it is hoped will gain credibility as its true greatness is discovered.

● TRACKS: *How The West Was Won And Where It Got Us; The Wake-Up Bomb; New Test Leper; Undertow; E-Bow The Letter; Leave; Departure; Bittersweet Me; Be Mine; Binky The Doormat; Zither; So Fast, So Numb; Low Desert; Electrolite.*

● FIRST RELEASED 1996
● UK PEAK CHART POSITION: 1
● USA PEAK CHART POSITION: 2

94 OLDER (–) ▲
GEORGE MICHAEL

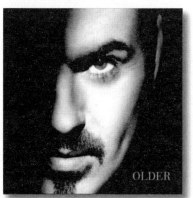

After his agonizing litigation with Sony, Michael could have gone under. He had put his recorded career on ice for some time, and pop is fickle and disloyal. *Older* was preceded by the single 'Jesus To A Child', which, although a substantial hit, disappointed. Over the past two years this track has grown as a song that has seeped into the consciousness. Together with the rest of the album, it has taken a while, but it is now seen as a very fine record. Michael is better at the slow ballads like 'Older' and 'To Be Forgiven', but 'Fastlove' brings back strong memories of that fresh-faced lad performing with whassisname in Wham! Michael is here for the long haul.

● TRACKS: *Jesus To A Child; Fastlove; Older; Spinning The Wheel; It Doesn't Really Matter; The Strangest Thing; To Be Forgiven; Move On; Star People; You Have Been Loved; Free.*

● FIRST RELEASED 1996
● UK PEAK CHART POSITION: 1
● USA PEAK CHART POSITION: 6

95 YOUNGER THAN YESTERDAY (148) ▲
THE BYRDS

With this album the Byrds proclaimed fully their musical genius. Distinctive three-part harmonies and chiming 12-string guitars affirmed the quartet's unique sound as a succession of superior compositions embraced folk, pop and country styles. Beguiling melodies nestled alongside experiment as the principals asserted an individuality while remaining aware of the strength of the whole. The acerbic wit of 'So You Wanna Be A Rock 'n' Roll Star' showed a group aware of commercial entrapment. On this set the Byrds rejected such advances and offered a beautiful altruism. Every individual song on this set has managed to grow in stature, especially those by Crosby and Hillman.

● TRACKS: *So You Want To Be A Rock 'N' Roll Star; Have You Seen Her Face; CTA-102; Renaissance Fair; Time Between; Everybody's Been Burned; Thoughts And Words; Mind Gardens; My Back Pages; The Girl With No Name; Why.*

● FIRST RELEASED 1967
● UK PEAK CHART POSITION: 37
● USA PEAK CHART POSITION: 24

96 **SUEDE** (228) ▲
SUEDE

Suede played intellectual high jinks with this, their debut album, employing provocative lyrics, a weighty, unknowing sexuality and the pointed angst of troubled teenagers the world over. The clever lure of their androgynous artwork combined tellingly with Brett Anderson's teasing flamboyance and dedicated (some might say studied) David Bowie air. However, they would have remained a one trick pony were it not for their stirring ability to put together some unashamedly great singles and adapt a host of subtle mood swings and arrangements that took Anderson's vocals to soaring new heights. Another bedsitter classic for indie lovers.

● TRACKS: *So Young; Animal Nitrate; She's Not Dead; Moving; Pantomime Horse; The Drowners; Sleeping Pills; Breakdown; Metal Mickey; Animal Lover; The Next Life.*

● FIRST RELEASED 1992
● UK PEAK CHART POSITION: 1
● USA PEAK CHART POSITION: did not chart

97 **SONGS FOR SWINGING LOVERS** (22) ▲
FRANK SINATRA

The most familiar Sinatra album and one that captured a generation of music lovers in the 50s; it is unquestionably his most perfect work. No album could begin to encapsulate quality lounge pop more than this. Quite apart from his graceful vocals, the orchestral arrangements are immaculate and crisp 40 years later. The band, conducted by Nelson Riddle, gave Sinatra such space and freedom that he was able to make already established songs his own. The 15 songs contained on this record should serve to educate élitists that pop music has to swing before it rocks. Nobody should be too proud to have this indispensable record in their collection.

● TRACKS: *You Make Me Feel So Young; It Happened In Monterey; You're Getting To Be A Habit With Me; You Brought A New Kind of Love To Me; Too Marvellous For Words; Old Devil Moon; Pennies From Heaven; Love Is Here To Stay; I've Got You Under My Skin; I Thought About You; We'll Be Together Again; Makin' Whoopee; Swingin' Down The Lane; Anything Goes; How About You;*

● FIRST RELEASED 1958
● UK PEAK CHART POSITION: 8 ● USA PEAK CHART POSITION: 2

98 **LITTLE EARTHQUAKES** (–) ▲
TORI AMOS

With this debut, Tori Amos rose above the inevitable Kate Bush/Joni Mitchell comparisons, producing a stunning set of brutally honest and emotionally wrought songs. A skilled and imaginative pianist, Amos also proved a versatile vocalist, moving from whisper to scream in an instant. She concentrates on intimate stories of her religious upbringing, childhood traumas, and predominantly, sex, self-discovery and unhappy relationships. 'Silent All These Years' was the first to hit a nerve with the public on single release, but all the tracks - memories of her father in 'Winter', the bittersweet 'Happy Phantom', the harrowing account of her own rape, 'Me And A Gun' - combine to make this inspiring, if rarely comfortable, listening.

● TRACKS: *Crucify; Girl; Silent All These Years; Precious Things; Winter; Happy Phantom; China; Leather; Mother; Tear In Your Hand; Me And A Gun; Little Earthquakes.*

● FIRST RELEASED 1992
● UK PEAK POSITION: 14
● USA PEAK POSITION: 54

99 SIAMESE DREAM (-) ▲
SMASHING PUMPKINS

The hardness of the grunge guitar and metal drums of the Pumpkins are always tempered by an incredibly mellow and soft centre. Corgan has a fantastic ability to find great chords to put in sequence, as in the opening track 'Cherub Rock'. This album received a new lease of life following the huge success of the *Mellon Collie* album. All the signs were here of a monster in the making. 'Quiet' is a joy and 'Hummer' has some wonderful peaks and troughs. Has anybody else ever noticed the incredible similarity in style between guitarist James Iha and the late Randy California of Spirit?

● TRACKS: *Cherub Rock; Quiet; Today; Hummer; Rocket; Disarm; Soma; Geek USA; Mayonaise; Spaceboy; Silverfuck; Sweet Sweet; Luna.*

● FIRST RELEASED 1993
● UK PEAK CHART POSITION: 4
● USA PEAK CHART POSITION: 89

100 PABLO HONEY (-) ▲
RADIOHEAD

Before the breakthrough that was *The Bends* and the colossal *OK Computer*, there was the quietly magnificent *Pablo Honey*. 'Creep' was the surprise hit single in the UK, but even that gave scant indication of how 'fuckin' special' this band would become. Benefiting from a raw production, the debut was undoubtedly less slick and accomplished than subsequent work, although Thom Yorke's vulnerable but impressive vocal styling was already in place on songs such as 'Stop Whispering'. Many of the compositions were somewhat simplistic, but in terms of musical maturity Radiohead were clearly years ahead of their time. An indispensable album, it should not be parted from its two big brothers.

● TRACKS: *You; Creep; How Do You?; Stop Whispering; Thinking About You; Anyone Can Play Guitar; Ripcord; Vegetable; Prove Yourself; I Can't; Lurgee; Blow Out.*

● FIRST RELEASED 1993
● UK PEAK CHART POSITION: 25
● USA PEAK CHART POSITION: 32

101 SPICE (–) ▲
SPICE GIRLS

If the column inches of Spice Girl press were placed end to end, they would encircle the world 18,000 times. Such was their power, and they did capture most people's attention, and many of their hearts. This album of pure pop has not one track less than great and it harks back to the days when children, grannies, milkmen and window-cleaners were all singing the Beatles' 'She Loves You'. This group of feisty women brought about girl power, but mostly they brought a smile back to angst-ridden pop music. 'Wannabe' and '2 Become 1' are classics of the art.

● TRACKS: *Wannabe; Say You'll Be There; 2 Become 1; Love Thing; Last Time Lover; Mama; Who Do Think You Are; Something Kinda Funny; Naked; If U Can't Dance.*

● FIRST RELEASED 1996
● UK PEAK CHART POSITION: 1
● USA PEAK CHART POSITION: 1

102 TAPESTRY (183) ▲
CAROLE KING

During the 60s Carole King was renowned for composing a succession of classic pop songs. A low-key recording career blossomed with the release of this album which successfully married this skill with the contemporary singer-songwriter movement. *Tapestry* is comprised of self-penned material and collaborations with either ex-husband Gerry Goffin or lyricist Toni Stern. King's unfussy vocal style enhances the simply stated yet astute material and in 'It's Too Late' the singer expresses the breakdown of a relationship with percipient incisiveness. Such skill ensures the album's lasting popularity.

● TRACKS: *I Feel The Earth Move; So Far Away; It's Too Late; Home Again; Beautiful; Way Over Yonder; You've Got A Friend; Where You Lead; Will You Love Me Tomorrow; Smackwater Jack; Tapestry; (You Make Me Feel Like) A Natural Woman.*

● FIRST RELEASED 1971
● UK PEAK CHART POSITION: 4
● USA PEAK CHART POSITION: 1

103 MARQUEE MOON (467) ▲
TELEVISION

New York's 70s punk was markedly different to that of Britain. Rather than reject the past, American groups deconstructed its forms and rebuilt them with recourse to the music's strengths. Television's leader, Tom Verlaine, professed admiration for Moby Grape and the folk rock of early Fairport Convention. Elements of the latter appear on this album's title track, which offers a thrilling instrumental break, built upon a modal scale. Verlaine's shimmering guitar style provides the set's focus, but his angular compositions are always enthralling. A sense of brooding mystery envelops the proceedings, and *Marquee Moon* retains its standing as one of the era's pivotal releases.

● TRACKS: *See No Evil; Venus; Friction; Marquee Moon; Elevation; Guiding Light; Prove It; Torn Curtain.*

● FIRST RELEASED 1977
● UK PEAK CHART POSITION: 28
● USA PEAK CHART POSITION: did not chart

104 IMAGINE (66) ▼
JOHN LENNON

Lennon's solo debut, although powerful, did not have the universal appeal of this album. Lennon veered from spitting anger in 'How Do You Sleep?', 'Give Me Some Truth' and cruel humour with 'Crippled Inside', yet the man was capable of intense romanticism as highlighted in 'Jealous Guy' and 'Oh My Love'. Those who resented John for being part of the Beatles break-up finally forgave him and began to love him again with this collection. The title track will stand as a classic of popular song and one that should be made part of the national curriculum, let alone the new national anthem.

● TRACKS: *Imagine; Crippled Inside; Jealous Guy; It's So Hard; I Don't Want To Be A Soldier; Give Me Some Truth; Oh My Love; How Do You Sleep?; How?; Oh Yoko!.*

● FIRST RELEASED 1971
● UK PEAK CHART POSITION: 1
● USA PEAK CHART POSITION: 1

105 LED ZEPPELIN II (26) ▼
LED ZEPPELIN

Having declared an individual brand of blues rock on their debut album, Led Zeppelin significantly expanded musical horizons on its successor. The opening riff to 'Whole Lotta Love' declared a strength of purpose and excitement and the song quickly achieved anthem-like proportions. *Led Zeppelin II* personifies the entire heavy metal spectrum, from guitar hero to virile vocalist. Sexual metaphor ('The Lemon Song') collides with musical dexterity ('Moby Dick') and the faintest whiff of sword and sorcery to create one of the most emphatic and celebratory heavy rock albums.

● TRACKS: *Whole Lotta Love; What Is And What Should Never Be; The Lemon Song; Thank You; Heartbreaker; Livin' Lovin' Maid (She's Just A Woman); Ramble On; Moby Dick; Bring It On Home.*

● FIRST RELEASED 1969
● UK PEAK CHART POSITION: 1
● USA PEAK CHART POSITION: 1

106 BEGGARS BANQUET (24) ▼
THE ROLLING STONES

The Rolling Stones emerged into the post-flower power age with this declamatory selection. Producer Jimmy Miller was instrumental in rekindling a musical power that possessed renewed forcefulness and focus. R&B remained rooted at the group's core - their reading of Robert Wilkins' 'Prodigal Son' is enthralling - while menace and anger ooze from what remain some of their finest compositions. Lascivious, malevolent, even politically impotent, they articulate a group freed from indecision and assured of direction. Their career as 'the world's greatest rock 'n' roll band' began with this release.

● TRACKS: *Sympathy For The Devil; No Expectations; Dear Doctor; Parachute Woman; Jig-Saw Puzzle; Street Fighting Man; Prodigal Son; Stray Cat Blues; Factory Girl; Salt Of The Earth.*

● FIRST RELEASED 1968
● UK PEAK CHART POSITION: 3
● USA PEAK CHART POSITION: 5

107 STICKY FINGERS (11) ▼
THE ROLLING STONES

The cheek and arrogance of the Stones came of age with this work, complete with zip-fly cover and 'up yours' tongue and lips. Crushing any doubts that they had gone soft with *Satanic Majesties*, the guitars of Keef and Mick Taylor rocked together while Jagger spat out some of his foxiest lyrics. Never had they sounded so loose, yet so together, with examples such as 'Bitch', 'Sister Morphine', the country-tinged 'Wild Horses' and the perennial 'Brown Sugar'. Downright dirty rock 'n' roll like this has still to be bettered and there is, as yet, no rival in sight.

● TRACKS: *Brown Sugar; Sway; Wild Horses; Can't You Hear Me Knocking; You Gotta Move; Bitch; I Got The Blues; Sister Morphine; Dead Flowers; Moonlight Mile.*

● FIRST RELEASED 1971
● UK PEAK CHART POSITION: 1
● USA PEAK CHART POSITION: 1

108 IN IT FOR THE MONEY (–) ▲
SUPERGRASS

Eagerly awaited by both fans and critics, *In It For The Money* was an energetic and accomplished second album that inexplicably failed to make a great impact with the record-buying public. Like their debut, virtually every track was worthy of single release, and the singles themselves, notably the blistering punk of 'Richard III' and the classy brass arrangements of 'Going Out', were outstanding. Never afraid of slowing down the pace at the right moment, ballads such as 'It's Not Me' were as impressive as the rockers. Humorous and imaginative throughout, revealing a remarkable grasp of melody and knack for hooklines, Supergrass promise much in the long haul of British pop music.

● TRACKS: *In It For The Money; Richard III; Tonight; Late In The Day; G-Song; Sun Hits The Sky; Going Out; It's Not Me; Cheapskate; You Can See Me; Hollow Little Reign; Sometimes I Make You Sad.*

● FIRST RELEASED 1997
● UK PEAK CHART POSITION: 1
● USA PEAK CHART POSITION: did not chart

109 ALL MOD CONS (678) ▲
THE JAM

Tagged punk by default, the Jam preferred 60s iconography, particularly the Mod movement, to the rattle of safety-pins. However, if the uniform was different, the sense of commitment was identical, and on *All Mod Cons*, the trio fused references and individuality. The spectres of the Who and Kinks remained, but songwriter Paul Weller restructured such influences to proclaim his own voice. Thus, a version of the latter's 'David Watts' introduces intent, rather than summarizing it and the set successfully explores several avenues postulated by the Jam's craft. Social comment, personal reflection and assured musicianship bind the album into a cohesive whole and laid down the contrasting paths the group members would later follow.

● TRACKS: *All Mod Cons; To Be Someone (Didn't We have A Nice Time); Mr. Clean; David Watts; English Rose; In The Crowd; Billy Hunt; It's Too Bad; Fly; The Place I Love; 'A' Bomb In Wardour Street; Down In The Tube Station At Midnight.*

● FIRST RELEASED 1978
● UK PEAK CHART POSITION: 6
● USA PEAK CHART POSITION: did not chart

110 HIS 'N' HERS (–) ▲
PULP

Pulp's breakthrough album arrived after an unbelievably long haul, and then Jarvis Cocker was suddenly sharing front pages of music magazines with Liam and Damon. Here, the songs explored now-familiar Pulp territory, social class, seedy sexual encounters, voyeurism ('Babies'), bad sex ('you bought a toy that can reach the places he never goes'), good sex, and lots more sex, all blessed with Cocker's humorous, touching and, conversely, often innocent lyrical observations. Capable of writing almost unbearably tender love songs and laments for wasted lives ('your hair is a mess and your eyes are just holes in your face'), Cocker's honesty and insight were distilled to perfection in the wonderful 'Do You Remember The First Time'.

● TRACKS: *Joyriders; Lipgloss; Acrylic Afternoons; Have You Seen Her Lately?; Babies; She's A Lady; Happy Endings; Do You Remember The First Time?; Pink Glove; Someone Like The Moon; David's Last Summer.*

● FIRST RELEASED 1994
● UK PEAK CHART POSITION: 9
● USA PEAK CHART POSITION: did not chart

111 UNKNOWN PLEASURES (493) ▲
JOY DIVISION

Joy Division's music inhabits an eerie, twilight world. Decay and alienation envelop singer Ian Curtis, whose cavernous, but dispassionate, voice belied the intensity he brought to bear. Rolling drum patterns, thudding bass lines and uncluttered synthesizer combine to create a dank, brooding atmosphere, chillingly supporting the songs' bleak lyrics. Yet listening to *Unknown Pleasures* is not a depressing experience. The group generate a terse excitement, emphasizing individual strengths and avoiding unnecessary embellishment. Their sense of commitment is utterly convincing and few debut albums can boast such unremitting power.

● TRACKS: *Disorder; Day Of The Lords; Candidate; Insight; New Dawn Fades; She's Lost Control; Shadow Play; Wilderness; Interzone; I Remember Nothing.*

● FIRST RELEASED 1979
● UK PEAK CHART POSITION: 71
● USA PEAK CHART POSITION: did not chart

112 APPETITE FOR DESTRUCTION (206) ▲
GUNS N'ROSES

Already a legend in its own meagre lifetime, this startling debut shrouded itself in controversy, from its original Robert Williams artwork to Axl Rose's unblinking accounts of LA's underbelly. This mawkish storytelling, combined with a brattish collective swagger and a surprisingly mature approach to their songs, guaranteed Guns N'Roses a speedy notoriety that was to serve their legend brilliantly. From the laconic 'Paradise City' to the achingly beautiful 'Sweet Child O' Mine', or the furious 'Welcome To The Jungle', the record brims with a brutal integrity. An album they could never surpass even if they had stayed together.

● TRACKS: *Welcome To The Jungle; It's So Easy; Nightrain; Out Ta Get Me; Mr. Brownstone; Paradise City; My Michelle; Think About You; Sweet Child O' Mine; You're Crazy; Anything Goes; Rocket Queen.*

● FIRST RELEASED 1987
● UK PEAK CHART POSITION: 5
● USA PEAK CHART POSITION: 1

MOONDANCE (152) ▲
VAN MORRISON

Where on previous recordings Van Morrison had implied soul and R&B roots, on *Moondance* he set them free. He had rarely sounded so relaxed, whether on the bubbling joy of 'And It Stoned Me', the finger-popping ease of the title track or the celebratory bliss of 'Caravan'. Morrison revelled in the music's tight arrangements, clearly enjoying the punchy horn section ('Glad Tidings') and empathizing with quieter, acoustic settings ('Crazy Love'). Where *Astral Weeks* was a cathartic stream-of-consciousness, *Moondance* shows an artist enraptured by a new-found musical freedom, from this moment on everything he sang had soul.

● TRACKS: *And It Stoned Me; Moondance; Crazy Love; Caravan; Into The Mystic; Come Running; These Dreams Of You; Brand New Day; Everyone; Glad Tidings.*

● FIRST RELEASED 1970
● UK PEAK CHART POSITION: 32
● USA PEAK CHART POSITION: 29

BLOODSUGARSEXMAGIK (–) ▲
RED HOT CHILI PEPPERS

With *BloodSugarSexMagik* the Chilis produced the defining moment of funk rock and the high point of their career. Raunchy and explicit from the first, the lyrical content was not for the easily offended and frequently strayed into misogyny. Musically, it straddled metal and funk with ease; in addition to the stomping, infectious rockers ('Give It Away', 'The Power Of Equality') and the downright funky ('Mellowship Slinky', 'Apache Rose Peacock'), all underpinned by Flea's virtuosic but unselfish basslines, the band also showed themselves capable of writing surprisingly melodic ballads ('Breaking The Girl', 'Under The Bridge'). Plagued by destructive drug problems and personnel changes, the Chilis have, sadly, never since equalled the achievements of this album.

● TRACKS: *The Power Of Equality; If You Have To Ask; Breaking The Girl; Funky Monks; Suck My Kiss; I Could Have Lied; Mellowship Slinky; The Righteous & The Wicked; Give It Away; BloodSugarSexMagik; Under The Bridge; Naked In The Rain; Apache Rose Peacock; The Greeting Song; My Lovely Man; Sir Psycho Sexy; They're Red Hot.*

● FIRST RELEASED 1991
● UK PEAK CHART POSITION: 25
● USA PEAK CHART POSITION: 3

THE SMITHS (75) ▼
THE SMITHS

As great first albums go, *The Smiths* remains a perfect bedsitter moment, cultivated from a batch of Morrissey's diaries then uplifted and exonerated on Marr's guitar. Their juxtaposing of a lopsided grin of gloom and the light doodling of an almost always perfectly placed guitar was virtually unheard of. Reference points were rare, apart from Morrissey's adopted Oscar Wilde demeanour, to which the press clung with a morbid fascination. It remains a delicate set of knowing quiffs and rounded, innocent eyes, beguiling the listener with some wonderfully crafted pop - when they weren't laughing behind their hands.

● TRACKS: *Reel Around The Fountain; You've Got Everything Now; Miserable Lie; Pretty Girls Make Graves; The Hand That Rocks The Cradle; Still III; Hand In Glove; What Difference Does It Make?; I Don't Owe You Anything; Suffer Little Children.*

● FIRST RELEASED 1984
● UK PEAK CHART POSITION: 2
● USA PEAK CHART POSITION: 150

OTIS BLUE (21) ▼
OTIS REDDING

The man who bought classic soul music to the white masses at the Monterey Pop Festival died later that year, just as he was really gearing up for a creative burst that included 'Dock Of The Bay'. This is the finest of many classic Otis albums in the soul genre and an automatic recommendation for anyone's playlist. Redding could make you dance and scream and the next minute have you crying yourself to sleep, such was his wide emotional range. Compare the power of 'Respect' and 'Shake' to the passion of 'I've Been Loving You Too Long' and 'My Girl'. Untouchable.

● TRACKS: *Ole Man Trouble; Respect; Change Gonna Come; Down In The Valley; I've Been Loving You Too Long; Shake; My Girl; Wonderful World; Rock Me Baby; Satisfaction; You Don't Miss Your Water.*

● FIRST RELEASED 1966
● UK PEAK CHART POSITION: 6
● USA PEAK CHART POSITION: 75

Jackson's domination of the world record market continued following *Thriller*, although by comparison it was an almighty flop with only 12 million sales. As Pink Floyd and Dire Straits have proved, one album can go completely sales haywire without necessarily being any better. The title track and the gorgeous 'Man In The Mirror' were substantial hits, but quality material such as 'Dirty Diana' and 'Liberian Girl' bolster a strong album. Jackson also seemed to have found the romance he seeks in 'I Just Can't Stop Loving You' and 'The Way You Make Me Feel'. Regardless of his press, history clearly shows that he has made a lot of people very, very happy.

● TRACKS: *Bad; The Way You Make Me Feel; Speed Demon; Liberian Girl; Just Good Friends; Another Part Of Me; Man In The Mirror; I Just Can't Stop Loving You; Dirty Diana; Smooth Criminal.*

● FIRST RELEASED 1987
● UK PEAK CHART POSITION: 1
● USA PEAK CHART POSITION: 1

---

118 **BRYTER LAYTER** (–) ▲
NICK DRAKE

Bryter Layter is the late Drake's most fully realized album, a beautifully melancholic and moving collection of songs featuring elegantly understated backing from the likes of Richard Thompson and John Cale. Although at times a deeply disturbing record, particularly on 'Hazey Jane II' and 'Fly', the album evokes an air of wistful calm with three delicate instrumentals framing the wry wit of 'Poor Boy', the studied isolation of 'At The Chime Of A City Clock' and the aching beauty of the matchless 'Northern Sky'. Almost thirty years after it was first released, *Bryter Layter* remains one of the most beautiful records ever made.

● TRACKS: *Introduction; Hazey Jane II; At The Chime Of A City Clock; One Of These Things First; Hazey Jane I; Bryter Layter; Fly; Poor Boy; Northern Sky; Sunday.*

● FIRST RELEASED 1970
● UK PEAK CHART POSITION: did not chart
● USA PEAK CHART POSITION: did not chart

---

119 **MTV UNPLUGGED IN NEW YORK** (–) ▲
NIRVANA

Recorded in November 1993, Kurt Cobain was dead by the time this beautiful record was released, shooting himself into notoriety as rock music's most significant casualty since John Lennon. *MTV Unplugged* is the acoustic antithesis of Nirvana's studio albums, casting the net wide to take in cover versions of songs by Lead Belly, David Bowie, the Meat Puppets and the Vaselines, alongside eloquent readings of songs from all three Nirvana albums. Though Cobain's voice struggles on several of the tracks, the overall atmosphere is of an intimate and wonderfully human recording, offering little indication of the tragedy that was to follow.

● TRACKS: *About A Girl; Come As You Are; Jesus Doesn't Want Me For A Sunbeam; The Man Who Sold The World; Pennyroyal Tea; Dumb; Polly; On A Plain; Something In The Way; Plateau; Oh Me; Lake Of Fire; All Apologies; Where Did You Sleep Last Night.*

● FIRST RELEASED 1994
● UK PEAK CHART POSITION: 1
● USA PEAK CHART POSITION: 1

---

120 **LOW** (216) ▲
DAVID BOWIE

The first (*Heroes* and *Lodger* would follow) of Bowie's three Berlin albums. Living there as a semi-recluse for three years, he worked with Svengali/producer Brian Eno and the results of their collaborations helped change the face of the European mainstream. Artists such as Gary Numan, Ultravox and OMD were indebted to the sound Bowie had created with the synthesizer to build a somewhat terse wall of sound. Critically acclaimed, but a relative commercial failure, apart from the surprise 'Sound And Vision' hit single, it remains as a pertinent reminder of Bowie's ability to surprise and enlighten.

● TRACKS: *Speed Of Life; Breaking Glass; What In The World; Sound And Vision; Always Crashing In The Same Car; Be My Wife; A New Career In A New Town; Warszawa; Art Decade; Weeping Wall; Subterraneans.*

● FIRST RELEASED 1977
● UK PEAK CHART POSITION: 2
● USA PEAK CHART POSITION: 11

121 **THE WHO SELL OUT** (–) ▲
THE WHO

One of the most memorable album cover images of the 60s is of baby-faced Roger Daltrey really sitting in a bath of cold baked beans. Apart from the cover, the music encapsulates London in the swinging 60s. The segments of pirate Radio London and the corny Rotosound strings are priceless. This album was and still is much more appreciated in the USA; maybe they saw something we failed to see. The CD reissue with extra tracks certainly proves the point. The track order and editing is faultless; 'Armenia City In The Sky' is followed by the sensational acoustic guitar of 'Mary Anne With The Shaky Hand' and the opening bass note of 'I Can See For Miles' is still euphoric.

● TRACKS: *Armenia City In The Sky; Heinz Baked Beans; Mary Anne With The Shaky Hand; Odorono; Tattoo; Our Love Was; I Can See For Miles; I Can't Reach You; Medac; Relax; Silas Stingy; Sunrise; Rael 1; Rael 2; Glittering Girl; Melancholia; Someone's Coming; Jaguar; Early Morning Cold Taxi; Hall Of Mountain King; Girl's Eyes; Mary Anne With The Shaky Hand (Alternate); Glow Girl.*

● FIRST RELEASED 1967
● UK PEAK CHART POSITION: 13
● USA PEAK CHART POSITION: 48

 122 **A LOVE SUPREME** (40) ▼
JOHN COLTRANE

John Coltrane's great masterpiece and one of the most profoundly moving records in all of jazz, *A Love Supreme* was recorded in 1964 by Coltrane's classic quartet (with pianist McCoy Tyner, bassist Jimmy Garrison and drummer Elvin Jones). It is a brilliantly integrated jazz suite examining four distinct stages of spiritual development, represented by four movements entitled 'Acknowledgement', 'Resolution', 'Pursuance' and 'Psalm'. The music is intense and gripping, and builds to a head on the fast and aggressive 'Pursuance' before the beautiful and soothing 'Psalm'. *A Love Supreme* is without doubt one of the most profound statements of religious conviction to emerge in this century.

● TRACKS: *Part 1 Acknowledgement; Part 2 Resolution; Part 3 Pursuance; Part 4 Psalm.*

● FIRST RELEASED 1967
● UK PEAK CHART POSITION: did not chart
● USA PEAK CHART POSITION: did not chart

 **123** **SO** (78) ▼
PETER GABRIEL

So consolidated Gabriel's reputation as an original and exciting composer, capable of projecting sophisticated lyrics on accessible melodies. 'Sledgehammer' was a massive hit (number one in the USA), as was 'Don't Give Up', with Kate Bush's vocals adding extra pathos. 'This Is The Picture' clearly shows the slightly surreal influence of co-writer Laurie Anderson, and the whole is given flight by Daniel Lanois' impeccable production. The towering achievement, however, is 'Mercy Street', a sparely orchestrated and perfectly constructed tribute to the late poet Anne Sexton. He has so far been unable to repeat the exercise.

● TRACKS: *Red Rain; Sledgehammer; Don't Give Up; That Voice Again; In Your Eyes; Mercy Street; Big Time; We Do What We're Told; This Is The Picture.*

● FIRST RELEASED 1986
● UK PEAK CHART POSITION: 1
● USA PEAK CHART POSITION: 2

124 **INNERVISIONS** (479) ▲
STEVIE WONDER

Uplifting and rolling, continuing a sequence of outstanding albums, Stevie Wonder again stamped his seal of importance during the early 70s. More than twenty years later, 'Living For the City' does sound a bit crass, especially rhyming pollution with solution, but that is a small carp when placed against the magnificence of 'He's Misstra Know-It-All', the out-and-out cleverness of 'Too High' and the graceful 'Golden Lady'. Stevie has an amazing conception of what vision is, something we take for granted when listening to the lyrics of 'Golden Lady', for example. Quite uncanny.

● TRACKS: *Too High; Visions; Living For The City; Golden Lady; Higher Ground; Jesus Children Of America; All In Love Is Fair; Don't You Worry 'Bout A Thing; He's Misstra Know-It-All.*

● FIRST RELEASED 1973
● UK PEAK CHART POSITION: 8
● USA PEAK CHART POSITION: 4

125 HATFUL OF HOLLOW (577) ▲
THE SMITHS

A composite of radio sessions and sundry early singles, *Hatful Of Hollow* provides an alternative snapshot of the Smiths' early career. Compiled in the wake of their debut album, it exhibited all of their considerable strengths, in particular Johnny Marr's ringing, expressive guitarwork. The riff he creates on 'How Soon Is Now' is thoroughly captivating. Vocalist Morrissey's distinctive croon and solipsistic lyrics are already unique and give the group its originality. At times ironic, at others wistful (as on 'Back To The Old House'), he takes the Smiths into new areas of expression and his contrasting visions are fully expressed herein.

● TRACKS: *William, It Was Really Nothing; What Difference Does It Make?; These Things Take Time; This Charming Man; How Soon Is Now?; Handsome Devil; Hand In Glove; Still Ill; Heaven Knows I'm Miserable Now; This Night Has Opened My Eyes; You've Got Everything Now; Accept Yourself; Girl Afraid; Back To The Old House; Reel Around The Fountain; Please, Please, Please Let Me Get What I Want.*

● FIRST RELEASED 1984
● UK PEAK CHART POSITION: 2
● USA PEAK CHART POSITION: did not chart

126 CROSBY STILLS & NASH (43) ▼
CROSBY, STILLS AND NASH

This beautiful example of 'wooden music' is pining for a reappraisal after being abused by critics in recent years in favour of the more varied *Déjà Vu*. Although the badly recorded bass still booms throughout, and yes, frankly Graham Nash is a bit twee, the quality of the harmonies remains breath-taking. Three youthful men singing songs about their relationships and changing partners deserve a better press in the 90s; they were, after all, brilliant. Graham Nash's coy 'Lady Of The Island' (about Joni Mitchell), Stills' opus-like 'Suite: Judy Blue Eyes' (about Judy Collins) and a slim Crosby singing of his sadly deceased sweetheart Christine on 'Guinevere'. Be brave, it's ok to own up to loving this timeless record.

● TRACKS: *Suite: Judy Blue Eyes; Marrakesh Express; Guinevere; You Don't Have To Cry; Pre Road Downs; Wooden Ships; Lady Of The Island; Helplessly Hoping; Long Time Gone; 49 Bye Byes*

● FIRST RELEASED 1969
● UK PEAK CHART POSITION: 25
● USA PEAK CHART POSITION: 6

127 IT'S GREAT WHEN YOU'RE STRAIGHT, YEAH! (–) ▲ BLACK GRAPE

Few could have been expecting great things from ex-Happy Monday Shaun Ryder, last seen drug-addled and artistically barren when that group fizzled out unceremoniously. However, his return was glorious - harnessing the remixing talents of Danny Saber and the croaky rapping of Kermit, *It's Great...* offered an instant high for party people. Ryder's slurred rantings and nonsense lyrics seemed more at home than ever: 'A Big Day In The North' most clearly recalled the Mondays sound, but the mighty 'Reverend Black Grape', 'Kelly's Heroes' and the irresistible invitation to 'Shake Your Money' defined the funky, in-yer-face Black Grape sound.

● TRACKS: *Reverend Black Grape; In The Name Of The Father; Tramazi Parti; Kelly's Heroes; Yeah Yeah Brother; A Big Day In The North; Shake Well Before Opening; Submarine; Shake Your Money; Little Bob.*

● FIRST RELEASED 1995
● UK PEAK POSITION: 1
● USA PEAK POSITION: did not chart

128 FUN HOUSE (427) ▲
THE STOOGES

The Stooges' minimalist approach to rock erupted fully on this, their second album. Simple riffs and splattered chords echo primitive R&B and provide a basic framework over which vocalist Iggy Pop tore the notion of 'singer' apart. Impulsive yelps and orgasmic moans punctuate a delivery that thrills and surprises in equal measure. Conventional structure disintegrates as the set progresses, culminating in the mayhem of a cacophonous finale into which recent addition, saxophonist Steve Mackay, adds a stream of notes implicit of Bedlam. Deranged yet free, *Fun House* destroyed preconceptions of 60s music and prepared a path for 70s punk.

● TRACKS: *Down On The Street; Loose; TV Eye; Dirt; 1970; Fun House; LA Blues.*

● FIRST RELEASED 1970
● UK PEAK CHART POSITION: did not chart
● USA PEAK CHART POSITION: did not chart

129 MAXINQUAYE (–) ▲
TRICKY

Tricky made a low-key entrance onto the music scene as a guest vocalist on Massive Attack's 1991 classic *Blue Lines*. There was little indication that he would resurface four years later with an album as powerfully unsettling as *Maxinquaye*. Accompanied by the sweet-voiced Martine, Tricky takes the listener on a tour of the dark corridors of his mind, dealing exclusively in paranoia and obsession. The striking rhythms of stand-out tracks 'Overcome', 'Hell Is Round The Corner' and 'Suffocated Love' merge seamlessly with a hard-rock reworking of Public Enemy's 'Black Steel In The Hour Of Chaos' and the warped soul of 'Abbaon Fat Tracks' to create one of the 90s' most compellingly atmospheric records.

● TRACKS: *Overcome; Ponderosa; Black Steel; Hell Is Round The Corner; Pumpkin; Aftermath; Abbaon Fat Tracks; Brand New You're Retro; Suffocated Love; You Don't; Strugglin'; Feed Me.*

● FIRST RELEASED 1995
● UK PEAK CHART POSITION: 3
● USA PEAK CHART POSITION: did not chart

130 THE VELVET UNDERGROUND (202) ▲
THE VELVET UNDERGROUND

Astonishingly this did not chart. Now affectionately known as 'the third album', it forms part of a catalogue that contains some of the most influential music of the rock era. Not even recouping its money when released, nor making the charts, it is astonishing how deeply this important band has seeped into our minds. Every track has huge merit, whether it is Maureen's innocent voice or Lou's drawl of sexuality on 'Some Kinda Love'; even the enthrallingly bizarre 'The Murder Mystery' still baffles. Like the cover, dark and decadent; like Lou Reed on the back cover, out of his head and upside-down.

● TRACKS: *Candy Says; What Goes On; Some Kinda Love; Pale Blue Eyes; Jesus; Beginning To See The Light; I'm Set Free; That's The Story Of My Life; The Murder Mystery; After Hours.*

● FIRST RELEASED 1969
● UK PEAK CHART POSITION: did not chart
● USA PEAK CHART POSITION: did not chart

131 IT TAKES A NATION OF MILLIONS TO HOLD US BACK (541) ▲ PUBLIC ENEMY

The title says it all. In 1988, when this album was released, Public Enemy's music cut with a wholly revolutionary edge. Rarely has fear, anger, paranoia and anxiety been so masterfully compressed onto a record's grooves. The Bomb Squad's artistry is the keynote to the hard, lean delivery, while Chuck D's supremely pointed lyrics leave no stone of the black experience unturned. It is not comfortable listening, but on tracks such as 'Don't Believe The Hype', 'Night Of The Living Baseheads' and 'Rebel Without A Pause' the listener is left in no doubt that they are facing a fantastically potent force.

● TRACKS: *Countdown To Armageddon; Bring The Noise; Don't Believe The Hype; Cold Lampin With Flavor; Terminator X To The Edge Of Panic; Mind Terrorist; Louder Than A Bomb; Caught, Can We Get A Witness?; Show Em Whatcha Got; She Watch Channel Zero?!; Night Of The Living Baseheads; Black Steel In The Hour Of Chaos; Security Of The First World; Rebel Without A Pause; Prophets Of Rage; Party For Your Right To Fight.*

● FIRST RELEASED 1988
● UK PEAK CHART POSITION: 8
● USA PEAK CHART POSITION: 42

132 LIVE AT THE APOLLO VOL.1 (36) ▼
JAMES BROWN

Superlatives abound when considering this seminal set. It has been called 'the greatest live album of all time' while Brown's position as the Godfather of Soul is almost indisputable. The singer was largely unknown outside black music circles prior to the release of this million-seller which fully captured the power and intensity of Brown in concert. It contains the cream of his releases to that point, each of which is injected with a passionate fervour. Brilliantly paced, the set grows in stature, as the famed Apollo audience responds to and, indeed, adds to the excitement. Brown towers majestically over the proceedings; pleading, extolling, proving himself not just the finest R&B singer of his generation, but one of the most distinctive in the history of popular music.

● TRACKS: *I'll Go Crazy; Try Me; Think; I Don't Mind; Lost Someone (Part 1); Lost Someone (Part 2); Please, Please, Please; You've Got The Power; I Found Someone; Why Do You Do Me Like You Do; I Want You So Bad; I Love You Yes I Do; Why Does Everything Happen To Me; Bewildered; Please Don't Go; Night Train.*

● FIRST RELEASED 1963
● UK PEAK CHART POSITION: did not chart
● USA PEAK CHART POSITION: 2

133 WHO'S NEXT (140) ▲
THE WHO

The follow-up to *Tommy* would always provide Pete Townshend with an artistic dilemma, and two years passed before the Who unleashed their next studio album. The wait proved worthwhile and taking the best from the aborted *Lifehouse* project, Townshend added a handful of urgent new songs to create one of his group's finest releases. Synthesizer obbligatos and acoustic guitars provide occasional counterpoints to the quartet's accustomed power, a contrast emphasizing their sense of dynamics. 'Won't Get Fooled Again', 'Behind Blue Eyes' and 'Baba O'Riley' were each destined to become integral parts of the Who's 70s lexicon, as vital as 'My Generation' had proved from the previous decade. *Who's Next* set a hard rock standard that even its creators struggled to emulate.

● TRACKS: *Baba O'Riley; Bargain; Love Ain't For Keeping; My Wife; Song Is Over; Getting In Tune; Going Mobile; Behind Blue Eyes; Won't Get Fooled Again.*

● FIRST RELEASED 1971
● UK PEAK CHART POSITION: 1
● USA PEAK CHART POSITION: 4

 ### 134 MOBY GRAPE (159) ▲
MOBY GRAPE

Time and time again this album is cited as the finest debut of all time. But just who were Moby Grape? They were a stellar San Francisco rock band who became appalling victims of record company hype followed by their own excesses, as they were lulled into believing they were more than they were. Loopy Skip Spence, growling Bob Mosely and talented bluesman Jerry Miller were but three-fifths of a great band. Every track could have been issued as a single, which is exactly what CBS did when they released five on the same day, with disastrous results. An indispensable collection and superseded in 1993 by the even more indispensable *Vintage Grape*.

● TRACKS: *Hey Grandma; Mr. Blues; Fall On You; 8.05; Come In The Morning; Omaha; Naked, If I Want To; Someday; Ain't No Use; Sitting By The Window; Changes; Lazy Me; Indifference.*

● FIRST RELEASED 1967
● UK PEAK CHART POSITION: did not chart
● USA PEAK CHART POSITION: 24

 ### 135 COUNTDOWN TO ECSTASY (–) ▲
STEELY DAN

Steely Dan were on a roll by the time this, their second album, was released. Already, they were the most critically favoured band of the 70s, and their star has never once dimmed. Prolific they were not, and quality not quantity was the order of the day. Jeff 'Skunk' Baxter added some tough meat to their smooth vegetables. This is never better demonstated than on 'My Old School'. This track has a series of almost-false guitar endings that the listener begs not to finish, even though he/she was probably smoking funny cigarettes at the time. Similarly gorgeous are 'The Boston Rag' and 'King Of The World'. And just who are those gloops on the album cover?

● TRACKS: *Bodhisattva; Razor Boy; The Boston Rag; Your Gold Teeth; Show Biz Kids; My Old School; Pearl Of The Quarter; King Of The World.*

● FIRST RELEASED 1973
● UK PEAK CHART POSITION: did not chart
● USA PEAK CHART POSITION: 35

 ### 136 NO OTHER (–) ▲
GENE CLARK

Clark's songwriting contribution to the early Byrds was a glorious asset that even they did not appreciate at the time. Many fans willed him to make this excellent album, if only to reinforce the respect and faith they had in his ability. Ill-health and booze kept him from repeating this solo effort and continuing his life as a songwriter. This paradoxical recording can be taken lightly (easy-on-the-ear songs) or as a heavy symbolic lyrical statement (deep stuff). More country rock than pop and like *Astral Weeks*, it has long-term hidden depths. The silk flares he wears on the cover have never been topped, by male or female.

● TRACKS: *Life's Greatest Fool; Silver Raven; No Other; Strength Of Strings; From A Silver Phial; Some Misunderstanding; The True One; Lady Of The North.*

● FIRST RELEASED 1974
● UK PEAK CHART POSITION: did not chart
● USA PEAK CHART POSITION: 144

137 THE SECOND COMING (–) ▲
STONE ROSES

Five fruitless years after the most acclaimed and influential album of the 80s, the Roses returned, having swapped Byrdsian guitar pop for swaggering Jimmy Page riffs. Predictably, the critics disapproved. Labelled overblown and self-indulgent, *The Second Coming* was woefully undervalued. Since its release, however, appreciation for this remarkable record has increased enormously: the sheer scope of 'Breaking Into Heaven' astonishes; the self-mocking 'Driving South', the sparkling 'Ten Storey Love Song', the frenzied 'Begging You' and the glorious 'Love Spreads' alone distinguish this album as a worthy successor. As the last, mighty gasp from a great band, all too aware of their own importance and on the verge of spectacular implosion, it stands as a fitting and poignant epitaph.

● TRACKS: *Breaking Into Heaven; Driving South; Ten Storey Love Song; Daybreak; Your Star Will Shine; Straight To The Man; Begging You; Tightrope; Good Times; Tears; How Do You Sleep; Love Spreads.*

● FIRST RELEASED 1994
● UK PEAK POSITION: 4
● USA PEAK POSITION: 47

 138 THE PIPER AT THE GATES OF DAWN
(–) ▲ PINK FLOYD

During the spring of 1967, while the Beatles were at Abbey Road finishing *Sgt. Pepper*, Pink Floyd were upstairs recording an album that would have a similarly immeasurable effect on the development of psychedelic rock. Its name taken from A.A. Milne's *The Wind in the Willows* (one of guitarist Syd Barrett's favourite books), *Piper At The Gates Of Dawn* was a child's garden of acid, an album-length exposition on the effects of LSD on a troubled mind. One of the first 'head' albums, it was rumoured that the tracks contained sounds — conversations, even — that one could only hear while tripping. 'Bike', however, brought it all back to basics with such profound lyrics as 'I've got a bike, you can ride it if you like'.

● TRACKS: *Astronomy Domine; Lucifer Sam; Matilda Mother; Flaming; Pow R. Toc H.; Take Up Thy Stethoscope And Walk; Interstellar Overdrive; Gnome; Chapter 24; Scarecrow; Bike.*

● FIRST RELEASED 1967
● UK PEAK CHART POSITION: 6
● USA PEAK CHART POSITION: 131

 **139** RAMONES (340) ▲
THE RAMONES

Wuntoofreefore. Described alternately as minimalists or cartoon characters, the Ramones brought both elements to their métier. Drawing upon the undying appeal of unpretentious 50s and 60s pop, the quartet reclaimed simplicity, adding to it a buzzsaw guitar and trash-culture values. Gore films, beach parties and solvent abuse are canonized in turn, but a sense of innocent self-deprecation prevents the charge of cheap sensationalism. Each track flirts around the two-minute watershed, the gaps between them barely discernible, the cumulative sense of fun and excitement as vital as ever. Over the years this formula has been acknowledged and loved and will continue to be passed down through recommendation.

● TRACKS: *Blitzkrieg Bop; Beat On The Brat; Judy Is A Punk; I Wanna Be Your Boyfriend; Chain Saw; Now, I Wanna Sniff Some Glue; I Don't Wanna Go Down To The Basement; Loudmouth; Havana Affair; Listen To My Heart; Fifty Third And Third; Let's Dance; I Don't Wanna Walk Around With You; Today Your Love, Tomorrow The World.*

● FIRST RELEASED 1976
● UK PEAK CHART POSITION: did not chart
● USA PEAK CHART POSITION: 111

 140 THE LEXICON OF LOVE (253) ▲
ABC

ABC are frequently described as purveyors of high-quality pop music, but this undervalues the elegance and attention to detail of their work. Although they have failed to repeat the success of *Lexicon Of Love*, it nevertheless represents an achievement to which many other artists can only aspire. The maturity of Trevor Horn's production created a remarkable debut album, yielding hits in 'Tears Are Not Enough', 'Poison Arrow', 'The Look Of Love' and 'All Of My Heart', with Martin Fry's talent as songwriter and vocalist delivering the goods with consistent aplomb. Probably the best ever example of 80s pop music.

● TRACKS: *Show Me; Poison Arrow; Many Happy Returns; Tears Are Not Enough; Valentine's Day; The Look Of Love (Part 1); Date Stamp; All Of My Heart; 4 Ever 2 Gether; The Look Of Love.*

● FIRST RELEASED 1982
● UK PEAK CHART POSITION: 1
● USA PEAK CHART POSITION: 24

141 GRIEVOUS ANGEL (770) ▲
GRAM PARSONS

Parsons' short life had already ended by the time his second album was released. An inevitable poignancy colours its content, but the singer's work was always charged with atmosphere. His subject matter followed accustomed country music precepts - broken hearts, stolen love and mortality - but Parsons' grasp of melody and lyrical intensity showed remarkable insight and ensured the lasting quality of his work. His duets with Emmylou Harris possess a heartfelt vulnerability and stand among the finest popular music has produced. Parsons' articulation of naked emotion is his final legacy. His status now is neither overblown or undeserved, he was a pioneer of the west.

● TRACKS: *Return Of The Grievous Angel; Hearts On Fire; I Can't Dance; Brass Buttons; $1000 Dollar Wedding; Medley Live From Northern Quebec: (a) Cash On The Barrelhead, (b) Hickory Wind; Love Hurts; Las Vegas; In My Hour Of Darkness.*

● FIRST RELEASED 1974
● UK PEAK CHART POSITION: did not chart
● USA PEAK CHART POSITION: 195

142 A HARD DAY'S NIGHT (–) ▲
THE BEATLES

This timeless album is only now being appreciated for what it is and not for what it purported to be. The 'songs from the motion picture' fayre was usually a hastily assembled group of songs for inclusion in a film. This film remains a classic of happy 60s naïvity. The songs flow like the absolute finest red wine. The title track leads to the glorious harmonica of 'I Should Have Known Better' (remember the guards van scene) to the powerfully poignant 'If I Fell' (remember Ringo suddenly relenting and picking up his drumsticks). This period represents the Beatles at their happiest. And the songs still are ridiculously good.

● TRACKS: *A Hard Day's Night; I Should Have Known Better; If I Fell; I'm Happy Just To Dance With You; And I Love Her; Tell Me Why; Can't Buy Me Love; Any Time At All; I'll Cry Instead; Things We Said Today; When I Get Home; You Can't Do That; I'll Be Back.*

● FIRST RELEASED 1964
● UK PEAK CHART POSITION: 1
● USA PEAK CHART POSITION: 1

143 IF ONLY I COULD REMEMBER MY NAME (288) ▲ DAVID CROSBY

Although this was a highly successful album, Crosby was later accused of being self-indulgent by some critics. In recent years that opinion has reversed, acknowledging that the amount of space he allowed to fellow musicians, makes this a wholly unselfish record. The cream of San Francisco assembled, and in no particular order, there are Jerry Garcia, Phil Lesh, Jack Casady, Paul Kantner, Joni Mitchell and Grace Slick. Crosby moves from the humour in his modern-day Jesse James story, 'Cowboy Movie', to wondrous spiritual voice excursions in 'I'd Swear There Was Somebody Here' and 'Tamalpais High'. The playing is faultless throughout and if you are not familiar with this wondrous record, please take the risk.

● TRACKS: *Music Is Love; Cowboy Movie; Tamalpais High; Laughing; What Are Their Names; Traction In The Rain; Song With No Words; Tree With No Leaves; Orleans; I'd Swear There Was Somebody Here.*

● FIRST RELEASED 1971
● UK PEAK CHART POSITION: 12
● USA PEAK CHART POSITION: 12

144 WHITE ON BLONDE (–) ▲
TEXAS

Texas were generally felt to have peaked with their debut album; *Rick's Road* continued a downward sales spiral, even though it contained some strong material. This album was a pleasant surprise, picking up awards everywhere and still selling in large quantities. For a band who might have been looking over their shoulders, this is a supremely confident album, full of good songs written by the band and, in particular, by Sharleen Spiteri and ex-Altered Image John McElhone. Respectable rock for the 90s, from the full production of tracks such as 'Halo' to the chiming tension created by 'Put Your Arms Around Me'.

● TRACKS: *0.34; Say What You Want; Drawing Crazy Patterns; Halo; Put Your Arms Around Me; Insane; Black Eyed Boy; Polo Mint City; White On Blonde; Postcard; 0.28; Ticket To Lie; Good Advice; Breathless.*

● FIRST RELEASED 1997
● UK PEAK CHART POSITION: 1
● USA PEAK CHART POSITION: did not chart

145 TUNNEL OF LOVE (–) ▲
BRUCE SPRINGSTEEN

Popular music as an art form has attained some of its greatest peaks when dealing with the thorny material of relationships. Bruce Springsteen's *Tunnel Of Love*, a powerful meditation on his own disintegrating marriage, represents a classic of its type. Predominantly an intimate solo recording the songs convey the gamut of emotions experienced in a long-term relationship, from desire ('Ain't Got You') through disquiet and deceit ('Tunnel Of Love' and 'Brilliant Disguise') to despair ('When You're Alone'), ending on a note of cautious optimism ('Valentine's Day'). Springsteen would never again be as nakedly emotional as he was on this beautiful and honest album.

● TRACKS: *Ain't Got You; Tougher Than The Rest; All That Heaven Will Allow; Spare Parts; Cautious Man; Walk Like A Man; Tunnel Of Love; Two Faces; Brilliant Disguise; One Step Up; When You're Alone; Valentine's Day.*

● FIRST RELEASED 1987
● UK PEAK CHART POSITION: 1
● USA PEAK CHART POSITION: 1

146 PLASTIC ONO BAND (259) ▲
JOHN LENNON

Now referred to as the primal scream album, Lennon allowed his tonsils and heart to bleed in a powerful exhumation of many of his demons. The plea for his lost mother in 'Mother' is as desperate as the realization expressed in 'I Found Out', with 'I've had religion from Jesus to Paul'. His Yoko songs are also a reassurance that, throughout this therapy, his Yoko was always there, and history has shown that it was his Yoko that helped him make it through. 'Working Class Hero' is another equally powerful track, even though John was not one. Essential listening for Beatles students with strong hearts.

● TRACKS: *Mother; Hold On; I Found Out; Working Class Hero; Isolation; Remember; Love; Well Well Well; Look At Me; God; My Mummy's Dead.*

● FIRST RELEASED 1970
● UK PEAK CHART POSITION: 11
● USA PEAK CHART POSITION: 10

147 IMPERIAL BEDROOM (37) ▼
ELVIS COSTELLO

Elvis clearly had a lot to get off his chest on this album dealing with emotional turmoil. While much of its lyrical brilliance deals with his thoughts, a small percentage slipped through with which we mortals could empathize. Now, having shown us he can tackle humour, politics and romance like no other, *Imperial Bedroom* was his most substantial album, as the issues covered will always be relevant and important. Chris Difford pitched in with one composition, 'Boy With A Problem'; perhaps Elvis found it too painful to write so directly about himself? Every track is powerful, simply read the lyrics. A gigantic record.

● TRACKS: *Beyond Belief; Tears Before Bedtime; Shabby Doll; The Long Honeymoon; Man Out Of Time; Almost Blue; And In Every Home; The Loved Ones; Human Hands; Kid About It; Little Savage; Boy With A Problem; Pidgin English; You Little Fool; Town Crier.*

● FIRST RELEASED 1982
● UK PEAK CHART POSITION: 6
● USA PEAK CHART POSITION: 30

148 AUGUST AND EVERYTHING AFTER (747) ▲
COUNTING CROWS

The Michael Stipe of this exciting outfit from California is Adam Duritz, whose dreadlocks and pained expressions belie his youth. He does sing and write some good and intense songs. This album remained on the US chart for an age and it can only be a matter of time before irresistible tracks such as 'Omaha' and 'Mr Jones' find their way onto 'classic rock tracks' playlists. Duritz is clearly a major talent but it is hoped that this sparkling debut is not his best shot. In time perhaps some of the whining angst can give way to happier times. For the record, this was a better debut than R.E.M., but maybe they have counted their crows before they have hatched.

● TRACKS: *Round Here; Omaha; Mr. Jones; Perfect Blue Building; Anna Begins; Time And Time Again; Rain King; Sullivan Street; Ghost Train; Raining In Baltimore; A Murder Of One.*

● FIRST RELEASED 1994
● UK PEAK CHART POSITION: 16
● USA PEAK CHART POSITION: 4

149 LIEGE AND LIEF (61) ▼
FAIRPORT CONVENTION

Where so much began. The advertisements ran: 'the first (literally) British folk rock LP ever.' It also represented a catharsis for the band, reconvening after a traumatic road accident that killed drummer Martin Lamble. Once again focused and with redoubtable folk fiddler Dave Swarbrick now permanently involved, they threw themselves into the electrification of ballads, myths and rollickin' jigs. The results were both innovative and stimulating. The union was blessed. If you sat down and tried to imagine a dream folk rock band, it still would not match the potential here. From the lusting pace of 'Matty Groves' to the tender cooing of 'Crazy Man Michael', Sandy Denny's voice is the perfect vehicle for this milestone. Imitated a thousand times, but never equalled.

● TRACKS: Come All Ye; Reynardine; Matty Groves; Farewell Farewell; The Deserter; The Lark In The Morning; Tamlin; Crazy Man Michael; Rakish Paddy; Foxhunters Jigs; Toss The Feathers.

● FIRST RELEASED 1970
● UK PEAK CHART POSITION: 17
● USA PEAK CHART POSITION: did not chart

151 EVERYBODY KNOWS THIS IS NOWHERE
(225) ▲ NEIL YOUNG

Neil Young's second solo album introduced his long-standing relationship with backing group Crazy Horse. The partnership allowed the singer greater musical flexibility and the understanding generated gave a unique synergy to his work. The combination could be concise, as on the chunky 'Cinnamon Girl', with its unusual timing and changes. The pivotal selections are the lengthy, guitar-based workouts, 'Down By The River' and especially 'Cowgirl In The Sand'. The group urge Young into textured, improvised playing, the appeal of which never palls. Elsewhere, the singer revisits his folk past and embraces country rock and pop, none better than the brilliant title track.

● TRACKS: Cinnamon Girl; Everybody Knows This Is Nowhere; Round & Round (It Won't Be Long); Down By The River; The Losing End (When You're On); Running Dry (Requiem For The Rockets); Cowgirl In The Sand.

● FIRST RELEASED 1969
● UK PEAK CHART POSITION: did not chart
● USA PEAK CHART POSITION: 34

150 I WANT TO SEE THE BRIGHT LIGHTS
TONIGHT (316) ▲ RICHARD AND LINDA THOMPSON

The debut album from Richard and Linda started a career that has placed Thompson in the 'forever to be a huge cult figure' bracket. They did everything on this album, bar make the charts and sell records. Folk, rock, country and pop are brilliantly covered in a tasteful and controlled package that is a delight from beginning to end, with Linda singing beautifully. Concert favourites such as 'The Calvary Cross' and 'When I Get To The Border' are to be found here. It is not flippant to say that Richard Thompson is a world class songwriter and guitarist, albeit totally under-appreciated.

● TRACKS: When I Get To The Border; The Calvary Cross; Withered And Died; I Want To See The Bright Lights Tonight; Down Where The Drunkards Roll; We Sing Hallelujah; Has He Got A Friend For Me; The Little Beggar Girl; The End Of The Rainbow; The Great Valerio.

● FIRST RELEASED 1974
● UK PEAK CHART POSITION: did not chart
● USA PEAK CHART POSITION: did not chart

152 CAN'T BUY A THRILL (169) ▲
STEELY DAN

Even the debut from Becker and Fagen put them stylistically a cut above the others. Played alongside the Doobie Brothers and the Eagles on smooth FM radio Steely Dan were linked immediately to the west coast music scene, a fact that was utterly wrong. This was and is, an east coast album; it is also assured, laid-back and layered with the jazz and soul influences that made their special kind of rock. Jeff 'Skunk' Baxter added the metal and David Palmer added pop vocal - but, from this sparkling debut we can clearly see Becker and Fagen in immaculate control. 'Do It Again' is of course, a diamond.

● TRACKS: Do It Again; Dirty Work; Kings; Midnite Cruiser; Only A Fool Would Say That; Reelin' In The Years; Fire In The Hole; Brooklyn (Owes The Charmer Under Me); Change Of The Guard; Turn That Heartbeat Over Again.

● FIRST RELEASED 1972
● UK PEAK CHART POSITION: 38
● USA PEAK CHART POSITION: 17

153 SUN COLLECTION (33) ▼
ELVIS PRESLEY

Elvis Presley's pivotal recordings for the Sun label almost venture beyond the realms of description. They not only define rockabilly's blend of country and R&B, but expose a singer whose unbridled style burst with freedom and sexual excitement. Material drawn from Arthur Crudup, Junior Parker and Arthur Gunter joins songs popularized by Bill Monore, Bob Wills and the Carter Family in a fervid melting pot that changed the course of pop forever. Rare masters from the same era join the five compelling singles Presley recorded for Sun before leaving for RCA. Rarely has history sounded so alive. This document is destined to last.

● TRACKS: *That's Alright; Blue Moon Of Kentucky; I Don't Care If The Sun Don't Shine; Good Rockin' Tonight; Milk Cow Blues Boogie; You're A Heartbreaker; I'm Left, You're Right, She's Gone; Baby Let's Play House; Mystery Train; I Forgot To Remember To Forget; I'll Never Let You Go; I Love You Because (first version); Tryin' To Get To You; Blue Moon; Just Because; I Love You Because (second version).*

● FIRST RELEASED 1975
● UK PEAK CHART POSITION: 16
● USA PEAK CHART POSITION: did not chart

154 PLACEBO (–) ▲
PLACEBO

An interesting combination of a Swede, a Swiss and an American, meeting in Luxembourg and sounding very British, in a post-punk sort of way. The group were signed for a reputed large advance, partly owing to the marketable, androgynous Brian Molko. However, the quality of their songwriting was demonstrated on their excellent debut. 'Nancy Boy', a surprising hit single, is in fact one of the lesser tracks on the album. There is much more depth to be found in 'Bionic', 'Come Home' and 'I Know', the latter complete with didgeridoo. After such a sparkling debut the cynical jury is already out.

● TRACKS: *Come Home; Teenage Angst; Bionic; 36 Degrees; Hang On To Your IQ; Nancy Boy; I Know; Bruise Pristine; Lady Of The Flowers; Swallow.*

● FIRST RELEASED 1996
● UK PEAK CHART POSITION: 40
● USA PEAK CHART POSITION: did not chart

155 STAND (59) ▼
SLY AND THE FAMILY STONE

Sly Stone was too busy having a good time and living life to the excess to begin to realize how influential his brand of funky soul would become. Early signs of rap also surfaced on this album. Confident, hard rocking and marvellously arrogant, the band were outrageous and exciting; even five minutes of a cappella handclapping was riveting. Two classics appear on this - 'I Want To Take You Higher' and 'Everyday People' - but the whole album is a necessary purchase for students of goodtime soul, dance, rap and funk. This family is the acknowledged leader.

● TRACKS: *Stand!; Don't Call Me Nigger, Whitey; I Want To Take You Higher; Somebody's Watching You; Sing A Simple Song; Everyday People; Sex Machine; You Can Make It If You Try.*

● FIRST RELEASED 1969
● UK PEAK CHART POSITION: did not chart
● USA PEAK CHART POSITION: 13

156 DISRAELI GEARS (65) ▼
CREAM

This is the power trio's perfect studio album which captured the dayglo spirit of psychedelic London as no other record could. As their blues influences waned, the hippie lyrics of Pete Brown came to the fore as the strident voice of Jack Bruce fused with Clapton's stinging and milky guitar and Baker's polyrhythmic drums. 'Tales Of Brave Ulysses', 'SWLABR' and 'Strange Brew' remain classics of their era, while 'Sunshine Of Your Love' has become one of rock's most imitated opening riffs. The Martin Sharpe album sleeve completes the package and displays Eric Clapton with the finest perm of 1967.

● TRACKS: *Strange Brew; Sunshine Of Your Love; World Of Pain; Dance The Night Away; Blue Condition; Tales Of Brave Ulysses; We're Going Wrong; Outside Woman Blues; Take It Back; Mother's Lament; SWLABR.*

● FIRST RELEASED 1967
● UK PEAK CHART POSITION: 5
● USA PEAK CHART POSITION: 4

157 THIRD/SISTER LOVERS (–) ▲
BIG STAR

After Big Star released *Radio City*, they fell apart, leaving Alex Chilton to record in 1975 what was later released as their *Third* (aka *Sister Lovers*). The album is strikingly different from everything Chilton has done before or since. With pained outpourings such as the haunting 'Holocaust', it holds its own against rock's greatest monuments to existential angst, from *Tonight's The Night* to *Bryter Layter*. It also ranks alongside the Beach Boys' *Smile* as perhaps the only 'classic' album with no set sequence. Chilton never bothered to sequence it because, upon its completion, no label wanted to release it. It finally came out four years later, and since then, while it has appeared on several labels, no two have used the same track order.

● TRACKS: *Stroke It Noel; For You; Kizza Me; You Can't Have Me; Nightime; Blue Moon; Take Care; Jesus Christ; Femme Fatale; O; Dana; Big Black Car; Holocaust; Kangaroo; Thank You Friends.*

● FIRST RELEASED 1978
● UK PEAK CHART POSITION: did not chart
● USA PEAK CHART POSITION: did not chart

158 OFF THE WALL (92) ▼
MICHAEL JACKSON

The album that moved Jackson out of juvenile pop, even though the suit he wears on the cover belies his still tender years untouched by facial butchery. Is it really 20 years ago that, along with the Clash, Jackson was deemed OK? The Quincy Jones production was immaculate and totally sympathetic to the 90s sound. Virtually the whole album holds up, with a thumbs-down for 'Burn This Disco Down', but remember that this does contain the perfection of 'Rock With You', the angst of 'She's Out Of My Life', Paul McCartney's 'Girlfriend' and the abandon of 'Get On The Floor/Off The Wall'. Absolutely harmlessly brilliant.

● TRACKS: *Don't Stop 'Til You Get Enough; Rock With You; Working Day And Night; Get On The Floor/Off The Wall; Girlfriend; She's Out Of My Life; I Can't Help It; It's The Falling In Love; Burn This Disco Down.*

● FIRST RELEASED 1979
● UK PEAK CHART POSITION: 5
● USA PEAK CHART POSITION: 3

159 TALKING BOOK (51) ▼
STEVIE WONDER

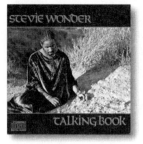

An even more mature album from the artist who confirmed everything promised on *Music Of My Mind*. Although he came dangerously close to AOR the quality of the songs and the remarkable choice of running order makes this an all-important Wonder album. Even if you choose to skip the MOR first track, 'You Are The Sunshine Of My Life', the beautifully relaxing sound will eventually force you to admit your romantic vulnerability. Jeff Beck sneaks in some subtle guitar on 'Lookin' For Another True Love' and Wonder plays some innovative Arp and Moog Sythesizers throughout.

● TRACKS: *You Are The Sunshine Of My Life; Maybe Your Baby; You And I (We Can Conquer The World); Tuesday Heartbreak; You've Got It Bad Girl; Superstition; Big Brother; Blame It On The Sun; Lookin' For Another Pure Love; I Believe (When I Fall In Love It Will Be Forever).*

● FIRST RELEASED 1972
● UK PEAK CHART POSITION: 16
● USA peak chart position: 3

160 FOR YOUR PLEASURE (271) ▲
ROXY MUSIC

MThe second album from the purveyors of art rock and glamour. Three out of five members appear to be left-handed, according to the inner sleeve. This put them way out of balance with the rest of the world, and for a while their wondrously inventive music put them out of step with the music being fed to us. The energy of tracks such as 'Editions Of You' still incites the need to dance. And how many times did you wait patiently for Ferry to get to the 'but you blew my mind' part of 'In Every Dream Home A Heartache', just so you could hear Manzanera's excellent phased guitar?

● TRACKS: *Do The Strand; Beauty Queen; Strictly Confidential; Editions Of You; In Every Dream Home A Heartache; The Bogus Man; Grey Lagoons; For Your Pleasure.*

● FIRST RELEASED 1973
● UK PEAK CHART POSITION: 4
● USA PEAK CHART POSITION: 193

161 LAYLA AND OTHER ASSORTED LOVE SONGS (138) ▼ DEREK AND THE DOMINOS

Studying the photographs inside the fold-out sleeve makes you question how such a wrecked bunch of musos could make such a great record. Excess was obviously the order of the day, yet excel was what they did. Everybody knows that 'Layla' is one of the best rock songs ever written, but here is the chance to strike a blow for Duane Allman's consistent guitar, especially on lost gems such as 'Anyday' and 'Key To The Highway'. Did anybody also notice how good Jim Gordon's drumming was? And the CD age means we can skip past the dreadful 'Thorn Tree In The Garden'.

● TRACKS: *I Looked Away; Bell Bottom Blues; Keep On Growing; Nobody Knows You; I Am Yours; Anyday; Key To The Highway; Tell The Truth; Why Does Love Got To Be So Sad; Have You Ever Loved A Woman; Little Sing; It's Too Late; Thorn Tree In The Garden; Layla.*

● FIRST RELEASED 1970
● UK PEAK CHART POSITION: did not chart
● USA PEAK CHART POSITION: 16

163 DÉJÀ VU (157) ▼ CROSBY, STILLS, NASH AND YOUNG

With the inspired decision to add Neil Young to the ranks, CSNY became one of America's biggest attractions for a short time. While the results on this excellent record show four individuals, rather than the vocal unity of the debut, it still holds up to repeated listening. Young contributed 'Country Girl', with a wonderful John Sebastian harmonica solo added, and the aching 'Helpless'. His colleagues pitched in with notable songs from Crosby ('Almost Cut My Hair'), Stills ('Carry On' and '4+20') and Nash, who has continuing radio play with 'Our House', and 'Teach Your Children' with Jerry Garcia's piercing but beautiful pedal steel guitar.

● TRACKS: *Carry On; Teach Your Children; Almost Cut My Hair; Helpless; Woodstock; Déjà Vu; Our House; 4+20; Country Girl; Everybody I Love You.*

● FIRST RELEASED 1970
● UK PEAK CHART POSITION: 5
● USA PEAK CHART POSITION: 1

162 HOTEL CALIFORNIA (171) ▲ THE EAGLES

A steady growth suddenly mushroomed into a monster as the Eagles, along with Fleetwood Mac, epitomized AOR in the early 70s. This record is supposedly a concept album but most of the purchasers merely enjoyed the accessible songs while driving down to the coast in their Volkswagen Caravanettes with 2.4 children. Joe Walsh was added to give gutsy guitar in the wake of the country flavour of Bernie Leaden, while Randy Meisner grew in stature as a writer with 'Try And Love Again' and 'New Kid In Town'. The title track still bites as Henley's voice blends with Walsh's epic solo.

● TRACKS: *Hotel California; New Kid In Town; Life In The Fast Lane; Wasted Time; Wasted Time (Reprise); Victim Of Love; Pretty Maids All In A Row; Try And Love Again; The Last Resort.*

● FIRST RELEASED 1976
● UK PEAK CHART POSITION: 2
● USA PEAK CHART POSITION: 1

164 THIS YEARS MODEL (67) ▼ ELVIS COSTELLO

Yet another collection from Elvis, surely the most prolific lyricist of the past two decades. This is a young, angry, and inexperienced Costello. He shouts and spits but always retains irresistible melody. 'Pump It Up' contains driving pop with a fine example of 'cheesy' organ, and is a high point. The Attractions sound like the best backing band in the world, and it is staggering to think that Costello had so much more bursting to get out when many of us would have been happy with this one album. Anyone who can rhyme Chelsea with Elsie and still sound cool has to be a bit special.

● TRACKS: *No Action; This Year's Girl; The Beat; Pump It Up; Little Triggers; You Belong To Me; Hand In Hand; (I Don't Want To Go To) Chelsea; Lip Service; Living In Paradise; Lipstick Vogue; Night Rally.*

● FIRST RELEASED 1978
● UK PEAK CHART POSITION: 4
● USA PEAK CHART POSITION: 30

165 METALLICA (234) ▲
METALLICA

For the band who helped change the traditional face of contemporary heavy metal, Metallica were never found wanting in innovation. Nevertheless, 1991's album of the same name appeared as a significant burst of ideas, surprising even their most ardent of fans. Songs were stripped down to comparatively palatable lengths and subtle orchestration was introduced, with vocalist James Hetfield dropping his infamous growl for a warm, accomplished vocal. 'Enter Sandman' and the lilting 'Nothing Else Matters' revealed both sides of their clever songwriting temperament, contributing to this unabashed masterstroke of sincerity and overwhelming musical confidence.

● TRACKS: *Enter Sandman; Sad But True; Holier Than Thou; The Unforgiven; Wherever I May Roam; Don't Tread On Me; Through The Never; Nothing Else Matters; Of Wolf And Man; The God That Failed; My Friend Of Misery; The Struggle Within.*

● FIRST RELEASED 1991
● UK PEAK CHART POSITION: 1
● USA PEAK CHART POSITION: 1

167 STARS (50) ▼
SIMPLY RED

Mick Hucknall is one of the most prodigious talents in the music business; anyone who disputes this statement need only listen without prejudice to *Stars*. His voice has a range, sensitivity and accuracy that puts others to shame, and enables him to journey between soul, hip-hop and jazz with alacrity. As if that were not enough, he has an almost Mozartian ability to compose melodies woven from the very essence of music. On *Stars* he left behind much of the narcissism of previous albums, gave the band high-quality material to develop and produced an enduring classic.

● TRACKS: *Something Got Me Started; Stars; Thrill Me; Your Mirror; She's Got It Bad; For Your Babies; Model; Freedom; How Could I Fall; Wonderland.*

● FIRST RELEASED 1991
● UK PEAK CHART POSITION: 1
● USA PEAK CHART POSITION: 76

166 PARALLEL LINES (108) ▼
BLONDIE

Madonna and Michael Jackson aside, this is supreme pop music and as good as the genre can ever get. Everybody loved Blondie; fans, children, critics, other musicians and senior citizens - and not just because the pouting little Debbie Harry was its frontperson. This is an unintentional greatest hits record that never lets up until the last note of 'Just Go Away' has died. If one wanted to carp, you could have asked for 'Denis' and 'Call Me' to have been included, but that would be just plain greedy. One of the greatest 'up' records of all time.

● TRACKS: *Fade Away; Hanging On The Telephone; One Way Or Another; Picture This; Pretty Baby; I Know But I Don't Know; 11.59; Will Anything Happen; Sunday Girl; Heart Of Glass; I'm Gonna Love You Too; Just Go Away.*

● FIRST RELEASED 1978
● UK PEAK CHART POSITION: 1
● USA PEAK CHART POSITION: 6

168 WITH THE BEATLES (19) ▼
THE BEATLES

Released as its creators evolved from pop group to phenomenon, *With The Beatles* both affirmed promise and proclaimed genius. A slew of memorable Lennon/McCartney compositions embraced pop at its most multi-faceted; robust, melancholic, excited and wistful. Their grasp of melody and harmony startled, yet for every unusual chord sequence employed, the Beatles' vigour and sense of purpose remained true. Influences and mentors were acknowledged by a handful of cover versions, but the strength of the album lies in the group's own creations. *With The Beatles* freed artists to record their own material, and the course of pop was irrevocably changed. And Ringo's ride cymbal work is hypnotic.

● TRACKS: *It Won't Be Long; All I've Got To Do; All My Loving; Don't Bother Me; Little Child; Till There Was You; Please Mister Postman; Roll Over Beethoven; Hold Me Tight; You Really Got A Hold On Me; I Wanna Be Your Man; (There's A) Devil In Her Heart; Not A Second Time; Money (That's What I Want).*

● FIRST RELEASED 1964
● UK PEAK CHART POSITION: 1
● USA PEAK CHART POSITION: 1

169 THE UNFORGETTABLE FIRE (18) ▼
U2

The title of this album was taken from an exhibition of paintings by survivors of Hiroshima and Nagasaki. It confirmed U2 as one of a handful of bands able to tackle such vast and emotive subjects with dignity and musical integrity. There are few artists capable of writing about religion, war, race, the Irish problem and life with such ferocity and global commercial success. 'Pride (In The Name Of Love)', a hymn to Martin Luther King, was a worldwide hit, and almost every track is an anthem sung by millions. The production by Brian Eno and Daniel Lanois was a taste of things to come.

● TRACKS: *A Sort Of Homecoming; Pride (In The Name Of Love); Wire; The Unforgettable Fire; Promenade; Fourth Of July; Bad; Indian Summer Sky; Elvis Presley And America; MLK.*

● FIRST RELEASED 1984
● UK PEAK CHART POSITION: 1
● USA PEAK CHART POSITION: 12

170 SECRETS (−) ▲
TONI BRAXTON

Braxton has the voice, Babyface has the words, and together they equal hot steamy sex - that is, if you happen to have the lyric sheet in front of you. If not, the intonation cleverly disguises the erotic content of songs such as 'You're Makin' Me High'. That aside, this is an overwhelmingly melancholic album, even though some of the songs are 'up' love songs, for example, 'Let It Flow'. Breaking hearts, love and sex, infidelity, 'how can I love again', and Kenny G are all present. Very much the way life has to be, for better or worse - apart from the Kenny G bit, that is.

● TRACKS: *Come On Over Here; You're Makin Me High; There's No Me Without You; Un-Break My Heart; Talking In His Sleep; How Could An Angel Break My Heart; Find Me A Man; Let It Flow; Why Should I Care; I Don't Want To; I Love Me Some Him; In The Late Of Night.*

● FIRST RELEASED 1996
● UK PEAK CHART POSITION: 4
● USA PEAK CHART POSITION: 2

171 THE KINKS ARE THE VILLAGE GREEN PRESERVATION SOCIETY (367) ▲ THE KINKS

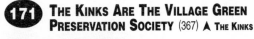

Although Pete Townshend's *Tommy* is seen as the first rock opera, Ray Davies actually conceived the idea with *Arthur* and this album. Taking the theme of England and its quaint Englishness, *Village Green* addresses Beeching's barbaric railway closures with 'The Last Of The Steam Powered Trains', and nostalgia in the title track; 'god save Donald Duck, vaudeville and variety'. 'Picture Book' describes growing old and 'Animal Farm' is a wonderful plea for rural sanity. The commercial failure of the album was in not having one outstanding song, but as a concept the collection is an absolute gem. Who else could use a lyric like 'we are the custard pie appreciation consortium' and get away with it.

● TRACKS: *The Village Green Preservation Society; Do You Remember Walter; Picture Book; Johnny Thunder; The Last Of The Steam-Powered Trains; Big Sky; Sitting By The Riverside; Animal Farm; Village Green; Starstruck; Phenomenal Cat; All My Friends Were There; Wicked Annabella; Monica; People Take Pictures Of Each Other.*

● FIRST RELEASED 1968
● UK PEAK CHART POSITION: did not chart
● USA PEAK CHART POSITION: did not chart

172 EVERY PICTURE TELLS A STORY
(320) ▲   ROD STEWART

Rod Stewart's third solo album brought the singer long-awaited commercial success. Its combination of strong, original songs and plum cover versions was finely judged as the artist paid tribute to mentors and declared his own craft. Members of Stewart's regular group, the Faces, provide intuitive support without the sense of compromise apparent on their own recordings. The singer's voice was rarely better; his interpretation of the Temptations' '(I Know I'm) Losing You' brought new dimensions to a Tamla/Motown classic. The highlight is, inevitably, 'Maggie May', one of the great pop anthems, but the remaining selections, such as 'Mandolin Wind' and Tim Hardin's beautiful 'Reason To Believe' contain a similar sense of purpose.

● TRACKS: *Every Picture Tells A Story; Seems Like A Long Time; That's All Right; Tomorrow Is A Long Time; Maggie May; Mandolin Wind; (I Know I'm) Losing You; Reason To Believe.*

● FIRST RELEASED 1971
● UK PEAK CHART POSITION: 1
● USA PEAK CHART POSITION: 1

173 THE GILDED PALACE OF SIN (849) ▲
FLYING BURRITO BROTHERS

The Gilded Palace Of Sin allowed two former Byrds, Gram Parsons and Chris Hillman, fully to explore country music. Several selections, notably 'Christine's Tune' and 'Wheels', succeeded in capturing the joys of Nashville-inspired rock, but the group proved equally adept at interpreting southern soul standards. Parsons' aching vocal on Dan Penn's 'Dark End Of The Street' articulated the dilemmas of infidelity, while on his own composition, 'Hot Burrito No. 1', he revealed a vulnerability unusual in a male singer. 'Sneeky' Pete Kleinow explored the sonic possibilities of the pedal steel guitar, rather than employ orthodox embellishments, and this desire to question preconceptions gives this album its unique qualities.

● TRACKS: *Christine's Tune; Sin City; Do Right Woman, Do Right Man; Dark End Of The Street; My Uncle; Wheels; Juanita; Hot Burrito No. 1; Hot Burrito No. 2; Do You Know How It Feels; Hippie Boy.*

● FIRST RELEASED 1969
● UK PEAK CHART POSITION: did not chart
● USA PEAK CHART POSITION: 164

 175 SURF'S UP (179) ▲
THE BEACH BOYS

Surf's Up established the Beach Boys as an 'albums' band without sacrificing their individuality. The group's harmonies are as peerless as ever, their grasp of evocative melody unerring, particularly on Bruce Johnson's 'Disney Girls'. The ecological tenor of several tracks was politically shrewd and by opting to revive the title song from the unit's fabled Smile project, the Beach Boys reminded the outside world of their innovative past. Carl Wilson emerged as a fine composer (Long Promised Road), ''Till I Die' showed Brian Wilson's gifts intact, and the result was an artistic triumph, enabling the group to progress unfettered by artistic preconceptions.

● TRACKS: *Don't Go Near The Water; Long Promised Road; Take A Load Off Your Feet; Disney Girls (1957); Student Demonstration Time; Feel Flows; Lookin' At Tomorrow (A Welfare Song); A Day In The Life Of A Tree; 'Till I Die; Surf's Up.*

● FIRST RELEASED 1971
● UK PEAK CHART POSITION: 15
● USA PEAK CHART POSITION: 29

 174 COMPUTER WORLD (–) ▲
KRAFTWERK

Although it coincided with their period of greatest commercial success and popularity, *Computer World* also marked the beginning of Kraftwerk's decline as a pioneering force in electronic music. Tracks such as 'Pocket Calculator' and 'It's More Fun To Compute' indicated that the seemingly endless musical inventiveness of Ralf Hütter and Florian Scheider was drying up, although the hypnotic beats of 'Numbers' put the group on the dancefloors courtesy of Afrika Bambaataa's sampling on his 'Planet Rock' the following year. Easily their most accessible collection, *Computer World* marked a slightly disappointing end to Kraftwerk's run of brilliant albums.

● TRACKS: *Computer World; Pocket Calculator; Numbers; Computer World 2; Computer Love; Homecomputer; It's More Fun To Compute.*

● FIRST RELEASED 1981
● UK PEAK CHART POSITION: 15
● USA PEAK CHART POSITION: 72

 **176** ZOOROPA (–) ▲
U2

If you study the wild computer graphics on the sleeve you could be expecting something frantic and electric. In fact, this is the most relaxing U2 album to date, and one on which they sound content to cruise instead of surmonizing. Brian Eno's prescence no doubt added the ambient feel that is present on most of the tracks. Bono sounds like Roland Gift (Fine Young Cannibals) on 'Lemon' and The Edge like a monosyllabic Lou Reed on 'Numb'. U2 took risks with this album because it broke a familiar pattern by not sounding like a U2 record. They sailed through the audition.

● TRACKS: *Zooropa; Babyface; Numb; Lemon; Stay (Faraway So Close); Daddy's Gonna Pay For Your Crashed Car; Some Days Are Better Than Others; The First Time; Dirty Day; The Wanderer.*

● FIRST RELEASED 1993
● UK PEAK CHART POSITION: 1
● USA PEAK CHART POSITION: 1

177 **L.A. WOMAN** (111) ▼
THE DOORS

The final Doors album to feature vocalist Jim Morrison reaffirmed the quartet's grasp of blues/rock. Beset by personal and professional problems, they retreated to a rehearsal room, cast such pressures aside and recorded several of their most memorable compositions. The musicianship is uniformly excellent, the interplay between guitarist Robbie Krieger and keyboard player Ray Manzarek exudes confidence and empathy, while the strength and nuances of Morrison's voice add an unmistakable resonance. His death within weeks of the album's completion inevitably casts a pall over its content, especially the eerie rain and the funereal electric piano of 'Riders On The Storm'.

● TRACKS: *The Changeling; Love Her Madly; Been Down So Long; Cars Hiss By My Window; L.A. Woman; L'America; Hyacinth House; Crawling King Snake; The W.A.S.P. (Texas Radio And The Big Beat); Riders On The Storm.*

● FIRST RELEASED 1971
● UK PEAK CHART POSITION: 28
● USA PEAK CHART POSITION: 9

 178 **MR TAMBOURINE MAN** (–) ▲
THE BYRDS

The only other major group of the 60s, other than the fab four, to elicit such universal love and approval are the Byrds (the famous five). They were originally seen as copyists, and were certainly slammed when they first came to hostile England. The great Byrdologist Johnny Rogan and most of us lesser mortals now realize their massive influence on popular music since 1965. The McGuinn 12-string Rickenbacker opening of the title track is still one of the greatest sounds in music! On this, Gene Clark showed us he was a genius songwriter. The CD reissue with bonus tracks is as essential and dutiful as breathing and smiling. Just like Crosby did in those days.

● TRACKS: *Mr Tambourine Man; I'll Feel A Whole Lot Better; Spanish Harlem Incident; You Won't Have To Cry; Here Without You; The Bells Of Rhymney; All I Really Want To Do; I Knew I'd Want You; It's No Use; Don't Doubt Yourself Babe; Chimes Of Freedom; We'll Meet Again; She Has A Way; You And Me.*

● FIRST RELEASED 1965
● UK PEAK CHART POSITION: 7
● USA PEAK CHART POSITION: 6

 179 **GOODBYE YELLOW BRICK ROAD** (30) ▼
ELTON JOHN

An ambitious and bold attempt to produce a double album with no fillers, and Elton succeeded better than most. This is a brilliant package of sadness and pathos, notably 'Funeral For A Friend', 'Love Lies Bleeding', 'Candle In The Wind' and 'Goodbye Yellow Brick Road'. Both Taupin and John were able to change mood for the perennial encore 'Benny And The Jets'. Quite why 'Benny' is so liked is a mystery, it is usually followed by 'Saturday Night's Alright For Fighting', which is a much more substantial song. Note that this album contains the original 'Candle In The Wind', written for Marilyn Monroe, not the 1997 version.

● TRACKS: *Funeral For A Friend; Love Lies Bleeding; Benny And The Jets; Candle In The Wind; Goodbye Yellow Brick Road; This Song Has No Title; Grey Seal; Jamaica Jerk Off; I've Seen That Movie Too; Sweet Painted Lady; Ballad Of Danny Bailey; Dirty Little Girl; All The Girls Love Alice; Your Sister Can't Twist (But She Can Rock 'N' Roll); Saturday Night's Alright For Fighting; Roy Rogers; Social Disease; Harmony.*

● FIRST RELEASED 1973
● UK PEAK CHART POSITION: 1
● USA PEAK CHART POSITION: 1

180 **TELLIN' STORIES** (–) ▲
THE CHARLATANS

One UK indie band to have well and truly lasted the course, the Charlatans are now seen as old lags of a new scene. With this, their most successful album to date, they lifted themselves from a pit of despair after the tragic death of keyboard player Rob Collins. Tragic and ironic because Collins gave their sound an original edge with his full-sounding Hammond organ. His replacement to complete the recording of this album was Martin Duffy from Primal Scream. Excellent songs such as 'North Country Boy' and 'How High' are minor classics and the final instrumental doodle, 'Rob's Theme', is a fitting tribute to Collins.

● TRACKS: *With No Shoes; North Country Boy; Tellin' Stories; One To Another; You're A Big Girl Now; How Can You Leave Us; Area 51; How High; Only Teethin'; Get On It; Rob's Theme.*

● FIRST RELEASED 1997
● UK PEAK CHART POSITION: 1
● USA PEAK CHART POSITION: did not chart

181 DARKNESS ON THE EDGE OF TOWN
(235) ▲ BRUCE SPRINGSTEEN

Springsteen rarely figures in favourite album lists nowadays; his pink Cadillac has stalled. This was the album after the famous Jon Landau statement came to pass, and although there are still many references to cars and girls it is a blistering album. It has a similar energy that was later to be found on *The River*. He states in 'Something In The Night', 'soon as you've got something they send someone to try and take it away'. He repeated the themes again and again, and we loved it; maybe his fall from grace is because we ultimately can get by with just one song about cars and girls.

● TRACKS: *Badlands; Adam Raised A Cain; Something In The Night; Candy's Room; Racing In The Street; The Promised Land; Factory; Streets Of Fire; Prove It All Night; Darkness On The Edge Of Town.*

● FIRST RELEASED 1978
● UK PEAK CHART POSITION: 16
● USA PEAK CHART POSITION: 5

183 LADY SOUL (85) ▼
ARETHA FRANKLIN

Aretha's Franklin's position as soul music's premier female vocalist was consolidated by this album. Her strident reading of Don Covay's 'Chain Of Fools' set the tone for a collection on which the singer unveiled several stellar original compositions and reinterpreted a batch of classic songs. Franklin's gospel roots were clearly displayed on the anthem-like 'People Get Ready' while her interpretation of 'Natural Woman' showed both vulnerable and assertive qualities. *Lady Soul* captures a performer at the peak of her power, restating her ability to take material and make it uniquely her own.

● TRACKS: *Chain Of Fools; Money Won't Change You; People Get Ready; Niki Hoeky; (You Make Me Feel Like) A Natural Woman; Since You've Been Gone (Sweet Sweet Baby); Good To Me As I Am To You; Come Back Baby; Groovin'; Ain't No Way.*

● FIRST RELEASED 1968
● UK PEAK CHART POSITION: 25
● USA PEAK CHART POSITION: 2

182 SURREALISTIC PILLOW (131) ▼
JEFFERSON AIRPLANE

One of a handful of albums epitomizing the 'Summer of Love', *Surrealistic Pillow*'s strengths lie in a gorgeous cross-section of folk, blues and acid-rock. Vocalists Grace Slick and Marty Balin interwove over a seamless instrumental section in which Jack Cassady (bass) and Jorma Kaukonen (guitar) enjoyed an almost telepathic understanding. The scope of the material is breathtaking, be it science fiction, Lewis Carroll or a succession of haunting, fragile love songs such as the exquisite 'Today'. Restrained when required, animated at others, but always challenging, the album succeeds through a collective determination.

● TRACKS: *She Has Funny Cars; Somebody To Love; My Best Friend; Today; Comin' Back To Me; 3/5 Mile In 10 Seconds; D.C.B.A-25; How Do You Feel; White Rabbit; Plastic Fantastic Lover; Embryonic Journey.*

● FIRST RELEASED 1967
● UK PEAK CHART POSITION: did not chart
● USA PEAK CHART POSITION: 3

184 HOT RATS (195) ▲
FRANK ZAPPA

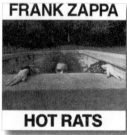

Having temporarily disbanded the Mothers Of Invention, Frank Zappa recorded this exceptional solo album. His group was renowned for musical satire, but here the artist opted to showcase his prowess on guitar. 'Willie The Pimp' apart, which features a cameo vocal by his old friend Captain Beefheart; the set is comprised of instrumentals. The players, who include Don 'Sugarcane' Harris, Jean-Luc Ponty and Ian Underwood, are uniformly excellent, combining to provide a solid jazz-rock platform for Zappa's always compulsive soloing. He relishes a freedom which, while acknowledging past achievements, prepared new territories for exploration. *Hot Rats* was a pivotal release in Zappa's misunderstood career.

● TRACKS: *Peaches En Regalia; Willie The Pimp; Son Of Mr. Green Genes; Little Umbrellas; The Gumbo Variations; It Must Be A Camel.*

● FIRST RELEASED 1969
● UK PEAK CHART POSITION: 9
● USA PEAK CHART POSITION: 173

185 ### GREEN (193) ▲
R.E.M.

The album that found the band sandwiched between being an important cult band on the verge of major success and being the world's most successful rock band of the 90s. A tricky situation, but this album made the breakthrough and mighty Warner Brothers were behind it. R.E.M. were able to get their folky mandolin material like 'You Are The Everything' accepted on an equal footing with great pop such as 'Stand' or 'Pop Song 89' (which could have been written by Jim Morrison and titled 'Hello I Love You'). 'Orange Crush' is already an FM radio favourite, and the rest is all recent history.

● TRACKS: *Pop Song 89; Get Up; You Are The Everything; Stand; World Leader Pretend; The Wrong Child; Orange Crush; Turn You Inside Out; Hairshirt; I Remember California; Untitled.*

● FIRST RELEASED 1988
● UK PEAK CHART POSITION: 27
● USA PEAK CHART POSITION: 12

 186 ### RAIN DOGS (212) ▲
TOM WAITS

Tom Waits discarded his bohemian sage persona with the radical *Swordfishtrombones*, and this follow-up release synthesized and developed themes from that groundbreaking album. Ever-shifting percussive textures are supported, where applicable, by horns or Farfisa organ and several guest musicians, including Rolling Stone Keith Richards, contribute to its mélange. Waits' bourbon-laced voice is as riveting as ever, intoning lyrics that are, at various times, touching, evocative, sly or simply funny. His off-kilter perceptions encompass country, polkas and heart-rending ballads, each of which he expresses with consummate ease. *Rain Dogs* is yet another strong statement from a highly innovative artist.

● TRACKS: *Singapore; Clap Hands; Cemetary Polka; Jockey Full Of Bourbon; Tango Till They're Sore; Big Black Maria; Diamonds And Gold; Hang Down Your Head; Time; Rain Dogs; Midtown; Ninth And Headpin; Gun Street Girl; Union Square; Blind Love; Walking Spanish; Downtown Train; Bride Of Raindog; Anywhere I Lay My Head.*

● FIRST RELEASED 1985
● UK PEAK CHART POSITION: 29
● USA PEAK CHART POSITION: 181

 187 ### IN A SILENT WAY (464) ▲
MILES DAVIS

Miles Davis's hushed masterpiece *In A Silent Way* was pieced together in the studio from a series of long stretches of quiet and intense collective improvisation. Masterfully demonstrating to the jazz world that rock's electric instruments were not necessarily harsh and noisy creatures, he again proved his creative and conceptual genius, fashioning the sound of fusion with the aid of Herbie Hancock, Chick Corea and Joe Zawinul on electric pianos and organ, John McLaughlin on electric guitar, Wayne Shorter on soprano saxophone, British bassist Dave Holland and drummer Tony Williams. This is a delicate and beautiful thing that has rarely been repeated.

● TRACKS: *Shhh; Peaceful; In A Silent Way; It's About That Time.*

● FIRST RELEASED 1969
● UK PEAK CHART POSITION: did not chart
● USA PEAK CHART POSITION: 134

 188 ### NEW BOOTS AND PANTIES!! (53) ▼
IAN DURY AND THE BLOCKHEADS

Ian Dury's one great album, so good that it overtakes major stars and million-selling supergroups. Dury portrayed the Essex man before Essex man was conceived, and brilliantly satirized it in 'Billericay Dickie' and 'Clevor Trever'. It is hard to imagine Dury the romantic, but there *is* a romantic in 'Wake Up And Make Love To Me' and 'I'm Partial To Your Abracadabra'; there is also sadness and regret in the beautiful 'My Old Man'. He should be remembered for his dynamite band the Blockheads and this necessary album - not his gold radio station albatross 'Hit Me With Your Rhythm Stick'.

● TRACKS: *Sweet Gene Vincent; Wake Up And Make Love To Me; I'm Partial To Your Abracadabra; My Old Man; Billericay Dickie; Clevor Trever; If I Was With A Woman; Plaistow Patricia; Blockheads; Blackmail Man.*

● FIRST RELEASED 1977
● UK PEAK CHART POSITION: 5
● USA PEAK CHART POSITION: 168

189 RUST NEVER SLEEPS (126) ▼
NEIL YOUNG AND CRAZY HORSE

Neil Young's lengthy recording career contains several landmark albums of which *Rust Never Sleeps* is one of the most vital. Half-acoustic, half-electric, it is bookended by contrasting versions of the same song which pays homage to Sex Pistols vocalist, Johnny Rotten. Long-time associates Crazy Horse support Young on the electric selections which exude white-noise power, marrying savage guitarwork with emphatic lyrics. The remaining selections offer a pastoral atmosphere. Part country, part folk, their gentle qualities invoke the atmosphere of Young's bestseller, *Harvest*, completing a set that provides a scintillating précis of the artist's eclectic work.

● TRACKS: *My My, Hey Hey (Out Of The Blue); Thrasher; Ride My Llama; Sail Away; Pocahontas; Powder Finger; Welfare Mothers; Sedan Delivery; Hey Hey, My My (Into The Black).*

● FIRST RELEASED 1979
● UK PEAK CHART POSITION: 13
● USA PEAK CHART POSITION: 8

191 THE NIGHTFLY (–) ▲
DONALD FAGEN

Quality will out. There was no need to put a great big Steely Dan sticker on this smooth little number, the radio programmers took care of that. Not surprisingly it sounded like another excellent album from the dildos. No tracks jar, each has a big-smile middle eight and although it may be just too slick for some people's taste, mostly it is a tremendous solo album. 'I.G.Y. (International Geophyical Year)', 'New Frontier' and the title track are gloriously easy on the ear. The cover version of Leiber and Stoller's 'Ruby Baby' is so good it sounds like a Fagen original.

● TRACKS: *I.G.Y.; Green Flower Street; Ruby Baby; Maine; New Frontier.*

● FIRST RELEASED 1982
● UK PEAK CHART POSITION: 44
● USA PEAK CHART POSITION: 11

190 #1 RECORD (–) ▲
BIG STAR

In mid-60s America, a typical AM radio station featured every style of music that was on the charts. Big Star grew up with that wide-ranging buffet on their transistor radios and could not tolerate the barriers that had arisen between pop and rock. On the Memphis quartet's luminous debut, *#1 Record*, they channelled the Beatles and the Byrds via the Who, layering high-decibel guitars over delicate folk-rock tunes. There was also a hint of Memphis soul, not surprising since one of the group's songwriter/guitarists, Alex Chilton, had led 60s hitmakers the Box Tops. While critics canonized it, poor distribution doomed it to the deletion bins.

● TRACKS: *Feel; The Ballad Of El Goodo; In The Street; Thirteen; Don't Lie To Me; The India Song; When My Baby's Beside Me; My Life Is Right; Give Me Another Chance; Try Again; Watch The Sunrise; ST100/6.*

● FIRST RELEASED 1972
● UK PEAK CHART POSITION: did not chart
● US PEAK CHART POSITION: did not chart

192 STEPHEN STILLS (295) ▲
STEPHEN STILLS

This outstanding solo debut came at a particularly successful and creative time for Stills. In the space of a couple of years he made two solo albums, released the superb Manassas double album and was part of CSNY. He was also living in Surrey, England, which explains the appearance of many UK-based musicians, from Eric Clapton to Ringo Starr and even Jimi Hendrix. This varied set shows Stills to be precociously talented as he tackled memphis soul, folk, blues, rock and goodtime pop with the still fresh-sounding 'Love The One You're With'. Equally arresting is 'Black Queen', allegedly recorded after Stills had downed a bottle of tequila, and was 'drunk as a skunk'.

● TRACKS: *Love The One You're With; Do For The Others; Church (Part Of Someone); Old Times, Good Times; Go Back Home; Sit Yourself Down; To A Flame; Black Queen; Cherokee; We Are Not Helpless.*

● FIRST RELEASED 1970
● UK PEAK CHART POSITION: 30
● USA PEAK CHART POSITION: 3

193 THE FREEWHEELIN' BOB DYLAN (80) ▼
BOB DYLAN

With this album Dylan emerged from the cloak of Woody Guthrie and proclaimed his own unique talent. No longer detached - the set was originally entitled 'Bob Dylan's Blues' - he personalized his songs, famously rejecting four from the final draft in favour of others reflecting his newer muse. Protest songs were given a wider resonance - the text of 'Masters Of War' remains as relevant some 30 years on - while his love songs are haunting, but universal, statements. Dylan injected black humour into the talking blues and railed against injustice in all forms with a perception encompassing the anger of a generation. *Freewheelin'* is a landmark in the development of folk and pop music.

● TRACKS: *Blowin' In The Wind; Girl From The North Country; Masters Of War; Down The Highway; Bob Dylan's Blues; Hard Rain's Gonna Fall; Don't Think Twice; Bob Dylan's Dream; Oxford Town; Talking World War III Blues; Corina Corina; Honey, Just Allow Me One More Chance; I Shall Be Free.*

● FIRST RELEASED 1964
● UK PEAK CHART POSITION: 1
● USA PEAK CHART POSITION: 22

194 TRANS-EUROPE EXPRESS (–) ▲
KRAFTWERK

Kraftwerk reached a creative peak on this 1977 masterpiece, whose second side was entirely devoted to a breathtaking aural recreation of an intercontinental train journey. The first side featured the shimmering beauty of 'Europe Endless' alongside the eerie, dislocated vocals of 'The Hall Of Mirrors' and 'Showroom Dummies', the latter track demonstrating the band's often unappreciated sly humour. Representing one of the pinnacles of 70s electronic music, it was a notable irony that the expressionless and mechanistic Kraftwerk went on to become, via Afrika Bambaataa's sampling of 'Trans-Europe Express' on his seminal 'Planet Rock' single, one of the early pioneers of dance music.

● TRACKS: *Europe Endless; The Hall Of Mirrors; Showroom Dummies; Trans-Europe Express; Metal On Metal; Franz Schubert; Endless Endless.*

● FIRST RELEASED 1977
● UK PEAK CHART POSITION: 49
● USA PEAK CHART POSITION: 119

195 COMING UP (–) ▲
SUEDE

Suede's third album, and their first without main songwriter Bernard Butler, lacked none of their trademark glam rock and catchy melodies, but, crucially, it discarded the pomposity and indulgence that marred *Dog Man Star*. Instead, boosted by Richard Oakes' inventive guitarwork and the arrival of Neil Codling on keyboards, they presented a sparsely produced collection of Bowie-tinged pop songs. Brett Anderson's favourite lyrical themes - bored youth, casual sex, seedy urban life ('peepshows and freakshows') and escape from it - enjoyed free rein, but were predominantly framed within raunchy rockers rather than gloomy ballads. With the likes of 'Trash', 'Filmstar' and 'She', Suede firmly established themselves as the godfathers of indie glam and offered some classic pop into the bargain.

● TRACKS: *Trash; Filmstar; Lazy; By The Sea; She; Beautiful Ones; Starcrazy; Picnic By The Motorway; The Chemistry Between Us; Saturday Night.*

● FIRST RELEASED 1996
● UK PEAK POSITION: 1
● USA PEAK POSITION: did not chart

196 HELP (112) ▼
THE BEATLES

Although *A Hard Day's Night* as a film captured more hearts than *Help*, both soundtrack albums are full of terrific songs. Half of this material was showcased in the movie. Who could forget the expertly filmed studio scene, as the boys record 'You're Going To Lose That Girl'. Prior to Ringo disappearing through the sawn-through floor with his drums, the engineer asks, 'boys are you buzzing?'. 'No thanks I've got the car', quips back John. The hit single 'Ticket To Ride' took on a new meaning as they skied down the mountain at night with flares. Beautiful, harmless stuff, and yet another album to testify to their greatness.

● TRACKS: *Help; The Night Before; You've Got To Hide Your Love Away; I Need You; Another Girl; You're Going To Lose That Girl; Ticket To Ride; Act Naturally; It's Only Love; You Like Me Too Much; Tell Me What You See; I've Just Seen A Face; Yesterday; Dizzy Miss Lizzy.*

● FIRST RELEASED 1965
● UK PEAK CHART POSITION: 1
● USA PEAK CHART POSITION: 1

197 FIVE LEAVES LEFT (130) ▼
NICK DRAKE

Nick Drake's debut album encapsulates a marriage between folk music and the singer-songwriter genre. Part Donovan, part Jim Webb, he articulated an aching romanticism at a time when progressive rock ran rampant. Beautiful melodies and fragrant accompaniment, in particular Robert Kirby's stunning string arrangements, enhance the artist's sense of longing in which warm, but understated, vocals accentuate the album's passive mystery. An aura of existential cool envelops the proceedings, accentuated by Danny Thompson's sonorous bass lines and Drake's poetic imagery. The result is a shimmering, autumnal collection, reflective but never morbid. It's a tragedy that Drake never lived to see how his stature has grown.

● TRACKS: *Time Has Told Me; River Man; Three Hours; Way To Blue; Day Is Done; 'Cello Song; The Thoughts Of Mary Jane; Man In A Shed; Fruit Tree; Saturday Sun.*

● FIRST RELEASED 1969
● UK PEAK CHART POSITION: did not chart
● USA PEAK CHART POSITION: did not chart

198 GARBAGE (–) ▲
GARBAGE

An exceptional debut that buried the quality of the music behind the attention that focused on lead singer Shirley Manson. She was outspoken and provocative visually and verbally, and the hacks rushed to kneel before her. From the opening 'Supervixen', the pace is set; the split-second pauses during this track are a powerful hook and grab the attention of the listener. Heavy and melodic, the band sound like a seasoned unit, bass and drum mixed together brilliantly, and the lead guitar never stealing the show, only complementing Manson's dusky vocals. Although much of the album utilizes loops and computer technology, the overall sound is that of a rock band.

● TRACKS: *Supervixen; Queer; Only Happy When It Rains; As Heaven Is Wide; Not My Idea; A Stroke Of Luck; Vow; Stupid Girl; Dog New Tricks; My Lover's Box; Fix Me Now; Milk.*

● FIRST RELEASED 1995
● UK PEAK CHART POSITION: 6
● USA PEAK CHART POSITION: 20

199 TONIGHT'S THE NIGHT (–) ▲
NEIL YOUNG

For many years this was the critics' favourite. The cognoscenti loved its rawness and the depression the album both portrayed and induced. The title track chronicles roadie Bruce Berry and Crazy Horse member Danny Whitten's deaths. Other songs address the fact that Young was just not a happy bunny at this time in his life. The sloppy piano and most guitar parts are played by Nils Lofgren. The bar-room atmosphere has been repeated on many Young albums over the years, but never as home-grown as this. Of all the excellent records Young has made, this is definitely not the one for sunny Sunday mornings.

● TRACKS: *Tonight's The Night; Speakin' Out; World On A String; Borrowed Tune; Come On Baby Let's Go Downtown; Mellow My Mind; Roll Another Number (For The Road); Albuquerque; New Mama; Lookout Joe; Tired Eyes; Tonight's The Night Part II.*

● FIRST RELEASED 1975
● UK PEAK CHART POSITION: 48
● USA PEAK CHART POSITION: 25

200 CATCH A FIRE (141) ▼
THE WAILERS

One of the biggest drawbacks of the CD age is the lack of potential for the covers. The original issue of this pivotal album came in the shape of a Zippo lighter, which opened with a rivetted flip-top (eventually) to reveal the cut out flame. Beyond the flame was the real fire: a superb collection of songs that stand up to repeated play over 20 years later. Even with the huge commercial success that Marley enjoyed with big-selling albums, the Wailers' followers and critics come back to this superb record time and time again. The first proper reggae album for any new collector.

● TRACKS: *Concrete Jungle; Slave Driver; 400 Years; Stop That Train; Rock It Baby; Stir It Up; Kinky Reggae; No More Trouble; Midnight Ravers.*

● FIRST RELEASED 1972
● UK PEAK CHART POSITION: did not chart
● USA PEAK CHART POSITION: 171

201 **HEJIRA** (438) ▲
JONI MITCHELL

Joni Mitchell draws freely on her heroes and influences, and in her turn inspires and informs the work of countless others; thus are the genes of our musical heritage passed on to new generations. The love of jazz glimpsed in *Court And Spark* and *The Hissing Of Summer Lawns* is wanton in *Hejira*. The arrangements are loose and the melodies seductively free-flowing. The lyrics, too, have broken free of rigid verse and rhyme structures and tend towards prose poetry. The cloak of introspection that weighs down on much of her work is lighter here; though far from mainstream. The chiming flanged guitar throughout, is inspired.

● TRACKS: *Coyote; Amelia; Furry Sings The Blues; Strange Boy; Hejira; Song For Sharon; Black Crow; Blue Motel Room; Refuge Of The Road.*

● FIRST RELEASED 1976
● UK PEAK CHART POSITION: 11
● USA PEAK CHART POSITION: 13

 202 **SURFER ROSA** (391) ▲
PIXIES

Now seen as an important alternative band of the 80s, it is a pity they were not more appreciated at the time. The Boston-based Pixies exploded into life with this abrasive selection. Produced by enfant terrible Steve Albini, the album emphasized the quartet's scratchy tension. A vicious drum sound underpins the group's uncanny blend of urgency and melody, where Black Francis's rabid intonation contrasts with Kim Deal's more gentle perspective. Obtuse lyrics and barely controlled guitar accentuate the Pixies' uncompromising visions and emphasize an approach that both excites and intrigues. Terse, exhilarating and single-minded, *Surfer Rosa* is an audacious collection.

● TRACKS: *Bone Machine; Break My Body; Something Against You; Broken Face; Gigantic; River Euphrates; Where Is My Mind?; Cactus; Tony's Theme; Oh My Golly!; Vamos; I'm Amazed; Brick Is Red.*

● FIRST RELEASED 1988
● UK PEAK CHART POSITION: did not chart
● USA PEAK CHART POSITION: did not chart

203 **CLEAR SPOT** (–) ▲
CAPTAIN BEEFHEART AND THE MAGIC BAND

After the unique *Trout Mask Replica*, Beefheart moved slowly to what we mortals would call music, very much like the stuff on *Safe As Milk*. His 'music from Venus' had never been quite so easy on the ear and *Clear Spot* was a hit album, of sorts. Nobody other than John Lennon has been able to approximate the English language so brilliantly as this man. How can you resist 'My Head Is My Only House Unless It Rains' or 'Her Eyes Are A Blue Million Miles'? The Captain can also fool us with a real love song, the sublime 'Too Much Time'.

● TRACKS: *Low Yo Yo Stuff; Nowadays A Woman's Gotta Hit A Man; Too Much Time; Circumstances; My Head Is My Only House Unless It Rains; Sun Zoom Spark; Clear Spot; Crazy Little Thing; Long Neck Bottles; Her Eyes Are A Blue Million Miles; Big Eyed Beans From Venus; Golden Birdies.*

● FIRST RELEASED 1972
● UK PEAK CHART POSITION: did not chart
● USA PEAK CHART POSITION: 191

204 **THE BLANTON-WEBSTER YEARS** (31) ▼
DUKE ELLINGTON

A special kind of magic surrounds the Ellington band that featured Ben Webster and Jimmy Blanton; the former's tenor solos, breathily romantic or fiercely swinging, the latter changing the role of the bass in jazz. Yet these two were far from being the only stars. Not least among others were the liquid beauty of Johnny Hodges's alto and Cootie Williams' plangent trumpet. In addition, there was always the

arranging-composing skills of Billy Strayhorn, another new arrival, and the maestro himself. Together, they brought to eternal life masterpieces such as 'Just A-Settin' And A-Rockin'', 'Ko-Ko', 'Jack The Bear', 'Cotton Tail' and 'Concerto For Cootie'.

● TRACKS: *You, You Darlin'; Jack The Bear; Ko Ko; Morning Glory; So Far, So Good; Conga Brava; Concerto For Cootie (Do Nothin' Till You Hear From Me); Me And You; Cotton Tail; Never No Lament; Dusk; Bojangles; A Portrait Of Bert Williams; Blue Goose; Harlem Air Shaft; At A Dixie Roadside Diner; All Too Soon; Rumpus In Richmond; My Greatest Mistake; Sepia Panorama; There Shall Be No Night; In A Mellow Tone; Five O'clock Whistle; Warm Valley; The Flaming Sword; Jumpin' Punkins; Across The Track Blues; John Hardy's Wife; Blue Serge; After All; Chloe; Bakiff; Are You Sticking?; I Never Felt This Way Before; Just A-Settin' And A-Rockin'; The Giddybug Gallop; The Sidewalks Of New York; Chocolate Shake; Flamingo; I Got It Bad (And That Ain't Good); Clementine; Brown Skin Gal; The Girl In My Dreams Tries To Look Like You; Jump For Joy; Moon Over Cuba; Take The 'A' Train; Five O'clock Drag; Rocks In My Bed; Blip Blip; Chelsea Bridge; Raincheck; What Good Would It Do?; I Don't Mind; Someone; My Little Brown Book; Main Stem; Johnny Come Lately; Hayfoot Strawfoot; Sentimental Lady; A Sip Of The Lip (Can Sink A Ship); Sherman Shuffle.*

● FIRST RELEASED 1987 ● RECORDED 1940-42
● UK PEAK CHART POSITION: did not chart
● USA PEAK CHART POSITION: did not chart

205 WE'RE ONLY IN IT FOR THE MONEY
(–) ▲ FRANK ZAPPA / MOTHERS OF INVENTION

The early Zappa albums were treasured by the few and totally misunderstood by the majority. The brilliant satire of the *Sgt. Pepper* cover should have garnered extra sales, but no. Zappa's scathing wit homed in on modern middle-class America and the west coast hippies. Nineteen vignettes of *avant garde*, doo-wop, some regular pop music and a lot of hilarious dialogue, which was so hip it has never dated. Zappa made us confront the obvious, and the results were alarming. These issues are best demonstrated on 'What's The Ugliest Part Of Your Body', 'Bow Tie Daddy' and 'The Idiot Bastard Son'.

● TRACKS: *Are You Hung Up; Who Needs The Peace Corps; Concentration Moon; Mom & Dad; Telephone Conversation; Bow Tie Daddy; Harry, You're A Beast; What's The Ugliest Part Of Your Body; Absolutely Free; Flower Punk; Hot Poop; Nasal Retentive Calliope Music; Let's Make The Water Turn Black; The Idiot Bastard Son; Lonely Little Girl; Take Your Clothes Off When You Dance; What's The Ugliest Part Of Your Body; Mother People; The Chrome Plated Megaphone Of Destiny.*

● FIRST RELEASED 1968
● UK PEAK CHART POSITION: did not chart
● USA PEAK CHART POSITION: 30

206 HERE COME THE WARM JETS (413) ▲
BRIAN ENO

Having left Roxy Music, Eno began his solo career with this idiosyncratic album. Robert Fripp, Paul Thompson and Phil Manzanera are among those appearing on a set of songs exhibiting a mischievous love of pure pop music. Macabre lyrics constantly subvert the quirky melodies, a feature fully expressed on 'Baby's On Fire', while the singer's cheeky vocals exaggerate the ambiguity. Savage guitar lines, erratic synthesizer and pounding drums provide exciting textures on a collection as beguiling as it is invigorating.

● TRACKS: *Needles In A Camel's Eye; The Paw Paw Negro Blowtorch; Baby's On Fire; Cindy Tells Me; Driving Me Backwards; On Some Faraway Beach; Blank Frank; Dead Finks Don't Talk; Some Of Them Are Old; Here Come The Warm Jets.*

● FIRST RELEASED 1974
● UK PEAK CHART POSITION: 26
● USA PEAK CHART POSITION: 151

207 MY AIM IS TRUE (46) ▼
ELVIS COSTELLO

'Oh I used to be disgusted, and now I try to be amused', sang a youngish Costello in 1977, as he opened what for many is his best album. The pent-up frustration of the first album was mixed with melancholy for this, his second offering. 'Alison' is a beautiful love song and could be (and should be) covered by Tony Bennett and Barbra Streisand, in the way that McCartney's 'Yesterday' became universal. Elsewhere, the wonderful Attractions support fine songs such as 'Mystery Dance', 'Red Shoes' and the paradoxical 'I'm Not Angry'. I wonder whether Costello knew how significant both he and this album would become?

● TRACKS: *Welcome To The Working Week; Miracle Man; No Dancing; Blame It On Cain; Alison; Sneaky Feelings; (The Angels Wanna Wear) My Red Shoes; Less Than Zero; Mystery Dance; Pay It Back; I'm Not Angry; Waiting For The End Of The World.*

● FIRST RELEASED 1977
● UK PEAK CHART POSITION: 14
● USA PEAK CHART POSITION: 32

208 AMERICAN BEAUTY (255) ▲
THE GRATEFUL DEAD

Following on from their beautiful country-tinged exercise in sounding like Crosby, Stills And Nash, the Dead gave us an even mellower set with this exemplary record. The album's stand-out track is the introspective 'Ripple'; for once, Jerry Garcia actually sings one of Robert Hunter's lyrics as though he means it. Other excellent supporting numbers are 'Box Of Rain' and the overwhelmingly sad 'Attics Of My Life'. Although the Grateful Dead remained a mellow band, they were never able to record another album that was as light and emotional. There are no overlong solos on this absolutely charming record, but tons of emotion when remembering Garcia.

● TRACKS: *Box Of Rain; Friend Of The Devil; Operator; Sugar Magnolia; Ripple; Brokedown Palace; Till The Morning Comes; Attics Of My Life; Truckin'.*

● FIRST RELEASED 1970
● UK PEAK CHART POSITION: did not chart
● USA PEAK CHART POSITION: 30

209 TURN! TURN! TURN! (–) ▲
THE BYRDS

Uncomfortably hot on the heels of their debut album, this record had no right to be so good. Once again Gene Clark had enough great songs to complement the Dylan and traditional material, especially 'Set You Free This Time' and 'It Won't Be Wrong'. Their cover of the title track is untouchable in terms of sound and emotion and just behind is the gorgeous 'Lay Down Your Weary Tune'. The excellent reissue contains among others the Crosby instrumental 'Stranger In A Strange Land'. Commercially, they had already peaked, but creatively they were just getting started. As good as this is, the best was still to come.

● TRACKS: *Turn! Turn! Turn!; It Won't Be Wrong; Set You Free This Time; Lay Down Your Weary Tune; He Was A Friend Of Mine; The World Turns All Around Her; Satisfied Mind; If You're Gone; The Times They Are A-Changin'; Wait And See; Oh! Susannah; The Day Walk (Never Before); She Don't Care About The Time; The Times They Are A Changin'; It's All Over Now, Baby Blue; She Don't Care About The Time; The World Turns All Around Her; Stranger In A Strange Land.*

● FIRST RELEASED 1965
● UK PEAK CHART POSITION: 11
● USA PEAK CHART POSITION: 17

210 GENERATION TERRORISTS (–) ▲
MANIC STREET PREACHERS

Those fans that discovered this album when it was first released deserve to feel ever so slightly smug. It took most of the rest of the world until *Everything Must Go* before this album was fully appreciated. Sounding like a cross between metal and punk, the energy and melody never lets up for one second. After the first three tracks are over, a quick lie-down is in order before you tackle the sentiment of 'Motorcycle Emptiness'. Lyrically, the Manics are giants; it is a great pity that their statements of ironic values of the 80s and 90s are not listened to more. Thank goodness this album was finally discovered.

● TRACKS: *Slash N' Burn; Nat West, Barclays, Midlands, Lloyds; Born To End; Motorcycle Emptiness; You Love Us; Love's Sweet Exile; Little Baby Nothing; Repeat (Stars And Stripes); Tennessee; Another Invented Disease; Stay Beautiful; So Dead; Repeat (UK); Spectators Of Suicide; Damn Dog; Crucifix Kiss; Methadone Pretty; Condemned To Rock N' Roll.*

● FIRST RELEASED 1992
● UK PEAK CHART POSITION: 13
● USA PEAK CHART POSITION: did not chart

211 RADIO CITY (–) ▲
BIG STAR

Big Star's level of influence is inversely proportionate to their sales. *Radio City*, the second album by the band from Memphis, Tennessee, is the greatest example of this phenomenon. When it was first released, practically the only people who knew about it were rock critics. Today, it is universally recognized as a major inspiration for the indie and alternative rock movements, influencing everyone from R.E.M. to Teenage Fanclub. Although the term 'power pop' had been kicking around for a while, *Radio City* defined the genre. Best-known (or least-obscure) of its tracks is the sparkling 'September Gurls', which has been covered by many artists, including the Bangles and the late-model Searchers. Still very modern in sound, it is a landmark of the second pop era.

● TRACKS: *O My Soul; Life Is White; Way Out West; What's Goin Ahn; You Get What You Deserve; Mod Lang; Back Of A Car; Daisy Glaze; She's A Mover; September Gurls; Morpha Too; I'm In Love With A Girl.*

● FIRST RELEASED 1974
● UK PEAK CHART POSITION: did not chart
● US PEAK CHART POSITION: did not chart

212 LED ZEPPELIN (209) ▼
LED ZEPPELIN

Led Zeppelin emerged from the ashes of the Yardbirds, but their self-assured debut album immediately established them in their own right. Faultless musicianship combined with strong material to create an emphatic statement of purpose. Blues standards are extensively reworked and original songs either acknowledge pop/rock structures or allow the quartet to extend itself musically. Guitarist Jimmy Page explores the instrument's potential with dazzling runs or sonic inventiveness, while Robert Plant takes the notion of vocalist into new realms of expression. *Led Zeppelin* announced the arrival of one of the most important groups of our time.

● TRACKS: *Good Times Bad Times; Babe I'm Gonna Leave You; You Shook Me; Dazed And Confused; Your Time Is Gonna Come; Black Mountain Side; Communication Breakdown; I Can't Quit You Baby; How Many More Times.*

● FIRST RELEASED 1969
● UK PEAK CHART POSITION: 6
● USA PEAK CHART POSITION: 10

213 AVALON (348) ▲
ROXY MUSIC

Like the Police, Roxy Music never outstayed their welcome and got out while they were on top. Their farewell album leaves a good taste in the mouth when remembering the doyens of art rock. By the time of this album they had become immaculate smoothies: Ferry had taken to suits, Eno was long gone and Andy Mackay had kept his quiff but grown an extra chin. Appearances aside, this is a lasting record and it proved to be one of their most successful. 'More Than This' and 'Take A Chance With Me' were both hit singles, as was the title track on which Ferry at his most seductive informs us 'now the party's over, I'm so tired'. A most agreeable exit.

● TRACKS: *More Than This; The Space Between; Avalon; India; While My Heart Is Still Beating; The Main Thing; Take A Chance With Me; To Turn You On; True To Life; Tara.*

● FIRST RELEASED 1982
● UK PEAK CHART POSITION: 1
● USA PEAK CHART POSITION: 53

215 BORN IN THE USA (70) ▼
BRUCE SPRINGSTEEN

Springsteen purists may well bemoan the overtly commercial stance taken on this record, but its catchiness, high toe-tapping factor and damn good songs cannot be denied. 'Darlington County' and 'Working On The Highway' are familiar Springsteen themes, but it is the incredible power of the title track's riff and the euphoria that 'Dancing In The Dark' still manages to convey that make this album special. It is felt that he peaked with this record, and his commercial standing has since plummeted, but *Born In The USA* still sparkles and above all, it still sounds like a good 80s rock album.

● TRACKS: *Born In The USA; Cover Me; Darlington County; Working On The Highway; Downbound Train; I'm On Fire; No Surrender; Bobby Jean; I'm Goin' Down; Glory Days; Dancing In The Dark; My Hometown.*

● FIRST RELEASED 1984
● UK PEAK CHART POSITION: 1
● USA PEAK CHART POSITION: 1

214 IT'S TOO LATE TO STOP NOW (340) ▲
VAN MORRISON

Having completed a sequence of peerless studio albums, Van Morrison embarked on an expansive tour with this searing live set. Drawing sterling support from the Caledonia Soul Orchestra, the singer performs some of his most popular songs, acknowledges influences and even pays homage to his hit group, Them, with a medley of their two most successful singles. Not content with simply recreating material, Morrison uses his instinctive gifts to change inflections and bring new emphases, reshaping each piece according to the moment's mood, rather than relying on previously recorded versions. His sense of timing on tracks such as the penultimate 'Caravan', is amazing; just to snap your finger and know the band can follow must be a great feeling.

● TRACKS: *Ain't Nothing You Can Do; Warm Love; Into The Mystic; These Dreams Of You; I Believe To My Soul; I've Been Working; Help Me; Wild Children; Domino; I Just Wanna Make Love To You; Bring It On Home; Saint Dominic's Preview; Take Your Hand Out Of My Pocket; Listen To The Lion; Here Comes The Night; Gloria; Caravan; Cypress Avenue.*

● FIRST RELEASED 1974
● UK PEAK CHART POSITION: did not chart
● USA PEAK CHART POSITION: 53

216 THERE'S A RIOT GOIN' ON (277) ▲
SLY AND THE FAMILY STONE

During the late 60s Sly And The Family Stone changed the nature of soul music by infusing it with elements of psychedelic pop. Their exciting, effervescent singles included 'Dance To The Music', 'Stand' and 'I Want To Take You Higher', but with the release of this album, group leader Sly Stone exorcised personal and cultural psychoses. Its brooding funk was distilled through a deep, somnambulist sound in which even the lightest of songs, 'Runnin' Away' or 'Family Affair', were tinged with discomfort. The set culminates with bitter, twisted rhythms, disembodied vocals and a ravaged intensity quite unlike anything previously heard in soul music.

● TRACKS: *Luv 'N' Haight; Just Like A Baby; The Poet; Family Affair; Africa Talks To You 'The Asphalt Jungle'; Brave And Strong; (You Caught Me) Smilin'; Time; Spaced Cowboy; Runnin' Away; Thank You For Talking To Me Africa.*

● FIRST RELEASED 1971
● UK PEAK CHART POSITION: 31
● USA PEAK CHART POSITION: 1

217 MASTER OF PUPPETS (625) ▲
METALLICA

Metallica's irresistible rise to the top continued with this enigmatic 1986 album. A constant touring unit by this point, their combination of light and dark and their deft staccato delivery, especially on the title-track, came brusquely through. Their ever-lengthening arrangements (three songs came in at over eight minutes), bolstered by the precise snap of Hetfield's vocals, testified to their undeniable power. The striding 'Battery', the darkly lit 'Welcome Home (Sanitarium)', as well as the complex instrumental, 'Orion', all gave powerful testament to their ever-developing skill and vision.

● TRACKS: Battery; Master Of Puppets; The Thing That Should Not Be; Welcome Home (Sanitarium); Disposable Heroes; Leper Messiah; Orion; Damage Inc.

● FIRST RELEASED 1986
● UK PEAK CHART POSITION: 41
● USA PEAK CHART POSITION: 29

218 AGAIN (227) ▲
BUFFALO SPRINGFIELD

A year after Sgt. Pepper came America's possible answer, both with the formidable talent within the band, including Stephen Stills, Richie Furay and Neil Young, and the varied content of folk, rock, country, soul and mild psychedelia. The strong egos within made their future an impossibility as the leaders went on to major success with CSNY and Poco. Hearing this record made David Crosby want to join them, while the UK rock cognoscenti prayed for them to stay together long enough to tour Britain. It was not to be, but this was a document to their great potential. A magnificent record to fulfil every desired emotion that quality music can provoke.

● TRACKS: Mr. Soul; A Child's Claim To Fame; Everydays; Expecting To Fly; Bluebird; Hung Upside Down; Sad Memory; Good Time Boy; Rock 'N' Roll Woman; Broken Arrow.

● FIRST RELEASED 1967
● UK PEAK CHART POSITION: did not chart
● USA PEAK CHART POSITION: 44

219 LUST FOR LIFE (–) ▲
IGGY POP

Iggy and Bowie at the height of their respective powers presented a formidable artistic engine, and Lust For Life sees them working up a full head of steam. Two songs will need little introduction - 'Lust For Life' and 'The Passenger' are as intrinsic to the tapestry of 70s rock music as sundry Beatles efforts were to the previous decade (their influence on 90s film soundtracks is a testament to their durability). Those monolithic jukebox favourites aside, listeners may also find space in their hearts for the swaggering 'Neighbourhood Threat' (shades of the Stooges, without the musical clatter) and the disquieting 'Turn Blue', written from the viewpoint of an overdosing junkie.

● TRACKS: Lust For Life; Sixteen; Some Weird Sun; The Passenger; Tonight; Success; Turn Blue; Neighbourhood Threat; Fall In Love With Me.

● FIRST RELEASED 1977
● UK PEAK CHART POSITION: 28
● USA PEAK CHART POSITION: 120

220 NEW YORK DOLLS (–) ▲
THE NEW YORK DOLLS

It's hard in retrospect, with all the alternative rock water that's passed under the bridge, to articulate the impact the New York Dolls' incendiary debut had on its release. The Stooges apart (and they were a different kettle of garage band entirely, in content as much as style), there simply hadn't been anything quite as confrontational, cocky and in-your-face as the New York Dolls before. From the classic Thunders/Johansen opener 'Personality Crisis' onwards, the Dolls revealed themselves as the new rock outsiders. The album's pungent undertones of low-life street hassle and edgy drug deals and sharply observed narcissism set them apart. And every subsequent punk rock icon, from Joey Ramone to Johnny Rotten, took note.

● TRACKS: Personality Crisis; Looking For A Kiss; Vietnamese Baby; Lonely Planet Boy; Frankenstein (Orig); Trash; Bad Girl; Subway Train; Pills; Private World; Jet Boy.

● FIRST RELEASED 1973
● UK PEAK CHART POSITION: did not chart
● USA PEAK CHART POSITION: did not chart

221 PINK MOON (−) ▲
NICK DRAKE

Drake arrived un-announced to drop the master tapes for this album into his record company's offices before disappearing back into self-imposed seclusion. *Pink Moon* can be listened to as a diary of its deeply troubled creator's state of mind, a defiantly stark and uncommercial record in marked contrast to the lush autumnal beauty of his first two albums. However, it is arguably Drake's most perfect musical expression. The eleven tracks achieve a haiku-like perfection, with only a piano overdub on the title track intruding on the exquisite stillness achieved by the razor-sharp recording of Drake's acoustic guitar and his delicate voice.

● TRACKS: *Pink Moon; Place To Be; Road; Which Will; Horn; Things Behind The Sun; Know; Parasite; Ride; Harvest Breed; From The Morning.*

● FIRST RELEASED 1972
● UK PEAK CHART POSITION: did not chart
● USA PEAK CHART POSITION: did not chart

222 IN THE WEE SMALL HOURS (199) ▼
FRANK SINATRA

As ever, Sinatra's collaboration with Nelson Riddle on this album is wholly successful, this time a magnificent statement in understated orchestration. Emotional and romantic Sinatra gently eases himself through another 16 classics of American popular song. Although he fails to swing he never ceases to move the listener, and images of comfy sofas, scotch on the rocks and radiograms spring to mind as we hear songs by Ellington, Rodgers and Hart, Van Heusen, Arlen and Harburg, and Porter. Mellow, rich and pure, and now universally acclaimed as one of the best albums Sinatra ever recorded. Friedwald, Martland and Dellar all agree.

● TRACKS: *In the Wee Small Hours Of The Morning; Mood Indigo; Glad To Be Unhappy; I Get Along Without You Very Well; Deep In A Dream; I See Your Face Before Me; Can't We Be Friends?; When Your Lover Has Gone; What Is This Thing Called Love; Last Night When We Were Young; I'll Be Around; Ill Wind; It Never Entered My Mind; Dancing On The Ceiling; I'll Never Be The Same; This Love Of Mine.*

● FIRST RELEASED 1955
● UK PEAK CHART POSITION: did not chart
● USA PEAK CHART POSITION: 2

223 FRANK SINATRA SINGS FOR ONLY THE LONELY (290) ▲   FRANK SINATRA

Asked to reveal the mood of this album prior to its release, Frank Sinatra (tongue-in-cheek) said: 'Put it this way - we discarded 'Gloomy Sunday' (the 'suicide' song) because it was too swingin'!' Bleak, it certainly is, but with the singer at the height of his powers singing a classy set of saloon songs, superbly arranged and conducted by Nelson Riddle, this is still the number 1 album of all time for many a Sinatra aficionado. Even in the 90s he was compelled to include one of the tracks, 'One For My Baby', complete with the distinctive piano introduction, in every concert performance. The album's cover, with its sad clown-face picture, won a Grammy Award.

● TRACKS: *Only The Lonely; Angel Eyes; What's New?; It's A Lonesome Old Town; Willow Weep For Me; Good-bye; Blues In The Night; Guess I'll Hang My Tears Out To Dry; Ebb Tide; Spring Is Here; Gone With The Wind; One For My Baby.*

● FIRST RELEASED 1958
● UK PEAK CHART POSITION: 5
● USA PEAK CHART POSITION: 1

224 COURT AND SPARK (145) ▼
JONI MITCHELL

Court And Spark continued Joni Mitchell's transition from folk-singer to sophisticated rock auteur. Crafted songs are bathed in a warm, textured backing, courtesy of Tom Scott's L.A. Express, a sinuous jazz-based combo. Her expressive voice weaves in and around engaging melodies that support and enhance the imagery suggested by evocative, personal lyrics. The title track alone is worth the price of admission, but the gorgeous lilt of 'Help Me' and the elegant sweep of 'Free Man In Paris' show an artist in firm control of her craft. A measured, thoughtful album, *Court And Spark* confirmed Mitchell as one of the most important and subtle talents of the rock era.

● TRACKS: *Court And Spark; Help Me; Free Man In Paris; People's Parties; The Same Situation; Car On A Hill; Down To You; Just Like This Train; Raised On Robbery; Trouble Child; Twisted.*

● FIRST RELEASED 1974
● UK PEAK CHART POSITION: 14
● USA PEAK CHART POSITION: 2

225 **FIFTH DIMENSION** (406) ▲
THE BYRDS

N ow seen as an album that was as far ahead as *Revolver*, released the same year. McGuinn's flirtation with space rock peaked on stunning tracks such as 'What's Happening?!?!' and the brilliant 'I See You'. The ultimate, however, is 'Eight Miles High', which over 30 years later constantly causes a shiver. The guitar solo is still a remarkable experience. Their mass market popularity had already peaked by the release of this album, and it has been left to the likes of biographer Johnny Rogan to re-emphasize their greatness over the years. The remastered CD is unmissable, as the original single version of 'Why' is also included.

● TRACKS: *5D (Fifth Dimension); Wild Mountain Thyme; Mr. Spaceman; I See You; What's Happening?!?!; I Come And Stand At Every Door; Eight Miles High; Hey Joe (Where You Gonna Go); Captain Soul; John Riley; 2-4-2 Fox Trot (The Lear Jet Song); Why (single version); I Know My Rider (I Know You Rider); Psychodrama City; Eight Miles High (alternate); Why (alternate); John Riley (instrumental).*

● FIRST RELEASED 1966
● UK PEAK CHART POSITION: 27
● USA PEAK CHART POSITION: 24

 226 **ACTUALLY** (207) ▼
PET SHOP BOYS

R eappraisal is always revealing, whether for good or bad. In the case of this album, the great revelation is the magnificent orchestration, even though it is created by synthesizers and keyboards. 'One More Chance' is blissfully symphonic and the favourite hits are still irritatingly effective. The production is shared between Julian Mendelsohn, David Jacob, Shep Pettibone and Stephen Hague and is mixed to digital perfection. Ultimately this album succeeds in delivering 'pop' exactly as it should be, but played too often it will begin to grate on your friends, as you will end up humming it all day and drive them to despair.

● TRACKS: *One More Chance; Shopping; Rent; Hit Music; What Have I Done To Deserve This?; It Couldn't Happen Here; It's A Sin; I Want To Wake Up; Heart; King's Cross.*

● FIRST RELEASED 1987
● UK PEAK CHART POSITION: 2
● USA PEAK CHART POSITION: 25

 227 **DUSTY IN MEMPHIS** (136) ▼
DUSTY SPRINGFIELD

N ot only is this Dusty's finest work it is unanimously acknowledged as one of the great soul albums. The secret is in the production; Jerry Wexler, Tommy Dowd and Arif Mardin enlisted the Sweet Inspirations for vocal support and the best Memphis session boys. Dusty's selection of material is exemplary, choosing songs by Randy Newman, Mann/Weill, Goffin King and Bacharach/David. This should have made her an international megastar; instead it scraped the US Top 100, failed to chart in the UK and started her slow decline. It is a faultless record on which we have, thankfully, now recognized she was far too ahead of her time for her own good.

● TRACKS: *Just A Little Lovin'; So Much Love; Son Of A Preacher Man; I Don't Want To Hear It Anymore; Don't Forget About Me; Breakfast In Bed; Just One Smile; The Windmills Of Your Mind; In The Land Of Make Believe; No Easy Way Down; I Can't Make It Alone.*

● FIRST RELEASED 1969
● UK PEAK CHART POSITION: did not chart
● USA PEAK CHART POSITION: 99

 228 **ELVIS PRESLEY** (49) ▼
ELVIS PRESLEY

A lthough five tracks remained from the Sun cellar this is usually known as Elvis's first RCA album, and what a lucky company they were, probably unaware that they had signed the greatest ever donor to their company pension scheme. No rock aficionado should be unaware of the tracks, although the album has long been replaced with compilations. It still is nominated by the majority of the cognoscenti who are old enough to remember this album plopping down on their Dansettes. It was a vitally important album, although now doomed by the age of CD, as there are much better compilations with many more tracks.

● TRACKS: *Blue Suede Shoes; I Love You Because; Tutti Frutti; I'll Never Let You Go; Money Honey; I'm Counting On You; I Got A Woman; One-Sided Love Affair; Just Because; Tryin' To Get To You; I'm Gonna Sit Right Down And Cry Over You; Blue Moon.*

● FIRST RELEASED 1956
● UK PEAK CHART POSITION: did not chart
● USA PEAK CHART POSITION: 1

229 **SWING EASY!** (56) ▼
FRANK SINATRA

For many Sinatra devotees this remains the best album above the populist *Songs For Swingin' Lovers*. Sinatra started 'swingin'' with this collection, albeit in a more relaxed mode akin to 40s dance bands rather than brassy 50s orchestration. Nelson Riddle is present here, adding golden touches to Cole Porter's 'Just One Of Those Things', in addition to further high-quality songs, chosen with care. Everybody knew Sinatra could sing, he just needed to find the right songs and the right arranger. This album, together with its sister, *Songs For Young Lovers* (included on the CD version), started it all.

● TRACKS: *Jeepers Creepers; Taking A Chance On Love; Wrap Your Troubles In Dreams; Lean Baby; I Love You; I'm Gonna Sit Right Down And Write Myself A Letter; Get Happy; All Of Me; Why Should I Cry Over You; Sunday; Just One Of Those Things.*

● FIRST RELEASED 1960
● UK PEAK CHART POSITION: 5
● USA PEAK CHART POSITION: did not chart

---

 230 **QUADROPHENIA** (–) ▲
THE WHO

To write and record one successful 'rock opera' is an achievement but to attempt it all over again and succeed is credit to Pete Townshend's determination and deep talent. *Tommy* was a naïve storyline compared to this, a story of a frustrated and angry mod in 1964. The band play blindingly good throughout and the remastered version in 1996 is outstanding. The fact that there is a storyline is almost irrelevant on a double album of excellent songs. '5:15' was the lone hit single, a sign that the pop charts were no longer a priority for Townshend; he wanted to be an artist. The subsequent film with Phil Daniels merely reinforced Townshend's vision.

● TRACKS: *I Am The Sea; The Real Me; Quadrophenia; Cut My Hair; The Punk And The Godfather; I'm One; The Dirty Jobs; Helpless Dancer; Is It In My Head?; I've Had Enough; 5:15; Sea And Sand; Drowned; Bell Boy; Doctor Jimmy; The Rock; Love Reign O'er Me.*

● FIRST RELEASED 1973
● UK PEAK CHART POSITION: 2
● USA PEAK CHART POSITION: 2

---

 231 **RATTUS NORVEGICUS** (186) ▼
THE STRANGLERS

Probably the most underrated of the new wave/punk bands, these non-too youthful Guildford brutes simply did not count, according to pundits such as Jon Savage, though that view may have been tempered by the fact that Jean Jaques Burnel gave him a kicking after a hostile review. The Stranglers combined a dark view of human nature with a musical legacy that stretched far beyond the year zero philosophy of others. *Rattus* offers a blend of cynicism, menace and antagonism unheard of since the Stooges (frequent comparisons to the Doors were misleading - they both had prominent keyboards). Stand-out tracks include the utterly venomous 'Ugly', the stage standard 'Hanging Around' and the elegiac 'Down In The Sewer'.

● TRACKS: *Sometimes; Goodbye Toulouse; London Lady; Princess Of The Streets; Hanging Around; Peaches; Get A Grip On Yourself; Ugly; Down In The Sewer: Falling; Down In The Sewer: Trying To Get Out Again; Rats Rally.*

● FIRST RELEASED 1977
● UK PEAK CHART POSITION: 4
● USA PEAK CHART POSITION: did not chart

---

232 **ALL CHANGE** (–) ▲
CAST

Although the list of UK 60s retro pop groups is growing at a frightening rate, the amount of really good ones is becoming similarly unmanageable. How many ways can you skin a G, D, C, Am, F sequence and still have room for a middle eight? At least another 12 ways, judging by this album. They sound familiar, but on 'Sandstorm' the hook is theirs, not to forget the wah-wah break, which, although Hendrix-derived, is still of their own making. Songs such as 'Finetime' and 'Alright' are instantly appealing, inducing a nagging 'where have I have I heard it before' in the head.

● TRACKS: *Alright; Promised Land; Sandstorm; Mankind; Tell It Like It Is; Four Walls; Finetime; Back Of My Mind; Walkaway; Reflections; History; Two Of A Kind.*

● FIRST RELEASED 1995
● UK PEAK CHART POSITION: 7
● USA PEAK CHART POSITION: did not chart

233 SAFE AS MILK (–) ▲
CAPTAIN BEEFHEART AND THE MAGIC BAND

The cover depicts four clean-cut kids in suits and tie; one is even wearing his father's hat. Is this not the most paradoxically bizarre cover ever, in relation to the music within? This sounded like music from Venus in 1967; now it just sounds remarkably good. Don van Vliet's Howlin' Wolf growl almost tears the speaker-cloth as he launches into 'Electricity'. Other marvellous excursions are 'Dropout Boogie', 'Plastic Factory' and 'Yellow Brick Road'. The latter should have opened the original album as the spoken 'the following tone is a reference tone' bit sets the tone for this unforgettable album.

● TRACKS: Sure 'Nuff'N Yes I Do; Zig Zag Wanderer; Call On Me; Dropout Boogie; I'm Glad; Electricity; Yellow Brick Road; Abba Zaba; Plastic Factory; Where There's A Woman; Grown So Ugly; Autumn's Child.

● FIRST RELEASED 1967
● UK PEAK CHART POSITION: did not chart
● USA PEAK CHART POSITION: did not chart

234 BIRTH OF THE COOL (42) ▼
MILES DAVIS

Although this album is credited to Davis, the importance of Gerry Mulligan's playing and, especially, his stellar compositions 'Jeru', 'Rocker' and the gorgeous 'Venus De Milo' make this 1956 album special. Although it is generally considered to be less accomplished than Kind Of Blue, this album is, arguably, in some ways more important. It would be churlish to say this was the birth of the cool, but the songs recorded by the legendary nonet and collected together here certainly mark the birth of something significant. Hearing all the tracks on the newly available CD version makes it more complete, and therefore, more necessary than ever. It is an utterly indispensable album.

● TRACKS: Move; Jeru; Moon Dreams; Venus De Milo; Budo; Deception; Godchild; Boplicity; Rocker; Israel; Rouge.

● FIRST RELEASED ?
● UK PEAK CHART POSITION: did not chart
● USA PEAK CHART POSITION: did not chart

235 A WIZARD/A TRUE STAR (–) ▲
TODD RUNDGREN

Even among Rundgren fans this album is likely to evoke a mixed response. Whether it is listened to as the recording peak of a maverick genius or a failed attempt to reproduce an acid trip on vinyl, A Wizard/A True Star is never less than interesting. The 22 tracks career wildly between the sublime ('International Feel', 'Zen Archer' and 'Sometimes I Don't Know What To Feel') and the ridiculous ('Rock And Roll Pussy', 'Dogfight Giggle', 'Just Another Onionhead'), via the inspired white soulboy medley on side two. In retrospect, A Wizard/A True Star should be honoured as an album where one of pop's godlike genii revealed his human frailties.

● TRACKS: International Feel; Never Never Land; Tic Tic Tic It Wears Off; You Need Your Head; Rock And Roll Pussy; Dogfight Giggle; You Don't Have To Camp Around; Flamingo; Zen Archer; Just Another Onionhead/Da Da Dali; When The Shit Hits The Fan/Sunset Blvd; Le Feel Internacionale; Sometimes I Don't Know What To Feel; Does Anybody Love You?; Medley: I'm So Proud/Ooh Baby Baby/La La Means I Love You/Cool Jerk; Hungry For Love; I Don't Want To Tie You Down; Is It My Name; Just One Victory.

● FIRST RELEASED 1973
● UK PEAK CHART POSITION: did not chart
● USA PEAK CHART POSITION: 86

236 TWELVE DREAMS OF DR SARDONICUS
(330) ▲ SPIRIT

The charismatic and legendary Randy California starred alongside his stepfather Ed Cassidy with the bare-chested and handsome Jay Ferguson. Together with Mark Andes and pianist John Locke this west coast band were one of the finest to come out of the late 60s movement. This is such an excellent album it is hard to imagine that Spirit were not a more successful band. They hit a peak with this suite of songs, right from the word go; 'Nothing To Hide' informs that the subject is married to the same bride, then on to 'Nature's Way', an ecological song where we are told that something is wrong with the planet. This is a masterful concept album from which nobody ever really understood what the concept was.

● TRACKS: Prelude-Nothing To Hide; Nature's Way; Animal Zoo; Love Has Found A Way; Why Can't I Be Free; Mr. Skin; Space Child; When I Touch You; Street Worm; Life Has Just Begun; Morning Will Come; Soldier.

● FIRST RELEASED 1970
● UK PEAK CHART POSITION: did not chart
● USA PEAK CHART POSITION: 63

237 LIKE A PRAYER (300) ▲
MADONNA

Madonna's exquisite sense of the pop song, and suitably stylish aesthetic to match, was pushed to the hilt for 1989's *Like A Prayer*. Sporting a bare midriff and a stylishly dark bob, she immediately set the Moral Majority up in arms with the title track's video, depicting, among other things, a negro Christ and a hillside of burning crosses. The song, however, was as strong and as dazzling as the images. Before deciding on utilizing a constant barrage of public sexuality over songs, Madonna made great records. Highlights here include the sexy bubble-gum of 'Cherish' and the delightful 'Express Yourself'. Great pop to go.

● TRACKS: *Like A Prayer; Express Yourself; Love Song; Till Death Us Do Part; Promise To Try; Cherish; Dear Jessie; Oh Father; Keep It Together; Spanish Eyes; Act Of Contrition.*

● FIRST RELEASED 1989
● UK PEAK CHART POSITION: 1
● USA PEAK CHART POSITION: 1

238 EXILE IN GUYVILLE (-) ▲
LIZ PHAIR

From Big Mama Thornton to Madonna, the sexually aggressive woman has always held a special fascination for pop fans. With *Exile In Guyville*, Liz Phair became the latest and by far the most foul-mouthed addition to the line. Her mission was to put a lacquered fingernail up the posterior of alternative rock's 'Guyville' establishment. Her model was the Rolling Stones' *Exile On Main Street* and its portrait of a lonely, nihilistic world. Phair's ingenuous voice, stripped-down arrangements, and catchy melodies made her sound like a female Jonathan Richman. However, it was her biting lyrics that drew the most attention, making *Exile In Guyville* one of the most critically acclaimed albums of 1993.

● TRACKS: *Six Foot One; Help Me Mary; Glory; Dance Of The Seven Veils; Never Said; Soap Star Joe; Explain It To Me; Canary; Mesmerizing; Fuck And Run; Girls, Girls, Girls; Divorce Song; Shatter; Flatter; Flower; Johnny Sunshine; Gunshy; Stratford-On-Guy; Strange Loop.*

● FIRST RELEASED 1993
● UK PEAK CHART POSITION: did not chart
● USA PEAK CHART POSITION: 196

239 SOLID AIR (125) ▼
JOHN MARTYN

He began as a folksy minstrel but seemed drawn to experimental, free form improvisation. *Solid Air* is where John Martyn's love affair with effects and echoplex became serious. The title track, dedicated to his close friend Nick Drake, became a eulogy, while the breezy 'Over The Hill' - one of the greatest songs ever written about a train journey - is a feathery delight. 'May You Never' and 'Don't Want To Know' continued the simple, stoned ballad approach, although it is his interpretation of Skip James's 'I'd Rather Be The Devil,' totally reshaped with hypnotic shifts, tidal echoes, and a slurred growl, which broods over the whole album. A record that remains Martyn's youthful zenith.

● TRACKS: *Solid Air; Over The Hill; Don't Want To Know; I'd Rather Be The Devil; Go Down Easy; Dreams By The Sea; May You Never; The Man In The Station; Easy Blues.*

● FIRST RELEASED 1974
● UK PEAK CHART POSITION: did not chart
● USA PEAK CHART POSITION: did not chart

240 SKETCHES OF SPAIN (-) ▲
MILES DAVIS

The third collaboration between Davis and Gil Evans was another work of two men who were musically plugged into each other. The orchestral score by Evans is both haunting and breathtaking when it bursts into life, while the understated playing from Davis is the parmesan on the pasta. The 16-minute 'Concierto De Aranjuez' is a stunning opening track. Many people stop the record at this point because there is so much to take in, and often one track will suffice. It sounds somewhat insulting to say that this album is the perfect background music for a dinner party. Conversation can continue, but it is the magnificent music that really captures the ears of the guests.

● TRACKS: *Concierto De Aranjuez; Will O' The Wisp; The Pan Piper; Saeta; Solea.*

● FIRST RELEASED 1960
● UK PEAK CHART POSITION: did not chart
● USA PEAK CHART POSITION: did not chart

241 SONGS OF LEONARD COHEN (52) ▼
LEONARD COHEN

Leonard Cohen's debut album encapsulated the performer's artistry. A successful poet and novelist, he came to music through the folk idiom and this set combines the aural simplicity and visual clarity of these two passions. Cohen's lugubrious voice brought an intensity to a haunting collection bound together by beautiful melodies and deeply personal lyrics. Members of contemporary group Kaleidoscope join producer John Simon in creating a delicate backdrop for some memorable love songs. Cohen's ability to be both intimate and universal is a rare gift and results in a body of work that is both timeless and enthralling, albeit a bit sombre.

● TRACKS: *Suzanne; Master Song; Winter Lady; The Stranger Song; Sisters Of Mercy; So Long, Marianne; Hey, That's No Way To Say Goodbye; Stories Of The Street Teachers; One Of Us Cannot Be Wrong.*

● FIRST RELEASED 1968
● UK PEAK CHART POSITION: 13
● USA PEAK CHART POSITION: 83

242 PRIVATE DANCER (25) ▼
TINA TURNER

Enlisting the help of notable producers such as Joe Sample, Martin Ware and Rupert Hine, Tina out-performed even the original artists as she strutted her way into rock music, having been on the periphery for years with her screaming R&B and her ex-husband's strong influence. Al Green's 'Let's Stay Together' is made her own and even without the thin-sounding organ on the Anne Peebles original, her interpretation of 'I Can't Stand The Rain' is wholly acceptable. Mark Knopfler's standing benefited from having written the title track, and if that isn't enough, there is also 'What's Love Got To Do With It'.

● TRACKS: *I Might Have Been Queen; What's Love Got To Do With It; Show Some Respect; I Can't Stand The Rain; Private Dancer; Let's Stay Together; Better Be Good To Me; Steel Claw; Help; 1984.*

● FIRST RELEASED 1984
● UK PEAK CHART POSITION: 2
● USA PEAK CHART POSITION: 3

243 A SWINGIN' AFFAIR (122) ▼
FRANK SINATRA

A further sequence of immaculate songs, chosen with an uncanny knowledge that they could be adapted for 'swingability' (my word): the set features four songs by Cole Porter, including 'Night And Day' and 'You'd Be So Nice To Come Home To', and further gems from Richard Rodgers and Lorenz Hart ('I Wish I Was In Love Again'), the Gershwin brothers and Duke Ellington's glorious 'I Got It Bad And That Ain't Good'. Those who will buy this in the age of the CD will find the bonus of 'The Lady Is A Tramp'. All 15 tracks are once again beautifully Nelson Riddled, giving space for the strings, trumpets and bassoons. For swingin' romantics only.

● TRACKS: *Night And Day; I Wish I Was In Love Again; I Got Plenty O' Nuttin'; I Guess I'll Have To Change My Plan; Nice Work If You Can Get it; Stars Fell On Alabama; No One Ever Tells You; I Won't Dance; Lonesome Road; At Long Last Love; You'd Be So Nice To Come Home To; I Got It Bad And That Ain't Good; From This Moment On; If I Had You; Oh Look At Me Now.*

● FIRST RELEASED 1957
● UK PEAK CHART POSITION: did not chart
● USA PEAK CHART POSITION: 2 or 44?

244 SWORDFISHTROMBONES (174) ▼
TOM WAITS

Tom Waits' early recordings cast him as a bohemian sage. Part Kerouac, part Bukowski, he infused beat culture with the sweep of Hollywood movie soundtracks and the precision of a Tin Pan Alley songsmith. Aware of a stylistic straitjacket, he cast it aside and produced this challenging album. Eschewing a traditional back-up group, Waits opted for a percussive sound based around marimbas, woodblocks and ever-shifting rhythm patterns. Elements of Captain Beefheart and *avant garde* composer Harry Parch can be heard as the singer roars, barks and growls through a series of adventurous compositions reliant on impression and suggestion for effect. Uncompromising and exciting, *Swordfishtrombones* is a remarkable achievement from an already unconventional sculptor.

● TRACKS: *Underground; Shore Leave; Dave The Butcher; Johnsburg, Illinois; 16 Shells From A 30.6; Town With No Cheer; In The Neighbourhood; Just Another Sucker On The Vine; Frank's Wild Years; Swordfishtrombones; Down, Down, Down; Soldier's Things; Gin Soaked Boy; Trouble's Braids; Rainbirds.*

● FIRST RELEASED 1983
● UK PEAK CHART POSITION: 62
● USA PEAK CHART POSITION: 167

245 **COME FLY WITH ME** (107) ▼
FRANK SINATRA

A mildly conceptual album that has lasted, with a choice of songs that takes the listener around the world in 45 minutes. Some of Sinatra's finest moments are on this album, notably with Sammy Cahn and Jimmy Van Heusen's uplifting 'Come Fly With Me' and 'It's Nice To Go Trav'ling'. This was Sinatra's first album arranged and conducted by Billy May, a relationship that produced further classic orchestrations. Once again the CD purchaser will greatly benefit from three bonus tracks with Nelson Riddle in charge; 'Chicago', 'South Of The Border' and 'I Love Paris'. Happy-go-lucky fare that we all need an infusion of from time to time.

● TRACKS: *Come Fly With Me; Around The World; Isle Of Capri; Moonlight In Vermont; Autumn In New York; On The Road To Madalay; Let's Get Away From It All; April In Paris; London By Night; Brazil; Blue Hawaii; It's Nice To Go Trav'ling.*

● FIRST RELEASED 1958
● UK PEAK CHART POSITION: 2
● USA PEAK CHART POSITION: 1

 246 **GET HAPPY!!** (187) ▼
ELVIS COSTELLO

T his album highlights the fine line between Elvis's pop/punk and R&B and soul. The impression is that he wrote, recorded and produced this album while on a creative roll of short, snappy, simple songs that go straight to the heart. Both he and the Attractions played with fiery energy without losing their great sense of melody. The contrasts are great, from the lyrical ingenuity of 'New Amsterdam' to the pace of 'I Stand Accused' and 'High Fidelity'. A record to which one should lie down and rest after digestion. Quite magnificent and even better with the extra tracks on the CD reissue.

● TRACKS: *Love For Tender; Opportunity; The Imposter; Secondary Modern; King Horse; Possession; Man Called Uncle; Clowntime Is Over; New Amsterdam; High Fidelity; I Can't Stand Up For Falling Down; Black And White World; Five Gears In Reverse; B Movie; Motel Matches; Human Touch; Beaten To The Punch; Temptation; I Stand Accused; Riot Act.*

● FIRST RELEASED 1980
● UK PEAK CHART POSITION: 2
● USA PEAK CHART POSITION: 11

 247 **BACK IN BLACK** (173) ▼
AC/DC

A fter the untimely death of former enigmatic vocalist Bon Scott, AC/DC finally chanced upon a worthy replacement in the shape of former Geordie frontman, Brian Johnson. The result was more than the formal pastiche some expected, with Johnson stamping his own personality, not to mention distinctive rasp, on the record. The band's staple lyrical diet of sex and the general pursuit of happiness, however, remained very much intact. Highlights include the stomping 'Hell's Bells', the quiet build of the title track, and the chuckling insolence of, 'Rock And Roll Ain't Noise Pollution'. A winning return.

● TRACKS: *Back In Black; Hell's Bells; Shoot To Thrill; Give The Dog A Bone; What Do You Do For Money Honey?; Rock And Roll Ain't Noise Pollution; Let Me Put My Love Into You; You Shook Me All Night Long; Shake A Leg; Have A Drink On Me.*

● FIRST RELEASED 1980
● UK PEAK CHART POSITION: 1
● USA PEAK CHART POSITION: 4

 248 **BLOOD, SWEAT & TEARS** (359) ▲
BLOOD, SWEAT & TEARS

T heir finest moment and a testimony to the best of the jazz/rock movement. Created by the legendary Al Kooper, the band was one of the major attractions throughout 1969. The album is bold, brassy and adventurous. Interpretations of Eric Satie music are followed by Traffic's 'Smiling Phases'. Hit singles galore were culled from this record - 'Spinning Wheel', You've Made Me So Very Happy', and 'And When I Die', not to forget a superb rendition of Billie Holiday's 'God Bless The Child'. Sadly BST and their magnificent early catalogue has fallen from favour. And where is the superb voice of David Clayton-Thomas to be found today?

● TRACKS: *Variations On A Theme By Eric Satie (1st & 2nd Movement); Smiling Phases; Sometimes In Winter; More And More; And When I Die; God Bless The Child; Spinning Wheel; You've Made Me So Very Happy/Blues Part II; Variations On A Theme By Eric Satie (1st Movement).*

● FIRST RELEASED 1969
● UK PEAK CHART POSITION: 15
● USA PEAK CHART POSITION: 1

249 **FACE TO FACE** (356) **▲**
THE KINKS

S adly, the long and magnificent career of one of the finest songwriters of our age, Ray Davies, is not truly represented on any one album, other than greatest hits packages. Many Kinks albums have appeared but the absolute five star gem was never made. So many albums, so prolific with the butter spread thinly. This record summed up swinging London in the 60s and like its great successor, *Something Else*, contained Ray's observations of ordinary people and situations. The album is strengthened by the classic 'Sunny Afternoon' but perceptive tracks such as 'Fancy', 'Dandy', 'Session Man' and 'Most Exclusive Residence For Sale' are gentle satires that give the record its heart.

● TRACKS: *Party Line; Rosy Won't You Please Come Home; Dandy; Too Much On My Mind; Session Man; Rainy Day In June; House In The Country; Holiday In Waikiki; Most Exclusive Residence For Sale; Fancy; Little Miss Queen Of Darkness; You're Looking Fine; Sunny Afternoon; I'll Remember.*

● FIRST RELEASED 1967
● UK PEAK CHART POSITION: 12
● USA PEAK CHART POSITION: 135

 250 **PRETZEL LOGIC** (110) **▼**
STEELY DAN

D onald Fagen and Walter Becker were session musicians and staff songwriters prior to founding Steely Dan in 1972. Their highly inventive music relied on a synthesis of styles, heard to perfection on this, their third album. Jazz, baion-based R&B and sumptuous west coast pop were fused together to create a sound greater than the sum of its parts and one that was uniquely 'Steely Dan'. Crafted session musicians brought a technical excellence to the set, but the strength of the duo's vision ensured that sterility did not supplant inspiration. Gorgeous melodies interweave with expertise to create a sumptuous tapestry satisfying head and heart.

● TRACKS: *Rikki Don't Lose That Number; Night By Night; Any Major Dude Will Tell You; Barrytown; East St. Louis Toodle-o; Parker's Band; Through With Buzz; Pretzel Logic; With A Gun; Charlie Freak; Monkey In Your Soul.*

● FIRST RELEASED 1974
● UK PEAK CHART POSITION: 37
● USA PEAK CHART POSITION: 8

 251 **WEST SIDE STORY** (55) **▼**
VARIOUS

E lectrifying on stage and screen - and just as exciting in superb stereo on this sensational album featuring Natalie Wood, Richard Beymer, Rita Moreno, Russ Tamblyn and George Chakiris. The singing voices of the first three of those artists were dubbed at various times by Marni Nixon, Jim Bryant and Betty Wand, respectively, and they more than lived up to the challenge of Leonard Bernstein and Stephen Sondheim's dynamic and breathtaking score. The figures are staggering - USA: 144 weeks in the Top 40, 54 of them at number 1; UK: 175 weeks in the Top 20, including 13 at number 1. Plus a US Grammy for best soundtrack album.

● TRACKS: *West Side Story - Prologue; Jet Song; Something's Coming; Dance At The Gym (Blues Promenade Jump); Maria; Tonight; America; Cool; One Hand, One Heart; Tonight; The Rumble; I Feel Pretty; Somewhere; Gee Officer Krupke; A Boy Like That; I Have A Love; West Side Story - Finale.*

● FIRST RELEASED 1962
● UK PEAK CHART POSITION: 1
● USA PEAK CHART POSITION: 1

 252 **JOHN WESLEY HARDING** (170) **▼**
BOB DYLAN

B ob Dylan's eighth album followed a lengthy hibernation in which the singer re-evaluated his art. He emerged with a set of stark simplicity and heartfelt intensity. Neither folk, nor rock, nor country, the selection boasts elements of all three, slipping into consciousness with a mesmerizing power belying its setting. A biblical purity encompasses the collection as Dylan paints graphic portraits of the disenfranchised - hobo, immigrant, drifter, messenger - articulating the uncertainty of the times. The mood lifts for the final track, a beautifully tender love song, suggesting that this is where salvation lies. *John Wesley Harding* repays repeated play with ever-unfolding metaphor and interpretation, including four hidden Beatles on the cover.

● TRACKS: *John Wesley Harding; As I Went Out One Morning; I Dreamed I Saw St. Augustine; All Along The Watchtower; The Ballad Of Frankie Lee And Judas Priest; Drifter's Escape; Dear Landlord; I Am A Lonesome Hobo; I Pity The Poor Immigrant; The Wicked Messenger; Down Along The Cove; I'll Be Your Baby Tonight.*

● FIRST RELEASED 1968
● UK PEAK CHART POSITION: 1
● USA PEAK CHART POSITION: 2

253 BITCHES BREW (523) ▲
MILES DAVIS

A thoroughly unsaintly concoction of jazz experimentation and rock psychedelia, *Bitches Brew* took the loose, exploratory, collective improvisation and rock beat approach that Miles Davis had developed on *In A Silent Way*, but painted it a slightly harsher and more sinister hue. This is a long work, first sold as a double album, with a mesmerizing feel to its collection of strange funk-rock grooves. Benny Maupin's bass clarinet adds an unnerving dimension to the group's sound, creaking threateningly from deep within, while Davis himself plays lean, but fragmented, trumpet lines. An inspired and intense work, *Bitches Brew* dramatically influenced the course of jazz history, and ushered in the dawn of the fusion movement.

● TRACKS: *Pharaoh's Dance; Bitches Brew; Spanish Key; John McLaughlin; Miles Runs The Voodoo Down; Sanctuary.*

● FIRST RELEASED 1970
● UK PEAK CHART POSITION: 71
● USA PEAK POSITION: 35

254 FRESH FRUIT FOR ROTTING VEGETABLES (799) ▲ THE DEAD KENNEDYS

W here most American groups formed in the Sex Pistols' wake adopted their image but none of their substance, the Dead Kennedys brought a new perspective to punk's Sturm und Drang. Group leader Jello Biafra attacked hypocrisy with a series of virulent anthems and, by extension, fought a tireless campaign against censorship. Bitter sarcasm is unleashed on 'Kill The Poor' and 'Holiday In Cambodia' while 'California Uber Alles' savages the 'new age' politics of contemporary governor Jerry Brown. Furious tempos and gunshot guitar emphasize the album's anger and frustration, and set a pattern for the ensuing hardcore movement. A hugely influential set.

● TRACKS: *Kill The Poor; Forward To Death; When Ya Get Drafted; Let's Lynch The Landlord; Drug Me; Your Emotions; Chemical Warfare; California Uber Alles; I Kill Children; Stealing People's Mail; Funland At The Beach; Ill In The Head; Holiday In Cambodia; Viva Las Vegas.*

● FIRST RELEASED 1980
● UK PEAK CHART POSITION: 33
● USA PEAK CHART POSITION: did not chart

255 NATTY DREAD (510) ▲
BOB MARLEY

O ut on his own following the defection of Bunny Wailer and Peter Tosh, this album saw Marley utilizing the talents of the I-Threes for the first time. There was still a nod to his past in the inclusion of a cover version of a Wailers tune, 'Lively Up Yourself', but elsewhere he revelled in his new found freedom, on 'Revolution' and most particularly, 'No Woman, No Cry', which has practically become a Jamaican national anthem since its release. If that song had an instantly universal appeal, Rasta themes were also brilliantly conveyed via 'Them Belly Full (But We Hungry)' and 'Rebel Music (Three O'Clock Roadblock)'. Marley had announced himself as one of the greats of modern music.

● TRACKS: *Lively Up Yourself; No Woman No Cry; Them Belly Full (But We Hungry); Rebel Music (3 O'Clock Roadblock); So Jah Seh; Natty Dread; Bend Down Low; Talkin' Blues; Revolution.*

● FIRST RELEASED 1975
● UK PEAK CHART POSITION: 75
● USA PEAK CHART POSITION: 28

256 THE TIMES THEY ARE A-CHANGIN'
(41) ▼ BOB DYLAN

O n his third album Bob Dylan both redefined and expanded his musical palate. Fêted as a protest singer, a nomenclature he rejected, he brought new insight to the genre, particularly with 'Only A Pawn In Their Game', in which he paints a wider canvas relating to the murder of civil rights leader Medgar Evers. Dylan's love songs herein are particularly poignant, their stark, acoustic setting enhancing a graphic lyricism. The title song boasts a wonderful ambiguity, managing to be political and personal, the latter aspect suggesting the changes Dylan would bring to his music. The last album as a folk artist *per se*, *The Times They Are A-Changin'* is yet another essential Dylan collection.

● TRACKS: *Times They Are A Changin'; The Ballad Of Hollis Brown; With God On Our Side; One Too Many Mornings; North Country Blues; Only A Pawn In Their Game; Boots Of Spanish Leather; When The Ship Comes In; Lonesome Death Of Hattie Carroll; Restless Farewell.*

● FIRST RELEASED 1964
● UK PEAK CHART POSITION: 4
● USA PEAK CHART POSITION: 20

257 **TOMMY** (423) ▲
THE WHO

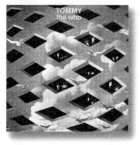

The definitive rock opera, *Tommy* liberated the Who from a 'singles band' stigma, and made them an international attraction. Composer Pete Townshend had flirted with the genre on two previous releases; here his vision was spread over two ambitious albums that played to his group's main strengths. Memorable songs were matched by pulsating musicianship, which emphasized the Who's internal kineticism, while the cast of characters unleashed revealed an unconventional imagination. Townshend even incorporates 'Eyesight To The Blind', first recorded by Sonny Boy Williamson, as part of his fable about the 'deaf, dumb and blind kid', a rare but successful reference to the past in what is a forward-looking achievement.

● TRACKS: *Overture; It's A Boy; 1921; Amazing Journeys; Sparks; Eyesight To The Blind; Miracle Cure; Sally Simpson; I'm Free; Welcome; Tommy's Holiday Camp; We're Not Gonna Take It; Christmas; Cousin Kevin; The Acid Queen; Underture; Do You Think It's Alright; Fiddle About; Pinball Wizard; There's A Doctor; Go To The Mirror; Tommy Can You Hear Me; Smash The Mirror; Sensation.*

● FIRST RELEASED 1969
● UK PEAK CHART POSITION: 2   ● USA PEAK CHART POSITION: 4

---

258 **MUSIC FROM BIG PINK** (163) ▼
THE BAND

The Band emerged from months of seclusion with this enthralling debut album. It followed a lengthy spell accompanying Bob Dylan, which culminated in sessions known as *The Basement Tapes*. Three songs herein were revived from those recordings, and the remainder showed a similar pastoral spirit. Where contemporaries sought expression in progressive music, the Band were largely reflective, creating atmosphere from traditional forms and distilling the results in an economic style. Their ensemble playing and rural voices were best captured on 'The Weight', an elliptical composition which displayed their craft to perfection. Americana of every hue can be gleaned from this collection, the depth of which left a marked impression on audiences and musicians alike.

● TRACKS: *Tears Of Rage; To Kingdom Come; In A Station; Caledonia Mission; The Weight; We Can Talk; Long Black Veil; Chest Fever; Lonesome Suzie; Wheels On Fire; I Shall Be Released.*

● FIRST RELEASED 1968
● UK PEAK CHART POSITION: did not chart
● USA PEAK CHART POSITION: 30

 **259** **LIVE!** (64) ▼
BOB MARLEY

Nobody who likes music could fail to be emotionally moved by this album, and not just because Marley is no longer with us. It was a special live treat before he died. The great thing about this record is the feeling that this is what it was like every night, unlike other live recordings which capture one or two gigs of a tour. Marley was extra special and a giant of popular music. Wallow in this vital record and listen to a man who had something to say and yet had fun while he said it. Most of the tracks you would want to be on the record are here, including the definitive version of 'No Woman No Cry' and a funky 'Lively Up Yourself'.

● TRACKS: *Trenchtown Rock; Burnin' And Lootin'; Them Belly Full (But We Hungry); Lively Up Yourself; No Woman No Cry; I Shot The Sheriff; Get Up, Stand Up.*

● FIRST RELEASED 1975
● UK PEAK CHART POSITION: 38
● USA PEAK CHART POSITION: 90

 **260** **MEDDLE** (–) ▲
PINK FLOYD

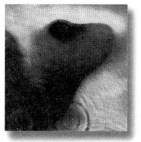

This famous 'inside the ear' cover is often put at the bottom of the Floyd pile in place of their many mega-selling others. *Meddle* is often remembered for the (admittedly impressive) 'Echoes', nearly 24 minutes of sweeping organ, building over clashing guitar. Equally good is the lilting 'A Pillow Of Winds', which is a delight, as is the easy-going 'Fearless', with some lovely chord changes. Waters also sings well as the whole band sound relaxed and more together than at any stage in their turbulent career. *Meddle* deserves reappraisal as the most therapeutic and enjoyable Floyd album.

● TRACKS: *One Of These Days; A Pillow Of Winds; Fearless; San Tropez; Seamus; Echoes.*

● FIRST RELEASED 1971
● UK PEAK CHART POSITION: 3
● USA PEAK CHART POSITION: 70

261 REMAIN IN LIGHT (135) ▼
TALKING HEADS

Led by the animated David Byrne and held together musically by a mathematically precise rhythm section of Tina Weymouth (bass) and Chris Frantz (drums), Talking Heads articulated America's post-60s cultural malaise. *Remain In Light*, their fourth album, consolidated a relationship with composer/producer Brian Eno, adding horns and guest performers to their intellectually based muse. Compositions and styles are deconstructed then reassembled afresh, no more so than on the exquisite 'Once In A Lifetime', which suggests a pan-international sound without expressing it aurally. Post-modern alienation was never so danceable.

● TRACKS: *Born Under Punches (The Heat Goes On); Crosseyed And Painless; The Great Curve; Once In A Lifetime; Houses In Motion; Seen And Not Seen; Listening Wind; The Overload.*

● FIRST RELEASED 1980
● UK PEAK CHART POSITION: 21
● USA PEAK CHART POSITION: 19

263 CLOSE TO THE EDGE (304) ▲
YES

Taken as a musical whole this suite of three parts is very sound, but what does begin to jar are some of the lyrics. In the 90s, even with the hippie revival and new age travellers, lyrics such as 'my eyes convinced eclipsed with the younger moon attained with love' do make you shake your head and say out loud, 'whaaaat are they talking about'? Yes have been shabbily treated by the press over the years yet their continuing popularity is in some way a vindication of their talent. Steve Howe's guitar sounds confident, Squire's bass wanders and thunks throughout, but what makes the album so good is the highly melodic theme that runs through it.

● TRACKS: *Solid Time Of Change; Total Mass Retain; I Get Up, I Get Down; Seasons Of Man; And You And I; Cord Of Life; Eclipse; The Preacher; Teacher; Siberian Khatru.*

● FIRST RELEASED 1972
● UK PEAK CHART POSITION: 4
● USA PEAK CHART POSITION: 3

262 DIAMOND LIFE (156) ▼
SADE

Sade crept up on the music market when they were least expecting it. The surprise hit 'Your Love Is King' was a very mature record for the singles market and one that opened the door to smooth soul-based pop. This album proved that she was no fluke and it became one of the most acclaimed debuts of all time. Sade rode out the publicity and coped with everything; for once the music did the talking. 'Smooth Operator' put her back in the pop charts but it was the overall class and confidence of the whole album that makes it so darn good. Her reading of Timmy Thomas's 'Why Can't We Live Together' is a highlight.

● TRACKS: *Smooth Operator; Your Love Is King; Hang On To Your Love; When Am I Gonna Make A Living; Frankie's First Affair; Cherry Pie; Sally; I Will Be Your Friend; Why Can't We Live Together.*

● FIRST RELEASED 1984
● UK PEAK CHART POSITION: 2
● USA PEAK CHART POSITION: 5

264 WHATEVER (380) ▲
AIMEE MANN

Perhaps the end of her relationship with Jules Shear gave Ms Mann a real kick to her songs, certainly the energy and the powerful lyrics succeed where *'Til Tuesday* failed. This won over many critics in 1993, both old and young - mainly those of us who love anything that sounds like the Byrds and others who see guitar indie pop as an extension of punk. Whatever, the album is a corker and memorable tracks such as 'I Should Have Known', 'Fifty Years After The Fair' and 'Stupid Thing' are classic quality guitar pop. P.S. Roger McGuinn guests on guitar as well. It's a pity she has faded after the promise of this album.

● TRACKS: *I Should've Known; Fifty Years After The Fair; 4th Of July; Could've Been Anyone; Put Me On Top; Stupid Thing; Say Anything; Jacob Marley's Chain; Mr Harris; I Could Hurt You Now; I Know There's A Word; I've Had It; Way Back When.*

● FIRST RELEASED 1993
● UK PEAK CHART POSITION: 39
● USA PEAK CHART POSITION: did not chart

265 KATE & ANNA MCGARRIGLE (149) ▼
KATE & ANNA MCGARRIGLE

These Canadian sisters unsuspectingly recorded this album, which, like Love's *Forever Changes*, is a huge critics' favourite, yet deserves much wider acceptance. Spotted and recorded by the canny Joe Boyd it is an album brimming with melancholy. Kate was formerly Mrs Loudon Wainwright, and the excellent 'Swimming Song' was written by him. Elsewhere, the evocative and anthemic '(Talk To Me Of) Mendocino' is a total joy and completely captures a feeling of being resigned to homesickness. Those who have not yet discovered this album will not be disappointed with this strong recommendation. Another quiet classic of great depth.

● TRACKS: *Kiss And Say Goodbye; My Town; Blues In D; Heart Like A Wheel; Foolish You; (Talk To Me Of) Mendocino; Complainte Pour Ste-Catherine; Tell My Sister; Swimming Song; Jigsaw Puzzle Of Life; Go Leave; Travellin' On For Jesus.*

● FIRST RELEASED 1975
● UK PEAK CHART POSITION: did not chart
● USA PEAK CHART POSITION: did not chart

266 THE MODERN DANCE (–) ▲
PERE UBU

It is hard to believe that such noises could come from so deep in America's heartland, played by a group named after a French absurdist playwright. The debut album by Pere Ubu, *The Modern Dance* is the realization of group leader David Thomas's (a.k.a. Crocus Behemoth) high-concept vision of a rock band whose sound was always just on the verge of falling apart. *Avant garde* and not terribly accessible, the album's noisy anarchy was a tonic for punks and intellectuals sick of the bloated, corporate sound that passed for commercial rock at the time. It became a major influence on the leading alternative bands of the following decade, including the Pixies and Hüsker Dü.

● TRACKS: *Non-Alignment Pact; The Modern Dance; Laughing; Street Waves; Chinese Radiation; Life Stinks; Real World; Over My Head; Sentimental Journey; Humor Me.*

● FIRST RELEASED 1977
● UK PEAK CHART POSITION: did not chart
● USA PEAK CHART POSITION: did not chart

267 THE WHO SINGS MY GENERATION
(–) ▲ THE WHO

The subject of some confusing history, which is a tragedy considering the importance of this album. Issued in the UK as *My Generation*, with 'I'm A Man' instead of 'Instant Party', the album is only available in the USA. A continuing legal stalemate with producer Shel Talmy is depriving many people of a truly excellent record. Townshend's short, sharp songs dominate. 'The Kids Are Alright' and 'A Legal Matter' are simple and direct with surprisingly mature lyrics of teenage angst. Daltrey, especially, sharpens his vocals on the two James Brown numbers, 'Please Please Please' and 'I Don't Mind'. A proper remastered reissue is demanded, now.

● TRACKS: *Out In The Street; I Don't Mind; The Good's Gone; La-La-La-Lies; Much Too Much; My Generation; The Kids Are Alright; Please Please Please; It's Not True; Instant Party; A Legal Matter; The Ox.*

● FIRST RELEASED 1965
● UK PEAK CHART POSITION: 5
● USA PEAK CHART POSITION: did not chart

268 SOMETHING/ANYTHING (–) ▲
TODD RUNDGREN

On only his third solo album, Rundgren confirmed his status as the new Brian Wilson with a superb collection of miniature pop masterpieces. The first three sides of this double album feature Rundgren alone in the studio tackling pure pop ('I Saw The Light', 'One More Day (No Words)'), power pop ('Couldn't I Just Tell You'), ballads ('Cold Morning Light', 'Sweeter Memories') and pop pastiche ('Wolfman Jack', 'I Went To The Mirror') with effortless skill and an unimpeachable grasp of melody. The fourth side is also wonderful, with Rundgren's most successful single, 'Hello It's Me', thrown nonchantly in among the sounds of a band jerking around in the studio.

● TRACKS: *I Saw The Light; It Wouldn't Have Made Any Difference; Wolfman Jack; Cold Morning Light; It Takes Two To Tango (This Is For The Girls); Sweeter Memories; Intro; Breathless; The Night The Carousel Burned Down; Saving Grace; Marlene; Song Of The Viking; I Went To The Mirror; Black Maria; One More Day (No Words); Couldn't I Just Tell You; Torch Song; Little Red Lights; Overture - My Roots: Money (That's What I Want)/Messin' With The Kid; Dust In The Wind; Piss Aaron; Hello It's Me; Some Folks Is Even Whiter Than Me; You Left Me Sore; Slut.*

● FIRST RELEASED 1972
● UK PEAK CHART POSITION: did not chart
● USA PEAK CHART POSITION: 29

269 **CHARLIE PARKER ON DIAL VOLS. 1-6**
(73) ▼ **CHARLIE PARKER**

Alto saxophonist Charlie Parker turned jazz on its head in the years following World War II, playing a thoroughly original and highly demanding music that furthered the emphasis on improvisation, and gave jazz a greater technical complexity and psychological depth. His numerous recordings for the west coast Dial label began in 1946, and represent one of the greatest bodies of work to be found anywhere in the music. The six volumes available today represent the complete works, and feature contributions by a host of leading musicians of the time, including Dizzy Gillespie, Miles Davis, Lucky Thompson, Errol Garner, Duke Jordan, Max Roach, Teddy Wilson, Red Norvo, and J.J. Johnson. Essential.
● TRACKS: *Volume 1 - Diggin' Diz; Moose The Mooche (three takes); Yardbird Suite (two takes); Ornithology (three takes); The Famous Alto Break; Night In Tunisia (two takes); Max Making Wax; Loverman; The Gypsy; Bebop. Volume 2 - This Is Always (two takes); Bird's Nest (three takes); Cool Blues (four takes). Volume 3 - Relaxin' At Camarillo; Cheers; Carvin' The Bird; Stupendous Theme Cooking (three takes). Volume 4 - Dexterity (two takes); Bongo Bop; Dewey Square (three takes); The Hymn (two takes); Bird Of Paradise (three takes); Embraceable You (two takes). Volume 5 - Bird Feathers; Klart-oveeseds-tere (two takes); Scrapple From The Apple; My Old Flame; Out Of Nowhere (three takes); Don't Blame Me; Moose The Mooche; Dark Shadows; Hallelujah. Volume 6 - Drying On A Reed (three takes); Quasimodo (two takes); Charlie's Wig (three takes); Bongo Beep; Crazeology (two excerpts); How Deep Is The Ocean (two takes).*
● FIRST RELEASED 1974   ● UK PEAK CHART POSITION: did not chart
● USA PEAK CHART POSITION: did not chart

270 **KING OF THE DELTA BLUES SINGERS**
(168) ▼ **ROBERT JOHNSON**

If you are a mountain climber you tackle Everest; if you are a blues lover you get to know this album very well. Very few had heard his music when this milestone album was first released in 1962, but it was evident that this was a body of work of fundamental importance to the development of postwar Chicago blues and blues in general. Little known in his lifetime, Johnson synthesized traditions represented by men like Charley Patton, Son House, Lonnie Johnson and Leroy Carr, and refined them through his unique interpretative skills. An accomplished guitarist with finger and slide, Johnson matched his virtuosity with a tortured vocal style that added deeper resonance to his words.
● TRACKS: *Crossroads Blues; Terraplane Blues; Come On In My Kitchen; Walking Blues; Last Fair Deal Gone Down; 32-20 Blues; Kindhearted Woman Blues; If I Had Possession Over Judgment Day; Preaching Blues; When You Got A Good Friend; Rambling On My Mind; Stones In My Passway; Traveling Riverside Blues; Milkcow's Calf Blues; Me And The Devil Blues; Hellhound On My Trail*
● FIRST RELEASED 1962
● UK PEAK CHART POSITION: did not chart
● USA PEAK CHART POSITION: did not chart

271 **LET'S GET IT ON** (597) ▲
MARVIN GAYE

Relishing the artistic freedom afforded by the success of *What's Goin' On*, Marvin Gaye recorded this sultry paean to sex. Where its predecessor relied on complex arrangements, the straightforward sound of *Let's Get It On* focused attention on its tight rhythms, strong melodies and Gaye's expressive singing. Either celebratory, as on the explicit title track, or reflective ('Distant Lover'), he explores a range of emotions with equal ease and intensity. Seductive sound matches seductive lyrics and attitudes at a time when Al Green, Barry White and Isaac Hayes laid claim to the 'lover man' sobriquet. *Let's Get It On* showed Marvin Gaye to be its undoubted master.

● TRACKS: *Let's Get It On; Please Don't Stay (Once You Go Away); If I Should Die Tonight; Keep Gettin' It On; Come Get To This; Distant Lover; You Sure Know How To Ball; Just To Keep You Satisfied.*

● FIRST RELEASED 1973
● UK PEAK CHART POSITION: 39
● USA PEAK CHART POSITION: 2

272 **PSYCHOCANDY** (74) ▼
JESUS AND MARY CHAIN

A love of classic pop songs and sonic terrorism conspire on this euphoric collection. Fuzz guitar, distortion and feedback drench almost every track, but beneath this assertive noise lies a gift for melody inspired by the Beach Boys and girl-group genre. The contrast is beguiling and if the constituent parts are not original, the audacity of such a combination is. Understated voices and nihilistic lyrics belie the intensity forged within. Created by passionate adherents of pop culture, *Psychocandy* is one of the 80s' landmark releases, inspiring some to follow a similar course, while others took similar influences to forge a quite different perspective.

● TRACKS: *Just Like Honey; The Living End; Taste The Floor; Hardest Walk; Cut Dead; In A Hole; Taste Of Cindy; Never Understand; Inside Me; Sowing Seeds; My Little Underground; You Trip Me Up; Something's Wrong; It's So Hard.*

● FIRST RELEASED 1985
● UK PEAK CHART POSITION: 31
● USA PEAK CHART POSITION: 188

273 **WAR** (105) ▲
U2

U2's strident march into rock 'n' roll legend took its first true steps with this record. *Boy* and *October* had given them an audience of hardcore devotees, but *War* gave them the full and rapt ear of the world. Their case was made with a record of contrasting moments; it is interesting to note that the lyrics printed on the gatefold sleeve are done so selectively. When this record breaks the silence, it roars, U2's now familiar outcry making itself apparent through dogmatic, but insatiable appeal. At the same time, 'Drowning Man' hinted at the texture and depth of work they would later produce.

● TRACKS: *Sunday Bloody Sunday; Seconds; Like A Song; New Years Day; Two Hearts Beat As One; The Refugee; Drowning Man; Red Light; '40'; Surrender.*

● FIRST RELEASED 1983
● UK PEAK CHART POSITION: 1
● USA PEAK CHART POSITION: 12

 274 **LOADED** (–) ▲
THE VELVET UNDERGROUND

The Velvet Underground were never ones to follow the crowd. In 1966, when catchy, lucid, three-minute pop tunes were the rule, they recorded their first album, which was dominated by dark celebrations of drug use. By 1970, when they recorded their fourth album, the vogue was for unwieldy drug anthems. Therefore, they made *Loaded*, an album dominated by catchy, lucid three-minute pop tunes. Their record label, expecting a wild, Warholesque romp, did not know what to make of the album, and it died a commercial death. Since then, it has gained respect from fans and critics as the source of many of Lou Reed's best compositions, including classics such as 'Rock And Roll' and 'Sweet Jane'.

● TRACKS: *Who Loves The Sun; Sweet Jane; Rock And Roll; Cool It Down; New Age; Head Held High; Lonesome Cowboy Bill; I Found A Reason; Train Round The Bend; Oh! Sweet Nuthin'.*

● FIRST RELEASED 1970.
● UK PEAK CHART POSITION: did not chart
● USA PEAK CHART POSITION: did not chart

 275 **THE RIVER** (139) ▼
BRUCE SPRINGSTEEN

Only Springsteen could have got away with releasing a double album with 19 tracks of what was basically the same song. Such was his standing that he did, and it worked like a dream. Almost all the tracks hit you in the stomach, with burning saxophone from Clarence Clemons and piercing wurlitzer organ. Bruce, meanwhile, sings of cars and girls and girls and cars, but at no stage does he forget that this is rock 'n' roll. With this release Springsteen completed a rite of passage. Described as 'the new Dylan' early in his career, the singer proved this tag a fallacy, drawing on Dansette pop - Phil Spector, Gary US Bonds, Mitch Ryder - rather than the folk tradition. The singer articulated the dilemmas of America's blue-collar workforce, encapsulating a generation trapped in a post-60s malaise. He does so with sumptuous melodies which draw in, rather than confront, the listener and show Springsteen not just as a magnetic showman, but as a pensive, literate songwriter.

● TRACKS: *The Ties That Bind; Sherry Darling; Jackson Cage; Two Hearts; Independence Day; Hungry Heart; Out In The Street; Crush On You; You Can Look (But You Better Not Touch); I Wanna Marry You; The River; Point Blank; Cadillac Ranch; I'm A Rocker; Fade Away; Stolen Car; Ramrod; The Price You Pay; Drive All Night; Wreck On The Highway.*

● FIRST RELEASED 1980
● UK PEAK CHART POSITION: 2
● USA PEAK CHART POSITION: 1

 **276** **BURNIN'** (262) ▼
BOB MARLEY AND THE WAILERS

Catch A Fire launched Jamaica's Wailers into international prominence with a brilliant cross of reggae and rock. Purists did fault its emphasis on the latter, a criticism answered with the earthier *Burnin'*. Stripped of session musicians, the group's frontline harmonies were supported by the sinewy Barrett brothers rhythm section which provided a dry counterpoint. Although Bob Marley was fully in control, the support of Bunny Livingston and Peter Tosh was crucial to the overall sound. Their vocal interplay mirrored that of the Impressions, but lyrically the Wailers proclaimed a vibrant militancy instantly heard on 'Get Up Stand Up'. Eric Clapton helped to popularize 'I Shot The Sherrif', but this album is noteworthy for its uncompromising blend of polemics and tough melodies.

● TRACKS: *Get Up Stand Up; Hallelujah Time; I Shot The Sheriff; Burnin' And Lootin'; Put It On; Small Axe; Pass It On; Duppy Conqueror; One Foundation; Rastaman Chant.*

● FIRST RELEASED 1975
● UK PEAK CHART POSITION: did not chart
● USA PEAK CHART POSITION: 151

277 SANDINISTA! (–) ▲
THE CLASH

Sprawling, self-important, yet strangely compelling, *Sandinista!* remains the most ambitious work by the group that deemed itself 'the only band that matters'. Although its broad scope left them open to criticisms of a lack of musical direction, no one could accuse them of having lost their political conviction. They made an agreement with their label, CBS, that they would relinquish their royalties on the first 200,000 copies sold if the label would release the triple album at the price of a double. Tackling a wide range of issues, from racism and unemployment to Cold War paranoia, the album's 36 songs include Clash classics such as 'Washington Bullets', 'The Magnificent Seven', and a witty remake of the Equals' 'Police On My Back'.

● TRACKS: *The Magnificent Seven; Hitsville U.K.; Junco Partner; Ivan Meets G.I. Joe; The Leader; Something About England; Rebel Waltz; Look Here; The Crooked Beat; Somebody Got Murdered; One More Time; One More Dub; Lightning Strikes (Not Once But Twice); Up In Heaven (Not Only Here); Corner Soul; Let's Go Crazy; If Music Could Talk; The Sound Of The Sinners; Police On My Back; Midnight Log; The Equaliser; The Call Up; Washington Bullets; Broadway; Lose This Skin; Charlie Don't Surf; Mensforth Hill; Junkie Slip; Kingston Advice; The Street Parade; Version City; Living In Fame; Silicone On Sapphire; Version Pardner; Career Opportunities; Shepherds Delight.*

● FIRST RELEASED 1980
● UK PEAK CHART POSITION: 19   ● USA PEAK CHART POSITION: 24

278 FEAR OF A BLACK PLANET (509) ▲
PUBLIC ENEMY

If Public Enemy's two previous albums had ruffled feathers, *Fear Of A Black Planet* set out its stall to exploit mainstream fears. Again, the title spoke volumes. This time they raged just as hard, but their political consciousness had grown. Professor Griff had been ejected from the band for his anti-Semitic stance, and much of the album's atmosphere is created by the bunker mentality of resultant clashes with the press. The siege mentality only underscores the group's hard-nosed, cut-and-paste sample technique and the eloquence of Chuck D. 'Fight The Power' still bites harder than just about any other track in rap's history.

● TRACKS: *Contract On The World Love Jam; Brothers Gonna Work It Out; 911 Is A Joke; Incident At 66.6 FM; Welcome To The Terrordome; Meet The G That Killed Me; Polywanacraka; Anti-nigger Machine; Burn Hollywood Burn; Power To The People; Who Stole The Soul; Fear Of A Black Planet; Revolutionary Generation; Can't Do Nuttin' For Ya Man; Reggie Jax; Leave This Off Your F***in' Charts; B Side Wins Again; War At Thirty Three And A Third; Final Count Of The Collision Between Us And Them.*

● FIRST RELEASED 1990
● UK PEAK CHART POSITION: 4
● USA PEAK CHART POSITION: 10

279 WHEELS OF FIRE (526) ▲
CREAM

Wheels Of Fire solved Cream's artistic dilemma whereby studio work was largely concise but live appearances centred on improvisation. This double set successfully offered both facets and captures the trio at their most ambitious. Where the in-concert section, in particular 'Crossroads', showed remarkable musical empathy, especially the dexterity of Bruce and the fluidity of Clapton. Pop songs and blues standards nestled together while cellos, viola and trumpet embellish certain selections as the group, in tandem with producer Felix Pappalardi, expanded Cream's oeuvre. Lyricist Pete Brown enhanced this experimental vision which defined the unit's creative peak.

● TRACKS: *White Room; Sitting On Top Of The World; Passing The Time; As You Said; Pressed Rat And Warthog; Politician; Those Were The Days; Born Under A Bad Sign; Deserted Cities Of The Heart; Crossroads; Spoonful; Train Time; Toad.*

● FIRST RELEASED 1968
● UK PEAK CHART POSITION: 3
● USA PEAK CHART POSITION: 1

280 MURMUR (–) ▲
R.E.M.

R.E.M.'s debut was a brilliant, original masterpiece, blending punk, garage and folk influences with their own inspired musical vision, and in the process creating a perplexing and organic whole. Stipe's muffled, mumbled vocals were the focus of attention, seemingly consisting of phonetic approximations of words rather than actual lyrics (significantly, 'conversation fear' was the only audible lyric in '9-9'). Buck's insistent Rickenbacker dominates the melodies, and the echoing vocal harmonies are precise throughout. Providing alternative radio anthems ('Radio Free Europe') as well as understated R.E.M. classics ('Perfect Circle'), this remains one of the band's best albums, and one of the greatest indie debuts in popular music history.

● TRACKS: *Radio Free Europe; Pilgrimage; Laughing; Talk About The Passion; Moral Kiosk; Perfect Circle; Catapult; Sitting Still; 9-9; Shaking Through; We Walk; West Of The Fields.*

● FIRST RELEASED 1983
● UK PEAK CHART POSITION: did not chart
● USA PEAK CHART POSITION: 36

281 **STEVE McQUEEN** (433) ▲
PREFAB SPROUT

While many felt that *Jordan: The Comeback* was their creative peak this remains the most popular choice. Recorded before the band's creative force Paddy MacAloon was hyped as the next big thing, it stands as a truly great pop album with enough complexity to make it special. The hit single, 'When Love Breaks Down', opened doors to a wider market and 'Faron Young' reawakened interest in the country music star of the same name. The jury is still out on their long-term prospects after so much promise and we wait to see whether MacAloon can surpass the quality of *Steve McQueen*.

● TRACKS: *Faron Young; Bonny; Appetite; When Love Breaks Down; Goodbye Lucille #1; Hallelujah; Moving The River; Horsing Around; Desire As; Blueberry Pies; When The Angels.*

● FIRST RELEASED 1985
● UK PEAK CHART POSITION: 21
● USA PEAK CHART POSITION: 178

 282 **WHITE LIGHT/WHITE HEAT** (239) ▼
THE VELVET UNDERGROUND

The difficult second album from one of rock's greatest influences was dusted off with little regard for trying to sell records. Blissfully unaware of how important this band was to become, their label Verve must have torn out their hair when presented with John Cale telling the story of Waldo over a guitar backdrop, on the eight minute plus 'The Gift', or 17 minutes of chunking and distorted heaven with 'Sister Ray', and Lou Reed extolling the virtues of 'searching for his mainline' or 'oh man I haven't got the time time, too busy sucking on his ding dong'.

● TRACKS: *White Light; White Heat; The Gift; Lady Godiva's Operation; Here She Comes Now; I Heard Her Call My Name; Sister Ray.*

● FIRST RELEASED 1968
● UK PEAK CHART POSITION: did not chart
● USA PEAK CHART POSITION: 171

 283 **ROXY MUSIC** (96) ▼
ROXY MUSIC

Totally original and a breath of bizarre air when released in 1972, it put the Brians Ferry and Eno at the forefront of the art-rock movement. The sheer style of the band gave rock music a powerful, brilliant injection after years of meandering British prog and American west coast lethargy. From the opening bars of 'Re-Make/Re-Model', and the bitter end of 'Bitters End', the album enthrals and holds the listener. You can almost believe that Ferry is sincere when he states, 'I would climb mountains, walk a thousand miles and put roses around our door'; almost, but not quite.

● TRACKS: *Bitters End; The Bob; Chance Meeting; If There Is Something; Ladytron; Re-Make/Re-Model; 2HB; Would You Believe?; Sea Breezes.*

● FIRST RELEASED 1972
● UK PEAK CHART POSITION: 10
● USA PEAK CHART POSITION: did not chart

 284 **STARSAILOR** (403) ▲
TIM BUCKLEY

Tim Buckley's work was always challenging, developing from that of a superior folk-singer to one encompassing many forms of expression. A growing jazz influence came to full fruition on *Starsailor*, which embraced the radical *avant garde* aspects of John Coltrane and Ornette Coleman. On several tracks the singer largely eschewed melody, giving full rein to his astonishing range, turning his voice into another instrument. Yet there were equal moments of gorgeous melancholia, no more so than on 'Song To The Siren', later popularized by This Mortal Coil. Supported only by muted electric guitar and eerie sound effects, Buckley sings with heartfelt emotion, resulting in one of his finest ever performances. The contrast between its ethereal atmosphere and the dense textures elsewhere result in an enthralling, intense collection.

● TRACKS: *Come Here Woman; I Woke Up; Monterey; Moulin Rouge; Song To The Siren; Jungle Fire; Starsailor; The Healing Festival; Down By The Borderline.*

● FIRST RELEASED 1970
● UK PEAK CHART POSITION: did not chart
● USA PEAK CHART POSITION: did not chart

285 IN THE COURT OF THE CRIMSON KING
(–) ▲ KING CRIMSON

One of the pioneering works of art-rock, and a musical and lyrical signpost for the pomposity of early 70s progressive rock music, *In The Court Of The Crimson King* is of lasting interest mainly thanks to the superb musicianship of Greg Lake, Ian McDonald and Michael Giles, and the wonderfully inventive guitarwork of the masterful Robert Fripp. Subtitled 'An Observation By King Crimson', the album flounders on Pete Sinfield's dreadful lyrics and the stilted dynamics of the multi-part arrangements. Anyone wishing to investigate the roots of Yes and Emerson, Lake And Palmer, however, should refer to this album.

● TRACKS: *21st Century Schizoid Man; I Talk To The Wind; Epitaph; Moonchild; The Court Of The Crimson King.*

● FIRST RELEASED 1969
● UK PEAK CHART POSITION: 5
● USA PEAK CHART POSITION: 28

286 ABRAXAS (120) ▼
SANTANA

Even though Santana now rarely roll off the tongue, their initial trio of albums still sound incredibly alive and exciting. *Abraxas* is the best of the three as it imbues the Latin fusion of their debut with smooth edges. The relaxed opening elegantly slips into 'Black Magic Woman', the finest ever interpretation of a Peter Green song. 'Se A Cabo', 'El Nicoya' and the memorable 'Oye Como Va' give us the quota of Latin rock. The album's star turn is the beautifully erotic 'Samba Pa Ti', which features a superb guitar solo that oozes the sexuality blatantly depicted by the Mati cover illustration.

● TRACKS: *Singing Winds, Crying Beasts; Black Magic Woman/Gypsy Queen; Oye Como Va; Incident At Neshabur; Se A Cabo; Mother's Daughter; Samba Pa Ti; Hope You're Feeling Better; El Nicoya.*

● FIRST RELEASED 1970
● UK PEAK CHART POSITION: 7
● USA PEAK CHART POSITION: 1

287 AJA (129) ▼
STEELY DAN

This represents the pinnacle of Steely Dan's gradual transition from rock band to their own brand of jazz-influenced white soul. Guitars were replaced by keyboards, and saxophones became more common. Walter Becker and Donald Fagen were only interested in spending time in the recording studios, while the fans pined and waited. The result set new standards in recorded excellence, and is regularly used as a hi-fi shop demonstration. The ambitious title track was deemed too difficult for radio play and only the two overtly accessible tracks 'Josie' and 'Peg', gave them valuable exposure. The song we have to blame for Deacon Blue was equally friendly on the ear.

● TRACKS: *Black Cow; Aja; Peg; Deacon Blues; Home At Last; I Got The News; Josie.*

● FIRST RELEASED 1977
● UK PEAK CHART POSITION: 5
● USA PEAK CHART POSITION: 3

288 SWEETHEART OF THE RODEO (832) ▲
THE BYRDS

Country music had always been an essential influence on the Byrds, but the decision to record an entire album in that style was controversial. Despite contemporary disquiet, *Sweetheart Of The Rodeo* has since become a landmark release, popularizing the notion of country rock. Traditional songs, standards, Bob Dylan compositions and original material were drawn together in a seamless whole, its continuity enhanced by crack Nashville session musicians. New group member Gram Parsons proved an adept catalyst; his departure soon after the album's release ensured it remained a one-off experiment. The Byrds moved elsewhere stylistically, but the influence of this recording is immeasurable.

● TRACKS: *You Ain't Goin' Nowhere; I Am A Pilgrim; The Christian Eye; You Don't Miss Your Water; You're Still On My Mind; Pretty Boy Floyd; Hickory Wind; One Hundred Years From Now; Blue Canadian Rockies; Life In Prison; Nothing Was Delivered.*

● FIRST RELEASED 1968
● UK PEAK CHART POSITION: did not chart
● USA PEAK CHART POSITION: 77

289 THE HISSING OF SUMMER LAWNS
(-) ▲ **JONI MITCHELL**

A continuing move towards jazz was the most striking element of this record when first released. Larry Carlton and Robben Ford became two names to bandy around and appear cool. Indeed, their guitar playing throughout is superlative. The real strength, however, is the way in which Mitchell reached new plateaux with graceful ease. The remarkable 'The Jungle Line' features the drums of Barundi and must be played loud to fully appreciate its *avant garde* quality. The opening line, 'Rousseau walk on trumpet paths', has the listener reaching for the *Dictionary Of Art*. As understated and lyrically deep as anything she has recorded, it is a stunning piece of work.

● TRACKS: *In France They Kiss On Main Street; The Jungle Line; Edith And The Kingpin; Don't Interrupt The Sorrow; Shades Of Scarlett Conquering; The Hissing Of Summer Lawns; The Boho Dance; Harry's House/Centerpiece; Sweet Bird; Shadows And Light.*

● FIRST RELEASED 1975
● UK PEAK CHART POSITION: 14
● USA PEAK CHART POSITION: 4

291 CAN'T SLOW DOWN (60) ▼
 LIONEL RICHIE

Mr Richie's brand of silky-smooth macho soul was the butt of some critics during the early 80s. A plethora of handsome studs with great voices, whopping great medallions, who just wanted to lurve all night long followed Richie. Yet another album crammed with hit singles, it was one of the 80s sales phenomena both in the USA and the UK - as was 'Hello'. Corny but delicious, and unashamedly romantic, and consequently, more couples have danced to his 'All Night Long (All Night)' than any other - and then 16 million couples went out and bought it.

● TRACKS: *Can't Slow Down; All Night Long (All Night); Penny Lover; Stuck On You; Love Will Find A Way; The Only One; Running With The Night; Hello.*

● FIRST RELEASED 1983
● UK PEAK CHART POSITION: 1
● USA PEAK CHART POSITION: 1

290 HISTORY PAST PRESENT AND FUTURE BOOK 1 (-) ▲ **MICHAEL JACKSON**

Jackson had a lot to do to regain his credibility at this point. He was canny in offering an irresistible greatest hits collection on disc one, so as to remind us how great he was. On disc two he gave us some new songs, many with lyrics that were more biting than usual. Jackson was angry in 'They Don't Really Care About Us' and 'Money', while in 'Earth Song' he attempts, and succeeds with the epic song of anti-pollution, anti-war. Quietly hidden on this disc is 'Stranger In Moscow', one of his best ever compositions. For all his quirks and failings, Jackson is still a major force.

● TRACKS: *Billie Jean; The Way You Make Me Feel; Black Or White; Rock With You; She's Out Of My Life; Bad; I Just Can't Stop Loving You; Man In The Mirror; Thriller; Beat It; The Girl Is Mine; Remember The Time; Don't Stop Til You Get Enough; Wanna Be Startin' Somethin'; Heal The World; Scream; They Don't Care About Us; Stranger In Moscow; This Time Around; Earth Song; D.S.; Money; Come Together; You Are Not Alone; Childhood (Theme From Free Willy); Tabloid Junkie; Bad; History; Little Susie; Smile.*

● FIRST RELEASED 1995
● UK PEAK CHART POSITION: 1
● USA PEAK CHART POSITION: 1

292 NEW GOLD DREAM (81, 82, 83, 84)
(155) ▼ **SIMPLE MINDS**

Simple Minds began their career indebted to Roxy Music, David Bowie and Magazine, but over successive releases emerged as a distinctive act. On *New Gold Dream* the group's ambitions came to full fruition, the awkward dissonance of early recordings replaced by a warm, textured sound. The content ranged from brash stadium rock to melodic ballad, but a singleness of purpose ensured such contrasts enhanced the set's overall cohesion. The quintet had never sounded so confident or assured and the resultant lush textures launched them into the international arena, fulfilling their undoubted promise. 'On Promised You A Miracle' did Kerr really sing 'guinea pigs are guinea pigs'?

● TRACKS: *Someone, Somewhere In Summertime; Colours Fly And Catherine Wheel; Promised You A Miracle; Big Sleep; Somebody Up There Likes You; New Gold Dream; Glittering Prize; Hunter And The Hunted; King Is White And In The Crowd.*

● FIRST RELEASED 1982
● UK PEAK CHART POSITION: 3
● USA PEAK CHART POSITION: 69

293 VAN HALEN (177) ▼
VAN HALEN

Quite simply put, no-one had seen or heard anything like it. Roth's flamboyant showmanship, with the microphone dangling provocatively between his legs on the cover, and Eddie Van Halen's monstrously inventive guitar playing became a textbook for air guitarists the world over. From the instrumental blow-out of 'Eruption', the gritty teen pop of 'Feel Your Love Tonight', to the strutting riff around which 'Ain't Talkin' 'Bout Love' was built and the grandiose reworking of The Kinks' 'You Really Got Me', Van Halen set their own absurd standards. One of the truly great rock and roll/metal debut albums.

● TRACKS: *You Really Got Me; Jamie's Cryin'; On Fire; Runnin' With The Devil; I'm The One; Ain't Talkin' Bout Love; Little Dreamer; Feel Your Love Tonight; Atomic Punk; Eruption; Ice Cream Man.*

● FIRST RELEASED 1978
● UK PEAK CHART POSITION: 34
● USA PEAK CHART POSITION: 19

294 DA CAPO (–) ▲
LOVE

Although *Forever Changes* is *the* Love album, there are enough supporters of *Da Capo* to make it a worthy second. 'Orange Skies' and 'She Comes In Colours' are both beautiful songs, but they are dwarfed by the unusual changes and acoustic beauty of 'The Castle', probably their greatest song. 'Seven & Seven Is' is also a stand-out; the energy put into this is phenomenal, climaxing with a nuclear ending that has been imitated but never bettered. The second side of the old vinyl album is now of course sequenced for CD. What has to be done is to programme only tracks 1 to 6. Track 7 is the 18-minute 'Revelation'. What should be revealed is that your CD player never need know about it. It is a self-indulgent dog of a track that does not know when to finish.

● TRACKS: *Stephanie Knows Who; Orange Skies; Que Vida!; Seven & Seven Is; The Castle; She Comes In Colours; Revelation.*

● FIRST RELEASED 1967
● UK PEAK CHART POSITION: did not chart
● USA PEAK CHART POSITION: 80

295 AFTERMATH (250) ▼
THE ROLLING STONES

The fourth Rolling Stones LP was the first to consist solely of Jagger/Richard compositions. As such, it reflected a switch from pure R&B, although the group's roots are still to the fore, particularly in Brian Jones's slide guitarwork. The same musician was also responsible for introducing exotica to the quintet's overall sound, marimbas, dulcimer, harpsichord and sitar being added at his behest. The result is a selection of unrivalled scope, where the Knightsbridge chic of 'Lady Jane' sits beside C&W ('High And Dry') and improvised workouts ('Goin' Home'). The desultory 'Under My Thumb' would, meanwhile, remain an integral part of the Stones' lexicon throughout the subsequent two decades. *Aftermath* confirmed that the directions suggested by 'The Last Time' and 'Satisfaction' could be successfully sustained.

● TRACKS: *Mother's Little Helper; Stupid Girl; Lady Jane; Under My Thumb; Doncha Bother Me; Goin' Home; Flight 505; High And Dry; Out Of Time; It's Not Easy; I Am Waiting; Take It Or Leave It; Think; What To Do.*

● FIRST RELEASED 1966
● UK PEAK CHART POSITION: 1
● USA PEAK CHART POSITION: 2

296 MEAT IS MURDER (378) ▲
THE SMITHS

The second Smiths album expanded upon the twin flight paths of its predecessor: singer Morrissey's unabashed solipsism and Johnny Marr's textured guitar playing. Opening with the plangent 'Headmaster's Ritual', *Meat Is Murder* brings both these facets into sharp focus with layers of sound supporting the singer's confessional, singsong style. Bittersweet humour and rampant profligacy mark the album's lyrical content, no more so than on the indignant, pro-vegetarian title track. Rhythm section Rourke and Joyce provide a supple spine for the group's two sparring partners, keeping both their potential excesses in check. Self-indulgent? Yes, but brilliantly so.

● TRACKS: *The Headmaster Ritual; Rusholme Ruffians; I Want The One I Can't Have; What She Said; Nowhere Fast; That Joke Isn't Funny Anymore; Well I Wonder; Barbarism Begins At Home; Meat Is Murder.*

● FIRST RELEASED 1985
● UK PEAK CHART POSITION: 1
● USA PEAK CHART POSITION: 110

297 ELECTRIC MUSIC FOR THE MIND AND BODY (416) ▲ COUNTRY JOE AND THE FISH

A lynchpin release in 1967, this album defined the genre known as acid-rock. Led by former folk musician Joe McDonald, the quintet combined engaging melodies with sharp, satirical lyrics encompassing different facets of the counter-culture. Drugs ('Bass Strings'), sex ('Porpoise Mouth') and politics ('Superbird') were detailed to pinpoint accuracy while the group contributed exquisite, subtle support. Guitarist Barry Melton brought shimmering majesty to the instrument, cutting through the verse with mercurial insight and soloing to perfection. The quiet power of this album continues to enthral those that are bothered to really listen. Others might just be bored.

● TRACKS: *Flying High; Not So Sweet Marsha Lorraine; Death Sound Blues; Happiness Is A Porpoise Mouth; Section 43; Superbird; Sad And Lonely Times; Love; Bass Strings; The Masked Marauder; Grace.*

● FIRST RELEASED 1967
● UK PEAK CHART POSITION: did not chart
● USA PEAK CHART POSITION: 39

298 MORRISON HOTEL (123) ▼
THE DOORS

F eted first as underground heroes, then reviled as teeny-bop stars, the Doors threw off such conundrums with this magnificent release. *Morrison Hotel* reaffirmed their blues roots, opening with the powerful 'Roadhouse Blues' before unfolding through a succession of songs showcasing all the group members' considerable strengths. Distinctively tight instrumental playing underscores memorable material, while Jim Morrison's authoritative vocal ranges from the demonstrative ('Maggie McGill') to the melancholic ('The Spy'). Despite contemporary problems, the Doors emerged with an album the equal of their first two stunning releases.

● TRACKS: *Roadhouse Blues; Waiting For The Sun; You Make Me Real; Peace Frog; Blue Sunday; Ship Of Fools; Land Ho; The Spy; Queen Of The Highway; Indian Summer; Maggie McGill.*

● FIRST RELEASED 1970
● UK PEAK CHART POSITION: 12
● USA PEAK CHART POSITION: 4

299 WORKINGMAN'S DEAD (–) ▲
GRATEFUL DEAD

N obody who had experienced the Dead's previous albums or live performances could have believed that they could go soft. In fact, they did it in such style that people hardly noticed. This folky gem is heavily influenced by Crosby, Stills, Nash And Young, and was their first major commercial success. Robert Hunter's lyrics dominate and suit the style and themes the record conjures up. Prior to this album the Dead could only jam. After this they were respected as also being able to sing, harmonize and play. A wonderfully rootsy album that is as American as the Band's self-titled record.

● TRACKS: *Uncle John's Band; High Time; Dire Wolf; New Speedway Boogie; Cumberland Blues; Black Peter; Easy Wind; Casey Jones.*

● FIRST RELEASED 1970
● UK PEAK CHART POSITION: did not chart
● USA PEAK CHART POSITION: 80

300 SEARCHING FOR THE YOUNG SOUL REBELS (878) ▲ DEXY'S MIDNIGHT RUNNERS

L ed by the abrasive and single-minded Kevin Rowland, Dexy's Midnight Runners spoke for an all-night culture immersed in northern soul. *Searching For The Young Soul Rebels* captures the original eight-piece group infusing passionate self-belief into songs based on 60s mentors Geno Washington and Jimmy James. Rowland's expressive voice is perfectly matched by pumping horns and punchy rhythms, but the intensity of their performance ensures the set never falls into pastiche. Each song bears the stamp of a manifesto, one that was largely Rowland's, a myopic vision that brought this line-up to an acrimonious, premature end. His commitment, however, ensured the lasting qualities of this album.

● TRACKS: *Burn It Down; Tell Me When My Lights Turn To Green; Teams That Meet In The Caffs; I'm Just Looking; Geno; Seven Day's To Long; I Couldn't Help It If I Tried; Thankfully Not Living In Yorkshire, It Doesn't; Keep It; Love Part One; There, There My Dear.*

● FIRST RELEASED 1980
● UK PEAK CHART POSITION: 6
● USA PEAK CHART POSITION: did not chart

WHAT WE DID ON OUR HOLIDAYS
(379) ▲   FAIRPORT CONVENTION

An album that revels in an embarrassment of influences which the band bind, making their own. This was the Fairport that ran with the psychedelic underground, flexing their muscles, a slumbering entity about to wake. This was their beatnik phase, producing such evergreens as Sandy Denny's beautiful 'Fotheringay', the first tangible examples of electrified trad in 'Nottamun Town' and 'She Moves Through The Fair' - neither song, incidentally, British. More significantly, Richard Thompson began to move in his own mysterious way, gifting 'Meet On The Ledge' which has since become their signature. Variety, as they say, is the spice of life and this collection adroitly exploits just that.

● TRACKS: *Fotheringay; Mr. Lacey; Book Song; The Lord Is In His Place; No Man's Land; I'll Keep It With Mine; Eastern Rain; Nottamun Town; Tale In Hard Time; She Moves Through The Fair; Meet On The Ledge; End Of A Holiday.*

● FIRST RELEASED 1969
● UK PEAK CHART POSITION: did not chart
● USA PEAK CHART POSITION: did not chart

302 RAW POWER (-) ▲
IGGY AND THE STOOGES

After Iggy Pop remixed *Raw Power* for CD release, he said that he believed the album held its own against the work of modern-day acts such as Smashing Pumpkins and Nirvana. Although he was referring to the album's unrelenting assault of loud, distorted guitars and gut-wrenching vocals, *Raw Power* has another quality that surpasses its modern-day emulators: melody. For all its noise, the album is surprisingly catchy, and tracks such as 'Search And Destroy' and the title track became singalong anthems for the punk generation. In light of the commercialization of alternative rock, *Raw Power's* combination of rebellion and accessibility fits in far better with today's alternative rock giants than it did in the somnolent past.

● TRACKS: *Search And Destroy; Gimme Danger; Your Pretty Face Is Going To Hell; Penetration; Raw Power; I Need Somebody; Shake Appeal; Death Trip.*

● FIRST RELEASED 1973
● UK PEAK CHART POSITION: 44
● USA PEAK CHART POSITION: 182

303 ELECTRIC WARRIOR (69) ▼
T. REX

Marc Bolan emerged from the petals of Britain's underground scene to become one of the 70s' bona fide rock stars. *Electric Warrior* followed the pattern of his group's highly successful singles wherein every track boasted nagging hooklines and incessant charm. Bolan understood pop history and his work drew on the immediacy of classic rock 'n' roll and the charm of its icons. He infused his music with an ebullient energy impossible to ignore, while offering a mythology to enhance its appeal. The antithesis of contemporaneous progressive rock, *Electric Warrior* was fresh and uncluttered and therein lies its continued attraction.

● TRACKS: *Mambo Sun; Cosmic Dancer; Jeepster; Monolith; Lean Woman Blues; Get It On; Planet Queen; Girl; The Motivator; Life's A Gas; Rip Off.*

● FIRST RELEASED 1971
● UK PEAK CHART POSITION: 1
● USA PEAK CHART POSITION: 32

304 LAZER GUIDED MELODIES (-) ▲
SPIRITUALIZED

Since *Lazer Guided Melodies* Spiritualized have had to endure the vagaries of indie credibility, but their musical blueprint has altered little from their powerful debut. Picking up where his former band Spaceman 3 had left off, Jason Pierce refined his exploration of trance-rock with elaborate arrangements and more sympathetic production values. The up-tempo 'Run' and 'Angel Sigh' hinted at the band's awesome live sound, but the album's true heart is found in the blissed-out nirvana of tracks such as 'Symphony Space', 'Sway' and '200 Bars'. This record virtually requires the listener be in a transcendental state while it is being played.

● TRACKS: *You Know It's True; If I Were With Her Now; I Want You; Run; Smiles; Step Into The Breeze; Symphony Space; Take Your Time; Shine A Light; Angel Sigh; Sway; 200 Bars.*

● FIRST RELEASED 1992
● UK PEAK CHART POSITION: 27
● USA PEAK CHART POSITION: did not chart

305 STATION TO STATION (–) ▲
DAVID BOWIE

Earmarking a more experimental phase *Station To Station* provided a more angular take on dance rhythms (most obvious on this album through the sublime funk bass of George Murray). Preference herein was for a more chilly, alienated dynamic, percolated through Bowie's heavily stylised vocals and increased use of electronica. The title-track takes over three minutes to announce 'the return of the Thin White Duke', its initial minimalism eventually crystallising into high-camp rock splendour. Over 10 minutes long, it is an intimidating introduction to what has often been perceived as Bowie's most bemusing work. 'Golden Years' is more yielding and easier on the ear. 'TVC15' betrays a rockier edge, leaving the aching beauty of the near-acoustic 'Wild Is The Wind' to finally steal the show.

● TRACKS: *Station To Station; Golden Years; Word On A Wing; TVC15; Stay; Wild Is The Wind; Word On A Wing (Live); Stay (Live)*

● FIRST RELEASED 1976
● UK PEAK CHART POSITION: 5
● USA PEAK CHART POSITION: 3

307 DOCUMENT (245) ▼
R.E.M.

R.E.M's later albums have sold by the container load, but they had to make albums like this to build a fan-base that brought them to notice. A number of critics place this record as their best. The band do sound as though they are having to work to be heard; there is significant energy in 'Finest Worksong' and their Byrdslike 'Welcome To The Occupation'. It has been some time since Michael Stipe had as many words to say as he did in 'It's the End Of The World As We Know It', and 'The One I Love' has to be one of their best songs of all time.

● TRACKS: *Finest Worksong; Welcome To The Occupation; Exhuming McCarthy; Disturbance At The Heron Houses; Strange; It's The End Of The World As We Know It (And I Feel Fine); The One I Love; Fireplace; Lightnin' Hopkins; King Of Birds; Oddfellows Local 151.*

● FIRST RELEASED 1987
● UK PEAK CHART POSITION: 28
● USA PEAK CHART POSITION: 10

306 OGDENS' NUT GONE FLAKE (366) ▲
THE SMALL FACES

Having begun their career as the archetypal Mod band, the Small Faces latterly embraced traces of flower-power's whimsy. Astute enough not to sacrifice their identity, the quartet retained a distinctive perspective, as evinced by a string of superb pop singles, including 'Here Comes The Nice' and 'Itchycoo Park'. A sense of pop melody and adventurism culminated on this album which encompassed tongue-in-cheek fun ('Lazy Sunday') and passionate love songs ('Afterglow'). Steve Marriott's voice remains completely self-assured and the group's characteristic organ-based swell is often enhanced by P.P. Arnold's emotional backing vocals. Eccentric comedian Stanley Unwin narrates the concept suite 'Hapiness Stan', but the music is strong enough to withstand the novelty tag. *Ogdens' Nut Gone Flake* was the Small Faces' swan-song, at least until an ill-starred reunion, but it proved a fitting end to a golden era.

● TRACKS: *Ogdens' Nut Gone Flake; Afterglow; Long Agos And Worlds Apart; Rene; Song Of A Baker; Lazy Sunday; Hapiness Stan; Rollin' Over; The Hungry Intruder; The Journey; Mad John; Happy Days Toy Town; Tin Soldier (live).*

● FIRST RELEASED 1967
● UK PEAK CHART POSITION: 1 ● USA PEAK CHART POSITION: 159

308 COPPER BLUE (332) ▲
SUGAR

Having disbanded the hugely influential Hüsker Dü, guitarist/vocalist Bob Mould embarked on a solo career during which he completed two contrasting albums. He then founded this power-packed trio, which resurrected the tone of his earlier group. *Copper Blue* sees Mould still firmly in control of his art, his barking voice enveloped by loud, crushing guitar and a succession of exhilarating hooklines. The album possesses awesome power and drive, but beyond the speed and distortion lies an understanding of the mechanics of classic pop songs, short, sharp and highly memorable. Mould is a crafted composer; 'Changes' is an awesome piece of hard pop.

● TRACKS: *The Act We Act; A Good Idea; Changes; Helpless; Hoover Dam; The Slim; If I Can't Change Your Mind; Fortune Teller; Slick; Man On The Moon.*

● FIRST RELEASED 1992
● UK PEAK CHART POSITION: 10
● USA PEAK CHART POSITION: did not chart

309 ARMED FORCES (236) ▼
ELVIS COSTELLO

Only recently has this album been reappraised favourably - this was, after all, his most commercial offering, yet its standing compared to *This Years Model* still indicates some cognoscenti resistance. Its political content should have given it credibility; lyrically it is as powerful as anything Costello has written. Even the overtly radio-friendly 'Oliver's Army' delivered some pretty uncompromising words, and exemplifies Costello's great strength: his ability to dress up a statement under the guise of a pop song. 'Green Shirt', 'Accidents Will Happen' and 'Goon Squad' are all as important as a pop song can be. Costello rarely wastes a lyric, and this album is no exception. The latest CD reissue has bonus tracks.

● TRACKS: *Accidents Will Happen; Senior Service; Oliver's Army; Big Boys; Green Shirt; Party Girl; Goon Squad; Busy Bodies; Sunday's Best; Moods For Moderns; Chemistry Class; Two Little Hitlers; (What's So Funny Bout) Peace Love And Understanding; My Funny Valentine; Tiny Steps; Clean Money; Talking In The Dark; Wednesday Week; Accidents Will Happen (Live); Alison (Live); Watching The Detectives.*

● FIRST RELEASED 1979
● UK PEAK CHART POSITION: 2
● USA PEAK CHART POSITION: 10

310 HOUSES OF THE HOLY (660) ▲
LED ZEPPELIN

Led Zeppelin at their most wilfully inventive. Displaying an eclectic irreverence for their recent history, they struck out with an assured astuteness that let them play what they felt. Consequently, the results were so genuinely original that the idea that they had any real musical contemporaries suddenly seemed absurd. 'The Crunge', played at funk rock years before the popular press had discovered and christened it, 'D'yer Mak'er' tossed reggae around for fun, while 'No Quarter' went on to be lifted wholesale by Pearl Jam predecessors, Mother Love Bone. At the heart of, and yet still ahead of, their time.

● TRACKS: *The Song Remains The Same; The Rain Song; Over The Hills And Far Away; The Crunge; Dancing Days; D'yer Mak'er; No Quarter; The Ocean.*

● FIRST RELEASED 1973
● UK PEAK CHART POSITION: 1
● USA PEAK CHART POSITION: 1

311 1962-66 (147) ▼
THE BEATLES

From the famous pair of red and blue, this one was always the poor relative, being one or two positions behind in the charts and selling one or two million fewer copies. Quite why will never be known, as the singles contained on this were bigger hits, and make for a better greatest hits package. You cannot tamper with the general opinion of the record buying public. What would be easier is that the every government throughout the world give every child a complete set of Beatles albums when they start school. Everybody reading this book must be familiar with every track on this album, even if they did not own it. They will always be the greatest popular 'beat combo' in the world.

● TRACKS: *Love Me Do; Please Please Me; From Me To You; She Loves You; I Want To Hold Your Hand; All My Loving; Can't Buy Me Love; A Hard Day's Night; And I Love Her; Eight Days A Week; I Feel Fine; Ticket To Ride; Yesterday; Help; You've Got To Hide Your Love Away; We Can Work It Out; Day Tripper; Drive My Car; Norwegian Wood; Nowhere Man; Michelle; In My Life; Girl; Paperback Writer; Eleanor Rigby; Yellow Submarine.*

● FIRST RELEASED 1973
● UK PEAK CHART POSITION: 3 ● USA PEAK CHART POSITION: 3

312 SLIPPERY WHEN WET (119) ▼
BON JOVI

Bon Jovi took a few faltering steps with their promising self-titled debut album and its shoddy *7800 Degrees Fahrenheit* follow-up. However, it was with this third record, a mixture of New Jersey storytelling and songwriter/collaborator Desmond Child's keen awareness of commercial appeal, that the perfect equation of songs and suss was established. The almost noble 'Wanted Dead Or Alive' spawned a thousand copycat monochrome, on-the-road videos, while the sure-fire snap of 'Livin' On A Prayer' and 'You Give Love A Bad Name' simply elevated the banner much higher.

● TRACKS: *Let It Rock; You Give Love A Bad Name; Livin' On A Prayer; Social Disease; Wanted Dead Or Alive; Raise Your Hands; Without Love; I'd Die For You; Never Say Goodbye; Wild In The Streets.*

● FIRST RELEASED 1986
● UK PEAK CHART POSITION: 6
● USA PEAK CHART POSITION: 1

GRACE & DANGER (435) ▲
JOHN MARTYN

Martyn shared the break-up of his marriage to Beverly by tearing open his heart and exposing all his emotions on record. Those listeners who were experiencing similar problems found it torturously compelling. The three emotional killers run consecutively - 'Sweet Little Mystery', 'Hurt In Your Heart' and 'Baby Please Come Home'. Each one pleads, begs and reasons and inevitably you ask, how on earth could she leave him? The answer is in the penultimate track where our John announces, 'I saved some for me' and 'I didn't give it all'. If you survived this album you can survive anything in later life, as our John has.

● TRACKS: *Some People Are Crazy; Grace And Danger; Lookin' On; Johnny Too Bad; Sweet Little Mystery; Hurt In Your Heart; Baby Please Come Home; Save Some For Me; Our Love.*

● FIRST RELEASED 1980
● UK PEAK CHART POSITION: 54
● USA PEAK CHART POSITION: did not chart

 FEATS DON'T FAIL ME NOW (243) ▼
LITTLE FEAT

If albums could be rolled and smoked, this would be one to keep for a special occasion, passed from friend to friend in a grin-inducing haze of contentment. Everything, from the Neon Park artwork to the sleeve notes, is goodtime. The line-up of the band on *Feats Don't Fail Me Now* works equally well on composition and playing. The songs, from the rhythmically chunky 'Rock And Roll Doctor' to the sprawlingly energetic 'Cold Cold Cold/Tripe Face Boogie', roll along without looking to left or right, and the arrangement is so tight you couldn't slide a Rizla in sideways. Country funk at its best, just remember not to inhale.

● TRACKS: *Rock And Roll Doctor; Oh Atlanta; Skin It Back; Down The Road; Spanish Moon; Feats Don't Fail Me Now; The Fan; Cold Cold Cold/Tripe Face Boogie.*

● FIRST RELEASED 1974
● UK PEAK CHART POSITION: did not chart
● USA PEAK CHART POSITION: 36

 THE FANTASTIC EXPEDITION OF DILLARD & CLARK (–) ▲ DILLARD AND CLARK

Gene Clark's major songwriting contribution to the Byrds is well documented and fully recognized. His solo work is highly rated, notably *No Other*. What should not be overlooked is his excellent two-album partnership with Doug Dillard and, not to be forgotten, future Eagle Bernie Leadon. This is the better of the two, and it features some high-standard gentle country-rock. Clark sounds very much at home with this material and if his life had been more settled, he could have been a giant country songwriter in the 90s. A comfortable, understated record that never diminishes, especially 'Train Leaves Here This Morning' and the best combination of strings and banjo ever with 'Why Not Your Baby'.

● TRACKS: *Out On The Side; She Darked The Sun; Don't Come Rollin'; Train Leaves Here This Morning; Why Not Your Baby; Lyin' Down The Middle; With Care From Someone; The Radio Song; Git It On Brother; In The Plain; Something's Wrong; Don't Be Cruel.*

● FIRST RELEASED 1969
● UK PEAK CHART POSITION: did not chart
● USA PEAK CHART POSITION: did not chart

316 **BLIZZARD OF OZ** (430) ▲
OZZY OSBOURNE

After the quiet implosion of Black Sabbath, the wise money was not on former vocalist, Ozzy, being the one to redeem himself musically. However, with shrewd management by his wife and a hotshot Californian in the shape of ex-Quiet Riot guitarist, Randy Rhoads, he reinvented himself and his musical persona, and created a startling debut album. Combining Rhoads' impetuous flurries of heavily stylized guitar, his own series of lyrical caricatures - 'Crazy Train' and 'Revelation (Mother Earth)' - and a healthy dose of controversy, citing renowned satanist Aleister Crowley as the subject matter for 'Mr. Crowley', he ensured himself acclaim and commerciality in equal measure.

● TRACKS: *I Don't Know; Crazy Train; Goodbye To Romance; Dee; Suicide Solution; Mr. Crowley; No Bone Movies; Revelation (Mother Earth); Steal Away (The Night).*

● FIRST RELEASED 1980
● UK PEAK CHART POSITION: 7
● USA PEAK CHART POSITION: 21

317 LIVE AT LEEDS (490) ▲
THE WHO

The Who forged their reputation as an exciting live attraction and elected to issue this set in the wake of the highly successful *Tommy*. Selections from that ground-breaking rock opera formed the core of this concert, but the group used the opportunity equally to restate past glories and acknowledge influences. Rock 'n' roll star Eddie Cochran had inspired the Who's Pete Townshend; the former's 'Summertime Blues' exploded with new fury within. 'Young Man Blues', first recorded by jazz singer Mose Allison, was given a new dimension through power chords, pulsating drumming and Roger Daltrey's expressive vocal. The CD reissue with bonus tracks is outstanding.

● TRACKS: *Magic Bus; My Generation; Shakin' All Over; Substitute; Summertime Blues; Young Man Blues.*

● FIRST RELEASED 1970
● UK PEAK CHART POSITION: 3
● USA PEAK CHART POSITION: 4

319 PRETENDERS (137) ▼
THE PRETENDERS

Former rock critic Chrissie Hynde launched the Pretenders with an engaging, yet passive, version of the Kinks' 'Stop Your Sobbing'. She unveiled her own persona fully on *The Pretenders*, which contains a series of excellent compositions marked by her sensual vocals and brilliant sense of dynamics. An understanding of pop's structures allowed Hynde to exploit them to her own ends while sympathetic support, particularly that of guitarist James Honeyman-Scott, used the excitement of rock without reference to its clichés. Tough and opinionated, Chrissie Hynde's first declaration of independence established the formula she proceeded to follow.

● TRACKS: *Precious; The Phone Call; Up The Neck; Tattooed Love Boys; Space Invader; The Wait; Stop Your Sobbing; Kid; Private Life; Brass In Pocket; Lovers Of Today; Mystery Achievement.*

● FIRST RELEASED 1980
● UK PEAK CHART POSITION: 1
● USA PEAK CHART POSITION: 9

318 GOODBYE AND HELLO (444) ▲
TIM BUCKLEY

Initially a folk-singer, Tim Buckley quickly defied stylistic categorization. *Goodbye And Hello* offers a rich musical vocabulary, from plaintive love song to free-form expressionism, with its core the artist's remarkable voice. Buckley glides and swoops around the melodies, colouring his material with raw emotion. His range is startling, from sonorous baritone to wild falsetto, but the intonation is never gratuitous. The beautiful 'Morning Glory' is on this record. He integrates with the song and musicians, most of whom were steeped in modern jazz. The haunting beauty of Tim Buckley's work is caught to perfection herein and continues to influence.

● TRACKS: *No Man Can Find The War; Carnival Song; Pleasant Street; Hallucinations; I Never Asked To Be Your Mountain; Once I Was; Phantasmagoria In Two; Knight-Errant; Goodbye And Hello; Morning Glory.*

● FIRST RELEASED 1967
● UK PEAK CHART POSITION: did not chart
● USA PEAK CHART POSITION: 171

320 I NEVER LOVED A MAN THE WAY I LOVE YOU (553) ▲   ARETHA FRANKLIN

Aretha Franklin emerged from years of often inappropriate recordings with Columbia with 'I Never Loved A Man', one of soul music's definitive performances. The song's simple, uncluttered arrangement allowed the singer free expression and her sense of artistic relief is palpable. The attendant album captured all of Franklin's gifts as she brings gospel fervour and individuality to a peerless collection of songs. Material drawn from Sam Cooke, Otis Redding and Ray Charles is infused with a rampant spirituality and given new perspectives when sung by this woman. The set also provides a showcase for Aretha's own compositional skills, as well as her propulsive piano playing which both employs and boosts the forcefulness of her singing. This album unleashed a major talent.

● TRACKS: *Respect; Drown In My Own Tears; I Never Loved A Man (The Way I Love You); Soul Serenade; Don't Let Me Lose This Dream; Baby, Baby, Baby; Dr. Feelgood (Love Is A Serious Business); Good Times; Do Right Woman Do Right Man; Save Me; A Change Is Gonna Come.*

● FIRST RELEASED 1967
● UK PEAK CHART POSITION: 36
● USA PEAK CHART POSITION: 2

321 STRANGE DAYS (224) ▼
THE DOORS

The Doors' second album redefined their uncompromising art. The disturbing timbre of Ray Manzarek's organ work provided the musical cloak through which guitarist Robbie Kreiger and vocalist Jim Morrison projected. Few singers in rock possessed his authority, where every nuance and inflection bore an emotional intensity. *Strange Days* contains some of the quartet's finest work, from the apocalyptical vision of 'When The Music's Over' to the memorable quirkiness of 'People Are Strange' and 'Moonlight Drive'. The graphic 'Horse Latitudes', meanwhile, confirmed Morrison's wish to be viewed as a poet, a stance ensuring the Doors were always more than just another rock band.

● TRACKS: *Strange Days; You're Lost Little Girl; Love Me Two Times; Unhappy Girl; Horse Latitudes; Moonlight Drive; People Are Strange; My Eyes Have Seen You; I Can't See Your Face In My Mind; When The Music's Over.*

● FIRST RELEASED 1967
● UK PEAK CHART POSITION: did not chart
● USA PEAK CHART POSITION: 3

322 FUMBLING TOWARDS ECSTASY (–) ▲
SARAH McLACHLAN

Despite the hokey synthesized drumbeats that dot such tracks as 'Mary', *Fumbling Towards Ecstasy* confirmed McLachlan's status as an heir to the tradition of Canadian bedsitter singer-songwriters that includes Gordon Lightfoot and Joni Mitchell. Her third album, it brought her to her widest audience yet, most notably in America, where it spent over a year on the charts and went gold. Written during a period of deep introspection, brought on by a harrowing charity trip to Cambodia and Thailand, most of the lyrics are laced with pain. However, the overall tone is that of a survivor, as in the title track, where she repeats over and over, 'I will not talk in class', 'I will not fear love.'

● TRACKS: *Possession; Wait; Plenty; Good Enough; Mary; Elsewhere; Circle; Ice; Hold On; Ice Cream; Fear; Fumbling Towards Ecstasy.*

● FIRST RELEASED 1994
● UK PEAK CHART POSITION: did not chart
● USA PEAK CHART POSITION: 50

323 HYSTERIA (607) ▲
DEF LEPPARD

Four years after *Pyromania*, Def Leppard were a comparative write-off. Dismissed by critics, seemingly dogged by bad luck, with drummer Rick Allen losing an arm in a car accident, *Hysteria* had to be an album to turn heads. In retrospect, it sounded like the first true hard rock record for the CD generation. Ambitious arrangements and remixes on songs such as 'Rocket' and 'Armaggedon It', a crisp single in 'Animal', and a dense paean to love with 'Love Bites', all bets were off. Def Leppard had created an intriguing language of ideas that still speaks volumes more than a decade on.

● TRACKS: *Women; Rocket; Animal; Love Bites; Pour Some Sugar On Me; Armaggedon It; Gods Of War; Don't Shoot Shot Gun; Run Riot; Hysteria; Excitable; Love And Affection; I Can't Let You Be A Memory.*

● FIRST RELEASED 1987
● UK PEAK CHART POSITION: 1
● USA PEAK CHART POSITION: 1

324 SAINT DOMINIC'S PREVIEW (241) ▼
VAN MORRISON

The cover depicts a troubled soul sitting on the church steps strumming his Martin guitar, probably unaware of the P.J. Proby split in his pants. The music inside is varied, as if Morrison is still feeling his way. He places the soul/jazz of 'Jackie Wilson Said' and 'I Will Be There' next to the delicious acoustic ramblings of 'Almost Independence Day' and 'Listen To The Lion'. It is the latter two that make this album so special. Van can knock off a soul song every time he opens his mouth, but 'Listen To The Lion' opens his soul. In addition to *Astral Weeks*, don't miss out on this album.

● TRACKS: *Jackie Wilson Said; Gypsy; I Will Be There; Listen To The Lion; St. Dominic's Preview; Redwood Tree; Almost Independence Day.*

● FIRST RELEASED 1972
● UK PEAK CHART POSITION: did not chart
● USA PEAK CHART POSITION: 15

325 BLUES AND THE ABSTRACT TRUTH
(540) ▲ OLIVER NELSON

Beautifully recorded and easily the best album of his career, which, early on, had included stints with Louis Jordan and Quincy Jones, and conducting and arranging for Jimmy Smith (notably 'Walk On The Wild Side'). The personnel on this record is formidable and probably enhances the album's high standing - Eric Dolphy (alto and flute), Bill Evans (piano), Roy Haynes (drums), Freddie Hubbard (trumpet), George Barrow (baritone) and Nelson (alto, tenor and writer/arranger). Lush arrangements on tracks such as 'Stolen Moments' are outstanding. It is hard to imagine that the man wholly behind this exceptional album was responsible for the *Six Million Dollar Man* television series theme.

● TRACKS: *Stolen Moments; Hoe Down; Cascades; Yearnin'; Butch And Butch; Teenie's Blues.*

● FIRST RELEASED 1961
● UK PEAK CHART POSITION: did not chart
● USA PEAK CHART POSITION: did not chart

326 AXIS: BOLD AS LOVE (198) ▼
THE JIMI HENDRIX EXPERIENCE

Live performances and the brilliant *Are You Experienced* established Jimi Hendrix as a guitarist nonpareil. This second set was largely less demonstrative, focusing on the artist's gifts as a songwriter. It included several reflective compositions, notably the haunting 'Little Wing'. This did not represent a radical change of emphasis - many of the tracks were actually recorded at sessions producing its predecessor - and the set simply offered another side to his talent. The guitarist's sonic creativity underscored 'If Six Was Nine' and 'Spanish Castle Magic' and although sometimes eclipsed by the albums issued on either side of it, *Axis: Bold As Love* brims with the same inventiveness. The 1997 MCA reissue is highly recommended.

● TRACKS: *EXP; Up From The Skies; Spanish Castle Magic; Wait Until Tomorrow; Ain't No Telling; Little Wing; If Six Was Nine; You've Got Me Floating; Castles Made Of Sand; She's So Fine; One Rainy Wish; Little Miss Lover; Bold As Love.*

● FIRST RELEASED 1967
● UK PEAK CHART POSITION: 5
● USA PEAK CHART POSITION: 3

327 SOME GIRLS (314) ▼
THE ROLLING STONES

One of the few latter period Stones albums that stands up to any real scrutiny in the light of their magnificent catalogue. Strolling out as the 70s were diminishing and punk was beginning to inflict a stranglehold and cultivate a disdain for anything over 30, the Stones once more enlivened their audience with the ability to surprise. Disregarding the contemporary mood and discarding their earlier R&B leanings, which they would later readopt, for funkier ground, irresistible undercurrents of rock 'n' roll patiently rumbled on, and 'Miss You' and the particularly excellent 'Beast Of Burden' showed them still capable of greatness.

● TRACKS: *Miss You; When The Whip Comes Down; Just My Imagination; Some Girls; Lies; Faraway Eyes; Respectable; Before They Make Me Run; Beast Of Burden; Shattered.*

● FIRST RELEASED 1978
● UK PEAK CHART POSITION: 2
● USA PEAK CHART POSITION: 1

328 SETTING SONS (–) ▲
JAM

After the creative *tour de force* and career regeneration that was *All Mod Cons*, the Jam continued their commercial ascendancy with *Setting Sons*. While it is not the band's most cohesive album ('Girl On The Phone' and 'Heatwave' are throwaway efforts at best), it did reveal further progress in Paul Weller's songwriting. There has never been a better song written about English class division than 'Eton Rifles'. Its sense of humour and self-deprecation is unique within Weller's usually austere songbook. Bruce Foxton also makes his key contribution to the Jam's arsenal with his best song, 'Smithers-Jones'. Weller's 'Thick As Thieves' and 'Saturday's Kids' are the other obvious crowd-pleasers.

● TRACKS: *Girl On The Phone; Thick As Thieves; Private Hell; Little Boy Soldiers; Wasteland; Burning Sky; Smithers-Jones; Saturday's Kids; The Eton Rifles; Heatwave.*

● FIRST RELEASED 1979
● UK PEAK CHART POSITION: 4
● USA PEAK CHART POSITION: 137

BLUE TRAIN (717) ▲
JOHN COLTRANE

Although it would seem that Alfred Lion's Blue Note label would have been the perfect home for a Bluetrane. Think of all those potentially great moody album shots. Surprisingly this is the only record he recorded for the label. Notwithstanding, it shows a confident Coltrane before he became a giant. The opening track is the leader; although a straightforward blues, it is a warming and familiar song. He is supported adequately by Lee 'Sidewinder' Morgan (trumpet), Kenny Drew (piano), Paul Chambers (bass), Curtis Fuller (trombone) and Philly Joe Jones (drums). Coltrane may have made more important albums, but none swung as much as this one.

● TRACKS: *Blue Train; Moments Notice; The Locomotion; I'm Old Fashioned; Lazy Bird.*

● FIRST RELEASED 1957
● UK PEAK CHART POSITION: did not chart
● USA PEAK CHART POSITION: did not chart

IN MY TRIBE (284) ▼
10,000 MANIACS

Natalie Merchant is one of those writers with an uncanny ability to portray the minutiae of life with pinpoint accuracy and detached humour. The songs on *In My Tribe* cover the difficulty of getting up in the morning ('Like The Weather'), her sister's wedding ('My Sister Rose') and childhood holidays ('Verdi Cries'), as well as relationships, drinking, corporal punishment and soldiering. Merchant writes free-flowing prose songs and performs them impeccably, ably assisted by the other Maniacs and the production of Peter Asher. All slightly off-the-wall, but none the worse for that.

● TRACKS: *What's The Matter Here?; Hey Jack Kerouac; Like The Weather; Cherry Tree; Painted Desert; Don't Talk; Peace Train; Gun Shy; My Sister Rose; A Campfire Song; City Of Angels; Verdi Cries.*

● FIRST RELEASED 1987
● UK PEAK CHART POSITION: did not chart
● USA PEAK CHART POSITION: 37

THE ORB'S ADVENTURES BEYOND THE ULTRAWORLD (–) ▲ THE ORB

The Orb lent new-found credibility to the concept album with the release of this impressively long debut in 1991. Having already pioneered ambient house music with the initial release of 'A Huge Ever Growing Pulsating Brain That Rules From The Centre Of The Ultraworld', Alex Patterson and his assorted collaborators constructed a whole double album's worth of blissed-out ambience that found favour with both the dance and rock communities. Based around the concept of a voyage to dimensions beyond normal consciousness, *Adventures Beyond The Ultraworld* was an almost perfect record for its time, providing an aural snapshot of acid house culture at its fleeting peak.

● TRACKS: *Little Fluffy Clouds; Earth (Gaia); Supernova At The End Of The Universe; Back Side Of The Moon; Spanish Castles In Space; Perpetual Dawn; Into The Fourth Dimension; Outlands; Star 6 & 7 8 9; A Huge Ever Growing Pulsating Brain That Rules From The Centre Of The Ultraworld: Live Mix Mk 10.*

● FIRST RELEASED 1991
● UK PEAK CHART POSITION: 29
● USA PEAK CHART POSITION: did not chart

RUM, SODOMY & THE LASH (273) ▼
THE POGUES

The Elvis Costello-produced *Rum, Sodomy & The Lash*, a title apparently taken from Winston Churchill's description of life in the Royal Navy, was the creative apex of their lolling, folky output. Shane MacGowan's rolling lilt was called to expound upon the rich lyrical tinges of 'A Pair Of Brown Eyes' and 'Dirty Old Town', while the band's ragged glory, dipping from a whisper to a powerful roar, shone through with 'The Old Main Drag' and 'I'm A Man You Don't Meet Every Day', utilizing their sometime sumptuous rasp. A fiercely unique record alive with abandon and a carefree soul.

● TRACKS: *The Sick Bed Of Cúchulainn; The Old Main Drag; Wild Cats Of Kilkenny; I'm A Man You Don't Meet Every Day; A Pair Of Brown Eyes; Sally Maclennane; Dirty Old Town; Jesse James; Navigator; Billy's Bones; The Gentleman Solder; And The Band Played Waltzing Matilda.*

● FIRST RELEASED 1985
● UK PEAK CHART POSITION: 13
● USA PEAK CHART POSITION: did not chart

333 PLEASE PLEASE ME (–) ▲
THE BEATLES

Recorded in between a cup of tea and a cigarette, this album is raw yet dazzling. Here were four lads, highly experienced on stage, but with little or no idea of what a recording studio was like. They were subtley marshalled by the much respected George Martin to deliver an entire album that was exactly what the fans wanted, but was still a surprise. Things were never as simple as this again, yet the genius is there - for example, Lennon's unmatchable rasping on 'Twist And Shout', McCartney's graceful ease in singing 'I Saw Her Standing There', Harrison's sparse but definite Gretsch chords and Starr's ace vocal on 'Boys'.

● TRACKS: *I Saw Her Standing There; Misery; Anna (Go To Him); Chains; Boys; Ask Me Why; Please Please Me; Love Me Do; P.S. I Love You; Baby Its You; Do You Want To Know A Secret; A Taste Of Honey; There's A Place; Twist And Shout.*

● FIRST RELEASED 1963
● UK PEAK CHART POSITION: 1
● USA PEAK CHART POSITION: record never released

334 BANDWAGONESQUE (448) ▲
TEENAGE FANCLUB

Teenage Fanclub emerged from a fraternal milieu centred on the Scottish town of Bellshill. A common love of pop tradition bound the quartet together and elements of their mentors abound on this collection. Neil Young and Big Star are obvious reference points, but the Fannies are not merely Byrds copyists. Dizzy melodies, long-hair guitar and unpretentiousness abound, the set's attraction ultimately residing in its cumulative, carefree charm. An impishness enhances the entire proceedings; only the churlish can resist its obvious attractions. Since this release they have been sorely taken for granted and have become an institution rather than stars. Everybody loves them but not enough to buy them.

● TRACKS: *The Concept; Satan; December; What You Do To Me; I Don't Know; Star Sign; Metal Baby; Pet Rock; Sidewinder; Alcoholiday; Guiding Star; Is This Music?.*

● FIRST RELEASED 1991
● UK PEAK CHART POSITION: 22
● USA PEAK CHART POSITION: 137

335 LET'S STAY TOGETHER (608) ▲
AL GREEN

The evocative title track that opens this glorious record sets a paradox. Al Green's remarkable voice, one that is hidden in the back of his throat, makes you constantly feel good. The subject matter of many of the songs on this album, however, is of sadness, lost love, frustration and confusion. Green was to popular soul in the 70s what Otis Redding was in the 60s; it was refreshing to see him performing and recording again in the early 90s. Perhaps the good reverend already knew in 1972 that he would be called to the church, because this collection has amazing healing powers.

● TRACKS: *Let's Stay Together; La-La For You; So You're Leaving; What Is This Feeling; Old Time Lovin'; I've Never Found A Girl; How Can You Mend A Broken Heart; Judy; It Ain't No Fun To Me.*

● FIRST RELEASED 1972
● UK PEAK CHART POSITION: did not chart
● USA PEAK CHART POSITION: 8

336 SYNCHRONICITY (113) ▼
THE POLICE

Fancy knowing you were going to break up and yet be able to record and produce this masterpiece. The world domination of the Police was as calculated and planned as was their departure. Each of the intervening albums have something special but the power of tracks such as 'Synchronicity II', and the haunting quality of 'Every Breath You Take' (you really believe Sting when he says, 'I'll be watching you') give this record the edge. The only tracks less than brilliant are Summers' and Copeland's offerings, a fact of which they must all have been aware. They bowed out while they were still winning.

● TRACKS: *Synchronicity I; Walking In Your Footsteps; O My God; Mother; Miss Gradenko; Synchronicity II; Every Breath You Take; King Of Pain; Wrapped Around Your Finger; Tea In The Sahara.*

● FIRST RELEASED 1983
● UK PEAK CHART POSITION: 1
● USA PEAK CHART POSITION: 1

337 **MAKING MOVIES** (128) ▼
DIRE STRAITS

The last album of their career that sounded as if they were trying to play, instead of going through the motions. David Knopfler had already departed from the band and brother Mark had a free rein, clear from any sibling rivalry. Every song stands up, apart from the dreadful 'Les Boys', hardly one of their show-stoppers. 'Solid Rock', 'Tunnel Of Love', Romeo And Juliet' and 'Skataway' would be on any decent greatest hits package. Following this artistic triumph they proceeded to release *Love Over Gold*, and we all know what album followed after that, don't we? Ho hum.

● TRACKS: *Tunnel Of Love; Romeo And Juliet; Skataway; Expresso Love; Hand In Hand; Solid Rock; Les Boys.*

● FIRST RELEASED 1980
● UK PEAK CHART POSITION: 4
● USA PEAK CHART POSITION: 19

 339 **GENIUS + SOUL = JAZZ** (76) ▼
RAY CHARLES

This is a difficult album to categorize. It is big band swing, jazz, soul, R&B, pop and blues, but mostly it is 'the genius' at work. This man has managed to stay hip for succeeding generations and also appeal to middle-class white America. This superb recording was made in 1961 shortly before he hit his commercial peak. Do not be put off by the big band: it is dynamic stuff, for example, 'Moanin'' and 'Strike Up The Band'. The CD reissue adds three live tracks from his *Genius Hits The Road* album to make this even more necessary and vital.

● TRACKS: *From The Heart; I've Got News For You; Moanin'; Let's Go; One Mint Julep; I'm Gonna Move To The Outskirts Of Town; Stompin' Room Only; Mister; Strike Up The Band; Birth Of The Blues.*

● FIRST RELEASED 1961
● UK PEAK CHART POSITION: did not chart
● USA PEAK CHART POSITION: 4

 338 **THE LOW SPARK OF HIGH HEELED BOYS** (184) ▼ **TRAFFIC**

The wandering jazzy music into which Traffic gradually flowed, hit a peak with this exceptional recording. The title track, with its perplexing lyrics, reaches numerous musical heights during its 12 minutes of life as it repeatedly comes back to Steve Winwood's accomplished vocal. Equally impressive, although shorter, is 'Hidden Treasure', highlighting what a good musician the late Chris Wood was. Finally, the band's loyal anchor, 'Gentleman' Jim Capaldi, takes lead on the cheeky (and sexist) 'Light Up Or Leave Me Alone'. The power of Traffic was in the atmosphere and space they created; this captures it.

● TRACKS: *Hidden Treasure; The Low Spark Of High Heeled Boys; Light Up Or Leave Me Alone; Rock 'N' Stew; Many A Mile To Freedom; Rainmaker.*

● FIRST RELEASED 1971
● UK PEAK CHART POSITION: did not chart
● USA PEAK CHART POSITION: 7

 340 **ANTHEM OF THE SUN** (432) ▲
THE GRATEFUL DEAD

Although much of this seminal record was taken from 15 live gigs it counts as a studio album because of the studio content and the remarkable tape splicing that removes any audience participation. 'The Faster We Go, The Rounder We Get' is one track, and 'the older we grow the easier it gets', is how we now view this work. Quite why it works is perplexing but there is incredible depth in the instrumentation, which reveals new facets after hundreds of plays. There is also a haunting beauty about the overall sound, especially the Hammond organ. It is an astonishingly good record that demands concentration. ¬

● TRACKS: *That's It For The Other One; Cryptical Envelopment; Quadlibet; For Tender Feet; The Faster We Go, The Rounder We Get; We Leave The Castle; Alligator; Caution (Do Not Stop On The Tracks).*

● FIRST RELEASED 1968
● UK PEAK CHART POSITION: did not chart
● USA PEAK CHART POSITION: 87

341 **UNHALFBRICKING** (480) ▲
FAIRPORT CONVENTION

T he transitional album before Fairport Convention invented folk rock with *Liege And Lief*, on this album they stretch out on longer numbers and introduce Dave Swarbrick, who plays some particularly fine fiddle on the lengthy 'A Sailor's Life'. Richard Thompson continued to mature with 'Genesis Hall' and 'Cajun Woman'. Equally impressive is Sandy's beautiful voice on her stellar composition 'Who Knows Where Time Goes'. Dylan abounds with three songs and 'Percy's Song' is a highlight. To round it up, a UK hit single, shock hórror, with Dylan's 'Si Tu Dois Partir'. Also a bold move for a little-known band was not having their name on the album sleeve.

● TRACKS: *Genesis Hall; Si Tu Dois Partir; Autopsy; A Sailor's Life; Cajun Woman; Who Knows Where The Time Goes; Percy's Song; Million Dollar Bash.*

● FIRST RELEASED 1969
● UK PEAK CHART POSITION: 12
● USA PEAK CHART POSITION: did not chart

342 **1967-70** (77) ▼
THE BEATLES

T he famous red and blue double albums were finally released on CD in 1994 to a public outcry, with complaints that the price was too high. The record company argued that it was the high

royalty negotiated with the artists that hiked up the price of a double CD. It made no difference whatsoever: both albums zoomed into the charts as everybody forked out £20 for the pleasure of buying tracks they already owned in some other shape or form - such is the power of the greatest pop group that ever was and will ever be. No discussion of the tracks is necessary - they are already part of our national heritage, and should be sung in morning assembly in every school in every part of the world.

● TRACKS: *Strawberry Fields Forever; Penny Lane; Sgt. Pepper's Lonely Hearts Club Band; With A Little Help From My Friends; Lucy In The Sky With Diamonds; A Day In The Life; All You Need Is Love; I Am The Walrus; Hello Goodbye; The Fool On The Hill; Magical Mystery Tour; Lady Madonna; Hey Jude; Revolution; Back In The USSR; While My Guitar Gently Weeps; Ob La Di Ob La Da; Get Back; Don't Let Me Down; Ballad Of John And Yoko; Old Brown Shoe; Here Comes The Sun; Come Together; Something; Octopus's Garden; Let It Be; Across The Universe; The Long And Winding Road.*

● FIRST RELEASED 1973
● UK PEAK CHART POSITION: 2
● USA PEAK CHART POSITION: 1

343 **HIGHWAY TO HELL** (-) ▲
AC/DC

I t will always be a mystery how a grown man can spend his life wearing a school tie and short trousers (pants in the USA) and receive adulation from the heavy metal fraternity. HM followers do not tolerate a cissy, yet the hugely talented Angus Young has become something of a hero. His riff-laden fills, combined with the tough vocals of the late Bon Scott, made AC/DC one of the genre's all-time leading lights. Bordering on the lighter side of metal, songs such as 'Love Hungry Man', 'Touch Too Much' and the title track will always delight.

● TRACKS: *Highway To Hell; Girl's Got Rhythm; Walk All Over You; Touch Too Much; Beating Around The Bush; Shot Down In Flames; Get It Hot; If You Want Blood (You've Got It); Love Hungry Man; Night Prowler.*

● FIRST RELEASED 1979
● UK PEAK CHART POSITION: 8
● USA PEAK CHART POSITION: 17

344 **THE STRANGER** (79) ▼
BILLY JOEL

D uring the late 70s many bemoaned the fact that Mr. Joel spent hours on our radio and years in the charts. Alexei Sayle even used his name in vain on 'Hello John Got A New Motor'. Two of his other albums, *An Innocent Man* and *52nd Street*, come close to greatness, but this monster of smooth AOR is the industry-standard Joel album that no comprehensive collection should be without. Layers of rich Fender Rhodes piano and crystal-clear vocals resulted in 16 million worldwide sales, even though Barry White recorded a better version of 'Just The Way You Are'.

● TRACKS: *Movin' Out (Anthony's Song); The Stranger; Just The Way You Are; Scenes From An Italian Restaurant; Vienna; Only The Good Die Young; She's Always A Woman; Get It Right The First Time; Everybody Has A Dream.*

● FIRST RELEASED 1978
● UK PEAK CHART POSITION: 25
● USA PEAK CHART POSITION: 2

ENDTRODUCING... (–) ▲
DJ SHADOW

The record-shop browsers pictured on the cover of *Endtroducing...* offered a fairly accurate indication of the contents: an obsessive and pointillistic amalgam of influences, ranging from hip-hop, through dance and jazz, to classical. A dark and brooding record, this album has quickly and quietly become a low-key classic. Subtly enveloping a core of old school hip-hop with layer upon layer of obscure samples, jazz vibes and moody instrumental and choral themes, Josh Davis's multitextured album attracted lavish critical praise and popular attention, and seemed a world away from the feisty rock of the more commercial dance artists.

● TRACKS: *Best Foot Forward; Building Steam With A Grain Of Salt; The Number Song; Changeling; What Does Your Soul Look Like (Part 4); Stem/Long Stem; Mutual Slump; Organ Donor; Why Hip Hop Sucks In '96; Midnight In A Perfect World; Napalm Brain/Scatter Brain; What Does Your Soul Look Like (Part 1 - Blue Sky Revisit).*

● FIRST RELEASED 1996
● UK PEAK POSITION: did not chart
● USA PEAK POSITION: did not chart

III (–) ▲
LED ZEPPELIN

They could do no wrong for many years, both in Britain and America. At the point of this album they were humungous, and, therefore, if they had gone into a recording studio and recited Enid Blyton stories, they would have topped the charts. *Led Zeppelin III* was only a good album by their standards, great by most of their imitators. It was a forerunner to the peerless *IV*, and remains overshadowed by it. Hints of acoustic material to follow came with 'Gallows Pole', first rehearsed with others at Bron-Y-Aur Stomp, the idyllic 'cottage in the country'. This is followed by the fat 12-string opening sound of 'Hats Off To (Roy) Harper', a composition by the mysterious Charles Obscure.

● TRACKS: *Immigrant Song; Friends; Celebration Day; Since I've Been Loving You; Out On The Tiles; Gallows Pole; Tangerine; That's The Way; Bron-Y-Aur Stomp; Hats Off To (Roy) Harper.*

● FIRST RELEASED 1970
● UK PEAK CHART POSITION: 1
● USA PEAK CHART POSITION: 1

FACE VALUE (71) ▼
PHIL COLLINS

The risk that Phil Collins took in displaying painful lyrics at an obviously harrowing time could have been taken as self-indulgence, but 18 years on this album is still seen as his best and most assured. The Genesis drummer displayed dynamic arrangements ('In The Air Tonight'), melancholy piano ('You Know What I Mean') and Philadelphia soul ('I Missed Again'), and wrapped up with a cover of 'Tomorrow Never Knows' at which even John Lennon would have tipped his hat. After this album Collins embarked on an extraordinarily busy career that included a rejuvenated Genesis, film roles and huge solo success. This will always be the album closest to his heart, with the paint pot on the piano.

● TRACKS: *In The Air Tonight; This Must Be Love; Behind The Lines; Roof Is Leaking; Droned; Hand In Hand; I Missed Again; You Know What I Mean; I'm Not Moving; If Leaving Me Is Easy; Tomorrow Never Knows; Thunder And Lightning.*

● FIRST RELEASED 1981
● UK PEAK CHART POSITION: 1
● USA PEAK CHART POSITION: 7

LIFES RICH PAGEANT (–) ▲
R.E.M.

For the first time in four albums, Michael Stipe evidently wanted the 'happy throngs' of listeners to hear and absorb his lyrics. On *Lifes Rich Pageant*, the band confidently tackled political and environmental issues, a direction more fully explored on the later *Document* and *Green*. Defiant and celebratory returns to their punk influences ('Just A Touch', 'These Days') were balanced by laments about US environmental policy and the folk tradition of the American South ('Swan Swan H'). Mills' and Berry's harmonies shone through, particularly on 'Fall On Me', still one of the best songs in the vast R.E.M. catalogue. A curiously sensitive and affecting album, packed with crafted pop songs, it marked a watershed for a group on the brink of unimagined worldwide success.

● TRACKS: *Begin The Begin; These Days; Fall On Me; Cuyahoga; Hyena; Underneath The Bunker; The Flowers Of Guatemala; I Believe; What If We Give It Away?; Just A Touch; Swan Swan H; Superman.*

● FIRST RELEASED 1986
● UK PEAK CHART POSITION: 43
● USA PEAK CHART POSITION: 21

349 DAYDREAM NATION (478) ▲
SONIC YOUTH

The double album that brought Sonic Youth to the attention of a wider audience and prompted the eager interest of a handful of major labels. *Daydream Nation*, with its sleepy single candle flickering silently on the gatefold cover, harnessed their reckless live favourite, 'Teenage Riot', while they ran gloriously roughshod over 'Rain King' and 'Silver Rocket', and offered the overtly camp glee of 'Trilogy', which came with parts a, b and z. Their assured ascension to festival billing and the giant Geffen label came as no surprise to anyone who had heard this album.

● TRACKS: *Teenage Riot; Silver Rocket; The Sprawl; 'Cross The Breeze; Eric's Trip; Total Trash; Hey Joni; Providence; Candle; Rain King; Kissability; Trilogy: a) The Wonder b) Hyperstation z) Eliminator Jr.*

● FIRST RELEASED 1988
● UK PEAK CHART POSITION: 99
● USA PEAK CHART POSITION: did not chart

350 NICE 'N' EASY (191) ▼
FRANK SINATRA

The perfect Sinatra album, which bridged both swing and gentle ballads, and yet another successful collaboration with Nelson Riddle and producer David Cavanaugh at Capitol Records. It is remarkable that ol' Blue Eyes continued to find exquisite songs to fill an album and not have to resort to any fillers that might have occurred when deadlines loomed. The title track sets the mood and he tackles 'Fools Rush In', 'Try A Little Tenderness' and Johnny Mercer's 'Dream'. Many of these songs were previously recorded when Sinatra was with Columbia as he prepared to depart for his own company Reprise.

● TRACKS: *Nice 'n' Easy; That Old Feeling; How Deep Is The Ocean; I've Got A Crush On You; You Go To My Head; Fools Rush In; Nevertheless (I'm In Love With You); She's Funny That Way; Try A Little Tenderness; Embraceable You; Mam'selle; Dream.*

● FIRST RELEASED 1960
● UK PEAK CHART POSITION: 4
● USA PEAK CHART POSITION: 1

351 FREAK OUT (221) ▼
FRANK ZAPPA/MOTHERS OF INVENTION

Led by the irascible Frank Zappa, the Mothers Of Invention were outsiders, even on this, their debut album. Older than most of their contemporaries, they brought a cynicism to their work that celebrated joys without recourse to nostalgia. Telling parodies of pop forms were as engaging as those upon which they drew, while experimental pieces, drawn from *avant garde* compositions by Edgar Varese and Stravinsky, took the notion of 'rock' into uncharted territory. Zappa's overview allowed such contrasting elements to function without disengagement, his skills as musician and engineer ensuring the innovative nature of this creation. It is also still great fun to listen to.

● TRACKS: *Hungry Freaks, Daddy; I Ain't Got No Heat; Who Are The Brain Police?; Go Cry On Somebody Else's Shoulder; Motherly Love; How Could I Be Such A Fool; Wowie Zowie; You Didn't Try To Call Me; Any Way The Wind Blows; I'm Not Satisfied; You're Probably Wondering Why I'm Here; Trouble Every Day; Help, I'm A Rock; The Return Of The Son Of Monster Magnet.*

● FIRST RELEASED 1967
● UK PEAK CHART POSITION: did not chart
● USA PEAK CHART POSITION: 130

352 AFTER BATHING AT BAXTER'S (–) ▲
JEFFERSON AIRPLANE

Always appreciated more in its homeland, *Baxter's* is a loose and challenging record. Transitional, as they left behind the folkiness of *Surrealistic Pillow* on their way to the surreal acidity of *Crown Of Creation*, it does have great charm. Love or hate the indulgence of Jack and Jorma's 'Spare Chaynge', it does sound good coming through large speakers. Kantner's 'Won't You Try' was his earliest anthem and set the pattern of much of his future work. This album is full of stoned innocence, the key being in the jumbled 'A Small Package Of Value Will Come To You Shortly'. They even giggle uncontrollably at the joke 'no man is an island, no man is a peninsula'!

● TRACKS: *Streetmasse: i The Ballard Of You & Me & Pooneil; ii A Small Package Of Value Will Come To You Shortly; iii Young Girl Sunday Blues; The War Is Over: i Martha; ii Wild Tyme; Hymn To An Older Generation: i The Last Wall Of The Castle; ii Rejoyce; How Suite It Is: i Watch Her Ride; ii Spare Chaynge; Shizoforest Love Suite: i Two Heads; ii Won't You Try/Saturday Afternoon.*

● FIRST RELEASED 1967
● UK PEAK CHART POSITION: did not chart
● USA PEAK CHART POSITION: 17

353 GRAND PRIX (–) ▲
TEENAGE FANCLUB

The adorable Fannies are in danger of becoming a 'much-loved institution' like the Kinks and XTC: great for warm-hearted feelings, but lousy for record sales. *Grand Prix* breaks the band's Byrdsian mould slightly, but there are enough jangly G chords to satisfy everyone. Virtually every song is a flawless gem, complete with the most precise harmonies; each rolls into the next with love and care, played, sung and produced with supreme clarity. With the fantastic boon of possessing three talented songwriters, TFC offer plenty of variety; in particular, Gerard Love's irresistible 'Sparky's Dream' achieves classic pop song status, and his 'Don't Look Back' is this accomplished album's highlight.

● TRACKS: *About You; Sparky's Dream; Mellow Doubt; Don't Look Back; Verisimilitude; Neil Jung; Tears; Discolite; Say No; Going Places; I'll Make It Clear; I Gotta Know; Hardcore/Ballad.*

● FIRST RELEASED 1995
● UK PEAK CHART POSITION: 7
● USA PEAK CHART POSITION: did not chart

 354 FUTURE DAYS (–) ▲
CAN

On *Future Days* Can fully explored the ambient direction they had introduced into their sound on the previous year's *Ege Bamyasi*, and in the process created a landmark in European electronic music. Apart from the delightfully concise single 'Moonshake', the album is comprised of just three long atmospheric pieces of music. The opening title track and 'Spray' build around the eerie vocals of Damo Suzuki as they weave in and out of the shimmering instrumental tracks. The closing 'Bel Air' is a gloriously expansive piece of music that progresses almost imperceptibly, before a sudden shock-ending after exactly 20 minutes.

● TRACKS: *Future Days; Spray; Moonshake; Bel Air.*

● FIRST RELEASED 1973
● UK PEAK CHART POSITION: did not chart
● USA PEAK CHART POSITION: did not chart

 355 SATURDAY NIGHT FEVER (293) ▼
VARIOUS

The disco revival came in the mid-90s and white suits, dodgy shirt collars and trousers with massive flares were once again the order of the day. While this album's success drove people mad as punk's enemy in the late 70s, it is now seen as a great piece of musical history. The Bee Gees did write some meaningful songs (with very high voices) on this but there is further perfect disco soul from Yvonne Elliman ('If I Can't Have You'), Tavares and Kool And The Gang. This is one soundtrack that is better than the film, well, only just.

● TRACKS: *Stayin' Alive; How Deep Is Your Love; Night Fever; Jive Talkin'; You Should Be Dancing; More Than A Woman; Calypso Breakdown; If I Can't Have You; A Fifth Of Beethoven; Open Sesame; Boogie Shoes; MFSB; K. Jee; Disco Inferno; Manhattan Skyline; Night On Disco Mountain; Salsation.*

● FIRST RELEASED 1978
● UK PEAK CHART POSITION: 1
● USA PEAK CHART POSITION: 1

 356 THE YES ALBUM (382) ▲
YES

OK, so much of Yes's output was pretentious, overblown and over-long. However, that does not detract from the volume of adventurous and technically brilliant work that lies buried beneath the less enduring (and endearing) stuff. *The Yes Album* benefits from having been recorded before Jon Anderson's lyrics became embarassingly obtuse, and before the producers lost the use of their fader fingers. The album opens with a storming 'Yours Is No Disgrace', Steve Howe excels on 'The Clap', the band take 'Starship Trooper' into orbit, and we all sing along to 'I've Seen All Good People'. It's really not all that proggy after all.

● TRACKS: *Yours Is No Disgrace; The Clap; Starship Trooper; Life Seeker; Disillusion; Wurm; I've Seen All Good People; Your Move; All Good People; A Venture; Perpetual Change.*

● FIRST RELEASED 1971
● UK PEAK CHART POSITION: 7
● USA PEAK CHART POSITION: 40

357 THE BUDDY HOLLY STORY (190) ▼
BUDDY HOLLY

Few artists have exercised such a profound influence in such a short space of time. Holly's untimely death robbed pop of a performer adept as a solo act and as leader of his group, the Crickets. He wrote, or co-wrote, most of his own material at a time when many singers relied on outside material, and his sparse, but effective, guitar style proved highly influential, particularly on British beat groups. *The Buddy Holly Story* abounds with songs now indisputably pop classics and confirms Holly's status as a major figure. The Beatles, Tex-Mex music and the singer-songwriter genre each owe Holly a debt, which is itself a lasting tribute to the quality of his work.

● TRACKS: *Raining In My Heart; Early In The Morning; Peggy Sue; Maybe Baby; Everyday; Rave On; That'll Be The Day; Heartbeat; Think It Over; Oh Boy; It's So Easy; It Doesn't Matter Any More.*

● FIRST RELEASED 1959
● UK PEAK CHART POSITION: 2
● USA PEAK CHART POSITION: 11

359 SUPERFLY (596) ▲
CURTIS MAYFIELD

As leader of the Impressions, Curtis Mayfield brought a lyricism to soul music. As a solo artist he chronicled society's travails and 'street' culture, which in turn inspired *Superfly*, the soundtrack to one of the era's most popular 'blaxploitation' movies. Mayfield's gift for combining light melody with simple, but chilling, wordplay ensured that the album stood up on its own terms without visual images, and its lynchpin selection, 'Freddy's Dead', was a million-selling single in its own right. Sympathetic but not sentimental, *Superfly* set new standards for soul music.

● TRACKS: *Little Child Runnin' Wild; Freddy's Dead; Give Me Your Love; Nothing On Me; Superfly; Pusherman; Junkie Chase; Eddie You Should Know; Think.*

● FIRST RELEASED 1972
● UK PEAK CHART POSITION: 26
● USA PEAK CHART POSITION: 1

358 GENIUS OF MODERN MUSIC VOLS. 1 & 2 (91) ▼ THELONIOUS MONK

Taken as a body of work these are two of the most important jazz albums of all time. Over the years Monk's importance grows, yet when these sessions were recorded his reputation was of cult status only. Monk has given us some outstanding compositions, and many are contained here. Naturally, the most recorded jazz song of all time, 'Round Midnight', is present, but so is the evergreen 'Ruby My Dear' and 'Monk's Mood'. And so on and so on; it reads like a greatest hits package. The CD versions are indispensable as there are many additional alternate takes.

● TRACKS: *Volume 1 - Round Midnight; Off Minor; Ruby My Dear; April In Paris; In Walked Bud; Thelonius; Epistrophy; Misterioso; Well You Needn't; Introspection; Humph. Volume 2 - Carolina Moon; Homin' In; Skippy; Let's Cool One; Suburban Eyes; Evonce; Straight No Chaser; Four In One; Nice Work If You Can Get It; Monk's Mood; Who Knows; Ask Me Now.*

● RECORDED 1947-52
● UK PEAK CHART POSITION: did not chart
● USA PEAK CHART POSITION: did not chart

360 COME DANCE WITH ME (233) ▼
FRANK SINATRA

On Sinatra's great records of the 50s and early 60s equal billing must be given to the conductors/arrangers. Sinatra was able to let loose and blossom with the confidence that the great songs he had chosen, together with his voice, would be enhanced by the orchestration. This album is another in a series of quite brilliant arrangements, this time by Billy May, giving new life to Johnny Mercer's 'Something's Gotta Give', Irving Berlin's 'Cheek To Cheek' and George Weiss's 'Too Close For Comfort'. In keeping with other Sinatra reissues the CD has four bonus tracks including two duets with Keely Smith.

● TRACKS: *Come Dance With Me; Something's Gotta Give; Just In Time; Dancing In The Dark; Too Close For Comfort; I Could Have Danced All Night; Saturday Night Is The Loneliest Night Of The Week; Day In, Day Out; Cheek To Cheek; Baubles, Bangles And Beads; The Song Is You; Last Dance.*

● FIRST RELEASED 1959
● UK PEAK CHART POSITION: 2
● USA PEAK CHART POSITION: 2

361 ON THE BEACH (–) ▲
NEIL YOUNG

Just how long should we tolerate the non-appearance of this album on CD? Sometimes the artist should be overruled. We don't care if Neil Young is unhappy with it, his public want it out and it is unfair to continue to deprive them. That said, this is one of Young's finest works, melodic, intense yet light, played exquisitely. Everything that some suggest *Harvest* lacks is present on this record. Young devotees read more into this album than the dark *Tonight's The Night*, such as the spectre of Charles Manson in 'Revolution Blues'. The real clincher is the autobiographical title track, with the simplistically powerful line 'the world is turning, I hope it don't turn away'.

● TRACKS: *Walk On; See The Sky About To Rain; Revolution Blues; For The Turnstiles; Vampire Blues; On The Beach; Motion Pictures; Ambulance Blues.*

● FIRST RELEASED 1974
● UK PEAK CHART POSITION: 42
● USA PEAK CHART POSITION: 16

362 A SALTY DOG (–) ▲
PROCOL HARUM

The powerful cover of this late 60s epic would still win awards. The brilliant spoof of a pack of Player's cigarettes no doubt gained extra sales, as seeing the pristine cover hanging in a record store was too much to pass on. The central theme is Keith Reid's infatuation with seafaring tales. The title track is a gigantic slab of pomp-rock that succeeds majestically. Other strong tracks are 'All This And More' and 'The Devil Came From Kansas'. Brooker's vocals could have benefitted from a more up-front mix, but minor carping aside, this is their finest album and one that is recommended.

● TRACKS: *A Salty Dog; The Milk Of Human Kindness; Too Much Between Us; The Devil Came From From Kansas; Boredom; Juicy John Pink; Wreck Of The Hesperus; All This And More; Crucifiction Lane; Pilgrim's Progress.*

● FIRST RELEASED 1969
● UK PEAK CHART POSITION: 27
● USA PEAK CHART POSITION: 32

363 THE NUMBER OF THE BEAST (229) ▼
IRON MAIDEN

A creative zenith for Iron Maiden. Capitalizing on new vocalist Bruce Dickinson and his rapturous wail, along with a keen eye for songwriting detail, *The Number Of The Beast* is an uncompromising, though surprisingly subtle, great hard rock record. Proudly displaying their *Boys' Own* Metal badge, subject matter includes *The Prisoner* television series as well as the plight of the native American in the Old West; they combine arch arrangements with a telling use of melody that, after the initial assault, lingers brilliantly in the mind.

● TRACKS: *The Invaders; Children Of The Damned; The Prisoner; 22, Acacia Avenue; The Number Of The Beast; Run To The Hills; Gangland; Hallowed Be Thy Name.*

● FIRST RELEASED 1982
● UK PEAK CHART POSITION: 1
● USA PEAK CHART POSITION: 33

364 BLUESBREAKERS WITH ERIC CLAPTON (210) ▼ JOHN MAYALL

The principals may have regarded the famous *Beano* cover album merely as a representation of their live work, but this album had as much to do with the British invasion of America's musical dominance as the Beatles or the Stones. Mayall willingly assumed the mantle of father of British blues that he had taken from Alexis Korner. Clapton was a blues purist who discovered other demons to drive his ambition, even if he could only emulate originals such as Freddie King, Buddy Guy, Otis Rush and Jimi Hendrix. Some maintain that Clapton has never played as well again, notwithstanding his current godlike status. Mayall has pursued a less notable but satisfying career, confident that this early achievement can never be bettered - by anyone.

● TRACKS: *All Your Love; Hideaway; Little Girl; Another Man; Double Crossin' Time; What'd I Say; Key To Love; Parchman Farm; Have You Heard; Ramblin' On My Mind; Steppin' Out; It Ain't Right.*

● FIRST RELEASED 1966
● UK PEAK CHART POSITION: 6
● USA PEAK CHART POSITION: did not chart

365 HAPPY TRAILS (765) ▲
QUICKSILVER MESSENGER SERVICE

If the quintessential San Francisco Sound is defined by lengthy improvised guitarwork and near-telepathic interplay, then *Happy Trails* crystallizes the genre on record. Taking cues from two Bo Diddley songs, the quartet introduce new realms of expression to rock music. Guitarists John Cipollina and Gary Duncan offer contrasting textures and sound, goading each other to greater heights. Largely recorded live in concert, *Happy Trails* encapsulates an era of experimentation, employing images that embodied the outlaw chic of the hippie subculture. Its strengths are not, however, bound to that era; the album's mesmerizing power remains as true as ever. The George Hunter cover painting is also indispensable.

● TRACKS: *Who Do You Love (Part One); When You Love; Where You Love; How Do You Love; Which Do You Love; Who Do You Love (Part Two); Mona; Maiden Of The Cancer Moon; Calvary; Happy Trails.*

● FIRST RELEASED 1968
● UK PEAK CHART POSITION: did not chart
● USA PEAK CHART POSITION: 27

367 ALADDIN SANE (270) ▼
DAVID BOWIE

Aladdin Sane was released as its creator's star was firmly ascending. A sprawling US tour inspired much of its content, particularly 'Drive In Saturday' and 'Panic In Detroit', but such images are infused with Bowie's contemporary interest in science fiction-styled alter egos. Regular backing group, the·Spiders From Mars, which included guitarist Mick Ronson, fuelled the compositions with an intuitive punch, although the diverse nature of the material showed Bowie's ever-present desire to challenge. Futuristic vistas are even harnessed to vintage R&B, as evinced on 'Jean Genie', which inspires comparisons with the Yardbirds and a reworking of the Stones' 'Let's Spend The Night Together'. The singer disbanded his group following this album, and *Aladdin Sane* thus marks a watershed in·his inventive career.

● TRACKS: *Watch That Man; Aladdin Sane; Drive In Saturday; Panic In Detroit; Cracked Actor; Time; The Prettiest Star; Let's Spend The Night Together; Jean Genie; Lady Grinning Soul.*

● FIRST RELEASED 1973
● UK PEAK CHART POSITION: 1
● USA PEAK CHART POSITION: 17

366 LATE FOR THE SKY (–) ▲
JACKSON BROWNE

Jackson Browne's early career was inextricably linked to the singer-songwriter movement of the 70s, and *Late For The Sky* has proved to be one of the era's strongest and most enduring albums. Browne's reflective song-writing style attained a new level of maturity on songs such as 'Fountain Of Sorrow' and 'For A Dancer', the latter a strikingly literate meditation on death. *Late For The Sky* is overshadowed by the title track and 'Before The Deluge', two brooding songs of personal and social apocalypse that book-end the album and serve as a textbook definition of the Californian mindset of the 70s.

● TRACKS: *Late For The Sky; Fountain Of Sorrow; Farther On; The Late Show; The Road And The Sky; For A Dancer; Walking Slow; Before The Deluge.*

● FIRST RELEASED 1974
● UK PEAK CHART POSITION: did not chart
● USA PEAK CHART POSITION: 14

368 L.A.M.F. (778) ▲
THE HEARTBREAKERS

The Heartbreakers revolved around two former members of the New York Dolls, Johnny Thunders and Jerry Nolan. Having decamped to London in 1976, they became an integral part of the early punk circuit, before their solitary studio album. Although hampered by an insubstantial mix, the set contains some of the era's most expressive songs, notably 'Born Too Loose' and 'Chinese Rocks', the latter a chilling account of heroin addiction, co-written with Dee Dee Ramone. Tight, unfussy playing emphasizes the power of material that proved pivotal in the development of the new music in both the UK and USA. Sadly, the featured line-up disintegrated soon afterwards and numerous permutations failed to recreate its strengths.

● TRACKS: *Born Too Loose; Baby Talk; All By Myself; I Wanna Be Loved; It's Not Enough; Chinese Rocks; Get Off The Phone; Pirate Love; One Track Mind; I Love You; Goin' Steady; Let Go.*

● FIRST RELEASED 1977
● UK PEAK CHART POSITION: 55
● USA PEAK CHART POSITION: did not chart

369 NOTHING'S SHOCKING (–) ▲
JANE'S ADDICTION

The instrumental track that opens the album reminds the listener of Randy California and his Spirit. Everything changes from then on; the lightness of Spirit gives way to harder stuff, much closer to Blue Cheer. Musically, it is easy to understand why the band were strongly tipped for great things; lyrically, there are some strange ramblings. 'Standing In The Shower' is a nice concept, but tells us nothing, and it is hard to agree with the paradox of 'Ted, Just Admit It' and just why 'sex is violent'. Maybe the art of enjoyment is to let the music wash over you at a high volume, because these chaps could certainly play.

● TRACKS: *Up The Beach; Ocean Size; Had A Dad; Ted, Just Admit It; Standing In The Shower, Thinking; Summertime Rolls; Mountain Song; Idiot's Rule; Jane Says; Thank You Boys; Pigs In Zen.*

● FIRST RELEASED 1988
● UK PEAK CHART POSITION: did not chart
● USA PEAK CHART POSITION: 103

 370 NEW YORK (–) ▲
LOU REED

In the world of contemporary Rock 'n' Roll, nobody has ever been able to sing about New York the way Reed can. Right from the decadent New York of the 60s with the Velvet Underground, Reed has had his finger on the nipple of what made it tick. He writes about the city as he views it from a dustbin. 'Romeo Had Juliette' has a great line, 'Manhattan's sinking like a rock into the filthy Hudson' and 'Halloween Parade' captures the downside of the glossy procession that takes place in Greenwich Village every year. It is no surprise that this album fared better outside the state of New York.

● TRACKS: *Romeo Had Juliette; Halloween Parade; Dirty Blvd; Endless Cycle; There Is No Time; Last Great American Whale; Beginning Of A Great Adventure; Busload Of Faith; Sick Of You; Hold On; Good Evening Mr. Waldheim; Xmas In February; Strawman; Dime Store Mystery.*

● FIRST RELEASED 1989
● UK PEAK CHART POSITION: 14
● USA PEAK CHART POSITION: 40

 **371 THE GENIUS OF RAY CHARLES** (87) ▼
RAY CHARLES

Neither pop nor jazz, once again Charles is hard to categorize even though many of the musicians have strong jazz credentials; Paul Gonsalves, Clark Terry, Zoot Sims and Bob Brookmeyer, for example. The album's strength (in addition to Brother Ray) lies in the choice of classic songs matched with lush orchestration. Ray's soulful voice will break hearts on 'Don't Let The Sun Catch You Cryin'', 'Just For A Thrill' and the ultimate song for hopeless romantics, Johnny Mercer and Harold Arlen's starry-eyed 'Come Rain Or Come Shine'. The excellent recording, particularly with Ray's up-front vocals, is the work of Jerry Wexler, Tom Dowd and Bill Schwartau.

● TRACKS: *Let The Good Times Roll; It Had To Be You; Alexander's Ragtime Band;.Two Years Of Torture; When Your Lover Has Gone; Deed I Do; Just For A Thrill; You Won't Let Me Go; Tell Me You'll Wait For Me; Don't Let The Sun Catch You Cryin'; Am I Blue; Come Rain Or Come Shine.*

● FIRST RELEASED 1959
● UK PEAK CHART POSITION: did not chart
● USA PEAK CHART POSITION: 17

 372 ATOMIC BASIE (–) ▲
COUNT BASIE

An inspired collaboration that worked so well, it is surprising that Basie and Neal Hefti did not form a long-term Sinatra/Riddle partnership. Hefti later found solace in writing musical opuses such as 'The Batman Theme'! Great for his bank balance, but little aid to his credibility. This, however, is a magnificent record that should always be played in its entirety. Basie rarely sounded so fresh and crisp. For a 1958 album, this is a staggering record. 'Splanky', in particular, spits out with an incredible force and their reading of 'Li'l Darlin' is definitive. The original engineer Bob Arnold deserves a special mention. The CD remastering is fabulous and comes with five bonus tracks.

● TRACKS: *The Kid From Red Bank; Duet; After Supper; Flight Of The Foo Birds; Double-O; Teddy The Toad; Whirly-Bird; Midnite Blue; Splanky; Fantail; Li'l Darlin'; Silks And Satins; Sleepwalker's Serenade; Sleepwalker's Serenade (alternate take); The Late Late Show; The Late Late Show (vocal version).*

● FIRST RELEASED 1958
● UK PEAK CHART POSITION: did not chart
● USA PEAK CHART POSITION: did not chart

373 SEPTEMBER OF MY YEARS (256) ▼
FRANK SINATRA

Released shortly before Frank Sinatra's 50th birthday, this album predictably found the singer in a warm and reflective mood. Conductor-arranger Gordon Jenkins provided a string-laden setting for a mixture of songs old and new, including Sammy Cahn and Jimmy Van Heusen's specially written title number. Released in the middle of the beat boom, it was awarded Grammys for album of the year and Sinatra's best male vocal performance on one of the tracks, 'It Was A Very Good Year' (Erwin Drake), and provided a great deal of musical comfort for many middle-aged, former 'Swingin' Lovers'.

● TRACKS: *September Of My Years; How Old Am I; Don't Wait Too Long; It Gets Lonely Early; This Is All I Ask; Last Night When We Were Young; The Man In The Looking Glass; It Was A Very Good Year; When The Wind Was Green; Hello Young Lovers; I See It Now; Once Upon A Time; September Song.*

● FIRST RELEASED 1965
● UK PEAK CHART POSITION: did not chart
● USA PEAK CHART POSITION: 5

374 LADY IN AUTUMN (86) ▼
BILLIE HOLIDAY

Without question the greatest jazz singer there has ever been (or will ever be), Holiday's unmistakable sound, her

inimitable phrasing, her faultless sense of what was right, helped mould an artist unique in the history of popular music. In the early years her joyous, youthful voice was backed by soloists of the calibre of Buck Clayton, her close friend Lester Young, and her ideal arranger, pianist Teddy Wilson. Towards the end of her life her voice was a flaking, fractured caricature of itself but her commanding artistry and musical integrity lent dignity and poignancy to her recordings.
● TRACKS: *Body And Soul; Strange Fruit; Trav'lin' Light; All Of Me; (There Is) No Greater Love; I Cover The Waterfront; These Foolish Things (Remind Me Of You); Tenderly; Autumn In New York; My Man; Stormy Weather; Yesterdays; (I Got A Man, Crazy For Me) He's Funny That Way; What A Little Moonlight Can Do; I Cried For You (Now It's Your Turn To Cry Over Me); Too Marvelous For Words; I Wished On The Moon; I Don't Want To Cry Anymore; Prelude To A Kiss; Nice Work If You Can Get It; Come Rain Or Come Shine; What's New?; God Bless The Child; Do Nothin' Till You Hear From Me; April In Paris; Lady Sings The Blues; Don't Explain; Fine And Mellow; I Didn't Know What Time It Was; Stars Fell On Alabama; One For My Baby (And One More For The Road); Gee Baby, Ain't I Good To You; Lover Man (Oh, Where Can You Be?); All The Way; Don't Worry 'bout Me.*
● FIRST RELEASED 1973
● UK PEAK CHART POSITION: did not chart
● USA PEAK CHART POSITION: did not chart

375 PARANOID (94) ▼
BLACK SABBATH

The murderous riff on which the title track hinges set the tone for this bruising album. Doom, death and destruction are Black Sabbath's staple diet, which they devour with numbing intensity. Repetition is at the heart of the album, sustained chords and ponderous bass often slowing tempos to crawling pace until, on 'War Pigs', they groan with suffocation. Guitarist Tony Iommi punctuates the sound with simple but lengthy solos, leaving vocalist Ozzy Osbourne to inject a sly cockiness. Pretenders have often grasped at their crown, but *Paranoid* shows that Black Sabbath remain the quintessential heavy metal band.

● TRACKS: *Paranoid; War Pigs; Planet Caravan; Iron Man; Electric Funeral; Hand Of Doom; Rat Salad; Fairies Wear Boots; Wicked World.*

● FIRST RELEASED 1970
● UK PEAK CHART POSITION: 1
● USA PEAK CHART POSITION: 12

376 FAITH (–) ▲
GEORGE MICHAEL

Before *Faith* George Michael was, to the record buyer, one half (or more) of Wham!, with its trite pop material and sexy teen image. *Faith* was crafted to establish him as a mature artist and serious lyricist, and it accomplished exactly that. Having had two years in gestation, it sold over 10 million copies and launched Michael's new personal and artistic image. 'I Want Your Sex' was a guaranteed number 1 hit after being widely banned, and was followed by five more hit singles. Although now seeming dated by its club-style production and spoilt by some embarrassing lyrics, it nevertheless marked the emergence of a major pop talent for the 90s.

● TRACKS: *Faith; Father Figure; I Want Your Sex, Pt. 1 & 2; One More Try; Hard Day; Hand To Mouth; Look At Your Hands; Monkey; Kissing A Fool; Hard Day; Last Request (I Want Your Sex, Pt. 3).*

● FIRST RELEASED 1987
● UK PEAK CHART POSITION: 1
● USA PEAK CHART POSITION: 1

377 **PARADE** (180) ▼
PRINCE AND THE REVOLUTION

Another soundtrack that fared more favourably than the movie, 'Under The Cherry Moon', from which it came, this was also the record that marked Prince's return to the live arena. The record itself came with a high camp video and guaranteed hit in the shape of 'Kiss' (which a collaboration of Tom Jones and the Art Of Noise would later cover), a delightfully funky little number around which the world threatened to dance. Elsewhere, both 'Girls And Boys' and 'Anotherloverholenyohead' charted. While the lifting strains of 'Sometimes It Snows In April' rounded off a wonderfully whole album, nothing could quite save the film.

● TRACKS: *Christopher Tracey's Parade; New Position; I Wonder U; Under The Cherry Moon; Girls And Boys; Life Can Be So Nice; Venus De Milo; Mountains; Do U Lie; Kiss; Anotherloverholenyohead; Sometimes It Snows In April.*

● FIRST RELEASED 1986
● UK PEAK CHART POSITION: 4
● USA PEAK CHART POSITION: 3

 378 **ONCE UPON A TIME** (88) ▼
SIMPLE MINDS

Simple Minds gained belated US chart success with '(Don't You) Forget About Me' and a distinctly transatlantic burr covered this, the ensuing album. Producers Jimmy Iovine and Bob Clearmountain sculpted an unambiguous sound where crowd-pleasing anthems invoked a genuine excitement. Loud, forthright and shorn of subtlety, *Once Upon A Time* shows the group's core trio - Jim Kerr (vocals), Charlie Burchill (guitar) and Mick McNeil (keyboards) - working together with genuine empathy, while a revamped rhythm section underpins the material with sinewy precision. They combine to create what many consider to be Simple Minds' most exciting and exhilarating release.

● TRACKS: *Once Upon A Time; All The Things She Said; Ghostdancing; Alive And Kicking; Oh Jungleland; I Wish You Were Here; Sanctify Yourself; Come A Long Way.*

● FIRST RELEASED 1985
● UK PEAK CHART POSITION: 1
● USA PEAK CHART POSITION: 10

 379 **COPPERHEAD ROAD** (860) ▲
STEVE EARLE

Steve Earle is one of the hip new stars who have given new country music acceptance with non-honky tonkers. Earle is a renegade who has been married almost as many times as the number of albums he has released. His songs are new country-Springsteen and he is not frightened to rock. The Pogues give great support to this memorable album. His career has faltered commercially since this release as his music has taken on a harder edge. The title track is a highlight, featuring some fine mandolin over an infectious beat; similar fare is 'You Belong To Me' and 'Back To The Wall'. Country purists may balk, but this album is destined to last. Earle is the Lemmy Motorhead of new country.

● TRACKS: *Copperhead Road; Snake Oil; Back To The Wall; The Devil's Right Hand; Johnny Come Lately; Even When I'm Blue; You Belong To Me; Waiting On You; Once You Love; Nothing But A Child*

● FIRST RELEASED 1988
● UK PEAK CHART POSITION: 44
● USA PEAK CHART POSITION: 56

 380 **OKLAHOMA!** (81) ▼
VARIOUS

Twelve years after it opened on Broadway, Richard Rodgers and Oscar Hammerstein II's first musical burst onto the screen in the Todd-AO widescreen process, with a fine cast that included Gordon MacRae, Shirley Jones, Charlotte Greenwood, Rod Steiger, Gloria Grahame, Gene Nelson and James Whitmore. All the marvellous songs heard in the stage production are here, with the highlights being 'Oh, What A Beautiful Mornin'', 'The Surrey With The Fringe On Top', 'People Will Say We're In Love', and the rousing title number. A spell of over four years in the US charts (four weeks at number 1) says it all.

● TRACKS: *Oklahoma Overture; Oh, What A Beautiful Morning; Surrey With The Fringe On Top; Kansas City; I Can't Say No; Many A New Day; People Will Say We're In Love; Poor Jud Is Dead; Out Of My Dreams; Farmer And The Cowman; All Or Nothin'; Oklahoma.*

● FIRST RELEASED 1955
● UK PEAK CHART POSITION: 4
● USA PEAK CHART POSITION: 1

381 ODESSEY & ORACLE (–) ▲
THE ZOMBIES

Reappraised, and now widely accepted as a masterpiece of late 60s pop, this is as timeless as it is faultless. Swirling Mellotron over Colin Blunstone's emotive voice, with every track to be cherished. It was a major success in the USA, where the Zombies were appreciated, and they put 'Time of The Season' near the top of the charts. The UK gave up on them after 'She's Not There'. Rod Argent went on to great success with Argent, Blunstone became a solo singer, but they have never forgotten their first love. The five Zombies are all alive and well, and are now bathing in the much-deserved praise this album now receives.

● TRACKS: *Care Of Cell 44; A Rose For Emily; Maybe After He's Gone; Beechwood Park; Brief Candles; Hung Up On A Dream; Changes; I Want Her She Wants Me; This Will Be Our Year; Butchers Tale (Western Front 1914); Friends Of Mine; Time Of The Season.*

● FIRST RELEASED 1968
● UK PEAK CHART POSITION: did not chart
● USA PEAK CHART POSITION: 95

382 EVERCLEAR (–) ▲
AMERICAN MUSIC CLUB

It is hard to imagine why American Music Club failed to chart in their homeland with any of their excellent records. Two of their albums did chart in the UK, but this was not one of them. Following their demise, Mark Eitzel has undertaken a solo career that seems to result in critical acclaim and zero sales. This is a beautiful record of great intensity and depth, and Eitzel's lyrics fit the mood of the instrumentation. He has clearly been around the block a few times with regard to relationships, and songs such as 'Ex-Girlfriend' will tug at a few 'been there, done that' hearts.

● TRACKS: *Why Won't You Stay; Rise; Miracle On 8th Street; Ex-Girlfriend; Crabwalk; The Confidential Agent; Sick Of Food; The Dead Part Of You; Royal Cafe; What The Pillar Of Salt Held Up; Jesus' Hands.*

● FIRST RELEASED 1991
● UK PEAK CHART POSITION: did not chart
● USA PEAK CHART POSITION: did not chart

383 THE POET (–) ▲
BOBBY WOMACK

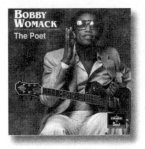

Mr Womack has been around forever, and even with his personal ups and downs (and he has had a few) he manages to survive. It's hard to think that this was the man who first recorded 'It's All Over Now' with the Valentinos in the early 60s, and word was spread by the Rolling Stones, who had a massive hit with it. He worked as a solo artist in the 70s and also with Linda Womack, as Womack And Womack. During the early 80s he hit a particularly fine seam of gold, and this was his most successful album. Falling somewhere between funk and Marvin Gaye sweet soul *The Poet* was a highly polished album.

● TRACKS: *So Many Sides Of You; Lay Your Lovin' On Me; Secrets; Just My Imagination; Stand Up; Games; If You Think You're Lonely; Where Do We Go From Here.*

● FIRST RELEASED 1981
● UK PEAK CHART POSITION: did not chart
● USA PEAK CHART POSITION: 29

384 TOO-RYE-AY (–) ▲
DEXY'S MIDNIGHT RUNNERS

After the Stax sound of *Searching For The Young Soul Rebels*, Dexys Midnight Runners abruptly switched styles for this excursion into what singer Kevin Rowland called 'Celtic soul'. The image, as ever with Dexys, was in keeping with the music as the group embraced hoedown gypsy chic, complete with dungarees and neckerchiefs. Musically, they combined fiddles with horns to create an exhilarating series of songs, updating Van Morrison's 'Jackie Wilson Said' and excavating key moments from Rowland's childhood, most notably in the invigorating 'Come On Eileen'. With the world at their command, Dexys could have cashed in with a carbon-copy sequel, but instead waited a tantalizing three years before emerging with the even more startling *Don't Stand Me Down.*

● TRACKS: *The Celtic Soul Brothers; Let's Make This Precious; All In All; Jackie Wilson Said; Old; Plan B; I'll Show You; Liars A To E; Until I Believe In My Soul; Come On Eileen.*

● FIRST RELEASED: 1982
● UK PEAK CHART POSITION: 2
● USA PEAK CHART POSITION: 14

385 3+3 (–) ▲
THE ISLEY BROTHERS

The day Ernie Isley picked up his electric guitar with a fuzzbox connected was the day the Isleys' fortunes changed for the better. The slick, besuited Tamla/Motown soul was replaced by funkier stuff with some truly spectacular guitar solos. The title track is present here in its full-length glory, as is the lengthy workout on 'Summer Breeze'. Ernie became a guitar hero with those two tracks and spawned a host of second-rate imitators. Other highlights are 'The Highways Of My Life' and James Taylor's 'Don't Let Me Be Lonely Tonight'. The version of the Doobie Brothers' 'Listen To The Music' can be dispensed with. Almost a rock album, but not quite soul.

● TRACKS: *That Lady; Don't Let Me Be Lonely Tonight; If You Were There; You Walk Your Way; Listen To The Music; What It Comes Down To; Sunshine (Go Away Today); Summer Breeze; The Highways Of My Life.*

● FIRST RELEASED 1973
● UK PEAK CHART POSITION: did not chart
● USA PEAK CHART POSITION: 8

386 DRY (532) ▲
PJ HARVEY

This West Country chanteuse with a credible line in extolling the virtues of sex, came with a wealth of emotional baggage that she was more than willing to share. Her public persona was a mix of nudity wrapped in clingfilm, or draped with a feather boa and arch, accentuated sunglasses, while her songs bristled with fragility and pain and occasionally, a surly inner strength. Now more widely acknowledged with her excellent *Rid Of Me* and *4 Track Demo*, *Dry* was the bedrock on which she built her tower of emotions. The gritty 'Victory', the surprisingly light 'Water', the evocative 'Happy And Bleeding' - all made for a crushing masterpiece.

● TRACKS: *Oh My Lover; O Stella; Dress; Victory; Happy And Bleeding; Sheela-Na-Gig; Hair; Joe; Plants And Rags; Fountain; Water.*

● FIRST RELEASED 1992
● UK PEAK CHART POSITION: 11
● USA PEAK CHART POSITION: did not chart

387 GOOD OLD BOYS (–) ▲
RANDY NEWMAN

Newman's first concept album tackled a typically controversial subject, the American south. The opening 'Rednecks' may have gained Newman notoriety (managing to offend everyone from southerners to northern liberals), but on tracks such as 'Marie', 'Louisiana 1927' and 'A Wedding In Cherokee Country', the tender heart beneath his withering irony was exposed. The album documents a complex mix of revulsion and empathy that touch on Newman's own New Orleans upbringing and his Jewishness. It was an unexpected irony, however, that the arch-satirist reached his songwriting peak on an album featuring the pick of America's session players and a glossy west coast production.

● TRACKS: *Rednecks; Birmingham; Marie; Mr. President (Have Pity On The Working Man); Guilty; Louisiana 1927; Every Man A King; Kingfish; Naked Man; A Wedding In Cherokee County; Back On My Feet Again; Rollin'.*

● FIRST RELEASED 1974
● UK PEAK CHART POSITION: did not chart
● USA PEAK CHART POSITION: 36

388 TEXAS FLOOD (–) ▲
STEVIE RAY VAUGHAN AND DOUBLE TROUBLE

Quite possibly the only electric blues/rock guitarist to come near rivalling Jimi Hendrix, Vaughan, who, like Hendrix, died tragically, was so good he was ridiculous. He was lacking in really good material, and his own compositions were mainly guitar workouts, such as 'Rude Mood', although he shows great feeling on the instrumental 'Lenny'. He is much more comfortable singing non-originals, and on this album he covers Buddy Guy's 'Mary Had A Little Lamb' and Howlin' Wolf's 'Tell Me', but the listener is still waiting for the bit where the guitar solo comes in. Poor Double Trouble barely get a look in.

● TRACKS: *Love Struck Baby; Pride And Joy; Texas Flood; Tell Me; Testify; Rude Mood; Mary Had A Little Lamb; Dirty Pool; I'm Cryin'; Lenny.*

● FIRST RELEASED 1983
● UK PEAK CHART POSITION: did not chart
● USA PEAK CHART POSITION: 38

BOOKENDS (160) ▼
SIMON AND GARFUNKEL

Over the years the overblown acclaim of *Bridge Over Troubled Water* has slightly lessened as the credibility of *Bookends* has grown. The gap deserves to narrow in future years as listeners discover some of Simon's most entertaining lyrics in 'Fakin' It', 'Punky's Dilemma' and 'Save The Life Of My Child' not to forget, "for God's sake, 'Mrs Robinson'" and the evocative 'America'. Sadly there is nothing to be done about still having to sit through 'Voices Of Old People', although CD technology makes this a programmable miss. Almost a perfect album, and for many critics, far superior than *Bridge*.

● TRACKS: *Bookends; Save The Life Of My Child; America; Overs; Voices Of Old People; Old Friends; Fakin' It; Punky's Dilemma; Hazy Shade Of Winter; At The Zoo; Mrs. Robinson.*

● FIRST RELEASED 1968
● UK PEAK CHART POSITION: 1
● USA PEAK CHART POSITION: 1

ALL THINGS MUST PASS (211) ▼
GEORGE HARRISON

A preponderance of timeless Lennon/McCartney songs ensured that George Harrison's contribution to the Beatles' catalogue was held in check. This backlog ensured that his 'official' debut set was teeming with strong material. 'Isn't It A Pity' and 'My Sweet Lord' are among his finest songs, despite the charge of plagiarism directed at the latter. A suitably lush Phil Spector production cocooned Harrison's sometimes one-dimensional voice, creating a tapestry enhanced by contributions by Eric Clapton and the group that would later become Derek And The Dominoes. Three albums made up a set that showed Harrison's gifts to be mature and indicated that his talents had been too long obscured.

● TRACKS: *I'd Have You Anytime; My Sweet Lord; Wah-wah; Isn't It A Pity; What Is Life; If Not For You; Behind That Locked Door; Let It Down; Run Of The Mill; Beware Of Darkness; Apple Scruffs; Ballad Of Sir Frankie Crisp (Let It Roll); Awaiting On You All; All Things Must Pass; I Dig Love; Art Of Dying; Isn't It A Pity; Hear Me Lord; Out Of The Blue; It's Johnny's Birthday; Plug Me In; I Remember Jeep; Thanks For The Peperoni.*

● FIRST RELEASED 1970
● UK PEAK CHART POSITION: 4
● USA PEAK CHART POSITION: 1

EXODUS (602) ▲
BOB MARLEY

Marley's consistent (certainly by reggae standards) album career has proffered many great songbooks, of which *Exodus* is just one good example. The singles 'One Love' and 'Jamming' will be familiar to anyone with even a passing acquaintance with Jamaican music, but just as vital are the touchingly vulnerable love song 'Waiting In Vain', the title track, and the splendid 'Guiltiness'. This was the first album to feature Junior Marvin on guitar, while the expressive use of horns adds new texture to the established quality of the Wailers' backing. Like most of his work, vital for a comprehensive collection.

● TRACKS: *Natural Mystic; So Much Things To Say; Guiltiness; The Heathern; Exodus; Jamming; Waiting In Vain; Turn Your Lights Down Low; Three Little Birds; One Love - People Get Ready.*

● FIRST RELEASED 1977
● UK PEAK CHART POSITION: 8
● USA PEAK CHART POSITION: 20

REGGATTA DE BLANC (242) ▼
THE POLICE

The career of the Police was planned, controlled and timed to perfection. The three talented individuals probably always knew that they would attempt to conquer the world and then disappear to pursue their own musical interests. This is the second of their five albums and contains two number 1 hits. Both are interesting little vignettes from the mind of Sting; 'Walking On The Moon', where he pleads 'I hope my legs don't break', and 'Message In A Bottle', which has a similarly desperate theme, with Sting observing 'seems I'm not alone in being alone, 100 billion castaways looking for a home'. Sting's theories do still hold water.

● TRACKS: *Message In A Bottle; Reggatta De Blanc; It's Alright For You; Bring On The Night; Deathwish; Walking On The Moon; On Any Other Day; The Bed's Too Big Without You; Contact; Does Everybody Stare; No Time This Time.*

● FIRST RELEASED 1979
● UK PEAK CHART POSITION: 1
● USA PEAK CHART POSITION: 25

TRACY CHAPMAN

Although she must be tired of the comparisons, Tracy did look like Joan Armatrading, and at times sounded like her. Even *Q Magazine* sneakily substituted her pen picture. She also debuted with an impressive album. Her career was given an irregular shot in the arm when she appeared at the Nelson Mandela concert. Her solo spot was extended at short notice because Stevie Wonder was unable to come on. She won over the crowd, who loved her brave vulnerability, and rose to the occasion, playing an immaculate and memorable set. This album leaped into the charts the following day and refused to be budged for many months.

● TRACKS: *Talkin' 'Bout A Revolution; Fast Car; Across The Lines; Behind The Wall; Baby Can I Hold You; Mountains O' Things; She's Got Her Ticket; Why?; For My Lover; If Not Now...; For You.*

● FIRST RELEASED 1988
● UK PEAK CHART POSITION: 1
● USA PEAK CHART POSITION: 1

CAN

Can were one of the most influential bands to emerge from Europe in the 70s, and this 1972 masterpiece marked a crucial stage in the development from the edgy experimentalism of their earlier albums to the softer ambience of their later work. 'Soup' and 'Pinch' were reminders of their wilder excesses, but on tracks such as 'One More Night' and 'Sing Swan Song' they demonstrated that they could be equally inventive within tighter song structures. 'I'm So Green' and 'Spoon' were almost conventional pop songs, to the extent that the latter provided the band with an unexpected chart-topper in their native Germany.

● TRACKS: *Pinch; Sing Swan Song; One More Night; Vitamin C; Soup; I'm So Green; Spoon.*

● FIRST RELEASED 1972
● UK PEAK CHART POSITION: did not chart
● USA PEAK CHART POSITION: did not chart

THE BEASTIE BOYS

Dismissed by some as zeitgeist-mugging white rap fakers after the huge commercial success of their debut album, the Beastie Boys' later work could hardly be said to reveal musical depth or sophistication either. However, thanks to an overdose of cultural reference points (via samples and lyrical cut-ups) and the Dust Brothers' pungent production, they were still big fun compared to hip-hop's new orthodoxy. At times ('Shake Your Rump', '3-Minute Rule') the sound is pure bedlam, but rap's most hilarious trio of b-boys just about keep the thread going through the montage of in-jokes and namechecks. Like all the best records, *Paul's Boutique* was a de facto commercial non-event.

● TRACKS: *To All The Girls; Shake Your Rump; Johnny Ryall; Egg Man; High Plains Drifter; The Sounds Of Science; 3-Minute Rule; Hey Ladies; 5-Piece Chicken Dinner; Looking Down The Barrel Of A Gun; Car Thief; What Comes Round; Shadrach; Ask For Janice; B-Boy Bouillabaisse a) 59 Christie Street b) Get On The Mic c) Stop That Train d) A Year And A Day e) Hello Brooklyn f) Dropping Names g) Lay It On Me h) Mike On The Mic i) A.W.O.L.*

● FIRST RELEASED 1989
● UK PEAK CHART POSITION: 44
● USA PEAK CHART POSITION: 14

THE BEACH BOYS

The aborted Smile project was replaced with a perplexing release that lost the band some of their surf and hot-rod fans, but endeared them to people who smoked funny cigarettes. Rumour has it that the band were so high they had to stay low, and recorded this album lying on the floor. Van Dyke Parks wove his wackiness around 'Heroes And Villains', 'Vegetables' and 'She's Going Bald'. The monumental 'Good Vibrations' was thrown in for good measure in glorious stereophonic sound. Now regarded as a classic and the album from which Brian Wilson would never recover; he was never quite the same man again.

● TRACKS: *Heroes And Villains; Vegetables; Fall Breaks And Back To Winter; She's Goin' Bald; Little Pad; Good Vibrations; With Me Tonight; Wind Chimes; Gettin' Hungry; Wonderful; Whistle In.*

● FIRST RELEASED 1967
● UK PEAK CHART POSITION: 9
● USA PEAK CHART POSITION: 41

DARE (395) ▼
THE HUMAN LEAGUE

This is the acceptable face of computerized pop. Four out of the six band members were playing nasty synthesizers. *Dare* was a commercial one-off and apart from one or two excellent singles, the Human League never came near to equalling such a collection of instantly recognizable melodies. Their later hits such as 'Mirror Man' and 'Human' were classy songs, but every track on this album can make you dance and sing along. This was one of Martin Rushent's finest productions and it is a pity that the Human League are not on our turntables any more. Maybe the fear of having to give up all those synthesizers for guitars was too scary.

● TRACKS: *Things That Dreams Are Made Of; Open Your Heart; The Sound Of The Crowd; Darkness; Do Or Die; Get Carter; I Am The Law; Seconds; Love Action (I Believe In Love); Don't You Want Me.*

● FIRST RELEASED 1981
● UK PEAK CHART POSITION: 1
● USA PEAK CHART POSITION: 3

398

ZUMA (–) ▲
NEIL YOUNG

Released to universally favourable reviews, *Zuma* has lasted as a favourite Young album. On this, he pleased guitar devotees by at last attempting to sound and play like he did on stage. The tone and volume he achieves on his old Gibson throughout this record is perfection. 'Drive Back' is a shining example of the style, played over a shuffling and changing tempo. Similarly evocative are 'Danger Bird' and 'Stupid Girl', but the album's *tour de force* is 'Cortez The Killer', a lengthy song that builds, noodles and droops but is never boring. CSN make a cursory appearance at the end with 'Through My Sails'.

● TRACKS: *Don't Cry No Tears; Danger Bird; Pardon My Heart; Lookin' For A Love; Barstool Blues; Stupid Girl; Drive Back; Cortez The Killer; Through My Sails.*

● FIRST RELEASED 1975
● UK PEAK CHART POSITION: 25
● USA PEAK CHART POSITION: 44

399

STRANDED (308) ▼
ROXY MUSIC

Roxy Music subverted a jaded progressive rock scene with an original blend of science fiction imagery, art-school nonce and eccentric music. Vocalist Bryan Ferry sang in a camp-styled croon, part Noël Coward, part Lou Reed, and having dismissed leadership rival Brian Eno, assumed full control of artistic direction for the group's third album. *Stranded* introduced violinist Eddie Jobson, whose contributions slotted in perfectly alongside reed player Andy Mackay and guitarist Phil Manzanera. A sense of cohesion permeates the set, group members contribute lyrically, but there was no denying that Roxy Music here represent Ferry's vision. Melodically strong, the album provides an ideal structure for his quirky intonation, resulting in a heady mix of experimentation and commercial acumen.

● TRACKS: *Street Life; Just Like You; Amazon; Psalm; Serenade; Song For Europe; Mother Of Pearl; Sunset.*

● FIRST RELEASED 1973
● UK PEAK CHART POSITION: 1
● USA PEAK CHART POSITION: 186

400

TEN SUMMONERS TALES (672) ▲
STING

Mr 'sheer profundity' delivered a stunning fourth solo album that probably surprised himself as well as the critics who were prepared to watch his fall from grace after the seeming failure of the intense *The Soul Cages*. Right from the opener, 'If I Ever Lose My Faith In You', the album holds its pace. That track will be seen as a classic in years to come, as will the beautiful 'Fields Of Gold' and 'Shape Of My Heart'. Sting is established as a major artist with a solo career that has now eclipsed his former supergroup.

● TRACKS: *Prologue (If I Ever Lose My Faith In You); Love Is Stronger Than Justice (The Munificent Seven); Fields Of Gold; Heavy Cloud No Rain; She's Too Good For Me; Seven Days; Saint Augustine In Hell; It's Probably Me; Everybody Laughed But You; Shape Of My Heart; Something The Boy Said; Epilogue (Nothing 'Bout Me).*

● FIRST RELEASED 1993
● UK PEAK CHART POSITION: 2
● USA PEAK CHART POSITION: 2

401 KING OF AMERICA (–) ▲
ELVIS COSTELLO

Costello's first album without the Attractions in tow also proved to be one of his best since 1980's *Get Happy*. A varied selection of musicians appear on the album, including legendary session veterans James Burton and Jerry Scheff, lending Costello's songs a distinctly American roots-rock feel. The songs, in turn, were some of the strongest he had ever written, from the finely observed character studies of 'American Without Tears' and 'Sleep Of The Just', to the scathing rants of 'Glitter Gulch' and 'Little Palaces'. On 'Our Little Angel', Costello sings about 'a chainsaw running through a dictionary', an apt description of the endlessly inventive lyricism that characterizes *King Of America*.

● TRACKS: *Brilliant Mistake; Lovable; Our Little Angel; Don't Let Me Be Understood; Glitter Gulch; Indoor Fireworks; Little Palaces; I'll Wear It Proudly; American Without Tears; Eisenhower Blues; Poisoned Rose; The Big Light; Jack Of All Parades; Suit Of Lights; Sleep Of The Just.*

● FIRST RELEASED 1986
● UK PEAK CHART POSITION: 11
● USA PEAK CHART POSITION: 39

 403 OMMADAWN (–) ▲
MIKE OLDFIELD

Ommadawn represents a creative peak for Oldfield that is often overshadowed by the huge commercial success of his debut *Tubular Bells*. Oldfield employed the same format he had used on his previous two albums, with both sides of the album comprising a lengthy instrumental collage. This time he drew on a greater range of musical styles, using recurring motifs that had recognizable African, Eastern European and Irish sources (Paddy Moloney of The Chieftains being responsible for the latter). The album was also notable for the way Oldfield collaborated with the other musicians, drawing attention away from his image as the self-styled studio recluse.

● TRACKS: *Ommadawn Part 1; Ommadawn Part 2.*

● FIRST RELEASED 1975
● UK PEAK CHART POSITION: 4
● USA PEAK CHART POSITION: 146

 402 HATS (–) ▲
BLUE NILE

Finding a category into which the critics can slot them has been a problem for this excellent Scottish band. File under 'very good quality pop' no longer exists on the record label. For the uninitiated, they have the soulful, wandering nature of John Martyn, mixed with some anthemic U2, plus a tolerable dose of Deacon Blue/Simply Red. A strong synthesizer backdrop may deter, but the lush arrangements are truly lovely. Paul Buchanan has an emotive voice that is well suited to his melancholic material. Three albums in nearly 15 years is hardly prolific, but they are critically acclaimed and quality is always better than quantity.

● TRACKS: *Over The Hillside; The Downtown Lights; Let's Go Out Tonight; Headlights On The Parade; From A Late Night Train; Seven A.M.; Saturday Night.*

● FIRST RELEASED 1989
● UK PEAK CHART POSITION: 12
● USA PEAK CHART POSITION: 108

404 WITH A LITTLE HELP FROM MY FRIENDS (–) ▲ **JOE COCKER**

Joe Cocker's debut built on the promise of the title track, a hit single the previous year, which had introduced the world to the singer's astonishing blues rasp of a voice and remains to this day one of the finest Beatles cover versions committed to vinyl. The vocal pyrotechnics of that song are muted on this album, with Cocker demonstrating his fine handling of more subtle material such as Bob Dylan's 'Just Like A Woman' and 'I Shall Be Released'. Backed by his own seasoned Grease Band and stellar session players Jimmy Page and Steve Winwood, Cocker sings with a soulful intensity that shone all too briefly during his wayward career.

● TRACKS: *Feeling Alright; Bye Bye Blackbird; Change In Louise; Marjorine; Just Like A Woman; Do I Still Figure In Your Life; Sandpaper Cadillac; Don't Let Me Be Misunderstood; With A Little Help From My Friends; I Shall Be Released.*

● FIRST RELEASED 1969
● UK PEAK CHART POSITION: did not chart
● USA PEAK CHART POSITION: 35

405 LOW-LIFE (446) ▲
NEW ORDER

New Order evolved from the rump of Joy Division following the death of vocalist Ian Curtis. The course they followed contrasted with that of their former incarnation, exploring a heady mix of techno-styled dance tracks and melodic soundscapes. *Low-Life* captured the quartet in eclectic mood, taking an electronic muse through diffuse material. It boasts two of New Order's finest ever songs, the ballad-styled 'Love Vigilantes' and the lush 'The Perfect Kiss', while elsewhere the quartet explore different facets of their sound without losing cohesion. This acclaimed release finally confirmed New Order as an act in its own right.

● TRACKS: *Love Vigilantes; The Perfect Kiss; This Time Of Night; Sunrise; Elegia; Sooner Than You Think; Sub-Culture; Face Up.*

● FIRST RELEASED 1985
● UK PEAK CHART POSITION: 7
● USA PEAK CHART POSITION: 94

---

406 LIVE AT FILLMORE EAST/THE FILLMORE
CONCERTS (–) ▲ THE ALLMAN BROTHERS BAND

The original *Fillmore East* album is one of the finest live documents of the rock era, capturing the original line-up of one of the 70s' tightest outfits before they were cruelly robbed of Duane Allman and Berry Oakley. Taken from five 1971 performances at New York's fabled Fillmore East, the extended and effortlessly melodic workouts of 'In Memory Of Elizabeth Reed' and 'Whipping Post' remain definitive recordings. The dual guitar interplay of Duane Allman and Dickey Betts glides effortlessly over the propulsive rhythm section of Oakley and twin drummers Jaimoe and Butch Trucks, while Greg Allman's powerful blues voice and melodic keyboard work provides the icing on the cake. The expanded *Fillmore Concerts* CD adds more tracks and digital clarity.

● TRACKS: *Statesboro Blues; Trouble No More; Don't Keep Me Wonderin'; In Memory Of Elizabeth Reed; One Way Out; Done Somebody Wrong; Stormy Monday; You Don't Love Me; Hot 'Lanta; Whipping Post; Mountain Jam; Drunken Hearted Boy.*

● FIRST RELEASED 1971
● UK PEAK CHART POSITION: did not chart
● USA PEAK CHART POSITION: 13

---

407 I AGAINST I (–) ▲
BAD BRAINS

Some people just don't 'get' Bad Brains. To be fair, their early recordings can be intimidating, and it is only when you familiarize yourself with the musical dialectics of tracks such as 'Pay To Cum' that you can really appreciate their kinetic aesthetic. Abandoning the speed-freak punk cum dub reggae crossover of old, Bad Brains now employed funk and conventional rock stylings. What they lost in 'edge' they more than compensated for in power, allowing temperamental vocalist H.R. to make the most of his famously elastic vocal range over the album's 31 minutes. The exception was 'Sacred Love', where H.R.'s vocals were phoned in from jail during recording sessions after being busted for marijuana possession.

● TRACKS: *Intro; I Against I; House Of Suffering; Re-Ignition; Secret 77; Let Me Help; She's Calling You; Sacred Love; Hired Gun; Return To Heaven.*

● FIRST RELEASED 1986
● UK PEAK CHART POSITION: did not chart
● USA PEAK CHART POSITION: did not chart

---

408 THE HANGMAN'S BEAUTIFUL
DAUGHTER (–) ▲ INCREDIBLE STRING BAND

Although it sounds élitist, 'you had to be there to really appreciate it'. Seeing them perform in 1968 and 1969 was a bizarre and rewarding sight. Medieval costumes, dancing maidens and an unbelievable array of instruments; to see the Incredibles perform was a remarkable experience. They epitomized the 'new age traveller' and as such are highly influential, and sadly under-appreciated. Thirty years later, their challenging folk music has not become any easier. Hearing the epic 13-minute 'A Very Cellular Song', with its many changes and parts, is still pretty formidable. Easy to poke fun at, but they were absolutely sincere, and very good at it.

● TRACKS: *Koeeaddi There; The Minotaur's Song; Witches Hat; A Very Cellular Song; Mercy I Cry City; Waltz Of The New Moon; The Water Song; Three Is A Green Crown; Swift As The Wind; Nightfall.*

● FIRST RELEASED 1968
● UK PEAK CHART POSITION: 5
● USA PEAK CHART POSITION: 161

409 **FREEDOM** (–) ▲
NEIL YOUNG

During the 80s Young managed to change his ways and confuse his audience. The last major album before this was the R&B-influenced *This Notes For You* - and just when everyone least expected it, he made a dynamite 'regular' Neil Young album. *Freedom* was the beginning of a run of acclaimed albums that now put Young up on a pedestal with Bob Dylan and Van Morrison as all-time great singing-troubadours. The difference, however, is that Young still rocks, and he likes his guitar to sound loud and dirty. *Freedom* was a restatement of his immense varied talent, still with enough new chord structures to make his familiar songs sound exciting and different.

● TRACKS: *Rockin' In The Free World; Crime In The City (Sixty To Zero Part 1); Don't Cry; Hangin' On A Limb; Eldorado; The Ways Of Love; Someday; On Broadway; Wrecking Ball; No More; Too Far Gone; Rockin' In The Free World.*

● FIRST RELEASED 1989
● UK PEAK CHART POSITION: 17
● USA PEAK CHART POSITION: 35

 410 **FEAR OF MUSIC** (–) ▲
TALKING HEADS

If there is any warning before The Bomb drops, you know that every radio is going to be blaring 'Life During Wartime', the best-known track on *Fear Of Music*, which was produced by Brian Eno, already well versed in the apocalypse through his work on David Bowie's *Low*. Talking Heads' third album showed them straying ever further from their roots in New York's CBGB's vehemently anti-disco scene, as they experimented with dance beats and African rhythms. Its black, industrial-looking cover reflected the bleak subject matter, with a high proportion of minor-key songs. David Byrne's cynical lyrics took a dim view of the effects of technology on humans, despite the group's increasing reliance on studio gadgetry.

● TRACKS: *I Zimbra; Mind; Paper; Cities; Life During Wartime; Memories Can't Wait; Air; Heaven; Animals; Electric Guitar; Drugs.*

● FIRST RELEASED 1979
● UK PEAK CHART POSITION: 33
● USA PEAK CHART POSITION: 21

 **411** **THE COMPLETE SAVOY SESSIONS**
(237) ▼ **CHARLIE PARKER**

Although they do not contain the number of classic sides found within the Dial collection, the importance of Charlie Parker's Savoy recordings is more than justified by the involvement of bebop piano genius Bud Powell (perhaps the only other true bebopper playing with the level of invention and profundity of Parker himself) and the fascinating play-off between a young and troubled Miles Davis and his own hero Dizzy Gillespie. The Savoy records include the legendary 'KoKo' (a breakneck torrent of improvisation based around the tricky 'Cherokee' chord sequence), and two classic blues in F major: 'Billie's Bounce' and 'Now's The Time'.

● TRACKS: *including - Billie's Bounce; Now's The Time i; Now's The Time ii; Thriving On A Riff i; Thriving On A Riff ii; Meandering; KoKo; Dizzy Boogie i; Dizzy Boogie ii; Flat Foot Floogie i; Flat Foot Floogie ii; Popity Pop; Slim's Jam.*

● FIRST RELEASED 1982
● UK PEAK CHART POSITION: did not chart
● USA PEAK CHART POSITION: did not chart

 412 **GIANT STEPS** (240) ▼
JOHN COLTRANE

As influential upon contemporaries and successors as were Armstrong and Parker, Coltrane divided critical comment. For his supporters he was both high priest of contemporary jazz and prophet of what was yet to come. The ultimate statement of Coltrane's early obsession with chord progressions, this album marks the moment before he changed direction. *Giant Steps* is a vibrant demonstration of his inventive, dazzling and relentless playing of bop. Hereafter, Coltrane sought and found an avenue for his restless exploratory zeal in modal jazz. The album is therefore both a landmark and turning point and is still a textbook for many young musicians.

● TRACKS: *Giant Steps; Cousin Mary; Countdown; Spiral; Syeeda's Song Flute; Mr. P.C.; Naima.*

● FIRST RELEASED 1959
● UK PEAK CHART POSITION: did not chart
● USA PEAK CHART POSITION: did not chart

413 STAND UP (–) ▲
JETHRO TULL

The vinyl sleeve reveals four cute little Tulls, who pop up to greet the listener; sadly, CD does not have this luxury. The music, however, is still as good. Tull reached a peak of heavy rock that was slowly to fade with subsequent albums as Ian Anderson discovered the acoustic guitar. This featured 'new' guitarist Martin Barre and he plays like a demon on powerful tracks such as 'A New Day Yesterday' and 'Nothing Is Easy'. The band have never sounded so together as they attempted Bach on the joyous, flute-led 'Bouree' and sprinkled some rustic humour with the acoustic 'Fat Man'.

● TRACKS: A New Day Yesterday; Jeffrey Goes To Leicester Square; Bouree; Back To The Family; Look Into The Sun; Nothing Is Easy; Fat Man; We Used To Know; Reasons For Waiting; For A Thousand Mothers.

● FIRST RELEASED 1969
● UK PEAK CHART POSITION: 1
● USA PEAK CHART POSITION: 20

414 THE HOT FIVES AND SEVENS 1-7
(109) ▼ LOUIS ARMSTRONG

More than seventy years on and still these recordings are breathtaking. The audacity of the virtuoso trumpeter, captured in the first full flush of his realization that he was the greatest, makes

clear why Armstrong in the 20s was the first true genius of jazz. An innovator, a pathfinder, not yet showman but with all the showman's qualities on tap, he surges triumphantly through a succession of masterpieces, minor and major. Above even these superlative surroundings is 'West End Blues' - endlessly imitated, never equalled. A monumental performance by a giant. Unmistakable, irreplaceable, unmissable, eternal music. At least one volume for every collection.

● TRACKS: Including - Memories Of You; You're Lucky To Me; Sweethearts On Parade; You're Drivin' Me Crazy; The Peanut Vendor; Just A Gigolo; Shine; Walkin' My Baby Back Home; I Surrender Dear; When It's Sleepytime Down South; Blue Again; Little Joe; I'll Be Glad When You're Dead; You Rascal You; Them There Eyes; When Your Lover Has Gone; Lazy River; Chinatown, My Chinatown; My Heart; (Yes!) I'm The Barrel; Gut Bucket Blues; Come Back, Sweet Papa; Georgia Grind; Heebie Jeebies; Cornet Chop Suey; Oriental Strut; You're Next; Muskrat Ramble; Don't Forget To Mess Around; I'm Gonna Gitcha; Droppin' Shucks; Who' Sit; King Of The Zulus; Big Fat Ma And Skinny Pa; Willie The Weeper; West End Blues; Wild Man Blues; Chicago Breakdown; Alligator Crawl; Potato Head Blues; Melancholy Blues; Weary Blues; Twelfth Street Rag.

● RECORDED 1925-28
● UK PEAK CHART POSITION: did not chart
● USA PEAK CHART POSITION: did not chart

415 CRAZY SEXY COOL (–) ▲
TLC

Worldwide sales exceed 15 million copies at the time of writing, remarkable by any standards. TLC (tender loving care) are a female urban R&B trio, Chilli, Left Eye and T-Boz, who mixed in some funk and hip-hop over their graceful and effortless voices. When they sing smooth soul they are unbeatable; take, for example, 'Red Light Special', 'Diggin' On You' and the hugely successful single 'Waterfalls', in which they warn 'don't go chasing waterfalls, please stick to the rivers and lakes that you're used to'. Highly commercial, slick, dead sexy, immaculately produced and, ultimately, impossible to fault.

● TRACKS: Intro-lude; Creep; Kick Your Game; Diggin' On You; Case Of The Fake People; CrazySexyCool; Interlude; Red Light Special; Waterfalls; Intermission-lude; Let's Do It Again; If I Was Your Girlfriend; Sexy - Interlude; Take Our Time; Can I Get A Witness; Switch; Sumthin' Wicked This Way Comes.

● FIRST RELEASED 1994
● UK PEAK CHART POSITION: 4
● USA PEAK CHART POSITION: 3

416 SWEET BABY JAMES (280) ▼
JAMES TAYLOR

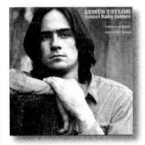

Taylor had already 'seen and been' enough by the time this album was released, having survived drug addiction and mental institutions by the age of 19, not to mention broken relationships. There was much for the listener to relate to during those heady days and this album made him a star, a status from which he tried to recoil. Two tracks from this album have been performed at every Taylor gig for 25 years - the irritating but necessary 'Steamroller' and his greatest song, 'Fire And Rain', which tells the story of his first 20 years in just over three minutes. Headphone-and-beanbag-friendly; remember to sit on the beanbag not the headphones.

● TRACKS: Sweet Baby James; Lo And Behold; Sunny Skies; Steamroller; Country Roads; Oh Susannah; Fire And Rain; Blossom; Anywhere Like Heaven; Oh Baby Don't You Lose Your Lip On Me; Suite For 20G.

● FIRST RELEASED 1970
● UK PEAK CHART POSITION: 7
● USA PEAK CHART POSITION: 3

417 HOLLAND (365) ▼
THE BEACH BOYS

Having finally rid themselves of a dated stripe-shirt image with the masterful *Surf's Up*, the Beach Boys continued the process with this ambitious album. The entire group had decamped to the Nederlands to record much of its content, a decision adding an emotional fission to its 'California Saga' trilogy. Although Brian Wilson's contribution was limited to two excellent songs, siblings Dennis and Carl rose to the occasion, with the latter's particularly impressive 'Trader'. The group's harmonies remain as distinctive as ever, while two recent additions to the line-up, Blondie Chaplin and Ricky Fataar, increased the vocal range and added new instrumental muscle. This became their best-selling album for six years, and *Holland* prepared the way for the Beach Boys' 70s comeback.

● TRACKS: *Sail On Sailor; Steamboat; California Saga : (i) Big Surf, (ii) The Beaks Of Eagles, (iii) California ; Trader; Leaving This Town; Only With You; Funky Pretty.*

● FIRST RELEASED 1973
● UK PEAK CHART POSITION: 20
● USA PEAK CHART POSITION: 36

418 GISH (–) ▲
SMASHING PUMPKINS

The Pumpkins' debut hit the music world at the height of the grunge phenomenon of the early 90s, and exhibited most of the usual characteristics - heavy rock riffs, often reminiscent of GN'R ('Siva', in particular), thrashing guitars and brooding, self-deprecating lyrics. However, *Gish* rose above the bulk of the college rock bands, revealing more refined songwriting sensibilities courtesy of Billy Corgan, and presenting astonishingly touching ballads ('Crush'). Clearly much more raw and naïve than the band's later work on the accomplished *Siamese Dream* and the ambitious *Mellon Collie...*, this album, nevertheless, set out the Pumpkins' agenda for rock and hinted at what was to come.

● TRACKS: *I Am One; Siva; Rhinoceros; Bury Me; Crush; Suffer; Snail; Tristessa; Window Paine; Daydream.*

● FIRST RELEASED 1991
● UK PEAK POSITION: did not chart
● USA PEAK POSITION: 195

419 MARCUS GARVEY (204) ▼
BURNING SPEAR

One of the most distinctive and original talents in the history of Reggae, Burning Spear - né Winston Rodney - was launched internationally with this striking album. His deep, preaching vocal is immediately arresting, a characteristic enhanced by a dense and brooding accompaniment. Taking cues from Rastafarian chants, Spear subtly builds an intensity, locking each track into a seamless whole. His knowledge of black history brings a chilling realism to the album's lyrics, resulting in what is incontestably a milestone in the development of reggae. Listening to it is an education itself. The CD reissue has the bonus of the dub version *Garvey's Ghost*.

● TRACKS: *Marcus Garvey; Slavery Days; Invasion; Live Good; Give Me; Old Marcus Garvey; Tradition; Jordan River; Red, Gold And Green; Resting Place.*

● FIRST RELEASED 1975
● UK PEAK CHART POSITION: did not chart
● USA PEAK CHART POSITION: did not chart

420 WEST SIDE STORY (100) ▼
ORIGINAL BROADWAY CAST

Record buyers who had not seen the show that opened on Broadway in 1957, could hardly believe their ears when this dramatic, early stereo album reached the stores soon afterwards. Classical composer Leonard Bernstein and newcomer Stephen Sondheim's spell-binding score combined exquisite ballads such as 'Maria' and 'Tonight' with streetwise numbers such as 'Gee, Officer Krupke' and the exhilarating 'America'. Carol Lawrence, Larry Kert and Chita Rivera led the superb young cast, and the album stayed for 120 weeks in the US chart but faired poorly on its UK release. In 1991 it was inducted into the NARAS Hall of Fame.

● TRACKS: *West Side Story Prologue; Jet Song; Something's Coming; Dance At The Gym (Blues Promenade Jump); Maria; Tonight; America; Cool; One Hand, One Heart; Tonight; The Rumble; I Feel Pretty; Somewhere; Gee, Officer Krupke; A Boy Like That; I Have A Love; West Side Story Finale.*

● FIRST RELEASED 1958
● UK PEAK CHART POSITION: 3
● USA PEAK CHART POSITION: 5

421 THE UNDERTONES (566) ▲
THE UNDERTONES

Having announced their arrival with the thrilling 'Teenage Kicks', one of the most perfect singles, the Undertones completed a debut album possessing all the charm of that first single. Innocent to the point of naïveté, the group deftly combine punk and pop with songs that articulate the angst of adolescence from within. Feargal Sharkey's braying voice cuts through the band's gutsy playing like a knife through butter, while simple, energetic hooklines emphasize the bubble-gum charm of 'Jimmy Jimmy' and 'Here Comes Summer'. Only the churlish could fail to be moved by this album's simplicity and verve.

● TRACKS: *Family Entertainment; Girls Don't Like It; Male Model; I Gotta Getta; Teenage Kicks; Wrong Way; Jump Boys; Here Comes Summer; Get Over You; Billy's Third; Jimmy Jimmy; True Confessions; She's A Runaround; I Know A Girl; Listening In.*

● FIRST RELEASED 1979
● UK PEAK CHART POSITION: 13
● USA PEAK CHART POSITION: 154

422 IN ROCK (117) ▼
DEEP PURPLE

Formed by discontented pop musicians, Deep Purple embraced progressive rock through judicious cover versions that drew acclaim at the expense of original material. Sensing a stylistic blind alley, Jon Lord (keyboards) and Ritchie Blackmore (guitar) brought new vocalist Ian Gillan into the line-up, a decision that irrevocably changed their fortunes. *In Rock* is one of the genre's definitive albums, combining hard-edged riffs with virtuoso technique, topped by Gillan's full-throated roar. Few singers could survive the instrumental power beneath him, but this he does with room to spare, reacting to and emphasizing his colleagues' musical prowess. Chock-full of material destined to become Deep Purple anthems, later releases were evaluated against this trail-blazing, heavy rock collection.

● TRACKS: *Speed King; Blood Sucker; Child In Time; Flight Of The Rat; Into The Fire; Living Wreck; Hard Lovin' Man.*

● FIRST RELEASED 1970
● UK PEAK CHART POSITION: 4
● USA PEAK CHART POSITION: 143

423 SUICIDE (-) ▲
SUICIDE

There is 'difficult music', there is 'difficult but rewarding music' and then there is *Suicide*. Greatness often arrives by chance - Rev's distinctive synthesizer squelch came via a broken Farfisa organ that the duo could not afford to repair. The key to their self-titled debut lies in the film noir communion of Vega's Manhattan blues growl with Vega's dissonant, repetitive, minimalist keyboard stabs. 'Ghost Rider' and 'Rocket U.S.A.' are, to the American underground at least, two of the most influential and enduring songs ever written. The urban paranoia/psychosis of 'Frankie Teardrop', meanwhile, is still mesmerizing, 20 years after the album's release. And, yes, still difficult to listen to.

● TRACKS: *Ghost Rider; Rocket U.S.A.; Cheree; Johnny; Girl; Frankie Teardrop; Ché; Cheree (Remix); Keep Your Dreams.*

● FIRST RELEASED 1977
● UK PEAK CHART POSITION: did not chart
● USA PEAK CHART POSITION: did not chart

424 SINGLES GOING STEADY (377) ▼
BUZZCOCKS

The Buzzcocks emerged from Manchester's thriving punk enclave with a succession of startling pop singles. Tight melodies and highly memorable hooklines were enveloped in a breathless group sound full of purpose and drive which contrasted with singer Pete Shelly's dispassionate, almost throwaway, delivery. These eight singles, both a-sides and flips, covered a variety of subject matter, from masturbation ('Orgasm Addict') to 1981 nuspeak ('Everybody's Happy Nowadays'), without recourse to obfuscation. Such seminal recordings have ensured the Buzzcocks' place in a lineage just a bit below the Kinks and the Smiths as one of the best purveyors of the 45 rpm.

● TRACKS: *Orgasm Addict; What Do I Get; I Don't Mind; Love You More; Ever Fallen In Love (With Someone You Shouldn't'ave); Promises; Everybody's Happy Nowadays; Harmony In My Head; Whatever Happened To; Oh Shit!; Autonomy; Noise Annoys; Just Lust; Lipstick; Why Can't I Touch It; Something's Gone Wrong Again; Love You More.*

● FIRST RELEASED 1981
● UK PEAK CHART POSITION: did not chart
● USA PEAK CHART POSITION: did not chart

425 SELLING ENGLAND BY THE POUND
(–) ▲   GENESIS

Considered by many to be the finest album of Peter Gabriel's tenure with Genesis, *Selling England By the Pound* was the first Genesis album to reach the UK Top 10 and their first ever to chart in America. It also gave them their first British hit single, with the inscrutable 'I Know What I Like (In Your Wardrobe)'. Heavily orchestrated, with Tony Banks' keyboards, in particular, often evincing classical pretensions, the dreamlike songs give earth-shaking importance to such real-world events as Essex boy gang fights ('The Battle Of Epping Forest') and grocery prices ('Aisle Of Plenty').

● TRACKS: *Dancing With The Moonlit Knight; I Know What I Like (In Your Wardrobe); Firth Of Fifth; More Fool Me; The Battle Of Epping Forest; After The Ordeal; The Cinema Show; Aisle Of Plenty.*

● FIRST RELEASED 1973
● UK PEAK CHART POSITION: 3
● USA PEAK CHART POSITION: 29

426 MANASSAS (–) ▲
STEPHEN STILLS MANASSAS

Originally a double album of four distinct sides, it was a well-planned package. Stills was bursting with ideas during his prolific period (1970-72). This supergroup was its real culmination. Chris Hillman added the occasional co-write, but this was sweet Stephen blue-eyes show. Showing he could write, sing and play country, blues, rock and pop, this is a rich and varied collection. Dallas Taylor, Paul Harris, Fuzzy Samuels, Jo Lala and Al Perkins completed the band, who were as great live as they were on record. It lasted only a few rockin' months until Stephen went home to Graham and David, and took a nap for the next twenty-five years.

● TRACKS: *The Raven; Song Of Love; Rock & Roll Crazies; Cuban Bluegrass; Jet Set (Sigh); Anyway; Both Of Us (Bound To Lose); Fallen Eagle; Jesus Gave Love Away For Free; Colorado; So Begins The Task; Hide It So Deep; Don't Look At My Shadow; It Doesn't Matter; Johnny's Garden; Bound To Fall; How Far; Move Around; The Love Gangster; What To Do; Right Now; The Treasure (Take One); Blues Man.*

● FIRST RELEASED 1972
● UK PEAK CHART POSITION: 30
● USA PEAK CHART POSITION: 4

427 THE ROLLING STONES (395) ▼
THE ROLLING STONES

A lowly position gained, presumably, because new product pushes it down the listings. It was, is and will always be a great white R&B record. Recorded swiftly and simply it smells of the London club scene of 1963. Admittedly crude by the Stones' later high standards it is still a vital and historically important album. They attempt Muddy Waters, 'I Just Want To Make Love To You', Jimmy Reed, 'Honest I Do', a frantic Chuck Berry, 'Carol', and even Marvin Gaye's 'Can I Get A Witness'. They even improve on Rufus Thomas's whistle on 'Walking The Dog'. Primitive but dazzling.

● TRACKS: *Route 66; I Just Want To Make Love To You; Honest I Do; I Need You Baby; Now I've Got A Witness; Little By Little; I'm King Bee; Carol; Tell Me (You're Coming Back); Can I Get A Witness; You Can Make It If You Really Try; Walking The Dog.*

● FIRST RELEASED 1964
● UK PEAK CHART POSITION: 1
● USA PEAK CHART POSITION: 11

428 SOMETHING ELSE BY THE KINKS
(–) ▲   THE KINKS

Often seen as the older-sister album to *The Village Green Preservation Society* and the one that saw the Kinks shift from being a raunchy beat combo to arty popsters. Ray Davies' notebook was bursting with observations of simple life and ordinary people at this particular time in his life. In addition to the monumental 'Waterloo Sunset', some of Davies' best songs are on this album. The recent remastered version is absolutely necessary, with the addition of eight tracks, including gems such as 'Act Nice And Gentle' and 'Autumn Almanac'. Dave Davies' excellent 'Susannah's Still Alive' is also included. These additions make an already perfect album just a bit more perfect.

● TRACKS: *David Watts; Death Of A Clown; Two Sisters; No Return; Harry Rag; Tin Soldier Man; Situation Vacant; Love Me Till The Sun Shines; Lazy Old Sun; Afternoon Tea; Funny Face; End Of The Season; Waterloo Sunset;* bonus tracks: *Act Nice And Gentle; Autumn Almanac; Susannah's Still Alive; Wonderboy; Polly; Lincoln County; There's No Life Without Love; Lazy Old Sun (alternate).*

● FIRST RELEASED 1967
● UK PEAK CHART POSITION: 35
● USA PEAK CHART POSITION: 153

429 BEGIN (–) ▲
THE MILLENNIUM

Many artists have sold more albums since their demise than they did while they were together. To the ranks of Big Star and the Velvet Underground, add the Millennium, psychedelic LA obscuros whose lone album found a new life in the digital age. They were the brainchild of Curt Boettcher, who produced the Association classics 'Along Comes Mary' and 'Cherish'. With future superstar producer Keith Olsen at his side and a cast of wildly creative performers (including future Crabby Appleton leader Michael Fennelly), Boettcher created a harmony-laden masterpiece of transcendent, sparkling pop music, often compared to the Beach Boys' *Smile* and Van Dyke Parks' *Song Cycle*. *Avant garde*, yet accessible, it was one of the first albums ever recorded with 16-track technology.

● TRACKS: *Prelude; To Claudia On Thursday; I Just Want To Be Your Friend; 5 A.M.; I'm With You; The Island; Sing To Me; It's You; Some Sunny Day; It Won't Always Be The Same; The Know-It-All; Karmic Dream Sequence #1; There Is Nothing More To Say; Anthem (Begin); Just About The Same; Blight.*

● FIRST RELEASED 1968
● UK PEAK CHART POSITION: did not chart
● USA PEAK CHART POSITION: did not chart

430 ORANGES & LEMONS (–) ▲
XTC

Using a 60s Milton Glaser-type cover illustration, this purported to be a retro album. In reality it was another extremely fine XTC album, their ninth in a series of classy, offbeat pop exercises from the musically fertile brain of Andy Partridge, who hated touring and loved to stay at home as a reclusive pop star. This is probably their best album and features Partridge's most complete and satisfying song. 'The Loving' and 'The Mayor Of Simpleton' are both excellent compositions, but they pale against the exceptional 'Chalkhills And Children'. On this, Partridge celebrates that his home (the nearby chalkhills) and children keep him sane and well-grounded against the possible excesses to which he would succumb as a touring popster.

● TRACKS: *Garden Of Earthly Delights; The Mayor Of Simpleton; King For A Day; Here Comes President Kill Again; The Loving; Poor Skeleton Steps Out; One Of The Millions; Scarecrow People; Merely A Man; Cynical Days; Across This Antheap; Hold Me My Daddy; Pink Thing; Miniature Sun; Chalkhills And Children.*

● FIRST RELEASED 1989
● UK PEAK CHART POSITION: 28
● USA PEAK CHART POSITION: 44

431 GREATEST HITS (189) ▼
ABBA

Everybody likes Abba, or at least no-one wishes to say anything against Sweden's greatest export since the Volvo. Abba appeal to the widest section of music critics and this album spent two and a half years in the UK chart. Since their well-documented personal break-up and professional parting, Abba's reputation has continued to grow. Television comedy sketches, Abba lookalikes and a further reissued collection, which also went to number 1, enhanced their reputation. This is the famous cover that graced a zillion homes, but only now do we realize that 'Knowing Me Knowing You', 'Dancing Queen' and 'Take A Chance On Me' are contained on volume 2.

● TRACKS: *SOS; He Is Your Brother; Ring Ring; Hasta Manana; Nina; Pretty Ballerina; Honey Honey; So Long; I Do I Do I Do; People Need Love; Bang A Boomerang; Another Town Another Train; Mamma Mia; Dance (While The Music Still Goes On); Waterloo; Fernando.*

● FIRST RELEASED 1976
● UK PEAK CHART POSITION: 1
● USA PEAK CHART POSITION: 48

432 A WALK ACROSS THE ROOFTOPS (–) ▲
THE BLUE NILE

The debut album from the enigmatic Blue Nile received tremendous reviews, yet barely scraped the chart. The promise was there, and it took shape on the second album *Hats*. Paul Buchanan's pleading voice is made for late-night listening in a cosy bedsitting room. Mulling over love lost, love found, happy times, sad times and kitchen sinks (I lied about the last bit, but you get the picture), a beautiful landscape of evocative music soaks in rather than hitting you first time. Blue Nile can be played over and over again, which is why they have only felt the need to put out three records in 15 years!

● TRACKS: *A Walk Across The Rooftops; Tinseltown In The Rain; From Rags To Riches; Stay; Easter Parade; Heatwave; Automobile Noise.*

● FIRST RELEASED 1983
● UK PEAK CHART POSITION: 80
● USA PEAK CHART POSITION: did not chart

433 **3 FEET HIGH AND RISING** (630) ▲
DE LA SOUL

The closest the rap world would come to the cartoon quality of Madness, with a similar musical integrity lurking beneath, De La Soul were warmly embraced both by hip-hop fans and chart-followers for their infectious, uninhibited blend of laconic rhymes and buoyant humour. Posdnous, Trugoy and Pasemaster Mase emerged from Long Island with an entirely different slant on rap's place in the scheme of things, piecing together this 1989 debut around the concept of a game show. The vitality of the single, 'Me Myself And I', was merely an appetizer for a carefree creative feast. Daisy Age Soul (Da Inner Sound, Y'all) had arrived, and everybody liked it very much.

● TRACKS: Intro; The Magic Number; Change In Speak; Cool Breeze On The Rocks; Can You Keep A Secret; Jenifa (Taught Me); Ghetto Thang; Transmitting Live From Mars; Eye Know; Take It Off; A Little Bit Of Soap; Tread Water; Say No Go; Do As De La Does; Plug Tunin'; De La Orgee; Buddy; Description; Me Myself And I; This Is A Recording For Living In A Fulltime Era; I Can Do Anything; D.A.I.S.Y. Age; Potholes In My Lawn.

● FIRST RELEASED 1989
● UK PEAK CHART POSITION: 13
● USA PEAK CHART POSITION: 24

 434 **OUT OF THE BLUE** (219) ▼
ELECTRIC LIGHT ORCHESTRA

Leader Jeff Lynne took his Lennon/Beatles sound to the extreme by releasing a double album of Beatlesque pop. Hit after hit followed and it is arguable that radio overplay made us sick of the sound of ELO and their subsequent fall from credibility. However, this would be unfair since Lynne is a master songwriter and this album is crammed full of great melodies and 'interesting twiddly bits'. Rather than recall the flogged hits, let us recall other corkers; 'Jungle', 'Standing In The Rain' and 'Birmingham Blues'. Who will own up to building the impossible cardboard cut-out space ship that came with the original, and how many still exist?

● TRACKS: Turn To Stone; It's Over; Sweet Talkin' Woman; Across The Border; Night In The City; Starlight; Jungle; Believe Me Now; Steppin' Out; Standing In The Rain; Summer And Lightning; Mr. Blue Sky; Sweet Is The Night; The Whale; Wild West Hero; Birmingham Blues.

● FIRST RELEASED 1977
● UK PEAK CHART POSITION: 4
● USA PEAK CHART POSITION: 4

 **435** **LIVE DEAD** (700) ▲
GRATEFUL DEAD

As the archetypal west coast band, famed for lengthy improvisation, the Grateful Dead found it difficult to translate their in-concert fire onto record. The group addressed this dilemma by recording Live Dead live in the studio, allowing free rein for guitarist Jerry Garcia's liquid flights. The twin drumming of Mickey Hart and Bill Kreutzman provides an imaginative platform, bassist Phil Lesh takes his instrument into new dimensions, while organist Pigen provides a distinctive swirling sound that envelops and enhances his colleagues' interplay. The last-named takes a vocal cameo on 'Turn On Your Lovelight', a performance showing the Dead's R&B roots, while 'Dark Star' exposes new levels of musical empathy. Such factors ensure this album's prominence in the group's canon.

● TRACKS: Dark Star; Death Don't Have No Mercy; Feedback; And We Bid You Goodnight; St. Stephen; Eleven; Turn On Your Lovelight.

● FIRST RELEASED 1970
● UK PEAK CHART POSITION: did not chart
● USA PEAK CHART POSITION: 64

 436 **CALYPSO** (201) ▼
HARRY BELAFONTE

Belafonte's third and most successful chart album was full of the kind of folksy and calypso-style songs that made him one of the showbusiness sensations of the 50s. Two of them, 'The Banana Boat Song (Day-O)' and 'Jamaica Farewell', were singles hits as well. The album itself spent 72 weeks in the US Top 40, 31 of them at number 1, and made history by becoming the first 33 rpm record by a solo artist to sell a million copies. It was only the beginning of Belafonte's phenomenal career on records, television and films. Love or hate the genre, this represents its commercial peak.

● TRACKS: The Banana Boat Song (Day-O); Jack-ass Song; Hosanna; Come Back Liza; I Do Adore Her; Dolly Dawn; Jamaica Farewell; Will His Love Be Like His Rum?; Man Smart; Star O; Brown Skin Girl.

● FIRST RELEASED 1956
● UK PEAK CHART POSITION: did not chart
● USA PEAK CHART POSITION: 1

437 **MILES SMILES** (104) ▼
MILES DAVIS

This was the last Miles album before his next plateau (or his next album), an occurrence that happened throughout his career. This is the quintet that moved into electronic music with *Bitches Brew*, Herbie Hancock, Wayne Shorter, Tony Williams, Ron Carter, an astonishing line-up and surely Miles's best post-Coltrane group. This is like music for the last supper; they all knew that Fender Rhodes pianos and Precision basses were coming and this is a superb farewell to acoustic jazz. All six tracks are rewarding, all different, yet the sound is the same. Much more appreciated today than when it was first released.

● TRACKS: *Orbits; Circle; Footprints; Dolores; Freedom Jazz Dance; Ginger Bread Boy.*

● FIRST RELEASED 1966
● UK PEAK CHART POSITION: did not chart
● USA PEAK CHART POSITION: did not chart

 438 **OUTLANDOS D'AMOUR** (151) ▼
THE POLICE

It is hard to imagine, after the sophistication of *Synchronicity* and Sting's excellent solo work, together with the new age/prog direction that Summers has taken, that the Police debut is a bit punky. This writer saw one of their first gigs supporting hippie darlings Spirit. They were energetic and raw but when they played 'So Lonely', 'Next To You' and 'Roxanne', you realized the potential of something really special. This album is underproduced and raw but it retains a quality that cannot be quantified. These are the real inventors of white reggae-flavoured punk pop. Derivative but innovative.

● TRACKS: *Next To You; So Lonely; Roxanne; Hole In My Life; Peanuts; Can't Stand Losing You; Truth Hits Everybody; Born In The 50s; Be My Girl - Sally; Masoko Tanga.*

● FIRST RELEASED 1979
● UK PEAK CHART POSITION: 6
● USA PEAK CHART POSITION: 23

439 **PRETENDERS II** (217) ▼
THE PRETENDERS

The band look magnificent on the cover as they pose with make-up or heavily retouched faces. They look confident, knowing that their follow-up is almost as good as the debut. Chrissie and Ray Davies were stepping out at this time, hence the opening track, 'The Adultress', as Hynde whispers her confession over a furious wall of sound, to be immediately followed by her reminder that 'Bad Boys Get Spanked'. If only Chrissie, if only. The album drives and dives, pausing for 'I Go To Sleep', another old Ray Davies song. There is not a bad track in sight.

● TRACKS: *The Adultress; Bad Boys Get Spanked; Messages Of Love; I Go To Sleep; Birds Of Paradise; Talk Of The Town; Pack It Up; Waste Not, Want Not; Day After Day; Jealous Dogs; English Rose; Louie Louie.*

● FIRST RELEASED 1981
● UK PEAK CHART POSITION: 7
● USA PEAK CHART POSITION: 10

 440 **MOVING PICTURES** (437) ▼
RUSH

The Canadian trio's new-found technological musing, which infuriated their more traditionally minded audience, came to glorious fruition with this record. The organic sensibilities of their quite excellent musicianship, combined with their dextrous inventiveness, made for a diverse and compelling record. Adopting a surprise reggae beat for 'Vital Signs', and with drummer Neil Peart's literary leanings much in evidence in a goggle-eyed adaptation of John Dos Passos' 'USA Trilogy' for the mini-epic 'The Camera Eye', Rush created a rich mesh of styles that is somehow both restrained and wildly evocative in the same instant. Reassuringly mature stuff.

● TRACKS: *Tom Sawyer; Red Barchetta; YYZ; Limelight; The Camera Eye; Witch Hunt (Part III Of Fear); Vital Signs.*

● FIRST RELEASED 1981
● UK PEAK CHART POSITION: 3
● USA PEAK CHART POSITION: 3

441 SAXOPHONE COLOSSUS (425) ▼
SONNY ROLLINS

A truly flawless album representing bop at its best, *Saxophone Colossus* is a quartet recording from 1956 led by the great Sonny Rollins on tenor saxophone and featuring pianist Tommy Flanagan, bassist Doug Watkins and drummer Max Roach. The record opens with the original, catchy and rousing version of Rollins' much-loved Caribbean-flavoured standard, 'St. Thomas', and includes a richly emotional 'You Don't Know What Love Is' and a superbly angular, side-long blues entitled 'Blue Seven'. Few musicians ever spoke the bebop language with such consistent inspiration and flair.

● TRACKS: *Moritat; Blue Seven; Strode Rode; St. Thomas; You Don't Know What Love Is.*

● FIRST RELEASED 1956
● UK PEAK CHART POSITION: did not chart
● USA PEAK CHART POSITION: did not chart

442 SPIRIT OF EDEN (–) ▲
TALK TALK

A s the album opens, you almost think that you have put on a Miles Davis album by mistake. The strains of trumpeter Henry Lowther are certainly convincing. Mark Hollis and his band moved on from the New Romantic tag and certainly produced a much more varied and ambitious album. 'The Rainbow' is a startling opener, and after Lowther's trumpet solo is a spooky harmonica solo from ex-Nine Below Zero ace, Mark Feltham. Other cameos convince the listener that Talk Talk have grown. The choice of musicians such as Nigel Kennedy, and the marvellous string bassist Danny Thompson, can do nothing but enhance their reputation. The City of Chelmsford choir are the icing on the cake.

● TRACKS: *The Rainbow; Eden; Desire; Inheritance; I Believe In You; Wealth.*

● FIRST RELEASED 1988
● UK PEAK CHART POSITION: 19
● USA PEAK CHART POSITION: did not chart

443 RED HEADED STRANGER (670) ▲
WILLIE NELSON

W illie Nelson stopped shaving, grew his hair, ditched his suits and found acceptance with the hippies who bought the country rock of the Flying Burrito Brothers. Like *Tommy*, *Red Headed Stranger* was a concept album, this time about a murderous preacher. His laid-back voice-and-guitar revival of 'Blue Eyes Cryin'' In The Rain' was a surprise US hit single, and Richard Thompson says, 'I like the fact that he plays these terrible solos and leaves them alone, which takes a lot of guts these days.'

● TRACKS: *Time Of The Preacher; I Couldn't Believe It Was True; Blue Rock Montana; Blue Eyes Crying In The Rain; Red Headed Stranger; Just As I Am; Denver; O'er The Waves; Down Yonder; Can I Sleep In Your Arms; Remember Me When The Candle Lights Are Gleaming; Hands On The Wheel; Bandera.*

● FIRST RELEASED 1975
● UK PEAK CHART POSITION: did not chart
● USA PEAK CHART POSITION: 28

444 DESPERADO (192) ▼
THE EAGLES

D rawing from their previous experience as hired musicians, the Eagles quickly became one of America's leading country rock attractions. *Desperado*, their second release, was an ambitious concept album wherein the outlaw was used as a metaphor for the rock performer. Recorded in London under the aegis of Glyn Johns, the set was marked by the quartet's highly measured playing and distinctive harmonies. Described at their inception as the 'new Buffalo Springfield', the Eagles certainly drew on Californian musical heritage, but on this album they proclaimed an original identity. Desperado is their most complete, and for many, their best album. It deserves at least equal billing with *Hotel California*.

● TRACKS: *Doolin Dalton; 21; Out Of Control; Tequila Sunrise; Desperado; Certain Kind Of Fool; Outlaw Man; Saturday Night; Bitter Creek.*

● FIRST RELEASED 1973
● UK PEAK CHART POSITION: 39
● USA PEAK CHART POSITION: 41

445 **I FEEL FOR YOU** (–) ▲
CHAKA KHAN

Just as people were beginning to think she had peaked (after the less than great *Chaka Khan*), she bounced back with this excellent set. Using a glut of producers - Mardin, Titleman, Foster and more - she attempted, and achieved, the combination of a great choice of material with the ability to keep her fans dancing. The Bacharach/Bayer Sager/Roberts 'Stronger Than Before' is beautifully performed, and la-di-da, ex-Spooky Tooth Gary Wright wrote 'My Love Is Alive'. Prince's 'I Feel For You' is another strong track, featuring the distinctive harmonica sound of Stevie Wonder. A pretty joyous album for dusting away cobwebs.

● TRACKS: *This Is My Night; Stronger Than Before; My Love Is Alive; Eye To Eye; La Flamme; I Feel For You; Hold Her; Through The Fire; Caught In The Act; Chinatown.*

● FIRST RELEASED 1984
● UK PEAK CHART POSITION: 15
● USA PEAK CHART POSITION: 14

---

 446 **RISQUÉ** (–) ▲
CHIC

They made two great albums, yet for some reason this one comes out on top over *C'est Chic*. They represented the pinnacle of late 70s disco music, with a brand of slick soul that was made for the dancefloor. Nile Rodgers and the late Bernard Edwards were the Babyfaces of their day. Their compositions, record production and sparing musicianship (guitar and bass, respectively) made Chic such a classy unit. Hard to imagine listening to this in a normal home environment as the fantasy of white suits and exotic cocktails is just too much to bear. 90s urban R&B owes everything to Chic.

● TRACKS: *Good Times; A Warm Summer Night; My Feet Keep Dancing; My Forbidden Lover; Can't Stand To Love You; Will You Cry (When You Hear This Song); What About Me.*

● FIRST RELEASED 1979
● UK PEAK CHART POSITION: 29
● USA PEAK CHART POSITION: 5

 **447** **RIO** (–) ▲
DURAN DURAN

Poor old Durannies: they have received more than their fair share of criticism during the 80s pop backlash, not so much because of their music, but because of what they appeared to stand for during the hedonistic, 'me me me' yuppie decade of Thatcherism. What is undeniable is, like ABC, they represented the very best of UK pop at that time, and *Rio* will stand as their one great album. They provoked resentment for their lifestyle, but what cynic or critic could resist wanting to swap places with them on that beautiful schooner, somewhere in the Indian Ocean, when they shot the video for the immaculate 'Save A Prayer'?

● TRACKS: *Rio; My Own Way; Lonely In Your Nightmare; Hungry Like The Wolf; Hold Back The Rain; New Religion; Last Chance On The Stairway; Save A Prayer; The Chauffeur.*

● FIRST RELEASED 1974
● UK PEAK CHART POSITION: 2
● USA PEAK CHART POSITION: 6

---

 448 **SPRING HILL FAIR** (–) ▲
THE GO-BETWEENS

The Go-Betweens were never as popular as their critical acclaim suggested they should have been, but their legacy has given the world albums such as this 1984 indie classic. With two equally brilliant songwriters in Grant McLennan and Robert Forster, the Go-Betweens always had an edge over other bands, and on *Spring Hill Fair* both men reached an early creative peak. Instant classics such as McLennan's 'Bachelor Kisses' and 'Slow Slow Music', and Forster's 'Part Company', 'Draining The Pool For You' and 'Man O'Sand To Girl O'Sea' should have broken the band commercially, but instead they continued to struggle in obscurity until their demise in 1989.

● TRACKS: *Bachelor Kisses; Five Words; The Old Way Out; You've Never Lived; Part Company; Slow Slow Music; Draining The Pool For You; River Of Money; Unkind & Unwise; Man O'Sand To Girl O'Sea.*

● FIRST RELEASED 1984
● UK PEAK CHART POSITION: did not chart
● USA PEAK CHART POSITION: did not chart

449 **VOLUNTEERS** (–) ▲
JEFFERSON AIRPLANE

The album that made relations with the then ultra-conservative RCA a little tense. Knowing that they had potentially one of America's biggest bands, the label had to let them use the 'f' word (on 'We Can Be Together'). A bigger problem was their left-of-centre political stance at that time. *Volunteers* is a fat album, full of great ideas but with a surplus of gastric juice. 'The Farm' doodles just half a minute too long, their version of 'Wooden Ships' just misses the mark and the Stephen Stills organ 'Meadowlands' is a waste. However, 'Eskimo Blue Day' and 'Good Shepherd' succeed, as does the blatant sexuality of 'Hey Frederick' when Grace sings 'either go away or go all the way in, look at what you hold'.

● TRACKS: *We Can Be Together; Good Shepherd; The Farm; Hey Frederick; Turn My Life Down; Wooden Ships; Eskimo Blue Day; A Song For All Seasons; Meadowlands; Volunteers.*

● FIRST RELEASED 1969
● UK PEAK CHART POSITION: 34
● USA PEAK CHART POSITION: 13

 450 **YOU CAN'T HIDE YOUR LOVE FOREVER** (–) ▲ **ORANGE JUICE**

Orange Juice was the leading attraction on Glasgow's fêted Postcard label. Critical plaudits followed the release of their first four singles and much was expected from this debut album. The insouciant charm of their windblown pop was emphasized by a clear production that focused on singer Edwyn Collins' sonorous croon. Songs echoing the strains of classic west coast pop deal with sorrow and rejection, a fragility matched by the group's still-untutored playing, in which their aspirations outstripped their technical abilities. The group's continued desire to broach preconceived barriers is what gives this album its implicit strength.

● TRACKS: *Falling And Laughing; Untitled Melody; Wan Light; Tender Object; Dying Day; L.O.V.E.; Intuition Told Me; Upwards And Onwards; Satellite City; Three Cheers For Our Side; Consolation Prize; Felicity; In A Nutshell.*

● FIRST RELEASED 1982
● UK PEAK CHART POSITION: 21
● USA PEAK CHART POSITION: did not chart

 451 **THERE GOES RHYMIN' SIMON** (197) ▼
PAUL SIMON

Was it really the tail-end of the 60s when Simon gave us this continuation of *Bookends*?, an album of a similar feel. After he parted from Garfunkel, Simon wrote songs without having to consider two-part harmonies, and this in turn gave his music a freer, less folk rock flavour. 'American Tune' remains one of his greatest compositions and would make a better alternative to 'America The Beautiful' as the national anthem. Simon had to wait a long time before he topped this record artistically, but he did it in style with *Graceland*. This is the other Paul Simon album to own.

● TRACKS: *Kodachrome; Tenderness; Take Me To The Mardi Gras; Something So Right; One Man's Ceiling Is Another Man's Floor; American Tune; Was A Sunny Day; Learn How To Fall; St. Judy's Comet; Loves Me Like A Rock.*

● FIRST RELEASED 1973
● UK PEAK CHART POSITION: 4
● USA PEAK CHART POSITION: 2

 452 **SHOOT OUT THE LIGHTS** (334) ▼
RICHARD AND LINDA THOMPSON

The world's most underrated songwriter, although Thompson must tire of hearing it so often. Together with his ex-wife Linda they made a series of quite brilliant albums that garnered heaps of praise and minimal sales. This is another slice of perfection that veers from whimsical fun in 'Wall Of Death' to desperate emotions in 'Shoot Out the Lights', which features the definitive Thompson guitar solo. Critics have often been accused of hyping artists, but try as they may, they can't do it with this one. Time will tell but this album should be in many more homes.

● TRACKS: *Don't Renege On Our Love; Walking On A Wire; Man In Need; Just The Motion; Shoot Out The Lights; Back Street Slide; Did She Jump Or Was She Pushed?; Wall Of Death.*

● FIRST RELEASED 1982
● UK PEAK CHART POSITION: did not chart
● USA PEAK CHART POSITION: did not chart

453 ALF (249) ▼
ALISON MOYET

Poor Alison Moyet may end up cursing this album for the rest of her career. Finding yourself with one of the year's biggest triumphs and rewarded by your record company with a large advance to put in your deposit account may sound satisfying, but for Alf it has not been an easy ride. The crisp Jolley/Swain production aided its success, and Moyet delivered a stunning voice to match strong material. Together they composed all the tracks bar one, Lamont Dozier's 'Invisible', the third hit single following on from 'Love Resurrection', and 'All Cried Out'. Powerful. High-quality pop which she has so far failed to match.

● TRACKS: *Love Resurrection; Honey For The Bees; For You Only; Invisible; Steal Me Blind; All Cried Out; Money Mile; Twisting The Knife; Where Hides Sleep.*

● FIRST RELEASED 1984
● UK PEAK CHART POSITION: 1
● USA PEAK CHART POSITION: 45

454 MACHINE HEAD (103) ▼
DEEP PURPLE

From the heady intro of 'Highway Star', written in a couple of hours on a bus between shows, to the lazy beat of 'Space Truckin'', *Machine Head* would have remained one of the classic line-up's (Glover, Paice, Gillan, Blackmore, Lord) great albums. However, the hand of fate took them to Montreux at the same time as Frank Zappa's Mothers Of Invention, and their witnessing of the burning down of the Casino, immortalized in 'Smoke On The Water' with Blackmore's plaintive riff, studied and dedicated to memory in a thousand guitar classes, and Gillan's simple retelling of events, elevated them and their record to legendary status. Da da da, dada dada, da da da, da da.

● TRACKS: *Highway Star; Maybe I'm A Leo; Pictures Of Home; Never Before; Smoke On The Water; Lazy; Space Truckin'.*

● FIRST RELEASED 1972
● UK PEAK CHART POSITION: 1
● USA PEAK CHART POSITION: 7

455 TUMBLEWEED CONNECTION (–) ▲
ELTON JOHN

Even though the atmospheric photograph of the old railway station that graces the cover is obviously English, the overwhelming theme of this album is Americana. Taupin's western lyrics complement Elton's bar-room piano perfectly on the more lively tracks such as 'Son Of Your Father', 'Burn Down The Mission' and 'Country Comfort'. The peaks, however, centre on two beautiful songs, 'Come Down In Time', with a brilliant string arrangement and the gentle acoustic duet with Lesley Duncan on 'Love Song', which she also wrote. Elton had not yet discovered the excesses of superstardom and this album retains little glamour and a lot of simple honesty.

● TRACKS: *Ballad Of A Well-Known Gun; Come Down In Time; Country Comfort; Son Of Your Father; My Father's Gun; Where To Now St. Peter?; Love Song; Amoreena; Talking Old Soldiers; Burn Down The Mission; Into The Old Man's Shoes; Madman Across The Water (original version).*

● FIRST RELEASED 1970
● UK PEAK CHART POSITION: 6
● USA PEAK CHART POSITION: 4

456 SPIKE (–) ▲
ELVIS COSTELLO

On his first album for Warner Brothers, Costello lived up to his new role as 'the beloved entertainer', moving further away from his new-wave background with a sprawling collection of songs in a diverse range of musical styles. *Spike* takes in pure pop ('Veronica'), cod-funk ('Chewing Gum'), gospel ('Deep Dark Truthful Mirror'), Irish folk ('Any King's Shilling') and rockabilly ('Pads, Paws And Claws'), alongside the venomous politicizing of 'Let Him Dangle' and 'Tramp The Dirt Down'. Not everything works, and in fact the strongest song on the album is the simple acoustic ballad 'Baby Plays Around', co-written with his wife Cait O'Riordan.

● TRACKS: *...This Town...; Let Him Dangle; Deep Dark Truthful Mirror; Veronica; God's Comic; Chewing Gum; Tramp The Dirt Down; Stalin Malone; Satellite; Pads, Paws And Claws; Baby Plays Around; Miss Macbeth; Any King's Shilling; Coal-Train Robberies; Last Boat Leaving.*

● FIRST RELEASED 1989
● UK PEAK CHART POSITION: 5
● USA PEAK CHART POSITION: 32

457 JOE'S GARAGE (-) ▲
FRANK ZAPPA

The superlative repackaging and remastering undertaken by Ryko has put the original three-part, two-record set of this magnificent nonsense tale together for the first time. This is back to the madness of *Freak Out*, with more pop and doo-wop bursting through all the complicated stuff, letting you know that Zappa could write a hit single, if he could be bothered to do so. *Joe's Garage* is a hoot and harmlessly pornographic. The sleeve-note states that it is 'a stupid story about how the government is trying to do away with music'. It is absolutely no coincidence that throughout, the listener mistakes the 'scrutinizer' as the 'scrotumizer'. Zappa was that rude, and that funny.

● TRACKS: *The Central Scrutinizer; Joe's Garage; Catholic Girls; Crew Slut; Fembot In A Wet T-Shirt; On The Bus; Why Does It Hurt When I Pee?; Lucille Has Messed My Mind Up; Scrutinizer Postlude; A Token Of My Extreme; Stick It Out; Sy Borg; Dong Work For Yuda; Keep It Greasy; Outside Now; He Used To Cut The Grass; Packard Goose; Watermelon In Easter Hay; A Little Green Rosetta.*

● FIRST RELEASED 1979
● UK PEAK CHART POSITION: 62 & 75
● USA PEAK CHART POSITION: 27 & 53

458 I WANT YOU (-) ▲
MARVIN GAYE

Another in a series of superb wandering groove albums from the premier sweet soul singer. He took the standard three-minute pop soul song and expanded the format. It is Gaye that is responsible for today's smooching urban R&B; he was for much of his career many years ahead of the game. This has been described as his 'oral sex' album, not that the others were not; this has the erotic edge. Built around the title track, the album is a theme album and as such should be played as a whole. There are no 'Too Busy Thinking Bout My Baby's on this; it is a much more challenging but satisfying work.

● TRACKS: *I Want You (Vocal); Come Live With Me Angel; After The Dance (Instrumental); Feel All My Love Inside; I Wanna Be Where You Are; I Want You (Intro Jam); All The Way Round; Since I Had You; Soon I'll Be Loving You Again; I Want You (Intro Jam); After The Dance (Vocal).*

● FIRST RELEASED 1976
● UK PEAK CHART POSITION: 22
● USA PEAK CHART POSITION: 4

459 JORDAN: THE COMEBACK (-) ▲
PREFAB SPROUT

Paddy MacAloon is arguably one of England's finest modern songwriters, and this 1990 release was a gloriously overlong mélange of styles, bound together by some of his most inspired melodies. The nineteen tracks cover a typically diverse range of subject matters, including a quartet of songs about the rise and fall of Elvis Presley that provide the album with its thematic core. Elsewhere, on songs such as 'We Let The Stars Go', 'All The World Loves Lovers' and 'Doo Wop In Harlem' MacAloon's songwriting hit new peaks. Never gaining the commercial success it deserved, *Jordan: The Comeback*'s heady brew even appeared to be a step too far for MacAloon, who did not release another album for seven years.

● TRACKS: *Looking For Atlantis; Wild Horses; Machine Gun Ibiza; We Let The Stars Go; Carnival 2000; Jordan: The Comeback; Jesse James Symphony; Jesse James Bolero; Moon Dog; All The World Loves Lovers; All Boys Believe Anything; The Ice Maiden; Paris Smith; The Wedding March; One Of The Broken; Michael; Mercy; Scarlet Nights; Doo Wop In Harlem.*

● FIRST RELEASED 1990
● UK PEAK CHART POSITION: 7
● USA PEAK CHART POSITION: did not chart

460 TODAY (222) ▼
THE BEACH BOYS

Although other Beach Boys albums have received greater critical acclaim, *Today* is almost unbeatable for its content of two-minute quality songs that are unpretentious and infectious. Their rock 'n' roll roots are revisited with 'Do You Wanna Dance' and 'Good To My Baby'. 'Dance, Dance, Dance' and 'Good To My Baby' are two underrated Brian Wilson songs and he complements them with more of his gorgeous ballads in 'She Knows Me Too Well' and 'Please Let Me Wonder'. The seeds of *Pet Sounds* were sewn with this impressive record.

● TRACKS: *Do You Wanna Dance; Good To My Baby; Don't Hurt My Little Sister; When I Grow Up; Help Me, Ronda; Dance, Dance, Dance; Please Let Me Wonder; I'm So Young; Kiss Me Baby; She Knows Me Too Well; In The Back Of My Mind; Bull Session With The Big Daddy.*

● FIRST RELEASED 1965
● UK PEAK CHART POSITION: 6
● USA PEAK CHART POSITION: 4

461 OAR (–) ▲
ALEXANDER 'SKIP' SPENCE

This is the product of a mad, tortured genius who took too many chemicals and lost it. Moby Grape had so much potential and Spence was a major figure in the band. This stark, disjointed collection is a classic 'cult' album, and will remain so as long as Syd Barrett, Roky Erickson, Peter Green and Spence continue to be written about. This is a challenging, brilliant, odd, lovable album that comes highly recommended. The Sony reissue in 1991 contains five bonus tracks. When Spence delivered this to Columbia Records, imagine the record executive listening to it, sitting back in his chair and saying, 'gee . . . I don't hear a hit single'.

● TRACKS: Little Hands; Cripple Creek; Diana; Margaret-Tiger Rug; Weighted Down (The Prison Song); War In Peace; Broken Heart; All Come To Meet Her; Book Of Moses; Dixie Peach Promenade; Lawrence Of Euphoria; Grey/Afro; This Time He Has Come; It's The Best Thing For You; Keep Everything Under Your Hat; Halo Of Gold; Doodle.

● FIRST RELEASED 1969
● UK PEAK CHART POSITION: did not chart
● USA PEAK CHART POSITION: did not chart

462 FUTURE GAMES (–) ▲
SPIRIT

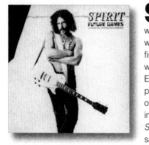

Subtitled 'A Magical Kahauna Dream', this was Randy California at his wackiest. Now seen as the first true sampled album, it is a work of perplexing genius. Each of the 22 tracks is preceded either by dialogue or snippets from TV or radio, including Kermit The Frog and Star Trek. The obscure sampled bites are lightened by California's gift for melody. Even though he was slightly out of his cosmic tree at the time, he never lost his gift for writing a beautiful song. This was a fairly barren time for the band, with only Ed Cassidy and California remaining from the first line-up. Consequently, this album was ignored by all but true spirits.

● TRACKS: CB Talk; Stars Of Love; Kahauna Dream; Buried In My Brain; Bionic Unit; So Happy Now; All Along The Watchtower; Would You Believe; Jack Bond Speaks; Star Trek Dreaming; Interlude XM; China Doll; Hawaiian Times; Gorn Attack; Interlude 2001; Detroit City; Freakout Frog; The Romulan Experience; Monkey See Monkey Do; Mt. Olympus; The Journey Of Nomad; Ending.

● FIRST RELEASED 1977
● UK PEAK CHART POSITION: did not chart
● USA PEAK CHART POSITION: did not chart

463 SAILOR (303) ▼
STEVE MILLER BAND

Long before Miller discovered the art of writing great short pop songs with infectious guitar licks he had a dynamite band that featured Boz Scaggs. This incandescent album was their last together and for the vast majority of Miller followers it remains the pinnacle. Sandwiched in-between Miller's love for the blues and R&B with 'Gangster Of Love' and 'You're So Fine', are great rock tracks such as 'Living In The USA' and 'Dime-A-Dance Romance'. The desert island choice, however, is the imaginative instrumental 'Song For Our Ancestors'; close your eyes and you can actually hear ferry boats entering the harbour, without needing artificial stimulants.

● TRACKS: Song For Our Ancestors; Dear Mary; My Friend; Living In The USA; Quicksilver Girl; Lucky Man; Gangster Of Love; You're So Fine; Overdrive; Dime-A-Dance Romance.

● FIRST RELEASED 1968
● UK PEAK CHART POSITION: did not chart
● USA PEAK CHART POSITION: 24

464 HEROES (–) ▲
DAVID BOWIE

The Germanic feel of this album is not surprising, as Bowie recorded it in Berlin during his infatuation with the city. It was a much more lively affair than Low and has the benefit of a title track that remains one of his best ever songs (in addition to excellent contributions from Fripp and Eno). 'Beauty And The Beast' was difficult to accept as a single, yet it works as the album's opener. 'Sense Of Doubt' is the opposite of 'Heroes' - dark and moody, as is 'Neukoln'. Even through the doom and gloom, this is an important Bowie album, and one to which critics return time and time again.

● TRACKS: Beauty And The Beast; Joe The Lion; Heroes; Sons Of The Silent Age; Blackout; V-2 Schneider; Sense Of Doubt; Moss Garden; Neukoln; The Secret Life Of Arabia.

● FIRST RELEASED 1977
● UK PEAK CHART POSITION: 3
● USA PEAK CHART POSITION: 35

465 ELTON JOHN (101) ▼
ELTON JOHN

Still learning his craft as a songwriter, this is the album that really made the critics take notice. Although recording techniques now make this (even on CD) sound dated, the quality of the songs and the mood they convey still have the ability to move us all. 'Your Song' will perennially be in the top 100 singles of all time. 'Border Song' and 'No Shoestrings On Louise' continue to show that Bernie Taupin should have been born in the Midwest, and romantics will still see the painful logic of 'I Need You To Turn To'. This is a remarkably mature album that often gets overlooked.

● TRACKS: *Your Song; I Need You To Turn To; Take Me To The Pilot; No Shoestrings On Louise; First Episode At Heinton; 60 Years On; Border Song; Greatest Discovery; The Cage; The King Must Die.*

● FIRST RELEASED 1970
● UK PEAK CHART POSITION: 11
● USA PEAK CHART POSITION: 4

466 SHAKE SOME ACTION (-) ▲
FLAMIN' GROOVIES

'**S**hake some action's what I need, to let me bust out at full speed. . . '. The words of a teenage rebel, set to the most aggressive mod music this side of 'My Generation' - except that, by the time San Francisco's Flamin' Groovies released the unrepentantly revivalist *Shake Some Action*, their average age was 30. Moreover, they were not rebelling against the older generation, but their own peers. Fortunately, their cries did not go unheard. Although *Shake Some Action* was not a mainstream hit, it was lauded by the press and became a huge influence on the punk and power-pop movements on both sides of the Atlantic.

● TRACKS: *Shake Some Action; Sometimes; Yes It's True; St. Louis Blues; You Tore Me Down; Please Please Girl; Let The Boy Rock 'n' Roll; Don't You Lie To Me; She Said Yeah; I'll Cry Alone; Misery; I Saw Her; Teenage Confidential; I Can't Hide.*

● FIRST RELEASED 1976
● UK PEAK CHART POSITION: did not chart
● USA PEAK CHART POSITION: 142

467 ROADMASTER (-) ▲
GENE CLARK

Although *Roadmaster* has the feel of a completed album, it is actually a collection of top-quality out-takes. It was originally released only in Europe, where Clark's previous album, *White Light*, had been a moderate success. It appeared seven years after Clark left the Byrds and has a laid-back, Sunday morning feel that was echoed in the Eagles' early work. However, beneath the languid rhythms are several songs that rank with Clark's best compositions. One track, 'Full Circle Song', was later performed by the Byrds on their reunion album, while two others, 'She's The Kind Of Girl' and the lovely 'One In A Hundred', *are* Byrds reunions.

● TRACKS: *She's The Kind Of Girl; One In A Hundred; Here Tonight; Full Circle Song; In A Misty Morning; Rough And Rocky; Roadmaster; I Really Don't Want To Know; I Remember The Railroad; She Don't Care About Time; Shooting Star.*

● FIRST RELEASED 1972
● UK PEAK CHART POSITION: did not chart
● USA PEAK CHART POSITION: did not chart

468 LIVE THROUGH THIS (-) ▲
HOLE

With the world and its dog besotted with the latest hybrid of punk rock (grunge) and its finest exponents (Nirvana), *Live Through This* almost slipped through the net. With Cobain dead a week before its release, journalists were more interested in his widow's reactions than her music. Little wonder - it was hard to overlook lyrics such as 'With a bullet, number one/Kill the family, save the son' ('Jennifer's Boy'). Courtney Love had just released the best album of her career. *Live Through This* saw Love's songwriting develop accessibility and personality. Most songs provided a happy halfway house between brash pop and blazing guitar workouts. There are some truly startling lyrical images what make *Live Through This* a thrilling experience.

● TRACKS: *Violet; Miss World; Plump; Asking For It; Jennifer's Body; Doll Parts; Credit In The Straight World; Softer, Softest; She Walks On Me; I Think That I Would Die; Gutless; Rock Star.*

● FIRST RELEASED 1994
● UK PEAK CHART POSITION: 13
● USA PEAK CHART POSITION: 52

469 SOUND AFFECTS (803) ▲
THE JAM

The most eloquent of punk rockers, the Jam may have had the energy and youthful fury of their musical contemporaries, but they also had the spirit, insight and wit of one Paul Weller. From the punning title to the easy storytelling, the set harboured an engrained bitterness and a quiet desperation that was to earmark much of Weller's work with the Jam. Lifting the Beatles' 'Taxman' almost wholesale for 'Start' may have seemed unforgiveable, but writing the flawless 'That's Entertainment' quite rightly absolved Weller of any blame. A great, great record.

● TRACKS: *Pretty Green; Monday; But I'm Different Now; Set The House Ablaze; Start; That's Entertainment; Dreamtime; Man In the Cornershop; Music For The Last Couple; Boy About Town; Scrape Away.*

● FIRST RELEASED 1980
● UK PEAK CHART POSITION: 2
● USA PEAK CHART POSITION: 72

471 LIKE A VIRGIN (102) ▼
MADONNA

The title track, which, combined with her overt sexuality, caused waves of controversy at the time, has now become part of movie folklore, with director Quentin Tarantino letting his brutish cast mull over the meaning of its lyrics for the opening sequence of the film *Reservoir Dogs*. It is somehow gratifying that the Madonna album that unleashed her on the world should have become a cultural icon and reference point for the 80s. A telling blend of lush pop songs and street suss - the snappy come-on of 'Into The Groove', the Monroe pastiche for 'Material Girl' - the dancing went on all through the night.

● TRACKS: *Material Girl; Shoo-bee-doo; Pretender; Stay; Angel; Like A Virgin; Over And Over; Love Don't Live Here Anymore; Into The Groove; Dress You Up.*

● FIRST RELEASED 1984
● UK PEAK CHART POSITION: 6
● USA PEAK CHART POSITION: 1

470 PEARL (302) ▼
JANIS JOPLIN

Released posthumously in 1971, *Pearl* is a startling, multi-coloured portrait of a major artist bestriding her material with consummate ease. From the chugging 'Move Over' to the portentous 'Get It While You Can', the power never wavers. 'Me And Bobby McGee' leaves all other versions at the starting blocks (it was a number 1 in the USA), while the a cappella 'Mercedes Benz' demonstrates that she only needed the Full Tilt Boogie Band to add colour, not depth. The balance is perfect on 'Half Moon', which sounds like Little Feat backing Grace Slick with laryngitis. If only there was more.

● TRACKS: *Move Over; Cry Baby; A Woman Left Lonely; Half Moon; Buried Alive In The Blues; Me And Bobby McGee; Mercedes Benz; Get It While You Can; Trust Me.*

● FIRST RELEASED 1971
● UK PEAK CHART POSITION: 50
● USA PEAK CHART POSITION: 1

472 LOVELESS (–) ▲
MY BLOODY VALENTINE

'The last word in noise-pop' was how this release was reviewed on release in 1991, but that is a somewhat simplistic response. Creation Records must have been relieved, having invested some £200,000 over three years indulging their notoriously workshy recluses. The results are well worth the price, at least in artistic terms. Eighteen sound engineers are credited on the LP sleeve and the group's huge, luminous soundscapes now involved everything from guitars to bagpipes. At one turn the Jesus And Mary Chain, at others Philip Glass or the Beach Boys, *Loveless* is a colossal achievement, and by necessity one constructed by the most ambitious studio band of their generation.

● TRACKS: *Only Shallow; Loomer; Touched; To Here Knows When; When You Sleep; I Only Said; Come In Alone; Sometimes; Blown A Wish; What You Want; Soon.*

● FIRST RELEASED 1991
● UK PEAK CHART POSITION: 24
● USA PEAK CHART POSITION: did not chart

473 SEAL (–) ▲
SEAL

Without prior knowledge of the artist, one might categorize this (his second) album as white blue-eyed soul - earnest, heartfelt, but lacking a certain grit. Some songs ('Prayer For The Dying') deal with tough emotional choices, but couched as they are in the lush romanticism of Trevor Horn's skilful production, you barely notice the pain expressed in the lyrics. The most intriguing song here, the choppy, complex 'Dreaming In Metaphors', would surely benefit from a more stripped-down presentation. Still, Seal is an immense talent and the music industry reveres him, and justifiably so - few others could make a stately baroque waltz like 'Kiss From A Rose' sound so damnably radio-friendly.

● TRACKS: *Bring It On; Prayer For The Dying; Dreaming In Metaphors; Don't Cry; Fast Changes; Kiss From A Rose; People Asking Why; Newborn Friend; If I Could; I'm Alive; Bring It On (reprise).*

● FIRST RELEASED 1994
● UK PEAK CHART POSITION: 1
● USA PEAK CHART POSITION: 15

474 THE HEALER (116) ▼
JOHN LEE HOOKER

When popular culture embraced John Lee, purists turned up their noses. They should have been pleased that the world's greatest living Delta bluesman was going to make some money before he turned up his toes. Teaming up with Carlos Santana, Bonnie Raitt, Los Lobos, Canned Heat (not for the first time) and others, lent Hooker's blues a contemporary gloss. It took the album to the upper reaches of the album charts around the world, brought him a number of Grammy awards and a new career in advertising. The blues is not only a healer, it drinks brandy and wears jeans. The Santana guitar solo on the title track is breathtaking and Hooker is the coolest senior citizen in the world.

● TRACKS: *The Healer; I'm In The Mood; Baby Lee; Cuttin' Out; Think Twice Before You Go; Los Lobos; Sally Mae; That's Alright; Rockin' Chair; My Dream; No Substitute.*

● FIRST RELEASED 1989
● UK PEAK CHART POSITION: 63
● USA PEAK CHART POSITION: 62

475 VEEDON FLEECE (–) ▲
VAN MORRISON

One of many Morrison albums that feature interesting but pointless covers, the besuited Van with country mansion and two large dogs gives no indication of the emotion and intensity contained on this album. *Veedon Fleece* is sadly ignored by all but the cognoscenti, even though the gap between this and *Astral Weeks* is not that great. 'Fair Play' is a magnificent, lilting opener, but the following 'Linden Arden Stole The Highlights' is a masterpiece, and a song that cries for another ten verses and five minutes length - a strange omission when you consider the many lengthy odes he has written. Exposure is all it needs (and a decent cover).

● TRACKS: *Fair Play; Linden Arden Stole The Highlights; Who Was That Masked Man; Streets Of Arklow; You Don't Pull No Punches, But You Don't Push The River; Bulbs; Cul De Sac; Comfort You; Come Here My Love; Country Fair.*

● FIRST RELEASED 1974
● UK PEAK CHART POSITION: 41
● USA PEAK CHART POSITION: 53

476 THE BASEMENT TAPES (–) ▲
BOB DYLAN AND THE BAND

In 1967 Dylan was recovering from his much publicized motorcycle crash, and with backing from the fledgling Band, he laid down dozens of rudimentary demo recordings. Eventually gaining an official release eight years later (with several delightful songs from a later Band session added), *The Basement Tapes* was a ragbag collection of alternately playful and serious acoustic songs that drew on a deep well of American tradition for their inspiration. Songs of the calibre of 'Tears Of Rage', 'Too Much Of Nothing', 'Nothing Was Delivered' and 'This Wheel's On Fire' only served to emphasize Dylan's startling fecundity and importance as a songwriter.

● TRACKS: *Odds And Ends; Orange Juice Blues (Blues For Breakfast); Million Dollar Bash; Yazoo Street Scandal; Goin' To Acapulco; Katie's Been Gone; Lo And Behold!; Bessie Smith; Clothes Line Saga; Apple Suckling Tree; Please, Mrs Henry; Tears Of Rage; Too Much Of Nothing; Yea! Heavy And A Bottle Of Bread; Ain't No More Cane; Crash On The Levee (Down In The Flood); Ruben Remus; Tiny Montgomery; You Ain't Goin' Nowhere; Don't Ya Tell Henry; Nothing Was Delivered; Open The Door, Homer; Long Distance Operator; This Wheel's On Fire.*

● FIRST RELEASED 1975
● UK PEAK CHART POSITION: 8 ● USA PEAK CHART POSITION: 7

477 BE YOURSELF TONIGHT (118) ▼
EURYTHMICS

This album replays like a greatest hits package, such is the content of full-blown memorable pop songs. The list is almost endless as this album is a chilling reminder of how good pop can be and how well Lennox and Stewart worked together. Even without the legendary Aretha Franklin on 'Sisters Are Doing It For Themselves' there is the pace and guts of 'I Love You Like A Ball And Chain' or the numerous confessional 'I'll be's' of 'It's Alright (Baby's Coming Back)'. This album stands up to repeated plays and will continue to improve with age. What perfection.

● TRACKS: *Would I Lie To You; There Must Be An Angel (Playing With My Heart); I Love You Like A Ball And Chain; Sisters Are Doing It For Themselves; Conditioned Soul; Adrian; It's Alright (Baby's Coming Back); Here Comes That Sinking Feeling; Better To Have Lost In Love (Than Never To Have Loved At All).*

● FIRST RELEASED 1985
● UK PEAK CHART POSITION: 3
● USA PEAK CHART POSITION: 9

478 LEGEND OF AMERICAN FOLK BLUES
(121) ▼ **WOODY GUTHRIE**

Folk-singer is too small a term to describe Woody Guthrie. Political activist, rambler, poet and commentator, he encapsulated the aura of Roosevelt's New Deal America. Guthrie spoke for the okie underclass in song the way Steinbeck chronicled their lives in novels and this superb selection compiles the best of his expansive output. The topical song was Guthrie's métier and his simple melodies and pungent lyrics left a huge impression on the 60s folk revival. Bob Dylan, Phil Ochs

and Tom Paxton owe him a considerable debt, but Guthrie's importance lies in the lasting quality of his own work. This CD has replaced *This Land Is Your Land* as the definitive Guthrie album.

● TRACKS: *This Land Is Your Land; Pastures Of Plenty; Pretty Boy Floyd; Take A Whiff On Me; Do Re Mi; Put My Little Shoes Away; Washington Talkin' Blues; Hard Travelin'; Jesus Christ; Whoopee Ti Yi Yo, Get Along Little Dogies; Grand Coulee Dam; A Picture From Life's Other Side; Talkin' Hard Luck Blues; Philadelphia Lawyer; I Ain't Got No Home; The Wreck Of The Old '97; Keep Your Skillet Good And Greasy; Dust Pneumonia Blues; Going Down That Road Feeling Bad; Goodnight Little Arlo (Goodnight Little Darlin'); So Long It's Been Good To Know You.*

● FIRST RELEASED 1992
● UK PEAK CHART POSITION: did not chart
● USA PEAK CHART POSITION: did not chart

479 TOYS IN THE ATTIC (319) ▼
AEROSMITH

A truly inventive Aerosmith album, still suffused with a gloriously raspy sense of the blues, but quietly evocative in its timbre and approach. It showed Tyler working out lyrics that were so much more than simple cars and girls fodder, 'Adam's Apple' theorizing that creation could quite possibly have occurred with an alien mothership landing on earth and setting the wheels of the human race in motion. 'Sweet Emotion' throbbed slowly into life, 'Big Ten Inch Record', a salty R&B work-out, while 'You See Me Crying' was heightened and given body by a warm orchestration. A clear steeple of great work amid a skyline of repeating successes.

● TRACKS: *Toys In The Attic; Uncle Salty; Adam's Apple; Walk This Way; Big Ten Inch Record; Sweet Emotion; No More No More; Round And Round; You See Me Crying.*

● FIRST RELEASED 1975
● UK PEAK CHART POSITION: did not chart
● USA PEAK CHART POSITION: 11

480 NEBRASKA (–) ▲
BRUCE SPRINGSTEEN

Dispensing with his famous E Street Band, Springsteen sat with only his guitar and a tape recorder (albeit a pretty good one). He recorded a series of barren songs, adding only a spooky harmonica and some reverb. This was the most atmospheric and naked album of the decade, and may have inspired the unplugged phenomenon of the 90s. He sounds like an 80s version of Johnny Cash, both in sound and in theme/content, although 'Used Cars' reveals his great weakness. It is impossible for the Boss to get through any album without making a reference to cars.

● TRACKS: *Nebraska; Atlantic City; Mansion On The Hill; Johnny 99; Highway Patrolman; State Trooper; Used Cars; Open All Night; My Father's House; Reason To Believe.*

● FIRST RELEASED 1982
● UK PEAK CHART POSITION: 3
● USA PEAK CHART POSITION: 3

481 **KING CREOLE** (484) ▲
ELVIS PRESLEY

King Creole was one of the very few Elvis films with good songs, recorded when he was first and foremost a rock 'n' roll singer. Although crudely recorded, the dated sound gives the album great bounce - thin guitar recorded in the bathroom, pudding drums and soggy stand-up bass - but the instrumentation complemented the King's quite magnificent voice. 'Hard Headed Woman' remains one of his liveliest tracks and the title track still has incredible moodiness, and even with 50s dance band brass it still works. The CD reissue announces a playing time of only 21.12, the only negative thing about the record.

● TRACKS: King Creole; As Long As I Have You; Hard Headed Woman; Trouble; Dixieland Rock; Don't Ask Me Why; Lover Doll; Crawfish; Young Dreams; Steadfast, Loyal And True; New Orleans.

● FIRST RELEASED 1958
● UK PEAK CHART POSITION: 4
● USA PEAK CHART POSITION: 2

 483 **MUSIC FOR A NEW SOCIETY** (–) ▲
JOHN CALE

Music For A New Society remains an uneasy listening experience 16 years after it was first released, a compelling aural snapshot of John Cale's chaotic state of mind in 1982. Harking back to his training in the avant garde, Cale used improvisational methods of composition learned from John Cage and LaMonte Young to provide a sparse musical backdrop to the emotional nihilism of his lyrics. On tracks such as 'Thoughtless Kind', 'If You Were Still Around', 'Damn Life' and 'Sanities', Cale fashioned some of modern music's most desperately passionate postcards from the edge. True to form, he followed it with the vacuous Caribbean Sunset.

● TRACKS: Taking Your Life In Your Hands; Thoughtless Kind; Sanities; If You Were Still Around; (I Keep) A Close Watch; Broken Bird; Chinese Envoy; Changes Made; Damn Life; Risé, Sam And Rimsky-Korsakov.

● FIRST RELEASED 1982
● UK PEAK CHART POSITION: did not chart
● USA PEAK CHART POSITION: did not chart

 482 **FOLLOW THE LEADER** (952) ▲
ERIC B & RAKIM

A New York team who met in 1985 and have gone on to become an important duo in Rap's short history. Their debut album, Paid In Full, caused great legal waves via its explicit use of samples (Eric B is often credited with putting the funk back into rap music via his James Brown signatures). Rakim was responsible for introducing a more relaxed, intuitive delivery which was a distinct advance on the thumping bravado of Run DMC and LL Cool J, and is best sampled on this influential and instructive album. The title track, 'Lyrics Of Fury' and 'Microphone Fiend' provided the fullest possible evidence of the duo's skill.

● TRACKS: Follow The Leader; Microphone Fiend; Lyrics Of Fury; Eric B Never Scared; Just A Beat; Put Your Hands Together; To The Listeners; No Competition; The R; Musical Massacre; Beats For The Listeners.

● FIRST RELEASED 1988
● UK PEAK CHART POSITION: did not chart
● USA PEAK CHART POSITION: 22

 484 **LADIES OF THE CANYON** (764) ▲
JONI MITCHELL

No longer the wistful folkie, Joni had by now joined the late 60s rock fraternity through her association with Graham Nash. Her lyrics had acquired an originality, which she expanded on Blue and For The Roses, but it was the quality of the songs that made them classics of the era. 'For Free' was recorded by David Crosby and the re-formed Byrds, and CSNY turned 'Woodstock' into a full-blown rock number. Joni's own definitive stamp remains on the much-covered 'The Circle Game', the ecology-conscious 'Big Yellow Taxi' and 'Willy', her song for her then 'old man' Nash.

● TRACKS: Morning Morgan Town; For Free; Conversation; Ladies Of The Canyon; Willy; The Arrangement; Rainy Night House; The Priest; Blue Boy; Big Yellow Taxi; My Old Man; Woodstock; The Circle Game.

● FIRST RELEASED 1970
● UK PEAK CHART POSITION: 8
● USA PEAK CHART POSITION: 27

485 THE LA'S (851) ▲
THE LA'S

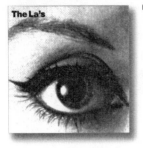

The perpetually dis-enchanted Liverpudlians grumbled their way through most of their interviews. Scathingly perfectionist, they dismissed most of their output with a metaphorical wave of the hand, compliments bounced off them in all directions, but for the La's, it was never enough. It is hard now to see why they were so dissatisfied; *The La's* is a graceful, sweeping and rather grand pop record, utterly charming and filled with a meek beauty typified by the wonderful 'There She Goes' single, the sincere 'I Can't Sleep' and the shining 'Timeless Melody'. Great moments.

● TRACKS: *Son Of A Gun; I Can't Sleep; Timeless Melody; Liberty Ship; There She Goes; Doledrum; Feeling; Way Out; IOU; Freedom Song; Failure; Lookin' Glass.*

● FIRST RELEASED 1990
● UK PEAK CHART POSITION: 30
● USA PEAK CHART POSITION: 196

486 DREADLOCKS DREAD (704) ▲
BIG YOUTH

This is the perfect Big Youth pop album: gone is the thundering sparse bass and in its place is a more orchestrated effort with shades of Marley and Burning Spear. 'Lightning Flash (Weak Heart Drop)' is sensational, while the happy-go-lucky 'Some Like It Dread' should have been a national hit. Only the power of his *Screaming Target* can top this album. His recorded output in recent years is meagre but this and *Screaming Target* should keep Youth's name alive long after any reggae boom has faded. He was after all the big name of 1973 (in Jamaica).

● TRACKS: *Train To Rhodesia; House Of Dreadlocks; Lightning Flash; Weak Heart; Natty Dread She Want; Some Like It Dread; Marcus Garvey; Big Youth Special; Dread Organ; Blackman Message; You Don't Care; Moving Away.*

● FIRST RELEASED 1975
● UK PEAK CHART POSITION: did not chart
● USA PEAK CHART POSITION: did not chart

487 FLY LIKE AN EAGLE (144) ▼
STEVE MILLER BAND

Miller forsook his love of the blues for this and its sister project *Book Of Dreams*. In turning to mainstream pop/rock he became a huge star and developed the knack of delivering high-quality three-minute songs that were perfect for FM radio. The album is linked by Miller's fascination with electronic sounds, sandwiched between the irresistible title track, the Bonnie and Clyde tale of 'Take The Money And Run', the irritatingly simple 'Rock 'n' Me' and the subdued 'The Window', with its quirky lyric 'ask my baby what she wants to be, she says a monkey in a tree'. His baby replies 'there's nothing greater than love', true enough. After all, it was Miller who rhymed 'northern California' with 'girls are warm yeah'.

● TRACKS: *Blue Odyssey; Dance, Dance, Dance; Fly Like An Eagle; Mercury Blues; Rock 'n' Me; Serenade; 2001; Sweet Marie; Take The Money And Run; Wild Mountain Honey; The Window; You Send Me.*

● FIRST RELEASED 1976
● UK PEAK CHART POSITION: 11
● USA PEAK CHART POSITION: 3

488 THE SINGLES 1969-1973 (305) ▼
CARPENTERS

Amost difficult album to admit to liking. Abba sounded positively hardcore punk compared to Karen and Richard, and yet just look at the sales and the position it gained. This album's popularity is represented by public opinion as well as reviewers and music biz types. The Carpenters' success was extraordinary and without explanation. The reissued/re-compiled CD also had incredible success when released. This will continue selling for as long as the record company keeps it in print. The lead guitar solo on 'Goodbye To Love' is still amazing though.

● TRACKS: *We've Only Just Begun; Top Of The World; Ticket To Ride; Superstar; Rainy Days And Mondays; Goodbye To Love; Yesterday Once More; It's Going To Take Some Time; Sing; For All We Know; Hurting Each Other; (They Long To Be) Close To You.*

● FIRST RELEASED 1974
● UK PEAK CHART POSITION: 1
● USA PEAK CHART POSITION: 1

489 THE BLACK SAINT AND THE SINNER LADY (178) ▼ CHARLES MINGUS

In many ways the essential Mingus album, *Black Saint* is a rich and powerful suite, embracing in one work the elements of blues, gospel, funk and Latin music that infused Mingus's sound and made it what it was. As well as featuring some of the best group arrangement outside the work of Ellington, it boasts superb contributions by pianist Jaki Byard and alto saxophonist Charlie Mariano. *Black Saint* is also revealing for its early use (in jazz) of studio dubbing, heard on the occasions when Mariano can be identified in the ensemble at the same time as he is soloing.

● TRACKS: *Solo Dancer (Stop! Look! And Listen, Sinner Jim Whitney); Duet Solo Dancers (Heart's Beat And Shades In Physical Embraces); Group Dancers ([Soul Fusion] Freewoman); Trio And Group Dancers (Stop! Look! And Sing Songs Of Revolutions!); Single Solos And Group Dance (Saint And Sinner Join In Merriment On Battle Front); Group And Solo Dance (Of Love, Pain, And Passioned Revolt, Then Farewell, My Beloved).*

● FIRST RELEASED 1963
● UK PEAK CHART POSITION: did not chart
● USA PEAK CHART POSITION: did not chart

491 MAIDEN VOYAGE (732) ▲ HERBIE HANCOCK

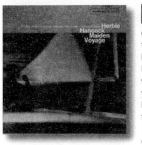

Probably the best in Herbie Hancock's series of fine Blue Note albums from the 60s, *Maiden Voyage* finds him in what is basically the Miles Davis band of the time, with Miles replaced by the young Freddie Hubbard. Hancock has always been a fine composer, but *Maiden Voyage* contains two classic compositions in particular - the beautiful 'Dolphin Dance', and the atmospheric and popular title track. Saxophonist George Coleman, bassist Ron Carter and drummer Tony Williams play as well throughout as they have ever played, and the whole record is marked with a timeless freshness and sense of creative tension.

● TRACKS: *Maiden Voyage; The Eye Of The Hurricane; Little One; Survival Of The Fittest; Dolphin Dance.*

● FIRST RELEASED 1964
● UK PEAK CHART POSITION: did not chart
● USA PEAK CHART POSITION: did not chart

490 461 OCEAN BOULEVARD (265) ▼ ERIC CLAPTON

It is really only 'Give Me Strength' that provides a hint of the emergence from anguish and peril represented by *461 Ocean Boulevard*. Clapton had descended into the depths of a serious heroin habit, invisible to the world for two years until Pete Townshend organized his comeback concert at the Rainbow. *461* followed, and showcases a relaxed Clapton, drawing as much on his songwriting ability and gentle vocal style as on his legendary guitar skills. Marley's 'I Shot The Sheriff' was a worldwide hit, and 'Let It Grow' and 'Get Ready' (written with Yvonne Elliman) are still regular concert favourites. This was Clapton's new dawn.

● TRACKS: *Get Ready; Give Me Strength; I Can't Hold Out Much Longer; I Shot The Sheriff; Let It Grow; Mainline Florida; Motherless Children; Please Be With Me; Steady Rollin' Man; Willie And The Hand Jive.*

● FIRST RELEASED 1974
● UK PEAK CHART POSITION: 3
● USA PEAK CHART POSITION: 1

492 WORLD MACHINE (143) ▼ LEVEL 42

Although it looks like Level 42 will never make another album, at least we have one which seems destined to endure. Mark King had already proved he could slap his bass better than almost anybody; now it was his turn to demonstrate his prowess as a classy songwriter. He succeeded in buoyant fashion with every track, very funky, very poppy and at times upliftingly wonderful, especially 'Something About You' and 'Coup D'Etat'. The winner for emotion, however, is the heartfelt 'Leaving Me Now'. Perfection, deliberately made for the age of the CD.

● TRACKS: *World Machine; A Physical Presence; Something About You; Leaving Me Now; I Sleep On My Heart; It's Not The Same For Us; Good Man In A Storm; Coup D'Etat; Lying Still.*

● FIRST RELEASED 1985
● UK PEAK CHART POSITION: 3
● USA PEAK CHART POSITION: 18

493 **HERE'S LITTLE RICHARD** (134) ▼
LITTLE RICHARD

The enigmatic Little Richard turned rock 'n' roll inside-out with a succession of highly expressive recordings during the mid-50s. Fuelled by an unfettered New Orleans backbeat, he combined gospel fervour and orgasmic delight in equal doses, singing without recourse to convention, hammering the piano keys with barely checked passion. *Here's Little Richard* abounds with essential performances that define an era and few collections offer such unremitting excitement. The pace barely relents, while almost every track has become an integral part of pop history, either in their own right, or through the countless cover versions they have inspired. It is an exceptional album from an exceptional talent.

● TRACKS: *Tutti Frutti; True, Fine Mama; Ready Teddy; Baby; Slippin' And Slidin'; Long Tall Sally; Miss Ann; Oh Why?; Rip It Up; Jenny Jenny; She's Got It; Can't Believe You Wanna Leave.*

● FIRST RELEASED 1957
● UK PEAK CHART POSITION: did not chart
● USA PEAK CHART POSITION: 13

 494 **LOVE IS THE THING** (132) ▼
NAT 'KING' COLE

Released in the days when albums were not promoted by extracting individual tracks and issuing them as singles, this was the first opportunity that young record-buyers had of hearing Nat Cole sing 'When I Fall In Love' and 'Stardust', songs with which he would forever be identified. Composer Hoagy Carmichael, who wrote 'Stardust' with Mitchell Parish, always maintained that this version, complete with the lovely verse, was his personal favourite. Of all the singer's varied albums - jazz, 'soft' country, easy listening - *Love Is The Thing*, which spent 55 weeks in the US Top 40, was the only one that went to number 1, where it stayed for eight weeks.

● TRACKS: *When I Fall In Love; The End Of A Love Affair; Stardust; Stay As Sweet As You Are; Where Can I Go Without You; Maybe It's Because I Love You Too Much; Love Letters; Ain't Misbehavin'; I Thought About Marie; At Last; It's All In The Game; When Sunny Gets Blue; Love Is The Thing.*

● FIRST RELEASED 1957
● UK PEAK CHART POSITION: did not chart
● USA PEAK CHART POSITION: 1

 495 **THE DIVISION BELL** (–) ▲
PINK FLOYD

At last, Gilmour and company rose majestically out of the sticky mire that had entrapped them and Roger Waters for years. It buried the ghost and enabled the new Floyd to be appraised separately, and, generally, very favourably. Gilmour had sharpened his singing almost to match his 'epic' guitar sound. 'What Do You Want From Me' had every necessary Floyd ingredient, without digging up the past. A cynic would analyze the lyrics of 'Poles Apart' and interpret them as a snide dig at Waters, if the reader so wanted, with lines such as 'why did we tell you then you were always the golden boy then'.

● TRACKS: *Cluster One; What Do You Want From Me; Poles Apart; Marooned; A Great Day For Freedom; Wearing The Inside Out; Take It Back; Coming Back To Life; Keep Talking; Lost For Words; High Hopes.*

● FIRST RELEASED 1994
● UK PEAK CHART POSITION: 1
● USA PEAK CHART POSITION: 1

 **496** **SCOTT 3** (–) ▲
SCOTT WALKER

Although it has been stated so many times, Scott Walker does have one of the greatest singing voices. Had he been born 30 years earlier he could have matched anything that Sinatra or Ella Fitzgerald attempted from the great American songbook. On this, the warm depth of the voice is complemented by the lush string arrangements, and tracks such as 'Rosemary' and 'Big Louise' are epic ballads of incredible maturity. The first 10 tracks are Engel originals and the last three are Jacques Brel poems. The latter artist provided an association that did much for Walker's credibility but little for his record sales. A beautifully comforting record.

● TRACKS: *It's Raining Today; Copenhagen; Rosemary; Big Louise; We Came Through; Butterfly; Two Ragged Soldiers; 30th Century Man; Winter Night; Two Weeks Since You've Gone; Sons Of; Funeral Tango; If You Go Away.*

● FIRST RELEASED 1969
● UK PEAK CHART POSITION: 3
● USA PEAK CHART POSITION: did not chart

497 SPIDERLAND (–) ▲
SLINT

Beloved of critics, ignored by the record-buying public, Slint stretched six tracks over 40 minutes and left an indelible impression on almost everyone. The songs on *Spiderland* evolve of their own accord, without reference to narrative structure. What at first glance appears meandering and prosaic ('For Dinner ...') becomes, on second and subsequent listenings, hypnotic, beatific and pan-dimensional. If Brian McMahon has a peer as alternative rock's most innovative guitarist it would have to be Steve Albini - who just happens to be the producer on *Spiderland*. The rear of the CD features the legend: 'This recording is meant to be listened to on vinyl', as if to ram home its left-field credentials. Whatever format you choose, *Spiderland* will not disappoint.

● TRACKS: *Breadcrumb Trail; Nosferatu Man; Don, Aman; Washer; For Dinner ...; Good Morning, Captain.*

● FIRST RELEASED 1990
● UK PEAK CHART POSITION: did not chart
● USA PEAK CHART POSITION: did not chart

498 GUITAR TOWN (–) ▲
STEVE EARLE

A much-loved album that is one of the key records in the development of 'new country'. The image of the immaculate, conservative, singing cowboy was completely ruined by Earle. He was bad, he loved substance abuse and he played loud, dirty, rock 'n' roll-laced country rock. Through all the past excess he has emerged a survivor, and is in reality the Bruce Springsteen of 'new country'. He sings of ordinary life and pick-up trucks instead of pink Cadillacs. 'Someday' highlights the perils of being trapped in a small town, with the last line giving some hope: 'someday I'll put her on that interstate and never look back'.

● TRACKS: *Guitar Town; Goodbye's All We've Got Left; Hillbilly Highway; Good Ol' Boy (Gettin' Tough); My Old Friend The Blues; Someday; Think It Over; Fearless Heart; Little Rock 'N' Roller; Down The Road; Good Ol' Boy (Gettin' Tough).*

● FIRST RELEASED 1986
● UK PEAK CHART POSITION: did not chart
● USA PEAK CHART POSITION: 89

499 THIS IS SOUL (142) ▼
VARIOUS

The finest sampler of soul music ever released, in terms of track selection (quite apart from the giveaway UK price of twelve shillings and sixpence), this record opened doors to the magnificent artists of Stax and Atlantic Records of the 60s. Every track could have topped the charts, and this album played end to end could still form the basis of any programme on soul music. Ben E King asks on one track 'what is soul?', the answer, as if you didn't know, is on this album. Only Aretha and Otis are missing from the original but thankfully added to the repackaged CD reissue.

● TRACKS: *Mustang Sally - Wilson Pickett; B-A-B-Y - Carla Thomas; Sweet Soul Music - Arthur Conley; When A Man Loves A Woman - Percy Sledge; I Got Everything I Need - Sam And Dave; What Is Soul? - Ben E. King; Fa Fa Fa Fa Fa (Sad Song) - Otis Redding; Knock On Wood - Eddie Floyd; Keep Looking - Solomon Burke; I Never Loved A Man (The Way I Love You) - Aretha Franklin; Warm And Tender Love - Percy Sledge; Land Of A Thousand Dances - Wilson Pickett.*

● FIRST RELEASED 1968
● UK PEAK CHART POSITION: 16
● USA PEAK CHART POSITION: 146

500 BAND ON THE RUN (311) ▼
WINGS

Paul McCartney's immediate solo career was largely viewed as lightweight. This album restated artistic strengths missing from earlier releases, reclaiming the artist's grasp of pop's dynamics and hooklines. From the pulsating abandonment of 'Jet' to the measured control of 'Let Me Roll It', *Band On The Run* is a tight, disciplined collection, full of contrast and commitment. McCartney's unfettered self-confidence permeates a selection that not only forced commentators to revise their views, but also asserted the singer's individual identity, rather than solely that of ex-Beatle.

● TRACKS: *Band On The Run; Jet; Bluebird; Mrs. Vandebilt; Let Me Roll It; Marmunia; No Words; Picasso's Last Words (Drink To Me); Nineteen Hundred And Eighty Five.*

● FIRST RELEASED 1973
● UK PEAK CHART POSITION: 1
● USA PEAK CHART POSITION: 1

501 **TRAFFIC** (146) ▼
TRAFFIC

On their second album the cottage dwellers from Berkshire refined their hippie pop into a looser and vastly mature work. Evocative tales of nonsense in the beautiful '40,000 Headmen', joyful malarkey with Mason's 'You Can All Join In' and one of his finest songs, 'Feelin Alright', which was a signpost to Mason's imminent departure. Throughout the record Capaldi's understated yet steady drums demonstrate just what a great rock drummer should do and Chris Wood's sound is everywhere, with trills on flute and blasts on saxophone. A record that will always be meant for glorious sunny days.

● TRACKS: *You Can All Join In; Pearly Queen; Don't Be Sad; Who Knows What Tomorrow May Bring; Feelin Alright; Vagabond Virgin; 40,000 Headmen; Cryin' To Be Heard; No Time To Live; Means To An End.*

● FIRST RELEASED 1968
● UK PEAK CHART POSITION: 9
● USA PEAK CHART POSITION: 17

502 **THE "CHIRPING" CRICKETS** (762) ▲
THE CRICKETS

Another great classic that failed to chart on both sides of the Atlantic; perhaps the name Crickets on the cover deterred purchasers who did not realize that this featured Mr Holly. The tracks speak for themselves, timeless pop-flavoured rock 'n' roll songs that still take some beating; 'Maybe Baby', 'That'll Be The Day' and 'Oh Boy' were the main hit singles, but the inclusion of 'Not Fade Away', 'It's Too late' and 'Send Me Some Lovin'' make this collection essential. The cover is a priceless timepiece from the days before real graphic designers were used, where a wonderful false sky has been dropped in behind four men who look like senior citizens, posing uncomfortably with guitars.

● TRACKS: *Oh Boy; Not Fade Away; You've Got Love; Maybe Baby; It's Too Late; Tell Me How; That'll Be The Day; I'm Looking For Someone To Love; An Empty Cup (And A Broken Date); Send Me Some Lovin'; Last Night; Rock Me My Baby.*

● FIRST RELEASED 1958
● UK PEAK CHART POSITION: did not chart
● USA PEAK CHART POSITION: did not chart

503 **THE CHRONIC** (–) ▲
DR DRE

The Chronic, you should be warned, has some of the most puerile lyrics ever to park their sorry ass (to use the vernacular) on vinyl. Yet it remains a high watermark recording in rap's turbulent history. Why? Because, musically, it works beautifully. Dr Dre is no rapper (he is helped out here by Snoop Doggy Dog). Instead he concentrates on what he's best at - engrossing, energized, multi-layered hip-hop. Pretty much the definitive soundtrack to the US urban environment of the early 90s, Dre's choppy soundclash mix-and-dash approach (and prodigious sampling of P-Funk era black music) founded a whole new genre, G-Funk. It also launched a few careers that should have been stillborn.

● TRACKS: *The Chronic (Intro); Wit Dre Day (And Everybody's Celebratin'); Let Me Ride; The Day The Niggaz Took Over; Nuthin' But A 'G' Thang; Deeez Nuuuts; Lil' Ghetto Boy; A Nigga Witta Gun; Rat-Tat-Tat-Tat; The $20 Sack Pyramid; Lyrical Gangbang; High Powered; The Doctor's Office; Stranded On Death Row; The Roach (The Chronic Outro).*

● FIRST RELEASED 1992
● UK PEAK CHART POSITION: did not chart
● USA PEAK CHART POSITION: did not chart

504 **TOUCH** (226) ▼
EURYTHMICS

This came at the end of 1983, a particularly prolific period for Stewart and Lennox - they had already spent most of the year in the chart with *Sweet Dreams*, released at the beginning of the year. This album shows less reliance on programmed instrumentation and a less 'Germanic' feel to the production. 'The First Cut' and 'Right By Your Side' indicate a loosening up and a more rootsy approach as Lennox discovers she has a great R&B/soul voice. 'Here Comes The Rain Again' and 'Who's That Girl?' exemplify the more familiar haunting Eurythmics sound.

● TRACKS: *Here Comes The Rain Again; Regrets; Right By Your Side; Cool Blue; Who's That Girl?; The First Cut; Aqua; No Fear, No Hate, No Pain (No Broken Hearts); Paint A Rumour.*

● FIRST RELEASED 1983
● UK PEAK CHART POSITION: 1
● USA PEAK CHART POSITION: 7

505 **STUTTER** (414) ▼
JAMES

Yet another product of Manchester's impressive scene, James offered this brash, folk-styled pop selection as their debut album following acclaimed singles for the Factory label. Produced by former Patti Smith Group guitarist Lenny Kaye, it opened with the eccentric 'Skullduggery' and proceeded in a quirky, unconventional manner. Complex arrangements and unorthodox lyrics abound, while vocalist Tim Booth accentuates the loose arrangements with highly stylized vocals that demand attention. An expanded line-up would gain commercial success with a very different sound, but *Stutter* captures James during their formative, experimental era.

● TRACKS: *Skullduggery; Scarecrow; So Many Ways; Just Hipper; John Yen; Summer Songs; Really Hard; Billy's Shirts; Why So Close; Withdrawn; Black Hole.*

● FIRST RELEASED 1986
● UK PEAK CHART POSITION: 68
● USA PEAK CHART POSITION: did not chart

---

 507 **JESUS OF COOL** (399) ▼
NICK LOWE

In America, presumably objecting to the title, they released this record with the title *Pure Pop For Now People*. In 1997, we 'now people' can continue to enjoy this little masterpiece. After serving his apprenticeship in Brinsley Schwarz, Lowe debuted during punk's heyday. He was fêted by the cognoscenti and his face regularly graced the pages of the UK music press. A 'surprise' hit single put Nick on *Top Of The Pops*, and the masses saw him only as the man who sang 'I Love The Sound of Breaking Glass'. It was a pity, because overlooked were gems such as 'So It Goes', 'Little Hitler' and the perceptive 'Music For Money'.

● TRACKS: *Music For Money; I Love The Sound Of Breaking Glass; Little Hitler; Shake And Pop; Tonight; So It Goes; No Reason; 36-inches High; Marie Provost; Nutted By Reality; Heart Of The City.*

● FIRST RELEASED 1978
● UK PEAK CHART POSITION: 22
● USA PEAK CHART POSITION: 127

---

 506 **MILESTONES** (158) ▼
MILES DAVIS

An album that has matured with age. Featuring the classic sextet with the personnel of Coltrane, Cannonball Adderley, Red Garland, Philly Joe Jones and Paul Chambers, it hints at what was to come with the phenomenal *Kind Of Blue* the following year. The modal jazz period was germinated here, particularly with 'Sid's Ahead', featuring one of Miles's finest solos, a tribute to late-night New York disc jockey Symphony Sid. Elsewhere the pace is swing and cool, with a unique drum sound on 'Billy Boy' and it closes with a superior reading of Monk's 'Straight No Chaser'.

● TRACKS: *Doctor Jekyll; Sid's Ahead; Two Bass Hits; Miles; Billy Boy; Straight No Chaser.*

● FIRST RELEASED 1958
● UK PEAK CHART POSITION: did not chart
● USA PEAK CHART POSITION: did not chart

---

 508 **ANIMALS** (–) ▲
PINK FLOYD

Equally famous for its ambitious cover, featuring the inflatable pig and Battersea Power station, *Animals* was a much more successful album than people now recall. Part of its invisibility is in not having a named single song. The album is divided into five parts and needs to be played as a whole; CD technology aids appreciation. 'Pigs (Three Different Ones)' is the most accessible song, even though the vitriolic lyrics aim to shock. UK censorship queen Mary Whitehouse comes in for some ridicule from Waters in the last verse. Among other things, she is described as a 'house proud town mouse'.

● TRACKS: *Pigs On The Wing 1; Dogs; Pigs (Three Different Ones); Sheep; Pigs On The Wing 2.*

● FIRST RELEASED 1992
● UK PEAK CHART POSITION: 2
● USA PEAK CHART POSITION: 3

509 **LONELY AT THE TOP** (458) ▼
RANDY NEWMAN

A criminally underrated man who has been writing poetical songs about American life for four decades. This is his greatest hits offering with the reality being that he only hit once with the misunderstood 'Short People'. Many of his early songs recorded by the likes of Dusty Springfield and Gene Pitney are still overlooked on this compilation, but we do have heartfelt ramblings and powerful understatements. To think that Newman can move us to tears of emotion with a lyric that merely states 'I think it's going to rain today' is remarkable. Please note the section 'did not chart'! Perhaps the next century will discover this man's genius.

● TRACKS: *Love Story; Living Without You; I Think It's Going To Rain Today; Mama Told Me Not To Come; Sail Away; Simon Smith And The Amazing Dancing Bear; Political Science; God's Song; Rednecks; Birmingham; Louisiana 1927; Marie; Baltimore; Jolly Coppers On Parade; Rider In The Rain; Short People; I Love L.A.; Lonely At The Top.*

● FIRST RELEASED 1987
● UK PEAK CHART POSITION: did not chart
● USA PEAK CHART POSITION: did not chart

 510 **PAWN HEARTS** (–) ▲
VAN DER GRAAF GENERATOR

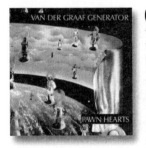

O f all the UK progressive bands of the late 60s, Van Der Graaf Generator is the one that is anathema to prog haters. Their name implies 'what on earth are you talking about', and the titles of some of their albums are equally as misleadingly pompous. This, however, is different; the title, for a start, is easy to remember. Prog stops and starts and has complicated time-changes and structures; this is prevalent on most tracks, which need an intelligent ear. The standard of musicianship is never in doubt; they weave and wander, but Banton, Evans and Jackson are a perfect foil to the eccentricities of Peter Hammil's alternative cosmos.

● TRACKS: *Lemmings (Including Cog); Man-Erg; A Plague Of Lighthouse Keepers; Eyewitness; Picture Lighthouse; Eyewitness; S.H.M.; Presence Of The Night; Kosmos Tours; (Custard's) Last Stand; The Clot Thickens; Land's End (Sineline); We Go Now.*

● FIRST RELEASED 1972
● UK PEAK CHART POSITION: did not chart
● USA PEAK CHART POSITION: did not chart

 511 **FIVE LIVE YARDBIRDS** (890) ▲
THE YARDBIRDS

F ew British Beat groups attempted in-concert recordings, but this proved a natural vehicle for the Yardbirds. One of the era's most popular live attractions, the set captures their exciting interpretation of British R&B. Their arrangements of blueswailing material by Howlin' Wolf, Bo Diddley and Slim Harpo are exceptional and their prowess as musicians is immediately self-evident. Keith Relf proves himself an accomplished harmonica player while Eric Clapton's guitarwork lays the foundation for his future recordings. Where many contemporaries struggled to complete wholly satisfying live albums, the Yardbirds did so with breath to spare.

● TRACKS: *Too Much Monkey Business; I Got Love If You Want It; Smokestack Lightning; Good Morning Little Schoolgirl; Respectable; Five Long Years; Pretty Girl; Louise; I'm A Man; Here 'Tis.*

● FIRST RELEASED 1964
● UK PEAK CHART POSITION: did not chart
● USA PEAK CHART POSITION: did not chart

 512 **JOHN BARLEYCORN MUST DIE** (–) ▲
TRAFFIC

T his was intended as the first Steve Winwood solo album following the stop-start-stop career of Traffic as a working unit. Capaldi and Wood were drafted in as session musicians. This logic sounds ridiculous now, as of course we always knew they would re-form. *Melody Maker* proclaimed 'TRAFFIC TO ROAR AGAIN'. The rest did them good, both physically and musically with two new Traffic standards added to their catalogue, the instrumental 'Glad' and 'Empty Pages'. The late Chris Wood was an exceptional flute player, never hogging the limelight. The subtlety of his playing excels on the title track. They held it together for four more years after this.

● TRACKS: *Glad; Freedom Rider; Empty Pages; Stranger To Himself; John Barleycorn; Every Mother's Son.*

● FIRST RELEASED 1970
● UK PEAK CHART POSITION: 11
● USA PEAK CHART POSITION: 5

513 **12 SONGS** (373) ▼
RANDY NEWMAN

Newman began his career as a contract songwriter, before embarking on a recording career renowned for sardonic wit. On this, his second album, the singer opted for simple accompaniment, his ragged voice and stylized piano supported largely by a crisp backing group that included Byrds guitarist Clarence White. Superb melodies were matched by an intense lyricism that embraced sometimes disquieting images previously unheard of in rock. Cynicism, bitterness and sexual perversion are unleashed in turn as Newman adopts different roles and personae. His dispassionate delivery demands decisions from the listener, an interaction that is as compulsive as it is disquieting.

● TRACKS: *Have You Seen My Baby?; Let's Burn Down The Cornfield; Mama Told Me Not To Come; Suzanne; Lover's Prayer; Lucinda; Underneath The Harlem Moon; Yellow Man; Old Kentucky Home; Rosemary; If You Need Oil; Uncle Bob's Midnight Blues.*

● FIRST RELEASED 1970
● UK PEAK CHART POSITION: did not chart
● USA PEAK CHART POSITION: did not chart

---

 514 **BIG HITS HIGH TIDE AND GREEN GRASS** (492) ▼ **THE ROLLING STONES**

Through The Past, Darkly was always the compilation to tuck under the arm, even though there is little to choose between the two records. This is slightly more bluesy. Mercifully the Stones are still with us and still trying to keep the critics happy after 35 controversial years . 'Hey you get offa mah cloud' in Jagger's worst Sidcup dialect still sounds magnificent, as does Brian's booming Vox pearl guitar on 'The Last Time' and Keef's opening chords to 'Not Fade Away'. To be handed down to your children as an important record from the 60s as the band who never went soft.

● TRACKS: *Have You Seen Your Mother, Baby, Standing In The Shadow; Paint It Black; It's All Over Now; The Last Time; Heart Of Stone; Not Fade Away; Come On; Satisfaction; Get Off My Cloud; As Tears Go By; 19th Nervous Breakdown; Lady Jane; Time Is On My Side; Little Red Rooster.*

● FIRST RELEASED 1966
● UK PEAK CHART POSITION: 4
● USA PEAK CHART POSITION: 3

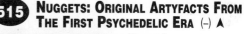 **515** **NUGGETS: ORIGINAL ARTYFACTS FROM THE FIRST PSYCHEDELIC ERA** (–) ▲
VARIOUS ARTISTS

A compilation that actually *defined* a genre, this sent out musical ripples that influenced innumerable bands, from the Damned to R.E.M. Compiler Lenny Kaye even gave the genre a name: punk. Although the music was later better known as 'garage', Kaye — himself about to pioneer 70s punk as Patti Smith's guitarist — was onto something when he asserted that America's aggressive teen bands of the mid-60s were the original punks. To prove that this was not an isolated, parochial movement, Kaye included not only Top 40 hits such as the Castaways' 'Liar, Liar' and the Count Five's 'Psychotic Reaction', but also buried treasures like the Remains' classic 'Don't Look Back' and the Chocolate Watch Band's 'Let's Talk About Girls'.

● TRACKS: *I Had Too Much To Dream (Last Night); Dirty Water; Night Time; Lies; Respect; A Public Execution; No Time Like The Right Time; Oh Yeah; Pushin' Too Hard; Moulty; Don't Look Back; Invitation To Cry; Liar, Liar; You're Gonna Miss Me; Psychotic Reaction; Hey Joe; Just Like Romeo And Juliet; Sugar And Spice; Baby Please Don't Go; Tobacco Road; Let's Talk About Girls; Sit Down I Think I Love You; Run Run Run; My World Fell Down; Open My Eyes; Farmer John; It's-A-Happening.*
● FIRST RELEASED: 1972
● UK PEAK CHART POSITION: did not chart
● USA PEAK CHART POSITION: did not chart

 **516** **DIVA** (154) ▼
ANNIE LENNOX

Nobody knew whether Annie Lennox could ever follow this outstanding solo debut; *Medusa* fell short of the mark. After contributing to the Tourists and being 50% of the Eurythmics she could be forgiven for getting writer's block, but no. This record is a credible work, Lennox' emotions pour forth in 'Why?', she reminds us to be wary on 'Walking On Broken Glass' and reaffirms the cliché on 'Money Can't Buy It'. While all this is going on, the listener can adore her talent, integrity and fantastic voice. She seems to have retired at the present time to a life of domesticity.

● TRACKS: *Why?; Walking On Broken Glass; Precious; Legend In My Living Room; Cold; Money Can't Buy It; Little Bird; Primitive; Stay By Me; Gift.*

● FIRST RELEASED 1992
● UK PEAK CHART POSITION: 1
● USA PEAK CHART POSITION: 23

517 CAN'T GET ENOUGH (–) ▲
BARRY WHITE

The man with the world's sexiest voice took a lot of flak, and was often parodied by those who were not soul disco fans. His fans thought differently, which made him one of the most successful acts of the 70s. For no apparent reason, in the 90s he suddenly became credible with the critics, and they were able fully to appreciate the quality of his Love Unlimited Orchestra, which gave substance to his supremely erotic songs of lurrve. The huge success of this album when first released was no fluke, and nearly 25 years later it holds up well against the new wave of smooth-talking soul singers.

● TRACKS: *Mellow Mood (Part 1); You're The First, The Last, My Everything; I Can't Believe You Love Me; Can't Get Enough Of Your Love, Babe; Oh Love, Well We Finally Made It; I Love You More Than Anything (In This World Girl); Mellow Mood (Part 2).*

● FIRST RELEASED 1974
● UK PEAK CHART POSITION: 4
● USA PEAK CHART POSITION: 1

518 COMPLETE BENNY GOODMAN VOLS. 1-7 (166) ▼ BENNY GOODMAN

Although there were jazzier bands than Goodman's, more musical and more creative bands, and bands that swung more, none had the popular and commercial appeal that his enjoyed for two or three glorious years in the 30s. After his breakthrough appearance at the Palomar Ballroom in Los Angeles on 21 August 1935, nothing could stop him. Labelled the 'King of Swing', Goodman offered the public what it wanted: punchy dance music, soloists like Harry James, magnetic showmen like Gene Krupa, and his own impeccable clarinet playing. The personnel was ever-changing thanks to Goodman's irascibility but the band thundered unmistakably on.

● TRACKS: *Including - He Ain't Got Rhythm; Never Should Have Told You; This Year's Kisses; You Can Tell She Comes From Dixie; Goodnight My Love; I Want To Be Happy; Chloe; Rosetta; Ida, Sweet As Apple Cider; Tea For Two; Runnin' Wild; Peckin'; Can't We Be Friends; Sing, Sing, Sing; Roll 'Em; When It's Sleepytime Down South; Afraid To Dream; Changes; Avalon; Handful Of Keys; The Man I Love; Smiles; Liza (All The Clouds Will Roll Away); Bob White; Sugarfoot Stomp; I Can't Give You Anything But Love Baby; Minnie The Moocher's Wedding Day; Let That Be A Lesson To You; Can't Teach My Old Heart New Tricks; I've Hitched My Wagon To A Star; Pop Corn Man.*
RECORDED 1935-39
● UK PEAK CHART POSITION: did not chart
● USA PEAK CHART POSITION: did not chart

519 STRANGER IN TOWN (175) ▼
BOB SEGER

Although this can be perceived as a dated album it is in the listings because of the importance it has in epitomizing American rock of the 70s. Seger had been around for some time, making his first record in 1965 and treading the boards, and must have found it mildly amusing to have such a colossal hit on his hands. As Seger was around first it is insulting to say he sounds like Springsteen, both in voice and in melody, but he does. 'Still The Same' still makes you melt and 'We've Got Tonight' is for those grown-up, macho, hopeless romantics who like motorbikes, but don't necessarily like getting on them.

● TRACKS: *Stranger In Town; Hollywood Nights; Still The Same; Old Time Rock 'n' Roll; Till It Shines; Feels Like A Number; Ain't Got No Money; We've Got Tonight; Brave Strangers; The Famous Final Scene.*

● FIRST RELEASED 1978
● UK PEAK CHART POSITION: 31
● USA PEAK CHART POSITION: 4

520 BODY AND SOUL (161) ▼
COLEMAN HAWKINS

The high regard this album still manages to command is enhanced by its having one of the most beautiful interpretations of the title track. Hawkins did not write it, but embossed his own soul into it, and by rights he should own it. However he played it, however or wherever it was recorded, the sparse breathy tone is, well, breathtaking. Without wishing to denigrate the other tracks on this record the title track remains as important as *Kind Of Blue* in assembling a record collection. Beautifully preserved from 10-inch disc and recorded in 1939, also contained is the 1956 recording, where you can hear the subtle click of the saxophone keys.

● TRACKS: *Meet Doctor Foo; Fine Dinner; She's Funny That Way; Body And Soul; When Day Is Done; The Sheik Of Araby; My Blue Heaven; Bouncing With Bean; Say It Isn't So; Spotlight; April In Paris; How Strange; Half Step Down Please; Jumping For Jane; I Love You; There Will Never Be Another You; Little Girl Blue; Dinner For One, Please James; I Never Knew; His Very Own Blues; Thirty Nine Inches; Bean Stalks Again; I'm Shooting High; Have You Met Miss Jones?; The Day You Came Along; The Essence Of You.*
● FIRST RELEASED 1958
● UK PEAK CHART POSITION: did not chart
● USA PEAK CHART POSITION: did not chart

521 **YOUNG AMERICANS** (260) ▼
DAVID BOWIE

David Bowie abandoned the glam/sci-fi personae of *Ziggy Stardust*, *Aladdin Sane* and *Diamond Dogs* with this radical departure. Recorded at Sigma Sound Studios, the home of Philadelphia International, it featured the label's crack house band and, as a result, confirmed the singer's growing love of soul and R&B. Pulsating dance grooves abound, in particular on the disco-influenced 'Fame', which topped the US singles chart. The song was co-written with John Lennon, a compliment Bowie repaid by reinventing the Beatles' 'Across The Universe' as a dancefloor classic. Such self-confidence abounds throughout this album which shows the singer firmly in command of yet another musical direction.

● TRACKS: *Young Americans; Win; Fascination; Right; Somebody Up There Likes Me; Across The Universe; Can You Hear Me; Fame.*

● FIRST RELEASED 1975
● UK PEAK CHART POSITION: 2
● USA PEAK CHART POSITION: 9

 523 **NEW MISERABLE EXPERIENCE** (–) ▲
GIN BLOSSOMS

This album stands as a sad memorial to Doug Hopkins' ability to craft winning songs out of the abject misery of his own life. Hopkins had been thrown out of the band he formed before *New Miserable Experience* was released, and by the time 'Hey Jealousy' and 'Found About You', two of his most engaging and self-deprecatory songs, had broken the band in America, he had taken his own life in a fit of depression. The album is not entirely about Hopkins (Jesse Valenzuela's 'Mrs Rita' and Robin Wilson's 'Allison Road' are also strong contenders), but it is his songs that remain longest in the memory.

● TRACKS: *Lost Horizons; Hey Jealousy; Mrs Rita; Until I Fall Away; Hold Me Down; Cajun Song; Hands Are Tied; Found About You; Allison Road; 29; Pieces Of The Night; Cheatin'.*

● FIRST RELEASED 1992
● UK PEAK CHART POSITION: 53
● USA PEAK CHART POSITION: 30

 522 **DIRE STRAITS** (286) ▼
DIRE STRAITS

They do look happy and innocent on the back of the sleeve, blissfully unaware of the mantle they would be thrown and of the millions of fans they would be expected to please. This, for many, is the only Dire Straits album to own, yet it sold only moderately and was dwarfed by *Brothers*. Knopfler sounded like he meant it on 'Sultans Of Swing' and who can forget the cheek of his lyric in the melancholic 'Wild West End'? 'I saw you walking out Shaftesbury Avenue, excuse me talking, I wanna marry you'. I hope Mark Knopfler has not forgotten this album.

● TRACKS: *Down To The Waterline; Water Of Love; Setting Me Up; Six Blade Knife; Southbound Again; Sultans Of Swing; In The Gallery; Wild West End; Lions.*

● FIRST RELEASED 1978
● UK PEAK CHART POSITION: 5
● USA PEAK CHART POSITION: 2

 524 **INGÉNUE** (360) ▼
K.D. LANG

Emerging from her ambivalent affair with country music, lang assembled a solid collection of material for this, her most commercially successful album. The opening lines: 'Save me/Save me from you/But pave me/The way to you', introduce a recurring theme - the agonizing conflict between the pain and the ecstasy of love. This is serious stuff; anthems of introspection and cries for honesty illuminated with startling imagery. There are lighter moments too, particularly in 'Miss Chatelaine', and the omnipresent Ben Mink ensures that the country influence is not totally abandoned. This will always be her best album, no matter how hard she tries.

● TRACKS: *Save Me; The Mind Of Love; Miss Chatelaine; Wash Me Clean; So It Shall Be; Still Thrives This Love; Season Of Hollow Soul; Outside Myself; Tears Of Love Is Recall; Constant Craving.*

● FIRST RELEASED 1992
● UK PEAK CHART POSITION: 3
● USA PEAK CHART POSITION: 18

525 METAL BOX (767) ▲
PiL

Determined to dispel musical preconceptions, former Sex Pistols singer Johnny Rotten undertook a radical path with his next venture. On *Metal Box* he unleashed a torrent of vocal styles, alternately pleading, moaning or wailing over a sound drawn equally from Jamaican dub or German experimentalists Can. Bassist Jah Wobble provides the fluid skeleton with throbbing, sinewy lines and patterns, while Keith Levene adds instinctive flourishes on both guitar and keyboards. Impressionistic rather than defined, the material owes its strength to the quartet's determination to challenge and their disavowal of compromise.

● TRACKS: *Albatross; Memories; Swan Lake; Poptones; Careeing; No Birds; Graveyard; The Suit; Bad Baby; Socialist; Chant; Radio 4.*

● FIRST RELEASED 1978
● UK PEAK CHART POSITION: 22
● USA PEAK CHART POSITION: did not chart

526 NO MORE HEROES (569) ▲
THE STRANGLERS

Punk's parents terribles, the Stranglers courted controversy throughout their early career. Caustic lyrics brought charges of misogyny, although the group suggested that outrage was merely part of the genre's tenet. They answered such criticism of their debut album with the even more uncompromising *No More Heroes*, a vengeful collection echoing the nihilism of its title. Role-playing apart, there was no denying a musical prowess compressing savage guitar, throbbing bass and swirling organ into vicious, driving sound. Hugh Cornwell's sneering intonation matched the aggression of his accompaniment, but the album also offered indications of the lighter pop style that the quartet would later follow.

● TRACKS: *I Feel Like A Wog; Bitching; Dead Ringer; Dagenham Dave; Bring On The Nubiles; Something Better Change; No More Heroes; Peasant In The Big Shitty; Burning Up Time; English Towns; School Mam; In The Shadows.*

● FIRST RELEASED 1977
● UK PEAK CHART POSITION: 2
● USA PEAK CHART POSITION: did not chart

527 TIM HARDIN 2 (407) ▼
TIM HARDIN

Tim Hardin's beguiling brand of jazz/folk, unveiled on his debut album, is equally prevalent on its follow-up. Although many of its songs last less than two minutes, they each possess a resonant beauty enhanced by the singer's smoky intonation. Always an introspective composer, Hardin takes the opportunity to extol pleasures discovered through family life, and few writers can expose such emotions without resorting to cliché. Sweet melodies and tinkling accompaniment reinforce the songs' fragility, underscoring the aura of gracefulness Hardin's best work generates. The CD reissue couples *Tim Hardin 1* as a bonus, making this essential listening.

● TRACKS: *Don't Make Promises; Green Rocky Road; Smugglin' Man; How Long; While You're On Your Way; It'll Never Happen Again; Reason To Believe; Never Too Far; Part Of The Wind; Ain't Gonna Do Without; Misty Roses; How Can We Hang On To A Dream; If I Were A Carpenter; Red Balloon; Black Sheep Boy; Lady Came From Baltimore; Baby Close It's Eyes; You Upset The Grace Of Living When You Lie; Speak Like A Child; See Where You Are And Get Out; It's Hard To Believe In Love For Long; Tribute To Hank Williams.*

● FIRST RELEASED 1967
● UK PEAK CHART POSITION: did not chart
● USA PEAK CHART POSITION: did not chart

528 DAMN THE TORPEDOES (172) ▼
TOM PETTY AND THE HEARTBREAKERS

It is encouraging to note that in compiling the superlative recent *Greatest Hits*, four tracks from this blinder of an album are included, more than from any of his others. This is the ideal starting point for Petty students, (and then you can acquire all his other albums). For those unfamiliar, he is a rock 'n' roll Roger McGuinn. Those who are already aware of him will know that he has the knack of writing some of the best middle eight hooks ever heard, plays a Rickenbacker, and that he has an addictive voice and a knock-out supporting band. Is that enough?

● TRACKS: *Refugee; Here Comes The Girl; Even The Losers; Century City; Don't Do Me Like That; What Are You Doin' In My Life?; Louisiana Rain.*

● FIRST RELEASED 1979
● UK PEAK CHART POSITION: 57
● USA PEAK CHART POSITION: 2

529 **WOODSTOCK** (165) ▼
VARIOUS

This album stands as the best live rock festival soundtrack. The story behind the festival is well known but the suggestion by Atco's marketing man, Johnny Bienstock, that 'you should put it out as a triple' was brave and bold. It worked of course, and thankfully the CD allows us to listen instead of changing sides. The best moments are here; Santana, 'Evil Ways', John Sebastian charming the crowd and the cataclysmic Joe Cocker with his stunning 'With A Little Help From My Friends'. Even the warts and all Crosby, Stills And Nash material is somehow charming, especially hearing that they were 'scared shitless'.

● TRACKS: *At The Hop; Coming Into Los Angeles; Dance To The Music; Drug Store Truck Drivin' Man; The Fish Cheer (medley); Freedom; Going Up The Country; I-Feel-Like-I'm-Fixin'-To-Die Rag (medley); I Had A Dream; I Want To Take You Higher; I'm Going Home; Joe Hill; Love March; Music Lover (medley); Purple Haze (medley); Rainbows All Over Your Blues; Rock And Soul Music; Sea Of Madness; Soul Sacrifice; Star Spangled Banner (medley); Suite: Judy Blue Eyes; Wooden Ships; We're Not Gonna Take It; With A Little Help From My Friends; Crowd Rain Chant; Volunteers.*

● FIRST RELEASED 1970
● UK PEAK CHART POSITION: 35 ● USA PEAK CHART POSITION: 1

 530 **TRES HOMBRES** (–) ▲
ZZ TOP

Few bands have endeared themselves to the public by maintaining a sound that has barely changed over a quarter of a century. ZZ Top didn't even bother to trim their beards. Even the Rolling Stones changed, even the Bee Gees changed, even Genesis. ZZ Top have been successfully stubborn, they have merely refined, as more recording tracks have become available in the studio. This is a superb heavy rock/boogie album, better than most of the competition in 1973, and because of their refusal to change, it sounds great in the 90s. Try this in addition to *Eliminator*.

● TRACKS: *Waitin' For The Bus; Jesus Just Left Chicago; Beer Drinkers & Hell Raisers; Master Of Sparks; Hot, Blue And Righteous; Move Me On Down The Line; Precious And Grace; La Grange; Shiek; Have You Heard.*

● FIRST RELEASED 1973
● UK PEAK CHART POSITION: did not chart
● USA PEAK CHART POSITION: 8

 531 **ENDLESS SUMMER** (542) ▲
THE BEACH BOYS

Just as everybody had written off the Beach Boys as *passé*, we were reminded of the colossal contribution that Brian Wilson had made to popular music with this inspired compilation. New Beach Boys albums were selling badly at the time of this release, and then somebody had the idea of packaging this superb collection of surf and car songs that reeked of sand, sea, sun and innocence. There is something special about 'catching a wave and you're sitting on top of the world', even though most followers have never been near a surfboard in their lives, let alone a clean beach.

● TRACKS: *Surfin' Safari; Surfer Girl; Catch A Wave; Warmth Of The Sun; Surfin' USA; Be True To Your School; Little Deuce Coup; In My Room; Shut Down; Fun Fun Fun; I Get Around; Girls On The Beach; Wendy; Let Him Run Wild; Don't Worry Baby; California Girls; Girl Don't Tell Me; Help Me Rhonda; You're So Good To Me; All Summer Long; Good Vibrations.*

● FIRST RELEASED 1974
● UK PEAK CHART POSITION: did not chart
● USA PEAK CHART POSITION: 1

532 **STAGE FRIGHT** (230) ▼
THE BAND

The third Band album reflected their trans-formation from studio ensemble to live act. Several selections, notably the title track, articulated the disquiet this engendered. The set still offered the quintet's mesmerizing cross-section of American music - soul, country R&B and pop - but where previous releases took a largely historical perspective, this collection brought together the past and present. Thus, the ribald, carnival atmosphere of 'W.S. Walcott Medicine Show' is set against 'The Rumor', in which songwriter Robbie Robertson sculpts a chilling portrait of the Nixon era. This ambitious panorama yielded a pivotal early 70s release.

● TRACKS: *Strawberry Wine; Sleeping; Time To Kill; Just Another Whistle Stop; All La Glory; The Shape I'm In; W.S. Walcott Medicine Show; Daniel And The Sacred Harp; Stage Fright; The Rumor.*

● FIRST RELEASED 1970
● UK PEAK CHART POSITION: 15
● USA PEAK CHART POSITION: 5

533 PETER GREEN'S FLEETWOOD MAC
(880) ▲ FLEETWOOD MAC

Now known as the 'dustbin' album, after its evocative cover, it is hard to believe that such an out-and-out blues album could have remained in the album charts for almost a year; but that is what this one achieved. The blues was on the crest of a wave in 1968; Eric Clapton had left John Mayall for Cream, but never really lost sight of the blues, and his successor, Peter Green, put together his ideal band with John McVie and Mick Fleetwood. Completing the band was the diminutive slide guitarist Jeremy Spencer. The album reflected their live appearances, with the 12 tracks shared between the two vocalists. At this remove, it is plain that Spencer's Elmore James imitations, while uncannily accurate, would quickly date. What has not dated are the sensitive songwriting and performances by the most accomplished blues guitarist this country has ever produced.

● TRACKS: My Heart Beat Like A Hammer; Merry Go Round; Long Grey Mare; Shake Your Moneymaker; Looking For Somebody; No Place To Go; My Baby's Good To Me; I Loved Another Woman; Cold Black Night; The World Keep On Turning; Got To Move.

● FIRST RELEASED 1968
● UK PEAK CHART POSITION: 4
● USA PEAK CHART POSITION: 198

534 DON'T SHOOT ME I'M ONLY THE PIANO PLAYER (182) ▼ ELTON JOHN

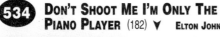

In writing reviews it is impossible to refer to this artist as John; it fits for some, but this subject has to be Elton, which immediately endears him to the public. He is one of the best-liked personalities in the music business, not tolerant of fools. This album, more than any, makes him loved, with the happiness/sadness of 'Daniel', to which we can relate, and the nostalgic sentiments of 'Teacher I Need You'. He rocks out and induces warmth with the irritatingly catchy 'Crocodile Rock' (we hate to love it), and on and on with 'Elderberry Wine'. Elton is generally seen as a good bloke, a view that sometimes clouds his huge talent as a musician and a music-lover.

● TRACKS: Daniel; Teacher I Need You; Elderberry Wine; Blues For My Baby And Me; Midnight Creeper; Have Mercy On The Criminal; I'm Going To Be A Teenage Idol; Texan Love Song; Crocodile Rock; High Flying Bird.

● FIRST RELEASED 1973
● UK PEAK CHART POSITION: 1
● USA PEAK CHART POSITION: 1

535 JOHNNY CASH AT FOLSOM PRISON
(604) ▲ JOHNNY CASH

Appearing at Glastonbury in 1994, it was clear that Johnny Cash has become an icon for the current generation. One reason is his alleged background of crime, although, in reality, Cash has only spent three days in jail - one of them for picking flowers. He is more like an old-time preacher, often finding his audiences in prisons. This classic album, which he had wanted to make for some years, brought out the best in his music. The audience is lively and quite unlike audiences anywhere else - listen to the applause when he sings, 'I shot a man in Reno just to watch him die.' There is the gallows humour of 'Twenty-Five Minutes To Go', the whimsy of 'Dirty Old Egg-Sucking Dog', a song written by one of the prisoners, 'Greystone Chapel', and a duet of 'Jackson' with June Carter. But the real star of the record is the audience: other albums have been recorded in prisons, and Johnny Cash has recorded in other prisons, but this album is special.

● TRACKS: Folsom Prison Blues; Dark As A Dungeon; I Still Miss Someone; Cocaine Blues; 25 Minutes To Go; Orange Blossom Special; The Long Black Veil; Send A Picture Of Mother; The Wall; Dirty Old Egg-Sucking Dog; Flushed From The Bathroom Of Your Heart; Jackson; Give My Love To Rose; I Got Stripes; Green Green Grass Of Home; Greystone Chapel.

● FIRST RELEASED 1968
● UK PEAK CHART POSITION: 8 ● USA PEAK CHART POSITION: 13

536 FABULOUS (185) ▼
LITTLE RICHARD

Little Richard's third album captured a singer building on his acknowledged style. He had forged a reputation based on undiluted R&B, typified on such expressive recordings as 'Tutti Frutti', 'Long Tall Sally' and 'Good Golly Miss Molly'. The Fabulous offered a wider musical perspective, although there was no denying the frantic fervour surrounding his versions of 'Kansas City' and 'Whole Lotta Shakin' Goin' On'. Such performances contrast with the more conciliatory 'Directly From My Heart', but the opportunity to broaden musical horizons suggested by this set was never fully taken up. In 1957 Richard denounced his work and joined the church, but although he later reversed that decision, this album closes his most creative period.

● TRACKS: Shake A Hand; Chicken Little Baby; All Night Long; The Most I Can Offer; Lonesome And Blue; Wonderin'; Whole Lotta Shakin' Goin' On; She Knows How To Rock; Kansas City; Directly From My Heart; Maybe I'm Right; Early One Morning; I'm Just A Lonely Guy.

● FIRST RELEASED 1958
● UK PEAK CHART POSITION: did not chart
● USA PEAK CHART POSITION: did not chart

537 **COUNTRY LIFE** (–) ▲
ROXY MUSIC

The sleeve proclaims 'the fourth Roxy Music album' and although it is the poor relative to the famous three, there is enough substance to merit a place in any collection. Guitarist Phil Manzanera is particularly inspired throughout; listen to his solo on 'Out Of the Blue'. Ferry makes his mark with expert delivery on the hit single 'All I Want Is You' and the heavily germanic 'Bitter Sweet'. The closing track is 'Prairie Rose', leaving one to ponder where do they go from here? Ferry could have been Englebert Humperdinck if he had not got into such a funk groove in his later albums.

● TRACKS: *The Thrill Of It All; Three And Nine; All I Want Is You; Out Of The Blue; If It Takes All Night; Bitter-Sweet; Triptych; Casanova; A Really Good Time; Prairie Rose.*

● FIRST RELEASED 1974
● UK PEAK CHART POSITION: 3
● USA PEAK CHART POSITION: 37

 538 **THE MAN AND HIS MUSIC** (514) ▼
SAM COOKE

Although Cooke never made an individually great album, this collection demonstrates his enormous catalogue of sweet soul music. The age of CD gave us this selection which is unbeatable in choice, ranging from his early days of gospel right through to the period before he was tragically killed. The fresh-faced man on the cover looks exactly as you imagine his music to sound; his voice was like cream in coffee. Most of the songs have been covered dozens of time by artists such as Cat Stevens, Rod Stewart, Aretha Franklin, Steve Miller and Otis Redding, but none has succeeded in interpreting any Cooke song as anything more than a humble tribute. Rod Stewart would be the first to admit this.

● TRACKS: *Touch The Hem Of His Garment; That's Heaven To Me; I'll Come Running Back To You; You Send Me; Win Your Love For Me; Just For You; Chain Gang; When A Boy Falls In Love; Only Sixteen; Wonderful World; Cupid; Nothing Can Change This Love; Rome Wasn't Built In A Day; Love Will Find Away; Everybody Loves To Cha Cha Cha; Another Saturday Night; Meet Me At Mary's Place; Having A Party; Good Times; Twistin' The Night Away; Shake; Somebody Have Mercy; Sad Mood; Ain't That Good News; Bring It On Home To Me; Soothe Me; That's Where It's At; A Change Is Gonna Come.*

● FIRST RELEASED 1986
● UK PEAK CHART POSITION: 8 ● USA PEAK CHART POSITION: 175

 539 **KINGS OF THE WILD FRONTIER** (–) ▲
ADAM AND THE ANTS

Adam succeeded in the pop charts with style as much as music. He rode the crest of some kind of post-punk new wave. His brand of pop leaned heavily on the drumming and chanting of African artists such as Barundi Black and was mostly highly original. 'Dog Eat Dog' and 'Antmusic' are two good examples of his genre. Tracks such as 'Feed Me To The Lions' are regular-sounding and, as such, fall short. The title track was the main hit, but spare a thought for the profound 'The Magnificent Five', with its opening lyric: 'long ago in London town, a man called Ant sat deeply sighing'.

● TRACKS: *Dog Eat Dog; Antmusic; Feed Me To The Lions; Los Rancheros; Ants Invasion; Killer In The Home; Kings Of The Wild Frontier; The Magnificent Five; Don't Be Square (Be There); Jolly Roger; Making History; The Human Beings.*

● FIRST RELEASED 1980
● UK PEAK CHART POSITION: 1
● USA PEAK CHART POSITION: 44

 540 **HEAVEN UP HERE** (589) ▲
ECHO AND THE BUNNYMEN

On their debut album this Liverpool quartet unveiled a sound crossing post-punk with psychedelic pop. Rather than repeat the formula, the group teased out the constituent parts of their sound to create *Heaven Up Here*. Alternately dreamlike and melancholically fragile, the set is marked by Ian McCulloch's arresting vocals which sweep across the textured sound with awesome confidence. The album exudes a cumulative power, building in atmosphere as it progresses, with Will Sergeant's plangent guitar emphasizing and supporting the drift of the singer's nuances. It is the final icing on an exquisite collection.

● TRACKS: *Show Of Strength; With A Hip; Over The Wall; It Was A Pleasure; A Promise; Heaven Up Here; The Disease; All My Colours; No Dark Things; Turquoise Days; All I Want.*

● FIRST RELEASED 1981
● UK PEAK CHART POSITION: 10
● USA PEAK CHART POSITION: 184

541 PIECE OF MIND (447) ▼
IRON MAIDEN

That nice little chap in the padded cell on the cover of this spunky album is clearly distressed by what is contained within. He should not be worried: it is first division metal, with the now departed Bruce Dickinson sounding in dynamic control. The CD version has the lead guitar strangely muted in the mix; this is especially noticeable on the driving 'Flight Of Icarus'. The twin guitars of Dave Murray and Adrian Smith blend together magnificently on 'The Trooper'. Sales of this album were boosted by crediting hundreds of people on the CD sleeve, including their many loyal early followers from east London.

● TRACKS: *Where Eagles Dare; Revelations; Flight Of Icarus; Die With Your Boots On; The Trooper; Still Life; Quest For Fire; Sun And Steel; To Tame A Land.*

● FIRST RELEASED 1983
● UK PEAK CHART POSITION: 3
● USA PEAK CHART POSITION: 14

542 THE DREAMING (–) ▲
KATE BUSH

Before *The Dreaming* Bush had released three eccentric but likeable albums, yet was still widely seen as a mainstream pop artist. Writing with the aid of a drum machine and producing herself for the first time, Bush let her imagination run wild with this album's dense, convoluted arrangements, premiered by the defiantly uncommercial single 'Sat In Your Lap'. Lyrically she shed her kooky teen image with songs inspired by Vietnam ('Pull Out The Pin'), Aboriginal culture ('The Dreaming') and film ('Get Out Of My House'). Even though it was a commercial failure, *The Dreaming* was a blueprint album for other studio-based artists in the 80s.

● TRACKS: *Sat In Your Lap; There Goes A Tenner; Pull Out The Pin; Suspended In Gaffa; Leave It Open; The Dreaming; Night Of The Swallow; All The Love; Houdini; Get Out Of My House.*

● FIRST RELEASED 1982
● UK PEAK CHART POSITION: 3
● USA PEAK CHART POSITION: 157

543 DIZZY HEIGHTS (–) ▲
LIGHTNING SEEDS

This album is one of those pop records that has something memorable in every track. Ian Broudie has the combined talent of pop eccentrics such as Andy Partridge and Paddy McAloon. However, the feeling is that the last two write great songs for themselves, whereas Broudie writes for a pop audience, with elements of Beach Boys, Beatles and late 60s summer fun songs mastered by writers like John Carter. It would be the ultimate treat to be able to read the lyrics supplied, but the typographic designer decided to make this just impossible. Fortunately, while we curse the CD sleeve, we still have our ears.

● TRACKS: *Imaginary Friends; You Bet Your Life; Waiting For Today To Happen; What If; Sugar Coated Iceberg; Touch And Go; Like You Do; Wishaway; Fingers And Thumbs; You Showed Me; Ready Or Not; Fish On The Line.*

● FIRST RELEASED 1996
● UK PEAK CHART POSITION: 11
● USA PEAK CHART POSITION: did not chart

544 EROTICA (–) ▲
MADONNA

She set out to shock and outrage and she absolutely succeeded. She pushed the obscenity law to the limit, with the stage act and with the photographs in the book that was published at the same time. The music, however, was pretty tame and was mainly innuendo, and nowhere near as overtly sexual as, say, Jen Tryin or PJ Harvey. *Erotica* succeeded when combined with Madonna's blush-inducing live show. Her version of Peggy Lee's classic 'Fever' is warm compared to the original breathy version, but the remaining material is highly charged disco pop. 'Where Life Begins' does challenge the listener to 'go down where it's warm inside', but the songs succeed on their own, without the contrived sex.

● TRACKS: *Erotica; Fever; Bye Bye Baby; Deeper And Deeper; Where Life Begins; Bad Girl; Waiting; Thief Of Hearts; Words; Rain; Why's It So Hard; In This Life; Secret Garden.*

● FIRST RELEASED 1992
● UK PEAK CHART POSITION: 2
● USA PEAK CHART POSITION: 2

545 KICK OUT THE JAMS (816) ▲
THE MC5

A true explosion of a record. Unfeasibly heady in its approach and delivery, it still stands today as one of the great, unabashed roars of bare, musical energy. Vocalist Rob Tyner crawls from a whisper to a scream, the tunnel of sound constructed around him both desperate and admirable. The title track is a manifestation of sound threatening to stumble and fall in on itself, and on the simply great 'Motor City Is Burning', the appropriately monikered guitarist, Fred 'Sonic' Smith, proves the power of his well-chosen nickname. Meanwhile, the eager sentiment of 'I Want You Right Now' speaks volumes about the tone of the album. One that will blow away your speaker covers, if you have not already removed them by now.

● TRACKS: *Ramblin' Rose; Kick Out The Jams; Come Together; Rocket Reducer No. 62 (Rama Lama Fa Fa Fa); Borderline; Motor City Is Burning; I Want You Right Now; Starship.*

● FIRST RELEASED 1969
● UK PEAK CHART POSITION: did not chart
● USA PEAK CHART POSITION: 30

546 ACE OF SPADES (614) ▲
MOTÖRHEAD

F êted by bikers, respected by punks, Motörhead exemplified rock's outlaw chic. On *Ace Of Spades* their speed-metal attack exploded with unparalleled fury. Thrashing guitars and primitive drums underpinned vocalist/bassist Lemmy, whose blooded-throat roar enhances the trio's aggression. Mind-numbingly basic and deafeningly loud, they savage rock's pomp and circumstance, rivalling 'Louie Louie' for simplicity and excitement. Chock-full of anthems for the dispossessed (witness '(We Are) The Road Crew'), *Ace Of Spades* is a classic of its genre. Motörhead exude the same cartoon personae as the Ramones, and as a result inspire a similar affection.

● TRACKS: *Ace Of Spades; Bite The Bullet; The Chase Is Better Than The Catch; Dance; Fast And Loose; Fire Fire; The Hammer; Jailbait; Live To Win; Love Me Like A Reptile; (We Are) The Road Crew; Shoot You In The Back.*

● FIRST RELEASED 1980
● UK PEAK CHART POSITION: 4
● USA PEAK CHART POSITION: did not chart

547 WELD (574) ▲
NEIL YOUNG AND CRAZY HORSE

Y oung hit yet another peak in the 90s and this blisteringly distorted album was the best. He out-grunges everybody with Crazy Horse, the best support band in the world (ask Ian McNabb). 'Cortez The Killer' is given new life, as is his gentle rocker 'Cinnamon Girl' from 1968. The excitement level of the double set is extraordinary as the gut-wrenching volume of playing fails to irritate - it only ignites the soul for more. The low point is the overlong and ponderous 'Farmer John', which should be left with the Searchers.

● TRACKS: *Hey Hey, My My (Into The Black); Crime In The City; Blowin' In The Wind; Welfare Mothers; Love To Burn; Cinnamon Girl; Mansion On The Hill; F*!#In' Up; Cortez The Killer; Powderfinger; Love And Only Love; Rockin' In The Free World; Like A Hurricane; Farmer John; Tonight's The Night; Roll Another Number.*

● FIRST RELEASED 1991
● UK PEAK CHART POSITION: 20
● USA PEAK CHART POSITION: 154

548 LET IT BE (–) ▲
REPLACEMENTS

T he Replacements were one of America's greatest bands of the 80s, irrespective of genre, though they received thin acknowledgement outside of informed critics during their lifetime. *Let It Be* demonstrates why they drove fans to devotion and critics to supplication. It was 1984, and the Replacements had left behind their sonic links to the Minneapolis punk scene. In particular, Paul Westerberg's songs had lost the timerity of old and he was increasingly willing to tackle subjects head on - 'Unsatisfied' is arguably the best song he ever wrote. However profundity aside, there is also a huge sense of fun about *Let It Be*, and even throwaway material like 'Gary's Got A Boner', and their cover of Kiss's 'Black Diamond', is enormous fun.

● TRACKS: *I Will Dare; Favorite Thing; We're Comin' Out; Tommy Gets His Tonsils Out; Androgynous; Black Diamond; Unsatisfied; Seen Your Video; Gary's Got A Boner; Sixteen Blue; Answering Machine.*

● FIRST RELEASED 1984
● UK PEAK CHART POSITION: did not chart
● USA PEAK CHART POSITION: did not chart

549 PERMANENT WAVES (–) ▲
RUSH

Falling somewhere in between heavy metal and AOR, Rush were one of the success stories of the period from 1976 to 1986 - all the more surprising because few Canadians manage to break out from the land of the maple leaf in this area of music. Much of their following idolized Alex Lifeson, who was a guitar hero with the technical ability of a Page or a Beck. Occasionally Neil Peart's lyrics leave a little to be desired: 'the shifting shafts of shining, weave the fabric of their dreams . . .' Jon Anderson from Yes was afflicted with the same condition of pretentiolyricitus. That aside, the music is faultless.

● TRACKS: *The Spirit Of Radio; Freewill; Jacob's Ladder; Entre Nous; Different Strings; Natural Science.*

● FIRST RELEASED 1980
● UK PEAK CHART POSITION: 3
● USA PEAK CHART POSITION: 4

551 SPIDERS (–) ▲
SPACE

Irritatingly infectious, the rumba-influenced pace of 'The Female Of The Species' or the contrived Steve Harley vocal on 'Neighbourhood' were singles that captured the ears. Space used imaginative arrangements for their sometimes strange pop. How they avoided litigation from the former UK Prime Minister John Major is a miracle. In 'Major Pager' they accuse a Mr. Major of selling Es to the Russians and state that he lied and took a wager. Obviously another Mr. Major. At least the Charlie Manson they sing about in 'Charlie M' is safely under lock and key. Interesting stuff, especially the charming concept of 'Me And You Vs The World'.

● TRACKS: *Neighbourhood; Mister Psycho; Female Of The Species; Money; Me And You Vs The World; Lovechild Of The Queen; No-One Understands; Voodoo Roller; Drop Dead; Dark Clouds; Major Pager; Kill Me; Charlie M; Growler.*

● FIRST RELEASED 1993
● UK PEAK CHART POSITION: 5
● USA PEAK CHART POSITION: did not chart

550 CLUB CLASSICS VOL. ONE (–) ▲
SOUL II SOUL

Where previous British translations of classic US black music styles had been hit and miss affairs, Jazzie B revolutionised contemporary soul music on both sides of the channel with the sublime (and occasionally ridiculous) *Club Classics*. Caron Wheeler's emotive performance on the opening track, 'Keep On Movin'' (the album's title in the US) set the tone of the album. It's not flawless - Jazzie B, genius producer and all-round music man, may be many things, but a rapper he is not. And a second great single, 'Back To Life', is included here only in 'a cappella' form. When Jazzie and Nellee Hooper's ideas and musical instincts coalesce the results boast a feel-good factor and warmth absent from recent soul music.

● TRACKS: *Keep On Movin'; Fairplay; Holdin' On; Feeling Free; African Dance; Dance; Feel Free; Happiness; Back To Life; Jazzie's Groove.*

● FIRST RELEASED 1989
● UK PEAK CHART POSITION: 1
● USA PEAK CHART POSITION: did not chart

552 THE DREAM OF THE BLUE TURTLES
(–) ▲ STING

Disbanding the Police at the height of their success was a bold move, but with a set of striking cheekbones and a McCartneyesque ear for melody Sting was always on to a winner with his solo career. Parts of his debut album came dangerously close to scuppering his pop kudos, as Sting and his all-star jazz sessionmen backing band (Branford Marsalis, Kenny Kirkland) dabbled in vapid jazz-rock fusion. The sublime, soulful pop of 'If You Love Somebody Set Them Free' and 'Fortress Around Your Heart' indicated a more profitable and appealing direction, one that Sting would pursue to great effect on 1993's *Ten Summoner's Tales*.

● TRACKS: *If You Love Somebody Set Them Free; Love Is The Seventh Wave; Russians; Children's Crusade; Shadows In The Rain; We Work The Black Seam; Consider Me Gone; The Dream Of The Blue Turtles; Moon Over Bourbon Street; Fortress Around Your Heart.*

● FIRST RELEASED 1985
● UK PEAK CHART POSITION: 3
● USA PEAK CHART POSITION: 2

553 BREAKFAST IN AMERICA (343) ▼
SUPERTRAMP

O ften forgotten, and when finally remembered it is usually for the often tedious, but huge-selling *Crime Of The Century*. This record cuts away the pomp and keeps it comparatively simple with some memorable pop songs and lyrics, for example, in the title track a simple statement, 'take a look at my girlfriend, she's the only one I've got', or the ridiculously simple rhymes in 'The Logical Song', and the painful truth of 'Goodbye Stranger' and 'Take The Long Way Home', which are further irritatingly catchy songs. Sadly Supertramp were not able to build on this excellent collection although they still have a loyal following.

● TRACKS: Gone Hollywood; The Logical Song; Goodbye Stranger; Breakfast In America; Oh Darling; Take The Long Way Home; Lord Is It Mine; Just Another Nervous Wreck; Casual Conversation; Child Of Vision.

● FIRST RELEASED 1979
● UK PEAK CHART POSITION: 3
● USA PEAK CHART POSITION: 1

554 1984 (535) ▼
VAN HALEN

V ocalist David Lee Roth's final record for the band and as such, the album stands as a testament of worth somewhere between high camp and high class. Eddie Van Halen's venerable, rolling guitar pulled immaculately into place, while his new-found love of the keyboard gave them their first international smash with 'Jump'. However, it is the quite demented rush of 'Panama', and the hilarious 'Hot For Teacher', with Roth exuding a droll litany of school-yard fantasies over a thunderous Alex Van Halen backbeat, that gives ultimate credence to the rock 'n' roll party that was the Roth/Van Halen partnership.

● TRACKS: Jump; Panama; Top Jimmy; Drop Dead Legs; Hot For Teacher; I'll Wait; Girl Gone Bad; House Of Pain.

● FIRST RELEASED 1984
● UK PEAK CHART POSITION: 15
● USA PEAK CHART POSITION: 2

555 GERRY MULLIGAN MEETS BEN WEBSTER
(196) ▼   GERRY MULLIGAN AND BEN WEBSTER

T his album combines the talents of two jazz giants. Saxophonist Ben Webster was one of the instrument's most influential exponents, primarily through his work with Duke Ellington. Mulligan, meanwhile, was an integral part of the 50s west coast movement and this set represents the confluence of two different generations. The featured quintet includes drummer Mel Lewis and bassist Leroy Vinnegar (who later played on the Doors' *The Soft Parade*), but the six tracks are noteworthy for the splendid empathy struck by Mulligan (baritone) and Webster (tenor). One of several collaborations between the former and notable guest artists, *Gerry Mulligan Meets Ben Webster* is a fine example of how two seemingly disparate musicians can perform together superbly.

● TRACKS: Chelsea Bridge; Cat Walk; Sunday; Who's Got Rhythm?; Tell Me When; Go Home.

● FIRST RELEASED 1960
● UK PEAK CHART POSITION: 15
● USA PEAK CHART POSITION: did not chart

556 BAND OF GYPSIES (–) ▲
JIMI HENDRIX

N o sooner had the Experience imploded than Hendrix was playing in another trio, this time with bassist Billy Cox and the very large ex-Electric Flag drummer Buddy Miles. This is the result of a live performance on New Year's Eve 1969, and although live albums are hard to recommend, this is one such album. Although the band seem underrehearsed and a little stodgy (especially Cox), the quality of Hendrix's playing is exceptional. Maybe the fact that he could rely on Miles for most of the vocals enabled him to concentrate purely on guitar. He is fluid and clear and the remastered CD issued in 1997 is excellent.

● TRACKS: Who Knows; Machine Gun; Changes; Power To Love; Message To Love; We Gotta Live Together.

● FIRST RELEASED 1970
● UK PEAK CHART POSITION: 6
● USA PEAK CHART POSITION: 5

557 BACK STABBERS (741) ▲
THE O'JAYS

With its in-house staff and recognizable sound, the Philadelphia International label was an early 70s equivalent of 60s Tamla/Motown. Flagship harmony act the O'Jays revelled in its sumptuous arrangements and flowing rhythms, as this excellent album testifies. Producers and songwriters Kenny Gamble and Leon Huff sculpted brilliant scenarios for the group; cautionary, in the case of the exhilarating title track, or clarion calls for universal brotherhood, as exemplified in 'Love Train'. The O'Jays brought many years of experience to these recordings, and on *Back Stabbers* found a spiritual home for their considerable talents. The orchestral arrangements are breathtaking.

● TRACKS: *When The World's At Peace; Back Stabbers; Who Am I; (They Call Me) Mr. Lucky; Time To Get Down; 992 Arguments; Listen To The Clock On The Wall; Shiftless, Shady, Jealous Kind Of People; Sunshine; Love Train.*

● FIRST RELEASED 1972
● UK PEAK CHART POSITION: did not chart
● USA PEAK CHART POSITION: 10

559 AVALON SUNSET (205) ▼
VAN MORRISON

Any one of a dozen Morrison titles could be recommended, so why this one? Maybe a few extra sales were made by having Sir Cliff Richard as co-vocalist on the overtly Christian 'Whenever God Shines His Light'. The overall themes are the same; the songs have that glorious quality of melancholy and Morrison sings as well as ever. The religion and spiritualism that have become a strong part of his work are here in large doses, yet there is never any hint than he is lecturing his public towards a better way. 'Have I Told You Lately' is a a perfect example of how Morrison can move the listener to tears.

● TRACKS: *Whenever God Shines His Light; Contacting My Angel; I'd Love To Write Another Song; Have I Told You Lately; Coney Island; I'm Tired Joey Boy; When Will I Ever Learn To Live In God; Orangefield; Daring Night; These Are The Days.*

● FIRST RELEASED 1989
● UK PEAK CHART POSITION: 13
● USA PEAK CHART POSITION: 91

558 COMPLETE & UNBELIEVABLE . . . THE DICTIONARY OF SOUL (274) ▼ OTIS REDDING

Soul giant Otis Redding crossed over into the pop charts with a version of the Temptations' 'My Girl'. This album followed that achievement and showed him bringing a wider perspective to R&B. Working in tandem with guitarist Steve Cropper, Redding tore up the blueprints of Beatles songs and standards, making them as much his own as the original songs the pair contributed. Never a subtle singer, Otis possessed a raw intensity, charging the material through the force of his personality. *Dictionary Of Soul* was the last album issued before the singer's untimely death; the artistic challenges it posed were sadly left unrealized.

● *Fa-Fa-Fa-Fa-Fa (Sad Song); I'm Sick Y'all; Tennessee Waltz; Sweet Lorene; Try A Little Tenderness; Day Tripper; My Lover; Prayer; She Put The Hurt On Me; Ton Of Joy; You're Still My Baby; Hang For You; Love Have Mercy.*

● FIRST RELEASED 1966
● UK PEAK CHART POSITION: 23
● USA PEAK CHART POSITION: 73

560 THE HARDER THEY COME (299) ▼
VARIOUS

The soundtrack to the groundbreaking film about Jamaican subcultures, this superb selection is also a synthesis of late 60s and early 70s reggae. Recordings by Jimmy Cliff, the movie's star, form the album's core and his contributions, notably 'Many Rivers To Cross', show his understated power to great effect. An important figure in the development of reggae, Cliff at last secured deserved acclaim with this collection. His work is ably supported by 'Pressure Drop', one of the finest songs the Maytals ever recorded, while the Melodians and Slickers prove equally strong. The latter's 'Johnny Too Bad' perfectly encapsulates the film's plot, one that helped launch reggae into the international arena.

● TRACKS: *You Can Get It If You Really Want It- Jimmy Cliff; Many Rivers To Cross - Jimmy Cliff; The Harder They Come - Jimmy Cliff; Sitting In Limbo - Jimmy Cliff; Draw Your Brakes - Scotty; Rivers Of Babylon - Melodians; Sweet And Dandy - Maytals; Pressure Drop - Maytals; Johnny Too Bad - Slickers; Shanty Town - Desmond Dekker.*

● FIRST RELEASED 1972
● UK PEAK CHART POSITION: did not chart
● USA PEAK CHART POSITION: 140

561 LET IT BE (–) ▲
THE BEATLES

On the back of the sleeve is the ironic note: 'This is a new phase Beatles album'. The new phase being, here are four maturing men growing apart and desperately needing a break from each other. The accompanying film is too painful to watch, as tempers fray and tension is in the air. In addition to the title track, only 'Get Back' and maybe 'Long And Winding Road' rate as great Beatles songs. The others are all brief entertainments and scraps of tunes. Lennon and Harrison had already moved on in their heads and McCartney was left to paste it together. The overwhelming feeling of this album is one of incredible sadness.

● TRACKS: *Two Of Us; Dig A Pony; Across The Universe; I Me Mine; Dig It; Let It Be; Maggie Mae; I've Got A Feeling; One After 909; The Long And Winding Road; For You Blue; Get Back.*

● FIRST RELEASED 1970
● UK PEAK CHART POSITION: 1
● USA PEAK CHART POSITION: 1

562 LADY IN SATIN (–) ▲
BILLIE HOLIDAY

This was her penultimate album, recorded when her body was telling her enough was enough. During the sessions with arranger Ray Ellis she was drinking vodka neat, as if it were tap water. Yet, for all her ravaged voice (the sweetness had long gone) she was still an incredible singer. The feeling she manages to put into almost every track sets this album as one of her finest achievements. 'You've Changed' and 'I Get Along Without You Very Well' are high art performances from the singer who saw life from the bottom upwards. The CD reissue masterminded by Phil Shaap is absolutely indispensable.

● TRACKS: *I'm A Fool To Want You; For Heaven's Sake; You Don't Know What Love Is; I Get Along Without You Very Well; For All We Know; Violets For Your Furs; You've Changed; It's Easy To Remember; But Beautiful; Glad To Be Unhappy; I'll Be Around; The End Of A Love Affair; I'm A Fool To Want You (Alternate tracks); The End Of A Love Affair (Alternate tracks); Pause Track.*

● FIRST RELEASED 1958
● UK PEAK CHART POSITION: did not chart
● USA PEAK CHART POSITION: did not chart

563 THE CARS (–) ▲
THE CARS

This ranks as one of the best debut albums from a rock band. The Cars are filed under rock, but they are closer to power pop than any other genre. Ric Ocasek sounded like a cross between the Raspberries and Television, punk sound with a pop attitude. The giveaway was the irresistible harmony-ridden hooks in just about every one of his songs. Listen again to 'You're All I've Got Tonight, 'Just What I Needed' or 'My Best Friend's Girl' and be thrilled. Lots of chunka chunka guitar and Mamas And Papas harmonies, and rarely a dull moment. They managed only six albums in 20 years, but they never bettered this.

● TRACKS: *Good Times Roll; My Best Friend's Girl; Just What I Needed; I'm In Touch With Your World; Don't Cha Stop; You're All I've Got Tonight; Bye Bye Love; Moving In Stereo; All Mixed Up.*

● FIRST RELEASED 1978
● UK PEAK CHART POSITION: 29
● USA PEAK CHART POSITION: 18

564 MINGUS MINGUS MINGUS MINGUS (–) ▲
CHARLES MINGUS

While Charles Mingus is rightly revered by the jazz world, he is yet to receive the universal blessing of the rock audience in the way that Coltrane and Miles have. This album is perfect for a Mingus primer. It is fat, gorgeous, accessible and often breathtaking. Suddenly, the swinging orchestra will pause its riff completely and a few notes of Mingus's growling bass will sneak in. For once the sleeve-note is right: 'he jolts with the unexpected'. 'II B.S.' is a stunning opener and from then on the listener can settle into a comfortable half-hour. A brilliant record.

● TRACKS: *II B.S.; I X Love; Celia; Mood Indigo; Better Get Hit In Yo' Soul; Theme For Lester Young; Hora Decubitus.*

● FIRST RELEASED 1963
● UK PEAK CHART POSITION: did not chart
● USA PEAK CHART POSITION: did not chart

565 PORNOGRAPHY (522) ▼
THE CURE

Before Cure founder Robert Smith drew up his archetype for eccentric pop and a fresh sense of lament that turned his band into an arena act in the USA, the Cure's leanings were more darkly felt. *Pornography*, a beautifully still and deep record, is a room full of shadows. Ambient in part, and occasionally challenging, its vision, even down to the oddly distorted photo on the cover, was one darkly wrapped. Smith's yelp of a vocal rose and fell in and out of the light, while 'The Hanging Garden' hinted at his as yet untapped, but clearly commercial, bent.

● TRACKS: *Pornography; The Hanging Garden; One Hundred Years; Siamese Twins; Figurehead; A Strange Day; Cold; A Short Term Effect.*

● FIRST RELEASED 1982
● UK PEAK CHART POSITION: 8
● USA PEAK CHART POSITION: did not chart

567 ELLA FITZGERALD SINGS THE COLE PORTER SONGBOOK (643) ▲ ELLA FITZGERALD

One of Fitzgerald's great assets was also, paradoxically, one of her failings as a jazz singer. Throughout her long career her voice was that of an innocent girl. This immaturity of sound, allied as it was to consummate musical mastery, weakened her jazz performances, especially in the blues where emotional intensity is of paramount importance. As if sensing this, Norman Granz heard in Ella's voice the ideal vehicle for a selection of readings from the Great American Songbook. Her coolly detached approach to lyrics is nowhere better displayed than on this album of songs by one of the most sophisticated American songwriters.

● TRACKS: *All Through The Night; Anything Goes; Too Darn Hot; In The Still Of The Night; I Get A Kick Out Of You; Do I Love You; Always True To You In My Fashion; Let's Do It; Just One Of Those Things; Every Time We Say Goodbye; All Of You; Begin The Beguine; Get Out Of Turn; I Am In Love; From This Moment On; I Love Paris; You Do Something To Me; Riding High; Easy To Love; It's Alright With Me; Why Can't You Behave; What Is This Thing Called Love; You're The Top; Love For Sale; It's D'Lovely; Night And Day; Ace In The Hole; So In Love; I've Got You Under My Skin; I Concentrate On You; Don't Fence Me In.*

● FIRST RELEASED 1956
● UK PEAK CHART POSITION: did not chart
● USA PEAK CHART POSITION: 15

566 THE CAPTAIN AND ME (434) ▼
THE DOOBIE BROTHERS

Boasting three strong vocalists, two expert guitarists and a brace of rhythmic drummers, the Doobie Brothers burst to national prominence with a sound crossing AM pop-rock, soul-tinged R&B and strong musicianship. Traces of Moby Grape, whom the group adored, can be heard in their vibrant harmonies and flowing hooklines, but *The Captain And Me* showed an act of singular purpose. The effervescent urgency propelling 'Long Train Running' and 'China Grove' into the US singles charts is apparent on every selection, where melody combines with twin-lead arpeggios to create an undoubted excitement. The unified sound emerging from this cross-section imbues this album with its lasting strength.

● TRACKS: *Natural Thing; Long Train Running; China Grove; Dark-eyed Cajun Woman; Clear As The Driven Snow; Without You; South City Midnight Lady; Evil Woman; Busted Down Around O'Connelly Corners; Ukiah; The Captain And Me.*

● FIRST RELEASED 1973
● UK PEAK CHART POSITION: did not chart
● USA PEAK CHART POSITION: 7

568 TRUST (–) ▲
ELVIS COSTELLO

Some of Costello's best songs are on this sometimes forgotten gem of a record. *This Years Model* and *My Aim Is True* are usually favoured by fans and critics, but who could fault the special middle-eight of 'You'll Never Be A Man', the great riff of 'Clubland', the smouldering 'Watch Your Step', the tragic 'Shot With His Own Gun' and the sheer pop simplicity of 'From A Whisper To Scream'. Lyrically, he packs them in ten to a dozen, leaving the literate listener's wide-open ears aching. A request that prolific writers should be forced to include lyric sheets with the CD is made. A blinder of an album.

● TRACKS: *Clubland; Lover's Walk; You'll Never Be A Man; Pretty Words; Strict Time; Luxembourg; Watch Your Step; New Lace Sleeves; From A Whisper To A Scream; Different Finger; White Knuckles; Shot With His Own Gun; Fish 'N' Chip Paper; Big Sister's Clothes.*

● FIRST RELEASED 1981
● UK PEAK CHART POSITION: 9
● USA PEAK CHART POSITION: 28

569 THIS NATION'S SAVING GRACE (468) ▼
THE FALL

As stubbornly maverick as ever, the Fall's tenth album hinges on their now-accustomed dissonance, into which a tighter, commercial edge was introduced. New guitarist Brix Smith, wife of leader Mark E., added a partly melodious sheen that brought an air of 60s subculture to the group's post-industrial rattle. Nothing was sacrificed in the process and while 'Bombast' hurtles with a vicious power, talismen Can were acknowledged in 'I Am Damo Suzuki', the name of the German band's Japan-born singer. Mark Smith towers over the proceedings, his voice prowling about the music, enhancing its intensity. This album shows the Fall extending stylistic barriers without sacrificing their individuality.

● TRACKS: *Mansion; Bombast; Barmy; What You Need; Spoilt Victorian Child; LA; Vixen; Couldn't Get Ahead; Gut Of The Quantifier; My New House; Paintwork; I Am Damo Suzuki; To NK Roachment: Yarbles; Petty (Thief) Lout; Rollin' Danyy; Cruisers Creek.*

● FIRST RELEASED 1985
● UK PEAK CHART POSITION: 54
● USA PEAK CHART POSITION: did not chart

570 THE SIDEWINDER (554) ▼
LEE MORGAN

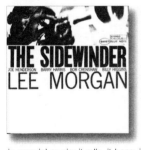

Simple and direct and somewhat of a runt album in the history of jazz. The solo on Art Blakey's recording of Bobby Timmons' 'Moanin'' is by Morgan, as is that on 'A Night In Tunisia'. By the time he came to record this album he had simplified his style, which appealed to the soul/jazz lovers of the 60s. To use the ultimate cliché, this is groovin' music; it rolls, it bops, it makes you feel good and its success is that it is refreshingly uncomplicated. Supported by Joe Henderson (tenor), Billy Higgins (drums), Barry Harris (piano) and Bob Cranshaw (bass).

● TRACKS: *The Sidewinder; Totem Pole; Gary's Notebook; Boy, What A Night!; Hocus Pocus.*

● FIRST RELEASED 1964
● UK PEAK CHART POSITION: did not chart
● USA PEAK CHART POSITION: 25

571 DAYS OF FUTURE PASSED (–) ▲
MOODY BLUES

From British R&B combo to classical pop with no transitional album in between, all they lost was lead singer Denny Laine and gained Lodge and Hayward. This was an ambitious record from a group who had stopped having hits in the UK, and their record company Decca/Deram should be applauded in allowing them down this untried road. This is the album that features Justin Hayward's epic song 'Nights In White Satin', together with some other fine, melancholic pop songs. What makes the album work is not the band, but the sensitive and rich orchestration throughout from the London Festival Orchestra and, in particular, the great contribution from conductor Peter Knight.

● TRACKS: *The Day Begins; Dawn, i Dawn Is A Feeling; The Morning, i Another Morning; Lunch Break, i Peak Hour; The Afternoon, i Forever Afternoon, ii Time To Get Away; Evening, i The Sun Set, ii Twilight Time; The Night, i Nights In White Satin.*

● FIRST RELEASED 1967
● UK PEAK CHART POSITION: 27
● USA PEAK CHART POSITION: 3

572 THE GENIUS HITS THE ROAD (–) ▲
RAY CHARLES

Contrary to the misleading title, this is not a live album. It is a journey through America with the titles acting as a travelogue. Many of the tracks are familiar, but it is Charles' unique touch that makes every song he attempts indelibly stamped. The best example is his golden touch on Hoagy Carmichael's gem 'Georgia'. Charles has made this his own with an emotional performance. Other credible covers are 'Moonlight In Vermont' and 'Basin Street Blues'. The 50th anniversary reissue CD contains some excellent bonus tracks, including the gritty and fittingly titled 'Hit The Road Jack'. This is an essential 'Brother Ray' album to own.

● TRACKS: *Alabamy Bound; Georgia On My Mind; Basin Street Blues; Mississippi Mud; Moonlight In Vermont; New York's My Home; California, Here I Come; Moon Over Miami; Deep In The Heart Of Texas; Carry Me Back To Old Virginny; Blue Hawaii; Chattanooga Choo-Choo. Sentimental Journey; Hit The Road Jack; Blue Moon Of Kentucky (Swingova); Rainy Night In Georgia; I'm Movin' On; Swanee River Rock (Talkin' Bout That River); Lonely Avenue.*

● FIRST RELEASED 1960
● UK PEAK CHART POSITION: did not chart
● USA PEAK CHART POSITION: 9

573 DREAD INNA BABYLON (–) ▲
U-Roy

A long with Big Youth, U Roy held the crown for Jamaica's greatest 'DJ's'. They were arguably *the* voices of the early 70s, and in their homeland were heard as often as Bob Marley. Repetitive though the DJ style is, it is nonetheless unforgettable and often hypnotic. U Roy has a voice that could recite the side of a cornflakes packet and still make it sound appealing. This is a more polished album than his earlier work, produced by Prince Tony, with the bass a little mixed down. The usual lyrics, however, sing out loud and clear; 'as I will say, good gosh, as I will tell you now'.

● TRACKS: *Runaway Girl; Chalice In The Palace; I Can't Love Another; Dreadlocks Dread; The Great Psalms; Natty Don't Fear; African Message; Silver Bird; Listen To The Teacher; Trench Town Rock.*

● FIRST RELEASED 1976
● UK PEAK CHART POSITION: did not chart
● USA PEAK CHART POSITION: did not chart

574 BIG ONES (–) ▲
AEROSMITH

A collection that can stand on its own as a bona fide album, *Big Ones* is a celebration of the survival of a rock band who have lived on the edge for many years. In the late 90s Tyler even manages to look more weathered than Keith Richard, and that must be the ultimate compliment. More than the Stones, more than Led Zeppelin, Aerosmith epitomize the attitude, lifestyle and sound of hard rock 'n' roll. This is the best introduction to Aerosmith and will no doubt lead to debauchery, non-stop partying and the rest of their outrageously great catalogue.

● TRACKS: *Walk On Water; Love In An Elevator; Rag Doll; What It Takes; Dude (Looks Like A Lady); Janie's Got A Gun; Cryin'; Amazing; Blind Man; Deuces Are Wild; The Other Side; Crazy; Eat The Rich; Angel; Livin' On The Edge; Dude (Looks Like A Lady) Live.*

● FIRST RELEASED 1994
● UK PEAK CHART POSITION: 7
● USA PEAK CHART POSITION: 6

575 SELECTED AMBIENT WORKS 1985-1992 (–) ▲ APHEX TWIN

V ery occasionally in music, something will come at you from so far out on the left field, that not only do you not note its immediate import, you scarcely recognize it as music at all. This is the record that cemented the media's fascination with Richard James, a Cornwall bedroom DJ. *Selected Ambient Works* is not an entirely representative recording, as these are essentially mood pieces, unlike the more instantaneous, dancefloor-targeted material that originally brought him to the nation's attention. Nevertheless if you are prepared to make the journey, and can see past the album's intimidating length and its lack of linear framework, there are some exquisite moments - ranging in texture from melodic delirium to sweeping melancholy.

● TRACKS: *Xtal; Tha; Pulsewidth; Ageispolis; Green CALX; Heliospan; We Are The Music Makers; Schotkey; Ptolemy; Hedphelym; Delphium; Actium; I.*

● FIRST RELEASED 1994
● UK PEAK CHART POSITION: did not chart
● USA PEAK CHART POSITION: did not chart

576 POSITIVE VIBRATION (–) ▲
BOB MARLEY AND THE WAILERS

T he overwhelming sadness of the song 'Johnny Was' seems to cling to the entire album like a sore. The power of Marley consoling a mother after her son has been pointlessly murdered is hard to forget, especially the lyric 'shot down in the street and died just because of the system'. Marley went some way to improving things by later getting the warring leaders Manley and Seaga at least to hold hands. This is Marley's deepest album and one that shows his compassion. On a lighter note, the superb background singing of the I Threes is, throughout, a constant uplift on an important album.

● TRACKS: *Positive Vibration; Roots, Rock, Reggae; Johnny Was; Cry To Me; Want More; Crazy Baldhead; Who The Cap Fits; Night Shift; War; Rat Race.*

● FIRST RELEASED 1976
● UK PEAK CHART POSITION: 15
● USA PEAK CHART POSITION: 8

577  ## CROSS ROAD (−) ▲
BON JOVI

Laid out side by side, track after track, the Bon Jovi catalogue is pretty formidable. Although this is a compilation, it is such a well-chosen selection, it sounds like a regular album. Lighter-sounding tracks such as 'Someday I'll Be Saturday Night' complement the rock anthem sound of 'Livin' On A Prayer'. Or how about the wonderful lyric of 'shot through the heart, and you're to blame, you give love a bad name'? How many thousands of spurned males and females have gone home and played that one very loud? The most highly accessible rock band currently around: loud, varied, melodic and great fun.

● TRACKS: *Livin' On A Prayer; Keep The Faith; Someday I'll Be Saturday Night; Always; Wanted Dead Or Alive; Lay Your Hands On Me; You Give Love A Bad Name; Bed Of Roses; Blaze Of Glory; In These Arms; Bad Medicine; I'll Be There For You; In And Out Of Love; Runaway; Never Say Goodbye.*

● FIRST RELEASED 1994
● UK PEAK CHART POSITION: 1
● USA PEAK CHART POSITION: 8

 579 ## PAID IN FULL (−) ▲
ERIC B. & RAKIM

The New York duo of DJ Eric Barrier and William Griffin Jr were early pioneers of rap. This was a highly influential album when first released, although nowadays it seems slighly tame. 'Eric B. Is President' created a stir when first issued and it was followed by the heavily remixed 'Paid in Full' (numerous versions were issued). Their sampling and scratching inspired a host of imitators. The use of funk backing caused James Brown to object, although in reality it rejuvinated Brown's career. They revelled in the plagiarism of other material, but in the light of what has happened since, they were angelicly innocent.

● TRACKS: *I Ain't No Joke; Eric B. Is On The Cut; My Melody; I Know You Got Soul; Move The Crowd; Paid In Full; As The Rhythm Goes On; Chinese Arithmetic; Eric B. Is President; Extended Beat.*

● FIRST RELEASED 1987
● UK PEAK CHART POSITION: 85
● USA PEAK CHART POSITION: 58

 578 ## PYROMANIA (439) ▼
DEF LEPPARD

The album that elevated Def Leppard to their now familiar superstar status. The combination of Mutt Lange's lush vocal arrangements and Def Leppard's hard-bitten, riffing approach to their music, gave them an endearing and instantly accessible formula of sometimes furious rock/pop, best typified by the excellent 'Photograph' and the enigmatic 'Comin' Under Fire'. Vocalist Joe Elliot's lyricism was also developing, with the thematic Vietnam War backdrop for 'Die Hard The Hunter' and the effect on its veterans in 'Billy's Got A Gun' hinting at the band's burgeoning songwriting maturity.

● TRACKS: *Rock Rock ('Til You Drop); Photograph; Stagefright; Too Late For Love; Die Hard The Hunter; Foolin'; Rock Of Ages; Comin' Under Fire; Action Not Words; Billy's Got A Gun.*

● FIRST RELEASED 1983
● UK PEAK CHART POSITION: 18
● USA PEAK CHART POSITION: 2

 580 ## REVENGE (203) ▼
EURYTHMICS

Having now made the transition into a full-blooded band that rocks, Lennox and Stewart could do no wrong and must be seen as one of the musical highlights of the 80s. To maintain such a high standard through six albums in four years takes some doing, yet here they go again, each time growing musically and adding that little extra, for example, the meaty harmonica opening on 'Missionary Man', the harder drum sound on all tracks, and finally Stewart back to playing lots of guitar and sounding as though he is having fun. Hypnotic, bouncy music that never threatens.

● TRACKS: *Let's Go; Take Your Pain Away; A Little Of You; Thorn In My Side; In This Town; I Remember You; Missionary Man; The Last Time; When Tomorrow Comes; The Miracle Of Love.*

● FIRST RELEASED 1986
● UK PEAK CHART POSITION: 3
● USA PEAK CHART POSITION: 12

581 TANGO IN THE NIGHT (421) ▼
FLEETWOOD MAC

Not having the mega-multi-million sales of *Rumours* allows this record greater credibility - the listener has the choice of discovering it. A worthy album, late in their career, many million miles away from the monster Peter Green created. It showed a much happier and cleaner Fleetwood Mac, having put much of their emotional baggage in the cupboard. The Bolivian coca trade had a surprisingly quiet year. Some of their strongest material is found here, Lindsey Buckingham's ambitious 'Big Love', Christine's beautiful 'Everywhere' and close second 'Little Lies'. Reappraising this record gives you a further chance to work out whether a rude word is repeated throughout 'Family Man'.

● TRACKS: *Big Love; Seven Wonders; Everywhere; Caroline; Tango In The Night; Mystified; Little Lies; Family Man; Welcome To The Room...Sara; Isn't It Midnight?; When I See You Again; You And I (Part Two)*.

● FIRST RELEASED 1987
● UK PEAK CHART POSITION: 1
● USA PEAK CHART POSITION: 7

582 FOR EVERYMAN (–) ▲
JACKSON BROWNE

Browne had already been applauded for his songwriting skills, but this was the album that consolidated his position as a singer after his debut album. This also showcases the finest band of LA musicians that session fees can buy, including Sneaky Pete, Russ Kunkel, Jim Keltner, Craig Doerge and Lee Sklar. Add to this harmony vocals from Bonnie Raitt, David Crosby, Don Henley and finally, the ever present guitar of the exceptional David Lindley. For once all these stars embellish rather than steal the show and Browne's happy/sad lyrics shine through a solid album. The title track is one of his great songs.

● TRACKS: *Take It Easy; Our Lady Of The Well; Colors Of The Sun; I Thought I Was A Child; These Days; Red Neck Friend; The Times You've Come; Ready Or Not; Sing My Songs To Me; For Everyman*.

● FIRST RELEASED 1973
● UK PEAK CHART POSITION: did not chart
● USA PEAK CHART POSITION: 43

583 UNLEASHED IN THE EAST (–) ▲
JUDAS PRIEST

The first real transatlantic breakthrough for Judas Priest came with this most unforgiving of live albums. Playing on their early success in the Far East, Judas Priest recorded a handful of shows in Tokyo on the back of their *Hell Bent For Leather* album. Their magnanimous success there made for a brutal and excited showing of live favourites that translated as a riotous success with the Japanese. Their inspired cover versions of Joan Baez's 'Diamonds And Rust' and Fleetwood Mac's 'Green Manalishi,' as well as such gruelling standards as 'Exciter' and 'Ripper', made for a convincing sweatpit of a show. One to raise your hands to.

● TRACKS: *Exciter; Running Wild; Sinner; Ripper; Green Manalishi (With The Two-Pronged Crown); Diamonds And Rust; Victim Of Changes; Genocide; Tyrant*.

● FIRST RELEASED 1979
● UK PEAK CHART POSITION: 10
● USA PEAK CHART POSITION: 70

584 DRESSED TO KILL (–) ▲
KISS

As outrageous as they looked, Kiss were pretty tame by today's Marilyn Manson standards. *Dressed To Kill* was the first album that found them being taken seriously as a commercial proposition. The clunky stack heels and the face paint undermined their ability as a straight-ahead heavy rock band. Basically, it's sex, drugs and glam rock 'n' roll. Similar happy-go-lucky themes are explored in 'Room Service' and the line 'baby I could use a meal', or in 'Ladies In Waiting' with 'and the meat looks good tonight'. Or, as they repeat at the end, 'I wanna rock and roll all nite and party every day'. Crank it up loud, it kicks ass.

● TRACKS: *Room Service; Two Timer; Ladies In Waiting; Getaway; Rock Bottom; C'mon And Love Me; Anything For My Baby; She; Love Her All I Can; Rock And Roll All Nite*.

● FIRST RELEASED 1975
● UK PEAK CHART POSITION: did not chart
● USA PEAK CHART POSITION: 32

585 THROWING COPPER (–) ▲
LIVE

Live sound like a cross between Nirvana and Counting Crows, with a lead vocalist (Ed Kowalczyk) who has definite shades of Michael Stipe (he even gets a credit on the sleeve). This album was one of the most successful of 1995 in the USA, where it is approaching sales of seven million copies. Although lyrically they were standard-fare 'angst' rock, one song managed to upset their hometown of York, in Pennsylvania. The song 'Shit Towne' did little to see the boys welcomed home after their success. They mostly succeed, however, and tracks such as 'All Over You' have no controversial content and are simply high-standard rock.

● TRACKS: *The Dam At Otter Creek; Selling The Drama; I Alone; Iris; Lightning Crashes; Top; All Over You; Shit Towne; T.B.D.; Stage; Waitress; Pillar Of Davidson; White Discussion.*

● FIRST RELEASED 1994
● UK PEAK CHART POSITION: 37
● USA PEAK CHART POSITION: 1

586 ALTERED BEAST (–) ▲
MATTHEW SWEET

Matthew Sweet has a great ability in being able to take a weighty list of influences and ingredients and make a good-quality blend of highly charged guitar-based pop. Anybody unfamiliar with his work, with a strong penchant for the electric Neil Young, the Raspberries, Gene Clark, Flamin' Groovies or Todd Rundgren will find this album utterly indispensable. Session men include guitarist Richard Lloyd, the brilliant fiddle player Byron Berline and the late Nicky Hopkins on piano. Sweet's work may be exclusively derivative but in the absence of the aforementioned artists, who else is there to carry the torch?

● TRACKS: *Dinosaur Act; Devil With The Green Eyes; The Ugly Truth; Time Capsule; Someone To Pull The Trigger; Knowing People; Life Without You; Intro; Ugly Truth Rock; Do It Again; In Too Deep; Reaching Out; Falling; What Do You Know?; Evergreen.*

● FIRST RELEASED 1993
● UK PEAK CHART POSITION: did not chart
● USA PEAK CHART POSITION: 75

587 VENGEANCE (917) ▲
NEW MODEL ARMY

Subsequently derided by the UK music press (seemingly because of little other than their Yorkshire roots), New Model Army were nevertheless in magnificent form for this debut mini-album, recorded before the departure of maestro bass player Stuart Morrow. Other efforts over the next decade or so have all had merit, often offering more in the way of considered songwriting. However, it was *Vengeance* that really gave NMA its huge fanbase. The lynchpin title track blew a hole straight through the side of traditional left-wing liberal tastes of protest rock music: 'I believe in justice, I believe in vengeance, I believe in GETTING the bastards'. Accusations of machismo were diffused by the stark questions posed in 'A Liberal Education', which homed in just as effectively on the lack of natural justice in the world.

● TRACKS: *Christian Militia; Notice Me; Smalltown England; A Liberal Education; Vengeance; Sex (The Black Angel); Running; Spirit Of The Falklands.*

● FIRST RELEASED 1984
● UK PEAK CHART POSITION: 73
● USA PEAK CHART POSITION: did not chart

588 PRETTY HATE MACHINE (–) ▲
NINE INCH NAILS

There are lyrics on Nine Inch Nails' 1989 debut album which you wouldn't want your children to recite and Trent Reznor, good looks notwithstanding, is hardly the sort you'd invite round to meet your parents. On this Reznor's despair, self-loathing and anxiety are animated by a fearful barrage of bone-crunching industrial noise. Parts of 'Something I Can Never Have', for example, could teach Motorhead a thing or two about the power riff. It's not all jet-propelled hate and fury, however, with varied producers (Flood, Adrian Sherwood, Keith LeBlanc) all bringing something new to the table. And if Reznor's nihilism clouds proceedings, his vitriol nevertheless produces some spectacular moments - 'Head Like A Hole', 'Sin' and 'Ring Finger' being prime examples.

● TRACKS: *Head Like A Hole; Terrible Lie; Down In It; Sanctified; Something I Can Never Have; Kinda I Want To; Sin; That's What I Get; The Only Time; Ring Finger.*

● FIRST RELEASED 1989
● UK PEAK CHART POSITION: 67
● USA PEAK CHART POSITION: 75

589 PETER GABRIEL 3 (–) ▲
PETER GABRIEL

The third of the former Genesis vocalist's self-titled releases, this is the album with Gabriel's melting face on the cover. Any vestiges of Gabriel's prog-rock tendencies were completely banished on this strikingly modern album, which explored the psychotic extremes of the human mind in intense, character-based songs such as 'Intruder', 'I Don't Remember' and 'Family Snapshot'. Gabriel's use of computer-controlled synthesizer and electronic rhythm tracks marked an important break with chord-based rock music, aided by Steve Lillywhite's stark production. The album also yielded two of Gabriel's most endearingly popular songs, the sardonic 'Games Without Frontiers' and 'Biko', a moving eulogy to the murdered South African anti-apartheid leader Steve Biko, which paved the way for a glut of inferior rock anthems to political oppression.

● TRACKS: Intruder; No Self Control; Start; I Don't Remember; Family Snapshot; And Through The Wire; Games Without Frontiers; Not One Of Us; Lead A Normal Life; Biko.

● First Released 1980
● UK PEAK CHART POSITION: 1
● USA PEAK CHART POSITION: 22

590 POUR DOWN LIKE SILVER (–) ▲
RICHARD AND LINDA THOMPSON

The serious-looking portraits of Sufi Richard and his loyal muslim wife could have put off the casual purchaser. The music is often profound, but within there are a number of classic Thompson songs. John Kirkpatrick's opening (just like Jimmy Shand) is a joy on 'Streets Of Paradise' where the tears fall down like whiskey and wine. Similarly strong are 'Night Comes In' and 'Beat The Retreat'. The final song, sung by Linda, is a beauty - a love song of immense depth, with the final lines 'I need you at the dimming of the day'. What a pity she has all but retired from singing.

● TRACKS: Streets Of Paradise; For Shame Of Doing Wrong; The Poor Boy Is Taken Away; Night Comes In; Jet Plane In A Rocking Chair; Beat The Retreat; Hard Luck Stories; Dimming Of The Day/Dargai.

● FIRST RELEASED 1975
● UK PEAK CHART POSITION: did not chart
● USA PEAK CHART POSITION: did not chart

591 SHOTGUN WILLIE (–) ▲
WILLIE NELSON

Prior to his major success as a founding father of the Outlaws (with Waylon Jennings), Nelson recorded for Atlantic. They were a record label who, among many things, were not renowned for country music. The production by Arif Mardin (with a little help from Jerry Wexler) has definite shades of southern soul and R&B. Nelson also has a great gift of singing in an incredibly unaffected way; he sings honestly as if he is singing for himself. This remarkable talent has endeared him to millions, and although this album failed to chart, it is one to return to, like an old friend, especially Leon Russell's 'A Song For You'.

● TRACKS: Shotgun Willie; Whiskey River; Sad Songs And Waltzes; Local Memory; Slow Down Old World; Stay All N ight (Stay A Little Longer); Devil In A Sleepin' Bag; She's Not For You; Bubbles In My Beer; You Look Like The Devil; So Much To Do; A Song For You

● FIRST RELEASED 1973
● UK PEAK CHART POSITION: did not chart
● USA PEAK CHART POSITION: did not chart

592 THE KÖLN CONCERT (212) ▼
KEITH JARRETT

Albums that sell vast quantities are not always to be recommended. This exceptional example of solo piano is the biggest selling record in the 25 year history of the pioneering jazz label ECM. It is an almost perfect recording of the art of piano dynamics, full of emotion, and throughout the hour or so duration the listener is never bored. Jarrett has repeated his concerts of improvisation hundreds of times, many have been recorded, and presumably, many routes of his spontaneity have led to blind alleys of jazz doodling. This is the best recorded example of the art, unlikely to be bettered.

● TRACKS: Part I; Part II a; Part II b; Part II c.

● FIRST RELEASED 1975
● UK PEAK CHART POSITION: did not chart
● USA PEAK CHART POSITION: did not chart

593 **LIVE AT THE REGAL** (483) ▼
B.B. KING

No matter how good the studio sessions were, B.B. King was at his best on stage in front of an appreciative, if not ecstatic, crowd. This set, recorded at Chicago's premier black theatre on 21 November 1964, delivered just that. Despite the less than perfect recording conditions, at a time when technology had yet to catch up with the demands placed upon it, the King of the Blues delivers a definitive performance in a programme that includes his then most recent single, 'Help The Poor', and a clutch of songs that were responsible for much of his success, 'Everyday I Have The Blues', 'Sweet Little Angel', 'It's My Own Fault', 'You Upset Me Baby' and 'Woke Up This Morning', among them. The band, including tenorman Johnny Board and organist Duke Jethro, is lean but tight, providing King with a springboard from which to leap into flights of immaculate guitar playing and singing.

● TRACKS: Everyday I Have The Blues; Sweet Little Angel; It's My Own Fault; How Blue Can You Get; Please Love Me; You Upset Me Baby; Worry, Worry; Woke Up This Morning; You Done Lost Your Good Thing Now; Help The Poor.

● FIRST RELEASED 1965
● UK PEAK CHART POSITION: did not chart
● USA PEAK CHART POSITION: 78

 594 **SUNFLOWER** (–) ▲
BEACH BOYS

Ah, if only the thousands who love Pet Sounds would discover this beautiful gem. Its sales and chart position are an insult - this is a sublime record of gigantic proportion. Try out the harmonic power of 'This Whole World', shed a tear at the beauty of 'Add Some Music To Your Day', be impressed with their early new-age discovery of 'Cool Cool Water', and be surprised that they can rock on 'Got To Know The Woman'. Brian is the acknowledged genius, but this album contains one of their greatest songs, written by Dennis: 'Forever' will make you melt, that is, if you have a romantic bone in your body.

● TRACKS: Slip On Through; This Whole World; Add Some Music To Your Day; Got To Know The Woman; Deirdre; It's About Time; Tears In The Morning; All I Wanna Do; Forever; Our Sweet Love; At My Window; Cool Cool Water.

● FIRST RELEASED 1970
● UK PEAK CHART POSITION: 29
● USA PEAK CHART POSITION: 151

 **595** **OH MERCY** (–) ▲
BOB DYLAN

The great Zim has been written off many times, and yet he can and will always come back and surprise us with another tremendous album. Much credit is given to producer Daniel Lanois, but don't forget, a producer cannot do much with pencil shavings. Some of Dylan's most cryptic statements are on this album. He was always better as a romantic than as a protest folkie, and the less obscure his lyrics become, the more he opens his heart. Take, for example, the simple 'Where Teardrops Fall'. Alternatively, the brilliant twist in the tail, 'Most Of The Time', is the deepest: 'Don't even remember what her lips felt like on mine, most of the time'.

● TRACKS: Political World; Where Teardrops Fall; Everything Is Broken; Ring Them; Man In The Long Black Coat; Most Of The Time; What Good Am I?; Disease Of Conceit; What Was It You Wanted; Shooting Star.

● FIRST RELEASED 1989
● UK PEAK CHART POSITION: 6
● USA PEAK CHART POSITION: 30

 596 **STRICTLY PERSONAL** (–) ▲
CAPTAIN BEEFHEART AND HIS MAGIC BAND

Raw yet accessible, like no other Beefheart album. It is his real blues album, and the closest any white boy came to the Mississippi without falling in. 'Gimme Dat Harp Boy' is pure Howlin' Wolf as Beefheart's voice and harmonica clones the Wolf. As usual there is great lyrical malarky at work, especially on 'Ah Feel Like Ahcid' and the ludicrous but brilliant 'Beatle Bones 'N' Smokin' Stones'. Much debate ensued about the merits of the phased or unphased versions; the former has finally won the day. This album should have been a commercial monster but it merely highlighted the sad fact that the world was not ready for such genius.

● TRACKS: Ah Feel Like Ahcid; Safe As Milk; Trust Us; Son Of Mirror Man - Mere Man; On Tomorrow; Beatle Bones 'N' Smokin' Stones; Gimme Dat Harp Boy; Kandy Korn.

● FIRST RELEASED 1968
● UK PEAK CHART POSITION: did not chart
● USA PEAK CHART POSITION: did not chart

597 WAITING FOR THE SUN (208) ▼
THE DOORS

The Doors' third album is one of contrast, capturing brash commerciality and political militancy. It survives the artistic dilemma this poses through a succession of excellent songs and many of singer Jim Morrison's most explicit lyrics. 'The Unknown Soldier' and 'Five To One' capture the Doors at their most politically strident, wherein music and image complement each other perfectly. Other selections show the quartet playful ('Hello I Love You'), wistful ('Summer's Almost Gone') or even peculiar ('My Wild Love'), but in each case the Doors proved themselves as intriguing as ever.

● TRACKS: *Hello I Love You; Love Street; Not To Touch; The Earth; Summer's Almost Gone; Winter Time Love; The Unknown Soldier; Spanish Caravan; My Wild Love; We Could Be So Good Together; Yes, The River Knows; Five To One.*

● FIRST RELEASED 1968
● UK PEAK CHART POSITION: 16
● USA PEAK CHART POSITION: 1

598 BANDSTAND (–) ▲
FAMILY

The album that almost made them major league stars, mainly because of the hit single 'Burlesque', which is still a radio-friendly track to this day. Elsewhere, their original ideas continued to abound - 'Bolero Babe', with its swirling violin, and the nostalgic 'Coronation' showed that Chapman and Whitney had so much in store. Humour was much more prevalent in Family lyrics than any other band of this era, sometimes buried under the rock. This time, it is 'Broken Nose' and the punchline, 'the day that I stopped loving you was the day you broke my nose'. Finally, the wonderful 'My Friend The Sun' is there to remind us of just what a great band they were, and they never felt the need to re-form.

● TRACKS: *Burlesque; Bolero Babe; Coronation; Dark Eyes; Broken Nose; My Friend The Sun; Glove; Ready To Go; Top Of The Hill.*

● FIRST RELEASED 1972
● UK PEAK CHART POSITION: 15
● USA PEAK CHART POSITION: 183

599 FLEETWOOD MAC (213) ▼
FLEETWOOD MAC

The loss of founding member Peter Green dealt a blow to Fleetwood Mac which it took them five years to assimilate. Numerous changes in personnel robbed them of focus until Californian singer-songwriters Stevie Nicks and Lindsay Buckingham joined the ranks. The duo introduced a new dynamism to the group, their bright, melodious compositions offsetting the earthier muse of pianist/vocalist Christine McVie. Buckingham's quicksilver guitarwork energized the group's pulsating rhythm section, regaining, at last, the sense of purpose marking early releases. Titling the album *Fleetwood Mac* suggested a new beginning, which indeed it was. This set saved the group from ignominy, and turned them into one of the world's leading rock bands.

● TRACKS: *Monday Morning; Warm Always; Blue Letter; Rhiannon; Over My Head; Crystal; Say You Love Me; Landslide; I'm So Afraid; World Turning; Sugar Daddy.*

● FIRST RELEASED 1975
● UK PEAK CHART POSITION: 23
● USA PEAK CHART POSITION: 1

600 SONG FOR MY FATHER (734) ▲
HORACE SILVER QUINTET

Yet another jazz steal; this time, Steely Dan borrowed the title track for 'Rikki Don't Lose That Number'. Horace Silver should take heart, this is his most successful album and one that finds its way onto many recommended lists, not just for the jazz fraternity. Its strength is its accessibility, and in keeping with many piano leader albums Silver does not seek to dominate. The quintet is completed by Carmell Jones (trumpet), Joe Henderson (tenor), Teddy Smith (bass) and Roger Humphries (drums). The reissued CD version contains four extra tracks from the same 1963/4 sessions.

● TRACKS: *Song For My Father; The Natives Are Restless Tonight; Calcutta Cutie; Que Pasa; Kicker; Lonely Woman.*

● FIRST RELEASED 1965
● UK PEAK CHART POSITION: did not chart
● USA PEAK CHART POSITION: 95

601 **THE DOCK OF THE BAY** (218) ▼
OTIS REDDING

Compiled in the wake of Redding's premature death, *The Dock Of The Bay* is a suitable testimony to a gigantic performer. The melancholic title track suggested a new musical blueprint and elements of the previously unissued 'Open The Door' show a similarly muted perspective. Tracks culled from *Otis Blue* and *The Soul Album* sit beside the playful 'Tramp', which represents the singer's brief partnership with Carla Thomas. The remaining material is drawn from various sources, including flip-sides and compilations and, taken as a whole, the album provides a précis of Redding's past, as well as intimating what was so sadly lost.

● TRACKS: *Shake; Mr. Pitiful; Respect; Love Man; (I Can't Get No) Satisfaction; I Can't Turn You Loose; Hard To Handle; Fa-Fa-Fa-Fa-Fa (Sad Song); My Girl; I've Been Loving You Too Long; Try A Little Tenderness; My Lover's Prayer; That's How Strong My Love Is; Pain In My Heart; A Change Is Gonna Come; (Sittin' On) The Dock Of The Bay.*

● FIRST RELEASED 1968
● UK PEAK CHART POSITION: 1
● USA PEAK CHART POSITION: 4

 602 **SHEER HEART ATTACK** (–) ▲
QUEEN

Although Queen's first and second albums both made the upper half of *Billboard*'s Top 200, *Sheer Heart Attack* was the one that broke them in America. It included their first US Top 40 single, 'Killer Queen', a melodramatic *tour de force* of multilayered harmonies, Noel Coward-style lyrics, wilfully erratic guitar crunches, and psychedelic phasing that laid the groundwork for such future hits as 'Bohemian Rhapsody'. Despite the album's Stateside success, it retained the quintessentially English sound and attitude that had marked the group's earlier efforts. Many American record buyers doubtlessly scratched their heads over the credit Brian May gave himself on the inner sleeve for playing the 'genuine George Formby ukelele-banjo'.

● TRACKS: *Brighton Rock; Killer Queen; Tenement Funster; Flick Of The Wrist; Lily Of The Valley; Now I'm Here; In The Lap Of The Gods; Stone Cold Crazy; Dear Friends; Misfire; Bring Back That Leroy Brown; She Makes Me (Stormtrooper In Stilettoes); In The Lap Of The Gods...Revisited.*

● FIRST RELEASED 1974
● UK PEAK CHART POSITION: 2
● USA PEAK CHART POSITION: 12

 603 **SUPERUNKNOWN** (–) ▲
SOUNDGARDEN

Although the world has overdosed on negative 'aaghhh feel my pain' and suicide lyrics, there is such a quality to the work of bands like Soundgarden it remains addictive. The overall sound and thick quality to *Superunknown* is rich beyond belief. It is possible merely to listen to the music and skip the lyrics, especially if it is a sunny happy day. Chris Cornell may have some internal demons and addictions from which to recover, but this has never clouded his ability to write some excellent music. Of course, if you are suicidal you might like to listen to this and contemplate living, just so that you can play it again and again.

● TRACKS: *Let Me Drown; My Wave; Fell On Black Days; Mailman; Superunknown; Head Down; Black Hole; Black Hole Sun; Spoonman; Limo Wreck; The Day I Tried To Live; Kickstand; Fresh Tendrils; 4th Of July; Half; Like Suicide; She Likes Surprises.*

● FIRST RELEASED 1994
● UK PEAK CHART POSITION: 4
● USA PEAK CHART POSITION: 1

 604 **PHIL SPECTOR'S CHRISTMAS ALBUM** (499) ▼ **VARIOUS**

Also known as *A Christmas Gift For You*, this album has grown in stature over the years and has been reissued countless times. If you have to own a record to play half a dozen times during the festive season, then this is the one and only. Featuring the amazing Spector production together with Darlene Love, The Crystals, The Ronettes, Bob B. Soxx And The Blue Jeans, even Leon Russell on piano and Sonny Bono on percussion, this is another timeless record that is unlikely ever to be surpassed as the greatest Christmas compilation of all time.

● TRACKS: *White Christmas; Frosty The Snowman; The Bells Of St. Marys; Santa Claus Is Coming To Town; Sleigh Ride; Marshmallow World; I Saw Mommy Kissing Santa Claus; Rudolph The Red Nosed Reindeer; Winter Wonderland; Parade Of The Wooden Soldiers; Christmas (Baby Please Come Home); Here Comes Santa Claus; Silent Night.*

● FIRST RELEASED 1963
● UK PEAK CHART POSITION; 19
● USA PEAK CHART POSITION: 6

605 GET A GRIP (–) ▲
AEROSMITH

On the opening track, 'Eat The Rich', Steven Tyler sounds like he is enjoying putting down the rich, even though there must be some element of ironic humour. Tyler and his band have certainly done their share of 'eating rich'. Elsewhere, there are plenty of similar moments of excess; 'Gotta Love It' has a psychedelic sandwich and 'Flesh' extols the virtues of pure, unadulterated sex. Aerosmith do nothing by halves; Tyler sings exactly what he thinks, good and bad. His mood is matched exactly by the energy of some excellent complementary guitar from Joe Perry. Not for those of a nervous disposition.

● TRACKS: *Intro; Eat The Rich; Get A Grip; Fever; Livin' On The Edge; Flesh; Walk On Down; Shut Up And Dance; Cryin'; Gotta Love It; Crazy; Line Up; Can't Stop Messin'; Amazing; Boogie Man.*

● FIRST RELEASED 1993
● UK PEAK CHART POSITION: 2
● USA PEAK CHART POSITION: 1

 ## 606 RAPTURE (–) ▲
ANITA BAKER

From the opening piano chords of 'Sweet Love', you know there is a good song coming. Ex-Chapter 8 vocalist Baker has an effortless delivery that swoops and dips like a swallow. 'Sweet Love' is just one of those soul songs that people who say they don't like soul music like. The choice of material is superb, and heart-tugging songs such as David Lasley's 'You Bring Me Joy' or Ken Hirsch and Marti Sharron's 'No One In The World' are only beaten by Baker's voice. The slower material is stronger and only 'Watch Your Step' and 'Same Ole Love' fail to hit the spot, simply because of the mood the other tracks set.

● TRACKS: *Sweet Love; You Bring Me Joy; Caught Up In The Rapture; Been So Long; Mystery; No One In The World; Same Ole Love; Watch Your Step.*

● FIRST RELEASED 1986
● UK PEAK CHART POSITION: 13
● USA PEAK CHART POSITION: 11

 ## 607 WILLIAM BLOKE (–) ▲
BILLY BRAGG

Bragg's fullest-sounding album so far does not cloud the continuing power of his songs. 'Upfield' masquerades as a 60s Motown pop song, but study the words and you will find he still has 'socialism of the heart'. 'Everybody Loves You Babe' is stripped bare so that only the lyric hits home. Heaven help the poor girl who is the subject of his wit. Bragg is at his best with guitar only; this is his real stage, from which he educates us with stinging irony in songs such as 'Northern Industrial Town'. Since *Life's A Riot*, Bragg has certainly grown but he has never sold out.

● TRACKS: *From Red To Blue; Upfield; Everybody Loves You Babe; Sugardaddy; A Pict Song; Brickbat; The Space Race Is Over; Northern Industrial Town; The Fourteenth Of February; King James Version; Goalhanger.*

● FIRST RELEASED 1996
● UK PEAK CHART POSITION: 16
● USA PEAK CHART POSITION: did not chart

 ## 608 KAYA (–) ▲
BOB MARLEY & THE WAILERS

Marley is in a mellow and happy mood as the album opens with 'excuse me while I light my spliff' on 'Easy Skanking' and maintains the feeling throughout. 'Kaya' has one of the best bass riffs of any Marley song (played by the wonderful Aston Family Man Barrett). The hit single 'Is This Love' is included and he sounds upbeat singing 'She's Gone', although the subject is that his lover has just left him. Nothing fazed him; he was able to address political and emotional subjects with the same degree of feeling and his manner was truly saintly. *Kaya* is one of his finest moments.

● TRACKS: *Easy Skanking; Kaya; Is This Love; Sun Is Shining; Satisfy My Soul; She's Gone; Misty Morning; Crisis; Running Away; Time Will Tell.*

● FIRST RELEASED 1978
● UK PEAK CHART POSITION: 4
● USA PEAK CHART POSITION: 50

609 **THESE DAYS** (–) ▲
BON JOVI

One of the best hard rock bands currently working, Bon Jovi have every ingredient in their music for customer satisfaction - softer than the hardest metal, but tougher than your standard AOR. Richie Sambora is a modern-day guitar hero, and certainly on a par with the 60s dinosaurs; - the Beck, Page and Blackmore crowd. He can play unobtrusively, as on 'These Days', or he can tear out your insides, like the solo on 'Damned'. High standards delivered seemingly with ease. And if they should decide to call it a day, Bon Jovi, with his drop-dead good looks, can make it as a movie star.

● TRACKS: Hey God; Something For The Pain; This Ain't A Love Song; These Days; Lie To Me; Damned; My Guitar Lies Bleeding In My Arms; It's Hard Letting You Go; Hearts Breaking Even; Something To Believe In; If That's What It Takes; Diamond Ring; All I Want Is Everything; Bitter Wine.

● FIRST RELEASED 1995
● UK PEAK CHART POSITION: 1
● USA PEAK CHART POSITION: 9

 610 **BY ALL MEANS NECESSARY** (705) ▲
BOOGIE DOWN PRODUCTIONS

The first post-Scott La Rock BDP release, By All Means Necessary is a fitting testament to KRS-1's former partner. With his brother Kenny Parker and D-Nice taking over the musical backdrop, samples ran from familiar funk to the heavy rock of Deep Purple. KRS-1 was again in supreme form, boasting a more sharply politicized edge, indicated by the cover image of the artist holding an Uzi in homage to the familiar Malcolm X image. Most pleasing of all was 'Stop The Violence', a call to inner city youth to stop destroying themselves, which rapidly became a movement. Sadly they listened but did not act on it.

● TRACKS: My Philosophy; Ya Slippin'; Stop The Violence; Illegal Business; Nervous; I'm Still Number 1; Part Time Success; Jimmy; P'Cha; Necessary.

● FIRST RELEASED 1988
● UK PEAK CHART POSITION: 38
● USA PEAK CHART POSITION: 75

 **611** **BOSTON** (–) ▲
BOSTON

Recorded on a simple 12-track recorder as a demo, it was so good that the record company released it. Tom Scholz masterminded the project in his spare time; little did he know that this record came to define AOR, and would become a hi-fi store standard demo disc. Since that time, this record-breaking debut has sold 15 million copies in its homeland. Sholtz put so much effort into making it, he has managed only three further records in 22 years. 'More Than A Feeling' still chills in a corny sort of way and the harmonies are pretty impressive.

● TRACKS: More Than A Feeling; Peace Of Mind; Foreplay/Long Time; Rock & Roll Band; Smokin'; Hitch A Ride; Something About You; Let Me Take You Home Tonight.

● FIRST RELEASED 1976
● UK PEAK CHART POSITION: 11
● USA PEAK CHART POSITION: 3

 612 **GIVE 'EM ENOUGH ROPE** (769) ▲
THE CLASH

Sensing the emollient rattle of punk was an artistic dead end, the Clash took an abrupt volte-face and invited American Sandy Pearlman to produce their second album. Respected for his work with Blue Oyster Cult and the Dictators, Pearlman introduced a sheen that disturbed purists but introduced the Clash to a wider audience. The clear sound brought a new emphasis to the quartet's internal interplay and allowed the material to stand up in its own right. Give 'Em Enough Rope contains several of the band's most popular songs, which range from the defiant 'Tommy Gun' to the sensitive 'Stay Free', a contrast confirming the Clash's wider musical ambitions.

● TRACKS: Safe European Home; English Civil War; Tommy Gun; Julie's Been Working For The Drug Squad; Last Gang In Town; Guns On The Roof; Drug-stabbing Time; Stay Free; Cheapstakes; All The Young Punks (New Boots And Contracts).

● FIRST RELEASED 1978
● UK PEAK CHART POSITION: 2
● USA PEAK CHART POSITION: 128

613 **EVERYBODY ELSE IS DOING IT, SO WHY CAN'T WE** (–) ▲ **THE CRANBERRIES**

It is impossible to be indifferent about the Cranberries. Dolores O'Riordan has a voice that either irritates like mad, or charms you into hopeless submission. Mixing her expressive yodelling against a chiming U2 guitar sound, the band could not fail. Strong folk elements remain, because of O'Riordan's dreamlike Celtic warbling. In the USA, where Irish music always finds a strong favour, they were huge in America before the British public really caught on. This album spent 130 weeks in the US chart and sold over five million copies there. Perfect songs that roll off the CD player, the only thing lacking is a lyric sheet.

● TRACKS: I Still Do; Dreams; Sunday; Pretty; Waltzing Back; Not Sorry; Linger; Wanted; Still Can't; I Will Always; How; Put Me Down.

● FIRST RELEASED 1993
● UK PEAK CHART POSITION: 1
● USA PEAK CHART POSITION: 1

 614 **AMERICAN DREAM** (–) ▲ **CROSBY STILLS NASH AND YOUNG**

A surprising late rally from a unique band who have received more than their fair share of criticism. Young always said he would return only when Crosby cleaned himself up. True to his word he did, and Crosby is probably the greatest survivor alive to tell his tale. His song 'Compass' is one of the highlights, and was written while in prison. Stills, in particular, shines with the fully produced 'That Girl' and the bluesy Stills/Young song 'Drivin' Thunder'. Another rare Stills/Young collaboration is the powerful 'Night Song' with the closing repeated lyric 'why not keep on singing anyway'. Why not indeed, an apt thought that closes an album that is better than we ever dared expect.

● TRACKS: American Dream; Got It Made; Name Of Love; Don't Say Goodbye; This Old House; Nighttime For Generals; Shadowland; Drivin' Thunder; Clear Blue Skies; That Girl; Compass; Soldiers Of Peace; Feel Your Love; Night Song.

● FIRST RELEASED 1988
● UK PEAK CHART POSITION: did not chart
● USA PEAK CHART POSITION: 16

615 **KISS ME KISS ME KISS ME** (–) ▲ **THE CURE**

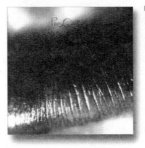

This hefty double album often sounds more like a compilation than a coherent whole, with musical ideas bouncing frantically back and forth. Nevertheless, in typical Cure style, Kiss Me Kiss Me Kiss Me successfully combined catchy pop with bitter despair. Through 17 immensely sensual songs, Robert Smith is at his most poetic ('strange as angels, dancing in the deepest ocean, twisting in the water, you're just like a dream') and vitriolic ('get your fucking voice out of my head . . . I never wanted any of this, I wish you were dead'). The joyous pop of 'Just Like Heaven' and 'The Perfect Girl' still delights, and the frisson provided by 'Shiver And Shake' reinforces the physical nature of this collection.

● TRACKS: The Kiss; Catch; Torture; If Only Tonight We Could Sleep; Why Can't I Be You?; How Beautiful You Are; The Snakepit; Just Like Heaven; All I Want; Hot Hot Hot!!!; One More Time; Like Cockatoos; Icing Sugar; The Perfect Girl; A Thousand Hours; Shiver And Shake; Fight.

● FIRST RELEASED 1987
● UK PEAK CHART POSITION: 6
● USA PEAK CHART POSITION: 35

616 **MONEY JUNGLE** (–) ▲ **DUKE ELLINGTON**

Although this excellent album is listed as a Duke Ellington, equal billing should be given to the participation of Charles Mingus and Max Roach. The remastered CD is outstanding, having been cleaned up from the original master tape. The CD also has the addition of six extra tracks, including four unheard Ellington originals: 'Very Special', 'Rem Blues', 'Switch Blade' and 'Backward Country Boy Blues'. He is as at home in the setting of a trio as he is with a wailing big-band, and as usual, he allows the other musicians to play. The trio version of 'Caravan' is exceptional, raucous and swinging.

● TRACKS: Very Special; A Little Max (Parfait); A Little Max (Parfait) Alternate Take; Fleurette Africaine (African Flower); Rem Blues; Wig Wise; Switch Blade; Caravan; Money Jungle; Solitude (Alternate Take); Solitude; Warm Valley; Backward Country Boy Blues.

● FIRST RELEASED 1963
● UK PEAK CHART POSITION: did not chart
● USA PEAK CHART POSITION: did not chart

617 LOVING YOU (215) ▼
ELVIS PRESLEY

Elvis Presley's first film, *Love Me Tender*, included music as an afterthought, but music was the priority in his next, *Loving You*. Four of the seven songs were hits, while 'Mean Woman Blues' has been recorded by Jerry Lee Lewis, Roy Orbison and many others. '(Let's Have A) Party' at 90 seconds is the shortest single ever to make the charts, a peculiar achievement as Elvis has an additional verse in the film. Fans used to send Elvis Presley teddy bears, hence the song of the same name. Jerry Leiber and Mike Stoller wrote one of their finest ballads with 'Loving You', a song comparable to Cole Porter's 'True Love' which, in turn, completed this 8-track, 10-inch album. In the USA, the album was issued in 12-inch format and the four additional tracks, including 'Blueberry Hill', were released on an EP in the UK.

● TRACKS: *Mean Woman Blues; (Let Me Be Your) Teddy Bear; Got A Lot O' Livin' To Do; Lonesome Cowboy; Hot Dog; (Let's Have A) Party; Blueberry Hill; True Love; Don't Leave Me Now; Have I Told You Lately That I Love You?; I Need You So; Loving You.*

● FIRST RELEASED 1957
● UK PEAK CHART POSITION: 24
● USA PEAK CHART POSITION: 1

618 IDLEWILD (–) ▲
EVERYTHING BUT THE GIRL

Through a sea of changes they moved, from sparse indie folk to jazz, and with this album, they slotted into the classy pop niche. Very much a cosy 80s album for those that had weathered the new wave of the late 70s, EBTG still have the Habitat/Ikea image in their front-room. This is unnecessary carping because the songs are quite excellent, from the romantic innocence of 'These Early Days' to the romantic experience of 'I Always Was Your Girl'. Thorn's voice is at last sounding fully in command and the choice of the late Danny Whitten's 'I Don't Want To Talk About It' is inspired.

● TRACKS: *I Don't Want To Talk About It; Love Is Here Where I Live; These Early Days; I Always Was Your Girl; Oxford Street; The Night I Heard Caruso Sing; Goodbye Sunday; Shadow On A Harvest Moon; Blue Moon Rose; Tears All Over Town; Lonesome For A Place I Know; Apron Strings.*

● FIRST RELEASED 1988
● UK PEAK CHART POSITION: 13
● USA PEAK CHART POSITION: did not chart

619 MIDDLE OF NOWHERE (–) ▲
HANSON

If you can forget the fact that this trio of brothers were not old enough to drive a car when the album was recorded, and still have their school lessons while on the road, you can enjoy it for what it is. Zac is the youngest, and plays drums and has great timing. Isaac is now 17 and is almost the grown-up, and Taylor is the perfect poser. Hanson are a phenomenon in the way the Jackson Five were; they are very, very good at what they do and show a scarily mature grasp of the fundamentals of writing a commercial pop/rock song. They could have a long future.

● TRACKS: *Thinking Of You; MMMBop; Weird; Speechless; Where's The Love; Yearbook; Look At You; Lucy; I Will Come To You; A Minute Without You; Madeline; With You In Your Dreams; Man From Milwaukee (Garage Mix).*

● FIRST RELEASED 1997
● UK PEAK CHART POSITION: 1
● USA PEAK CHART POSITION: 1

620 I'M YOUR MAN (–) ▲
LEONARD COHEN

A strange juxtaposition of biting lyrics, haunting melodies, world-weary vocals, and dinky production, *I'm Your Man* was Leonard Cohen's best-received album in years, making the UK Top 50 and earning kudos from critics across the globe. The lead-off track, 'First We Take Manhattan', immediately sets the mood, as Cohen intones sinisterly, 'They sentenced me to twenty years of boredom' but then, to borrow from Lou Reed, the coloured girls sing, and we're in Las Vegas. However, despite Cohen's dodgy self-production, the songs, and his unmistakable delivery, quickly take centre-stage. One stand-out is 'Everybody Knows', a love-gone-wrong tune full of angst.

● TRACKS: *First We Take Manhattan; Ain't No Cure For Love; Everybody Knows; I'm Your Man; Take This Waltz; Jazz Police; I Can't Forget; Tower Of Song.*

● FIRST RELEASED 1988
● UK PEAK CHART POSITION: 48
● USA PEAK CHART POSITION: did not chart

621 BERLIN (-) ▲
LOU REED

This album missed the bus in the USA but was his most successful album in the UK. One theory is that his association with David Bowie kicked it into action. Another is that the overtly European theme appealed to more people outside the USA. Over the years this has all changed; *Berlin* is now viewed as a tremendous work, and second only to his albatross, *Transformer*. Reed's rich patina vocal may be flat but on tracks such as 'Caroline Says II' and 'Sad Song', it benefits the song. The darkness of the album is best exemplified by the powerful suicide of 'The Bed'. Reed is at his most moribund, yet sings with a childlike skip in his voice.

● TRACKS: *Berlin; Lady Day; Men Of Good Fortune; Caroline Says I; How Do You Think It Feels; Oh Jim; Caroline Says II; The Kids; The Bed; Sad Song.*

● FIRST RELEASED 1973
● UK PEAK CHART POSITION: 7
● USA PEAK CHART POSITION: 98

622 PRONOUNCED LEH-NERD-SKIN-NERD (-) ▲ LYNYRD SKYNYRD

More rock than Little Feat, but with a similar southern boogie feel and absolute top-notch musicianship. Most of the members of this record are now dead even though the band plays on. Al Kooper produced this record, which explains the sensitive use of strings and piano. Although tracks such as 'I Ain't The One', 'Simple Man' and 'Tuesday's Gone' are outstanding, the one to wait for is 'Free Bird', a song that rivals 'Stairway To Heaven' for hard rock credibility. The nine-minute epic starts with organ and slide and builds in a similar way, but at 4.44 it changes into fifth gear and the air guitars are out in force.

● TRACKS: *I Ain't The One; Tuesday's Gone; Gimme three Steps; Simple Man; Things Goin' On; Mississippi Kid; Poison Whiskey; Free Bird.*

● FIRST RELEASED 1973
● UK PEAK CHART POSITION: did not chart
● USA PEAK CHART POSITION: 27

623 SEVENTH SOJOURN (-)· ▲
MOODY BLUES

It is difficult to imagine that this album was recorded through difficult times - the band were fragmenting. This was to be their last album for a few years as they closed the second phase of their career (the first being the Denny Laine R&B years). Musically, it was a strong album, because in addition to the hit singles 'Isn't Life Strange' and 'I'm Just a Singer', there is Justin Hayward's stirring 'New Horizons' and the punchy 'You And Me'; the latter could have been a third hit single, had it been released. One or two lapses only, the main offender being the fey 'For My Lady'.

● TRACKS: *Lost In A New World; New Horizons; For My Lady; Isn't Life Strange; You And Me; The Land Of Make-Believe; When You're A Free Man; I'm Just A Singer (In A Rock And Roll Band).*

● FIRST RELEASED 1972
● UK PEAK CHART POSITION: 5
● USA PEAK CHART POSITION: 1

624 REPUBLIC (-) ▲
NEW ORDER

Their cult years behind them, 1993 saw New Order put their best commercial foot forward with this, their major label debut. By this time they were an act geared to mainstream appetites, and the lighter tone and preponderance of upbeat synthesizer hooks on *Republic* suggested a group who had identified their strengths and weaknesses in the four-year interval since their last album. The vibrant tunesmithery that has always been the group's trademark was augmented by a typically polished Stephen Hague production. 'Regret' duly became their first major US radio hit. Other effective tracks include set-closer 'Avalanche', and 'World', the record's most feisty interlude.

● TRACKS: *Regret; World; Ruined In A Day; Spooky; Everyone Everywhere; Young Offender; Liar; Chemical; Times Change; Special; Avalanche.*

● FIRST RELEASED 1993
● UK PEAK CHART POSITION: 1
● USA PEAK CHART POSITION: 11

625 READY TO DIE (–) ▲
NOTORIOUS B.I.G.

There can have been few more prophetic album titles in the history of music than the one that accompanied Notorious B.I.G.'s 1994 debut. The larger-than-life Brooklyn denizen had turned to hip-hop after making a dodgy living on the streets - a fact celebrated in many of his lyrics. The tone is resolutely grim throughout street narratives such as 'Gimme The Loot', though most hip-hop fans came to Notorious through his cruder, lewder material ('Big Poppa', 'Me & My Bitch'). The album-closer, 'Suicidal Thoughts', in light of his subsequent murder, is an awe-inspiring exercise in fatalistic social realism - 'When I die, I want to go to hell/'Cos I'm a piece of shit, it ain't hard to fuckin' tell'.

● TRACKS: Intro; Things Done Changed; Gimme The Loot; Machine Gun Funk; Warning; Ready To Die; One More Chance; Fuck Me (Interlude); The What -; Juicy; Everyday Struggle; Me & My Bitch; Big Poppa; Respect; Friend Of Mine; Unbelievable; Suicidal Thoughts.

● FIRST RELEASED 1994
● UK PEAK CHART POSITION: did not chart
● USA PEAK CHART POSITION: 15

626 DIRTY MIND (–) ▲
PRINCE

Nowhere near as famous as numerous other Prince albums, and not nearly as commercially successful, but Dirty Mind is the pot-boiler. It hung around the US album chart for a year, just straying inside the top 50. It flows as an album better than most Prince recordings, and is best appreciated as a whole, rather like the way the Beach Boys' Sunflower is now viewed. Understated but wholly satisfying, with easy-on-the-ear songs such as 'Do It All Night' and 'Gotta Broken Heart Again'. Delightful sounds like an inappropriate word when discussing Prince, but this is his 'delightful' album. It will grow in stature.

● TRACKS: Dirty Mind; When You Were Mine; Do It All Night; Gotta Broken Heart Again; Uptown; Head; Sister; Partyup.

● FIRST RELEASED 1980
● UK PEAK CHART POSITION: did not chart
● USA PEAK CHART POSITION: 45

627 FULFILLINGNESS' FIRST FINALE (–) ▲
STEVIE WONDER

Having to follow Talking Book and Innervisions was a massive task, and yet a year later, with hardly a pause he did it. This period of his career is the most prolific and most fertile in terms of ideas. Overall this is a beautifully mellow album, for example the opening track 'Smile Please' is understated, and similarly relaxed is 'It Ain't No Use'. 'You Haven't Done Nothing' is dangerously similar in sound to 'Superstition' Wonder can be forgiven for such a small lapse. He ends with a pleading love song 'Please Don't Go', with yet another great middle hook. He finds more chords on the piano than anybody else.

● TRACKS: Smile Please; Heaven Is 10 Zillion Light Years Away; Too Shy To Say; Boogie On Reggae Woman; Creepin'; You Haven't Done Nothin'; It Ain't No Use; They Won't Go When I Go; Bird Of Beauty; Please Don't Go.

● FIRST RELEASED 1974
● UK PEAK CHART POSITION: 5
● USA PEAK CHART POSITION: 1

628 DON'T STAND ME DOWN (–) ▲
DEXY'S MIDNIGHT RUNNERS

Kevin Rowland's career was based around the idea of being wilfully perverse, but even ardent followers were baffled by this album. The immaculately dressed band on the record sleeve gives little indication of the bizarre nature of the music within. Songs drift along for several minutes as Rowland talks with guitar player Billy Adams about his feelings. Suddenly the talk stops, and the songs burst spectacularly into life, most notably on the brilliant 'This Is What She's Like', in its full ten-minute glory. Don't Stand Me Down remains Rowland's definitive artistic statement, but it also managed to destroy his commercial standing in one fell swoop.

● TRACKS: The Occasional Flicker; This Is What She's Like; Knowledge Of Beauty; One Of Those Things; Reminisce Part Two; Listen To This; The Waltz.

● FIRST RELEASED 1985
● UK PEAK CHART POSITION: 22
● USA PEAK CHART POSITION: did not chart

PERMANENT VACATION (–) ▲
AEROSMITH

Their second release for Geffen Records, and the album that saw them crawl out of the indifferent route they had been following for a few years. Aerosmith's rise from the ashes is a great tale of rock 'n' roll excess, and one for which Geffen must thank their lucky stars. This album has the sparkle and energy of *Rocks* and the chorus of *Toys in The Attic*. 'Magic Touch' climbs and soars, the crude beat of 'Rag Doll' creeps under the skin and 'Dude (Looks Like A Lady)' is a reworked tale of the Kinks' 'Lola'. They have not looked back since this album.

● TRACKS: *Heart's Done Time; Magic Touch; Rag Doll; Simoriah; Dude (Looks Like A Lady); St. John; Hangman Jury; Girl Keeps Coming Apart; Angel; Permanent Vacation; I'm Down; The Movie.*

● FIRST RELEASED 1987
● UK PEAK CHART POSITION: 37
● USA PEAK CHART POSITION: 11

 WORKER'S PLAYTIME (–) ▲
BILLY BRAGG

Few singers in recent history have the honesty to sing as they sound. There is no false American twang, no hip angst vocals and no lo-fi intensity. Bragg sings like a geezer from Barking, Essex, which is exactly what he is. He is, however, blessed with a knack for writing powerful political songs of lyrical truth and romantic ballads of heart-rending openness. Long after Bragg has hung up his Burns guitar, other people with twangy American accents and plenty of angst will record songs such as 'She's Got A New Spell' and 'The Price I Pay', and they will have huge hits with them.

● TRACKS: *She's Got A New Spell; Must I Paint You A Picture; Tender Comrade; The Price I Pay; Little Time Bomb; Rotting On Remand; Valentine's Day Is Over; Life With The Lions; The Only One; The Short Answer; Waiting For The Great Leap Forwards.*

● FIRST RELEASED 1988
● UK PEAK CHART POSITION: 17
● USA PEAK CHART POSITION: 198

 FONTANELLE (–) ▲
BABES IN TOYLAND

Fontanelle was a revelation on release in 1992, a caustic but compelling extrapolation of the dark side of the female psyche. With Maureen Herman taking over on bass from Michelle Leon, it upped the ante following Babes In Toyland's impressive but less cohesive debut, *Spanking Machine*. Kat Bjelland (the project's co-producer in tandem with Lee Ranaldo) is the perfect conduit for these abrasive songs, by turns cajoling and accusing. At times you can almost hear Bjelland's vocal chords disintegrate under the strain she puts on them ('Handsome Gretel'). That song is also typical of the Babes' nursery rhymes-gone-sour lyrical thematic. To sustain that intensity over 15 songs without ever descending into metal/punk cliché was quite an achievement.

● TRACKS: *Bruise Violet; Right Now; Bluebell; Handsome Gretel; Blood; Magick Flute; Won't Tell; Quite Room; Spun; Jungle Train; Pearl; Red Eyes; Mother; Gone.*

● FIRST RELEASED 1992
● UK PEAK CHART POSITION: 24
● USA PEAK CHART POSITION: did not chart

 PRAYERS ON FIRE (–) ▲
BIRTHDAY PARTY

Nick Cave is widely acknowledged as one of our most mature songwriting talents these days, but there was a time when he seemed to be the most unhinged soul in Christendom. The Birthday Party's performances, whether in the studio or on stage, were always compelling, and they left behind no more powerful document than this shattering record. *Prayers On Fire*, an intense, disquieting effort, was their first international release after relocating to London from Australia. While the violence of the group's urban rockabilly rumbles underneath, often to no obvious linear structure, Cave's lyrics are informed, acute, but utterly unyielding and savage. Check the no-compromise ferocity of 'Nick The Stripper' and 'King Ink', still among his best songs.

● TRACKS: *Zoo-Music Girl; Cry; Capers; Nick The Stripper; Ho-Ho; Figure Of Fun; King Ink; A Dead Song; Yard; Dull Day; Just You And Me; Blundertown; Kathy's Kisses.*

● FIRST RELEASED 1981
● UK PEAK CHART POSITION: did not chart
● USA PEAK CHART POSITION: did not chart

BLACK SABBATH (232) ▼
BLACK SABBATH

The archetypal heavy metal band, Black Sabbath unleashed a debut album marked by basic riffs, power chords and the faintest whiff of satanism. Its crushing atmosphere of doom proved intense and relentless; the cumulative effect was dubbed 'downer rock', but it proved immediately popular with a disaffected, often working-class, audience. Their fierce loyalty was fuelled by the negative response this album garnered from many rock critics who proved immune to its single-minded power. Singer Ozzy Osbourne already possessed one of the most distinctive voices in rock and proved the ideal frontman for his group's unremitting attack. Still dug out, dusted off, and played.

● TRACKS: Black Sabbath; The Wizard; Behind The Walls Of Sleep; NIB: Evil Woman; Sleeping Village; Warning.

● FIRST RELEASED 1970
● UK PEAK CHART POSITION: 8
● USA PEAK CHART POSITION: 23

 THE BLASTERS (–) ▲
THE BLASTERS

The second album by these California boys (but the first to reach a wide audience) makes an in-contestable claim for them as the quintessential roots-rock band of the '80s. At a time when their contemporaries were indulging in injudicious amounts of eyeliner and synthesizers, brothers Phil and Dave Alvin and their cohorts were making college radio safe for the likes of Little Willie John and Jimmie Rodgers. Alvin was the only post-punk songwriter who ever successfully picked up where Chuck Berry left off. As they put it on the manifesto 'American Music'; 'We got the Louisiana boogie and delta blues/Country swing and rockabilly too'. Enough to make the Stray Cats run off with their tails between their legs.

● TRACKS: Marie Marie; No Other Girl; I'm Shakin'; Border Radio; American Music; So Long Baby Goodbye; Hollywood Bed; Never No More Blues; This Is It; Highway 61; I Love You So; Stop The Clock.

● FIRST RELEASED: 1981
● UK PEAK CHART POSITION: did not chart
● USA PEAK CHART POSITION: 36

 ANOTHER SIDE OF BOB DYLAN (938) ▲
BOB DYLAN

On this album it was clear that the almighty Bobness was becoming bored with straight folk. Although still acoustic, his left-thinking devotees began to raise an eyebrow at subtle lyrical shifts, yet this album was to be raided time and again - particularly by the Byrds - in 1965's folk rock boom. There is much free-spirited music, as if Dylan was somehow aware of the acceptance that was around the corner, and it has been noted that here were the first signs of the trademark vocal so prevalent through the rest of the 60s. Take your pick: most of the offerings are striking. 'My Back Pages', 'All I Really Want To Do', 'It Ain't Me Babe', and even a last nod to protest, 'The Chimes Of Freedom': how can one man be so prolific?

● TRACKS: All I Really Want To Do; Black Crow Blues; Spanish Harlem Incident; Chimes Of Freedom; I Shall Be Free; To Ramona; Motorpsycho Nightmare; My Back Pages; I Don't Believe You; Ballads In Plain D; It Ain't Me Babe.

● FIRST RELEASED 1964
● UK PEAK CHART POSITION: 8
● USA PEAK CHART POSITION: 43

 APRIL IN PARIS (–) ▲
COUNT BASIE

It is wonderful albums like this that really benefit from the age of the CD. This was crying out for reissue, and apart from the cardboard sleeve, Verve have treated one of the Count's greatest albums with utmost respect. The lush swing of the Basie band has never sounded happier and the addition of alternate takes is a joy to behold. Listeners will be reminded just how good this band was as they stroll through 'Sweety Cakes', add a sheen to Frank Foster's 'Shiny Stockings' and rip it apart with Neal Hefti's magnificent 'Dinner With Friends'. A highly recommended album just bursting with joy.

● TRACKS: April In Paris; Corner Pocket; Didn't You?; Sweetie Cakes; Magic; Shiney Stockings; What Am I Here For?; Midgets; Mambo Inn; Dinner With Friends; April In Paris; Corner Pocket; Didn't You; Magic; Magic; What Am I Here For?; Midgets.

● FIRST RELEASED 1961
● UK PEAK CHART POSITION: did not chart
● USA PEAK CHART POSITION: did not chart

637 SHE'S SO UNUSUAL (-) ▲
CYNDI LAUPER

O nce the orange-haired Lauper dropped the contrived, dumb, cutesy, lispy broad persona, Cyndi Lauper was seen as a credible artist, and has subsequently become highly respected as a terrific songwriter. On this, her pen was sharpened with the magnificent song of unconditional love, 'Time After Time', a track that has since been recorded by others, including beautiful cover versions by Miles Davis and the jazz husband-and-wife duo, Tuck And Patti. Less sophisticated, but of equal fun, is 'She Bop', and then there are well-chosen covers such as Jules Shear's 'All Through The Night' and Prince's 'When You Were Mine'.

● TRACKS: *Money Changes Everything; Girls Just Want To Have Fun; When You Were Mine; Time After Time; She Bop; All Through The Night; Witness; I'll Kiss You; He's So Unusual; Yeah Yeah.*

● FIRST RELEASED 1983
● UK PEAK CHART POSITION: 16
● USA PEAK CHART POSITION: 4

638 ELLINGTON INDIGOS (-) ▲
DUKE ELLINGTON

A n extraordinary man, with an equally extraordinary small group. Among the other masterful musicians are Harry Carney, Jimmy Hamilton, Johnny Hodges, Paul Gonsalves, Shorty Baker, Clark Terry and Ray Nance. This was probably his finest band since the Blanton-Webster days. They play with relaxed beauty on numbers that many of them knew how to play in their sleep. The Gonsalves solo on 'Where Or When' is beautiful, and the balance the band strike on 'Mood Indigo' is exemplary. The reissued CD comes with two additional tracks, both superb; Cole Porter's 'Night And Day' and Hammerstein and Kern's 'All The Things You Are'.

● TRACKS: *Solitude; Where Or When; Mood Indigo; Night And Day; Prelude To A Kiss; All The Things You Are; Willow Weep For Me; Tenderly; Dancing In The Dark; Autumn Leaves; The Sky Fell Down.*

● FIRST RELEASED 1958
● UK PEAK CHART POSITION: did not chart
● USA PEAK CHART POSITION: did not chart

639 SWEET DREAMS (352) ▼
EURYTHMICS

S till finding their way after a disjointed debut album following the break-up of the Tourists, Annie and Dave found commercial success with this, their 'programmed' album. The electronic drums and keyboards fit well into the eerie and mysterious qualities of the songs (Edward de Bono is thanked on the sleeve). For those who thought synthesizer pop was the answer during the lull of the 80s, then the Eurythmics embodied it, and did it better than most. It will be good to see these songs performed by a live band when they eventually re-form, perhaps in the 21st century.

● TRACKS: *Love Is A Stranger; I've Got An Angel; Wrap It Up; I Could Give You (A Mirror); The Walk; Sweet Dreams (Are Made Of This); Jennifer; This Is The House; Somebody Told Me; This City Never Sleeps.*

● FIRST RELEASED 1983
● UK PEAK CHART POSITION: 3
● USA PEAK CHART POSITION: 15

640 HEAVEN OR LAS VEGAS (582) ▼
COCTEAU TWINS

A band who have had to endure the term 'ethereal' being bandied about around their name more than any other. With their soulful and quite blissful meanderings, their music has a sustainable beauty free of regard for contemporaries or peers. *Heaven Or Las Vegas* saw vocalist Elizabeth Fraser substituting the occasional obscure lyric in place of her uniquely visionary wall of sound, and the single, 'Ice Blink Luck', even had a near-recognizable structure and a very tempting hook. Their unearthly wealth of ideas remains undiminished even though Fraser has suffered greatly from problems with her voice in recent years.

● TRACKS: *Cherry-coloured Funk; Pitch The Baby; Ice Blink Luck; Fifty-fifty Clown; Heaven Or Las Vegas; I Wear Your Ring; Fotzepolitic; Wolf In The Breast; River, Road And Rail; Frou-frou Foxes In Midsummer Fires.*

● FIRST RELEASED 1990
● UK PEAK CHART POSITION: 7
● USA PEAK CHART POSITION: 99

641 FUTURE GAMES (–) ▲
FLEETWOOD MAC

Not a Mac album that springs readily to mind, when you consider the multi-billion sellers in the catalogue. This was during their 'lost period', when they were neither a boy or a girl. Greeny had long departed and Stevie Nicks was not even a twinkle in Mick Fleetwood's eye. Bob Welch was the frontman, and shared the songs with Chrsuitne Mcvie and Danny Kirwan. McVie's 'Morning Rain' is a strong song, spoilt by messy production. The album's jewel is Welch's title track. Had he not been discredited for a marital indiscretion within the band, this is a song the latest Fleetwood Mac could easily justify doing today.

● TRACKS: *Woman Of 1000 Years; Morning Rain; What A Shame; Future Games; Sands Of Time; Sometimes; Lay It All Down; Show Me A Smile.*

● FIRST RELEASED 1971
● UK PEAK CHART POSITION: did not chart
● USA PEAK CHART POSITION: 91

643 SPACE RITUAL ALIVE (–) ▲
HAWKWIND

Surely the ultimate 'head' album, a double album (and CD) of gigantic, cosmic nonsense. Put Hawkwind, namely poet Bob Calvert, together with his USA equivalent Paul Kantner, and you have space rock nirvana, galactic eldorado and interplanetary mumbo jumbo of the highest order. If anybody cares to knock these lords of the cosmos just take note that they have charted in the UK with no less than, 23 albums. Pulsating science fiction has never been better translated or, as the sleeve note says, 'we were born to go as far as we can fly, turn electric dreams into reality'. They laugh all the way to the bank of Andromeda.

● TRACKS: *Earth Calling; Born To Go; Down Through The Night; The Awakening; Lord Of Light; Black Corridor; Space Is Deep; Electronic No 1; Orgone Accumulator; Upside Down; Seconds Of Forever; Brainstorm; 7 By 7; Sonic Attack; Time We Left This World Today; Master Of The Universe; Welcome To The Future; You Shouldn't Do That; Master Of The Universe; Born To Go.*

● FIRST RELEASED 1973
● UK PEAK CHART POSITION: 9
● USA PEAK CHART POSITION: 179

642 SINATRA AT THE SANDS (–) ▲
FRANK SINATRA

Very few live albums equal the original recording, and generally live albums do not capture the performance. This one does. You can sense immediatly that Frankie was in a good mood the minute he stepped on the stage. His patter is spot on and he is able to go from great humour into classy love songs (such as 'The Shadow Of Your Smile') with great ease. The Quincy Jones arrangements and the Count Basie orchestra are both faultless. Although critics have suggested he was past his peak by 1966, there is little to prove their case on this album. The tinkling glasses and coughs are also a bonus.

● TRACKS: *Come Fly With Me; I've Got A Crush On You; I've Got You Under My Skin; The Shadow Of Your Smile; Street Of Dreams; One For My Baby (And One More For The Road); Fly Me To The Moon; One O'Clock Jump; Monologue; You Make Me Feel So Young; All Of Me; The September Of My Years; Get Me To The Church On Time; It Was A Very Good Year; Don't Worry Bout Me; Makin' Whoopee!; Where Or When; Angel Eyes; My Kind Of Time; Monologue; My Kind Of Town (Reprise).*

● FIRST RELEASED 1966
● UK PEAK CHART POSITION: 7
● USA PEAK CHART POSITION: 9

644 LIFE (231) ▼
INSPIRAL CARPETS

The Inspiral Carpets emerged from Manchester's rave/club scene alongside the Stone Roses and Happy Mondays. Each of these groups fused a dance groove to 60s-styled pop, the Carpets' brand of psychedelia fashioned by Clint Boon's Vox-styled organ work. Taking inspiration from garage bands and the Doors, he adds a distinctive flourish to the band's grasp of simple, commercial melodies. *Life* is the unit's first full-length album, following three EPs and a selection drawn from John Peel sessions. It captures their enthusiastic slant on a genre briefly in vogue, and one to which they brought humour and a refreshing eclecticism.

● TRACKS: *Real Thing; Song For A Family; This Is How It Feels; Directing Traffik; Besides Me; Many Happy Returns; Memories Of You; She Comes In The Fall; Monkey On My Back; Sun Don't Shine; Inside My Head; Move; Sackville.*

● FIRST RELEASED 1990
● UK PEAK CHART POSITION: 2
● USA PEAK CHART POSITION: did not chart

645 I'M ALIVE (-) ▲
JACKSON BROWNE

An album that saw Browne return to high-quality songs brought about by the familiar chestnut 'relationship problems'. Much media attention was given to his break-up with actress Darryl Hannah, and Browne seemed to come off worse. However, he deserves the last laugh because it prompted stellar songs such as the title track, 'My Problem Is You' and the light reggae beat of 'Everywhere I Go'. Few contemporary songwriters can analyze and discuss their own problems and failings through songs as openly and, apparently honestly, as Jackson Browne. Anybody that wrote him off as one of 'those 70s singer songwriters' should lend an ear to this album, especially those with marital problems.

● TRACKS: *I'm Alive; My Problem Is You; Everywhere I Go; I'll Do Anything; Miles Away; Too Many Angels; Take This Rain; Two Of Me, Two Of You; Sky Blue And Black; All Good Things.*

● FIRST RELEASED 1993
● UK PEAK CHART POSITION: 35
● USA PEAK CHART POSITION: 40

646 NIGHT AND DAY (310) ▼
JOE JACKSON

Jackson's great New York album, full of atmosphere, high-quality musicianship and mature arrangements, put him way beyond the pop of his first two albums. The cosmopolitan flavour is captured on the Latin-styled 'Cancer', Jackson's romantic nature is exposed on the beautiful 'Would You Be My Number Two' and the album's headliner is the modern classic 'Steppin' Out', with its unforgettable bass and piano intro. This album should have been a platform to make Jackson an international artist, but for some reason his career faltered and he was eventually dropped by his record company. Repeated radio play of 'Steppin' Out' should keep this album in print.

● TRACKS: *Another World; Chinatown; TV Age; Target; Would You Be My Number Two; Steppin' Out; Breaking Us In Two; Cancer; Real Men; Slow Song.*

● FIRST RELEASED 1982
● UK PEAK CHART POSITION: 3
● USA PEAK CHART POSITION: 4

647 JONI MITCHELL (-) ▲
JONI MITCHELL

Known by the cognoscenti as *Song To A Seagull*, this David Crosby-produced album is a sparse and beautiful folk album. This was her debut, yet already it was apparent that here was an immense lyrical talent. Her great songwriting melodies came later, as these are standard-fare folky items. Few writers had used such a conversational style in song, and for that alone, this was a milestone of a record. The listener was encouraged and welcomed into a stream of dialogue and tales without needing to know what they were all about. However, in the last track, we do know the identity of the man who sails and takes her to his schooner: he has a walrus moustache and is very large.

● TRACKS: *I Had A King; Michael From Mountains; Night In The City; Marcie; Nathan La Franeer; Sisotowbell Lane; The Dawntreader; The Pirate Of Pennance; Song To A Seagull; Cactus Tree.*

● FIRST RELEASED 1968
● UK PEAK CHART POSITION: did not chart
● USA PEAK CHART POSITION: 189

648 JUDY AT CARNEGIE HALL (223) ▼
JUDY GARLAND

The sleeve note begins: 'On the evening of April 23, 1961, 3,165 privileged people packed the world famous Carnegie Hall beyond its capacity, and witnessed what was to be probably the greatest evening in show business history.' This souvenir of that remarkable occasion is said to contain the complete concert, during which Judy Garland sang 26 songs and mesmerized the audience with her sensational all-round performance. The album won Grammys for album of the year, best female vocal performance, best engineering and best cover. It was in the US chart for 73 weeks, 13 of them at number 1.

● TRACKS: *When You're Smiling; Almost Like Being In Love (medley); Who Cares?; Puttin' On The Ritz; How Long Has This Been Going On; Just You, Just Me; The Man That Got Away; San Francisco; That's Entertainment; Come Rain Or Come Shine; You're Nearer; A Foggy Day; If Love Were All; Zing Went The Strings Of My Heart; Stormy Weather; You Made Me Love You (medley); Rockabye Your Baby With A Dixie Melody; Over The Rainbow; Swanee; After You've Gone; Chicago; The Trolley Song (overture); Over The Rainbow (overture); The Man That Got Away (overture); Do It Again; You Go To My Head; Alone Together; I Can't Give You Anything But Love.*

● FIRST RELEASED 1961
● UK PEAK CHART POSITION: 13   ● USA PEAK CHART POSITION: 1

649 **HOTTEST NEW GROUP IN JAZZ** (–) ▲
LAMBERT, HENDRICKS AND ROSS

Hard to choose between the three fantastic albums they recorded for Columbia, but the great technology of the CD puts all three in one package (*Sing Ellington* and *High Flying*). Those unfamiliar with LH&R need to know that they sang jazz like no other, before or since. The combination of the three magnificent voices; the sweet scat of Annie Ross, the cool husky Hendricks and the clean and well-pitched Lambert. Fabulous renditions of 'Moanin' (written by Hendricks and Bobby Timmons) and 'Summertime' are only just beaten by Ross's classic 'Twisted' (revamped by Joni Mitchell on *Court And Spark*). The coolest, hippest jazz vocal album ever.

● TRACKS: *Charleston Alley; Moanin'; Twisted; Bijou; Cloudburst; Centrepiece; Gimme That Wine; Sermonette; Summertime; Everybody's Boppin'; Cottontail; All Too Soon; Happy Anatomy; Rocks In My Bed; Main Stem; I Don't Know What Kind Of Blues I've Got; Things Ain't What They Used To Be; Midnight Indigo; What Am I Here For?; In A Mellow Tone; Caravan; Come On Home; The New ABC; Farmer's Market; Cookin' At The Continental; With Malice Toward None; Hi-Fly; Home Cookin' Halloween Spooks; Popity Pop; Blue; Mr P. C.; Walkin'; This Here (Dis Hyunh); Swingin' Till The Girls Come Home; Twist City; Just A Little Bit Of Twist; A Night In Tunisia.*
● FIRST RELEASED 1960
● UK PEAK CHART POSITION: did not chart
● USA PEAK CHART POSITION: did not chart

 650 **THE LAST RECORD ALBUM** (261) ▼
LITTLE FEAT

Many remember their Little Feat albums by which wonderful Neon Park illustration was on the cover. The famous giant jelly graces this one. The music within is equally delectable, with the horizontal mambo on 'Romance Dance' and 'All That You Dream', as they celebrate by singing 'I've Been Down But Not Like This Before'. The album's star is the tear-jerking, beautiful ballad 'Long Distance Love'. Very probably Lowell George's greatest song, its gentle understatement and simplicity is pure genius; 'ah her toes were so pretty, and her life so sweet'. An essential Little Feat album. The CD reissue contains two extra tracks from the live album *Waiting For Columbus*.

● TRACKS: *Romance Dance; All That You Dream; Long Distance Love; Day Or Night; One Love; Down Below The Borderline; Somebody's Leavin'; Mercenary Territory.*

● FIRST RELEASED 1975
● UK PEAK CHART POSITION: 36
● USA PEAK CHART POSITION: 36

 651 **TROUBLE MAN** (–) ▲
MARVIN GAYE

Tenuous though it is, history books list it as a Marvin Gaye album. Those who did not see the film (from which this is a soundtrack) might unsuspectingly think Marvin might sing on it. In fact he does on one track, the title song. The film was another low-budget blaxploitation detective movie that fell short of both *Superfly* (Curtis Mayfield) and *Shaft* (Isaac Hayes). Musically, however, the remaining instrumental music is hard to fault, even though it sounds very much of its era. Approach with some degree of caution, but expect to be pleasantly surprised.

● TRACKS: *Main Theme From Trouble Man; T Plays It Cool; Poor Abbey Walsh; The Break In (Police Shoot Big); Cleo's Apartment; Trouble Man; Theme From Trouble Man; T Stands For Trouble; Main Theme From Trouble Man; Life Is A Gamble; Deep-In-It.*

● FIRST RELEASED 1972
● UK PEAK CHART POSITION: did not chart
● USA PEAK CHART POSITION: 14

 652 **WE ARE ONE** (–) ▲
MAZE (FEATURING FRANKIE BEVERLY)

Maze were formed in Philadelphia at the height of the Philly sound, yet they failed to achieve any degree of success until they moved out to San Francsico (hardly the mecca of sweet soul). Ten years later they made this, their best and most successful album. Beverly's vocals are clearly a strong focus, a cross between Al Green and Marvin Gaye, but the musical strength of Maze is excellent. Covering the ground between funk and rock, there are enough understated musical trills to make this an album for musicians as well as hopeless romantics. It all comes together as one on 'I Wanna Thank You', complete with Doobie Brothers harmonies.

● TRACKS: *Love Is The Key; Right On Time; Your Own Kind Of Way; I Wanna Thank You; We Are One; Never Let You Down; I Love You Too Much; Metropolis.*

● FIRST RELEASED 1983
● UK PEAK CHART POSITION: 38
● USA PEAK CHART POSITION: 25

653 TIGERLILY (–) ▲
NATALIE MERCHANT

Its a pity that the record company felt the need to sticker the cover with 'former singer songwriter with 10,000 Maniacs'. Such is the fickle and forgetful pop public. The understated and underrated Merchant has a distinctive voice, and with concentration, this is a rewarding collection of songs that hark back to the Band's *Music From Big Pink* album. Not surprisingly, it was recorded down the road in Bearsville. Perhaps all back-catalogue 10,000 Maniacs albums should be stickered with 'featuring the highly original and talented Natalie Merchant, future solo singer and songwriter'. And maybe she does not want to sell as many records as Celine Dion.

● TRACKS: *San Andreas Fault; Wonder; Beloved Wife; River; Carnival; I May Know The Word; The Letter; Cowboy Romance; Jealousy; Where I Go; Seven Years.*

● FIRST RELEASED 1995
● UK PEAK CHART POSITION: 39
● USA PEAK CHART POSITION: 13

654 RAM (–) ▲
PAUL AND LINDA McCARTNEY

On *Ram* McCartney moved further away from the studio polish of the Beatles' swan-song, *Abbey Road*, with a wonderfully unforced and ramshackle collection of songs. On 'Smile Away' and 'Monkberry Moon Delight', he proved that he could still play the unrepentant rocker, while 'Uncle Albert/Admiral Halsey' was an utterly charming slice of McCartney whimsy that managed to avoid the tweeness that was sometimes his bugbear. The closing track, 'The Back Seat Of My Car', contained more hooks than are usually found on the average album, proving that even at his most spontaneous McCartney was still melodic to the core.

● TRACKS: *Too Many People; 3 Legs; Ram On; Dear Boy; Uncle Albert/Admiral Halsey; Smile Away; Heart Of The Country; Monkberry Moon Delight; Eat At Home; Long Haired Lady; Ram On; The Back Seat Of My Car.*

● FIRST RELEASED 1971
● UK PEAK CHART POSITION: 1
● USA PEAK CHART POSITION: 2

655 A KIND OF MAGIC (272) ▼
QUEEN

Produced, in part, for the film *Highlander*, *A Kind Of Magic* celebrated Queen as intelligent, speculative travellers, utilizing new-found technology with their instantly recognizable body of harmony and pointed arrangements. The title track, with its accompanying part animated/part action video, was a finger-clicking build that spiralled gorgeously into whoops of sheer delight. 'One Vision' celebrated their dazzling, show-stealing set at Live Aid, while 'Who Wants To Live Forever' yearned majestically. 'Friends Will Be Friends' was a guaranteed, arm-waving crowd-pleaser. A gracious and graceful pleasure.

● TRACKS: *Princes Of The Universe; A Kind Of Magic; One Year Of Love; Pain Is So Close To Pleasure; Friends Will Be Friends; Who Wants To Live Forever; Gimme The Prize; Don't Lose Your Head; One Vision.*

● FIRST RELEASED 1986
● UK PEAK CHART POSITION: 1
● USA PEAK CHART POSITION: 46

656 BLACK AND BLUE (–) ▲
ROLLING STONES

One in a series of their 70s 'groove' albums, and one of the best, even though they had obviously been listening to far too many James Brown albums judging by the opening track, 'Hot Stuff'. More traditionally Stones-sounding is 'Hand Of Fate', full of Keef's chiming barred chords. 'Cherry Oh Baby' could have been skipped in favour of more riff. 'Memory Road' comes close to AOR but 'Fool To Cry' is a gem, demonstrating how far from Dartford their music and Jagger's accent have travelled. Even when they are coasting, and they seem to be doing so on this, they still knocked out most of the opposition. And they still do.

● TRACKS: *Hot Stuff; Hand Of Fate; Cherry Oh Baby; Memory Motel; Hey Negrita; Melody; Fool To Cry; Crazy Mama.*

● FIRST RELEASED 1976
● UK PEAK CHART POSITION: 2
● USA PEAK CHART POSITION: 1

657 THIRD (–) ▲
SOFT MACHINE

When Kevin Ayers left the band, Soft Machine moved into deep jazz/rock - so deep that they rarely rocked. The mercurial Robert Wyatt became occasional vocalist, although they were now effectively an instrumental unit of great originality. *Third* is generally regarded as their peak recording, a wandering foray using Elton Dean's soprano saxophone and Mike Ratledge's keyboards as the foundation to their sound. 'Moon In June' features Wyatt's frail, high-pitched voice, and is still talked about by cultists for the fact that he rarely sang the same words from one performance to another. Difficult music, but well worth the effort, especially after a vat of wine.

● TRACKS: *Facelift; Slightly All The Time; Moon In June; Out-Bloody-Rageous.*

● FIRST RELEASED 1970
● UK PEAK CHART POSITION: 18
● USA PEAK CHART POSITION: did not chart

658 TALKING HEADS: 77 (–) ▲
TALKING HEADS

The first album from this hard-to-categorize quartet has been constantly available since release. They bucked the trend of American rock bands by sounding different and strangely British. This hybrid sound, with a mix of punk, reggae and funk, induced curiosity, and ultimately they became one of the most influential bands of the latter part of the decade, even though their own sound was itself derivative. Twenty years on, this sounds a little vapid compared to their later work, although the power of some songs is retained. 'Psycho Killer', 'The Book I Read' and the ironic lyrical jollity of 'Don't Worry About The Government' still have the ability to sting.

● TRACKS: *Uh-Oh Love Comes To Town; New Feeling; Tentative Decisions; Happy Day; Who Is It?; No Compassion; The Book I Read; Don't Worry About The Government; First Week/Last Week, Carefree; Psycho Killer; Pulled Up.*

● FIRST RELEASED 1977
● UK PEAK CHART POSITION: 60
● USA PEAK CHART POSITION: 97

659 EVERYTHING'S DIFFERENT NOW (–) ▲
'TIL TUESDAY

The least successful of 'Til Tuesday's three albums, *Everything's Different Now* is also the best loved. By the time it was released, 'Til Tuesday was no longer extant, having trimmed down to Aimee Mann and whomever she was collaborating with that week. As a result, *Everything's Different Now* is for all intents and purposes Mann's first solo album, displaying themes that would become familiar in her later work: micro-analyses of failed relationships in general and her failed relationship with songwriter Jules Shear in particular ("J' for Jules'), contrasted with her steadfast belief in true love ('(Believed You Were) Lucky'). *Everything's Different Now* nearly lives up to its title, as Mann augments her trademark sound with acoustic guitars and her catchiest hooks yet.

● TRACKS: *Everything's Different Now; R.I.P. In Heaven; Why Must I; 'J' for Jules; (Believed You Were) Lucky; Limits To Love; Long Gone (Buddy); The Other End (Of The Telescope); Crash And Burn; How Can You Give Up?*

● FIRST RELEASED 1988
● UK PEAK CHART POSITION: did not chart
● USA PEAK CHART POSITION: 124

660 ENTER THE WU-TANG (36 CHAMBERS) (–) ▲ WU-TANG CLAN

Staten Island's Wu-Tang Clan made their 1993 debut with an album that single-handedly rectified regional imbalance in US rap. New York had given the world hip-hop but by the early 90s it was dominated by west coast artists, and Ices T and Cube, in particular. *Enter The Wu-Tang (36 Chambers)* introduced the world to Prince Rakeem - alongside Dr Dre the most talented and prolific producer in hip-hop. On top of Rakeem's lovingly assembled collages of urban strife, the Wu-Tang's numerous retinue of rappers laid siege to the microphone. At times an achievement of head-spinning musical intensity (and language that is not so much bad as grievous), when the component pieces work coherently, the formula makes for spectacular listening.

● TRACKS: *Bring Da Ruckus; Shame On A Nigga; Clan In Da Front; Wu-Tang: 7th Chamber; Can It Be All So Simple; Intermission; Da Mystery Of Chessboxin'; Wu-Tang Clan Ain't Nuthing Ta F' Wit; C.R.E.A.M.; Method Man; Protect Ya Neck; Tearz; Wu-Tang: 7th Chamber - Part II; Method Man (Remix) Skunk Mix.*

● FIRST RELEASED 1993
● UK PEAK CHART POSITION: did not chart
● USA PEAK CHART POSITION: 41

HOW DARE YOU ! (–) ▲
10CC

They gave it the ludicrous moniker, '70s art rock'. Over twenty years later it simply sounds like a very good pop album, which is what it was in the first place. Gouldman was already a polished veteran on catchy 60s pop songs and Eric Stewart was an early Mindbender. They gelled perfectly with Godley and Creme and produced some excellent hit singles. This is their best album, which features two of their huge hits, 'Art For Art's Sake' and 'I'm Mandy Fly Me' (nothing to do with the withdrawn drug Mandrax, of course). 10CC had lots of middle-eights, hooks, melodies and twiddly bits, and they still sound very, very good.

● TRACKS: How Dare You; Lazy Ways; I Wanna Rule The World; I'm Mandy Fly Me; Iceberg; Art For Art's Sake; Rock 'N' Roll Lullaby; Head Room; Don't Hang Up; Get It While You Can.

● FIRST RELEASED 1976
● UK PEAK CHART POSITION: 5
● USA PEAK CHART POSITION: 47

DIRT (–) ▲
ALICE IN CHAINS

Brutal and hard but exciting and surprisingly melodic, Dirt made Alice In Chains national stars in 1992 after being around the Seattle alternative rock scene for many years. They produce a blindingly together sound, with the bass of Mike Starr able to switch between following the bass drum beat and cloning Layne Staley's guitar note for note, albeit a few octaves lower. They have such polish that they are often reminiscent of the heyday of Led Zeppelin. Lyrically they plow the familiar angst furrow with tracks such as 'Junkhead', 'Sickman' and 'God Smack'. Equally satisfying are 'Them Bones' and 'Rooster', which saw them start in a direction that led to Jar Of Flies two years later.

● TRACKS: Them Bones; Dam That River; Rain When I Die; Sickman; Rooster; Junkhead; Dirt; God Smack; Hate To Feel; Angry Chair; Down In A Hole; Would?

● FIRST RELEASED 1992
● UK PEAK CHART POSITION: 4
● USA PEAK CHART POSITION: 42

ROCKS (370) ▼
AEROSMITH

One of the reasons why Aerosmith, after a number of creatively lean years, are still given legendary credence and an eager ear with each new release, Rocks encapsulated the very essence of rock 'n' roll. They may have been the target of detractors who still pinned them as nothing more than a poor man's Rolling Stones, but Rocks pioneered a strength and swagger and real depth that remains very nearly unsurpassed. From the slowly escalating 'Back In The Saddle' to the dying strains of 'Home Tonight', this album held the full spirit and soul of Aerosmith in both hands.

● TRACKS: Back In The Saddle; Last Child; Rats In The Cellar; Combination; Sick As A Dog; Nobody's Fault; Get The Lead Out; Lick And A Promise; Home Tonight.

● FIRST RELEASED 1976
● UK PEAK CHART POSITION: did not chart
● USA PEAK CHART POSITION: 3

WALTZ FOR DEBBY (580) ▼
BILL EVANS

Recorded on the same night as Sunday At The Village Vanguard, Waltz For Debby captures one of the most important and well-integrated piano trios in the history of jazz, working on a superbly inspired night. It is clear, listening to this record, that bassist Scott Lafaro had a very special rapport with Evans, and drummer Paul Motian's subtle, improvised accompaniments and eccentric, quirkily quiet swing was the perfect engine for this subtle, impressionistic pianist. Check out the lovely, gentle 'My Foolish Heart', and the lively 'Milestones' and, of course, 'Waltz For Debby'.

● TRACKS: My Foolish Heart; Waltz For Debby; Detour Ahead; My Romance; Some Other Time; Milestones.

● FIRST RELEASED 1961
● UK PEAK CHART POSITION: did not chart
● USA PEAK CHART POSITION: did not chart

665 **BOB DYLAN** (–) ▲
BOB DYLAN

The first album from the greatest musical poet of the 20th century gave little indication of what was to come. Although released in 1961, it reeks of the 50s folk/protest movement. Many of the standards covered by Dylan had been sung by a thousand troubadours throughout the McCarthy era and the anti-war movement. Dylan sings on this like an innocent angel, and makes Ric Von Schmidt's 'Baby, Let Me Follow You Down' sound so sweet. The seeds of greatness were apparent in the sensitive original 'Song To Woody', a sadly overlooked song in the massive Dylan catalogue. A wonderful exercise in what was then and what is not now.

● TRACKS: You're No Good; Talkin' New York; In My Time Of Dyin'; Man Of Constant Sorrow; Fixin' To Die; Pretty Peggy-O'; Highway 51; Gospel Plow; Baby, Let Me Follow You Down; House Of The Risin' Sun; Freight Train Blues; Song To Woody; See That My Grave Is Kept Clean.

● FIRST RELEASED 1962
● UK PEAK CHART POSITION: 13
● USA PEAK CHART POSITION: did not chart

 666 **RECKLESS** (244) ▼
BRYAN ADAMS

Bryan Adams was played a great deal on the radio in 1984/5; his music was the most radio-friendly rock to have been heard in a long time. Revisiting this album more than a decade later still confirms this; if anything, hearing him less makes you like him more. The hit singles still sound consistently good - 'Somebody', 'Summer Of '69' and 'Run To You' - but although he has a clearly recognizable style and sound all the other tracks sound fresh. Adams never needs to top this record as there is enough grist on this to keep him playing live forever.

● TRACKS: The Only One; Take Me Back; This Time; Straight From The Heart; Cuts Like A Knife; I'm Ready; What's It Gonna Be; Don't Leave Me Lonely; The Best Was Yet To Come; One Night Love Affair; She's Only Happy When She's Dancin'; Run To You; Heaven; Somebody; Summer Of '69; Kids Wanna Rock; It's Only Love; Long Gone; Ain't Gonna Cry.

● FIRST RELEASED 1984
● UK PEAK CHART POSITION: 7
● USA PEAK CHART POSITION: 1

 667 **LAST TIME AROUND** (–) ▲
BUFFALO SPRINGFIELD

Although this album is effectively the potato peelings of a delicious meal, the fragmentation of the band is no longer apparent thirty years later. Reappraising this record puts it still behind Again, but there is a gentle quality about the whole record. As Messina and Furay took control (later together as Poco), the album develops a country rock feel. Young's premier contribution is 'I Am A Child' and the then prolific Stills hits the button with four gems: the plea for world unity, 'Uno Mundo', the song of a fugitive, 'Four Days Gone', 'Special Care' and the original 'Questions'. A much better album than we could have expected from this outstanding group.

● TRACKS: On The Way Home; It's So Hard To Wait; Pretty Girl Why; Four Days Gone; Carefree Country Day; Special Care; The Hour Of Not Quite Rain; Questions; I Am A Child; Merry-Go-Round; Uno Mundo; Kind Woman.

● FIRST RELEASED 1968
● UK PEAK CHART POSITION: did not chart
● USA PEAK CHART POSITION: 42

 668 **LICK MY DECALS OFF, BABY** (988) ▲
CAPTAIN BEEFHEART AND THE MAGIC BAND

Beefheart's second recording for Frank Zappa's Straight label consolidated the artistic freedom expressed on its predecessor Trout Mask Replica. Avant garde rock and free jazz melt into a seamless whole, jagged guitars and ravaged saxophone splinter through the mix while ex-Mothers Of Invention drummer Artie Tryp, herein renamed Ed Marimba, brings new rhythmic possibilities to the Captain's heady brew. Beefheart prowls around the proceedings with consummate ease, his expressive voice, which echoes bluesman Howlin' Wolf, emphasizing the adventurism of both music and lyrics. By demolishing previous notions of tonality and structure, Captain Beefheart inspired a whole generation of post-punk disciples, from Pere Ubu to Sonic Youth. A CD release please.

● TRACKS: Lick My Decals Off, Baby; Doctor Dark; I Love You, You Big Dummy; Peon; Bellerin' Plain; Woe-Is-Uh-Me-Bop; Japan In A Dishpan; I Wanna Find A Women That'll Hold My Big Toe Till I Have To Go; Petrified Forest; One Rose That I Mean; The Buggy Boogie Woogie; The Smithsonian Institute Blues (Or The Big Dig); Space-Age Couple; The Clouds Are Full Of Wine (Not Whiskey Or Rye); Flash Gordon's Ape.

● FIRST RELEASED 1970
● UK PEAK CHART POSITION: 20
● USA PEAK CHART POSITION: did not chart

669 COSMO'S FACTORY (362) ▼
CREEDENCE CLEARWATER REVIVAL

Described as the consummate singles act, Creedence Clearwater Revival enhanced this reputation when three of the tracks included herein, 'Travelin' Band', 'Up Around The Bend' and 'Looking Out My Back Door', each achieved gold status. Such recordings fully captured the group's exciting brand of 50s-orientated rock 'n' roll, its urgency enhanced by the expressive voice of lead singer/songwriter John Fogerty. His ability to harness traditional pop but express it in a contemporary manner had been established over four previous albums and *Cosmos Factory* was no exception. Two extended selections, 'Ramble Tamble' and 'I Heard It Through The Grapevine', show a penchant for guitar workouts unexplored since the quartet's debut album, and the combination of economy and experimentation captures an act at a creative peak.

● TRACKS: *Ramble Tamble; Before You Accuse Me; Travelin' Band; Ooby Dooby; Lookin' Out My Back Door; Run Through The Jungle; Up Around The Bend; My Baby Left Me; Who'll Stop The Rain; I Heard It Through The Grapevine; Long As I Can See The Light.*

● FIRST RELEASED 1970
● UK PEAK CHART POSITION: 1
● USA PEAK CHART POSITION: 1

 ### 670 REPERCUSSION (-) ▲
THE DB'S

In 1981, when the New York (via North Carolina) group the dB's released this, their second album, it did not sound like anything else around. Today, it *still* does not sound like anything else. As performers and songwriters, the dB's' affections lay largely with 60s acts such as the Lovin' Spoonful and the Association. However, they recognized that the album was a separate and unique medium from the single, and they treated it as such. Each song shows a different facet of the central theme: breaking up. Together, they form a rare gem. As with the best 60s pop tunes, the sad songs sound happy (the glorious janglefest 'Neverland') and the happy ones sound sad ('I Feel Good (Today)').

● TRACKS: *Happenstance; We Were Happy There; Living A Lie; From A Window To A Screen; Ask For Jill; Amplifier; Neverland; Storm Warning; Ups And Downs; Nothing Is Wrong; In Spain; I Feel Good (Today).*

● FIRST RELEASED 1981.
● UK PEAK CHART POSITION: did not chart
● USA PEAK CHART POSITION: did not chart

 ### 671 SUNSHINE SUPERMAN (-) ▲
DONOVAN

It is incredible to think that 'Sunshine Superman', the proto-psychedelic classic that boasts a Jimmy Page guitar solo, was actually recorded in 1965. It is as though Donovan had barely hung up his much-criticized Dylan cap before emerging, fully fledged, as the UK's Flower Child Number One. The rest of the album, recorded closer to its September 1966 release, is similarly cutting-edge, especially the haunting 'Season Of The Witch', which Al Kooper, Stephen Stills, and Mike Bloomfield covered on *Super Session*. On another track, 'Bert's Blues', he paid tribute to his greatest influence outside of Dylan, folk guitarist/songwriter Bert Jansch. And the Green Lantern received a mention in a song.

● TRACKS: *Sunshine Superman; Legend Of A Girl Child Linda; Three King Fishers; Ferris Wheel; Bert's Blues; Season Of The Witch; The Trip; Guinevere; The Fat Angel; Celeste.*

● FIRST RELEASED 1966
● UK PEAK CHART POSITION: 25
● USA PEAK CHART POSITION: 11

672 AT NEWPORT (247) ▼
DUKE ELLINGTON

This concert marked the so-called rebirth of Ellington. Of course, it was the jazz audience that had lost sight of the band, and Newport saw the end of temporary obscurity. Irritated by the place on the programme and his musicians' habitual tardiness, Ellington began the second set in a do-or-die mood. They did not die. Wonderful solos by the likes of Clark Terry and Johnny Hodges, propulsive drumming, and the incredible marathon solo by Paul Gonsalves that links the two parts of 'Diminuendo In Blue' and 'Crescendo In Blue', make this an evening that will live forever in the annals of jazz.

● TRACKS: *Newport Jazz Festival Suite - a) Festival Junction b) Blues To Be There c) Newport Up; Jeep's Blues; Diminuendo And Crescendo In Blue.*

● FIRST RELEASED 1957
● UK PEAK CHART POSITION: did not chart
● USA PEAK CHART POSITION: 14

673 ONE SIZE FITS ALL (–) ▲
FRANK ZAPPA / MOTHERS OF INVENTION

Unusual for a Zappa album to open with the star turn; he usually waits until midway. 'Inca Road' is a superb piece that reaffirms, should it be necessary, that Zappa was an astonishingly great lead guitarist. The quality of the guitar solo is matched throughout by some skilful keyboards from George Duke. Having said that, the solo on 'Po-Jama People' is also pretty nifty. This was a high-charting album for Zappa (in the USA), and for once justice was done, as other similarly great Zappa albums failed completely. This is one of 71 necessary FZ albums to own!

● TRACKS: Inca Roads; Can't Afford No Shoes; Sofa No 1; Po-Jama People; Florentine Pogen; Evelyn, A Modified Dog; San Ber'dino; Andy; Sofa No. 2.

● FIRST RELEASED 1975
● UK PEAK CHART POSITION: did not chart
● USA PEAK CHART POSITION: 26

 675 THE KICK INSIDE (275) ▼
KATE BUSH

Discovered and nurtured by Pink Floyd's Dave Gilmour, Kate Bush burst into an unsuspecting world with the dramatic 'Wuthering Heights'. The ambitiousness of this startling single was carried over into the singer's debut album where already imaginative compositions were enriched by her evocative falsetto. Bush's intonation expressed a variety of emotions. Alternately coy, playful and sensual, she uses her voice to swoop and glide around the material, enhancing the imagery posed by graphic lyrics. Sympathetic accompaniment added weight to a collection in which the artist's purposeful single-mindedness was already apparent.

● TRACKS: Moving; Saxophone Song; Strange Phenomena; Kite; The Man With The Child In His Eyes; Wuthering Heights; James And The Cold Gun; Feel It; Oh To Be In Love; L'Amour Looks Something Like You; Them Heavy People; Room For The Life; The Kick Inside.

● FIRST RELEASED 1978
● UK PEAK CHART POSITION: 3
● USA PEAK CHART POSITION: did not chart

 674 THE REVOLUTION WILL NOT BE TELEVISED (–) ▲ GIL SCOTT-HERON

Unconsciously, Scott-Heron was one of the first rappers. The title track is a strong attack on the way the racist media can manipulate and distort. Cutting and humorous, he gets to the heart of the matter and his literate delivery explains why he wrote his first book at the age of 12. What is not often addressed is his fabulous voice, a cross between Mark Murphy and Jackie Wilson, full of soul, especially emotive on 'The Get Out Of The Ghetto Blues'. He has chosen to use his voice to educate, and his crystal-clear diction (he is a regular public performer of his work at poetry readings) makes listening wholly pleasurable.

● TRACKS: The Revolution Will Be Televised; Sex Education-Ghetto Style; The Get Out Of The Ghetto Blues; No Knock; Lady Day And John Coltrane; Pieces Of A Man; Home Is Where The Hatred Is; Brother; Save The Children; Whitey On The Moon; Did You Hear What They Said; When You Are Who You Are; I Think I'll Call It Morning; A Sign Of The Ages; Or Down You Fall; The Needle's Eye; The Prisoner.

● FIRST RELEASED 1970-72
● UK PEAK CHART POSITION: did not chart
● USA PEAK CHART POSITION: did not chart

 676 SONGS OF LOVE AND HATE (789) ▲
LEONARD COHEN

Leonard Cohen was already established as a denizen of 'bedsitter music' by the time this third album was issued. Deftly balanced between newly written material and older songs, it contains several of the singer's most graphic and literate compositions. Allegory vies with personal recollection to create a set of unparalleled depth while Cohen's grasp of melody stays as secure as ever. His unconventional voice remains fixedly morose, but its individuality ensures a bewitching resonance, particularly on 'Famous Blue Raincoat' and 'Joan Of Arc'. Cohen's poetic imagery was never as striking or as moving.

● TRACKS: Avalanche; Last Year's Man; Dress Rehearsal Rag; Diamonds In The Mine Field; Love Calls You By Your Name; Famous Blue Raincoat; Sing Another Song, Boys; Joan Of Arc.

● FIRST RELEASED 1971
● UK PEAK CHART POSITION: 4
● USA PEAK CHART POSITION: 145

677 DAYDREAM (306) ▼
THE LOVIN' SPOONFUL

At least one album from this stellar New York pop band should be in every collection and *Daydream* narrowly pipped *Do You Believe In Magic* and *Hums Of*. John Sebastian was a lyrical genius and master craftsman of short, humorous love songs. Lengthy titles said exactly what they meant, with 'Didn't Want To Have To Do It' or 'You Didn't Have To Be So Nice' (an unforgettable intro), are both glorious. Sebastian, Boone, Yanovsky and Butler were no slouches at goodtime blues either, for example, 'Bald Headed Lena' and 'Jug Band Music'. It is, however, the title track that brings the biggest smiles and happiest memories. As indispensable as the Beatles.

● TRACKS: *Daydream; There She Is; It's Not Time Now; Warm Baby; Day Blues; Let The Boy Rock & Roll; Jug Band Music; Didn't Want To Have To Do It; You Didn't Have To Be So Nice; Bald Headed Lena; Butchie's Tune; Big Noise From Speonk.*

● FIRST RELEASED 1966
● UK PEAK CHART POSITION: 8
● USA PEAK CHART POSITION: 10

679 MODERN LOVERS (–) ▲
MODERN LOVERS

One of the great 'lost' albums in rock history, *Modern Lovers* offered listeners a bridge between the Velvet Underground and the birth of punk. It also introduced them to Jonathan Richman, a most underrated songwriter. The Modern Lovers' only proper album is actually a collection of demos recorded with John Cale in the early 70s. They were never released until 1976, by which time the band had long passed. The classic tracks available here include 'Pablo Picasso', 'She Cracked' and 'Roadrunner', the subliminal influence at work behind Cornershop's 'Brimful Of Asha'. Richman's aching vocals, often seemingly on the point of collapse, provide the sort of direct emotional connection that great rock 'n' roll has always been about.

● TRACKS: *Roadrunner; Astral Plane; Old World; Pablo Picasso; I'm Straight; She Cracked; Hospital; Someone I Care About; Girl Friend; Modern World; Dignified And Old; Government Center.*

● FIRST RELEASED 1976
● UK PEAK CHART POSITION: did not chart
● USA PEAK CHART POSITION: did not chart

678 SPIRIT OF DJANGO (–) ▲
MARTIN TAYLOR

Something about this album captured more than just the core of jazz buffs and fans of Taylor's exquisite acoustic jazz guitar. It sold remarkably well and was universally applauded. Taylor is supported by Alec Dankworth (bass), Dave O'Higgins (sax), Jack Emblow (accordion) and guitarist John Goldie. The concept of paying homage by playing in Django's style, but not necessarily following his songs, is highly original. To choose to Djangoize Gershwin's 'Lady Be Good' and Cole Porter's 'Night And Day was clever. To Djangoize Robert Palmer's 'Johnny And Mary' and Pat Metheny's James Taylor tribute, 'James', was inspiring.

● TRACKS: *Chez Fernand; Minor Swing; Night And Day; Nuages; James; Double Top; Django's Dream; Swing; Lady Be Good; Honeysuckle Rose; Johnny And Mary.*

● FIRST RELEASED 1994
● UK PEAK CHART POSITION: did not chart
● USA PEAK CHART POSITION: did not chart

680 MESSAGE FROM THE COUNTRY (–) ▲
THE MOVE

At the time that Roy Wood and Jeff Lynne were recording this album, most of their artistic energy was going into the creation of the Electric Light Orchestra. Wood's 'It Wasn't My Idea To Dance' has the same dissonance that characterized the first ELO album, and, with a little cello, could easily pass as a track from that record. The pop sensibility that shone through the Move's early work was still there, but the group was losing its artistic focus, although as a performing unit it was at its peak. When they set their sights on a specific goal, such as 'The Minister', with its 'Paperback Writer' feel, or the title track, with its Beach Boys a cappella coda, the results were magical.

● TRACKS: *It Wasn't My Idea To Dance; The Minister; Message From The Country; Words Of Aaron; Ben Crawley Steel Company; Until Your Mama's Gone; No Time; Ella James; Don't Mess Me Up; My Marge.*

● FIRST RELEASED 1971.
● UK PEAK CHART POSITION: did not chart
● USA PEAK CHART POSITION: did not chart

681 SUBSTANCE (–) ▲
NEW ORDER

NEW
ORDER
—
SUBSTANCE
1987

Career retrospectives are usually shoddy affairs, ignored by weary bands with little concern for the integrity of their discography, and overseen instead by haphazard record company execs trying to wring the last penny from their fading stars. *Substance* deflects both potential criticisms - the music is overwhelmingly strong and the presentation superior. Listening to this collection of singles and b-sides, it is impossible not to admire both the continuity and consistency of New Order's sound. Every fan will have their own favourites, from the group's sublime debut single through to the mature synth-pop of 'True Faith', but it is hard to identify a single dud a-side, and some of the flip-sides included on the second CD are also pretty remarkable.

● TRACKS: CD1: *Ceremony; Everything's Gone Green; Temptation; Blue Monday; Confusion; Thieves Like Us; Perfect Kiss; Subculture; Shellshock; State Of The Nation; Bizarre Love Triangle; True Faith CD2: In A Lonely Place; Procession; Mesh; Hurt; The Beach; Confused Instrumental; Lonesome Tonight; Murder; Thieves Like Us Instrumental; Kiss Of Death; Shame Of The Nation; 1963.*

● FIRST RELEASED 1987
● UK PEAK CHART POSITION: 3
● USA PEAK CHART POSITION: 36

682 STRAIGHT OUTTA COMPTON (561) ▼
NWA

MThey might have lacked Chuck D's dexterity, but when Ice Cube, Dr Dre, MC Ren, Eazy-E, *et al.* arrived on the scene in 1988 they did so with irresistible force. The intensity of the music, the brutality of the rhymes and the explicit violence of the lyrics single-handedly triggered gangsta rap. There had been historical precedents, notably Schooly D, but we have *Straight Outta Compton* to blame for everything from the Geto Boys to Snoop Doggy Dogg (whom Dre would produce). Unlike Public Enemy, NWA were unable to maintain the momentum, and after this album their influence would dissipate with the defection of chief lyricist Cube. However, this album even provoked the interest of the FBI.

● TRACKS: *Straight Outta Compton; Fu** The Police; Gangsta Gangsta; If It Ain't Rough It Ain't Me; Parental Discretion Is Advised; Express Yourself; I Ain't The One; Dopeman; Compton's In The House; 8 Ball.*

● FIRST RELEASED 1989
● UK PEAK CHART POSITION: 41
● USA PEAK CHART POSITION: 37

683 MY FAIR LADY (246) ▼
ORIGINAL BROADWAY CAST

By the early 90s this superb album of what some still consider to be the most perfect stage musical ever, had spent a record-breaking 292 weeks in the US Top 40 - 15 of them at number 1. It also stayed in the upper reaches of the UK chart for 129 weeks. The album was recorded in mono, and Alan Jay Lerner and Frederick Loewe's wonderful score, and a cast headed by Rex Harrison, Julie Andrews and Stanley Holloway, were not nearly so effective in the subsequent stereo version. Just 10 years after its initial release sales were estimated to be well over six million, and the album was inducted into the NARAS Hall of Fame in 1977.

● TRACKS: *Overture; Why Can't The English; Wouldn't It Be Loverly?; With A Little Bit Of Luck; I'm An Ordinary Man; Just You Wait; The Rain In Spain; I Could Have Danced All Night; Ascot Gavotte; On The Street Where You Live; You Did It; Show Me; Get Me To The Church On Time; Hymn To Him; Without You; I've Grown Accustomed To Her Face.*

● FIRST RELEASED 1956
● UK PEAK CHART POSITION: 2
● USA PEAK CHART POSITION: 1

684 THE PATSY CLINE SHOWCASE (864) ▲
PATSY CLINE

Astonishingly, only three albums were released during Patsy Cline's lifetime, this being the best one. Although she was a competent up-tempo performer, she excelled with tear-jerking ballads like 'I Fall To Pieces' and Willie Nelson's 'Crazy'. Producer Owen Bradley bathed her throbbing vocals with echo, added a vocal group (the Jordanaires) and a gentle beat, sweetened by strings. Thus, they created the template for country music of the 60s. Patsy's male counterpart was Jim Reeves and in 1981, their versions of 'Have You Ever Been Lonely?' and 'I Fall To Pieces' were merged for duet recordings. LeAnn Rimes would not be singing today if it were not for the songs of Patsy Cline.

● TRACKS: *I Fall To Pieces; Foolin' Round; The Wayward Wind; South Of The Border; I Love You So Much It Hurts; Seven Lonely Days; Crazy; San Antonio Rose; True Love; Walking After Midnight; A Poor Man's Roses.*

● FIRST RELEASED 1963
● UK PEAK CHART POSITION: did not chart
● USA PEAK CHART POSITION: 74

685 HEAVY SOUL (–) ▲
PAUL WELLER

As Paul Weller gets better, so his critics start coming out of the woodwork. *Heavy Soul* received black and white reviews, none were grey. Prolonged listening draws out more from the material. It continues his late 60s flirtation that developed on *Stanley Road*. This time the guitar is heavier, although it never clouds the obvious quality of songs such as 'Peacock Suit' and the title track. Weller reveals the pitfalls of neglecting a relationship in the beautiful 'I Should Have Been There To Inspire You'. Further revelatory lyrics can be found in 'Science' with 'I've got a pick in my pocket does that make me a player?'. That is for the listener to make up his or her mind.

● TRACKS: *Heavy Soul Pt 1; Peacock Suit; Up In Suzes' Room; Brushed; Driving Nowhere; I Should Have Been There To Inspire You; Heavy Soul Pt 2; Friday Street; Science; Golden Sands; As You Lean Into The Light; Mermaids.*

● FIRST RELEASED 1997
● UK PEAK CHART POSITION: 2
● USA PEAK CHART POSITION: did not chart

686 BOSSANOVA (462) ▼
PIXIES

With a keen sense of the absurd, Black Francis's (now Frank Black) Pixies were the consummate darlings of the music press - no surprise, with their refreshing mix of overblown guitars, discreet nods to the surreal and a vibrant grasp of pure pop that offered a luscious blow to the senses on execution. 'Cecilia Ann' stood somewhere between spandex metal and 'Beach Blanket Bingo', while the deranged singalong of 'Is She Weird' sat alongside the first single, 'Velouria', underlining their ability to write timeless singles that filled the head and sent toes tapping incessantly out of time. A recent compilation confirmed their standing.

● TRACKS: *Cecilia Ann; Velouria; Is She Weird; All Over The World; Down To The Well; Blown Away; Stormy Weather; Rock Music; Allison; Ana; Dig For Fire; The Happening; Hang Wire; Havalina.*

● FIRST RELEASED 1990
● UK PEAK CHART POSITION: 3
● USA PEAK CHART POSITION: 70

687 A DAY AT THE RACES (238) ▼
QUEEN

Another UK number 1 for Queen, *A Day At The Races* celebrated their diversity and colourfully flamboyant sense of the unreal. Stylistically, the adoption of any one musical form over the other was simply beneath them. They flirted with a passion, dipping and whimsical with 'Good Old Fashioned Lover Boy', grand, entranced and eloquent with 'Somebody To Love', while 'Tie Your Mother Down', with its sense of mischief, scathing wit and a shrill, delighted laugh, put its foot through the floor and a fist through the ceiling. To paraphrase *The Times*, a work of sheer bloody poetry.

● TRACKS: *Long Away; The Millionaire Waltz; You And I; Somebody To Love; White Man; Good Old Fashioned Lover Boy; Drowse; Teo Torriate (Let Us Cling Together); Tie Your Mother Down; You Take My Breath Away.*

● FIRST RELEASED 1976
● UK PEAK CHART POSITION: 1
● USA PEAK CHART POSITION: 5

688 HAND OF KINDNESS (944) ▲
RICHARD THOMPSON

Richard Thompson's position as Britain's premier chronicler of pain, loving and most things dark, was on the line here, his first album minus wife of a decade Linda - hers a voice guaranteed to lift any music - and with much to prove. He did it with considerable panache and a trusted band of old mates. The collection is a two-headed demon, combining rock with an acoustic intimacy. The songs are of a vintage, with 'A Poisoned Heart And A Twisted Memory', 'Hand Of Kindness' itself, and his greatest ever folk song, 'Devonside'. Hungry music that should be force fed to those who have not yet discovered their Thompson appetite.

● TRACKS: *Tear Stained Letter; How I Wanted To; Both Ends Burning; A Poisoned Heart And A Twisted Memory; The Wrong Heartbeat; Hand Of Kindness; Devonside; Two Left Feet.*

● FIRST RELEASED 1983
● UK PEAK CHART POSITION: did not chart
● USA PEAK CHART POSITION: 186

689 CRIME OF THE CENTURY (–) ▲
SUPERTRAMP

The punishment befits the crime, and a quarter of a century later, Supertramp have been forgiven by critics. Quite why they induced such negative press seems unjustified, as 'Bloody Well Right' and 'Dreamer' sound as fresh as ever. The electric piano cuts through the speakers like a knife through butter, the treble at times hurting the ear like a heavy rock guitar solo. Both Hodgson's and Davies' voices sound rich and confident, although both are quite different. Maybe the pace slackens with the slightly indulgent 'If Everyone Was Listening' and the title track, but there are enough musical highlights to recommend this for any would-be 90s progster's wants list.

● TRACKS: School; Bloody Well Right; Hide In Your Shell; Asylum; Dreamer; Rudy; If Everyone Was Listening; Crime Of The Century.

● FIRST RELEASED 1974
● UK PEAK CHART POSITION: 4
● USA PEAK CHART POSITION: 38

690 TANX (–) ▲
T. REX

There were more successful T. Rex albums, notably The Slider, but without any hit singles, this collection seems to win favour as the most cohesive and interesting. The reissued CD on Edsel has the generous bonus of seven tracks, including the largely ignored single 'Children Of The Revolution'. The expanded booklet has excellent sleeve notes from Bolanologist Mark Paytress; unfortunately, the designer decided to make them totally unreadable with ludicrous overprinting. This album clearly demonstrates there is more to the Bolan catalogue than the radio-flogged 'Get It On' and 'Telegram Sam'. He was a fascinating lyricist, who could hope to put the line 'myxomatosis is an animal's disease' in a song and succeed.

● TRACKS: Tenement Lady; Rapids; Mister Mister; Broken-Hearted Blues; Shock Rock; Country Honey; Electric Slim & The Factory Hen; Mad Donna; Born To Boogie; Life Is Strange; The Street & Babe Shadow; Highway Knees; Left Handed Luke & The Beggar Boys; Children Of The Revolution; Jitterbug Love; Sunken Rags; Solid Gold Easy Action; Xmas Message; 20th Century Boy; Free Angel.

● FIRST RELEASED 1972
● UK PEAK CHART POSITION: 4 ● USA PEAK CHART POSITION: 102

691 FLOOD (–) ▲
THEY MIGHT BE GIANTS

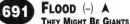

It is fair to say that listening to this, their second album, in one hit is a little hard on the ear. Individually, the pathos and humour these chaps manage to put into every song is admirable - very much like a 90s version of Tom Lehrer, but without the satire. The jokes are ironic rather than obvious. Their commercial success is, of course, due to the songs' accessibility, the most commercial being the wonderful 'Birdhouse In Your Soul', a deserved hit single. The story of a back-stabbing office ogre is chronicled in the shape of 'Someone Keeps Moving My Chair'. Some tracks are clearly private jokes and pass by the listener, although self-interpretation can come into play.

● TRACKS: Theme From Flood; Birdhouse In Your Soul; Lucky Ball & Chain; Istanbul (Not Constantinople); Dead; Your Racist Friend; Particle Man; Twisting; We Want A Rock; Someone Keeps Moving My Chair; Hearing Aid; Minimum Wage; Letterbox; Whistling In The Dark; Hot Cha; Women & Men; Sapphire Bullets Of Pure Love; They Might Be Giants; Road Movie To Berlin.

● FIRST RELEASED 1990
● UK PEAK CHART POSITION: 14
● USA PEAK CHART POSITION: 75

692 SOUTH PACIFIC (248) ▼
VARIOUS

The blockbuster film starring Mitzi Gaynor, Rossano Brazzi and John Kerr spawned this record-breaking album full of some of Richard Rodgers and Oscar Hammerstein II's most popular songs. Opera singer Giorgio Tozzi dubbed for Brazzi's singing voice on the beautiful 'Some Enchanted Evening' and others, but Mitzi Gaynor provided her own vocals on songs such as the famous 'I'm Gonna Wash That Man Right Outa My Hair', 'I'm In Love With A Wonderful Guy', and the delightful 'Honey Bun'. The statistics are frightening - USA: 161 weeks in the chart, 31 of them at number 1; UK: a total of 115 weeks at number 1, 70 of them consecutively. The UK figures are (to date) a record.

● TRACKS: South Pacific Overture; Dites Moi; Cockeyed Optimist; Twin Soliloquies; Some Enchanted Evening; Bloody Mary; There Is Nothin' Like A Dame; Bali Ha'i; I'm Gonna Wash That Man Right Outa My Hair; I'm In Love With A Wonderful Guy; Younger Than Springtime; This Is How It Feels; Entr'acte; Happy Talk; Honey Bun; You've Got To Be Carefully Taught; This Nearly Was Mine.

● FIRST RELEASED 1958
● UK PEAK CHART POSITION: 1
● USA PEAK CHART POSITION: 1

693 SOUND OF MUSIC (263) ▼
ORIGINAL BROADWAY CAST

Multi-million sales, a spell of 16 weeks at the top of the US chart, and winning Gold Disc and Grammy Awards were fitting rewards for this memorable recording of Richard Rodgers and Oscar Hammerstein II's much-loved musical which opened on Broadway in November 1959. The show's stars, Mary Martin and Theodore Bikel, were in fine vocal form, and led the excellent cast through the score's highlights, which included 'My Favourite Things', 'Do-Re-Mi', and 'Edelweiss' - the last song that Rodgers and Hammerstein wrote together before the latter's death in 1960.

● TRACKS: *Preludium; The Sound Of Music; Maria; A Bell Is No Bell; I Have Confidence In Me; Do-Re-Mi; Sixteen Going On Seventeen; My Favourite Things; The Lonely Goatherd; How Can Love Survive; So Long, Farewell; Climb Every Mountain; Something Good; Wedding Sequence; Maria (Reprise); Concert Do-Re-Mi (Reprise); Edelweiss; So Long, Farewell (Reprise); Climb Every Mountain (Reprise).*

● FIRST RELEASED 1960
● UK PEAK CHART POSITION: 4
● USA PEAK CHART POSITION: 1

695 C'MON KIDS (–) ▲
THE BOO RADLEYS

A consistently imaginative album and one that reveals at least one clever hook or twist in every track. Returning to the spirit of *Giant Steps* after their recent chart forays, a screeching wall-of-guitar noise dominates the title track, which leads into increasingly strange subject matter ('Meltin's Worm') and fresh musical ideas throughout. The dub feel of 'Fortunate Son' recalls the mighty 'Lazarus', and the Simon And Garfunkel-style harmonies of 'New Brighton Promenade' emphasize the Boos' stunning ability to write crafted, melodic pop songs. Overall a highly uncommercial album, it nevertheless restored the band's reputation as inspired pop experimenters.

● TRACKS: *C'mon Kids; Meltin's Worm; Melodies For The Deaf (Colours For The Blind); Get On The Bus; Everything Is Sorrow; Bullfrog Green; What's In The Box (See Whatcha Got); Four Saints; New Brighton Promenade; Fortunate Son; Shelter; Ride The Tiger; One Last Hurrah.*

● FIRST RELEASED 1996
● UK PEAK CHART POSITION: 1
● USA PEAK CHART POSITION: did not chart

694 AFRICAN HERBSMAN (–) ▲
BOB MARLEY AND THE WAILERS

Prior to the universal success that Marley later experienced, he was already a giant at home. Having worked with all the legendary producers, he still could not find the key to expand his territory. This album represents his work with Lee Perry at the end of the 60s and up to *Catch A Fire*. Many of the songs he later re-recorded, and the latter versions are the familiar ones. These, however, have authenticity; they are less polished but sound Jamaican. 'Lively Up Yourself', '400 Years' and 'Kaya' sound smoother than their famous relatives. The bass is rounder and Marley's vocals are mixed in, rather than up-front. Historically indispensable.

● TRACKS: *Lively Up Yourself; Small Axe; Duppy Conquerer; Trench Town Rock; African Herbsman; Keep On Moving; Fussing And Fighting; Stand Alone; All In One; Don't Rock The Boat; Put It On; Sun Is Shining; Kaya; Riding High; Brain Washing; 400 Years.*

● FIRST RELEASED 1974
● UK PEAK CHART POSITION: did not chart
● USA PEAK CHART POSITION: did not chart

696 DAMN RIGHT, I'VE GOT THE BLUES
(507) ▼ BUDDY GUY

And in 1991, he had good reason. At that point, Guy had not made a studio album for a decade. The fact that Eric Clapton, who made sure that Buddy was a regular guest on his Royal Albert Hall blues nights, had called him the world's greatest guitarist still had not gained him a recording contract. Silvertone put that right with sessions that included the best session men from Britain and America, with guest appearances by Clapton, Jeff Beck and Mark Knopfler. The album showed all sides of Guy's talent, the blues singer, the soul man and the extravagantly gifted guitarist. A reluctant star, he has nevertheless taken full advantage of his new-found status as the uncrowned King of Chicago Blues.

● TRACKS: *Damn Right I Got The Blues; Where Is The Next One Coming From; Five Long Years; Missing Sally; There Is Something On Your Mind; Early In The Morning; Too Broke To Spend The Night; Let Me Love You Baby; Rememberin' Stevie.*

● FIRST RELEASED 1991
● UK PEAK CHART POSITION: 43
● USA PEAK CHART POSITION: 136

697 **TEASER AND THE FIRECAT** (595) ▼
CAT STEVENS

Following in the tradition of his previous effort, with a similar cover design and feel, Cat continued his painful journey through life. Even then, there was a sadness linked to his happy songs such as 'Moonshadow', 'How Can I Tell You' and 'Tuesday's Dead'. Our favourite school hymn was also given the treatment - how did he manage to make such a happy verse sound so sad? The answer, as we have all seen, was in himself; he was a rare songwriter but he was mostly a very troubled soul, something he seems to have resolved through his conversion to the Muslim faith. He won, we lost him.

● TRACKS: *The Wind; Rubylove; If I Laugh; Changes IV; How Can I Tell You; Tuesday's Dead; Morning Has Broken; Bitterblue; Moonshadow; Peace Train.*

● FIRST RELEASED 1971
● UK PEAK CHART POSITION: 3
● USA PEAK CHART POSITION: 2

 698 **MINGUS AH UM** (536) ▼
CHARLES MINGUS

One of the five essential Mingus albums to own, and even if you are not a jazz fan this is still worthy of being in any comprehensive collection. The opening track, 'Better Git It In Your Soul', rushes along at a furious pace and then there is a wonderful change of tempo into an a cappella and handclap pause. It rolls on, of course, but the nature of this track reflects the nature of Mingus who never failed to experiment (even though sometimes he failed). The personnel comprises John Handy III, Shafi Hadi and Booker Ervin (saxophones), Horace Parlan Jr (piano), Willie Dennis and James Knepper (trombones) and Charles Richmond (drums). Mingus whoops, shouts and holds it all together and then turns the pace majestically on numbers such as 'Goodbye Pork Pie Hat'.

● TRACKS: *Better Git It In Your Soul; Goodbye Pork Pie Hat; Boogie Stop Shuffle; Self-Portrait In Three Colours; Open Letter To Duke; Bird Calls; Fables Of Faubus; Pussy Cat Dues; Jelly Roll*

● FIRST RELEASED 1960
● UK PEAK CHART POSITION: did not chart
● USA PEAK CHART POSITION: did not chart

 699 **CHICAGO TRANSIT AUTHORITY** (–) ▲
CHICAGO

This debut has surprisingly endured, whereas all their following 18,000 albums with the same title (other than a number change) have little or no credibility in the public's memory. This album can be interchanged with the second and third Blood Sweat And Tears album; all represent the very best of late 60s American jazz/rock. The band changed their name soon afterwards as they ploughed a successful path into smooth AOR. Lengthy tracks such as 'South California Purples' and their excellent cover version of Spencer Davis Group's 'I'm A Man' prove beyond doubt that these chaps can really play. Maybe they were smarter than most in seeing the limitations of jazz/rock and moving on to play Russian roulette.

● TRACKS: *Introduction; Does Anybody Really Know What Time It Is?; Beginnings; Questions 67 & 68; Listen; Poem 58; Free Form Guitar; South California Purples; I'm A Man; Prologue, August 29, 1968; Someday August 29 1968; Liberation.*

● FIRST RELEASED 1969
● UK PEAK CHART POSITION: 9
● USA PEAK CHART POSITION: 17

 700 **CROCODILES** (529) ▼
ECHO AND THE BUNNYMEN

Echo And The Bunnymen was formed by vocalist Ian McCulloch on sundering his partnership with Julian Cope in the Crucial Three. The singer's mélange of Jim Morrison and Lou Reed is encapsulated on this engaging album, which matched persuasive melodies to a moody air of doom. It included a re-recording of the quartet's first single, 'Pictures On My Wall', and the anthem-like 'All That Jazz', but while the musicians invested each track with a taut precision, especially guitarist Will Sergeant, *Crocodiles'* strength is derived from McCulloch's stylish vocals. He adds a new dimension to already strong material, a factor investing the set with its lasting appeal.

● TRACKS: *Going Up; Stars Are Stars; Pride; Monkeys; Crocodiles; Rescue; Villiers Terrace; Pictures On My Wall; All That Jazz; Happy Death Men.*

● FIRST RELEASED 1980
● UK PEAK CHART POSITION: 17
● USA PEAK CHART POSITION: did not chart

TELL MAMA (473) ▼
ETTA JAMES

Having already been an established leading soul singer for 13 years and having 18 R&B hits to her name, in 1967 Etta went to record in Alabama at the legendary Muscle Shoals studio. The result was her most accomplished album, on which her voice had been mixed to perfection, allowing her to sound strong on the previously distorted high notes. James was rightly seen in a different light as one of the great soul voices of all time as she belted out powerful tracks such as 'The Love Of My Man' and 'Watch Dog'. Her slower numbers were equally arresting, including the wonderful 'I'd Rather Go Blind'.

● TRACKS: Tell Mama; I'd Rather Go Blind; Watch Dog; The Love Of My Man; I'm Gonna Take What He's Got; The Same Rope; Security; Steal Away; My Mother-In-Law; Don't Lose Your Good Thing; It Hurts Me So Much; Just A Little Bit.

● FIRST RELEASED 1968
● UK PEAK CHART POSITION: did not chart
● USA PEAK CHART POSITION: 82

 SHIFT WORK (488) ▼
THE FALL

Shift Work is divided into two parts, both exhuming the doom that was prevalent for the unprivileged during Thatcher's reign. Mark Smith illuminates his feelings with some of his finest sneering and slurred vocals. Part 1, 'Earth's Impossible Day' and Part 2, 'Notebooks Out Plagiarists', are both essential listening. The Fall churn out great albums, quickly and quietly - they need to be noisy so that the rest of the world can catch up with an incredible band who should stand alongside the Smiths as giants of thinking people's irreverent music. Mark E. Smith's time will surely come, even though he is leaving it rather late.

● TRACKS: "Earths Impossible Day": So What About It?; Idiot Joy Showland; Edinburgh Man; Pittsville Direkt; The Book Of Lies; High Tension Line; The War Against Intelligence; "Notebooks Out Plagiarists": Shift-Work; You Haven't Found It Yet; The Mixer; White Lightning; A Lot Of Wind; Rose; Sinister Waltz.

● FIRST RELEASED 1991
● UK PEAK CHART POSITION: 17
● USA PEAK CHART POSITION: did not chart

703 **ROCK AND ROLLIN' WITH** (254) ▼
FATS DOMINO

Antoine 'Fats' Domino's brand of New Orleans R&B had scarcely changed since his first record, 'The Fat Man', in 1949 but with the advent of rock 'n' roll, his record label encouraged him to push the rhythm, drop the blues, beef up the saxes, write teenage lyrics and call it rock 'n' roll. Fats did not mind: he simply loved playing music. This collection included older material such as 'Please Don't Leave Me', but still justified the rock 'n' roll tag. Fats' wife is the subject of 'Rosemary' and they had eight children, each of which was christened with a name beginning with 'A'. Perhaps Fats' records had plenty of bounce because he used to work in a bedsprings factory?

● TRACKS: Tired Of Crying; Rosemary; All By Myself; You Said You Love Me; Ain't It A Shame; The Fat Man; Poor Me; Bo Weevil; Don't Blame It On Me; Goin' Home; Going To The River; Please Don't Leave Me.

● FIRST RELEASED 1956
● UK PEAK CHART POSITION: did not chart
● USA PEAK CHART POSITION: 17

704 **LUMPY GRAVY** (–) ▲
FRANK ZAPPA

Was it that Zappa's music was so far ahead of its time, or was it just not what we thought a weirdo genius like him should be doing? Either way, since his death, his stature as a serious composer has grown. Lumpy Gravy missed most by a mile because it was the first of Zappa's 'challenging' orchestral pieces, and not what his audience had come to expect. Performed by the Abnuceals Emuukha Electric Symphony Orchestra & Chorus, it was a lengthy instrumental suite broken up by equally 'challenging' dialogue. On the back cover, Frank looks out and asks, 'is this phase 2 of We're Only In It For The Money?'. No, we don't think so.

● TRACKS: Part One: The Way I See It Barry; Duodenum; Oh No; Bit Of Nostalgia; It's From Kansas; Bored Out 90 Over; Almost Chinese; Switching Girls; Oh No Again; At The Gas Station; Another Pickup; I Don't Know If I Can Go Through This Again; Part Two; Very Distraughtening; White Ugliness; Amen; Just One More Time; A Vicious Circle; King Kong; Drums Are Too Noisy; Kangaroos; Envelops The Bath Tub; Take Your Clothes Off.

● FIRST RELEASED 1968
● UK PEAK CHART POSITION: did not chart
● USA PEAK CHART POSITION: 159

705 GETTING READY... (548) ▼
FREDDIE KING

Although a Texas boy, King came to musical maturity on Chicago's West Side, along with Magic Sam, Otis Rush and Buddy Guy. During the early 60s, he made a groundbreaking series of records, vocal and instrumental, 'Have You Ever Loved A Woman' and 'Hideaway' later became standards during the British blues boom. In 1966, he made a couple of lacklustre records before signing with Leon Russell's Shelter label. Russell had a deep appreciation of King's music and knew how to combine traditional material with contemporary arrangements. It showed that Freddie's talents were still intact on a set of standard blues that included 'Dust My Broom', and 'Key To The Highway'. The diamond, however, is 'Going Down', with the world's greatest descending riff.

● TRACKS: *Same Old Blues; Dust My Broom; Worried Life Blues; Five Long Years; Key To The Highway; Going Down; Living On The Highway; Walking By Myself; Tore Down; Palace Of The King; Gimme Some Lovin'; Send Someone To Love.*

● FIRST RELEASED 1971
● UK PEAK CHART POSITION: did not chart
● USA PEAK CHART POSITION: did not chart

706 BLUEJEAN BOP! (453) ▼
GENE VINCENT

In May 1956, the two-and-a-half minutes of 'Be Bop A Lula' marked the astonishing recording debut of Gene Vincent, and the following month Gene was back in Owen Bradley's studio in Nashville for his first album, *Bluejean Bop*. Producer Ken Nelson flipped the echo switch to maximum and created a space-age sound for 'Who Slapped John?', in particular. Gene's voice was softer than most rock 'n' rollers and his tender versions of 'Ain't She Sweet?' and 'Up A Lazy River' display an inkling to become an all-round entertainer. His country roots are covered in 'Waltz Of The Wind' but it is the extraordinary rock 'n' roll numbers such as 'Bluejean Bop' and 'Bop Street' (don't be fooled by the slow start!) that make the album so remarkable and created a guitar hero out of Cliff Gallup. Gene Vincent rocks, the Bluecaps roll and the result is uninhibited magic.

● TRACKS: *Bluejean Bop; Jezebel; Who Slapped John?; Ain't She Sweet?; I Flipped; Waltz Of The Wind; Jump Back, Honey, Jump Back; That Old Gang Of Mine; Jumps, Giggles, And Shouts; Up A Lazy River; Bop Street; Peg O' My Heart.*

● FIRST RELEASED 1956
● UK PEAK CHART POSITION: did not chart
● USA PEAK CHART POSITION: 16

707 THE SOUND OF 65 (861) ▲
THE GRAHAM BOND ORGANIZATION

Of the many groups that developed from Blues Incorporated, this was probably the most musically talented. Led by the larger-than-life Graham Bond on organ, the Organization consisted of Jack Bruce, Ginger Baker and Dick Heckstall-Smith. Every member of the band came from a jazz background and brought a much more open and improvisational approach to their blues playing, which had a harder edge than that heard from similar groups led by Georgie Fame and Brian Auger. Their repertoire ranged from crowd-pleasers like 'Hoochie Coochie Man' and 'Got My Mojo Working' to Ramsey Lewis's 'Wade In The Water'. This album was pressed in very small quantities, and is now a collectors' item. Whether or not they were the sound of 65, Bond never achieved the equivalent success of Bruce and Baker before his life ended under the wheels of an Underground train in May 1974.

● TRACKS: *Hoochie Coochie Man; Baby Make Love To Me; Neighbour Neighbour; Early In The Morning; Spanish Eyes; Oh Baby; Little Girl; I Want You; Wade In The Water; Got My Mojo Working; Train Time; Baby Be Good To Me; Half A Man; Tammy.*

● FIRST RELEASED 1965
● UK PEAK CHART POSITION: did not chart
● USA PEAK CHART POSITION: did not chart

708 DOOKIE (–) ▲
GREEN DAY

Green Day took all the good elements of grunge and mixed them with a fine blend of 70s power pop. That way, they managed to appeal to a wide range of listeners and it probably goes a long way to explain why they sell a damn sight more records than the Pleasers, the Shoes, Flamin' Groovies, Jane's Addiction and Sebadoh put together. *Dookie* has sold 10 million copies in their homeland, and probably half that again worldwide. Their huge success cannot be explained; they are merely a very good pop punkster band with catchy songs and some adrenalin-rush middle-eights. And 'Basket Case' is such a great song.

● TRACKS: *Burnout; Having A Blast; Chump; Long View; Welcome To Paradise; Pulling Teeth; Basket Case; She; Sassafras Roots; When I Come Around; Coming Clean; Emenius Sleepus; In The End; F.O.D.*

● FIRST RELEASED 1994
● UK PEAK CHART POSITION: 13
● USA PEAK CHART POSITION: 2

709 THE IDIOT (–) ▲
IGGY POP

Iggy's solo debut following the end of the Stooges, *The Idiot* is often overlooked in favour of his second epistle, *Lust For Life*. Great album though the latter may be, *The Idiot* served to remind rock's better-informed fans that one of its most original talents was still alive and kicking. Produced by Bowie, *The Idiot* contains two compositions, 'Funtime' and 'China Girl', that he later recorded himself. Another highlight is the electronics-driven 'Nightclubbing' (a certifiable post-punk classic) and the meandering 'Dum Dum Boys' (a precursor to 'The Passenger'). An album that proved Iggy did not need to be flanked by guitars to retain his edge and menace.

● TRACKS: *Sister Midnight; Nightclubbing; Funtime; Baby; China Girl; Dum Dum Boys; Tiny Girls; Mass Production.*

● FIRST RELEASED 1977
● UK PEAK CHART POSITION: 30
● USA PEAK CHART POSITION: 72

711 CROWN OF CREATION (–) ▲
JEFFERSON AIRPLANE

A rich and varied collection showing off the different talents of the main songwriters. Their major breakthrough was still to come with *Volunteers* a year or so later; this is most certainly their *Revolver*. Among the many memorable moments are Slick's beautiful vocal on 'Lather', the band's sensitive cover version of David Crosby's 'Triad' and Jorma Kaukonen's stunning wah-wah solo on 'If You Feel'. Add to this the intense lyrics, such as the drug problems of Grace's subject in 'Greasy Heart', and Balin and Kantner's consistently strong vocals throughout. Finally, although under-recorded compared to his Hot Tuna work, Jack Casady shows his remarkable dexterity on bass.

● TRACKS: *Lather; In Time; Triad; Star Track; Share A Little Joke; Chushingura; If You Feel; Crown Of Creation; Ice Cream Phoenix; Greasy Heart; The House At Pooneil Corners.*

● FIRST RELEASED 1968
● UK PEAK CHART POSITION: did not chart
● USA PEAK CHART POSITION: 6

710 BETWEEN THE LINES (–) ▲
JANIS IAN

A breakthrough album of considerable stature, Janis Ian joined the bedsitter songwriter set with a collection of powerful and beautiful songs with beautifully understated arrangements. 'At Seventeen' was the hit single, a magnificent, mature song about the pains of growing up. Elsewhere, similar sentiments of elusive love are offered with 'When The Party's Over' and the promise of a one-night stand with 'The Come-On'. There were no veiled obsure lyrics here; Ian spoke out loudly and clearly to an audience that could closely relate to at least one of the songs. This album still retains that great quality.

● TRACKS: *When The Party's Over; At Seventeen; From Me To You; Bright Lights And Promises; In The Winter; Water Colors; Between The Lines; The Come On; Light A Light; Tea & Sympathy; Lover's Lullaby.*

● FIRST RELEASED 1975
● UK PEAK CHART POSITION: did not chart
● USA PEAK CHART POSITION: 1

712 JOE COCKER! (–) ▲
JOE COCKER

Still riding high on the American success of his debut album and a show-stopping appearance at the Woodstock festival, Joe Cocker hastily recorded a follow-up with his Grease Band and guest musicans including Leon Russell and Clarence White. Remarkably, it sustained the quality of his debut, with Cocker barnstorming his way through Russell's instant classic 'Delta Lady' and 'Hitchcock Railway', and reworking two more Beatles songs. As on *With A Little Help From My Friends*, it was the more restrained material that revealed most about Cocker's interpretative talents, with sensitive readings of Leonard Cohen's 'Bird On A Wire' and John Sebastian's 'Darlin Be Home Soon' being particularly impressive.

● TRACKS: *Dear Landlord; Bird On The Wire; Lawdy Miss Clawdy; She Came In Through The Bathroom Window; Hitchcock Railway; That's Your Business; Something; Delta Lady; Hello, Little Friend; Darling Be Home Soon.*

● FIRST RELEASED 1969
● UK PEAK CHART POSITION: did not chart
● USA PEAK CHART POSITION: 11

713 JOY OF A TOY (–) ▲
KEVIN AYERS

Ayers left the Soft Machine for a solo career when his basic pop leanings appeared at odds with the intense jazz/rock of his former colleagues. This album was a cult favourite at the end of the 60s for no reason other than that Ayers was well liked because he was ever so slightly mad. Take a look and listen at the content of this album: 'Song For Insane Times', 'Eleanor's Cake (Which Ate Her)' and 'Stop This Train (Again Doing It)'. Through the haze of quirkiness there is a strong light melodic feel to much of the music, and Ayers did possess a heartbreaker voice that prompted one woman to state, 'he is the sexiest man in the world'.

● TRACKS: *Joy Of A Toy Continued; Town Feeling; The Clarietta Rag; Girl On A Swing; Song For Insane Times; Stop This Train (Again Doing It); Eleanor's Cake (Which Ate Her); The Lady Rachel; Oleh Oleh Bandu Bandong; All This Crazy Gift Of Time.*

● FIRST RELEASED 1969
● UK PEAK CHART POSITION: did not chart
● USA PEAK CHART POSITION: did not chart

714 THE KINGSTON TRIO AT LARGE
(587) ▼ THE KINGSTON TRIO

As if to prove a point, this was the second album by the Trio that went to number 1 in the same year, in thir homeland. Back in post-McCarthy America, the folk song had been far less complicated and more immediate. This was an era when right-on students and town dwellers began to look to folk as a focal point for social comment. Recreators such as the Kingstons, as well as authentic rural performers, opened up folk to an ever-expanding audience. With albums like this, folk for 'pop thinkers' was being created and a whole movement had its foundations in back-to-basics, quickly formulated recordings. *At Large* is a credit to its genre.

● TRACKS: *MTA; All My Sorrows; Blew Ye Winds; Carey, Carey; The Seine; I Bowled; Good News; Getaway John; The Long Black Rifle; Early Mornin'; Scarlet Ribbons (For Her Hair); Remember The Alamo.*

● FIRST RELEASED 1959
● UK PEAK CHART POSITION: did not chart
● USA PEAK CHART POSITION: 1

715 THE MAN-MACHINE (–) ▲
KRAFTWERK

The *Man-Machine* and its predecessor, 1977's *Trans-Europe Express*, deserve their exalted position in the pantheon of modern music, if only for their importance in shaping the future development of hip-hop and dance music. The concept behind *The Man-Machine* took Kraftwerk's mechanistic vision of humanity to its logical extreme, but the music within captured the group at their most engagingly melodic. Instantly memorable, 'The Model' reached number 1 in the UK singles chart three years later, and proved to be a direct inspiration for the wave of gloomy electronic bands that quickly followed. However, none of them ever came close to grasping the subtle human touch that lay behind Kraftwerk's faceless exterior.

● TRACKS: *The Robots; Spacelab; Metropolis; The Model; Neon Lights; The Man-Machine.*

● First Released 1978
● UK PEAK CHART POSITION: 9
● USA PEAK CHART POSITION: 130

716 NEW YORK TENDABERRY (829) ▲
LAURA NYRO

Laura Nyro, who died in 1997, found fame when her compositions were covered by other artists, including Blood, Sweat And Tears, Barbra Streisand and the Fifth Dimension. Drawing inspiration from Broadway's Tin Pan Alley, R&B and Brill Building acolytes Carole King and Ellie Greenwich, she wrote material echoing these elements without ever sounding derivative. *New York Tendaberry* shows her skills to full effect, combining brassy, up-tempo pop with plaintive, introspective musings. Nyro's emotional voice swoops and dives at will, emphasizing the intensity of her songwriting. Uncompromising and challenging, this album showcases the art of a painfully underrated performer.

● TRACKS: *You Don't Love Me When I Cry; Captain For Dark Mornings; Tom Cat Goodby; Mercy On Broadway; Save The Country; Gibsom Street; Time And Love; Sweet Lovin Baby; Capatain Saint Lucifer; New York Tendaberry.*

● FIRST RELEASED 1969
● UK PEAK CHART POSITION: did not chart
● USA PEAK CHART POSITION: 32

717 SONGS FROM A ROOM (451) ▼
LEONARD COHEN

Leonard Cohen's second album maintained the haunting strengths of its predecessor. His hypnotic, murmured voice retains its compelling power and the content on *Songs From A Room* proves equally resonant. Where another pensive singer-songwriter might warp his craft with bathos, Cohen injects his work with mature insight, using metaphor and poetic insight to enhance his craft. Superb acoustic guitarwork weaves a path throughout the bewitching melodies, enhancing the singer's spell, although Cohen's self-deprecating humour is equally prevalent, particularly on the singalong 'Tonight Will Be Fine'. *Songs From A Room* captures every facet of Cohen's inestimable talent.

● TRACKS: Bird On A Wire; Story Of Isaac; A Bunch Of Lonesome Heroes; Seems So Long Ago; Nancy; The Old Revolution; The Butcher; You Know Who I Am; Lady Midnight; Tonight Will Be Fine.

● FIRST RELEASED 1969
● UK PEAK CHART POSITION: 2
● USA PEAK CHART POSITION: 63

718 SAILIN' SHOES (264) ▼
LITTLE FEAT

A band that received nothing but praise and is rightly remembered with great affection. The re-formed version of the 90s with Craig Fuller does not come near the magical unit led by the late Lowell George. Most of their albums are recommended as a band that band should sound like. 'Easy To Slip' opens with George smacking chords from his acoustic guitar as his partners fall in line, loose yet totally together. Little Feat were one of the finest bands of the 70s - only now do we really appreciate just how great they were. And yes, this is the one that has 'Willin'' on it.

● TRACKS: Easy To Slip; Cold Cold Cold; Trouble; Tripe Face Boogie; Willin'; A Apolitical Blues; Sailin' Shoes; Teenage Nervous Breakdown; Got No Shadow; Cat Fever; Texas Rose Cafe.

● FIRST RELEASED 1972
● UK PEAK CHART POSITION: did not chart
● USA PEAK CHART POSITION: did not chart

719 VIVID (-) ▲
LIVING COLOUR

One of the most innovative and exciting live acts ever to emerge from New York City, Living Colour vaulted into the spotlight with this debut recording. Critically acclaimed and embraced by fans, *Vivid* defies categorization even 10 years after its release. It transcends genres and fuses disparate musical formats while providing a solid rhythmic foundation for Vernon Reid's impressive guitar work. 'Broken Hearts' is an inventive fusion of hip-hop with a country twang. 'Funny Vibe' juxtaposes hardcore with funk and a biting commentary. 'Cult Of Personality' and 'Which Way To America' are both relentless rockers that provide a compelling backdrop (complete with media sound bites) for Reid's often amazing guitar solos.

● TRACKS: Cult Of Personality; I Want To Know; Middle Man; Desperate People; Open Letter (To A Land Lord); Funny Vibe; Memories Can't Wait; Broken Hearts; Glamour Boys; What's Your Favorite Color? (Theme Song); Which Way To America.

● FIRST RELEASED 1988
● UK PEAK CHART POSITION: did not chart
● USA PEAK CHART POSITION: 6

720 HERE MY DEAR (-) ▲
MARVIN GAYE

A concept album of some magnitude, although the subject matter could hardly have been comfortable listening for Anna, Marvin Gaye's ex-wife. She was the subject of Gaye's public 'divorce album', a clever idea if there were no real people involved. The illustration on the sleeve depicts love, marriage, pain and divorce, in addition to the scales of justice (equal). This lengthy album (originally a double vinyl) was poorly received by the critics, although now it has grown in stature, and it really does have considerable depth and melody. Let's face it, if Gaye sang a gardening seed catalogue from cover to cover it would be brilliant.

● TRACKS: Here, My Dear; I Met A Little Girl; When Did You Stop Loving Me, When Did I Stop Loving You; Anger; Is That Enough; Everybody Needs Love; Time To Get It Together; Sparrow; Anna's Song; When Did You Stop Loving Me, When Did I Stop Loving You (Instrumental); A Funky Space Reincarnation; You Can Leave, But It's Going To Cost You; Falling In Love Again; When Did You Stop Loving Me, When Did I Stop Loving You (Reprise).

● FIRST RELEASED 1978
● UK PEAK CHART POSITION: did not chart
● USA PEAK CHART POSITION: 26

721 **DANGEROUS** (-) ▲
MICHAEL JACKSON

Alfter a lengthy gap of nearly five years, Jackson had to pull something out of the bag. *Bad* was, after all, a difficult act to follow, and the press were trying to prove he was bonkers. This was a pretty decent attempt and fell in with the hard dance beat of the early 90s. 'Heal The World' was much like the old melodic Jackson, and it became a major hit. 'Black Or White' was the best of the rest, a well-constructed song in which he attempted to repeat 'Ebony And Ivory' in the context of 90s dance music. All was well until he jarred when he rhymed 'nations' with 'relations'.

● TRACKS: *Jam; Why You Wanna Trip On Me; In The Closet; She Drives Me Wild; Remember The Time; Can't Let Her Get Away; Heal The World; Black Or White; Who Is It; Give In To Me; Will You Be There; Keep The Faith; Gone Too Soon; Dangerous.*

● FIRST RELEASED 1991
● UK PEAK CHART POSITION: 1
● USA PEAK CHART POSITION: 1

 722 **IN SEARCH OF THE LOST CHORD**
(-) ▲ **MOODY BLUES**

Alfter the success of *Days Of Future Passed*, the Mark II Moodies knew that they had hit upon a winning formula. Once again, mellotrons swirled around each member's contributions, a truly democratic band at this stage. 'Voices In The Sky' became a hit single, but here it is one part of a trilogy that includes 'Visions Of Paradise' and the hypnotic 'The Best Way To Travel'. Whatever 'beep' they created to simulate a spaceship travelling through the cosmos, it works. The throwaway 'Dr Livingstone I Presume' does not, but can be programmed out in the CD age. 'Ride My See-Saw' proved that they had not gone completely soft, and could still rock.

● TRACKS: *Departure; Ride My See-Saw; Dr. Livingstone I Presume; House Of Four Doors; Legend Of A Mind; House Of Four Doors (Part Two); Voices In The Sky; The Best Way To Travel; Visions Of Paradise; The Actor; The Word; Om.*

● FIRST RELEASED 1968
● UK PEAK CHART POSITION: 5
● USA PEAK CHART POSITION: 23

 **723** **VIVA HATE** (267) ▼
MORRISSEY

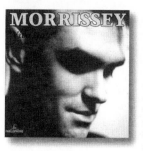

When internal strife killed off the Smiths, attention focused on ex-lead singer Morrissey. His response was a self-assured debut album in which echoes of his former group, notably on 'Suedehead', largely gave way to softer, orchestrated material. Aided by Durutti Column guitarist Vini Reilly and sometime Smiths producer Stephen Street, Morrissey crooned in now-accustomed fashion, toying with melody lines and articulating high-camp angst for a wan generation. The ambition of 'Late Night, Maudlin Street' is balanced by the crispness of 'Everyday Is Like Sunday' and for those worried that Morrissey would flounder without Smiths foil Johnny Marr, *Viva Hate* is a singularly confident riposte.

● TRACKS: *Alsation Cousin; Little Man, What Now?; Everyday Is Like Sunday; Bengali In Platforms; Angel, Angel, Down We Go Together; Late Night, Maudlin Street; Suedehead; Break Up The Family; The Ordinary Boys; I Don't Mind If You Forget Me; Dial A Cliché; Margaret On The Guillotine.*

● FIRST RELEASED 1988
● UK PEAK CHART POSITION: 1
● USA PEAK CHART POSITION: 48

 724 **MOTT THE HOOPLE** (-) ▲
MOTT THE HOOPLE

From the brilliant cover illustration by M.C. Escher to what nearly every critic called a 'straightfaced' version of Sonny Bono's 'Laugh At Me' (as though it was impossible to perform it any other way), Mott The Hoople's debut album showed that they were clearly no ordinary post-psychedelic British band. Their original material, particularly guitarist Mick Ralph's 'Rock And Roll Queen', presaged the glam sound for which they would later become renowned. Appropriately, *Mott The Hoople* was produced by the inventive (and seriously whacked) Guy Stevens. A decade later, the Clash, who were strongly influenced by Mott The Hoople, called upon him to produce *London Calling*.

● TRACKS: *You Really Got Me; At The Crossroads; Laugh At Me; Backsliding Fearlessly; Rock And Roll Queen; Rabbit Foot And Toby Time; Half Moon Bay; Wrath And Wroll.*

● FIRST RELEASED 1971
● UK PEAK CHART POSITION: did not chart
● USA PEAK CHART POSITION: 191

725 **Vs** (495) ▼
PEARL JAM

The second album from Pearl Jam saw them attempt to establish their own identity - previously they had trailed in the wake of Nirvana as 'Seattle's other band'. If *Ten* had seen them arrive from nowhere, then by the advent of this follow-up everyone knew who they were. The album entered the US chart at number 1, and recorded the highest one week sales total in history - after which a critical commentary on the merits or otherwise of the album is rendered utterly irrelevant. It was, however, another rock-solid performance, substituting *Ten's* verve for greater coherence. The opening track 'Go' should convince after approximately 57 seconds.

● TRACKS: *Go; Animal; Daughter; Glorified G; Dissident; WMA; Blood; Rearviewmirror; Rats; Elderly Woman Behind The Counter In A Small Town; Leash; Indifference.*

● FIRST RELEASED 1993
● UK PEAK CHART POSITION: 2
● USA PEAK CHART POSITION: 1

 726 **WHEN A MAN LOVES A WOMAN** (269) ▼ **PERCY SLEDGE**

Had it not been for two highly memorable singles this album might have found it's way into the bins. 'When A Man Loves A Woman' and 'Warm And Tender Love' are still classic radioplay fodder. They established Sledge as a master soul balladeer and the voice for teenage romantics. UK radio presenter Johnny Walker, broadcasting from the pirate ship Radio Caroline in the 60s, used both songs regularly for his 'Frinton flashers': couples parked on the Essex coast would flash car lights in anticipation of Percy Sledge being played. Other highlights on this underrated album are 'It Tears Me Up' and 'Take Time To Know Her', both great examples of southern soul.

● TRACKS: *I'll Be Your Everything; If This Is the Last Time; Hard To Be Friends; Blue Water; Love Away People; Take Time To Know Her; Out Of Left Field; Warm And Tender Love; It Tears Me Up; When A Man Loves A Woman; Walkin' In The Sun; Behind Closed Doors; Make It Good And Make It Last; The Good Love; I Believe In You; My Special Prayer.*

● FIRST RELEASED 1966
● UK PEAK CHART POSITION: did not chart
● USA PEAK CHART POSITION: 37

 727 **HELLO, I MUST BE GOING** (252) ▼
PHIL COLLINS

The omnipresent Phil took two years to follow *Face Value*, which cynics believed to be a fluke and fans willed him to repeat. This album rocketed him back to the top, together with a number 1 single, 'You Can't Hurry Love', and a superb video featuring Phil in triplicate with a tonic mohair suit and Blues Brother shades. The rest is in a similar vein to his debut, albeit with a happier theme running throughout. The album's finale is the touching 'Why Can't It Wait 'Til Morning', a sentence we have all used in the same way at some time in our lives.

● TRACKS: *I Don't Care Anymore; I Cannot Believe It's True; Like China; Do You Know, Do You Care?; You Can't Hurry Love; It Don't Matter To Me; Thru' These Walls; Don't Let Him Steal His Heart Away; The West Side; Why Can't It Wait 'Til Morning.*

● FIRST RELEASED 1982
● UK PEAK CHART POSITION: 2
● USA PEAK CHART POSITION: 8

728 **RECKONING** (–) ▲
R.E.M.

The murmuring continued with this, R.E.M.'s second album, recorded in only two weeks, and yet critical acclaim and a growing fanbase had not made the music any less elusive. From the cover depiction of a winding river/snake, the jangly music within was similarly ambiguous, drenched in alternately murky, then dazzlingly clear, images. The water theme predominates throughout side one's five-song suite, with talk of harbours, oceans and water towers, crowned by the sublime lament of 'So. Central Rain'. Later, the melancholic eulogy of 'Camera' sits comfortably beside the cod-country of '(Don't Go Back To) Rockville' and the brisk but disillusioned tour around 'Little America'. An astonishingly assured and uncommercial half-sibling to *Murmur.* file under water.

● TRACKS: *Harborcoat; 7 Chinese Brothers; So. Central Rain; Pretty Persuasion; Time After Time (Annelise); Second Guessing; Letter Never Sent; Camera; (Don't Go Back To) Rockville; Little America.*

● FIRST RELEASED 1984
● UK PEAK CHART POSITION: 91
● USA PEAK CHART POSITION: 27

729 LITTLE CRIMINALS (-) ▲
RANDY NEWMAN

Newman's most commercially successful album opens with his misunderstood masterpiece, 'Short People'. Of course he is not being derogatory towards people of restricted growth, that's just the way it seems. Those who understand Mr. Newman's brilliant pathos and irony know he has a heart of gold. After all, what heart of stone could write evocative material such as 'Baltimore' and 'I'll Be Home'. It is widely known that Newman is one of America's greatest ever songwriters - if only his music could be more widely known and appreciated, and not have to rely on 'helping hands' of the Eagles to escalate its US sales and chart position.

● TRACKS: Short People; You Can't Fool The Fat Man; Little Criminals; Texas Girl At The Funeral Of Her Father; Jolly Coppers On Parade; In Germany Before The War; Sigmund Freud's Impersonation Of Albert Einstein In America; Baltimore; I'll Be Home; Rider In The Rain; Kathleen (Catholicism Made Easier); Old Man On The Farm.

● FIRST RELEASED 1977
● UK PEAK CHART POSITION: did not chart
● USA PEAK CHART POSITION: 9

730 ARC OF A DIVER (278) ▼
STEVE WINWOOD

With a glorious voice that sounds as if he has just swallowed a jar of cod liver oil of malt, Winwood has the advantage of instant recognition; add to this a musicianship that has been employed in dozens of sessions over the past four decades, and the result is a prodigious talent that runs like a vein of gold through rock music since the Spencer Davis Group. Arc Of A Diver, released at the end of 1980 after a long period of self-imposed retreat, is a triumphant resurgence. With lyrical contributions by Viv Stanshall (the rich imagery of the title track) and Will Jennings, Winwood never falls into the trap of shaming the music with sub-standard words. Another musical genius.

● TRACKS: While You See A Chance; Second Hand Woman; Slowdown Sunset; Spanish Dancer; Night Train; Dust; Arc Of A Diver.

● FIRST RELEASED 1980
● UK PEAK CHART POSITION: 13
● USA PEAK CHART POSITION: 3

731 RATTLE AND HUM (257) ▼
U2

The album of the movie, or the movie of the album? U2's trip into the America of myths and legends took them into the musical heartland of their heroes. Jamming and recording with both B.B. King and Bob Dylan in Sun Studios, the Irish four-piece doffed their metaphorical hats in respect and not some little awe. Hendrix's 'The Star Spangled Banner' stood alone, quietly dignified, towards the end of the set. It now seems a long way from Mephisto's Zoo TV antics, and perhaps, in retrospect, that is not such a bad thing.

● TRACKS: Helter Skelter; Hawkmoon 269; Van Dieman's Land; Desire; Angel Of Harlem; I Still Haven't Found What I'm Looking For; When Love Comes To Town; God Part II; Bullet The Blue Sky; Silver And Gold; Love Rescue Me; Heartland; The Star Spangled Banner; All I Want Is You; Freedom For My People; All Along The Watchtower; Pride (In The Name Of Love).

● FIRST RELEASED 1988
● UK PEAK CHART POSITION: 1
● USA PEAK CHART POSITION: 1

732 HYMNS TO THE SILENCE (-) ▲
VAN MORRISON

A double CD at this stage of his career came as a surprise, but a double CD this good, came as a shock. Morrison had a great deal to say in 1991 about his childhood and his faith; much of it came through on this record in a much less oblique way than we had been used to. The spoken dialogue on 'On Hyndford Street' is intensely personal and revealing. For once, we were hearing Morrison's thoughts. Morrison clearly has religion but on this riveting record he refused to preach. Georgie Fame continued to add familiarity to the sound and this was the best Morrison album for many, many years.

● TRACKS: Professional Jealousy; I'm Not Feeling It Anymore; Ordinary Life; Some Peace Of Mind; So Complicated; I Can't Stop Loving You; Why Must I Always Explain; Village Idiot; See Me Through Part II (Just A Closer Walk With Thee); Take Me Back; By His Grace; All Saints Day; Hymns To The Silence; On Hyndford Street; Be Thou My Vision; Carrying A Torch; Green Mansions; Pagan Streams; Quality Street; It Must Be You; I Need Your Kind Of Loving.

● FIRST RELEASED 1991
● UK PEAK CHART POSITION: 5
● USA PEAK CHART POSITION: 99

733 EASY RIDER (268) ▼
VARIOUS

Several films have captured the mood of the 60s generation; *Easy Rider* chronicled the dying embers of the hippie dream. Plot and characterization apart, its appeal is also due to a carefully structured soundtrack that not only enhanced the celluloid imagery, but stands as a strong collection in its own right. Material is drawn from a wide range of artists and musical styles, be it the Byrds' superior folk rock, the proto-heavy metal of Steppenwolf, the orchestrated Mass of the Electric Prunes or the hallucinogenic madness of the Holy Modal Rounders. Late-60s rock in microcosm, the set is a brilliant snapshot in time. The only gripe remains in choosing McGuinn's solo 'Ballad Of Easy Rider' over the superior version by his band. Easily the best album of its type.

● TRACKS: *The Pusher - Steppenwolf; Born To Be Wild - Steppenwolf; The Weight - Band; I Wasn't Born To Follow - Byrds; If You Want To Be A Bird - Holy Modal Rounders; Don't Bogart Me - Fraternity Of Man; If Six Was Nine - Jimi Hendrix Experience; Kyrie Eleison Mardi Gras - Electric Prunes; It's Alright Ma (I'm Only Bleeding) - Roger McGuinn; Ballad Of Easy Rider - Roger McGuinn.*

● FIRST RELEASED 1969
● UK PEAK CHART POSITION: 2
● USA PEAK CHART POSITION: 6

734 VIOLENT FEMMES (-) ▲
VIOLENT FEMMES

A band with a surfeit of natural charm, the Violent Femmes can also boast of a prodigious back catalogue of easily accessible, effortlessly original songs. And this is the best place to start. Their ramshackle Milwaukee hillbilly punk is complemented by Gordon Gano's geek with attitude lyrics, by turns hilarious and tragic, often within a few lines. Sample the emotional simplicity of 'Kiss Off' or 'Please Do Not Go'. Unlike so many of their contemporaries, you feel nobody else on the planet could have written or performed something like 'Gone Daddy Gone', which single-handedly redefines the essential elements of a great pop song (imagine Brian Wilson writing his surf instrumentals on a xylophone).

● TRACKS: *Blister In The Sun; Kiss Off; Please Do Not Go; Add It Up; Confessions; Prove My Love; Promise; To The Kill; Gone Daddy Gone; Good Feeling.*

● FIRST RELEASED 1991
● UK PEAK CHART POSITION: did not chart
● USA PEAK CHART POSITION: 171

735 PINK FLAG (496) ▼
WIRE

Wire's furious interpretation of punk was encapsulated on this primitive, minimalist debut. Abrasive and disjointed, these 21 tracks exude a fury impossible to ignore and one enhanced by their very brevity. Tracks halt, sometimes abruptly, when the point has been made, creating an ever-changing mélange of sound and texture. While generally aggressive, *Pink Flag* also boasts two wonderful pop songs ('Ex-Lion Tamer' and 'Mannequin'), suggesting that Wire would not be constrained by stylistic expectations. The album's mixture of polemics and pointedness would influence several US groups, including R.E.M., who later covered 'Strange'. Its perceptive urgency grows with time.

● TRACKS: *Reuters; Field Day For The Sundays; Three Girl Rhumba; Ex Lion Tamer; Lowdown; Start To Move; Brazil; It's So Obvious; Surgeon's Girl; Pink Flag; The Commercial; Straight Line; 106 Beats That; Mr. Suit; Strange; Fragile; Mannequin; Different To Me; Champs; Feeling Called Love; 12 X U.*

● FIRST RELEASED 1977
● UK PEAK CHART POSITION: did not chart
● USA PEAK CHART POSITION: did not chart

736 FRAGILE (-) ▲
YES

This marked the period when Yes left the planet and took up residence on one of artist Roger Dean's far-off lands. The musical transition is apparent with longer instrumental passages taking over from the three-minute song format. No longer could they be seen playing in clubs for five bob. Lengthy pieces open and close the album, and both songs have become Yes chestnuts. 'Heart Of The Sunrise' and 'Roundabout' are strong tracks musically, with the latter winning out as being more accessible. Without detracting from Anderson, Howe, Bruford and Wakeman, Chris Squire's bass playing is superlative throughout.

● TRACKS: *Roundabout; Cans And Brahms; We Have Heaven; South Side Of The Sky; Five Per Cent For Nothing; Long Distance Runaround; The Fish (Shindleria Praematurus); Mood For A Day; Heart Of The Sunrise.*

● FIRST RELEASED 1972
● UK PEAK CHART POSITION: 7
● USA PEAK CHART POSITION: 4

737 ELEPHANT MOUNTAIN (-) ▲
THE YOUNGBLOODS

This was the closest that the Youngbloods came to making a fully realized album. It remains their finest work, even though fans and critics felt, and still feel, that they were capable of something much better. The disposable snippets and vignettes help to fill up an album of a 'few great songs'. 'Darkness Darkness' is one of the great ones, with a guitar break that seems to go above the last fret on the neck. 'Quicksand', 'Ride the Wind' and 'Beautiful' are further examples of clever but unpretentious pop masquerading as rock. Jesse Colin Young was a fine songwriter and the undisputed brains behind Bauer and Banana.

● TRACKS: *Darkness Darkness; Smug; On Sir Francis Drake; Sunlight; Double Sunlight; Beautiful; Turn It Over; Rain Song; Trillium; Quicksand; Black Mountain Breakdown; Sham; Ride The Wind.*

● FIRST RELEASED 1969
● UK PEAK CHART POSITION: did not chart
● USA PEAK CHART POSITION: 118

739 NINE LIVES (-) ▲
AEROSMITH

Just like the Doctor Seuss-styled top hat that Steven Tyler pops out of on stage, Aerosmith conjured up an unexpectedly great album. Sounding rejuvenated, there are enough strong new songs to add permanently to their (still) magnetic stage show. Standard Aerosmith rock comes in the shape of the excellent title track, and the album's first hit single, 'Falling In Love'. Equally good, but more interesting, are the mantic-styled 'Taste Of India' and the cheeky sexual innuendo in the many shades of 'Pink'. Lyrics such as 'pink as the bing on your cherry' show that Tyler still has a sense of humour.

● TRACKS: *Nine Lives; Falling In Love; Hole In My Soul; Taste Of India; Full Circle; Something's Gotta Give; Ain't That A Bitch; The Farm; Crash; 10; Pink; Falling Off; Attitude Adjustment; Fallen Angels.*

● FIRST RELEASED 1997
● UK PEAK CHART POSITION: 4
● USA PEAK CHART POSITION: 1

738 FOR THOSE ABOUT TO ROCK (283) ▼
AC/DC

Brian Johnson's second album as AC/DC's frontman, and as such helped them create a phenomenal commercial success, with both singles, 'Let's Get It Up' and the title track, charting on both sides of the Atlantic. The album went on to sell over a million copies worldwide and the title track became an immediate live favourite, complete with a cannon-fire salute stage show that became instant encore material. Elsewhere, their familiar rattle remained intact, with 'Night Of The Long Knives' and 'Breaking The Rules' forging a familiar piece of metal.

● TRACKS: *For Those About To Rock (We Salute You); Put The Finger On You; Let's Get It Up; Inject The Venom; Snowballad; Evil Walk; COD; Breaking The Rules; Night Of The Long Knives; Spellbound.*

● FIRST RELEASED 1981
● UK PEAK CHART POSITION: 3
● USA PEAK CHART POSITION: 1

740 BAD COMPANY (297) ▼
BAD COMPANY

This is not heavy metal, this is not rock, this is heavy rock. There is a difference and Bad Company embodied it. Coming out of the blues-based band Free, Paul Rodgers immediately found good company with the talented Mick Ralphs. Although subsequent albums reworked the same basic theme, this is the standard by which Bad Company should be judged. Tightly structured songs, driving beat, immaculate guitar and, of course, the definitive vocals of Rodgers. Just replay 'Can't Get Enough', 'Bad Company' and 'Ready For Love' as a reminder, and finish with the gentle 'Seagull', one of Rodgers/Ralphs' finest compositions.

● TRACKS: *Can't Get Enough; Rock Steady; Ready For Love; Don't Let Me Down; Bad Company; The Way I Choose; Movin' On; Seagull.*

● FIRST RELEASED 1974
● UK PEAK CHART POSITION: 3
● USA PEAK CHART POSITION: 1

741 STAR (–) ▲
BELLY

Few informed critics would ever say that Tanya Donelly was the real talent behind Throwing Muses, but over the years the Rhode Island guitarist and songwriter did contribute some of the group's best songs. Her defection to Belly (named after her favourite word) was encouraged by the lack of writing opportunities in the Muses, following a brief sojourn in the Breeders. Belly secured immediate commercial rewards when 'Feed The Tree' became an international bestseller. The rest of the material on *Star* shares that song's essential components - intoxicating guitar breaks and poppy hooks masking decidedly unpoppy lyrical sentiments (self-disgust, perversity, cynicism). Though there are no substandard songs in sight, the harrowing rape narrative of 'Dusted' is a particular stand-out.

● TRACKS: *Someone To Die For; Angel; Dusted; Every World; Gepetto; Witch; Slow Dog; Low Red Moon; Feed The Tree; Full Moon, Empty Heart; White Belly; Untogether; Star; Sad Dress; Stay.*

● FIRST RELEASED 1993
● UK PEAK CHART POSITION: 2
● USA PEAK CHART POSITION: 59

742 NICK OF TIME (420) ▼
BONNIE RAITT

Although famed primarily for her interpretation of compositions by the likes of Joni Mitchell, John Hiatt, James Taylor and Paul Brady, *Nick Of Time* includes two fine Raitt-penned songs. 'The Road's My Middle Name' is an up-tempo blues number, harking back to her early career performing alongside Son House and Mississippi Fred McDowell. The title track is one of her best, a sensitive examination of the traumas of ageing. Throughout the album her voice is haunting and controlled, bringing new meaning and depth to a varied range of material. Bonnie turned 40 gracefully with this album and it gave her unexpected massive success just in the nick of time.

● TRACKS: *Nick Of Time; A Thing Called Love; Love Letters; Cry On My Shoulder; Real Man; Nobody's Girl; Have A Heart; Too Soon To Tell; I Will Not Be Denied; I Ain't Gonna Let You Break My Heart Again; The Road's My Middle Name.*

● FIRST RELEASED 1989
● UK PEAK CHART POSITION: 51
● USA PEAK CHART POSITION: 1

743 SOCIAL LIVING (–) ▲
BURNING SPEAR

If Bob Marley was the populist spokesman of the Rastafarianism movement, then Burning Spear (Winston Rodney) was clearly, through his music, the intellectual spin doctor. His albums are gentle history lessons in black culture; they tend to inform rather than preach. This is one of a number of excellent albums built around his theme of Marcus Garvey, the great leader of the Back To Africa movement. Spear is surrounded by the finest session musicians in Jamaica, in addition to Sly and Robbie. In assembling a record collection there are always a few token Marley records included. At least one Burning Spear album should be made compulsory.

● TRACKS: *Marcus Children Suffer; Come; Social Living; Marcus Say Jah No Dead; Marcus Senior; Nyah Keith; Institution; Mister Garvey; Civilise Reggae.*

● FIRST RELEASED 1978
● UK PEAK CHART POSITION: did not chart
● USA PEAK CHART POSITION: did not chart

744 TEA FOR THE TILLERMAN (298) ▼
CAT STEVENS

The series of albums Yusuf Islam (formerly Mr. Stevens) made following this magnificent introspective set were all of similar but gradually declining quality. What was totally original became less so, even though his voice retained its sad quality and his acoustic guitar was as wooden as ever. This record has been played so many hundreds of times that the running order seems automatic: the long intro on 'Where Do The Children Play', into 'Hard Headed Woman', and then on track 3 wait for the middle eight - 'oh baby baby it's a wild world'. Turn it over and you still have 'Father And Son' yet to come.

● TRACKS: *Where Do The Children Play; Hard Headed Woman; Wild World; Sad Lisa; Miles From Nowhere; But I Might Die Tonight; Longer Boats; Into White; On The Road To Find Out; Father And Son; Tea For The Tillerman.*

● FIRST RELEASED 1970
● UK PEAK CHART POSITION: 20
● USA PEAK CHART POSITION: 8

745 **I FEEL LIKE I'M FIXIN' TO DIE** (–) ▲
COUNTRY JOE AND THE FISH

A part from the 'lets look weird' cover shot, this is merely a dressed-up folk rock album made unusual by some stinging guitar from the talented Barry Melton. It was his sound more than Country Joe's voice that gave them a unique psych sound. In fact, sometimes the guitar is so laid-back a non-stoned listener could doze off. This is the one with the famous Woodstock anthem and anti-war song rolled into one, 'The Fish Cheer & I Feel Like I'm Fixing To Die Rag'. Sadly it all sounds just a little bit twee and dated, apart from the aforementioned Melton guitar.

● TRACKS: *The Fish Cheer & I Feel Like I'm Fixing To Die Rag; Who Am I; Pat's Song; Rock Coast Blues; Magoo; Janis; Thought Dream; Thursday; Eastern Jam; Colours For Susan.*

● FIRST RELEASED 1967
● UK PEAK CHART POSITION: did not chart
● USA PEAK CHART POSITION: 67

 746 **DISINTEGRATION** (–) ▲
THE CURE

D ark, dreamlike and magical, *Disintegration* surely represents one of the Cure's finest hours. Although retaining the darkest elements of the earlier albums, it pointed the way towards the band's later, more commercial work on *Wish*. The intoxicating music draws the listener inexorably downwards, but somehow one remains buoyant - rarely since this album has Robert Smith surpassed the beauty and yearning of 'Pictures Of You', or the poignant pop of 'Love Song'. The nightmarish 'Lullaby', however, increases the pressure, and by the final tracks, all hope quite literally disintegrates. A unique and emotionally raw album, *Disintegration* evokes the sensation of inevitable, but desirable, death by drowning.

● TRACKS: *Plainsong; Pictures Of You; Closedown; Love Song; Last Dance; Lullaby; Fascination Street; Prayers For Rain; The Same Deep Water As You; Disintegration; Homesick; Untitled.*

● FIRST RELEASED 1990
● UK PEAK POSITION: 3
● USA PEAK POSITION: 12

 **747** **DAMNED DAMNED DAMNED** (289) ▼
THE DAMNED

T he first British punk band to release a single ('New Rose'), the Damned followed this achievement with the genre's debut album. *Damned Damned Damned* captured its furious rattle of basic chords and angry sentiments, delivered at amphetamine-like speed. Producer Nick Lowe ensured the quartet's primal scream was not modified by prevailing attitudes of musical correctness and the set's success is as due to his detached overview as the group's fevered nihilism. Their energy is exciting, the sense of freedom and mischief unrelenting, *Damned Damned Damned* defined punk both aurally and philosophically. The downstroke E-minor chord in 'Fan Club' is nectar.

● TRACKS: *Neat Neat Neat; Fan Club; I Fall; Born To Kill; Stab Your Back; Feel The Pain; New Rose; Fish; See Her Tonite; 1 Of The 2; So Messed Up; I Feel Alright.*

● FIRST RELEASED 1977
● UK PEAK CHART POSITION: 36
● USA PEAK CHART POSITION: did not chart

 748 **HYPOCRISY IS THE GREATEST LUXURY**
(527) ▼ DISPOSABLE HEROES OF HIPHOPRISY

O ften berated as the group that it is OK for non-rap fans to like, the Disposable Heroes' solitary album proper represents much more than that might imply. Shades of Michael Franti and Rono Tse's previous incarnation, as part of the Beatnigs, resurface in the collision of samples, noise and breakbeats. Tse's technique is exemplary. However, it is Franti's fiercely intelligent narratives that carry the day. Where bombast and finger-pointing had been the order of the day in hip-hop, Franti includes his own inadequacies (notably calling himself a 'jerk' in 'Music And Politics') in his diagnosis of the problem.

● TRACKS: *Satanic Reverses; Famous And Dandy (Like Amos 'N' Andy); Television, The Drug Of The Nation; Language Of Violence; The Winter Of The Long Hot Summer; Hypocrisy Is The Greatest Luxury; Everyday Life Has Become A Health Risk; Ins Greencard A-19 191 500; Socio-Genetic Experiment; Music And Politics; Financial Leprosy; California Über Alles; Water Pistol Man.*

● FIRST RELEASED 1992
● UK PEAK CHART POSITION: 40
● USA PEAK CHART POSITION: did not chart

749 THE GEORGE AND IRA GERSHWIN SONGBOOK (696) ▼ ELLA FITZGERALD

The paradox of Ella Fitzgerald's prominence in the history of jazz singing and her lack of emotional intensity is much less apparent on this album. George Gershwin's affinity with jazz, and the corresponding delight jazz musicians take in performing his material, allow the singer to fly with the music. As for brother Ira's lyrics, they receive their due as cheerful, tender and always delightful examples of the lyricist's art. The Songbook series remains one of Ella Fitzgerald's major contributions - among many - to American popular music and this in particular is one of the best of the sizeable bunch.

● TRACKS: *Including - Sam And Delilah; But Not For Me; My One And Only; Let's Call The Whole Thing Off; I've Got Beginners Luck; Lady Be Good; Nice Work If You Can Get It; Things Are Looking Up; Just Another Rhumba; How Long Has This Been Going On; S'wonderful; Man I Love; That Certain Feeling; By Strauss; Who Cares; Someone To Watch Over Me; Real American Folk Song; They All Laughed; Looking For A Boy; My Cousin From Milwaukee; Somebody From Somewhere; Foggy Day; Clap Yo' Hands; For You, For Me, Forever More; Stiff Upper Lip; Strike Up The Band; Soon; I've Got A Crush On You; Bidin' My Time; Aren't You Kind Of Glad We Did; Of Thee I Sing; Half It Dearie Blues; I Was Doing It Right; He Loves And She Loves; Love Is Sweeping The Country; Treat Me Rough; Love Is Here To Stay; Slap That Bass; Isn't It A Pity; Shall We Dance.*
● FIRST RELEASED 1959 ● UK PEAK CHART POSITION: did not chart
● USA PEAK CHART POSITION: 111

750 BLOOD AND CHOCOLATE (285) ▼ ELVIS COSTELLO

On this album the Attractions are fronted by Napoleon Dynamite. They perform with him as if they have played together for years. Napoleon trots out another powerful stream of angst, emotion and vitriol. Costello had so much lyrical frustration, he should be commissioned to write the entire Top 40. 'I Want You' is one of the most intense songs he has ever written; he really does open up his soul, and makes a public statement set over a simple melody, accompanied by Nick Lowe on acoustic guitar. The album is similar in feel to *Imperial Bedroom* and a record that needs the lyric sheet to be read, digested and acted upon. Costello might end up working for Relate.

● TRACKS: *Uncomplicated; I Hope You're Happy Now; Tokyo Storm Warning; Home Is Anywhere You Hang Your Head; I Want You; Honey Are You Straight Or Are You Blind; Blue Chair; Battered Old Bird; Crimes Of Paris; Poor Napoleon; Next Time Round.*

● FIRST RELEASED 1986
● UK PEAK CHART POSITION: 16
● USA PEAK CHART POSITION: 84

751 BRAIN SALAD SURGERY (–) ▲ EMERSON, LAKE AND PALMER

Much maligned, although it is hard to understand why. They merely took what the Nice did one stage further as Palmer became the songwriter in place of Lee Jackson. The two sides of ELP were adaptations of classical pieces, which usually worked well. On this, 'Jerusalem' and 'Toccata' are given the prog treatment. The longer original suite 'Karn Evil' allows Emerson to let loose on his organ and piano. He is astonishingly fluid and imaginative. A wholly successful album, apart from the dreadful Chas & Dave, cor blimey singalonga ELP 'Benny The Bouncer'. Somebody, at some stage, must have thought it was a good idea.

● TRACKS: *Jerusalem; Toccata; Still . . You Turn Me On; Benny The Bouncer; Karn Evil 9; Karn Evil 9.*

● FIRST RELEASED 1973
● UK PEAK CHART POSITION: 2
● USA PEAK CHART POSITION:11

752 EDEN (–) ▲ EVERYTHING BUT THE GIRL

Tracy Thorn and Benn Watt decided to step forward with this album and shed the twee 'not quite in tune' indie image that permeated much of their early work. Using tasteful arrangements and some excellent session players, Eden was an important transitional record. Pete King, Nigel Nash and Dick Pearce added some fine reed and brass that made good songs such as 'Tender Blue' and the bossa nova 'Each And Every One' sound positively great. The stand-out track is 'Another Bridge', which has a gentle hammond organ doodling over a fat acoustic G chord throughout. They became chart stars long after this album.

● TRACKS: *Each And Every One; Bittersweet; Tender Blue; Another Bridge; The Spice Of Life; The Dustbowl; Crabwalk; Even So; Frost And Fire; Fascination; I Must Confess; Soft Touch.*

● FIRST RELEASED 1984
● UK PEAK CHART POSITION: 14
● USA PEAK CHART POSITION: did not chart

753 MUSIC IN A DOLL'S HOUSE (-) ▲
FAMILY

From the opening Jim King falsetto on 'The Chase' to the quirky 'God Save The Queen' ending, *Music From A Doll's House* never flags. In 1968 King's saxophone and Ric Grech's violin were imaginative additions to the standard band profile, and their playing was skin-tight. With the strangled vibrato of Roger Chapman's vocals - still one of rock's most astonishing performers - Family created a power that has rarely been matched. 'Old Songs New Songs' is a great rocker in anyone's book (why fade it in mid-flight?), and 'Voyage' presents a classic slice of psychedelia. Over-produced (by Dave Mason) it may be, but as a debut album there are few equals of its time.

● TRACKS: *The Chase; Mellowing Grey; Never Like This; Me My Friend; 'Variation On A Theme Of' Hey Mr Policeman; Winter; Old Songs New Songs; 'Variation On A Theme Of' The Breeze; Hey Mr. Policeman; See Through Windows; 'Variation On A Theme Of' Me My Friend; Peace Of Mind; Voyage; Breeze; 3 X Time.*

● FIRST RELEASED 1968
● UK PEAK CHART POSITION: 35
● USA PEAK CHART POSITION: did not chart

754 THE SCORE (-) ▲
FUGEES

Combining traditional hip-hop with melodic soul, the Fugees was one of the most refreshing surprises of 1996. Released with little fanfare, the album succeeded on its merit alone, and picked up many awards in addition to several million sales. The success of the singles 'Ready Or Not' and their excellent version of Bob Marley's 'No Woman No Cry' helped to change the general public's previous negative reaction to rap. Joining the mainstream was further aided with the even more successful interpretation of Roberta Flack's 'Killing Me Softly'. A superb version over a steady, slow snare drum beat, it became a major hit all over the world. The clever use of sampling and overall 'good vibe' feel made for a formidable record.

● TRACKS: *Red Intro; How Many Mics; Ready Or Not; Zealots; The Beast; Fu-Gee-La; Family Business; Killing Me Softly; The Score; The Mask; Cowboys; No Woman, No Cry; Manifest/Outro; Fu-Gee-La; Fu-Gee-La; Mista Mista; Fu-Gee-La.*

● FIRST RELEASED 1996
● UK PEAK CHART POSITION: 3
● USA PEAK CHART POSITION: 1

755 BREEZIN' (651) ▼
GEORGE BENSON

Benson earned his reputation as a superior jazz guitarist through his partnership with soul/jazz organist Brother Jack McDuff. Several solo albums for the CTI label ensued before a switch to the giant Warner Brothers resulted in extraordinary chart success with this release. Benson's remake of the title track, originally a hit for fellow guitarist Gabor Szabo, set the tone for the entire set wherein mellifluous funk underscores the artist's sweet voice and soft-touch technique. Like Nat 'King' Cole before him, Benson left jazz to court a wider audience and with *Breezin'* he did so with considerable aplomb.

● TRACKS: *This Masquerade; Six To Four; Breezin'; So This Is Love; Lady; Affirmation.*

● FIRST RELEASED 1976
● UK PEAK CHART POSITION: did not chart
● USA PEAK CHART POSITION: 1

756 FROM THE MARS HOTEL (-) ▲
GRATEFUL DEAD

Set off by the beautiful Kelly/Mouse cover with the lonely hotel and the indecipherable lettering - that is until somebody has the wacky idea of holding the album up against a mirror so you can read the lettering back to front. Some of their long-standing live favorites are on this exemplary record. The highly commercial 'Scarlet Begonias' and the infectious 'Loose Lucy' are both here. The beautiful 'Ship Of Fools' is only bettered by the jazzy 'Unbroken Chain'. A mellow and beautifully articulate record that still retains shades of the Crosby, Stills And Nash influence left over from *American Beauty*.

● TRACKS: *U.S. Blues; China Doll; Unbroken Chain; Loose Lucy; Scarlet Begonias; Pride Of Cucamonga; Money Money; Ship Of Fools.*

● FIRST RELEASED 1974
● UK PEAK CHART POSITION: 47
● USA PEAK CHART POSITION: 16

757 OLD NO. 1 (843) ▲
GUY CLARK

Having retreated from Texas psychedelia to front a guitar repair shop, Guy Clark was saved from a journeyman life when several of his songs were covered by Jerry Jeff Walker. A recording contract ensued, which Clark embraced with this country/folk masterpiece. Mature lyricism and captivating melodies mark an intimate set enhanced by the singer's raspy, lived-in intonation. These largely autobiographical songs are never introverted and address scenarios of love, longing and ageing in a compelling, haunting manner. The evocative 'Desperados Waiting For A Train' exemplifies the skills of a crafted songsmith who reclaimed the art of the singer-songwriter at a time when it seemed doomed to self-pity.

● TRACKS: *Rita Ballou; LA Freeway; She Ain't Goin' Nowhere; A Nickel For The Fiddler; That Old Time Feeling; Texas 1947; Desperados Waiting For A Train; Like A Coat From The Cold; Instant Coffee Blues; Let Him Roll.*

● FIRST RELEASED 1971
● UK PEAK CHART POSITION: did not chart
● USA PEAK CHART POSITION: did not chart

758 PILLS 'N' THRILLS AND BELLYACHES (364) ▼ HAPPY MONDAYS

The sound of Madchester baggydom could be heard going to the wall with this album, which represented a creative peak for the whole scene and the Mondays especially. Shaun Ryder's laconic vocal dips created some real ambience and body for their swaying and almost graceful dancing backdrops. It was his clever, almost punning wordplay and sometimes wonderfully obscure vocal and lyrical chatter, combined with Mark Day's surprisingly credible guitarwork, that helped create a stylish, if loose-fitting album. 'Kinky Afro', 'Step On', 'Holiday', were all charming and charmed, long before anyone could see them falling away.

● TRACKS: *Kinky Afro; God's Cop; Donovan; Grandbag's Funeral; Loose Fit; Dennis And Lois; Bob's Yer Uncle; Step On; Holiday; Harmony.*

● FIRST RELEASED 1990
● UK PEAK CHART POSITION: 4
● USA PEAK CHART POSITION: 89

759 TUESDAY NIGHT MUSIC CLUB (738) ▼
SHERYL CROW

Her previous credentials included working with Eric Clapton, then suddenly she stepped forward and delivered an album of such breathtaking maturity that it sounded as if she had been making albums forever. Furthermore, she also sounds like we have been listening to her for 20 years. However, this debut album has tended to be overplayed on mainstream rock radio. The full-bodied anguish of 'Run, Baby, Run' complements the cutesy Ricky Lee Jones voice on 'All I Wanna Do'; her lyrics are honest, original and never dull, and are wrapped around immediate songs. She is a notable 'newish' talent, and now has a difficult third album to make.

● TRACKS: *Run, Baby, Run; Leaving Las Vegas; Strong Enough; Can't Cry Anymore; Solidify; No One Said It Would Be Easy; What I Can Do For You; All I Wanna Do; We Do What We Can; I Shall Believe.*

● FIRST RELEASED 1994
● UK PEAK CHART POSITION: 8
● USA PEAK CHART POSITION: 3

760 THE PRETENDER (287) ▼
JACKSON BROWNE

Jackson Browne's literate Californian music reached a creative peak with this exceptional release. A pensive, introspective song-writer, he combines a poetic perceptiveness with subtle melodies, resulting in an engaging music reliant on suggestion, rather than power. *The Pretender* contains several of his finest songs, particularly the lengthy title track and the melancholic 'Here Come Those Tears Again'. Superb support from guitarist David Lindley emphasizes the nuances in Browne's work, gently adding to its poignancy. Recorded following the suicide of the singer's wife, *The Pretender* provided Browne with an artistic catharsis that never slips into self-pity.

● TRACKS: *The Fuse; Your Bright Baby Blues; Linda Paloma; Here Comes Those Tears Again; Only Child; Daddy's Tune; Sleep's Dark And Silent Gate; The Pretender.*

● FIRST RELEASED 1976
● UK PEAK CHART POSITION: 26
● USA PEAK CHART POSITION: 5

761 ## JOAN BAEZ IN CONCERT (294) ▼
JOAN BAEZ

The 'queen of folk' was an accomplished live performer as this, the first of two *In Concert* albums proved. Accompanying herself on acoustic guitar, Baez brought her pure, virginal soprano to contrasting material. Her interpretations of Childe ballads 'Matty Groves' and 'The House Carpenter' are particularly moving, but an empathy with American folklore, including Woody Guthrie and the Carter Family, is equally apparent. Baez's reading of Malvina Reynolds' protest song, 'What Have They Done To The Rain', is especially arresting and inspired a later pop hit for the Searchers. This album helped take folk music out of the coffee-house circuit and into national consciousness.

● TRACKS: Babe; I'm Gonna Leave You; Geordie; Copper Kettle; Kubaya; What Have They Done To The Rain; Black Is The Colour Of My True Love's Hair; Danger Water; Gospel Ship; The House Carpenter; Pretty Boy Floyd; Lady Mary; Ate Amanha; Matty Groves.

● FIRST RELEASED 1962
● UK PEAK CHART POSITION: did not chart
● USA PEAK CHART POSITION: 10

 762 ## A HARD ROAD (576) ▼
JOHN MAYALL AND THE BLUESBREAKERS

Following Eric Clapton's departure after the magnificent *Bluesbreakers* album, Mayall plugged the gap with Peter Green. Little did anyone know (except Green) that he would almost equal Clapton in the minds of fans and the cognoscenti. Two instrumentals on this collection, Freddie King's 'The Stumble' and Green's 'The Super-Natural', clearly demonstrate the clean and sparing sound of his Gibson Les Paul. The line-up is completed by bassist John McVie and Aynsley Dunbar on drums. Ex-commercial artist Mayall also designed and painted the cover, which itself is a fine piece of art-work and is probably rotting in some printer's basement, long forgotten. The remastered CD reissue is quite superb.

● TRACKS: A Hard Road; It's Over; You Don't Love Me; The Stumble; Another Kinda Love; Hit The Highway; Leaping Christine; Dust My Blues; There's Always Work; The Same Way; The Super-Natural; Top Of The Hill; Someday After A While (You'll Be Sorry), Living Alone.

● FIRST RELEASED 1967
● UK PEAK CHART POSITION: 10
● USA PEAK CHART POSITION: did not chart

 763 ## FACING YOU (828) ▲
KEITH JARRETT

The stunning ECM debut that unleashed one of the greatest piano players of our time. Using jazz as an excuse, Jarrett initiated and indoctrinated us with improvised solo piano, something to which listeners would become used over the next three decades. *Facing You* is boogie-woogie, country hoedown, blues, folk, rock 'n' roll-flavoured jazz, and is still an astonishing album. The music press at the time of issue were bereft of ideas about how to categorize him; it would have been much simpler just to wallow in the music. Much of Jarrett's and Manfred Eicher's future musical philosophy started out with this important record.

● TRACKS: In Front; Ritooria; Lalene; My Lady: My Child; Landscape For Future Earth; Starbright; Vapallia; Semblence.

● FIRST RELEASED 1972
● UK PEAK CHART POSITION: did not chart
● USA PEAK CHART POSITION: did not chart

 764 ## AUTOBAHN (279) ▼
KRAFTWERK

Germanic in approach and delivery this record gets under the skin and infuriates as you find yourself compelled to hum the melodies. A significant record in the development of electronic music, and not to be confused with other 'kraut rock' efforts from the school of mid-70s prog, this is the album from which countless bands borrowed riffs - passages of the Cure, Depeche Mode, Joy Division, and New Order are to be found among the five lengthy tracks. Don't be fooled: Kraftwerk were there at least five years in advance. Great for driving on the motorway in Europe, incidentally!

● TRACKS: Autobahn; Kometenmelodie 1; Kometenmelodie 2; Mitternacht; Morgenspaziergang.

● FIRST RELEASED 1974
● UK PEAK CHART POSITION: 4
● USA PEAK CHART POSITION: 5

765 ROCK 'N' ROLL ANIMAL (276) ▼
LOU REED

Lou turned from the minimalist fuelled on anger and betrayal to full-blown, heavy metal superstar for this album, producing a gloriously live revamping and work-out of his older hits, filled with a strutting confidence that his audience had never fully experienced before. Ferocity was at a premium with tough reworkings of 'White Light', 'White Heat,' 'Sweet Jane' and 'Lady Day', among others, all recorded as part of a set at New York's Academy Of Music. The following year in 1974, *Lou Reed Live* appeared, culled from the same set. Purists may have been galled by his approach, but *Animal* went on to earn Reed his first gold disc.

● TRACKS: *Intro; Sweet Jane; White Light; White Heat; Heroin; Lady Day; Rock And Roll.*

● FIRST RELEASED 1974
● UK PEAK CHART POSITION: 26
● USA PEAK CHART POSITION: 45

 **767** 100% FUN (–) ▲
MATTHEW SWEET

'Sick Of Myself', the first single from this, Matthew Sweet's follow-up to *Altered Beast*, captured the mood of a time when artists from Beck to Green Day were vying to capture self-hatred on record. Although ex-Television guitarist Richard Lloyd was given freer reign this time around, the songs were still short - averaging less than three-and-a-half minutes - and snappy, with hooks and harmonies aplenty. Continuing his obsession with 60s pop, he added such instruments as harpsichord, electric piano, clavinet and theremin to his usual army of 12-string guitars. He has still to write the classic pop song of which he is capable.

● TRACKS: *Sick Of Myself; Not When I Need It; We're The Same; Giving It Back; Everything Changes; Lost My Mind; Come To Love; Walk Out; I Almost Forgot; Super Baby; Get Older; Smog Moon.*

● FIRST RELEASED 1995
● UK PEAK CHART POSITION: did not chart
● USA PEAK CHART POSITION: 65

 766 WHAT'S THE 411? (–) ▲
MARY J. BLIGE

The opening track 'Leave A Message' is an immediately intriguing hook for the listener. A series of answerphone messages over a funky drum beat does not fail, even though most callers insist on saying 'peace' instead of 'goodbye' at the end of every call. The artist first appears on track two, and stays in control throughout an album of high-quality urban R&B/soul. Highly commercial, yet it never sinks to the blandness of some other 90s female pop acts. Tracks such as 'Real Love' lend more to the best of Aretha Franklin pop flirtations than to 90s R&B. Blige is Aretha's heir apparent.

● TRACKS: *Leave A Message; Reminisce; Real Love; You Remind Me; Intro Talk; Sweet Thing; Love No Limit; I Don't Want To Do Anything; Slow Down; My Love; Changes I've Been Going Through; What's The 411?*

● FIRST RELEASED 1992
● UK PEAK CHART POSITION: 53
● USA PEAK CHART POSITION: 6

 768 MY FUNNY VALENTINE (788) ▲
MILES DAVIS

One of the finest live albums in the history of jazz, *My Funny Valentine* presents the Miles Davis Quintet live at the Lincoln Centre's Philharmonic Hall in 1964. Surrounded by the vibrant and youthful rhythm section of Herbie Hancock (piano), Ron Carter (bass) and Tony Williams (drums), Davis was enjoying a strong new surge of creativity, and played with a stunning level of invention and passion throughout. The resonance of the long title track - one of those flawless performances that happens only very occasionally - dominates the record. Front-line partner George Coleman (tenor saxophone) chose a good evening to play some of the most beautiful solos of his life.

● TRACKS: *My Funny Valentine; All Of You; Stella By Starlight; All Blues; I Thought About You.*

● FIRST RELEASED 1964
● UK PEAK CHART POSITION: did not chart
● USA PEAK CHART POSITION: 138

769 SHOUT AT THE DEVIL (692) ▼
MÖTLEY CRÜE

The Crüe's first attempt at major label stardom after the success of their independent debut, *Too Fast For Love*, Elektra Records went all out for infamy with a gatefold sleeve package, complete with a translucent pentagram adorning their logo. Musically, it was more of the same - the anthemic title track, the instant clarity of 'Looks That Kill', with its wasteland and warriors video - while their troubled history with the LAPD was raked over for 'Knock 'Em Dead Kid'. All of this and a trashy cover of 'Helter Skelter' - their capacity for stardom seemed infinite.

● TRACKS: *In The Beginning; Shout At The Devil; Looks That Kill; Bastard; Knock 'Em Dead Kid; Danger; Too Young To Fall In Love; Helter Skelter; Red Hot; Ten Seconds 'Til Love; God Bless The Children Of The Beast.*

● FIRST RELEASED 1983
● UK PEAK CHART POSITION: did not chart
● USA PEAK CHART POSITION: 17

770 TEXAS FEVER (-) ▲
ORANGE JUICE

Texas Fever was the group's third album, and a long way from their innocent beginnings as a fractious indie enterprise with Postcard Records. Despite this being the best of Orange Juice's handful of records, it was recorded amid inter-band turmoil. Luckily, such problems could not dilute the group's escalating musical sophistication. *Texas Fever* saw the group create some elaborate and hugely entertaining pop-funk. Credit reggaemeister Dennis Bovell's production and Zeke Manyika's superb rhythmic flow. Given that the original album was recorded in less than ideal conditions and encompassed a mere six tunes, it is amazing they retain such confidence and urgency. 'Bridge' (alongside 'Felicity', the group's best single) and 'A Sad Lament' still sound like great contemporary pop a decade and a half down the line.

● TRACKS: *Bridge; Craziest Feeling; Punch Drunk; The Day I Went Down To Texas; A Place In My Heart; A Sad Lament; Leaner Period; Out For The Count; Move Yourself.*

● FIRST RELEASED 1984
● UK PEAK CHART POSITION: 34
● USA PEAK CHART POSITION: did not chart

771 THE PAUL SIMON SONGBOOK (639) ▼
PAUL SIMON

Having begun his singing career as half of be-bop duo Tom And Jerry, Paul Simon embraced folk music during a spell domiciled in Brentwood, Essex, England, and returned there in 1965 to record this haunting solo album. Fellow singer Al Stewart produced the set, on which Simon accompanied himself solely on acoustic guitar. This simple setting enhances the self-penned compositions, many of which would be re-recorded when the artist rejoined his erstwhile partner, Art Garfunkel. The pair gained early success with new renditions of 'The Sound Of Silence' and 'I Am A Rock', but these first versions are equally persuasive, possessing a quiet maturity that permeates this entire album.

● TRACKS: *I Am A Rock; Leaves That Are Green; A Church Is Burning; April Come She Will; The Sound Of Silence; A Most Peculiar Man; He Was My Brother; Kathy's Song; The Side Of A Hill; A Simple Desultory Philippic; Flowers Never Bend With The Rainfall; Patterns.*

● FIRST RELEASED 1965
● UK PEAK CHART POSITION: did not chart
● USA PEAK CHART POSITION: did not chart

772 EQUAL RIGHTS (-) ▲
PETER TOSH

Tosh was the second lieutenant with Bob Marley in the Wailers, and knew that to establish himself, he had to break loose from the greatest band in the history of reggae. *Legalize It* was his first major move, and this follow-up is equally strong; in particular, it contains his suberb composition 'Get Up Stand Up', surely one of the great anthems of Jamaican music. The album's weight is bolstered from the excellent support throughout of fellow Wailer Bunny Livingston, and the peerless session men, Sly and Robbie. Tosh's hard-edged protest was curtailed when he was gunned down in 1987.

● TRACKS: *Get Up, Stand Up; Downpressor Man; I Am That I Am; Stepping Razor; Equal Rights; African; Jah Guide; Apartheid.*

● FIRST RELEASED 1977
● UK PEAK CHART POSITION: did not chart
● USA PEAK CHART POSITION: did not chart

773 **RANDY NEWMAN** (–) ▲
RANDY NEWMAN

Although the back cover of *Randy Newman* boasted 'Randy Newman Creates Something New Under the Sun', his songwriting talent was nothing new to the music industry who had long admired him. Unfortunately, even with the release of this, his debut, it would still be some time before the secret would become known to the record-buying public. Its commercial failure is astonishing in light of how many of its songs went on to become classics; 'Living Without You', 'So Long Dad', 'Love Story', and especially the heartbreaking 'I Think It's Going To Rain Today'. Vocally, too, Newman is at the top of his game, bending notes as only he can and demonstrating the strong influence of his New Orleans home-town.

● TRACKS: *Love Story; Bet No One Ever Hurt This Bad; Living Without You; So Long Dad; I Think He's Hiding; Linda; Laughing Boy; Cowboy; The Beehive State; I Think It's Going To Rain Today; Davy The Fat Boy.*

● FIRST RELEASED 1971
● UK PEAK CHART POSITION: did not chart
● USA PEAK CHART POSITION: 191

---

 774 **GAUCHO** (–) ▲
STEELY DAN

Probably the most critically revered band of the 70s, Steely Dan's brand of slick pop with a dose of jazz/funk left a meagre but vital catalogue to cling on to. This was their last gasp at the onset of the 80s. Perhaps they were aware of the fact that they were too 70s for the 80s. This was their least accessible and most mature album (no criticism is intended), as the content washes over the listener like a warm shower. 'Hey Nineteen' is the hit single from this set, a radio-friendly nostalgic look at 1967, impeccable in production and with evocative lyrics. Lots of echoey Fender Rhodes and sensitive brass. This is a sanitized record that cannot be faulted.

● TRACKS: *Babylon Sisters; Hey Nineteen; Glamour Profession; Gaucho; Time Out Of Mind; My Rival; Third World Man.*

● FIRST RELEASED 1980
● UK PEAK CHART POSITION: 27
● USA PEAK CHART POSITION: 9

---

775 **DREAM LETTER (LIVE IN LONDON 1968)** (–) ▲ **TIM BUCKLEY**

Buckley's London debut was recorded shortly after the release of the pivotal *Happy Sad*, on which he had broken away from folk music and embraced a more expressive, jazz-based style. The respectful audience at the Queen Elizabeth Hall reserve their warmest applause for standard singer-songwriter fare like 'Morning Glory' and 'Once I Was', but Buckley himself seems more at ease on lengthier vocal workouts such as 'Love From Room 109/Strange Feeling' and 'Carnival Song/Hi Lily, Hi Lo', enjoying the new-found freedom of expression afforded his remarkable multi-octave voice. The musical accompaniment is superb, Buckley's 12-string backed by guitar, vibes and bass. The only mystery is why this recording did not gain an official release until 1990.

● TRACKS: *Introduction; Buzzin' Fly; Phantasmagoria In Two; Morning Glory; Dolphins; I've Been Out Walking; The Earth Is Broken; Who Do You Love; Pleasant Street/You Keep Me Hanging On; Love From Room 109/Strange Feelin'; Carnival Song/Hi Lily, Hi Lo; Hallucinations; Troubadour; Dream Letter/Happy Time; Wayfaring Stranger/You Got Me Runnin'; Once I Was.*

● FIRST RELEASED 1990
● UK PEAK CHART POSITION: did not chart
● USA PEAK CHART POSITION: did not chart

---

776 **OLIVER!** (309) ▼
VARIOUS

Ron Moody recreates his magnificent stage performance as Fagin on this soundtrack album of what must be the best British musical film ever. Shani Wallis replaced Georgia Brown as Nancy, and, together with Mark Lester (Oliver), Jack Wild (Artful Dodger) and Oliver Reed (the sinister Bill Sikes), gives Lionel Bart's marvellous score the full treatment. Highlights are impossible to select; Oliver's tender 'Where Is Love?' and Fagin's 'You've Got To Pick A Pocket Or Two' linger in the memory, but the complete set is as fresh now as when it was released over 25 years ago. In those pre-Lloyd-Webber days, musicals had lots of strong songs, not just one.

● TRACKS: *Overture; Food Glorious Food; Boy For Sale; Where Is Love?; You've Got To Pick A Pocket Or Two; Consider Yourself; I'd Do Anything; Be Back Soon; As Long As He Needs Me; Who Will Buy; It's A Fine Life; Reviewing The Situation; Oom Pah Pah; Finale.*

● FIRST RELEASED 1968
● UK PEAK CHART POSITION: 4
● USA PEAK CHART POSITION: 20

777 HEAVY WEATHER (−) ▲
WEATHER REPORT

Probably the best fusion album ever made, and the coming together of five precociously talented musicians. Joe Zawinul and Wayne Shorter assembled the unit with little knowledge that the complex music would become so accessible. Two compostions stand out; the graceful 'A Remark You Made', an evocative love song without words, and the hit single 'Birdland' (so successful it was even used by Akai for a major advertising campaign). On these two Zawinul compostions their genius bass player Jaco Pastorius gives a taste of what he was capable of. He bent the notes to make them talk, and that high octave solo on 'Birdland' is still a treasured moment.

● TRACKS: *Birdland; A Remark You Made; Teen Town; Harlequin; Rumba Mama; Palladium; The Juggler; Havona.*

● FIRST RELEASED 1977
● UK PEAK CHART POSITION: 43
● USA PEAK CHART POSITION: 30

---

 779 MISPLACED CHILDHOOD (−) ▲
MARILLION

Marillion were at the forefront of the brief progressive rock revival of the 80s, and as such had to endure constant critical carping about their similarities to Genesis. Led at this stage of their career by Fish, they reached a creative and commercial peak with this 1985 release, a concept album based loosely around the singer's childhood. What saved the album from empty bombast was Marillion's sudden emergence as a skilled and melodic rock group, exemplified by the UK hit single 'Kayleigh'. While nothing else on the album was quite able to match this song, the rest is still worthy of re-investigation.

● TRACKS: *Pseudo Silk Kimono; Kayleigh; Lavender; Bitter Suite; Heart Of Lothian; Waterhole (Expresso Bongo); Lords Of The Backstage; Blind Curve; Childhoods End?; White Feather.*

● FIRST RELEASED 1985
● UK PEAK CHART POSITION: 1
● USA PEAK CHART POSITION: 47

---

 778 GOODBYE JUMBO (−) ▲
WORLD PARTY

This is a fine album that paradoxically owes much of its originality to its up-front eclecticism. Karl Wallinger's undoubted talent and experience (musical director of *The Rocky Horror Show*, ex-Waterboys) are applied to create a powerful tribute to his 60s influences. The opening 'Is It Too Late' is reminiscent of Them's 'Baby Please Don't Go', and is followed by 'Way Down Now', complete with 'Sympathy For The Devil'-style 'woo-woos'. It is difficult to keep track of all the styles cleverly woven into the fabric, but the Beatles abound - Wallinger even had his studio built to reproduce the Abbey Road sound for the equally strong follow-up, *Bang!*

● TRACKS: *Is It Too Late; Way Down Now; When The Rainbow Comes; Put The Message In The Box; Ain't Gonna Come Till I'm Ready; And I Fell Back Alone; Take It Up; God On My Side; Show Me To The Top; Love Street; Sweet Soul Dream; Thank You World.*

● First Released 1990
● UK PEAK CHART POSITION: 36
● USA PEAK CHART POSITION: 73

 **780** JANET (−) ▲
JANET JACKSON

Although Janet Jackson's sleeve note dedication to her fans, 'who made me what I am', might seem a little over the top, those fans responded by buying millions of copies. Although there are 27 listed tracks, many merely constitute a few-second segue. Nevertheless, the album showed increasing confidence aligned with a desire to explore a wider variety of styles, not always successfully - perfect production, good voice, but somehow lacking in heart and soul. Can 10 million fans be wrong? Perhaps the promise of an album is greater than the content. Oh, and Janet, the top button and zip on your Levis have inadvertently come undone.

● TRACKS: *Morning; That's The Way Love Goes; You Know; You Want This; Be A Good Boy; If; Back; This Time; Go On Miss Janet; Throb; What'll I Do; The Lounge; Funky Big Band; Racism; New Agenda; Love pt 2; Because Of Love; Wind; Again; Another Lover; Where Are You Now; Hold On Baby; The Body That Loves You; Rain; Any Time Any Place; Are You Still Up; Sweet Dreams.*

● FIRST RELEASED 1993
● UK PEAK CHART POSITION: 1
● USA PEAK CHART POSITION: 1

781 THE SKY IS CRYING (456) ▼
STEVIE RAY VAUGHAN AND DOUBLE TROUBLE

Vaughan's death on 27 August 1990 brought to a tragic end the surging wave of his popularity. The album he had made with his brother Jimmie, *Family Style*, had just been released and this album, prepared by Jimmie from the various album sessions, was not expected to amount to much.

In fact, this was at least as good as any of them - and better than *Live Alive*. 'Little Wing' was perhaps his best adaptation of a Jimi Hendrix song. His take on the Elmore James title song was also a fitting tribute to both the writer and the performer. There are bound to be further compilations and live recordings released, but these studio recordings are testimony to Stevie Ray's devotion to his craft.

● TRACKS: *Boot Hill; The Sky Is Crying; Empty Arms; Little Wing; Wham; May I Have A Talk With You; Close To You; Chittlins Con Carne; So Excited; Life By The Drop.*

● FIRST RELEASED 1991
● UK PEAK CHART POSITION: did not chart
● USA PEAK CHART POSITION: 10

782 OPERATION RADICATION (–) ▲
YELLOWMAN

Originally released on vinyl only, this vital CD reissue covers the early part of Winston Foster's career. The tall, imposing figure of a black albino is now seen as a sex-symbol; in his schooldays he was often an outcast as people found it hard to come to terms with the way he looked. Sly and Robbie give all the tracks here the edge of professionalism, although the secret of being able to appreciate Yellowman is the depth of his humour. Subtly hidden, his humour, often very rude, is a joy to discover. Take 'Even Tide Fire' as a perfect example. Highly rewarding.

● TRACKS: *11 + 11; Shorties; Morning Ride; Even Tide Fire; Operation Radication; Couchie; Out A Hand; Mad Over Me; Lovers Corner; Bim & Bam; Badness; My Possie.*

● FIRST RELEASED 1980
● UK PEAK CHART POSITION: did not chart
● USA PEAK CHART POSITION: did not chart

783 ESCAPE (281) ▼
JOURNEY

One of America's biggest rock bands of all time, Journey managed to achieve a perfect blend of spirited and soulful AOR that brought them both commercial and critical success. With Steve Perry's blistering vocal range and Neal Schon's colourful shading of sounds, they created an album that was neither understated or overblown. Their songwriting skill as a band was extraordinary, passing quickly from fond balladeering to hard rock in an assured instant. From the astounding 'Don't Stop Believing' to the quiet sanctity of 'Open Arms', their all-round ability still astounds even though their overall credibility appears low.

● TRACKS: *Don't Stop Believing; Stone In Love; Who's Crying Now; Keep On Running; Still They Ride; Escape; Lay It Down; Dead Or Alive; Mother, Father; Open Arms.*

● FIRST RELEASED 1981
● UK PEAK CHART POSITION: 32
● USA PEAK CHART POSITION: 1

784 MIDNIGHT LOVE (–) ▲
MARVIN GAYE

Leaving the safety and familiarity of Tamla/ Motown has seen many artists take a flight to obscurity. Gaye turned it on its head and made his most successful album for over ten years. The pivotal track is 'Sexual Healing', an idea given to him by his biographer David Ritz and co-written with Odell Brown. This track alone is worth the price of the album (even though it was a single). It oozes greatness with every second and was the last great Marvin Gaye song. And for the record, he played drums, piano, organ, bells, synths and bongos. A premier voice lost to the world.

● TRACKS: *Midnight Lady; Sexual Healing; Rockin' After Midnight; 'Til Tomorrow; Turn On Some Music; Third World Girl; Joy; My Love Is Waiting.*

● FIRST RELEASED 1982
● UK PEAK CHART POSITION: 10
● USA PEAK CHART POSITION: 7

785 HEART (282) ▼
HEART

The other Wilson sisters strode wilfully back into the international charts with their self-titled debut for Capitol Records. Now seen as the first female AOR classic. Drawing on outside writers to help develop the project, they created an album of enormous musical wealth that charted internationally with a host of successful spin-off singles. With Ron Nevison's lush production and the Wilsons' soulful vocals, tracks such as 'What About Love', 'Never', and the yearning 'These Dreams' were guaranteed sellers, while the band still rocked majestically for 'If Looks Could Kill' and 'Wolf', in particular.

● TRACKS: *If Looks Could Kill; What About Love; Never; These Dreams; Wolf; All Eyes; Nobody Home; Nothin' At All; What He Don't Know; Shellshock.*

● FIRST RELEASED 1985
● UK PEAK CHART POSITION: 19
● USA PEAK CHART POSITION: 1

786 GOING FOR THE ONE (–) ▲
YES

It seemed very strange to see a Yes album without Roger Dean's colourful, ipsy-dipsy land of fantasy on the cover. The replacement is a concrete jungle of grey skyscrapers, but do not fear, the music is still the same. The reassuring chorus on the title track and Howe's beautiful acoustic guitar on 'Turn Of The Century' comfort the listener that some things never change. After a gap of three years, the Yes boys refused to say no and came back with one of the best albums of their lengthy career. The real unanswered question, however: is that Jon Anderson's cute little bottom on the album cover?

● TRACKS: *Going For The One; Turn Of The Century; Parallels; Wonderous Stories; Awaken.*

● FIRST RELEASED 1977
● UK PEAK CHART POSITION: 1
● USA PEAK CHART POSITION: 8

787 BRING THE FAMILY (–) ▲
JOHN HIATT

Hiatt was already a seasoned performer and songwriter by the time this album was released. He was 'the songwriter's songwriter' and destined for critically acclaimed cult status. This is just one of a series of excellent collections of songs that have been recorded by dozens of artists from Bonnie Raitt to Joe Cocker. The simple piano accompanying the gravel-voiced 'Have A Little Faith In Me' makes the hairs stand up on end. Hiatt's fine supporting musicians are Jim Keltner (drums), Ry Cooder (guitar) and Nick Lowe (bass). This unsung genius is the Randy Newman of roots-rock.

● TRACKS: *Memphis In The Meantime; Alone In The Dark; Thing Called Love; Lipstick Sunset; Have A Little Faith In Me; Thank You Girl; Tip Of My Tongue; Your Dad Did; Stood Up; Learning How To Love You.*

● FIRST RELEASED 1987
● UK PEAK CHART POSITION: did not chart
● USA PEAK CHART POSITION: 107

788 I JUST CAN'T STOP IT (–) ▲
THE BEAT

Along with Madness and the Specials, the Beat were the best of the late 70s two-tone movement. Left-of-centre politics were coupled to a sensitive grasp of ska and blue beat. Their debut is virtually a greatest hits package with the sparkling 'Mirror In The Bathroom', 'Hands Off She's Mine' and 'Twist And Crawl'. Additionally there are great covers of Andy Williams' smooth ballad 'Can't Get Used To Losing You' and a wonderful rude 'Rough Rider' first heard in 1968 from Prince Buster. Singer Dave Wakeling left in 1983 to form General Public and the band fell apart.

● TRACKS: *Mirror In The Bathroom; Hands Off She's Mine; Two Swords; Twist & Crawl; Rough Rider; Click Click; Big Shot; Whine & Grine/Stand Down Margaret; Noise In This World; Can't Get Used To Losing You; Best Friend; Jackpot.*

● FIRST RELEASED 1980
● UK PEAK CHART POSITION: 3
● USA PEAK CHART POSITION: did not chart

789 BEATLES FOR SALE (–) ▲
THE BEATLES

Released at the end of an exhausting 12 months, the fab four were a little jaded when they recorded this. Still, the genius comes through with some classic Lennon/McCartney songs such as 'Eight Days A Week', 'Baby's in Black' and Lennon's early hint at the trough he was in with 'I'm A Loser'. When he sang 'although I laugh and I act like a clown, beneath this mask I am wearing a frown', he was not just being flippant. McCartney delivered the beautifully compact 'I'll Follow The Sun' and brilliantly belted out Lieber and Stoller's 'Kansas City'. Even when they were sub-par, they were better than the rest.

● TRACKS: No Reply; I'm A Loser; Baby's In Black; Rock And Roll Music; I'll Follow The Sun; Mr Moonlight; Kansas City; Hey Hey Hey Hey; Eight Days A Week; Words Of Love; Honey Don't Every Little Thing; I Don't Want To Spoil The Party; What You're Doing; Everybody's Trying To Be My Baby.

● FIRST RELEASED 1964
● UK PEAK CHART POSITION: 1
● USA PEAK CHART POSITION: did not chart

790 THE AUDIENCE WITH BETTY CARTER
(324) ▼ BETTY CARTER

For Betty Carter, songs are vehicles for her talent. If something does not fit her conception of how her performance should be, then she changes it. Nothing is sacred; and yet, somehow, nothing is profaned. Standards from the Great American Songbook are reworked with seemingly dismissive ease. The album title is significant: woe betide any audience that risks not being 'with' Betty Carter. In command, on display, this tough, restless tigress of jazz overshadows her contemporaries, What is more, her statement that she can see no-one coming along to challenge her superiority, looks increasingly true as the years pass by.

● TRACKS: Sounds (Movin' On); I Think I Got It Now; Caribbean Sun; The Trolley Song; Everything I Have Is Yours; I'll Buy You A Star; I Could Write A Book; Can't We Talk It Over; Either It's Love Or It Isn't; Deep Night; Spring Can Really Hang You Up The Most; Tight; Fake; So; My Favourite Things; Open The Door.

● FIRST RELEASED 1979
● UK PEAK CHART POSITION: did not chart
● USA PEAK CHART POSITION: did not chart

791 ONE FOR ALL (586) ▼
BRAND NUBIAN

From the Bronx, New York, and led by Grand Puba Maxwell, Brand Nubian's debut album was as cool and classy as anything in the genre. Backed by Lord Jamar, Sadat X and DJ Alamo, Puba kicked out reams of Muslim-influenced thinking, backed by steals from some of the great moments of soul music. Despite the creed of the Five Percent Nation, which was so manifest within its grooves, it was by no means humourless (highlighted by name-checks for people such as Englebert Humperdink), while samples of James Brown and Roy Ayers spiced up the backing tracks. In 1991 Puba left to go solo, taking DJ Alamo with him, and although Brand Nubian have persevered with a new line-up and recorded two well-received albums, they have yet to match this achievement.

● TRACKS: All For One; Feels So Good; Concerto In X Minor; Ragtime; To The Right; Dance To My Ministry; Drop The Bomb; Wake Up; Step To The Rear; Slow Down; Try To Do Me; Who Can Get Busy Like This Man; Grand Puba, Positive And LG; Brand Nubian; Wake Up; Dedication.

● FIRST RELEASED 1991
● UK PEAK CHART POSITION: did not chart
● USA PEAK CHART POSITION: 130

792 MR. MENTION (–) ▲
BUJU BANTON

Buju Banton emerged in the early 90s as the most exciting new voice on the ragga scene since Shabba Ranks. Mr. Mention effectively collects together Banton's early dancehall hits, recorded at Donovan Germain's Penthouse Studio. 'Love Mi Browning' caused some controversy by announcing Banton's love for light-skinned girls, to which he replied with the self-explanatory 'Love Black Woman'. Other cuts defining the dancehall fashions of the moment included 'Batty Rider' and 'Woman Nuh Fret', while 'Who Say' and 'Bonafide Love' featured vocal contributions from Beres Hammond and Wayne Wonder, respectively. The focal point, however, is always Banton's mesmerizingly deep, gruff voice and his sharp DJing skills.

● TRACKS: Batty Rider; Love How The Gal Flex; Love Black Woman; Look How You Sweet; Woman Nuh Fret; Have To Get You Tonight; Dickie; Love Mi Browning; Buju Moving; Who Say; The Grudge; How The World A Run; Buju Love You To The Max; Man Fe Dead; Bonafide Love.

● FIRST RELEASED 1991
● UK PEAK CHART POSITION: did not chart
● USA PEAK CHART POSITION: did not chart

Popular music is almost unthinkable without the influence of Chuck Berry. He combined the economy of R&B with a brilliant gift for lyricism that encapsulated adolescent spirit in a manner no other performer has matched. The three opening tracks on this album define Berry's gifts; each one is now an integral part of pop's lexicon. Intriguingly, these compositions can be heard in the early work of the Beach Boys, Rolling Stones and Beatles, which itself is a tribute to Berry's enormous influence. His unique guitar style is showcased on 'Blue Ceiling' and 'Guitar Boogie', resulting in a set that expresses the artist's talent to the full. Compilations have superseded this vinyl release.

● TRACKS: *Sweet Little Sixteen; Blue Feeling; La Jaunda; Guitar Boogie; Oh Baby Doll; In-Go; Rock At The Philharmonic; Reelin' And Rockin; Rock & Roll Music; It Don't Take But A Few Minutes; Low Feeling; How You've Changed.*

● FIRST RELEASED 1958
● UK PEAK CHART POSITION: did not chart
● USA PEAK CHART POSITION: did not chart

Creedence Clearwater Revival were part of a second wave of San Francisco groups, but unlike their geographical contemporaries, the quartet offered a disciplined music, indebted to 50s rock 'n' roll and southern 'swamp' styles. Leader, singer and songwriter John Fogerty possesses one of rock's most distinctive voices, his hoarse, urgent intonation matched by his group's mathematically precise drive. *Green River*, their third album, includes two million-selling singles, the title track and 'Bad Moon Rising', both of which encapsulate the Creedence métier. Remaining selections expose a similar economy, crammed with punchy hooklines, tight playing and incisive lyrics, taking inspiration from traditional styles, but in the process creating something unique.

● TRACKS: *Bad Moon Rising; Cross-tie Walker; Sinister Purpose; Night Time Is The Right Time; Green River; Commotion; Tombstone Shadow; Wrote A Song For Everyone; Lodi.*

● FIRST RELEASED 1969
● UK PEAK CHART POSITION: 20
● USA PEAK CHART POSITION: 1

David Ackles' first album announced the arrival of an original songwriting talent. Drawing from previous experience in film and theatre, he produced a highly literate music in which stories unfolded with vivid detail. His dispassionate vocal encouraged songs to unfold with brooding intensity, but unlike many contemporaries, Ackles was not a confessional composer. He spoke for the rootless drifter ('The Road To Cairo'), the unrequited lover ('Down River') or the dreamer whose hopes were inevitably dashed ('When Love Is Gone'). Backing group Rhinocerous provide intuitively understanding support in a set that maintains its stature, albeit as a cult item.

● TRACKS: *The Road To Cairo; When Love Is Gone; Sonny Come Here; Blue Ribbons; What A Happy Day; Down River; Laissez-Faire; Lotus Man; His Name Is Andrew; Be My Friend.*

● FIRST RELEASED 1968
● UK PEAK CHART POSITION: did not chart
● USA PEAK CHART POSITION: did not chart

Bowie's best work since *Heroes* at that time, and the critics responded with relief as much as anything else. The Nile Rogers production was an inspired partnership as Bowie entered another phase in his chameleon-like career - this time rock/disco. Even Stevie Ray Vaughan was added to sharpen the guitar parts, although the overall impression is that this is not a guitar album. Had that been the case then surely Mick Ronson would have been hired. Rarely has an album opened with three similarly blockbusting tracks, 'Modern Love', 'China Girl' and the title track.

● TRACKS: *Modern Love; China Girl; Let's Dance; Without You; Ricochet; Criminal World; Cat People (Putting Out Fire); Shake It.*

● FIRST RELEASED 1983
● UK PEAK CHART POSITION: 1
● USA PEAK CHART POSITION: 4

797 MUSIC FOR THE MASSES (–) ▲
DEPECHE MODE

One of the bands that not only dominated the charts for most of the 80s, but they also typified the type of music that will be looked back on as 'the sound of the 80s'. Their sometimes Germanic electronic pop became softer on this album. They were becoming more of a band, and they were 'rockin', just a little. keyboards still dominated but the melody seemed less regimented. Vocalist Dave Gahan excelled, as his voice grew in power. In a year or two they would become stadium rock stars, and change forever. The reissued CD had a number of excellent bonus tracks including some interesting remixed material.

● TRACKS: *Never Let Me Down Again; The Things You Said; Strangelove; Sacred; Little 15; Behind The Wheel; I Want You Now; To Have And To Hold; Nothing; Pimpf; Agent Orange; Never Let Me Down Again (Aggro Mix); To Have And To Hold (Spanish Taster); Pleasure Little Treasure (Glitter Mix).*

● FIRST RELEASED 1987
● UK PEAK CHART POSITION: 10
● USA PEAK CHART POSITION: 35

798 OUR MAN IN PARIS (318) ▼
DEXTER GORDON

One of the most successful of Blue Note's 'blue' period and an album that remains his finest work. Although his tenor sax occasionally grates, this is a brilliant example of late bebop. Supported by Bud Powell (piano), Kenny Clarke (drums) and Pierre Michelot (bass), the simple quartet sound coolly in control. 'Willow Weep For Me' is played with great beauty and 'A Night in Tunisia' is yet another well-crafted version. The wonderful bonus of 'Our Love Is Here To Stay' and 'Like Someone In Love' (from Powell's Alternate Takes) on the CD reissue puts this album in the first division.

● TRACKS: *Scrapple From The Apple; Willow Weep For Me; Stairway To The Stairs; A Night In Tunisia; Our Love Is Here To Stay; Like Someone In Love; Broadway.*

● FIRST RELEASED 1963
● UK PEAK CHART POSITION: did not chart
● USA PEAK CHART POSITION: did not chart

799 CAPTAIN FANTASTIC AND THE BROWN DIRT COWBOY (–) ▲ ELTON JOHN

In the pre-punk era, where severely inflated egos and ludricous concept albums were *de rigeur*, Elton John and Bernie Taupin's account of their rise from struggling penury to the peak of superstardom is one of rock's better attempts at self-mythology. The original vinyl record was an elaborate package in itself, and the music within is on a suitably grandiose and self-indulgent scale. At times, John's music and Taupin's lyrics struggle to gel, but when they come together on tracks such as 'Someone Saved My Life Tonight' and 'Gotta Get A Meal Ticket', John carries the concept with suitable aplomb.

● TRACKS: *Captain Fantastic And The Brown Dirt Cowboy; Tower Of Babel; Bitter Fingers; Tell Me When The Whistle Blows; Someone Saved My Life Tonight; (Gotta Get A) Meal Ticket; Better Off Dead; Writing; We All Fall In Love Sometimes; Curtains.*

● FIRST RELEASED 1975
● UK PEAK CHART POSITION: 2
● USA PEAK CHART POSITION: 1

800 ELVIS (346) ▼
ELVIS PRESLEY

While Private Elvis Presley was gaining his stripes in Germany, RCA was desperate for new material. They kept the pot boiling by taking his first UK album, *Rock 'n' Roll No.I*, substituting three tracks and adding two more. Although critics sometimes regard his Sun tracks in a different light to his RCA ones, they sit well together. 'I Was The One', the b-side of 'Heartbreak Hotel' and one of Elvis's favourite songs, could easily have been recorded at Sun. 'Lawdy, Miss Clawdy', written and originally recorded by Lloyd Price, remains one of Presley's best-ever performances: the lyrics do not mean much but there is tremendous commitment from Elvis. Lloyd Price's original version had Fats Domino on piano: this one had Elvis himself. Elvis always enjoyed his recording sessions and you can sense this in the good-natured 'Money Honey'.

● TRACKS: *That's All Right; Lawdy, Miss Clawdy; Mystery Train; Playing For Keeps; Poor Boy; Money Honey; I'm Counting On You; My Baby Left Me; I Was The One; Shake, Rattle And Roll; I'm Left, You're Right, She's Gone; You're A Heartbreaker; Trying To Get You; Blue Suede Shoes.*

● FIRST RELEASED 1959
● UK PEAK CHART POSITION: did not chart
● USA PEAK CHART POSITION: 1

801 PIECES OF THE SKY (–) ▲
EMMYLOU HARRIS

The title of Emmylou Harris's first major-label solo album comes from a line in one of its songs, 'Before Believing': 'How would you feel if the world was falling all apart all around you?'. She knew how it felt. Two years earlier, she had been devastated by the death of her partner Gram Parsons. Nine of its ten songs are cover versions, with the lone original, 'Boulder To Birmingham', standing as a poignant tribute to Parsons (it has become her signature tune). A milestone in the development of the genre that became 'New Country', the album was a critical success. One track, a cover of the Louvin Brothers' 'If I Could Only Win Your Love', became the first of Harris's many US country hits.

● TRACKS: Bluebird Wine; Too Far Gone; If I Could Only Win Your Love; Boulder To Birmingham; Before Believing; Bottle Let Me Down; Sleepless Nights; Coat Of Many Colours; For No One; Queen Of The Silver Dollar.

● FIRST RELEASED 1975
● UK PEAK CHART POSITION: did not chart
● USA PEAK CHART POSITION: 45

802 OUT TO LUNCH! (315) ▼
ERIC DOLPHY

Although a difficult album for those not seeped in jazz, it is still regarded as a milestone of recorded jazz. Featuring Freddie Hubbard (trumpet), Bobby Hutcherson (vibes), Tony Williams (drums) and Richard Davis (bass), this recording shows a unit hell-bent on pushing forward the perimeters of jazz, with extraordinary success. Dolphy's various saxophones, flute and chilling bass clarinet are literally all over the place without ever detracting from the quite outstanding performances from his supporting musicians. Although it won't be played as often as Kind Of Blue your collection would be all the poorer without it.

● TRACKS: Hat And Beard; Something Sweet, Something Tender; Gazzelloni; Out To Lunch; Straight Up And Down.

● FIRST RELEASED 1964
● UK PEAK CHART POSITION: did not chart
● USA PEAK CHART POSITION: did not chart

803 CONCERT BY THE SEA (323) ▼
ERROLL GARNER

Garner's place in the history of jazz piano is unusual. He demonstrates no obvious influences of any other pianist, he appears to have influenced no-one; and yet his is such a thoroughly engaging, happy, always enjoyable style. Here, he deftly picks his way through a sprightly selection of songs. Throughout, the Elf happily indulges his love for lengthy introductions that defy listeners to identify the coming tune, yet, when he finally arrives at the song as the composer wrote it, everything seems just right. Ageless music in an impishly droll style that defies categorization; it's just Erroll's way. Ask Dudley Moore, he'll tell you.

● TRACKS: I'll Remember April; Teach Me Tonight; Mambo Carmel; It's Alright With Me; Red Top; April In Paris; They Can't Take That Away From Me; Where Or When; Erroll's Theme.

● FIRST RELEASED 1958
● UK PEAK CHART POSITION: did not chart
● USA PEAK CHART POSITION: 12

804 DRAGNET (–) ▲
FALL

With the Fall currently taking up more shelf space in your local record emporium than any other credible modern rock act, it is easy to overlook some of their earlier material. Dragnet was Mark E. Smith's second long-playing outing, and it contains two bona fide Fall greats - 'Spectre Versus Rector' and 'Psykick Dancehall'. As far as this writer is concerned, you can also add 'Dice Man' and 'Printhead' to that ever-expanding list. Smith's observations are by turns vindictive and hilarious, and sometimes so obscure in meaning they may as well be encrypted. It is also the first album to feature Craig Scanlon's distinctive scraped-bowel guitar-work, and is therefore more representative of the early model Fall than Live At The Witch Trials, which preceded it earlier in 1979.

● TRACKS: Before The Moon Falls; Muzorewi's Daughter; A Figure Walks; Psykick Dancehall; Spectre Versus Rector; Your Heart Out; Flat Of Angles; Dice Man; Choc-Stock; Put Away; Printhead.

● FIRST RELEASED 1979
● UK PEAK CHART POSITION: did not chart
● USA PEAK CHART POSITION: did not chart

805 THIS IS FATS DOMINO (322) ▼
FATS DOMINO

Despite the cheapo-cheapo cover, this is one of the most potent rock 'n' roll albums of the 50s. Fats' revival of Louis Armstrong's 'Blueberry Hill' was so successful that nearly everyone now regards it as Fats' song. He and his producer Dave Bartholomew wrote many straightforward conversational rock 'n' roll songs, including 'Ain't It A Shame', now known as 'Ain't That A Shame'. (Pat Boone, an English graduate, originally had not wanted to cover a song with the word 'Ain't' in the title.) 'Blue Monday', which Fats sang in *The Girl Can't Help It*, is one of the first songs about the drudgery of the working week. He sent himself up in 'The Fat Man's Hop'. Why were people so concerned when Elvis put on weight? Fats Domino always looked the same and was much heavier than Elvis.

● TRACKS: *Blueberry Hill; Honey Chile; What's The Reason I'm Not Pleasing You; Blue Monday; So Long; La La; Troubles Of My Own; You Done Me Wrong; Reeling And Rocking; The Fat Man's Hop; Poor Poor Me; Trust In Me.*

● FIRST RELEASED 1957
● UK PEAK CHART POSITION: did not chart
● USA PEAK CHART POSITION: 19

806 WEASELS RIPPED MY FLESH (–) ▲
FRANK ZAPPA / MOTHERS OF INVENTION

Once attracted by the irresistibly sinister Neon Park album cover illustration, the new owner has to play it. And once again, unless you are already familiar with this wacky genius, the results can be challenging. From the perplexing Germanic interlude of the opener, 'Didja Get Any Onya?', to the complex xylophone changes of 'The Eric Dolphy Memorial Barbecue', Zappa's music should always have been played loud. As background music at a normal volume it serves only to irritate, except for almost normal rock tracks, such as the interpretation of Little Richard's 'Directly From My Heart To You'. It ends with some brilliant free-form something or other. All this was 25 years before Pat Metheny's *Zero Tolerence For Silence*.

● TRACKS: *Didja Get Any Onya?; Directly From My Heart To You; Prelude To The Afternoon Of A Sexually Aroused Gas Mask; Toad Of The Short Forest; Get A Little; The Eric Dolphy Memorial Barbecue; Dwarf Nebula Processional March & Dwarf Nebula; My Guitar Wants To Kill Your Mama; Oh No; The Orange County Lumber Truck; Weasels Ripped My Flesh.*

● FIRST RELEASED 1970
● UK PEAK CHART POSITION: did not chart
● USA PEAK CHART POSITION: 189

807 GENE CLARK WITH THE GOSDIN BROTHERS (–) ▲   GENE CLARK

This, Gene Clark's first solo album, was released the same week in March 1967 as the Byrds' first album since his departure, *Younger Than Yesterday*. However, as one magazine noted, the Byrds' album made the upper reaches of *Billboard*'s Top 200, while this record did not even make the bottom 100. Such was the fate of a man ahead of his time. Besides the excellent Everly Brothers-style harmonies of the Gosdin Brothers, there are elements of nascent psychedelia (the over-amped 'So You Say You Lost Your Baby'), pre-*Sgt. Pepper* orchestral pop ('Echoes'), and buoyant garage rock ('Elevator Operator'). An eminently listenable, beautifully crafted album, its status as a minor classic is well deserved.

● TRACKS: *Echoes; Think I'm Gonna Feel Better; Tried So Hard; Is Yours Is Mine; Keep On Pushin'; I Found You; So You Say You Lost Your Baby; Elevator Operator; The Same One; Couldn't Believe Her; Needing Someone.*

● FIRST RELEASED 1967.
● UK PEAK CHART POSITION: did not chart
● USA PEAK CHART POSITION: did not chart

808 SPLIT (–) ▲
THE GROUNDHOGS

Always a bit unfashionable, Tony TS McPhee and his Groundhogs made a number of albums in the late 60s that succeeded purely on their instrumental ability. After the aptly named *Blues Obituary* album they moved on to guitar prog. *Split* was a huge success; the opus-like length and popularity at live gigs guaranteed a good sale to fans. This spread as word of mouth went around that McPhee was an 'amazing guitar'. In reality he was, and is, pretty nifty: he used his wah-wah in all the right places in 1971. The reissued CD from BGO contains the fascinating hallucinatory tale behind 'Split', and explains just what it is all about.

● TRACKS: *Split Part One; Split Part Two; Split Part Three; Split Part Four; Cherry Red; A Year In The Life; Junkman; Groundhog.*

● FIRST RELEASED 1971
● UK PEAK CHART POSITION: 5
● USA PEAK CHART POSITION: did not chart

809 HOT BUTTERED SOUL (749) ▼
ISAAC HAYES

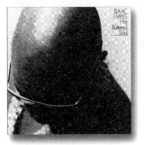

A staff songwriter with the legendary Stax label, Isaac Hayes, with partner David Porter, composed material for many of the company's artists, including Sam And Dave, Carla Thomas and Johnnie Taylor. Frustrated with this backroom role, he began recording in his own right, and with *Hot Buttered Soul*, redefined the notion of soul music. Although the tracks were lengthy, there was no sense of self-indulgence, each one evolving over sensual rhythms and taut arrangements. Hayes' vocal anticipated the 'rap' genre of Barry White and Millie Jackson without slipping into self-parody, lending an air of sophistication to a highly influential collection.

● TRACKS: *Walk On By; Hyperbolicsyllaciscesquedalymistic; One Woman; By The Time I Got To Phoenix.*

● FIRST RELEASED 1969
● UK PEAK CHART POSITION: did not chart
● USA PEAK CHART POSITION: 8

810 YOU GOT MY MIND MESSED UP
(436) ▼ JAMES CARR

F or lovers of vintage soul James Carr is god. Totally underrated with only a few compilation albums available, it is a mystery why this man is so overlooked. Carr, like Johnnie Taylor, was also a member of the legendary Soul Stirrers until he went solo for the Goldwax label. His deep and powerful 'You've Got My Mind Messed Up' was a huge R&B hit in the USA and this album followed it. There is not a bad track on the album, and one further high point is the definitive reading of Dan Penn and Spooner Oldham's 'Dark End Of The Street', the greatest ever country-meets-soul song. This album begs reissue.

● TRACKS: *Pouring Water On A Drowning Man; Love Attack; Coming Back To Me Baby; I Don't Want To Be Hurt Anymore; That's What I Want To Know; These Ain't Raindrops; Dark End Of The Street; I'm Going For Myself; Lovable Girl; Forgetting You; She's Better Than You.*

● FIRST RELEASED 1965
● UK PEAK CHART POSITION: did not chart
● USA PEAK CHART POSITION: did not chart

811 BLOWS AGAINST THE EMPIRE (–) ▲
JEFFERSON STARSHIP

B efore the Airplane metamorphosed into a Starship, there was a loose conglomeration assembled by science-fiction devotee Paul Kantner. This was a vehicle to release his great concept album. Friends such as David Crosby, Graham Nash and the Grateful Dead were roped in, and apart from one or two pompous lyrics ('Mau Mau (Amerikon)') the project was a success critically and commercially. Highlights, however, are the slower acoustic melodies that have great atmosphere, such as 'A Child Is Coming' and 'Have You Seen The Stars Tonite'. The idea was to hijack a starship, leave the Earth and live happily ever after. 'Yeah, wow, great man, but like, where do we get our drugs from?'

● TRACKS: *Mau Mau (Amerikon); The Baby Tree; Let's Go Together; A Child Is Coming; Sunrise; Hijack; Home; Have You Seen The Stars Tonite; XM; Starship.*

● FIRST RELEASED 1970
● UK PEAK CHART POSITION: did not chart
● USA PEAK CHART POSITION: 20

812 ORGAN GRINDER SWING (693) ▼
JIMMY SMITH

U sing the monicker 'Incredible' was no flash banner, it was true. Smith defined the Hammond organ as a jazz instrument and milked and bled it to its limit. The sub-credit for guitarist Kenny Burrell and drummer Grady Tate is also well deserved. This is the ultimate groovy, smokey jazz trio record that Smith made. The title track has been used for countless radio trailers over the years, while the often covered Duke Ellington classic, 'Satin Doll', is given extra special effort. Burrell has worked with Smith more than any other musician. His mellow tone and Smith's treble notes blend like cucumber and salmon.

● TRACKS: *The Organ Grinder's Swing; Oh, No, Babe; Blues For J; Greensleeves; I'll Close My Eyes; Satin Doll.*

● FIRST RELEASED 1965
● UK PEAK CHART POSITION: did not chart
● USA PEAK CHART POSITION: 15

813 FOR THE ROSES (-) ▲
JONI MITCHELL

A gigantic leap from the frail folky to a major writer of breathtaking depth. Critics were unanimous in recognizing the first icon of 70s singer-songwriters. Combining folk roots with pop sensibility and delicately laced with jazz (just listen to the soprano saxophone at the end of 'Cold Blue Steel And Sweet Fire' by Tom Scott), this marked the first in a series of classic albums from Mitchell. The outstanding use of metaphors in 'Electricity' comparing love to electricity has rarely been bettered. Using lines such as 'the masking tape tangles, it's sticky and black' and 'but the lines overloaded and the sparks started flying', Mitchell was on a roll. Similarly stunning was 'You Turn Me On I'm A Radio'.

● TRACKS: Banquet; Cold Blue Steel And Sweet Fire; Barangrill; Lesson In Survival; Let The Wind Carry Me; For The Roses; See You Sometime; Electricity; You Turn Me On I'm A Radio; Blonde In The Bleachers; Woman Of Heart And Mind; Judgement Of The Moon And Stars (Ludwig's Tune).

● FIRST RELEASED 1972
● UK PEAK CHART POSITION: did not chart
● USA PEAK CHART POSITION: 11

814 COOKIN' (-) ▲
MILES DAVIS

O ne of a series of important albums recorded for Prestige during the 50s that also included the excellent *Workin'* and *Steamin'*. Davis's dream quintet also included John Coltrane and Red Garland (piano), Paul Chambers (bass) and the breathing brushwork of Philly Joe Jones. Of the dozens of line-ups over many years, this unit is still spoken of with sparkling eyes by those who saw them play during their two years together. One of his best recordings of 'My Funny Valentine' is on this disc, as well as a definitive 'Blues By Five'. The title was Davis's: 'after all, that's what we did, came in and cooked'.

● TRACKS: My Funny Valentine; Blues By Five; Airegin; Tune Up.

● FIRST RELEASED 1957
● UK PEAK CHART POSITION: did not chart
● USA PEAK CHART POSITION: did not chart

815 THE MARBLE INDEX (-) ▲
NICO

A t the time that Nico released her first album, *Chelsea Girl*, in 1968, she was the toast of the Warhol crowd, a familiar face in the society pages, featuring in fashion magazines throughout the Western world. By the time *The Marble Index* appeared the following year, her record label advances went largely towards medical bills, as her beauty and talent diminished in the face of something very familiar to the Warhol crowd: a heroin habit. Produced by former Velvet Underground bandmate John Cale, *The Marble Index* established Nico as a songwriter. Her gothic compositions, intoned in her unearthly voice, captured all too well the angst of one whose much-heralded looks hid a soul that was unable to allow itself to feel or express love.

● TRACKS: Prelude; Lawns Of Dawns; No One Is There; Air's Song; Facing The Wind; Julius Caesar; Frozen Warnings; Evening Of Light.

● FIRST RELEASED 1969
● UK PEAK CHART POSITION: did not chart
● USA PEAK CHART POSITION: did not chart

816 LIFE AFTER DEATH (-) ▲
THE NOTORIOUS B.I.G.

F abulous arrangements, thoughtful samples and production by Sean 'Puffy' Combs make this ambitious double CD easy on the ear. B.I.G. had a hip-hop voice that never grated; in fact, he had the ability to lapse into smooth soul so easily, he could have been Luther Vandross. Rap has come a long way since the angry shouters, and this takes the genre to a peak of perfection; listeners who feel that rap is not for them should start with this as a sampler. The sermonizing is there, and much of it is relevant, but there is so much cool soul that the record is easy on the ear. Tragically, B.I.G. posed for the album cover standing beside a hearse.

● TRACKS: Life After Death Intro; Somebody's Gotta Die; Hypnotize; Kick In The Door; !@ You Tonight; Last Day; I Love The Dough; What's Beef; B.I.G. Interlude; Mo Money Mo Problems; Niggas Bleed; I Got A Story To Tell; Notorious Thugs; Miss U; Another; Going.Back To Cali; Ten Crack Commandments; Playa Hater; Nasty Boy; Sky's The Limit; The World Is Filled; My Downfall; Long Kiss Goodnight; You're Nobody (Til Somebody Kills You).

● FIRST RELEASED 1997
● UK PEAK CHART POSITION: 23
● USA PEAK CHART POSITION: 1

817 THE SOUND OF MUSIC (313) ▼
ORIGINAL BROADWAY CAST

Multi-million sales, a spell of 16 weeks at the top of the US chart, and winning Gold Disc and Grammy Awards were fitting rewards for this memorable recording of Richard Rodgers and Oscar Hammerstein II's much-loved musical which opened on Broadway in November 1959. The show's stars, Mary Martin and Theodore Bikel, were in fine vocal form, and led the excellent cast through the score's highlights, which included 'My Favourite Things', 'Do-Re-Mi', and 'Edelweiss' - the last song that Rodgers and Hammerstein wrote together before the latter's death in 1960.

● TRACKS: Preludium; The Sound Of Music; Maria; A Bell Is No Bell; I Have Confidence In Me; Do-Re-Mi; Sixteen Going On Seventeen; My Favourite Things; The Lonely Goatherd; How Can Love Survive; So Long, Farewell; Climb Every Mountain; Something Good; Wedding Sequence; Maria (Reprise); Concert Do-Re-Mi (Reprise); Edelweiss; So Long, Farewell (Reprise); Climb Every Mountain (Reprise).

● FIRST RELEASED 1960
● UK PEAK CHART POSITION: 4
● USA PEAK CHART POSITION: 1

818 THE SOUL ALBUM (656) ▼
OTIS REDDING

The Soul Album is often overlooked when examining Redding's output. No singles were culled from its content, but this does not diminish the quality of the excellent songs it contains. The original material reveals the strength of the singer's partnership with guitarist Steve Cropper, and the cover versions show Redding's gift for reinterpretation. Sam Cooke, the Temptations and Wilson Pickett are each acknowledged in turn, while Otis also takes shots at two contemporary hits, Roy Head's 'Treat Her Right' and Slim Harpo's 'Scratch My Back'. The Soul Album is as strong as any other records issued by the singer during his short lifetime.

● TRACKS: Just One More Day; It's Growing; Cigarettes And Coffee; Chain Gang; Nobody Knows You (When You're Down And Out); Good To Me; Scratch My Back; Treat Her Right; Everybody Makes A Mistake; Any Ole Way; 634-5789.

● FIRST RELEASED 1966
● UK PEAK CHART POSITION: 22
● USA PEAK CHART POSITION: 54

819 QUEEN 2 (321) ▼
QUEEN

The first of two Queen albums released in 1974 that elevated them high into the British consciousness. As mystically embracing as their self-titled debut, references to ogres and fairies and, unsurprisingly, queens, abounded. However, it was their sense of musical adventure, May's evocative guitar sound and daring arrangements, combined with Mercury's sense of the grandiose and unique vocal style that indicated early on that they were not a band who were afraid of innovation. 'Funny How Love Is' and the successful 'Seven Seas Of Rhye' hinted at an album and band quite capable of changing the face of musical history.

● TRACKS: Procession; Father To Son; White Queen (As It Began); Some Day One Day; The Loser In The End; Ogre Battle; The Fairy Feller's Master Stroke; Nevermore; The March Of The Black Queen; Funny How Love Is; Seven Seas Of Rhye.

● FIRST RELEASED 1974
● UK PEAK CHART POSITION: 5
● USA PEAK CHART POSITION: 49

820 BUENA VISTA SOCIAL CLUB (-) ▲
RY COODER & THE BUENA VISTA SOCIAL CLUB

Ry Cooder produced and played with a loose conglomeration of Cuban musicians, some of them elderly veterans, on this 1996 album, recorded in Havana. However, unlike other cultural tourists (Paul Simon on Graceland, David Byrne on Rei Momo) who appropriate foreign musical styles and fashion their own songs around them, Cooder wants the Cubans to play their own material. Is this, nevertheless, a Ry Cooder album? Debatable. Regardless, it is a lovely, often stirring collection, encompassing various styles. The musicologist in Cooder would be gratified to have made the point that Cuban music is far more than a single entity.

● TRACKS: Chan: De Camino A La Vereda; El Cuarto De Tula; Pueblo Nuevo; Dos Gardenias; Y Tu Que Has Hecho?; Veinte Anos; El Carretero; Candela; Amor De Loca Juventad; Orgullecida; Murmullo; Beuna Vista Social Club; La Batamesa.

● FIRST RELEASED 1997
● UK PEAK CHART POSITION: did not chart
● USA PEAK CHART POSITION: did not chart

821 **POCKET FULL OF KRYPTONITE** (312) ▼
SPIN DOCTORS

The Steve Miller Band of the 90s has made a small impression with this irresistible package. Crammed full of great riffs and licks, tight playing and singing with enthusiasm. The title track together with the wry 'Little Miss Can't Be Wrong' were both hit singles in the wake of the excellent 'Two Princes', one of the few occasions where the cliché of rhyming 'baby' with 'maybe' was completely acceptable. On the European edition the three extra tracks show off their ability as a live band. Unpretentious rock music for the 90s and a memorable debut that they could never come near again.

● TRACKS: *Jimmy Olsen's Blues; What Time Is It?; Little Miss Can't Be Wrong; Forty Or Fifty; Refrigerator Car; Two Princes; Off My Line; How Could You Want Him (When You Could Have Me?); Shinbone Alley; Yo Mamas A Pajama; Sweet Widow; Stepped On A Crock.*

● FIRST RELEASED 1992
● UK PEAK CHART POSITION: 2
● USA PEAK CHART POSITION: 3

 822 **IT'S MY LIFE** (–) ▲
TALK TALK

An early band of New Romantics, they spent some time trying to shake off the image. Vocalist Mark Hollis has a problem insofar that his voice is very much of the New Romantic era, the pristine, pitch-perfect singing style similar to Tony Hadley (Spandau Ballet) and Martin Fry (ABC). Hollis's distinctive voice made some good pop songs sound great. The title track, for example, has every synth gimmick under the sun but cannot fail in its infectious spirit. Some splendid old-timers are added to the proceedings; jazz trumpeter Henry Lowther wails beautifully and guitarist Robbie McIntosh excels. Splendid, unchallenging stuff.

● TRACKS: *Dum Dum Girl; Such A Shame; Renée; It's My Life; Tomorrow Started; The Last Time; Call In The Night Boy; Does Caroline Know?; It's You.*

● FIRST RELEASED 1984
● UK PEAK CHART POSITION: 35
● USA PEAK CHART POSITION: 42

 823 **STOP MAKING SENSE** (327) ▼
TALKING HEADS

A live album made for the film of the same name, and one that deserves to survive, as it is one of the finest 'rock' concert recordings ever made. The quality is such that the listener can be lulled into forgetting it is live; only the up-front and raw drums give the game away. Elsewhere, Byrne performs majestically, giving new life to old masters. Both 'Psycho Killer' and' Once In A Lifetime' benefit from fresher versions, and the hypnotic, lengthy finale, 'Take Me To The River', is guaranteed to stay in your head for days. Talking Heads sound better on this than they do on record, if you get my drift.

● TRACKS: *Psycho Killer; Swamp; Slippery People; Burning Down The House; Girlfriend Is Better; Once In A Lifetime; What A Day That Was; Life During Wartime; Take Me To The River.*

● FIRST RELEASED 1984
● UK PEAK CHART POSITION: 37
● USA PEAK CHART POSITION: 41

824 **TIM HARDIN 1** (780) ▼
TIM HARDIN

Normally classed as a folk-singer, Tim Hardin brought a jazz/blues perspective to the genre. His relaxed, languid voice mirrored the ease of his stylish compositions, the strongest of which show-cased a highly original talent. Fragile lyrics, romanticism, tender melodies and haunting instrumentation combine to perfection on a collection of enchanting songs, several of which have become pop standards, notably 'Reason To Believe'. Although known for wistful ballads, Hardin was equally adept with up-tempo material, a combination fully exploited herein. His highly personal reflections left their mark on a generation of singer-songwriters.

● TRACKS: *Don't Make Promises; Green Rocky Road; Smugglin' Man; How Long; While You're On Your Way; It'll Never Happen Again; Reason To Believe; Never Too Far; Part Of The Wind; Ain't Gonna Do Without; Misty Roses; How Can We Hang On To A Dream.*

● FIRST RELEASED 1966
● UK PEAK CHART POSITION: did not chart
● USA PEAK CHART POSITION: did not chart

825 INTO THE GREAT WIDE OPEN (–) ▲
TOM PETTY AND THE HEARTBREAKERS

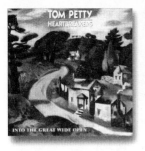

Petty once represented the new wave of pop in the late 70s. There was an edge of punkiness to his music and that has served him well throughout his career. Very few stars as unassuming as Petty have courted all audiences and succeeded. This is a Jeff Lynne production, which would usually have had pundits making a heretic cross with their fingers. Fortunately, it was listened to for what it was: an excellent album of Petty songs played by the best support band in the world. 'Learning To Fly', for example, has a simple repeated four-chord pattern, F C Am G, and out of this Petty has woven the perfect pop song. One of many.

● TRACKS: *Learning To Fly; Kings Highway; Into The Great Wide Open; Two Gunslingers; The Dark Of The Sun; All Or Nothing; All The Wrong Reasons; Too Good To Be True; Out In The Cold; You And I Will Meet Again; Makin' Some Noise; Built To Last.*

● FIRST RELEASED 1991
● UK PEAK CHART POSITION: 3
● USA PEAK CHART POSITION: 13

---

 826 LABOUR OF LOVE (–) ▲
UB40

Playing reggae and supporting the UK Labour Party during a decade of Thatcherism and racism demonstrated that these chaps had morals and guts. They eventually prospered (good ultimately conquers bad) and they can now look back and taste their achievement. In the UK, UB40 have done as much to popularize reggae as Bob Marley did for the rest of the world. This is their most refined album and contains some of their major hits. They make a point in the sleeve-notes of informing the listener that all these songs had been recorded by Jamaican artists. No apology is needed - their 'Cherry Oh Baby' and 'Red Red Wine' have become classics for this band. Much respect, irie.

● TRACKS: *Cherry Oh Baby; Keep On Moving; Please Don't Make Me Cry; Sweet Sensation; Johnny Too Bad; Red Red Wine; Guilty; She Caught The Train; Version Girl; Many Rivers To Cross.*

● FIRST RELEASED 1983
● UK PEAK CHART POSITION: 1
● USA PEAK CHART POSITION: 14

---

827 IN STEP (–) ▲
STEVIE RAY VAUGHAN

The album opens with an unashamedly simple rock 'n' roll track, 'The House Is Rockin', well chosen, because it sets the tone for an album that you feel Mr Vaughan dusted off before breakfast, such is his fluidity. Most of the tracks maintain a lively R&B feel, although Buddy Guy's 'Leave My Girl Alone' is a slow blues that Vaughan relishes and plays with sparing care. The final track is another of his brilliant solo instrumentals (as was his previous version of 'Little Wing'); this time 'Riviera Paradise' gets the nine-minute treatment. His guitar shimmers through a glorious, moody, romantic piece.

● TRACKS: *The House Is Rockin'; Crossfire; Tightrope; Let Me Love You Baby; Leave My Girl Alone; Travis Walk; Wall Of Denial; Scratch-N-Sniff; Love Me Darlin'; Riviera Paradise.*

● FIRST RELEASED 1989
● UK PEAK CHART POSITION: 63
● USA PEAK CHART POSITION: 33

---

828 ARETHA NOW (374) ▼
ARETHA FRANKLIN

Aretha Now opens with the explosive 'Think', an ecstatic performance propelled by the singer's gospel-like fervour and punchy piano playing. It set the tone for yet another self-assured selection, in which Franklin brought her expressive voice to bear on a series of excellent songs. She brings new authority to material first recorded by Sam Cooke ('You Send Me'), Don Covay ('See-Saw') and Dionne Warwick ('I Say A Little Prayer'), investing each with a ferocious pride and zeal. The original songs are equally strong, resulting in one of the most accomplished soul albums of the 60s. She is the Queen of soul.

● TRACKS: *Think; I Say A Little Prayer; See-Saw; Night Time Is The Right Time; You Send Me; You're A Sweet Sweet Man; I Take What I Want; Hello Sunshine; A Change; I Can't See Myself Leaving You.*

● FIRST RELEASED 1968
● UK PEAK CHART POSITION: 6
● USA PEAK CHART POSITION: 3

829 JACK ORION (329) ▼
BERT JANSCH

Where Jansch's previous albums were largely comprised of self-penned material, this third set was drawn from traditional songs, bar an instrumental reading of Ewan MacColl's 'First Time Ever I Saw Your Face'. The artist's highly original guitar style underpins the lengthy title track and the enthralling 'Black Water Side'. Jimmy Page is only one of many musicians expressing a debt to Jansch and the latter track provided the template for 'Black Mountain Side' on *Led Zeppelin I*. Bert's languid interpretation of 'Nottamun Town' inspired a later version by Fairport Convention, but they struggled to match the enthralling atmosphere created here. *Jack Orion* is a mesmerizing selection from a hugely influential performer.

● TRACKS: *The Waggoner's Lad; The First Time I Ever Saw Your Face; Jack Orion; The Gardener; Nottamun Town; Henry Martin; Blackwaterside; Pretty Polly.*

● FIRST RELEASED 1966
● UK PEAK CHART POSITION: did not chart
● USA PEAK CHART POSITION: did not chart

830 CHEAP THRILLS (355) ▼
BIG BROTHER AND THE HOLDING COMPANY

This ramshackle, sparkling and ear-shattering album from the band 'featuring' lead vocalist Janis Joplin came out of the San Francisco rock scene in 1968. The full-blown vocals from Janis sparred with the loose electric guitar of Sam Andrew and the finger-picking style of James Gurley, and kept them apart from other bands in the area who courted folk and psychedelia. Both 'Piece Of My Heart' and 'Ball And Chain' are classics of their time and place and although the recording is flawed the atmosphere Joplin creates is riveting and has never been bettered by any of the Janisalike rock chicks of the past three decades.

● TRACKS: *Combination Of The Two; I Need A Man To Love; Summertime; Piece Of My Heart; Turtle Blues; Oh Sweet Mary; Ball And Chain.*

● FIRST RELEASED 1968
● UK PEAK CHART POSITION: did not chart
● USA PEAK CHART POSITION: 1

831 DON'T TRY THIS AT HOME (–) ▲
BILLY BRAGG

Perhaps more aptly titled, 'Don't Try Humming These Alone', on this set the prolific Bragg squeezed his impressive and thoughtful lyrics into 16 extraordinarily tight and melodic songs. It briefly made him a chart star, largely helped by the lush arrangements (Cara Tivey's keyboards and Mary Ramsey's violas, in particular), catchy choruses and Bragg's own street-cred humour. Who else could sing about 'drinking with Thomas Paine', who said that 'revolutions ... are as different as the cultures/That give them birth', and still produce three hits ('Sexuality', 'Accident Waiting To Happen', 'You Woke Up My Neighbourhood') from the same album?

● TRACKS: *Accident Waiting To Happen; Moving The Goalposts; Everywhere; Cindy Of A Thousand Lives; You Woke Up My Neighbourhood; Trust; God's Footballer; The Few; Sexuality; Mother Of The Bride; Tank Park Salute; Dolphins; North Sea Bubble; Rumours Of War; Wish You Were Her; Body Of Water.*

● FIRST RELEASED 1991
● UK PEAK CHART POSITION: 8
● USA PEAK CHART POSITION: did not chart

832 THE SERPENT'S EGG (–) ▲
DEAD CAN DANCE

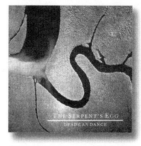

By the time this album was released in 1988, the group had moved steadily away from conventional modern rock (in so far as they were ever a part of that movement), exploring Celtic, Middle Eastern and medieval traditions in the process. It is the latter which dominates this album which begins with the beatific 'The Host Of Seraphim', arguably Lisa Gerrard's finest recorded moment. Accusations of new-agey hokum bedevilled the project's critical reception, but the artistry and songwriting sleight of hand distinguishes them from the run-of-the-mill Gregorian chant. 'Severance' sounds like Ian McCulloch at confession, and album-closer 'Ullyses' is furnished not only with an aromatic medieval cadenza, but another of the alluringly wistful vocals to be found throughout the album.

● TRACKS: *The Host Of Seraphim; Orbis De Ignis; Severance; The Writing On My Father's Hand; In The Kingdom Of The Blind The One-Eyed Are Kings; Chant Of The Paladin; Song Of Sophia; Echolalia; Mother Tongue; Ullyses.*

● FIRST RELEASED 1988
● UK PEAK CHART POSITION: did not chart
● USA PEAK CHART POSITION: did not chart

833 FROM ELVIS IN MEMPHIS (556) ▼
ELVIS PRESLEY

Years trapped making facile films and equally poor soundtrack albums dented Presley's popularity without tarnishing the myth. Convincing material would rekindle his reputation. *From Elvis In Memphis* was issued in the wake of the spellbinding *Elvis' TV Special* and it offered a similar sense of musical adventure. Recorded at Chips Moman's American Recording Studio, it featured the crack house band behind hits for the Box Tops, Aretha Franklin and Sandy Posey. Presley's first sessions in Memphis for 14 years result in a thrilling set that captures the singer at his finest. Like *Elvis Is Back*, his immediate post-army release, this spirited album proves that Presley could turn on his talent when the mood or opportunity took him.

● TRACKS: *Wearin' That Loved On Look; Only The Strong Survive; I'll Hold You In My Heart; Long Black Limousine; It Keeps Right On A-Hurtin'; I'm Moving On; Power Of My Love; Gentle On My Mind; After Loving You; True Love Travels On A Gravel Road; Any Day Now; In The Ghetto.*

● FIRST RELEASED 1969
● UK PEAK CHART POSITION: 1
● USA PEAK CHART POSITION: 13

834 UNPLUGGED (336) ▼
ERIC CLAPTON

The clear leader of the unplugged fashion and one of Clapton's finest efforts. A wonderful relaxed atmosphere oozes through the record as the listener can read his mind: 'I don't have to do this'. A set of beautifully played acoustic blues, strongly sung and well supported by his regulars, including second guitarist Andy Fairweather Low and acrobatic percussionist Ray Cooper, MTV probably did not know what they were starting with this. When the 'sitting down' fashion fades, as it certainly will, this album will always be regarded as its vanguard. This put Clapton back on track to his blues roots.

● TRACKS: *Signe; Before You Accuse Me; Hey Hey; Tears In Heaven; Lonely Stranger; Nobody Knows You When You're Down And Out; Layla; Running On Faith; Walkin' Blues; Alberta; San Francisco Bay Blues; Malted Milk; Old Love; Rollin' And Tumblin'.*

● FIRST RELEASED 1992
● UK PEAK CHART POSITION: 2
● USA PEAK CHART POSITION: 2

835 BADUIZM (–) ▲
ERYKAH BADU

In describing Badu's voice as sensational, there is no exaggeration. It is effortless, smooth and expressive, and she is stunning live. This album was one of the 1997's surprises and nearly topped the US album chart. Described as African R&B, she veers from light hip-hop ('On & On') to sweet soul ('Otherside Of The Game'). She has such an expressive style that she could attempt blues, jazz, soul, rap, even pop and still wipe the floor. The only negative side is the corny spoken dialogue, which just sticks in the back of the throat. That aside, a sensational debut.

● TRACKS: *Rimshot (Intro); On & On; Appletree; Otherside Of The Game; Sometimes (Mix #9); Next Lifetime; Afro (Freestyle Skit); Certainly; 4 Leaf Clover; No Love; Drama; Sometimes; Certainly (Flipped It); Rimshot (Outro).*

● FIRST RELEASED 1997
● UK PEAK CHART POSITION: 18
● USA PEAK CHART POSITION: 2

836 THE WONDERFUL AND FRIGHTENING WORLD OF (397) ▼ THE FALL

The eighth Fall album consolidated the abrasive sextet's relationship with producer John Leckie, who helped expand their musical palate without sacrificing individuality. The presence of guitarist Laura Elise, better known as Brix Smith, expanded the unit's tonal capabilities, but they remain firmly a vehicle in which singer Mark E. Smith vented his spleen. His vitriolic lyrics were as uncompromising as ever, even if now-accustomed dissonance is occasionally paired with neo-psychedelic nuances. *The Frightening World* captures the Fall as they expanded their frame of reference, and in the process, gained recognition for their highly original music.

● TRACKS: *Lay Of The Land; 2 x 4; Copped It; Elves; Oh! Brother; Draygo's Guilt; God-box; Clear Off; C.R.E.E.P.; Pat-Trip Dispenser; Slang King; Bug Day; Stephen Song; Craigness; Disney's Dream Debased; No Bulbs.*

● FIRST RELEASED 1984
● UK PEAK CHART POSITION: 62
● USA PEAK CHART POSITION: did not chart

837 FOO FIGHTERS (–) ▲
FOO FIGHTERS

Formed by ex-Nirvana drummer Dave Grohl, this was a much better album than anybody expected outside of the band circle. Much lighter than the oppressive direction grunge was taking, it contained some fabulous moments. Sounding like a cross between Sugar and the Pixies, Grohl moved to guitar and blossomed as a songwriter, mixing heavy riffs over classic 60s pop chord changes, such as the stunning 'I'll Stick Around'. The legacy of his former famous past has already been eclipsed by the success of this band and, in particular, in the way he acted fast and redirected the media's attention. A remarkable debut.

● TRACKS: *This Is A Call; I'll Stick Around; Big Me; Alone + Easy Target; Good Grief; Floaty; Weenie Beenie; Oh, George; For All The Cows; X-Static; Watershed; Exhausted.*

● FIRST RELEASED 1995
● UK PEAK CHART POSITION: 3
● USA PEAK CHART POSITION: 23

838 UNCLE MEAT (–) ▲
FRANK ZAPPA / MOTHERS OF INVENTION

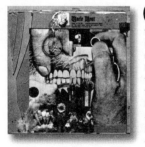

Over the two-record set, Zappa manages to cover the entire spread of his interests. Masquerading as a movie in progress, it is a way of highlighting the struggle of trying to keep the band together against a pretty hostile, or worse, apathetic audience. The frustration of putting something out that is artistically brilliant has a particular significance, as music and film go hand in hand. The film dialogue is either hilarious or it will leave you cold. The former is the general consensus. Zappa was so far ahead that his earth life ended before we caught up with him. Weird but highly recommended.

● TRACKS: *Uncle Meat; The Voice Of Cheese; Nine Types Of Industrial Pollution; Zolar Czakl; Dog Breath In The Year Of The Plague; The Legend Of The Golden Arches; Louie Louie; The Dog Breath Variations; Sleeping In A Jar; Our Bizarre Relationship; The Uncle Meat Variations; Electric Aunt Jemima; Prelude To King Kong; God Bless America; A Pound For A Brown On The Bus; Ian Underwood Whips It Out; Mr Green Genes; We Can Shoot You; If We'd All Been Living In California; The Air; Project X; Cruising For Burgers; Uncle Meat Film Excerpt Part 1; Tengo Na Minchia Tanta; Uncle Meat Film Excerpt Part 2; King Kong Itself; King Kong; 1-5.*

● FIRST RELEASED 1969
● UK PEAK CHART POSITION: did not chart
● USA PEAK CHART POSITION: 43

839 CITY TO CITY (–) ▲
GERRY RAFFERTY

Often mistaken with *Night Owl*, as they both had similar subject matter and beautiful Patrick Byrne covers, the main difference is that this is the one with 'Baker Street', probably the most flogged song of the past two decades, and one that now does his credibility no good. Missing out in the memory bank is the powerful 'The Ark', and the often ignored, radio-friendly title track. It also includes two of his finest open love songs - 'Right Down The Line' and the innocently profound 'Whatever's Written In Your Heart' (is all that matters), with the line 'so we agree to disagree, at least we got our memories'.

● TRACKS: *The Ark; Baker Street; Right Down The Line; City To City; Stealin' Time; Mattie's Rag; Whatever's Written In Your Heart; Home And Dry; Island; Waiting For The Day.*

● FIRST RELEASED 1978
● UK PEAK CHART POSITION: 6
● USA PEAK CHART POSITION: 1

840 IN THE DARK (–) ▲
GRATEFUL DEAD

The great comeback album, or at least an album that no deadhead expected at this stage in their career. Garcia had been seriously ill for some time, and was not expected to recover. Suddenly, a new studio album was announced, as a seemingly fit Garcia started to tour and was reputedly appalled when they had a huge hit single with the autobiographical 'Touch Of Grey'. Other strong tracks are Weir's 'Hell In A Bucket' and the magnificent 'Black Muddy River' written by Garcia and Hunter. With such a strong bunch of songs it is amazing that the underwhelming 'Tons Of Steel', by the late Brent Mydland, was even considered.

● TRACKS: *Touch Of Grey; Hell In A Bucket; When Push Comes To Shove; West L.A. Fadeaway; Tons Of Steel; Throwing Stones; Black Muddy River.*

● FIRST RELEASED 1987
● UK PEAK CHART POSITION: 57
● USA PEAK CHART POSITION: 6

841 MY FAVORITE THINGS (333) ▼
JOHN COLTRANE

One of John Coltrane's (many) extraordinary talents was his ability to drastically transcend the material he chose to play, and often infuse the trivial or frivolous with something altogether very profound. Under the spell of the quartet (with pianist McCoy Tyner, temporary bassist Steve Davis and drummer Elvin Jones), 'My Favorite Things' becomes an almost religious celebration of life, brought to a series of ecstatic climaxes by Coltrane's nasal, Eastern-sounding soprano saxophone and Jones's propulsive, 6/8 clatter. This popular album also contains 'But Not For Me', a breakneck version of 'Summertime' and a beautiful 'Every Time We Say Goodbye'.

● TRACKS: *My Favorite Things; Every Time We Say Goodbye; Summertime; But Not For Me.*

● FIRST RELEASED 1960
● UK PEAK CHART POSITION: did not chart
● USA PEAK CHART POSITION: did not chart

842 SHADOWS AND LIGHT (680) ▼
JONI MITCHELL

Although this incredible live unit never recorded a proper studio album we do have this as a reminder of just what is possible. Joni the folkie briefly became Ms Mitchell the jazz singer, supported by the formidable talents of Pat Metheny, Lyle Mays, Jaco Pastorius, Michael Brecker and Don Alias. Many of Mitchell's jazz flirtations are given the full treatment with musicians who understood both her and the genre. It is a staggering marriage of talents and wholly successful. There are even obligatory bonus solos from Pat and Don. They should have stayed together for at least another album.

● TRACKS: *In France They Kiss On Main Street; Edith And The Kingpin; Coyote; Goodbye Pork Pie Hat; The Dry Cleaner From Des Moines; Amelia; Pat's Solo; Hejira; Black Crow; Don's Solo; Dreamland; Free Man In Paris; Band Intro; Furry Sings The Blues; Why Do Fools Fall In Love; Shadows And Light; God Must Be A Boogie Man; Woodstock.*

● FIRST RELEASED 1975
● UK PEAK CHART POSITION: 34
● USA PEAK CHART POSITION: 2

843 BIG SCIENCE (–) ▲
LAURIE ANDERSON

A brilliant narration of modern America with profound and biting wit that is so true it is just not funny. Modern technology has now made the subjects of this extraordinary album outdated - computers and answerphones are now old hat. At the time, 'O Superman', the main track, was weird and challenging, yet highly commercial, and it was a surprising hit single. The vocoder-repeated 'uh, uh, uh, uh, uh, uh, uh' is numbing. Less musical but more revealing is the description of a pilot informing his passengers that the plane is crash-landing; he asks them to follow all the safety rules. A deadly perceptive *avant garde* album.

● TRACKS: *From The Air; Big Science; Sweaters; Walking & Falling; Born, Never Asked; O Superman (For Massenet); Example #22; Let X=X; It Tango.*

● FIRST RELEASED 1982
● UK PEAK CHART POSITION: 29
● USA PEAK CHART POSITION: 124

844 DIXIE CHICKEN (–) ▲
LITTLE FEAT

The great Neon Parks album paintings were anticipated almost as much as the next collection from Little Feat, the band with which his work became inextricably linked. This album found them at a musical peak as a stellar 70s rock band who had oodles of swamp blues and funk, with a loose shambling style that came with confidence not sloppiness. Lowell George was singing better than ever on this collection, notably with the sublime 'Roll Um Easy' where his voice was chillingly expressive. Bill Payne and Richie Haywood play their respective keyboard and drums with calm and precision. There are no weak tracks here, and this is another vital album, in keeping with all recordings with which George was involved.

● TRACKS: *Dixie Chicken; Two Trains; Roll Um Easy; On Your Way Down; Kiss It Off; Fool Yourself; Walkin All Night; Fat Man In The Bathtub; Juliette; Lafayette Railroad.*

● FIRST RELEASED 1973
● UK PEAK CHART POSITION: did not chart
● USA PEAK CHART POSITION: did not chart

845 **MISS AMERICA** (–) ▲
MARY MARGARET O'HARA

S ounding like a cross between Laurie Anderson (on the low notes) and Dolores from the Cranberries (on the high notes), Mary Margaret is yet another troubadour with something to say. It was recorded in 1988 and is now something of a cult item. Canadian singer O'Hara exhorts her romantic frustrations· through some pretty powerful lyrics. 'There is but one love, but one love won't do' (on 'When You Know Why You're Happy') and 'I miss you and you give me something to cry about' ('To Cry About') should keep the tears flowing in bedsits across the land. A translucent album.

● TRACKS: *To Cry About; Year In Song; Body's In Trouble; Dear Darling; A New Day; When You Know Why You're Happy; My Friends Have; Help Me Lift You Up; Keeping You In Mind; Not Be Alright; You Will Be Loved Again.*

● FIRST RELEASED 1988
● UK PEAK CHART POSITION: did not chart
● USA PEAK CHART POSITION: did not chart

 **847** **OLIVER!** (390) ▼
ORIGINAL LONDON CAST

A perfect souvenir of Lionel Bart's celebrated stage musical which was a smash hit in London and on Broadway in the early 60s. All the drama and exuberance of Peter Coe's breathtaking original production is captured perfectly on this album, with stand-out performances from Ron Moody (Fagin), Georgia Brown (Nancy) and Keith Hamshere (Oliver Twist). The 1989 reissue on CD is a timely reminder that, although there have been many stage revivals over the past 30 years - and an excellent film version in 1968 - this cast laid down the definitive version of Bart's masterpiece (although Robert Lindsay came close). Once again, it is all about great, great songs.

● TRACKS: *Food Glorious Food; Oliver; I Shall Scream; Boy For Sale; That's Your Funeral; Where Is Love?; Consider Yourself; You've Got To Pick A Pocket Or Two; It's A Fine Life; Be Back Soon; Oom Pah Pah; My Name; As Long As He Needs Me; I'd Do Anything; Who Will Buy?; Reviewing The Situation; Finale.*

● FIRST RELEASED 1960
● UK PEAK CHART POSITION: 4
● USA PEAK CHART POSITION: did not chart

 846 **ROUND ABOUT MIDNIGHT** (–) ▲
MILES DAVIS

A n important album that saw Miles and the his best ever quintet (Coltrane, Garland, Jones and Chambers) move to the mighty Columbia. It was while at Columbia that he grew to be the biggest name in jazz, and with their marketing, even made the pop chart. This debut is also musically very fine; with production by George Avakian, the quintet breeze through six tracks that include excellent readings of 'Tadd's Delight' and, from his Charlie Parker apprenticeship, the familiar 'Ah-Leu-Cha'. The title track is just a shade too dry, but nevertheless credible. This album started a 30-year relationship with Columbia Records.

● TRACKS: *Round Midnight; Ah-Leu-Cha; All Of You; Bye Bye Blackbird; Tadd's Delight; Dear Old Stockholm.*

● FIRST RELEASED 1957
● UK PEAK CHART POSITION: did not chart
● USA PEAK CHART POSITION: did not chart

 **848** **TRAVELS** (328) ▼
PAT METHENY

A double album that flirts with rock, folk, country and Latin - but is emphatically a jazz album. Metheny is equipped with probably his best ever live group; Steve Rodby, Dan Gottlieb, Nana Vasconcelos, and his right arm, keyboard virtuoso Lyle Mays. The recording exudes warmth, and often improves on tracks already issued on studio albums; for example, 'Phase Dance' is played with more verve and 'Song For Bilbao' sounds more passionate in a live context. The diamond in the mine, however, is the shortest piece - the glorious and delicate title track - worth the price of the album alone.

● TRACKS: *Are You Going With Me?; The Fields, The Sky; Goodbye; Phase Dance; Straight On Red; Farmer's Trust; Extradition; Goin' Ahead; As Falls Wichita, So Falls Wichita Falls; Travels; Song For Bilbao; San Lorenzo.*

● FIRST RELEASED 1983
● UK PEAK CHART POSITION: did not chart
● USA PEAK CHART POSITION: 62

849 **THE FINAL CUT** (–) ▲
PINK FLOYD

This is not a pretty album. Described as 'a requiem for the post war drama' it is Pink Floyd at their most miserable. In addition to the sombre lyrics and themes explored by Roger Waters, it was recorded while the band were so fragmented, they had effectively broken up. Gilmour and Waters' feud has been well documented and this could well have been titled *The Final Straw*. The only hint of lightness and humour throughout is in 'Not Now John', but only in the shape of irony ('Can't stop lose job mind gone silicon'). Not an album to be played at parties or anniversaries.

● TRACKS: *The Post War Dream; Your Possible Pasts; One Of The Few; The Heroes' Return; The Gunner's Dream; Paranoid Eyes; Get Your Filthy Hands Off My Desert; The Fletcher Memorial Home; Southampton Dock; The Final Cut; Not Now John; Two Suns In The Sunset.*

● FIRST RELEASED 1983
● UK PEAK CHART POSITION: 1
● USA PEAK CHART POSITION: 6

 851 **STEEL WHEELS** (–) ▲
ROLLING STONES

The *Steel Wheels* tour of 1989 was the biggest-grossing in the USA, and was noteworthy for this fact rather than for the quality of the material on offer. *Steel Wheels* represented the Stones' response to persistent rumours of their demise. After a well-publicized spat, both Jagger and Richards had released solo albums, and some reassurance was clearly needed. The opening riff of 'Sad Sad Sad' provided it; unmistakable Stones stuff, as is the rest of the album. A critical and radio success, *Steel Wheels* yielded a few minor hits in 'Mixed Emotions', 'Rock And A Hard Place' and 'Almost Hear You Sigh'.

● TRACKS: *Sad Sad Sad; Mixed Emotions; Terrifying; Hold On To Your Hat; Hearst For Sale; Blinded By Love; Rock And A Hard Place; Can't Be Seen; Almost Hear You Sigh; Continental Drift; Break The Spell; Slipping Away.*

● FIRST RELEASED 1989
● UK PEAK CHART POSITION: 2
● USA PEAK CHART POSITION: 3

 850 **HOKEY POKEY** (–) ▲
RICHARD AND LINDA THOMPSON

A brave follow-up to their masterful *I Want To See The Bright Lights Tonight*, this attempts to encapsulate various British working-class musical styles - folk, brass band, playground songs and pub singalongs - much as the Band did for indigenous American genres. The Thompsons do not always succeed; *Hokey Pokey* sometimes feels like a theoretical exercise. Nevertheless, the tension between the songs' jaunty surfaces and the neurotic undercurrent of Richard's blistering guitar is beguiling. The one undeniably great track (other than the jaunty title track) is 'A Heart Needs A Home', sung by Linda with grave beauty and authority. It is inexplicably buried deep towards the end as if an afterthought.

● TRACKS: *Hokey Pokey; I'll Regret It In The Morning; Smiffy's Glass Eye; The Egypt·Room; Never Again; Georgie On A Spree; Old Man Inside A Young Man; The Sun Never Shines On The Poor; A Heart Needs A Home; Mole In A Hole.*

● FIRST RELEASED 1975
● UK PEAK CHART POSITION: did not chart
● USA PEAK CHART POSITION: did not chart

 852 **BORN UNDER A BAD SIGN** (–) ▲
ALBERT KING

The giant left-handed guitarist was no stranger to the recording studio by 1966, but Albert King had still to make his mark with the record-buying public. When he linked up with the cream of Stax's Memphis musicians, including Booker T. And The MGs and the Memphis Horns, that connection was made. 'Laundromat Blues', 'Oh, Pretty Woman' and 'Crosscut Saw' set the scene for 'Born Under A Bad Sign' and 'The Hunter', which quickly found their way into the repertoires of Cream and Free. The convolutions of his guitar style were perfectly complemented by the trademark Stax funk rhythms. The team went on to make many more singles and albums, none of which could surpass the achievements of their first meeting.

● TRACKS: *Laundromat Blues; Oh, Pretty Woman; Crosscut Saw; Down Don't Bother Me; Born Under A Bad Sign; Personal Manager; Kansas City; The Very Thought Of You; The Hunter; Almost Lost My Mind; As The Years Go Passing By.*

● FIRST RELEASED 1967
● UK PEAK CHART POSITION: did not chart
● USA PEAK CHART POSITION: did not chart

853 A DUB EXPERIENCE: REGGAE GREATS

(–) ▲ SLY & ROBBIE

The influence that these two session men have had on reggae is unmatched in the history of popular music. They have been the backbone rhythm section for countless records that have come out of Kingston. This is a graceful dub record full of surprises and crying out to be played on a good sound system. Dennis Brown's 'Assault On Station' is dreamy and moody while 'Demolition City' has some wonderful spacy phasing and torn-apart brass sections. It is no surprise that outside Jamaica they are in constant demand from the likes of Bob Dylan and Lester Bowie. They are unique.

● TRACKS: *Destination Unknown; Assault On Station; Joy Ride; Demolition City; Computer Malfunction; Jailbreak; Skull And Crossbones; Back To Base.*

● FIRST RELEASED 1985
● UK PEAK CHART POSITION: did not chart
● USA PEAK CHART POSITION: did not chart

854 SONNY ROLLINS VOL. 2 (354) ▼

SONNY ROLLINS

The famous Harold Feinstein cover borrowed by Joe Jackson ('how dare he', said the purists) for *Body And Soul* also announces 'Monaural' Sonny Rollins. Did we ever have a 'Stereophonic' Charlie Parker; do we care? This is a blisteringly good album that never once loses pace. The formidable line-up is Jay Jay Johnson (trombone), Horace Silver and Thelonious Monk (piano), Art Blakey (drums) and Paul Chambers (bass). Wonderful versions of Monk's 'Misterioso' and 'Reflections' are included, plus Rollins' own 'Why Don't I' and 'Wail March'. The finest 'monaural' record Rollins ever made.

● TRACKS: *Why Don't I; Wail March; Misterioso; Reflections; You Stepped Out Of A Dream; Poor Butterfly.*

● FIRST RELEASED 1957
● UK PEAK CHART POSITION: did not chart
● USA PEAK CHART POSITION: did not chart

855 EAST SIDE STORY (363) ▼

SQUEEZE

In one of the smartest free transfer deals ever, Squeeze were able to plug the massive midfield gap left by the departing Jools Holland with the nimble-fingered Paul Carrack. They gained an extra vocalist in the process, but there seems to have been little room for Carrack's underrated and expressive voice. For many, the album's best track was 'Tempted', with Carrack taking lead vocal (with help from producer Elvis Costello). Close behind in the queue is 'Someone Else's Bell', 'Is That Love', 'In Quintessence' - in fact the whole set, except possibly the uncomfortable chord/key change of 'F-Hole', which leads back to the hypnotically great 'Tempted'.

● TRACKS: *In Quintessence; Someone Else's Heart; Tempted; Piccadilly; There's No Tomorrow; A Woman's World; Is That Love; F-hole; Labelled With Love; Someone Else's Bell; Mumbo Jumbo; Vanity Fair; Messed Around.*

● FIRST RELEASED 1981
● UK PEAK CHART POSITION: 19
● USA PEAK CHART POSITION: 44

856 THE SLIDER (–) ▲

T.REX

Bolan could string together the most ridiculous words and make them sound a) like poetry, and b) like they always belonged together. This precociously talented Elf left a huge mark on 70s pop so that 'Metal guru, is it you' sounded as normal as 'tea for two' did forty years earlier. Other lyrical pairings are the rocking 'Chariot Choogle' and the acoustic 'Spaceball Ricochet', two totally different styles that Bolan could have swapped and they would still have worked. He sang 'my little baby she's a tip-a-toed vamp rider', and even he didn't know what it meant. Surely that is genius?

● TRACKS: *Metal Guru; Mystic Lady; Rock On; The Slider; Baby Boomerang; Spaceball Ricochet; Buick Mackane; Telegram Sam; Rabbit Fighter; Baby Strange; Ballrooms Of Mars; Chariot Choogle; Main Man; Cadillac; Thunderwing Lady.*

● FIRST RELEASED 1972
● UK PEAK CHART POSITION: 4
● USA PEAK CHART POSITION: 17

857 ## MORE SONGS ABOUT BUILDINGS AND FOOD (-) ▲ TALKING HEADS

Even though this was recorded at the beautiful Compass Point studio in the Caribbean, this album manages to retain the concrete urbanism of the American city, the subject of many of Byrne's songs. Again produced by the mercurial Brian Eno; he and David Byrne did work particularly well together. Eno's elaborate arrangements never once clouded the clarity of some of those simple pop riffs (especially some of those guitar trills on 'With Our Love'). Talking Heads seemed arty and complex at the time. More than twenty years later they seem less awesome but much more accessible and enjoyable. This album, in particular, holds up well.

 TRACKS: *Thank You For Sending Me An Angel; With Our Love; The Good Thing; Warning Sign; The Girls Want To Be With The Girls; Found A Job; Artists Only; I'm Not In Love; Stay Hungry; Take Me To The River; The Big Country.*

● FIRST RELEASED 1978
● UK PEAK CHART POSITION: 21
● USA PEAK CHART POSITION: 29

858 ## FULL MOON FEVER (338) ▼ TOM PETTY

This album is just damn good fun - a great collection of easy-going rock songs, crafted not to change the world, but certainly to make it just a little brighter. Petty's first solo project (without the Heartbreakers), *Full Moon Fever* shares the goodtime feel of the Traveling Wilburys' contemporary 'Handle With Care'. This is not altogether surprising; Jeff Lynne co-produced and George Harrison and Roy Orbison guest. The only non-Petty composition is a version of Gene Clark's 'Feel A Whole Lot Better', while 'Zombie Zoo', a bewildered parent's diatribe on the kids of today, comes perilously close to social commentary.

 TRACKS: *Free Fallin'; I Won't Back Down; Love Is A Long Road; A Face In The Crowd; Runnin' Down A Dream; Feel A Whole Lot Better; Yer So Bad; Depending On You; The Apartment Song; Alright For Now; A Mind With A Heart Of It's Own; Zombie Zoo.*

● FIRST RELEASED 1989
● UK PEAK CHART POSITION: 8
● USA PEAK CHART POSITION: 3

 **859** ## REGGAE GREATS (-) ▲ TOOTS AND THE MAYTALS

Second only to the Wailers, the Maytals were rumoured to have been the band that Chris Blackwell wanted to sign in preference to the Wailers. True or false, they are a magnificent band and this album confirms their standing as a pivotal influence on 'reggay', as they spelt it. '54-56 That's My Number' is still the best rocksteady track ever released and is a natural choice for any reggae compilation. Equally effective are the soulful 'Just Like that' and probably the best treatment of John Denver's 'Take Me Home, Country Roads'. Toots has one of the best voices to come out of Jamaica, bar none.

● TRACKS: *54-56 (That's My Number); Reggae Got Soul; Monkey Man; Just Like That; Kunky Kingston; Sweet & Dandy; Take Me Home Country Roads; Time Tough; Spiritual Healing; Pressure Drop; Peace Perfect Peace; Bam Bam.*

● FIRST RELEASED 1988
● UK PEAK CHART POSITION: did not chart
● USA PEAK CHART POSITION: did not chart

860 ## MR FANTASY (-) ▲ TRAFFIC

Released at the height of flower power, Traffic were originally the perfect 'tangerine candy coloured bicycle' group. Mason's hippie ditties blended with Winwood's more ambitious musical aspirations. Although they were given the same title, the US and UK albums had different track-listings. The US version has the edge because it includes the hit singles 'Hole In My Shoe' and 'Paper Sun' as well as 'Smiling Phases', which was covered by Blood Sweat And Tears. The UK version has 'Utterly Simple' and 'Hope I Never Find Me There' in their place. Mercifully, both versions include the magnificent title track with the definitive Winwood guitar solo (or was it Mason?).

● TRACKS: *Paper Sun; Dealer; Coloured Rain; Hole In My Shoe; No Face, No Name, No Number; Heaven Is In Your Mind; House For Everyone; Berkshire Poppies; Giving To You; Smiling Phases; Dear Mr Fantasy.*

● FIRST RELEASED 1967
● UK PEAK CHART POSITION: 8
● USA PEAK CHART POSITION: 88

861 VAN HALEN II (341) ▼
VAN HALEN

Dismissed as the poor relation to their thrilling debut on its release, it has only been with the passage of time that *Van Halen II* has been afforded any kind of classic stature. Roth's impertinent, sly humour is still in place, but it is Eddie Van Halen's easy experimentation that takes this record to another level. His daring and frantic switches in styles set him aside as the most versatile of players. He still worked the effusive pop for 'Dance The Night Away', but his brush strokes, particularly within 'DOA' and 'You're No Good', were now much more adventurous and wide.

● TRACKS: *You're No Good; Dance The Night Away; Somebody Get Me A Doctor; Bottoms Up; Outta Love Again; Light Up The Sky; DOA; Women In Love; Spanish Fly; Beautiful Girls.*

● FIRST RELEASED 1979
● UK PEAK CHART POSITION: 23
● USA PEAK CHART POSITION: 6

862 GREASE (465) ▼
VARIOUS

Three of the first four tracks on this double album, 'Summer Nights', 'Hopelessly Devoted To You' and 'You're The One That I Want', all went on to become big hits in the USA and UK for the new disco sensation John Travolta and his co-star Olivia Newton-John. Frank Valli also took the title song into the upper reaches of charts all over the world. As for this album, it lingered for 12 weeks at number 1 in America, and topped the British chart for a lucky 13. Even in the 90s several of these tracks are still guaranteed floor-fillers at many a party night, and once again it is showing at a cinema near you.

● TRACKS: *Grease; Summer Nights; Hopelessly Devoted To You; Sandy; Look At Me, I'm Sandra Dee; Greased Lightning; It's Raining On Prom Night; You're The One That I Want; Beauty School Dropout; Alone At The Drive In Movie; Blue Moon; Rock 'N' Roll Is Here To Stay; Those Magic Changes; Hound Dog; Born To Hand Jive; Tears On My Pillow; Mooning; Rock 'N' Roll Party Queen; Freddy My Love; There Are Worse Things I Could Do; Look At Me, I'm Sandra Dee (Reprise); We Go Together; Love Is A Many Spendoured Thing; Grease (Reprise).*

● FIRST RELEASED 1978
● UK PEAK CHART POSITION: 1   ● USA PEAK CHART POSITION: 1

863 WHITNEY HOUSTON (–) ▲
WHITNEY HOUSTON

Although she has now been eclipsed by younger urban R&B female stars, Houston will stand as the first to bring this type of clean soul music to the world. In the USA alone, this record stayed in the charts for four years, sold fifteen million copies and spent fourteen weeks on top of the charts. It would be churlish to offer any criticism when most of the world would disagree. The immaculate production is by Jermaine Jackson, bank manager is Clive Davis and even the bathing suit on the back cover gets a credit. It is however, with all its slickness, an indispensable soul album.

● TRACKS: *You Give Good Love; Thinking About You; Someone For Me; Saving All My Love For You; Nobody Loves Me Like You Do; How Will I Know; All At Once; Take Good Care Of My Heart; Greatest Love Of All; Hold Me.*

● FIRST RELEASED 1985
● UK PEAK CHART POSITION: 2
● USA PEAK CHART POSITION: 1

864 GERMFREE ADOLESCENTS (389) ▼
X RAY SPEX

Punk with a twist that was very nearly animated. Cartoon characters embroiled in the new wave, although the posturing, aggression and a collective two fingers to the world mentality that proliferated elsewhere, seemed to have bypassed X Ray Spex. They were the deliberate underachievers, poking fun at the establishment as opposed to the heavy reprimands of their contemporaries. 'The Day The World Turned Dayglo', 'Warrior In Woolworths', and the title track all typified their brash indulgences in punk/pop. A theme park equivalent to their more stern-faced counterparts and a colourful explosion of sound.

● TRACKS: *The Day The World Turned Dayglo; Obsessed With You; Genetic Engineering; Identity; I Live Off You; Germfree Adolescents; Art-I-Ficial; Let's Submerge; Warrior In Woolworths; I Am A Poseur; I Can't Do Anything; Highly Inflammable; Age; Plastic Bag; I Am A Cliche; Oh Bondage Up Yours!*

● FIRST RELEASED 1978
● UK PEAK CHART POSITION: 30
● USA PEAK CHART POSITION: did not chart

865 ELIMINATOR (409) ▼
Z.Z. TOP

1983 was the year Z.Z. Top went from being everyone's favourite bar-room boogie band to international superstars. Graced with mind-boggling and incredibly photogenic beards, a very neat trilogy of sexy videos and a collective ear for a quite distinct and highly stylized, if somewhat grizzled blues/pop, the sudden enormity of their success seems in retrospect like no real surprise. MTV had never quite seen the like and the attention given to the excellent 'Gimme All Your Lovin'' single was quickly repeated for both 'Sharp-Dressed Man' and the quite irreverent 'Legs'. It still sounds fresh, innovative and fun today in the wake of many imitators.

● TRACKS: *Gimme All Your Lovin'; Got Me Under Pressure; Sharp-dressed Man; I Need You Tonight; I Got The Six; Legs; Thug; TV Dinners; Dirty Dog; If I Could Only Flag Her Down; Bad Girl.*

● FIRST RELEASED 1983
● UK PEAK CHART POSITION: 3
● USA PEAK CHART POSITION: 9

866 THE ORIGINAL AMERICAN DECCA RECORDINGS (337) ▼ COUNT BASIE

These recordings capture all the fire, energy and raw excitement of the Basie band as it roared out of Kansas City to startle the jazz world. Talented players occupy every chair, many of them

awesome soloists: Buck Clayton, Harry Edison, Dicky Wells, Earle Warren, Herschel Evans, and the sublime and trend-setting Lester Young; all were buoyed and spurred along by the All-American Rhythm Section of Basie, Freddie Green, Walter Page and Jo Jones. If this were not enough, the band singer was the great Jimmy Rushing. Not surprisingly, after this, big band jazz was never quite the same again. Indeed, it might even be argued that later Basie bands never recaptured this early magic.

● TRACKS: *Including - Honeysuckle Rose; Pennies From Heaven; Swinging At The Daisy Chain; Roseland Shuffle; Exactly Like You; Boo Hoo; Glory Of Love; Boogie Woogie (I May Be Wrong); Smarty (You Know It All); One O'clock Jump; Listen My Children And You Shall Hear; Jon's Idea; Goodmorning Blues (1st take); Goodmorning Blues (2nd take); Our Love Was Meant To Be; Time Out; Topsy; I Keep Remembering; Out Of The Window; Don't You Miss Your Baby; Let Me Dream; Georgianna; Blues In The Dark; Sent For You Yesterday; Every Tub; Now Will You Be Good?; Swingin' The Blues; Mama Don't Want No Peas 'N' Rice 'N' Coconut Oil; Blue And Sentimental; Doggin' Around; Stop Beatin' Around The Mulberry Bush (1st take); Stop Beatin' Around The Mulberry Bush (2nd take); London Bridge Is Falling Down; Texas Shuffle.*

● RECORDED 1937-39
● UK PEAK CHART POSITION: did not chart
● USA PEAK CHART POSITION: did not chart

867 ONE OF THESE NIGHTS (–) ▲
THE EAGLES

This marked the transition from a nifty country rock band to a rock combo with the potential for world domination. The music was a tad sweeter and less ironic, a morsel rockier with Top 40 friendliness. Tracks such as 'Take It To The Limit' and 'Lyin' Eyes' have been played far too much on the radio. They need to be rested in place of Bernie Leadon's unusual instrumental, 'Journey Of The Sorcerer' (used as the theme to BBC Television's *Hitchhiker's Guide To The Galaxy*), or the other great Leadon song, 'I Wish You Peace'. Financially, the Eagles never looked back after this, but the critical snipers were out in force.

● TRACKS: *One Of These Nights; Too Many Hands; Hollywood Waltz; Journey Of The Sorcerer; Lyin' Eyes; Take It To The Limit; Visions; After The Thrill Is Gone; I Wish You Peace.*

● FIRST RELEASED 1975
● UK PEAK CHART POSITION: 8
● USA PEAK CHART POSITION: 1

868 SAVAGE (–) ▲
EURYTHMICS

Annie Lennox, the visual chameleon puts another face on; this time she is a blonde Barbie. Under the covers she is very much the familiar voice that became one of the most listened to throughout the 80s. This came towards the end, and as such is not the usual greatest hits package that many of their regular albums sounded like. Stewart was beginning to experiment with electronic sound (again) as Lennox seemed to want to sing more. In 'I Need A Man', Annie sings of the type of man she does not want, in 'Shame' she mourns nostalgia, while in 'Savage' there is sadness, bitterness and anger. This sounds like it was a difficult album to make.

● TRACKS: *Beethoven (I Love To Listen To); I've Got A Lover (Back In Japan); Do You Want To Break Up?; You Have Placed A Chill In My Heart; Shame; Savage; I Need A Man; Put The Blame On Me; Heaven; Wide Eyed Girl; I Need You; Brand New Day.*

● FIRST RELEASED 1987
● UK PEAK CHART POSITION: 7
● USA PEAK CHART POSITION: 41

869 GREAT BALLS OF FIRE! (335) ▼
JERRY LEE LEWIS

It is astonishing to note that this record failed to make the charts on either side of the Atlantic. Although the singles have become classics, this album was released at a time when Lewis' country roots were taking over. Fortunately, his rock 'n' roll material is now back in favour and most of the vital piano-bashing gems are included here. Lewis was the first white rock 'n' roller to give new meaning to the word 'sweat'. At live performances as he progressed further into his greatest hits catalogue, his hair would curl and flop down, as buckets of the stuff poured onto his keyboard. Phew!

● TRACKS: *Whole Lotta Shakin' Going On; It'll Be Me; Lewis Boogie; Drinkin' Wine Spo-Dee-O-Dee; Rock 'N' Roll Ruby; Matchbox; Ubangi Stomp; Great Balls Of Fire; You Win Again; Mean Woman Blues; Milkshake Mademoiselle; Breathless; Down The Line; Good Rockin' Tonight; Jambalaya (On The Bayou).*

● FIRST RELEASED 1964
● UK PEAK CHART POSITION: did not chart
● US PEAK CHART POSITION: did not chart

871 MADONNA (–) ▲
MADONNA

Now manufactured as *The First Album*, this marked the debut of the biggest new star of the 80s, and one that will be followed throughout her life, regardless of any new music. Madonna was *the* female pop icon that the world had always sought. As for the music, this is a credible debut of familiar-sounding pop that broke no barriers. Today, the 80s drum machine and synths sound stodgy and dated. More significant was the clear signal of a major new artist in the making - not only was she outspoken and outrageously confident but she wrote all her own songs, and it is the songs that stand, regardless of the production.

● TRACKS: *Lucky Star; Borderline; Burning Up; I Know It; Holiday; Think Of Me; Physical Attraction; Everybody.*

● FIRST RELEASED 1982
● UK PEAK CHART POSITION: 6
● USA PEAK CHART POSITION: 8

870 DUKE (347) ▼
GENESIS

Genesis still have a credibility problem which at present just trails the present standing of ex-drummer/vocalist Philip Collins. *Duke* was the record that shed their 'heavy prog' image and found them beginning to loosen up. Collins had grown in confidence following Peter Gabriel's departure and the band immediately became much tighter musically. In addition to the hit singles 'Duchess', the buoyant 'Turn It On Again' and realism of a situation in 'Misunderstanding', there is the painful honesty of 'Please Don't Ask'. There have been many bigger Genesis albums, but none have anywhere near as much heart.

● TRACKS: *Behind The Lines; Duchess; Guide Vocal; Man Of Our Times; Misunderstanding; Heathaze; Turn It On Again; Alone Tonight; Cul-de-sac; Please Don't Ask; Duke's Travels; Duke's End.*

● FIRST RELEASED 1980
● UK PEAK CHART POSITION: 1
● USA PEAK CHART POSITION: 11

872 GRIS GRIS (–) ▲
DR. JOHN

Spooky and difficult to classify, especially when it was first released in 1968. Dr John was immediately hailed as yet another psychedelic tangerine bicycle head. He was not, of course, and over the past 30 years has become a giant of New Orleans funky jazz. Nothing has really changed except that his piano playing is much more predominant now. Then he used his mysterious voice as an original tool. 'Gris Gris Gumbo Ya Ya' and 'I Walk On Guilded Splinters' still sound magnificent after all these years. If you don't buy this album he might just turn you into a snake.

● TRACKS: *Gris-Gris Gumbo Ya Ya; Danse Kalinda Ba Doom; Mama Roux; Danse Fambeaux; Croker Courtbullion; Jump Sturdy; I Walk On Guilded Splinters.*

● FIRST RELEASED 1968
● UK PEAK CHART POSITION: did not chart
● USA PEAK CHART POSITION: did not chart

873 **JOHNNY CASH AT SAN QUENTIN** (326) ▼ JOHNNY CASH

A giant of country music, Johnny Cash retained respect for the travails of the audience that elevated him to that position. Recorded live at one of America's most notorious prisons, this album displays an empathy bereft of condescension and captures a performer combining charisma with natural ease. The material is balanced between established favourites and new material, including 'Wanted Man', an unrecorded Bob Dylan song, and the light-hearted hit 'A Boy Named Sue'. It was not the first time Cash had recorded in a penal institution, but this appearance, at a time when American values were being vociferously questioned, suggested the artist's rebelliousness had not diminished.

● TRACKS: *Wanted Man; Wreck Of Old 97; I Walk The Line; Darling Companion; Starkville City Jail; San Quentin; A Boy Named Sue; Peace In The Valley; Folsom Prison Blues.*

● FIRST RELEASED 1969
● UK PEAK CHART POSITION: 2
● USA PEAK CHART POSITION: 1

 874 **ONE STEP BEYOND** (–) ▲ MADNESS

M adness were at the forefront of the UK ska revival at the end of the 70s, very much a regional thing. Madness were very London and they soon shed the two-tone image and became one of the most consistent UK chart groups of the following decade. This debut shows both sides, from the excellent blue beat signature tune 'Chipmunks Are Go!' and a first class cover of Prince Buster's 'One Step Beyond' to their own masterful pop, and in particular the highly polished 'My Girl'. What Lindisfarne are to Newcastle, and Fairport Convention are to Cropredy, so Madness are to Finsbury Park.

● TRACKS: *One Step Beyond; My Girl; Night Boat To Cairo; Believe Me; Land Of Hope And Glory; The Prince; Tarzan's Nuts; In The Middle Of The Night; Bed & Breakfast; Razor Blade Alley; Swan Lake; Rockin' In A Flat; Mummy's Boy; Chipmunks Are Go!*

● FIRST RELEASED 1979
● UK PEAK CHART POSITION: 2
● USA PEAK CHART POSITION: 128

 **875** **BURN** (342) ▼ DEEP PURPLE

T he first Deep Purple album to feature Glenn Hughes and David Coverdale, and as such, resulted in a much more bluesy effort all round. Coverdale's throaty roar, combined with Hughes' soaring vocal, made for a heartfelt, rootsy record. 'Might Just Take Your Life' was a hit single, and the album featured a series of extended jams, which worked most spectacularly with the elongated 'Mistreated', later resurrected by Coverdale as a live favourite with Whitesnake. The title track and 'Lay Down, Stay Down' gave vent to their more familiar refrains and emphasized the strength of their songwriting.

● TRACKS: *Burn; Might Just Take Your Life; Lay Down, Stay Down; Sail Away; You Fool No-one; What's Goin' On Here?; Mistreated; 'A' Zoo.*

● FIRST RELEASED 1974
● UK PEAK CHART POSITION: 3
● USA PEAK CHART POSITION: 9

 876 **MYSTERY GIRL** (–) ▲ ROY ORBISON

W ho could have known that the much-loved Orbison would record his best album at this late stage in his career; furthermore, that he would be dead a few months later. The success of his role in the Traveling Wilburys gave him a much-deserved boost. Orbison had *the* great voice of pop and after many years of indifferent material he finally hit gold with great songs such as 'You Got It' (written with Lynne and Petty), 'Careless Heart' (written with Diane Warren) and 'A Love So Beautiful' (written with Lynne). Orbison's tragic dedication to us when he finished this album was 'don't give up before the miracle happens'.

● TRACKS: *You Got It; In The Real World; Dream You; A Love So Beautiful; California Blue; She's A Mystery To Me; The Comedians; The Only One; Windsurfer; Careless Heart.*

● FIRST RELEASED 1989
● UK PEAK CHART POSITION: 2
● USA PEAK CHART POSITION: 5

877 BLESS THE WEATHER (–) ▲
JOHN MARTYN

I diosyncratic, difficult, lovable genius. Many other plaudits have been laid at the feet of this enigmatic giant. *Bless The Weather* was a gorgeous transitional record from folk to jazzier material, and features, among others, Richard Thompson and the mercurial Danny Thompson, arguably Martyn's greatest sparring partner. In addition to the hopelessly romantic title track and 'Head And Heart', there is a wonderful interpretation of 'Singin' In The Rain'. The experimental 'Glistening Glyndebourne' showed our John's developing interest in the 'echoplex' sound in which he was to immerse himself over the next few years. Other words that spring to mind are wayward, boozer, cheeky, passionate and, once more, genius.

● TRACKS: *Go Easy; Bless The Weather; Sugar Lump; Walk On The Water; Just Now; Head And Heart; Let The Good Things Come; Back Down The River; Glistening Glyndebourne; Singin' In The Rain.*

● FIRST RELEASED 1971
● UK PEAK CHART POSITION: did not chart
● USA PEAK CHART POSITION: did not chart

878 THIS WAS (–) ▲
JETHRO TULL

A debut of incredible maturity that fitted in nicely between blues and prog. Mick Abrahams was the darling of the clubs, and for a brief moment held a candle to Clapton, especially with his showpiece 'Cat's Squirrel'. Abrahams soon left to form Blodwyn Pig. Anderson, the undisputed leader, wore A great coat, played flute and stood like a pretty flamingo (not). Live they were tremendous, and on record they got even better than this. 'Song For Jeffrey' was the choice single. Other interesting tracks are the flute-led 'Serenade For a Cuckoo' (written by Roland Kirk) and 'Dharma For One', with a drum solo that is not boring.

● TRACKS: *My Sunday Feeling; Some Day The Sun Won't Shine For You; Beggar's Farm; Move On Alone; Serenade To a Cuckoo; Dharma For One; It's Breaking Me Up; Cat's Squirrel; A Song For Jeffrey; Round.*

● FIRST RELEASED 1968
● UK PEAK CHART POSITION: 10
● USA PEAK CHART POSITION: 62

879 OUT OF THE COOL (491) ▼
GIL EVANS

A much admired and loved man, of all the many brilliant orchestration projects this was his finest in his own right. He teases us with the opening of 'La Nevada' until the gorgeous repeated four-bar riff finally bursts on our ears with orgasmic delight. There are wonderful brass solos from John Coles, Tony Studd and Budd Johnson and a bass showcase for Ron Carter. As the opening track peters out after 15 minutes the listener enjoys the smug realization that there are a further four outstanding pieces to come. Too much of Evans's fame came through Miles Davis and Jimi Hendrix.

● TRACKS: *La Nevada; Where Flamingoes Fly; Bilbao Song; Stratusphunk; Sunken Treasure.*

● FIRST RELEASED 1960
● UK PEAK CHART POSITION: did not chart
● USA PEAK CHART POSITION: did not chart

880 FEARLESS (–) ▲
FAMILY

A lthough Family never received commercial success, their standing as a premier late 60s prog rock band is still considerable. Their blistering live shows revolved around the manic Roger Chapman, who in addition to pelting the audience with tambourines, had the most incredible vibrato and vocal range. *Fearless* maintained the quality songs that Chapman and Charlie Whitney had developed over the previous four albums, and all were sung with passion and subtle humour. The odd man out here is the beautiful 'Larf And Sing', written by violinist Polly Palmer. Family's worthy catalogue has been sensitively remastered by Castle, and this is an album of hidden depth and character.

● TRACKS: *Between Blue And Me; Sat'd-Y Barfly; Larf And Sing; Spanish Tide; Save Some For Thee; Take Your Partners; Children; Crinkley Grin; Blind; Burning Bridges.*

● FIRST RELEASED 1971
● UK PEAK CHART POSITION: 14
● USA PEAK CHART POSITION: 177

881 ## SINATRA AND SWINGIN' BRASS (-) ▲
FRANK SINATRA

Recorded at a time when Sintara was 'going for it'. He had to prove that his own record label could sell his own records better than Capitol could. In 1962 he was singing particularly well, and on this his unusually 'belting' voice was complimented by some sensational arrangements from Neil Hefti. It is surprising that they did not record together more often. The sharp jazzy brass of 'Goody Goody' and 'You Can't Take That Away From Me' are wonderful. He even had a hit single in the shape of 'Everybody's Twistin', included as a bonus track on the CD. A champagne record, and one of his jazziest.

● TRACKS: Goody Goody; They Can't Take That Away From Me; At Long Last Love; I'm Beginning To See The Light; Don'cha Go 'Way Mad; I Get A Kick Out Of You; Tangerine; Love Is Just Around The Corner; Ain't She Sweet; Serenade In Blue; I Love You; Pick Yopurself Up; Everybody's twistin'; Nothing But The Best; You Bought A New Kind Of Love To Me.

● FIRST RELEASED 1962
● UK PEAK CHART POSITION: 14
● USA PEAK CHART POSITION: 18

 882 ### FIRE AND WATER (331) ▼
FREE

Free emerged from the British blues boom with a tight, muscular style that framed Paul Rodgers' throaty voice. Guitarist Paul Kossoff provides the perfect foil with incisive, measured solos exemplified by his contribution to 'All Right Now'. This successful single transformed the group from club to festival status. Free's unhurried, careful intensity is captured perfectly on the album's title track and 'Oh I Wept', two songs charged with emotion. Where many contemporaries tended towards excess, Free implied a resonant power, particularly through Andy Fraser's liquid bass work, which weaves between the melody lines, rather than asserting them. *Fire And Water* is a high spot in heavy rock; rather than merely asserting masculine qualities, this album also shows a rare vulnerability.

● TRACKS: Oh I Wept; Remember; Heavy Load; Fire And Water; Mr. Big; Don't Say You Love Me; All Right Now.

● FIRST RELEASED 1970
● UK PEAK CHART POSITION: 2
● USA PEAK CHART POSITION: 17

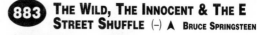 **883** ## THE WILD, THE INNOCENT & THE E STREET SHUFFLE (-) ▲ BRUCE SPRINGSTEEN

Although Springsteen's world domination has waned noticeably in recent years, he does have a back-catalogue of considerable power. This sleeper contains at least two Springsteen classics in the shape of the lovely '4th Of July, Asbury Park (Sandy)' and the powerful concert encore 'Rosalita (Come Out Tonight)', on which saxophonist Clarence Clemons demonstrated what an asset he is to Springsteen's sound. The album failed to chart when released in 1973, and made the lists during his breakthrough year of 1975. That year, *Born To Run* turned him into a superstar, and the down-home friendliness that this record had was lost forever. The album's title summed up everything.

● TRACKS: The E Street Shuffle; 4th Of July, Asbury Park (Sandy); Kitty's Back; Wild Billy's Circus Story; Incident On 57th Street; Rosalita (Come Out Tonight); New York City Serenade.

● FIRST RELEASED 1973
● UK PEAK CHART POSITION: 33
● USA PEAK CHART POSITION: 59

 884 ### AGENTS OF FORTUNE (-) ▲
BLUE OYSTER CULT

Fêted by heavy metal fans, this was a much broader album that put them in touch with AOR radio, and consequently took them out of their heavy rock ghetto. The ace in their tarot pack was the entrancing and enchanting 'Don't Fear The Reaper' - the greatest song that the original Byrds never wrote. Flowing and chiming it put the band in the pop charts with a song of rare quality and consequently pushed this album's sales. The other tracks struggle to compete with the Reaper, but there are moments, especially with 'The Revenge Of Vera Gemini', on which Patti Smith narrates.

● TRACKS: This Ain't The Summer Of Love; True Confessions; (Don't Fear) The Reaper; E.T.I.; The Revenge Of Vera Gemini; Sinful Love; Tattoo Vampire; Morning Final; Tenderloin; Debbie Denise.

● FIRST RELEASED 1980
● UK PEAK CHART POSITION: 26
● USA PEAK CHART POSITION: 29

885 BLIND FAITH (–) ▲
BLIND FAITH

One magnificent super-group, one tasteless cover, one album, one tour; that's all folks. Contrary to popular myth, they were very, very good; Clapton and Winwood found corners of the stage in which they could hide as they tried to shun the spotlight under which Cream and Traffic had put them. And that is why the fans rebelled. They wanted lots of Clapton guitar solos and another 'Dear Mr Fantasy'. What they got was a collection that improves with age; a delightfully ramshackle 'Well All Right', a great Clapton song, 'In The Presence Of The Lord', and a sparse but powerful Winwood on 'Can't Find My Way Home'. The CD reissue includes two bonus tracks.

● TRACKS: Had To Cry Today; Can't Find My Way Home; Well All Right; Presence Of The Lord; Sea Of Joy; Do What You Like; Exchange And Mart; Spending All My Days.

● FIRST RELEASED 1969
● UK PEAK CHART POSITION: 1
● USA PEAK CHART POSITION: 1

 ## 886 NASHVILLE SKYLINE (–) ▲
BOB DYLAN

It is hard to recall now how deeply unfashionable country music was in 1969 - Dylan's label, Columbia, dismayed at his apparent retrogression, begged him to remove the word 'Nashville' from the album's title. However, as usual, he proved ahead of the game; his embrace of country ushered in Gram Parsons, the Flying Burrito Brothers and scores of subsequent artists under the Americana banner. Prescient too was his nod to Johnny Cash, with whom he duets on the gorgeous 'Girl From The North Country'. Most tracks are pleasant and enduring; the chart hit 'Lay Lady Lay' remains the Dylan song of choice for non-fans.

● TRACKS: Girl From The North Country; Nashville Skyline Rag; To Be Alone With You; I Threw It All Away; Peggy Day; Lay Lady Lay; One More Night; Tell Me That It Isn't True; Country Pie; Tonight I'll Be Staying Here With You.

● FIRST RELEASED 1969
● UK PEAK CHART POSITION: 1
● USA PEAK CHART POSITION: 3

 ## 887 SAUCERFUL OF SECRETS (–) ▲
PINK FLOYD

Hearing this played live in 1967 must have been quite an experience. Nobody was doing music like this, quite like this; although there were a few purple tangerine chocolate bicycle machines around. Part of the affection that this album still holds is nostalgic affection; the other part is the audience were as out of it as the band were. The Floyd have since stretched recording technique to perfection and this recording now sounds lame in terms of production. The songs, however, still maintain great character of times past; 'Remember A Day' still provokes a hum and 'Set The Controls' evokes those dodgy light shows.

● TRACKS: Let There Be More Light; Remember A Day; Set The Controls For The Heart Of The Sun; Corporal Clegg; A Saucerful Of Secrets; See-saw; Jugband Blues.

● FIRST RELEASED 1968
● UK PEAK CHART POSITION: 9
● USA PEAK CHART POSITION: did not chart

 ## 888 FREE PEACE SWEET (–) ▲
DODGY

The music on the punning Free Peace Sweet, the third album by London trio Dodgy, owes at least as much to west coast America as it does to northern England. Beach Boys-style harmonies are matched by clean, intricate and solid rock arrangements, similar to Who's Next-era Who. However, Dodgy refuse to be purists or revivalists; the album's 'Intro' has a trip-hop beat, while the UK Top 5 hit 'Good Enough' evokes classic brassy Motown. Although the US branch of A&M inexplicably declined to release the album, it was quite deservedly Dodgy's breakthrough in their home country, where it went platinum.

● TRACKS: Intro; In A Room; Trust In Time; You've Gotta Look Up; If You're Thinking Of Me; Good Enough; Ain't No Longer Asking; Found You; One Of Those Rivers; Prey For Drinking; Jack The Lad; Long Life; U.K.R.I.P.; Homegrown.

● FIRST RELEASED 1996
● UK PEAK CHART POSITION: 7
● USA PEAK CHART POSITION: did not chart

889 ### EAGLES (–) ▲
THE EAGLES

Their least commercially successful record still retains qualities that make it one of their best. Their classic reading of Jackson Browne and Glen Frey's 'Take It Easy' never drags, and Henley's sex-charged vocal on 'Witchy Woman' still sounds convincing. Other delights are Leadon and Gene Clark's 'Train Leaves Here This Morning' and Jack Tempchin's memorable 'Peaceful Easy Feeling'. This was rock/country, as opposed to Poco and the Burritos' country/rock. Nothing would be as simple and uncomplicated for the Eagles ever again, and this album retains a great charm and innocence that soon disappeared from their career. A truly stunning debut album.

● TRACKS: *Take It Easy; Witchy Woman; Chug All Night; Most Of Us Are Sad; Nightingale; Train Leaves Here This Morning; Take The Devil; Earlybird; Peaceful Easy Feeling; Tryin'.*

● FIRST RELEASED 1972
● UK PEAK CHART POSITION: did not chart
● USA PEAK CHART POSITION: 22

 891 ### PIECES OF YOU (–) ▲
JEWEL

An extraordinary debut, both in terms of maturity and sales. Produced by ex-Neil Young cohort Ben Keith, the album, subtitled *What We Call Human Nature In Actuality Is Human Habit,* was one of the surprises of 1997. Lyrically between Suzanne Vega and Beth Orton, the album is full of surprises on the ear, not all of them sweet. The title track is meant to hurt with its ironic cruelty. Jewel has the range of Joni Mitchell, Joan Baez and Emmylou Harris in a contemporary setting. She is definitely a major new talent, providing there are more stories like these ones to tell.

● TRACKS: *Who Will Save Your Soul; Pieces Of You; Little Sister; Foolish Games; Near You Always; Painters; Morning Song; Adrian; I'm Sensitive; You Were Meant For Me; Don't; Daddy; Angel Standing By; Amen; Foolish Games.*

● FIRST RELEASED 1997
● UK PEAK CHART POSITION: did not chart
● USA PEAK CHART POSITION: 4

 890 ### HEX ENDUCTION HOUR (–) ▲
THE FALL

To use the word challenging seems patronising when describing the Fall's work. Leader Mark E Smith does not tolerate fools gladly and he would verbally lash such pompous observations. However, it is a difficult album to love as it is lyrically uncompromising and musically spartan. This was the first of many Fall albums to chart, thanks to regular plugs from Fall-father John Peel, and as such it remains a favourite. 'Just Step S'Ways' is the track that remains in the head, although 'Who Makes The Nazis?' is a disturbingly accurate dialogue of what was to come throughout the 80s in the UK with right-wing factions.

● TRACKS: *The Classical; Jawbone And The Air-Rifle; Hip Priest; Fortress/Deer Park; Mere Pseud Mag. Ed; Winter (Hostel Maxi); Winter 2; Just Step S'Ways; Who Makes The Nazis?; Iceland; And This Day.*

● FIRST RELEASED 1982
● UK PEAK CHART POSITION: 71
● USA PEAK CHART POSITION: did not chart

 892 ### COLTRANE JAZZ (375) ▼
JOHN COLTRANE

Released shortly after the groundbreaking *Giant Steps, Coltrane Jazz* features a number of takes from the 'Naima' session, with Wynton Kelly, Paul Chambers and Jimmy Cobb, as well as a track with Cedar Walton and Lex Humphries and an early outing by his newly formed quartet featuring pianist McCoy Tyner, Steve Davis and Elvin Jones. While lacking the conceptual strength of many of Coltrane's greatest works, *Coltrane Jazz* captures the saxophonist during one of his interesting periods of change, and includes some memorable original tunes. Particularly worth investigating are 'Harmonique', an unusual theme involving polyphonics (more than one note played simultaneously), and a beautiful ballad performance of 'I'll Wait And Pray'.

● TRACKS: *Little Old Lady; Village Blues; My Shining Hour; Fifth House; Harmonique; Like Sonny; I'll Wait And Pray; Some Other Blues.*

● FIRST RELEASED 1961
● UK PEAK CHART POSITION: did not chart
● USA PEAK CHART POSITION: did not chart

893 HERE WE GO AGAIN! (361) ▼
THE KINGSTON TRIO

Admirers of left-wing, thinking songsters such as Woody Guthrie and the Weavers, the Kingston Trio - Nick Reynolds, Bob Shane and Dave Guard - were the alternative. They cared, but also laced concern with commercial appeal. There was an intelligent market just waiting to sympathize, and for some four years The Trio were top dogs as far as folk-singing was concerned. Successful with a campfire rendering of 'Tom Dooley' they rattled out albums at a hell of a lick. Have guitars will record? *Here We Go Again*, probably exactly how they felt in the liberal whirlwind that surrounded them, is not only a fine slice of 50s American folkloric sound but a document of a period when acoustic music began inching towards acceptance.

● TRACKS: *Molly Dee; Across The Wide Missouri; Haul Away; The Wanderer; 'Round About The Mountain; Oleanna; The Unfortunate Miss Bailey; San Miguel (Inn Taton); Rollin' Stone; Goober Peas; A Worried Man.*

● FIRST RELEASED 1959
● UK PEAK CHART POSITION: did not chart
● USA PEAK CHART POSITION: 1

 894 BEDTIME STORIES (-) ▲
MADONNA

Madonna changed her image from sex and erotica to looking like a cross between Marilyn Monroe and Barbara Cartland. Musically, she was growing and expanding her sound, and this album was her classiest to date. Less pop and more soul, resulting in wholly satisfying tracks such as 'Secret' and 'I'd Rather Be Your Lover'. The co-opted writers/producers no doubt helped in giving the songs and production greater depth, notably Dallas Austin, Dave Hall and, especially, Babyface, with the excellent 'Forbidden Love' and 'Take A Bow'. A wonderfully rich and creamy album that should stand as one of her best achievements.

● TRACKS: *Survival; Secret; I'd Rather Be Your Lover; Don't Stop; Inside Of Me; Human Nature; Forbidden Love; Love Tried To Welcome Me; Sanctuary; Bedtime Story; Take A Bow.*

● FIRST RELEASED 1994
● UK PEAK CHART POSITION: 2
● USA PEAK CHART POSITION: 3

 895 NO SLEEP 'TIL HAMMERSMITH (353) ▼
MOTÖRHEAD

Unlike many heavy metal contemporaries, Motörhead leader Lemmy possesses self-deprecating humour. Stripped of pretension, he goads the basic three-chord trick with a full-throated bellow, emphasizing his trio's vicious racket. On this live selection the group reprise the cream of their back catalogue with untrammelled venom, in the process destroying already power-packed studio counterparts. Continuing a line from the MC5 and Stooges, rather than gothic fantasy, the band understand the excitement of noise and exploit it to its full potential. Thrash metal and hardcore owe them a debt but, as this album proves, there is only one Motörhead.

● TRACKS: *Ace Of Spades; Stay Clean; The Metropolis Hammer; Iron Horse; No Class; Overkill; The Road Crew; Capricorn; Motörhead.*

● FIRST RELEASED 1981
● UK PEAK CHART POSITION: 1
● USA PEAK CHART POSITION: did not chart

 896 THE SHAPE OF JAZZ TO COME (372) ▼
ORNETTE COLEMAN

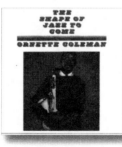

As the 50s ended, Ornette Coleman became the new herald of the future of jazz, surpassing for a time, even John Coltrane. Intent on feeling and with often scant regard for technique, he plunged headlong into a musical form that defied categorization and dismayed orthodox musicologists. Especially aware of the blues, Coleman eschewed a rigid structure in the music and favoured instead explorations of its poetic content. Free jazz to Coleman and his followers was jazz freed not only from musical restraints but also from sociological and cultural parameters. This album demonstrates his radicalism and his awareness of both past and future jazz.

● TRACKS: *Lonely Woman; Eventually; Peace; Focus On Sanity; Congeniality Chronology.*

● FIRST RELEASED 1960
● UK PEAK CHART POSITION: did not chart
● USA PEAK CHART POSITION: did not chart

897 SLANTED AND ENCHANTED (–) ▲
PAVEMENT

The punk era had already posited the notion that limited production values and/or technique could exist in inverse proportion to good music. Pavement, then, were the first Americans of note to conceptualize the message as the medium, accentuating perceived shortcomings. This stance had several advantages - their stripped-and-raw aesthetic pushed the group's hooky songs to the forefront. Unlike their earlier recordings, which were too scattershot and tentative to be easily accessible, *Slanted And Enchanted* saw the recently expanded line-up at their best. 'Chesley's Little Wrists' and 'No Life Singed Her' are just two examples of the songwriting's high-quality threshold. America's answer to the Fall was a long time coming, but proved to be well worth the wait.

● TRACKS: *Summer Babe (Winter Version); Trigger Cut; Wounded-Kite At: 17; No Life Singed Her; In The Mouth A Desert; Conduit For Sale!; Zurich Is Stained; Chesley's Little Wrists; Loretta's Scars; Here; Two States; Perfume-V; Flame Throwa; Jackals, False Grails: The Lonesome Era; Our Singer.*

● FIRST RELEASED 1991
● UK PEAK CHART POSITION: 72
● USA PEAK CHART POSITION: did not chart

898 INTO THE PURPLE VALLEY (856) ▼
RY COODER

Guitarist Cooder was a respected session musician prior to launching a solo career. His distinctive style blossomed fully on this, his second album, which is a brilliant compendium of American country/folk styles. Tight, but sparse accompaniment takes the artist through songs largely drawn from the Dustbowl Ballads of the Depression era. An unerring empathy is heard throughout, particularly on Woody Guthrie's 'Vigilante Man'. Cooder's ungainly voice captures the pervasive atmosphere, but it is his chilling slide guitarwork for which this album is renowned.

● TRACKS: *How Can You Keep On Moving; Billy The Kid; Money Honey; FDR In Trinidad; Teardrops Will Fall; Denomination Blues; On A Monday; Hey Porter; Great Dreams Of Heaven; Taxes On The Farmer Feeds Us All; Vigilante Man.*

● FIRST RELEASED 1971
● UK PEAK CHART POSITION: did not chart
● USA PEAK CHART POSITION: 113

899 SCOTT 2 (368) ▼
SCOTT WALKER

Although it opens with the up-tempo strains of 'Jackie', Scott Walker's second solo album generally courts the dark existentialism of its predecessor. Four enigmatic original songs, of which 'The Bridge' is particularly dramatic, match the moody intensity of the singer's Jacques Brel interpretations. Walker's reading of 'Next', the tale of a mobile army brothel, is particularly riveting. He invests material by Tim Hardin and Burt Bacharach with the same dark power, using his deep, resonant voice to majestic effect, buoyed by imaginative orchestral arrangements from, among others, Peter Knight and Reg Guest. *Scott 2* is an astonishing work, confirming Walker as one of the finest singers in pop.

● TRACKS: *Jackie; Best Of Both Worlds; Black Sheep Boy; The Amorous Humphrey Plug; Next; The Girls From The Street; Plastic Palace People; Wait Until Dark; Windows Of The World; The Bridge; Come Next Spring.*

● FIRST RELEASED 1968
● UK PEAK CHART POSITION: 1
● USA PEAK CHART POSITION: did not chart

900 CHAIRS MISSING (612) ▼
WIRE

A euphemism for insanity, *Chairs Missing* is an apt summation of Wire's disturbing music. A product of London's punk scene, the quartet nonetheless owed a debt to the art-school experimentation of the mid-60s, a contrast that gave their craft originality. Oblique pop songs, including 'Outdoor Miner' and 'I Am The Fly', exemplify Wire's development from the abrasive minimalism of earlier releases, while their widening musical perspectives are reflected in the edgy 'Practice Makes Perfect'. Producer Mike Throne adds keyboards and synthesizer to the group's guitar-based attack as *Chairs Missing* established Wire as one of the most innovative bands of their era.

● TRACKS: *Practice Makes Perfect; French Film Blurred; Another The Letter; Men Second; Marooned; Sand In My Joints; Being Sucked In Again; Heartbeat; Mercy; Outdoor Miner; I Am The Fly; I Feel Mysterious Today; From The Nursery; Used To; Too Late.*

● FIRST RELEASED 1978
● UK PEAK CHART POSITION: 48
● USA PEAK CHART POSITION: did not chart

901 ## BLUES BROTHERS (424) ▼
VARIOUS

A film that stands up to repeated viewing is complemented by an album that has the same effect. The musical stars make cameos to perform one track each, Aretha as the waitress in a diner tears into 'Think' while Cab Calloway dons his best white suit for a spectacular 'Minnie The Moocher'. The 'brothers' are supported by most of Booker T. And The MGs and they deliver some rousing numbers including a bottle-throwing 'Rawhide' and a loose 'Gimme Some Lovin''. Aykroyd and Belushi could have become the Sam And Dave of the 80s. Aykroyd tried it again in 1998 with reasonable success.

● TRACKS: *Shake A Tail Feather; Think; Minnie The Moocher; Rawhide; Jailhouse Rock; She Caught The Katy; Gimme Some Lovin'; Old Landmark; Sweet Home Chicago; Peter Gunn; Everybody Needs Somebody To Love.*

● FIRST RELEASED 1980
● UK PEAK CHART POSITION: 4
● USA PEAK CHART POSITION: 13

902 ## SHAZAM (–) ▲
THE MOVE

Although *Shazam* is generally considered the Move's least 'pop' effort, in many ways it is the most pop of all their releases. *Shazam* begins with 'Hello Suzie', a concise slice of Blue Cheer-style heavy rock, and ends with Tom Paxton's 'The Last Thing On My Mind', in an arrangement that is a homage to the Byrds (the backing track emulates '5-D', the backwards guitar, 'Thoughts And Words'). Even on the epic 'Cherry Blossom Clinic Revisited', they are tight and disciplined, a perfect counterpoint to the insanity of the song's protagonist. Perhaps the most masterly work of Roy Wood's career, that track seamlessly binds passages from Bach and Tchaikovsky with Lewis Carroll-style lyrics and fat acoustic guitars.

● TRACKS: *Hello Susie; Beautiful Daughter; Cherry Blossom Clinic Revisited; Fields Of People; Don't Make My Baby Blue; The Last Thing On My Mind.*

● FIRST RELEASED 1970
● UK PEAK CHART POSITION: did not chart
● USA PEAK CHART POSITION: did not chart

903 ## CALIFORNIA BLOODLINES (–) ▲
JOHN STEWART

Such a genuine record, recorded with little pomp, and yet every track is special. It is a very even list of sitting on a porch with guitar songs. Pop with folk and country overtones with the beautiful voice of Stewart in effortless command. This, after all, is the man who wrote 'Daydream Believer' for the Monkees and nearly a quarter of a century later was in the pop charts duetting with Stevie Nicks on 'Gold'. In between he released a number of gentle country rock albums of which this is the star turn. The See For Miles reissue has bonus tracks. Underrated both as a songwriter and as a fine singer.

● TRACKS: *California Bloodlines; Razor Back Woman; She Believes In Me; Omaha Rainbow; The Pirates Of Stone County Road; Shackles And Chains; Mother Country; Lonesome Picker; You Can't Look Back; Missouri Birds; July, You're A Woman; Never Goin' Back; Heart Full Of Woman And A Bellyfull Of Tennessee; Willard; Big Joe, Friend Of Jesus; Marshall Wind.*

● FIRST RELEASED 1969
● UK PEAK CHART POSITION: did not chart
● USA PEAK CHART POSITION: 193

904 ## JANET JACKSON'S RHYTHM NATION 1814 (–) ▲ ### JANET JACKSON

Little did you know that the American national anthem, 'God Bless America', was written in 1814. Janet did, and she sets out in 'Rhythm Nation' to dish out a bit of 'let's all work together for a better world and improve our way of life type thing'. This vein continues for a number of tracks, and admirable though it is, she sounds so much more convincing singing a good old-fashioned love song. The Jacksons were meant to dance, not to sermonize. That said, 'Miss You Much', 'Lonely' and 'Come Back To Me' are fabulous. Slick, sweet soul sung and played perfectly.

● TRACKS: *Interlude: Pledge; Rhythm Nation; Interlude: TV; State Of The World; Interlude: Race; The Knowledge; Interlude: Let's Dance; Miss You Much; Interlude: Come Back; Love Will Never Do (Without You); Livin' In A World (They Didn't Make); Alright; Interlude: Hey Baby; Escapade; Interlude: No Acid; Black Cat; Lonely; Come Back To Me; Someday Is Tonight; Interlude: Livin' In Complete Darkness.*

● FIRST RELEASED 1989
● UK PEAK CHART POSITION: 4
● USA PEAK CHART POSITION: 1

905 NIGHT OWL (-) ▲
GERRY RAFFERTY

Ex-Humblebum Rafferty took a while to find success, especially after the managerial problems of his previous band, Stealers Wheel. It all came good with *City To City* and 'Baker Street', and this album came shortly after that success. His songwriting was at a peak with easily flowing songs such as 'Get It Right Next Time' and 'Take The Money And Run'. Much of the rancour of his previous band spills over into these lyrics, and of the way he was trying to hold his relationship together. This, therefore, is an honest album from a time in his life that he had difficulty putting behind him. Trauma does produce good songs.

● TRACKS: *Days Gone Down; Night Owl; The Way That You Do It; Why Won't You Talk To Me; Get It Right Next Time; Take The Money And Run; Family Tree; Already Gone; The Tourist; It's Gonna Be A Long Night.*

● FIRST RELEASED 1979
● UK PEAK CHART POSITION: 9
● USA PEAK CHART POSITION: 29

906 THE BEAST INSIDE (345) ▼
INSPIRAL CARPETS

Never regarded as the artistic élite of the Madchester scene (although, of course, they were not actually from Manchester itself), the Inspiral Carpets have nevertheless produced a body of work which, if not paralleling the one-off impact of the Stone Roses, has marked them out as consistent achievers. The best of their albums are *Life* and this one, which maintains the group's traditions (a big organ sound, character-based lyrics, bad haircuts), yet also saw a bolder, more introspective songwriting effort, expanding on the narrative style expressed on their debut album.

● TRACKS: *Caravan; Please Be Cruel; Born Yesterday; Sleep Well Tonight; Grip; Beast Inside; Niagara; Mermaid; Further Away; Dreams Are All We Have.*

● FIRST RELEASED 1991
● UK PEAK CHART POSITION: 5
● USA PEAK CHART POSITION: did not chart

907 HANDFUL OF EARTH (900) ▼
DICK GAUGHAN

Fiercely political, this was the work that cemented Gaughan's reputation for outspoken topicality and burning Scots nationalism. It is a milestone and traditional music would doubtlessly be the poorer without it. The mix of vitriol and conciliation is startling: there are no punches pulled in 'The World Turned Upside Down', yet contrast that with the tender 'Snows They Melt The Soonest' or the hands-across-the-water brotherhood expressed in 'Both Sides The Tweed.' The unobtrusive, atmospheric backing allows Gaughan to range freely across the principles and influences by which he still stands as loyally to this day. A truly passionate record.

● TRACKS: *Erin Go Bragh; Now Westlin' Winds; Craigie Hill; The World Turned Upside Down; The Snows That Melt The Soonest; Lough Erne; First Kiss At Parting; Scojun Waltz; Randers Hopsa; A Song For Ireland; The Worker's Song; Both Sides The Tweed.*

● FIRST RELEASED 1981
● UK PEAK CHART POSITION: did not chart
● USA PEAK CHART POSITION: did not chart

908 VIOLATOR (-) ▲
DEPECHE MODE

Following a lenghty gap between this and the last album *Music For The Masses*, the band had now become a huge attraction in the USA. They were the only group to take what was very much European music, to the USA. The synthesizers and keyboards still dominated the sound but there was a greater depth to the lyrics, or at least more was read into them. Religion, that red rag to a rock 'n' roller, had taken over. Gahan additionally was heading down a dark path of drugs, as Marin Gore attempted to hold the band together. Their unresolved problems permeated through this dramatic album.

● TRACKS: *World In My Eyes; Sweetest Perfection; Personal Jesus; Halo; Waiting For The Night; Enjoy The Silence; Policy Of Truth; Blue Dress; Clean.*

● FIRST RELEASED 1990
● UK PEAK CHART POSITION: 2
● USA PEAK CHART POSITION: 7

909 MADE IN JAPAN (371) ▼
DEEP PURPLE

Recorded on the Japanese tour of 1972, Deep Purple created the most effortless of great live albums. Labouring under the *Machine Head* tour and with inter-band relationships that saw both Gillan and Glover feuding with the sometimes difficult Blackmore and quitting the band early the following year, the record, for its part, does not suffer from the personnel inconsistencies, the band playing what would become, in retrospect, a greatest hits set. The consistency of the material - 'Child In Time', 'Strange Kind Of Woman', 'Space Truckin'' - was, and still is, astounding, matched only by the arch standards of Purple's live performance.

● TRACKS: *Highway Star; Child In Time; Smoke On The Water; The Mule; Strange Kind Of Woman; Lazy; Space Truckin'*.

● FIRST RELEASED 1973
● UK PEAK CHART POSITION: 16
● USA PEAK CHART POSITION: 6

910 TIME OUT (388) ▼
DAVE BRUBECK

Second only to *Jazz Samba* by Stan Getz, as the most commercially successful jazz record of all time (it even contained a single for the pop charts, Paul Desmond's magnificent 'Take Five'), Brubeck brilliantly popularized jazz and offered it as a palatable alternative to Bobby Vee. This album sold by the trunkload and made Brubeck a popular star. Those jazz critics who shunned him for becoming too commercial must eat their words, as this is a monumental album of the finest modern jazz. 'Blue Rondo A La Turk' and 'Kathy's Waltz' demonstrate this man's graceful, nonchalant class.

● TRACKS: *Blue Rondo A La Turk; Strange Meadow Lark; Take Five; Three To Get Ready; Kathy's Waltz; Everybody's Jumpin'; Pick Up Sticks*.

● FIRST RELEASED 1959
● UK PEAK CHART POSITION: 11
● USA PEAK CHART POSITION: 2

911 TALKING WITH THE TAXMAN ABOUT POETRY (357) ▼ BILLY BRAGG

Agitpop's aggrieved and finely humoured singer-songwriter, Billy Bragg gave full vent to his impassioned view of the world with the excellent *Talking With The Taxman About Poetry*. Less fully blown in execution than *Brewing Up*, or his mini-album *Life's A Riot With Spy Vs Spy*, his finally honed angst nevertheless remained intact, with his pungent and almost always topical material sitting comfortably alongside a new and instantly more accessible batch of songs. The wonderfully arch 'Greetings To The New Brunette' and the uplifting 'Levi Stubbs Tears' were indicative of Bragg's rapidly developing craft.

● TRACKS: *Greetings To The New Brunette; Train Train; The Marriage; Ideology; Levi Stubbs Tears; Honey I'm A Big Boy Now; There Is Power In A Union; Help Save The Youth Of America; Wishing The Days Away; The Passion; The Warmest Room; The Home Front*.

● FIRST RELEASED 1986
● UK PEAK CHART POSITION: 8
● USA PEAK CHART POSITION: did not chart

912 THE LOW-END THEORY (–) ▲
A TRIBE CALLED QUEST

With their second album in 1991, they became serious contenders for Public Enemy's (until then) undisputed crown as hip-hop's cultural leaders. However, where their debut was propelled by a disparate array of samples, *The Low-End Theory* was built on a stricter musical doctrine - its spine provided by bebop jazz. Though jazz-rap crossover would become a staple of popular music in the mid-90s (Gang Starr, Jazzmatazz, etc.), this album played a substantial part in breaking down barriers between genres. Phife Dog and Q-Tip are on great form too, making the most of Quest's energetic production with cool asides and insightful observations ('The Infamous Date Rape', 'Showbusiness').

● TRACKS: *Excursions; Buggin' Out; Rap Promoter; Butter; Verses From The Abstract; Showbusiness; Vibes And Stuff; The Infamous Date Rape; Check The Rhime; Everything Is Fair; Jazz (We've Got); Skypager; What?; Scenario*.

● FIRST RELEASED 1991
● UK PEAK CHART POSITION: 58
● USA PEAK CHART POSITION: 45

913 JAILBREAK (386) ▼
THIN LIZZY

Not true heavy metal perpetrators, more out-and-out rockers, with a feeling for pop. The late Phil Lynott has a growing core of younger fans, as word is passed down that even though he had his demons he was an outstanding performer. This is their best studio album and it contains two classics; 'The Boys Are Back In Town' and the title track. Both spit and crackle, bass and lead guitar burst out of the speaker at loud volume, and throughout, the gentle, laconic voice of Lynott delivers his poetry. Don't allow his death to see Thin Lizzy fade from the memory.

● TRACKS: *Angel From The Coast; The Boys Are Back In Town; Cowboy Song; Emerald; Fight Or Jail; Jailbreak; Romeo And The Lonely Girl; Running Back; Warriors.*

● FIRST RELEASED 1976
● UK PEAK CHART POSITION: 10
● USA PEAK CHART POSITION: 18

914 THE RAVEN (–) ▲
STRANGLERS

While not forsaking the belligerence of yester-year, by 1979 and *The Raven*, the most despised band in the UK rock firmament had at least refined their combative zeal. The Stranglers' sound had now evolved into something that combined eloquence with grandeur take the title track, or the neo-operatic flourishes to Dave Greenfield's 'Genetix'. Elsewhere, this was the last Stranglers album where principal songwriters Cornwell and Burnel worked in relative harmony together. While the former indulged his fascination with all things Eastern ('Ice'), the latter unveiled his abiding (and somewhat unfortunate) interest in aliens ('Meninblack'). The best tracks are the acidic put-down of Americana ('Dead Los Angeles') and the group's first genuine pop song, 'Duchess'.

● TRACKS: *Longships; The Raven; Dead Los Angeles; Ice; Baroque Bordello; Nuclear Device; Shah Shah A Go Go; Don't Bring Harry; Duchess; Meninblack; Genetix; Bear Cage.*

● FIRST RELEASED 1979
● UK PEAK CHART POSITION: 4
● USA PEAK CHART POSITION: did not chart

915 E.1999 ETERNAL (–) ▲
BONE THUGS-N-HARMONY

By the time Bone Thugs-N-Harmony released their 1994 debut, *Creepin On Ah Come Up*, gangsta rap was rapidly becoming an embarrassing cliché. With their much more considered follow-up, the group worked within the considerations to produce something fresh, resonant and invigorating. Drawing on hip-hop's old school conventions, the group weld lyrical and vocal gymnastics (at times akin to scat jazz) to samples and restrained beats. Take the opening track, where the scene is set with constant rainfall, or 'Budsmokers Only', where DJ Uneek employs an old Earth Wind & Fire sample to propel the group's advocacy of 'weed'. Or try '1st Of That Month', which showcases the group's ability to shift gears between classic R&B high harmonies and an authentic contemporary rap aesthetic.

● TRACKS: *Da Introduction; East 1999 Eternal; Crept And We Came; Down 71 (The Getaway); Mr Bill Collector; Budsmokers Only; Crossroad; Me Killa; Land Of That Heartless; No Shorts, No Loses; 1st Of That Month; Buddah Lovaz; Die Die Die; Mr Ouija 2; Mo' Murda; Shotz To Tha Double Glock; Tha Crossroads (DJ U-Neek's Mo Thug Remix).*

● FIRST RELEASED 1995
● UK PEAK CHART POSITION: did not chart
● USA PEAK CHART POSITION: 1

916 SAIL AWAY (–) ▲
RANDY NEWMAN

On *Sail Away* Newman returned to the lush orchestration of his debut album, but here the strings framed a more substantial collection of songs. *Sail Away* opens with the now infamous title track, where Newman voices the pitch of a slave trader to his cargo of slaves over one of his most beautiful melodies. Elsewhere on the album, the targets of 'Political Science', 'Burn On' and 'God's Song' may have been easy pickings for a satirist of Newman's stature, but the winning character sketches of 'Simon Smith And His Dancing Bear' and 'Dayton, Ohio - 1903' showcased a songwriter close to his peak.

● TRACKS: *Sail Away; Lonely At The Top; He Gives Us All His Love; Last Night I Had A Dream; Simon Smith And The Amazing Dancing Bear; Old Man; Political Science; Burn On; Memo To My Son; Dayton, Ohio - 1903; You Can Leave Your Hat On; God's Song (That's Why I Love Mankind).*

● FIRST RELEASED 1972
● UK PEAK CHART POSITION: did not chart
● USA PEAK CHART POSITION: 163

917 END OF THE CENTURY (–) ▲
RAMONES

'T his is rock 'n' roll radio, come on lets rock 'n' roll with the Ramones, the opening track informs the listener. On 'Do You Remember Rock 'N' Roll Radio?' the band sound more like Roy Wood's Wizzard than wacky punksters, and maybe they were always out of their time. The Ramones were always too much fun to be taken seriously. In the midst of the angry punk uprising they merely barred their chords and encouraged dancing and a good time. This is a great, great album for breaking the ice at parties, and because of the Phil Spector production it requires only a Dansette-quality CD player.

● TRACKS: *Do You Remember Rock 'N' Roll Radio?; I'm Affected; Danny Says; Chinese Rock; The Return Of Jackie And Judy; Let's Go; Baby I Love You; Make It On Time; This Ain't Havana; Rock 'N' Roll High School; All The Way; High Risk Insurance.*

● FIRST RELEASED 1980
● UK PEAK CHART POSITION: 14
● USA PEAK CHART POSITION: 44

918 MONSTER (–) ▲
R.E.M.

A lthough not the chart monster the record company expected, this album nevertheless contained enough hit singles to satisfy. There was a self-consciously harder edge to the recording, although the trademark melodies and haunting hooks were present in small doses. 'Crush With Eyeliner' was the commercial highlight, and tracks such as 'Star 69' harked back to the punk feel of the early R.E.M. albums. The tremelo tone of Peter Buck's guitar is constant throughout, irritating some, but also reflecting the band's desire to move as far as possible from the mandolin-dominated ballads of their most recent work. Stipe's vocals were also mixed down, a perplexing move for what the band had planned as their all-out rock album.

● TRACKS: *What's The Frequency, Kenneth?; Crush With Eyeliner; King Of Comedy; I Don't Sleep, I Dream; Star 69; Strange Currencies; Tongue; Bang And Blame; I Took Your Name; Let Me In; Circus Envy; You.*

● FIRST RELEASED 1994
● UK PEAK CHART POSITION: 1
● USA PEAK CHART POSITION: 1

919 GOLD AGAINST THE SOUL (–) ▲
MANIC STREET PREACHERS

A band who can be as heavy as Metallica and as poppy as Simple Minds is no mean feat. The Manics fit the bill, with James Bradfield's stretched tonsils never having to resort to a scream to fill in for some words, such as wooooahhhh or yeahhhhhhhh. Bradfield never wastes a second, because he has a lot to say, and that is what makes the Manics a bit different from the pack; their lyrics are bitingly good, even the ones shrouded in mystery; at least they are interesting. Particular attention can be paid to 'Life Becomes A Landslide' and the observant title track.

● TRACKS: *Sleepflower; From Despair To Where; La Tristesse Durere (Scream To A Sigh); Yourself; Life Becoming A Landslide; Drug Drug Druggy; Roses In The Hospital; Nostalgic Pushead; Symphony Of Tourette; Gold Against The Soul.*

● FIRST RELEASED 1993
● UK PEAK CHART POSITION: 8
● USA PEAK CHART POSITION: did not chart

920 THE SCREAM (679) ▼
SIOUXSIE AND THE BANSHEES

D espite evolving from a group of Sex Pistols fans, Siouxsie And The Banshees eschewed the clichés of punk, offering instead an austere and bleak music. Bassist Steve Severin and drummer Kenny Morris provide simple, Teutonic-style patterns over which Siouxsie Sioux wails in the manner of former Velvet Underground chanteuse Nico. Unremitting original songs are joined by a version of the Beatles' 'Helter Skelter', which the Banshees interpret with the full knowledge of its inspiration for murderer Charles Manson. *The Scream* is an apt title for such desolate music.

● TRACKS: *Pure; Jigsaw Feeling; Overground; Carcass; Helter Skelter; Mirage; Metal Postcard; Nicotine Stain; Surburban Relapse; Switch.*

● FIRST RELEASED 1978
● UK PEAK CHART POSITION: 12
● USA PEAK CHART POSITION: did not chart

921 **BOYS FOR PELE** (–) ▲
TORI AMOS

T he artist challenges the listener to work out the hidden depths to this powerful album. The double entendre and sexual imagery of the lyrics are as much to do with the listener's imagination as with Amos's intention. This makes it work in so far as both male and female perspectives can be construed. If animals could read, they too would find this an agreeable record. The harpsichord and piano offer dramatic and sometimes brutally stark backgrounds, but for once the lyrics rule the song and the music becomes secondary. A special-edition CD features the Armand's Star mix of 'Professional Widow', the lightest moment of an intense but excellent record.

● TRACKS: *Horses; Blood Roses; Father Lucifer; Professional Widow; Professional Widow (Armand's Star Trunk Funkin' Mix); Mr Zebra; Marianne; Caught A Lite Sneeze; Muhammad My Friend; Hey Jupiter; Way Down; Little Amsterdam; Talula (The Tornado Mix); Not The Red Baron; Agent Orange; Doughnut Song; Putting The Damage On; Twinkle.*

● FIRST RELEASED 1996
● UK PEAK CHART POSITION: 39
● USA PEAK CHART POSITION: 2

 922 **YOUR ARSENAL** (501) ▼
MORRISSEY

P roduced by the late Mick Ronson, this record has incredible tension, long before the overblown and un-necessary Morrissey/Rogan feud started. Beat group echoes, doom-laden lyrics and a full atmosphere that conjures up memories of Johnny Kidd And The Pirates, the Ventures and the Pretenders. Solo artists often mellow out and mature, but on this superlative recording, Morrissey paradoxically rocks more than ever and shows further creative maturity. 'You're Gonna Need Someone On Your Side' and 'Glamorous Glue' are only two reasons to buy this album. How many more lyrical odes does he have left?

● TRACKS: *You're Gonna Need Someone On Your Side; Glamours Glue; We'll Let You Know; The National Front Disco; Certain People I Know; We Hate It When Our Friends Become Successful; You're The One For Me, Fatty; Seasick, Yet Still Docked; I Know It's Gonna Happen Someday.*

● FIRST RELEASED 1993
● UK PEAK CHART POSITION: 4
● USA PEAK CHART POSITION: 21

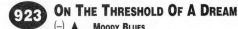
923 **ON THE THRESHOLD OF A DREAM**
(–) ▲ **MOODY BLUES**

I f you disregard the precious sleeve-note introduction written by friend of the band Lionel Bart, and ignore the spoken-word 'therefore I am' twaddle at the beginning, this is arguably their best album. The band are oozing ideas and the contrast between Ray Thomas's songs and Justin Hayward's is as refreshing as the difference between Mike Pinder's 'So Deep Within You' and John Lodge's 'To Share Our Love'. The last segment is the album's peak; Pinder's sensitive 'Have You Heard' and 'The Voyage' sum up the whole album. Never had the Mellotron been used so well and it is a great pity they became so unfashionable.

● TRACKS: *In The Beginning; Lovely To See You; Dear Diary; Send Me No Wine; To Share Our Love; So Deep Within You; Never Comes The Day; Lazy Day; Are You Sitting Comfortably; The Dream; Have You Heard Part 1; The Voyage; Have You Heard Part 2.*

● FIRST RELEASED 1969
● UK PEAK CHART POSITION: 1
● USA PEAK CHART POSITION: 20

 924 **IMPRESSIONS** (412) ▼
JOHN COLTRANE

S o this is the source of the Byrds' 'Eight Miles High'? (Yes, listen to 'India'.) Coltrane continued to influence and break barriers both within his own highly fickle cognoscenti and outside in the rock world during the mid-60s, as his contemporaries cited his massive influence. Four exquisite excursions with McCoy Tyner (piano), Jimmy Garrison and Reggie Workman (bass), Elvin Jones and Roy Haynes (drums) and Eric Dolphy playing some extraordinary bass clarinet on the aforementioned 'India'. The other *tour de force* is the similarly explorative 'Impressions'. Not easy, but absolutely worthwhile.

● TRACKS: *India; Up Against The Wall; Impressions; After The Rain.*

● FIRST RELEASED 1963
● UK PEAK CHART POSITION: did not chart
● USA PEAK CHART POSITION: did not chart

925 MONTEREY INTERNATIONAL POP FESTIVAL (384) ▼ JIMI HENDRIX / OTIS REDDING

'Yeah dig brother, it's really outasite here, didn't even rain, no buttons to push' - the opening words from Jimi Hendrix at the legendary festival as he introduces 'Like A Rolling Stone' with great humour and plays it with casual ease. The two artists on this album are probably the greatest of their genre. Both are black, one plays rock, one sings soul, one charms as the other sweats. Both were outstanding stars at this festival, and although both are dead they remain towering giants of music. Even when first released in 1970 the subtitle *Historic Performances* already expressed the importance of this album.

● TRACKS: *Like A Rolling Stone; Rock Me, Baby; Can You See Me; Wild Thing; Shake; Respect; I've Been Loving You Too Long; (I Can't Get No) Satisfaction; Try A Little Tenderness.*

● FIRST RELEASED 1970
● UK PEAK CHART POSITION: did not chart
● USA PEAK CHART POSITION: 16

927 BACK FROM RIO (−) ▲ ROGER McGUINN

McGuinn can trade off his influential work with the Byrds until he chooses to retire. He is a legendary figure and commands our respect. Finding a record deal for his newer songs took quite a while as he was without a contract for many years. This was a credible return, reminding us his distinctive sound was truly original. The chiming Rickenbacker is strongly featured, and on 'Car Phone' he even teases with a spluttering burst of the phenomenal 'Eight Miles High' guitar solo. Elsewhere he sings Elvis Costello ('You Bowed Down') and Jules Shear ('If We Never Meet Again'). For a man who had every right to be tired, this was an energetic return.

● TRACKS: *Someone To Love; Car Phone; You Bowed Down; Suddenly Blue; The Trees Are All Gone; King Of The Hill; Without Your Love; The Time Has Come; Your Love Is A Gold Mine; If We Never Meet Again.*

● FIRST RELEASED 1991
● UK PEAK CHART POSITION: did not chart
● USA PEAK CHART POSITION: 44

926 MAGICAL MYSTERY TOUR (−) ▲ THE BEATLES

The Americans saw the sense in making this an album, with a few extra tracks. In the UK it was released as a double EP, highly original but a pain to keep turning over four sides. The CD stopped all that, and we can universally benefit from some high-quality Beatles music. This album deserves better appreciation because it does contain three of Lennon's finest - the swirling 'Baby You're A Rich Man', the staggering lyrics of 'I Am The Walrus' and the pinnacle, 'Strawberry Fields Forever'. The film may have disappointed but there is enough great material here to keep any dissenter quiet.

● TRACKS: *Magical Mystery Tour; The Fool On The Hill; Flying; Blue Jay Way; Your Mother Should Know; I Am The Walrus; Hello Goodbye; Strawberry Fields Forever; Penny Lane; Baby You're A Rich Man; All You Need Is Love.*

● FIRST RELEASED 1967
● UK PEAK CHART POSITION: 31
● USA PEAK CHART POSITION: 1

928 BLUE (−) ▲ LEANN RIMES

Much fuss was made about the fact that she was only fourteen when this album hit the charts. She has a remarkably mature voice, very similar to Patsy Cline's, yet unlike in it in that she has little or no experience in affairs of the heart or bottle. 'Blue' was one of the most successful country songs for many years, and clearly kick-started this album's phenomenal chart run. Mom and Dad get plenty of thanks on the album, but it is their daughter who wins the Grammys and has an incredible delivery and talent that should be around for the next fifty years or so.

● TRACKS: *Blue; Hurt Me; One Way Ticket (Because I Can); My Baby; Honestly; The Light In Your Eyes; Talk To Me; I'll Get Even With You; Cattle Call; Good Lookin' Man; Fade To Blue.*

● FIRST RELEASED 1996
● UK PEAK CHART POSITION: did not chart
● USA PEAK CHART POSITION: 3

929 ITS A SHAME ABOUT RAY (–) ▲
LEMONHEADS

The band's leader Evan Dando received an immense amount of media coverage between this and their next album, *Come On Feel The Lemonheads*. The press saw another self-destructive rock 'n' roller in the making and hounded him about his drug habit. This album, however, is a delight and has the same feel as a Big Star record, or the rolling melody of the early Byrds, but much more sloppy and loose. Dando is a fine songwriter and the first 12 songs on this record feel like one great track. The unlucky 13th track is Paul Simon's 'Mrs Robinson', which you will either love or hate.

● TRACKS: *Rockin Stroll; Confetti; It's A Shame About Ray; Rudderless; Buddy; The Turnpike Down; Bit Part; Alison's Starting To Happen; Hannah & Gabi; Kitchen; Ceiling Fan In My Spoon; Frank Mills; Mrs Robinson.*

● FIRST RELEASED 1992
● UK PEAK CHART POSITION: 33
● USA PEAK CHART POSITION: 68

 930 THE BLUES OF LIGHTNIN' HOPKINS
(387) ▼ **LIGHTNIN' HOPKINS**

Hopkins had been a prolific recording artist in the decade following his first sessions in 1948. His stark, functional guitar style and rich Texas drawl made his work instantly recognizable. The inheritor of a blues tradition that went back to Blind Lemon Jefferson and Texas Alexander, he was an idiosyncratic musician, at his best when playing alone. His predecessors' work was reflected in his first album session, recorded by Sam Charters in January 1959. Not having recorded commercially for several years, Lightnin' was in serious mood, resulting in a set of masterful performances that carried more weight than his later, frequently arbitrary sessions. Later CD reissues have surpassed this work, simply by having more tracks.

● TRACKS: *Penitentiary Blues; Bad Luck And Trouble; Come Go Home With Me; Trouble Stay 'Way From My Door; See That My Grave Is Kept Clean; Goin' Back To Florida; Reminiscenses Of Blind Lemon; Fan It; Tell Me, Baby; She's Mine.*

● FIRST RELEASED 1959
● UK PEAK CHART POSITION: did not chart
● USA PEAK CHART POSITION: did not chart

 931 THE LOUIS ARMSTRONG STORY 1-7
(398) ▼ **LOUIS ARMSTRONG**

Legendary New Orleans trumpeter and vocalist Louis 'Satchmo' Armstrong was jazz's first instrumentalist soloist. An immensely gifted technician with a profoundly lyrical melodic conception and ringing, celebratory tone, he broke away from the entirely polyphonic New Orleans tradition to play a music that shifted the emphasis onto his (and sometimes others') individual solos. This skilfully compiled seven-volume set starts in November 1925 and ends in March 1931, and features his celebrated Hot Fives and Hot Sevens recordings, his brilliant early big band work, and the start of the concurrent interest in his extraordinary vocals.

● TRACKS: *Including - When You're Smiling; Some Of These Days; On The Sunny Side Of The Street; Solitude; When The Saints Go Marching In; Ain't Misbehavin'; Jeepers Creepers; I Want A Little Girl; Someday You'll Be Sorry; Lazy River; I Love Jazz; Mack The Knife; Muskat Ramble; Tiger Rag; When It's Sleepy Time Down South; Cabaret; Volare; Indiana; A Kiss To Build A Dream On; Hello Dolly; Blueberry Hill; St. James Infirmary; Tenderly; You'll Never Walk Alone; Mop Mop.*

● FIRST RELEASED 1988
● UK PEAK CHART POSITION: did not chart
● USA PEAK CHART POSITION: did not chart

 932 DIESEL AND DUST (–) ▲
MIDNIGHT OIL

The opening track, 'Beds Are Burning', has an infectious middle eight that goes: 'how can we dance when our earth is turning, how do we sleep while our beds are burning'. This seemingly harmless song offers irony about the plight of minority races in Australia. It continues with the second track, 'Put Down That Weapon'. By the time the record is finished the listener has learnt something about a part of the world that would not normally get any exposure. This is a clever way of getting their message across. Were the songs not so good, this could be like going back to school.

● TRACKS: *Beds Are Burning; Put Down That Weapon; Dreamworld; Arctic World; Warakurna; The Dead Heart; Whoah; Bullroarer; Sell My Soul; Sometimes; Gunbarrel Highway.*

● FIRST RELEASED 1987
● UK PEAK CHART POSITION: 19
● USA PEAK CHART POSITION: 21

933 THE MONKEES (393) ▼
THE MONKEES

Created to perform roles in a television series, the Monkees were greeted with scepticism by certain sections of the rock fraternity. The quartet may not have played the instruments on their debut album, but this does not diminish the appeal of its content. Excellent songs by Tommy Boyce and Bobby Hart formed its core, while contributions by Carole King, David Gates and group member Mike Nesmith ensure that the quality remains consistently high. Mickey Dolenz possesses the ideal pop voice and the enthusiasm generated on each performance is completely captivating. The Monkees' grasp of teen angst and melodrama is sure and, now divorced from contemporary travails, this album stands as one of the era's most entertaining debuts.

● TRACKS: *Theme From The Monkees; Saturday's Child; I Wanna Be Free; Tomorrow's Gonna Be Just Another Day; Papa Gene's Blues; Take A Giant Step; Last Train To Clarksville; This Just Doesn't Seem To Be My Day; Let's Dance On; I'll Be True To You; Sweet Young Thing; Gonna Buy Me A Dog.*

● FIRST RELEASED 1966
● UK PEAK CHART POSITION: 1
● USA PEAK CHART POSITION: 1

934 BREWING UP WITH (–) ▲
BILLY BRAGG

A man seemingly made redundant/irrelevant by the final defeat of the UK Conservative Party, there was always more to Billy Bragg's agit-prop acoustic punk songs than lefty bluster. Equally divided between Thatcher-baiting and schoolyard romance, his early works demonstrated an affinity for songwriting built on commendable empathy for his subjects. The fact that his singularly unrounded Barking accent made him incomprehensible to Americans added to his appeal for many. Though it lacks his trademark 'A New England', *Brewing Up* slightly edges out its precursor by dint of its honesty and intimacy ('The Myth Of Trust'), political instinct ('Island Of No Return' was one of a mere handful of songs to criticize the government's position in the Falklands War) and the innate adolescent charm of 'The Saturday Boy'.

● TRACKS: *It Says Here; Love Gets Dangerous; From A Vauxhall Velox; The Myth Of Trust; The Saturday Boy; Island Of No Return; This Guitar Says Sorry; Like Soldiers Do; St Swithin's Day; Strange Things Happen; A Lover Sings.*

● FIRST RELEASED 1984
● UK PEAK CHART POSITION: 16
● USA PEAK CHART POSITION: did not chart

935 THE SOUTHERN HARMONY AND MUSICAL COMPANION (404) ▼
THE BLACK CROWES

Given the sub-Stones boogie of their debut, *Shake Your Money Maker*, *The Southern Harmony* came as a quietly accomplished body of work, apparently way beyond their relative youth and experience. The *Exile On Main Street* references were still intact, but the predominant swagger and sashay had been abandoned in favour of a soulful interpretation of their roots, rather than a parody of their influences. Chris Robinson's Jagger pastiche was replaced by a more gutsy, honest strut, while brother Rich plays with an aplomb and spirit that struck darkly at the heart of their songs. A very grown-up record indeed.

● TRACKS: *Sting Me; Remedy; Thorn In My Pride; Bad Luck Blue Eyes Goodbye; Sometimes Salvation; Hotel Illness; Black Moon Creepin'; No Speak, No Slave; My Morning Song; Time Will Tell.*

● FIRST RELEASED 1992
● UK PEAK CHART POSITION: did not chart
● USA PEAK CHART POSITION: 1

936 PIANO MAN (–) ▲
BILLY JOEL

The first album to bring Joel international attention, it set down principles that marked his later career: clarity of production, annoyingly memorable tunes and distinctly suspect lyrics - like Steve Miller, Joel is not above inverting 'gin and tonic' to 'tonic and gin' for the purposes of rhyming. His vocal style was blustery even back in 1975: it is as if he bullies listeners into going along for the ride. Still, he has undeniable skill - *Piano Man* is easier to admire than to love, but few other artists ploughing the AOR furrow deliver the goods as effectively.

● TRACKS: *Travelin' Prayer; Piano Man; Ain't No Crime; You're My Home; Ballad Of Billy The Kid; Worse Comes To Worst; Stop In Nevada; If Only I Had The Words (To Tell You); Somewhere Along The Line; Captain Jack.*

● FIRST RELEASED 1973
● UK PEAK CHART POSITION: 98
● USA PEAK CHART POSITION: 27

937 **BRAVE NEW WORLD** (–) ▲
THE STEVE MILLER BAND

Although Miller no longer sells in vast quantities he does have a massive back catalogue of high-quality albums. This was during his first musical peak and followed the landmark *Sailor*. There are no weak tracks, and many are now Miller classics. He was able to move from anthemic pop with 'Kow Kow' (who had himself a pet alligator) to the acoustic 12-string simplicity of 'Seasons'. 'My Dark Hour' features an illicit cameo from Paul McCartney, a favour Miller returned nearly 30 years later on *Flaming Pie*. A memorable, foot-tapping, happy album, with some great, short, nifty guitar breaks. It is a pity the space cowboy lost his knack.

● TRACKS: *Brave New World; Celebration Song; Can't You Hear Your Daddy's Heartbeat; Got Love 'Cause You Need It; Kow Kow; Seasons; Space Cowboy; LT's Midnight Dream; My Dark Hour.*

● FIRST RELEASED 1969
● UK PEAK CHART POSITION: did not chart
● USA PEAK CHART POSITION: 22

 938 **RING A DING DING!** (–) ▲
FRANK SINATRA

The most eagerly awaited Sinatra album for a decade was in anticipation of the material that he was saving for this, his debut release on Reprise (his own label). Good as it was, it fell short of *Nice 'N' Easy*, a year earlier, which was a hard act to follow. Sinatra cruises rather than belts, as if the relief of getting away from Capitol Records had sapped his vocal strength. The Johnny Mandel arrangements are a delight and the choice of material is superb. In addition to the wonderful 'I've Got My Love To Keep Me Warm', there are two Nelson Riddle bonus tracks on the CD reissue.

● TRACKS: *Ring A Ding Ding; Let's Fall In Love; Be Careful It's My Heart; A Foggy Day; A Fine Romance; In The Still Of The Night; The Coffee Song; When I Take My Sugar To Tea; Let's Face The Music And Dance; You'd Be So Easy To Love; You And The Night And The Music; I've Got My Love To Keep Me Warm; Zing! Went The Strings Of My Heart; The Last Dance; The Second Time Around.*

● FIRST RELEASED 1961
● UK PEAK CHART POSITION: 8
● USA PEAK CHART POSITION: 4

 939 **PROMENADE** (–) ▲
THE DIVINE COMEDY

The Divine Comedy is the brainchild of Neil Hannon, a Scott Walker for the 90s, with a welcome side-order of arch humour thrown in. *Promenade* remains his most satisfying work, a concept album loosely based around a day in the life of two young lovers. With arrangements inspired by Michael Nyman and lyrics that quote freely from literature and film, *Promenade* continually borders on the pretentious. However, when Hannon's lush orchestral pop reaches its grand peaks on 'The Summerhouse' and the closing segue of 'Ten Seconds To Midnight' and 'Tonight We Fly', his overreaching ambition is spectacularly justified.

● TRACKS: *Bath; Going Downhill Fast; The Booklovers; A Seafood Song; Geronimo; Don't Look Down; When The Lights Go Out All Over Europe; The Summerhouse; Neptunes Daughter; A Drinking Song; Ten Seconds To Midnight; Tonight We Fly.*

● FIRST RELEASED 1994
● UK PEAK CHART POSITION: did not chart
● USA PEAK CHART POSITION: did not chart

 940 **THE B-52's** (383) ▼
THE B-52's

Formed in Athens, Georgia, the B-52's emerged from this nominal outback with 'Rock Lobster', a quirky pop song that drew critical praise and engendered a major recording contract. *The B-52's* maintained the originality of that debut single, with staccato voices, vox guitar and surreal lyrics. Drawing on 60s kitsch ephemera, both aurally and visually, the quintet created a unified image, but one reflecting post-modernism rather than nostalgia. A cracked sense of humour lay at the core of this album, but the group's infectious joy and sense of purpose blend with danceable rhythms to ensure a quality more enduring than mere wackiness.

● TRACKS: *Planet Claire; 52 Girls; Dance This Mess Around; Rock Lobster; Lava; There's A Moon In The Sky (Called Moon); Hero Worship; 6060-842; Downtown.*

● FIRST RELEASED 1979
● UK PEAK CHART POSITION: 22
● USA PEAK CHART POSITION: 59

941 **AKOUSTIC BAND** (–) ▲
CHICK COREA

Of the many albums that Corea has recorded and played on, and of all the many styles that he has tackled with success, none have delighted as much as this offering. A wholly satisfying union of exemplary musicians - Corea, Dave Weckl (drims) and John Patitucci (bass). Piano, bass and drum rarely fail as the perfect jazz trio and the light but meaty covers of classics such as Mercer/Kozma/Prevert's 'Autumn Leaves', Ellington's 'Sophisticated Lady' and Coltrane's 'Bessie's Blues' are gently inspired. Corea's four compositions blend into the collection like Cinderella's slipper, with Patitucci's playing particularly inspired on 'Circles'.

● TRACKS: *Bessie's Blues; My One And Only Love; So In Love; Sophisticated Lady; Autumn Leaves; Someday My Prince Will Come; Morning Sprite; T.B. C. (Terminal Baggage Caim); Circles; Spain.*

● FIRST RELEASED 1989
● UK PEAK CHART POSITION: did not chart
● USA PEAK CHART POSITION: did not chart

 943 **SONGS FROM THE WOOD** (–) ▲
JETHRO TULL

Ian Anderson's folk leanings had always crept into Tull's work. The proggy instrumental sections of albums such as *Benefit* and *Aqualung* were more medieval folk than heavy rock. He came out of the closet with this excellent album. Flute and acoustic guitar had never sounded more fitting, and there was just enough grit in Anderson's voice ('Jack-In-The-Green') to remind listeners that he was a rock 'n' roller after all. They sound like they looked on the cover of *This Was*, which was the album on which they looked like they sound on this. An undeniably earthy record from a fertile soil.

● TRACKS: *Songs From The Wood; Jack-In-The-Green; Cup Of Wonder; Hunting Girl; Ring Out, Solstice Bells; Velvet Green; The Whistler; Pibroch (Cap In Hand); Fire At Midnight.*

● FIRST RELEASED 1977
● UK PEAK CHART POSITION: 13
● USA PEAK CHART POSITION: 8

 942 **LOVE CHRONICLES** (–) ▲
AL STEWART

Stewart was part of the late 60s bedsitter folkies who went electric. John Martyn, Ralph McTell and Michael Chapman spring to mind. Stewart was a credible songwriter with a hint of a camp lisp in his voice. Women loved it, men clearly felt threatened by it. Years before 'Year Of The Cat', Stewart recorded his mammoth track 'Love Chronicles', a sort of up-tempo 'Sad Eyed Lady Of The Lowlands'. Even better was the woeful tale of a young girl falling into prostitution through a series of unlucky circumstances - 'Old Compton Street Blues' is a superb song, well worth your attention as 'the circle it turns and turns and turns so mad little girl'.

● TRACKS: *In Brooklyn; Old Compton Street Blues; Ballad Of Mary Foster; Life And Life Only; You Should Have Listened To Al; Love Chronicles.*

● FIRST RELEASED 1969
● UK PEAK CHART POSITION: did not chart
● USA PEAK CHART POSITION: did not chart

 944 **THE PAPAS AND THE MAMAS** (–) ▲
MAMAS AND PAPAS

Surprising that of the five proper Mamas And Papas albums, this one comes out on top as the one with greatest appeal. Their catalogue is now superseded by whatever 'greatest hits' package is currently available and not too many are on this. This is their understated dark album, underlining the disintegrating relationships within the band. John Philips is at his deepest, even though it is well disguised with 'Meditation Mama' and the shiny 'Safe In My Garden'. Additionally, there is proof of their remarkable vocal prowess with 'Gemini Child' and a touch of doo-wop on 'Ivy'. Whatever problems they were having does not spoil the listening pleasure, and yes, this is the best complete Mamas And Papas album.

● TRACKS: *The Right Somebody To Love; Safe In My Garden; Meditation Mama; For The Love Of Ivy; Dream A Little Dream Of Me; Mansions; Gemini Child; Nothing's Too Good For My Little Girl; Too Late; Twelve Thirty; Rooms; Midnight Voyage.*

● FIRST RELEASED 1983
● UK PEAK CHART POSITION: did not chart
● USA PEAK CHART POSITION: 50

SMASH (–) ▲
OFFSPRING

When America re-discovered punk rock in the early 90s, Offspring and Green Day were the two most obvious beneficiaries. Nostalgics they might have been, but of the two bands the Offspring always sounded more authentic, truer to the original spirit. *Smash* has some terrific, high-velocity/melodic songs. After the spoken-word pastiche 'Time To Relax', the album hits its stride with 'Nitro (Youth Energy)', a kinetic trad punk slammer with Dexter Holland doing a fearfully good imitation of the Damned's Dave Vanian. The run of songs from 'Something To Believe In' (old-style hardcore), 'Come Out And Play' (featuring cute work by Noodles) and 'Self Esteem' is pure punk rock Valhalla.

● TRACKS: *Time To Relax; Nitro (Youth Energy); Bad Habit; Gotta Get Away; Genocide; Something To Believe In; Come Out And Play; Self Esteem; It'll Be A Long Time; Killboy Powerhead; What Happened To You?; So Alone; Not The One; Smash.*

● FIRST RELEASED 1994
● UK PEAK CHART POSITION: 21
● USA PEAK CHART POSITION: 4

 MOANIN' THE BLUES (411) ▼
HANK WILLIAMS

The strong blues thread in Hank Williams' music is partially the result of having learned guitar playing from a black musician, Tee-Tot. He also suffered a great deal, and proved that real suffering has to be endured before the artist can write convincingly about misery. Songwriting does not come any better than the compact, aching poetry of 'I'm So Lonesome I Could Cry'. It is not all doom and gloom, however, on this 8-track, 10-inch album: there is the unusual chording of 'Honky Tonk Blues' and the playful yodels of 'Lovesick Blues' and 'Long Gone Lonesome Blues'. Hank Williams is the most influential man country music has ever produced, or is ever likely to. Essential.

● TRACKS: *Moanin' The Blues; I'm So Lonesome I Could Cry; My Sweet Love Ain't Around; Honky Tonk Blues; Lovesick Blues; The Blues Come Around; I'm A Long Gone Daddy; Long Gone Lonesome Blues.*

● FIRST RELEASED 1952
● UK PEAK CHART POSITION: did not chart
● USA PEAK CHART POSITION: did not chart

 CAN I HAVE MY MONEY BACK (–) ▲
GERRY RAFFERTY

Rafferty seems to have spent his life writing about his tribulations with the music business and the problems it caused with his relationships. This was the first of many albums, including those with Stealers Wheel, to address this subject. That should not cloud the enjoyment because some of his gentlest moments are here, such as 'Didn't I' and the lovely 'Mary Skeffington'. 'Sign On The Dotted Line', written with Joe Egan, is the first of the 'business' songs. Nowadays, 'Baker Street' pays the mortgage, but in the innocent times of 1971 Rafferty needed every record sale he could get. Sadly this underexposed gem of a record let him down.

● TRACKS: *New Street Blues; Didn't I; Mr Universe; Mary Skeffington; Long Way Round; Can I Have My Money Back?; Sign On The Dotted Line; Make You, Break You; To Each And Everyone; One Drink Down; Don't Count Me Out; Half A Chance; Where I Belong.*

● FIRST RELEASED 1971
● UK PEAK CHART POSITION: did not chart
● USA PEAK CHART POSITION: did not chart

LICENSED TO ILL (–) ▲
THE BEASTIE BOYS

Wholly original, the first and the best rap group to make the genre universally palatable. These Brooklyn boys succeed with a combination of tremendously exciting backgrounds, from straight riff metal (on 'Rhymin' & Stealin'' and 'She's Crafty') to sample ('The New Style'). Having learnt their art by observing rather than participating while at NYU, they sound street-cred, even though some members are positively middle-class. The Volkswagen badge-stealing craze was unknowingly started by the band, who wore the pendant in order to mock the hippies who had worn the ban-the-bomb medallion. The rap album for people who think they don't like rap.

● TRACKS: *Rhymin' & Stealin'; The New Style; She's Crafty; Posse In Effect; Slow Ride; Girls; Fight For Your Right; No Sleep Till Brooklyn; Paul Revere; Hold It Now, Hit It; Brass Monkey; Slow And Low; Time To Get Ill.*

● FIRST RELEASED 1986
● UK PEAK CHART POSITION: 7
● USA PEAK CHART POSITION: 1

949 SINATRA SWINGS (–) ▲
FRANK SINATRA

Just another in a series of indispensable albums from the master. The orchestration is predicably faultless, conducted by Billy May. Sinatra continued this run of great albums through to 1965; this time his own record company Reprise benefited, although Capitol still had a back-catalogue of classics. Opening with the familiar Rodgers and Hart's 'Falling In Love With Love', he also covered lesser-known songs such as 'Granada', previously a hit for Frankie Laine. His interpretation, with May's sparkling arrangement, was so good that they issued it as a single, and it was a sizeable hit. The album is also known as *Swing Along With Me*, to create total confusion.

● TRACKS: *Falling In Love With Love; The Curse Of An Aching Heart; Don't Cry Joe; Please Don't Talk About Me When I'm Gone; Love Walked In; Granada; I Never Knew; Don't Be That Way; Moonlight On The Ganges; It's A Wonderful World; Have You Met Miss Jones?; You're Nobody 'Til Somebody Loves You.*

● FIRST RELEASED 1961
● UK PEAK CHART POSITION: 8
● USA PEAK CHART POSITION: 6

950 MORE OF THE MONKEES (415) ▼
THE MONKEES

Clearly they were not America's answer to the Beatles, even though at the time moptop fans seethed and decided to boycott them. They were the best manufactured pop group ever, and in Michael Nesmith had a musical semi-genius. Their second album, apart from the wretched 'Your Auntie Grizelda', carries on from their debut. It contains the mantric '(I'm Not Your) Steppin' Stone', Neil Diamond's chunka-chunka-chunk 'Look Out (Here Comes Tomorrow)', the funky 'Mary Mary' and the paragon, 'I'm A Believer', also written by Neil Diamond. Euphoric and nostalgic and completely marijuana-free.

● TRACKS: *When Love Comes Knockin' (At Your Door); Mary, Mary; Hold On Girl; Your Auntie Grizelda; (I'm Not Your) Steppin' Stone; Look Out (Here Comes Tomorrow); The Kind Of Girl I Could Love; The Day We Fall In Love; Sometime In The Morning; Laugh; I'm A Believer.*

● FIRST RELEASED 1967
● UK PEAK CHART POSITION: 1
● USA PEAK CHART POSITION: 1

951 THE FAMILY THAT PLAYS TOGETHER
(–) ▲   SPIRIT

Still overlooked, the magnificent Spirit, under their guiding light Randy California, released many albums. It is their Columbia/Ode work that contains the golden age. This and *The Twelve Dreams Of Doctor Sardonicus* are the first ones to own. Here the band sound united and in full flow as the tracks blend like an opera. John Locke's piano is particularly rewarding, but then so are the songs; the jazzy summer-day feel of 'It Shall Be', the epic build-up of 'It's All The Same', the guitar-laden finale of 'Aren't You Glad' and the winsome 'Darlin' If'. The excellent CD reissue has five bonus tracks to savour.

● TRACKS: *I Got A Line On You; It Shall Be; Poor Richard; Silky Sam; Drunkard; Darlin' If; It's All The Same; Jewish; Dream Within A Dream; She Smiles; Aren't You Glad; Fog; So Little To Say; Mellow Fellow; Now Or Anywhere; Space Chile.*

● FIRST RELEASED 1968
● UK PEAK CHART POSITION: did not chart
● USA PEAK CHART POSITION: 22

952 COULDN'T STAND THE WEATHER
(684) ▼   STEVIE RAY VAUGHAN AND DOUBLE TROUBLE

Stevie Ray was already the hottest act in Austin, Texas, way before David Bowie used his guitar on 'Let's Dance'. Vaughan's 1983 debut album, *Texas Flood*, had alerted the world to a new guitar phenomenon who combined the blues power of Freddie and Albert King with the inspired ferocity of Jimi Hendrix. He made the Hendrix connection plain with his take on 'Voodoo Chile (Slight Return)', which rapidly became a concert highlight. At the other extreme was 'Tin Pan Alley', a slow blues made famous by Jimmy Wilson but now associated with the Texas hotshot. This was the time when Stevie Ray's celebrity and status among his peers was at least the equal of Eric Clapton. The pitfalls were beckoning.

● TRACKS: *Scuttle Buttin'; Couldn't Stand The Weather; Things That I Used To Do; Voodoo Chile (Slight Return); Cold Shot; Tin Pan Alley; Honey Bee; Stang's Swang.*

● FIRST RELEASED 1984
● UK PEAK CHART POSITION: did not chart
● USA PEAK CHART POSITION: 31

953 **HOW WILL THE WOLF SURVIVE** (–) ▲
LOS LOBOS

The critical breakthrough album for a refreshing sound that created Tex-Mex rock 'n' roll. The band were already a highly efficient live band by the time of this release and their confidence flows as they tackle different styles, from straight rock 'n' roll on 'I Got Loaded' to traditional Mexican folk with 'Serenata Nortena'. 'Evangeline' and 'Don't Worry Baby' are also strong album tracks, with the latter featuring a piercingly good guitar solo over a furious drum beat. The title track is the peak - the best vocal performance that Steve Winwood never sang; the resemblance to Winwood on this track is uncanny.

● TRACKS: Don't Worry Baby; A Matter Of Time; Corrido No 1; Our Last Night; The Breakdown; I Got Loaded; Serenata Nortena; Evangeline; I Got To Let You Know; Lil King Of Everything; Will The Wolf Survive.

● FIRST RELEASED 1984
● UK PEAK CHART POSITION: 77
● USA PEAK CHART POSITION: 47

955 **MODERN SOUNDS IN COUNTRY AND WESTERN MUSIC** (875) ▼ RAY CHARLES

Ray Charles had dabbled with country music at Atlantic, notably 'I'm Movin' On', but the move to ABC-Paramount prompted him to record a full album. His version of Don Gibson's 'I Can't Stop Loving You' was a transatlantic number 1 and not far behind his bittersweet performance of Eddy Arnold's 'You Don't Know Me'. Ray's own favourite was 'I Love You So Much It Hurts'. The album was so successful that he recorded a second volume and had hits with 'Take These Chains From My Heart' and 'Cryin' Time'. Although the album showed that black soul and white country could be merged, Ray Charles lost his momentum, tending to cruise along on the same theme and never again writing a song to equal 'What'd I Say'.

● TRACKS: Bye Bye Love; You Don't Know Me; Half As Much; I Love You So Much It Hurts; Just A Little Lovin'; Born To Lose; Worried Mind; It Makes No Difference Now; You Win Again; Careless Love; I Can't Stop Loving You; Hey Good Lookin'.

● FIRST RELEASED 1962
● UK PEAK CHART POSITION: 6
● USA PEAK CHART POSITION: 1

954 **NO JACKET REQUIRED** (401) ▼
PHIL COLLINS

No Jacket Required reached number 1 in more countries than you can shake a drumstick at, and shows Collins at his most mature and versatile. 'Sussudio' opens the album with the familiar death-by-drums intro, setting the pattern of strong arrangements and attacking vocals. 'Only You Know And I Know' and 'Who Said I Would' explore this territory with the vibrant assistance of the Phoenix Horns, while the massive 'One More Night' provides an elegant contrast. Surely the strongest track, however, is the elegaic 'Long Long Way To Go', which brought tears to a billion pairs of eyes as one of the highlights of Live Aid.

● TRACKS: Sussudio; Only You Know And I Know; Long Long Way To Go; Don't Want To Know; One More Night; Don't Lose My Number; Who Said I Would; Doesn't Anybody Stay Together Anymore?; Inside Out; Take Me Home.

● FIRST RELEASED 1985
● UK PEAK CHART POSITION: 1
● USA PEAK CHART POSITION: 1

956 **BERT JANSCH** (460) ▼
BERT JANSCH

Bert Jansch was the figurehead of the British 60s folk movement. An excellent composer, the owner of a remarkably expressive voice and an immensely influential guitarist, he brought an earthy, blues-based perspective to the genre which took it out of the traditional circuit without sacrificing its strengths to commerciality. This album is little short of breathtaking. Jansch combines an arresting technique, as displayed on Davey Graham's 'Angie', with a gift for graphic lyricism, chillingly exhibited on 'Needle Of Death'. Artists as diverse as Jimmy Page and Donovan (who recorded 'Do You Hear Me Now?') cited Jansch as an influence. Bert Jansch proves why.

● TRACKS: Strolling Down The Highway; Smokey River; Oh How Your Love Is Strong; I Have No Time; Finches; Rambling's Gonna Be The Death Of Me; Veronica; Needle Of Death; Do You Hear Me Now?; Alice's Wonderland; Running From Home; Courting Blues; Casbah; Dreams Of Love; Angie.

● FIRST RELEASED 1965
● UK PEAK CHART POSITION: did not chart
● USA PEAK CHART POSITION: did not chart

957 BEDSITTER IMAGES (394) ▼
AL STEWART

Stewart achieved commercial success during the 70s with a AOR style exemplified on *Year Of The Cat*. Yet he began his career as a folk singer, aiding the early work of Paul Simon and John Martyn, and recording several excellent albums, of which this was his first. Taking a cue from Donovan, Stewart sang in a light, restrained manner, describing scenes in meticulous detail and with a keenly romantic eye. Stewart's grasp of simple melody is always true and if the orchestrations are a shade overblown, they do not undermine the material's quiet strength. British folk rock took many cues from this engaging collection.

● TRACKS: *Bedsitter Images; Swiss Cottage Manoeuvres; Scandinavian Girl; Pretty Golden Hair; Denise At 16; Samuel, Oh How You've Changed!; Cleave To Me; A Long Way Down From Stephanie; Ivich; Beleeka Doodle Day.*

● FIRST RELEASED 1967
● UK PEAK CHART POSITION: did not chart
● USA PEAK CHART POSITION: did not chart

959 BELLYBUTTON (–) ▲
JELLYFISH

History has shown that there will always be a market for McCartneyesque popsters, such as Squeeze and Crowded House. However, it has also shown that said market does not chartbusters make. And so it went, when San Francisco's Jellyfish landed on the beach in 1990 with *Bellybutton*, eliciting raves from pop-starved critics and enjoying an MTV hit with 'The King Is Half-Undressed', but failing to reach the grunge-caked upper reaches of the US charts. Although writers compared them with 60s artists such as the Beatles and the Beach Boys, their hearts were in the 70s, as evidenced by their overt Queen references and their choice of Albhy Galuten, who had worked with the disco-era Bee Gees, as their producer.

● TRACKS: *The Man I Used To Be; That Is Why; The King Is Half-Undressed; I Wanna Stay Home; She Still Loves Him; All I Want Is Everything; Now She Knows She's Wrong; Bedspring Kiss; Baby's Coming Back; Calling Sarah.*

● FIRST RELEASED 1990
● UK PEAK CHART POSITION: did not chart
● USA PEAK CHART POSITION: 124

958 MUDDY WATERS AT NEWPORT (482) ▼
MUDDY WATERS

The old cover photograph of Muddy clutching John Lee Hooker's guitar gave the impression that he was at a Folk Festival rather than the prestigious Newport Jazz Festival. However, the record revealed the King of Chicago blues at his very best, shouting his music above the discordant wail of a band that included Otis Spann, James Cotton, Pat Hare and Francis Clay. Film of the event shows a sharply dressed Muddy shimmying and jiving around the stage with the energy of a man half his age. Some of that atmosphere is apparent on the record, in a programme that includes 'Hoochie Coochie Man', Big Bill Broonzy's 'I Feel So Good', recent singles 'I Got My Brand On You' and 'Soon Forgotten', and a massive 'Got My Mojo Working'. The set ends in poignant mood with the announcement of the end of the Festival and Otis Spann's improvised 'Goodbye Newport Blues'.

● TRACKS: *I Got My Brand On You; I'm Your Hoochie Koochie Man; Baby, Please Don't Go; Soon Forgotten; Tiger In Your Tank; I Feel So Good; Got My Mojo Working; Got My Mojo Working Part 2; Goodbye Newport Blues.*
● FIRST RELEASED 1960
● UK PEAK CHART POSITION: did not chart
● USA PEAK CHART POSITION: did not chart

960 BELONGING (584) ▼
KEITH JARRETT

The spine on the CD cites Keith Jarrett as the recording artist, but many regard this as a Jan Garbarek album. Jarrett was the non-Scandinavian in a superb quartet that comprised Garbarek (saxophones), Pelle Danielson (bass) and Jon Christensen (drums). Garbarek and Jarrett constantly interplay, offering melancholy, romance, sadness and emotional, musical bliss on 'Spiral Dance' and 'Blossom', and manage to groove along with the out-of-character 'Long As You Know You're Living Yours'. One of the finest moments from ECM's exceptional and now sizeable catalogue, perhaps Jarrett and Garbarek need to work together sporadically in order to spark and recharge each other.

● TRACKS: *Spiral Dance; Blossom; Long As You Know You're Living Yours; Belonging; The Windup; Solstice.*

● FIRST RELEASED 1974
● UK PEAK CHART POSITION: did not chart
● USA PEAK CHART POSITION: did not chart

961 REGGAE GREATS (-) ▲
BLACK UHURU

Duckie Simpson founded his first freedom group (Uhuru means freedom) in 1975, with little success. When the brilliant music doctors Sly And Robbie became involved, Uhuru's fortunes changed. Most of the cuts on this excellent collection are produced by the dynamic duo, and it shows. That they are such a crucial part of Black Uhuru is a testament to their ability to change the shape and sound of everything they touch. Overwhelmingly good are 'Happiness', 'Push Push' and 'World Is Africa', but the most powerful song in the catalogue is 'Youth Of Eglington'. They observed the troubled times of racial disharmony in Brixton better than most.

● TRACKS: *Happiness; World Is Africa; Sponji Reggae; Youth Of Eglington; Darkness; What Is Life; Bull In The Pen; Elements; Push Push; Right Stuff.*

● FIRST RELEASED 1985
● UK PEAK CHART POSITION: did not chart
● USA PEAK CHART POSITION: did not chart

963 JAZZ SAMBA (594) ▼
STAN GETZ

The album that launched Jobim's now classic 'Desafinado', *Jazz Samba* was released in 1962, in the early days of America's bossa nova craze and before the music lost its charm to cliché. Joined by fellow Latin jazz pioneer Charlie Byrd on classical guitar, and a discreet bass and drums team, tenor saxophonist Getz makes light and elegant music out of a collection of catchy bossas and sambas. His virtuosity, bluesy drive and smooth, soft tone make the music cook like bossa jazz rarely has since. There are still enough surprises to make this record more than just a period piece, and it stands as a fine example of Getz's lyrical genius.

● TRACKS: *Desafinado; Samba Dees Days; O Pato; Samba Triste; Samba De Uma Nota So; E Luxo So; Baia.*

● FIRST RELEASED 1962
● UK PEAK CHART POSITION: 15
● USA PEAK CHART POSITION: 1

962 THE KING AND I (519) ▼
VARIOUS

Considered by many to be an improvement on the Original Cast album that followed the show's 1951 Broadway production, this record features the unmistakable tones of the definitive 'King', Yul Brynner, but his co-star Deborah Kerr's singing voice is skilfully dubbed by one of the undisputed mistresses of that art, Marni Nixon. It is difficult to spot the point at which Kerr stops speaking and Nixon begins singing on lovely songs such as 'Shall We Dance?' and 'Getting To Know You', but, after listening to the score again on the 1993 CD reissue, it is easy to understand the album's long tenure in the UK (103 weeks) and US (178 weeks) bestsellers lists.

● TRACKS: *I Whistle A Happy Tune; My Lord And Master; Hello, Young Lovers; March Of The Siamese Children; A Puzzlement; Getting To Know You; We Kiss In A Shadow; I Have Dreamed; Shall I Tell You What I Think Of You?; Something Wonderful; Song Of The King; Shall We Dance?; Something Wonderful.*

● FIRST RELEASED 1956
● UK PEAK CHART POSITION: 4
● USA PEAK CHART POSITION: 1

964 RID OF ME (-) ▲
PJ HARVEY

The album opens with a moodily strummed guitar that builds to a climax. 'Lick my lips I'm on fire' is highly charged sexuality, yet each time the title track is played, its shocking power never fails. Other similar fare is on offer as Harvey's voice writhes like her body. This is an artist who you feel takes absolutely no prisoners, a black widow of lyricism that threatens and makes you blush with painful honesty. The only oddball is Dylan's 'Highway 61 Revisited'; her sexuality fails to work on a song that belongs to his Bobness only. Johnny Winter tried and failed as well.

● TRACKS: *Rid Of Me; Missed; Legs; Rub 'Til It Bleeds; Hook; Man-Size Sextet; Highway '61 Revisited; 50ft Queenie; Yuri-G; Man-Size; Dry; Me-Jane; Snake; Ecstasy.*

● FIRST RELEASED 1993
● UK PEAK CHART POSITION: 3
● USA PEAK CHART POSITION: 158

965 STOP THE WORLD I WANT TO GET OFF (571) ▼ ORIGINAL LONDON CAST

It was not a 'coach party' show, and this album only stayed in the UK chart for 14 weeks, but *Stop The World* proved to be the launching pad for authors and songwriters Anthony Newley and Leslie Bricusse, and remains a remarkable piece of work. Newley and his co-star Anna Quayle share some marvellous songs on this recording, including 'Typically English' and 'Someone Nice Like You', but it is the enormous hits, such as 'What Kind Of Fool Am I?', 'Once In A Lifetime', and 'Gonna Build A Mountain', for which the show is inevitably remembered. After more than 30 years, worn-out copies can now be replaced by the 1989 CD reissue.

● TRACKS: ABC; I Wanna Be Rich; Typically English; Lumbered; Gonna Build A Mountain; Glorious Russian; Melinki Meilchick; Typische Deutsche; Nag Nag Nag; All-American; Once In A Lifetime; Mumbo Jumbo; Someone Nice Like You; What Kind Of Fool Am I?

● FIRST RELEASED 1961
● UK PEAK CHART POSITION: 8
● USA PEAK CHART POSITION: did not chart

966 SOMEDAY MY PRINCE WILL COME (-) ▲ MILES DAVIS

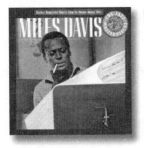

Quintessential Miles, laid-back, confident and spacious, together with, for many, his best musical unit of John Coltrane, Wynton Kelly, Paul Chambers and Philly Joe Jones, further augmented by Hank Mobley (tenor) and Jimmy Cobb. Although Coltrane was only guesting, his strong spirit is felt and his vignettes are faultless. The title track builds beautifully until a wonderful drone-like, booming bass line closes it. The other stand-out tracks are 'Pfrancing', with some glorious light fingers from Kelly and on 'Teo' the groove is very much in the *Kind Of Blue* mould. This is an exceptional Miles album that often gets overlooked.

● TRACKS: Someday My Prince Will Come; Old Folks; Pfrancing; Drad-Dog; Teo; I Thought About You.

● FIRST RELEASED 1961
● UK PEAK CHART POSITION: did not chart
● USA PEAK CHART POSITION: did not chart

967 KILL 'EM ALL (559) ▼ METALLICA

Occasionally one album can be pinpointed as the turning point in a musical genre. *Kill 'Em All* is one such album and, boy, did the heavy metal genre need a transfusion of new blood. Herein trad metal was stripped of its late-70s pomposity and reduced to its base element of brutal sonic force. The rhythm section of Burton and Ulrich do a masterful job, as does rhythm guitar ace and vocalist James Hetfield, on a set that owes a debt to punk as much as to Iron Maiden and Judas Priest. The phantasmagorical allusions are still there in the lyrics, as are some long-winded guitar solos, but otherwise *Kill 'Em All* promised a creative rebirth for hard rock.

● TRACKS: Hit The Lights; The Four Horsemen; Motorbreath; Jump In The Fire; (Anesthesia) - Pulling Teeth; Whiplash; Phantom Lord; No Remorse; Seek & Destroy; Metal Militia.

● FIRST RELEASED 1983
● UK PEAK CHART POSITION: did not chart
● USA PEAK CHART POSITION: 155

968 ESP (-) ▲ MILES DAVIS

Probably the best of a number of edgy and exciting albums recorded during one of Miles Davis's most creative periods, *ESP* dates from 1965 and features one of his greatest bands. The daring, youthful sense of adventure that tenor saxophonist Wayne Shorter, pianist Herbie Hancock, bassist Ron Carter and drummer Tony Williams brought to Davis helped relaunch his career and put him in touch with the experimental jazz spirit of the period. The new music was looser, freer, and featured abrupt changes of direction and rhythm, as the musicians responded to each other as much as to any preset scheme.

● TRACKS: ESP; Eighty One; Little One; RJ; Agitation; Iris; Mood.

● FIRST RELEASED 1965
● UK PEAK CHART POSITION: did not chart
● USA PEAK CHART POSITION: did not chart

969 STANDARDS VOL 1 (−) ▲
KEITH JARRETT

Not to forget the equal billing of drummer Jack DeJohnette and bassist Gary Peacock, without doubt Jarrett's most critically acclaimed line-up. They just know how to play together and feed off their respective dynamics. Most of Jarrett's best non-solo work has been with these two peerless musicians. Their inter-pretations are stunning, especially Bobby Troup and Leah Worth's 'Meaning Of The Blues' and an astonishingly good version of Billie Holiday's 'God Bless The Child', which after 15 minutes never once drags. Jarrett also sounds positively buoyant on the tracks he scats. *Standards Vol 2* and *Standards Live* are also essential.

● TRACKS: *Meaning Of The Blues; All The Things You Are; It Never Entered My Mind; The Masquerade Is Over; God Bless The Child.*

● FIRST RELEASED 1983
● UK PEAK CHART POSITION: did not chart
● USA PEAK CHART POSITION: did not chart

971 ELLA AND LOUIS (−) ▲
ELLA FITZGERALD & LOUIS ARMSTRONG

An inspired collaboration, masterminded by producer Norman Granz. Both artists were riding high at this stage in their careers. Granz assembled a stellar quartet of Oscar Peterson (piano), Buddy Rich (drums), Herb Ellis (guitar) and Ray Brown (bass). Equally inspired was the choice of material, with the gruffness of Armstrong's voice blending like magic with Fitzgerald's stunningly silky delivery. Outstanding are Irving Berlin's 'Cheek To Cheek' and 'Isn't This A Lovely Day', and everything else works like a dream, with the golden star going to the Gershwin brothers' 'They Can't Take That Away From Me'. Gentle and sincere, this is deserving of a place in every home.

● TRACKS: *Can't We Be Friends; Isn't This A Lovely Day; Moonlight In Vermont; They Can't Take That Away From Me; Under A Blanket Of Blue; Tenderly; A Foggy Day; Stars Fell On Alabama; Cheek To Cheek; The Nearness Of You; April In Paris.*

● FIRST RELEASED 1957
● UK PEAK CHART POSITION: did not chart
● USA PEAK CHART POSITION: 12

970 HAIR (677) ▼
ORIGINAL BROADWAY CAST

The first and best musical of the hippie peace and love generation, with a score by Gerome Ragni, James Rado and composer Galt Macdermot. The show and the album were quite different to the usual Broadway fare, but songs such as 'Aquarius', 'Good Morning Starshine', 'Let The Sunshine In' and the title number, soon went on to have a life of their own. The album spent 59 weeks in the US Top 40, 13 of them at number 1, and also did well in the UK. It was also awarded a Grammy for 'best score from an Original Cast album'.

● TRACKS: *Aquarius; Donna; Hashish; Sodomy; Colored Spade; Manchester, England; I'm Black; Ain't Got No; Air; Initials; I Got Life; Hair; My Conviction; Don't Put It Down; Frank Mills; Be-In; Where Do I Go?; Black Boys; White Boys; Easy To Be Hard; Walking In Space; Abie Baby; Three-Five-Zero-Zero; What A Piece Of Work Is Man; Good Morning Starshine; Flesh Failures (Let The Sunshine In).*

● FIRST RELEASED 1968
● UK PEAK CHART POSITION: 29
● USA PEAK CHART POSITION: 1

972 BARE WIRES (408) ▼
JOHN MAYALL

One of Mayall's bravest and best changes of style and line-ups. He enlisted some of the cream of the British jazz movement (Henry Lowther, Dick Heckstall-Smith, Chris Mercer) who, together with drummer Jon Hiseman, made a formidable, brassy album. Mayall's lyrics, although often obscured by the great musicianship, were also notable, as this was a highly reflective time in his life. The album is best enjoyed complete, as the links between songs are vital to its enjoyment, especially the Bare Wires suite containing the sad but beautiful 'I Know Now'. Guitarist Mick Taylor added the obligatory but indispensable lead breaks. Very probably his finest album.

● TRACKS: *Bare Wires Suite; Where Did I Belong; Start Walking; Open A New Door; Fire; I Know How; Look In The Mirror; I'm A Stranger; No Reply; Hartley Quits; Killing Time; She's Too Young; Sandy.*

● FIRST RELEASED 1968
● UK PEAK CHART POSITION: 3
● USA PEAK CHART POSITION: 59

973 **THROUGH THE PAST, DARKLY** (408) ▼
THE ROLLING STONES

The Stones went from being a great R&B band to the world's greatest rock 'n' roll band. Both titles are slightly dubious because much of the material on this vital package consists simply of good pop songs. This will probably also be the last time this record and its sister, *High Tide & Green Grass*, make their way into any recommendations. The recent CD packages have a bigger and better selection. CD does not yet have age on its side, unlike this record. This is the Stones (mostly) in transition, with Brian Jones still present. The hexagonal cover was brilliant but a severe pain to own as it soon began to tear.

● TRACKS: *Paint It Black; Ruby Tuesday; She's A Rainbow; Jumpin' Jack Flash; Mother's Little Helper; Let's Spend The Night Together; Honky Tonk Woman; Dandelion; 2000 Light Years From Home; Have You Seen Your Mother, Baby, Standing In The Shadow; Street Fighting Man.*

● FIRST RELEASED 1969
● UK PEAK CHART POSITION: 2
● USA PEAK CHART POSITION: 2

 975 **MIDNIGHT BLUE** (636) ▼
KENNY BURRELL

From the first sight of Reid Miles' brilliant typography on the cover you know what you are getting. Smooth smootchy jazz guitar played at the pace of a slow loris - quite magnificent in its sparing qualities. Mr. Burrell, together with Grant Green and Wes Montgomery, defined this style. 'Chitlins Con Carne' is a late-night feast while 'Midnight Blue' is smokey and soulful, and yes, Van Morrison did borrow the intro for 'Moondance'. There is subtle support from Major Holley Jnr. (bass), Bill English (drums), Ray Barretto (conga) and lustrous understated tenor from the omnipresent Stanley Turrentine.

● TRACKS: *Chitlins Con Carne; Mule; Soul Lament; Midnight Blue; Wavy Gravy; Gee Baby Ain't I Good To You; Saturday Night Blues.*

● FIRST RELEASED 1963
● UK PEAK CHART POSITION: did not chart
● USA PEAK CHART POSITION: did not chart

974 **HELLO, DOLLY!** (835) ▼
ORIGINAL BROADWAY CAST

Carol Channing had her greatest Broadway role (to date) in this hit Broadway show, and her scatty style and unmistakable squeaky voice came over perfectly on this album. The many highlights from Jerry Herman's stunning score included the tender 'It Only Takes A Moment' and 'Put On Your Sunday Clothes', but it was the title number, a good old-fashioned rouser, that won the Grammy for song of the year - in the middle of the beat boom! The album itself lingered for 58 weeks in the US Top 40, peaking at number 1.

● TRACKS: *I Put My Hand In; It Takes A Woman; Put On Your Sunday Clothes; Ribbons Down My Back; Dancing; Motherhood March; Before The Parade Passes By; Elegance; Hello, Dolly!; It Only Takes A Moment; So Long Dearie; Hello Dolly Finale.*

● FIRST RELEASED 1964
● UK PEAK CHART POSITION: did not chart
● USA PEAK CHART POSITION: 1

976 **BURGERS** (–) ▲
HOT TUNA

The magnificent, though sometimes top-heavy, splinter group formed by Jack Casady and Jorma Kaukonen from the Jefferson Airplane, Hot Tuna allowed two exceptional musicians to stretch out and explore their love of old blues. It also stopped them becoming bored while Grace Slick and Paul Katner gazed at the ocean. A strong feature of this Tuna album was the violin of Papa John Creach. They successfully mixed beautifully evocative instrumentals such as 'Highway Song' with traditional numbers like 'True Religion'. Their own blues sounded authentic, notably with the most agreeable 'Keep On Truckin''. Make a note of its tongue-in-cheek fishy lyrics, which only a Hot Tuna could sing.

● TRACKS: *True Religion; Highway Song; 99 Year Blues; Sea Child; Keep On Truckin'; Water Song; Ode For Billy Dean; Let Us Get Together Right Down Here; Sunny Day Strut.*

● FIRST RELEASED 1972
● UK PEAK CHART POSITION: did not chart
● USA PEAK CHART POSITION: 68

977 ELLA FITZGERALD SINGS THE RODGERS AND HART SONGBOOK (668) ▼ ELLA FITZGERALD

Richard Rodgers' tuneful music and Lorenz Hart's wittily amusing lyrics form a very special part of American popular music. So too does Ella Fitzgerald, and their meeting - under the benign influence of Norman Granz - is a high-water mark in the story of popular singing. The singer's unworldly and ingenuous charm suits the material and transports the listener to times without care; until, that is, the occasional tartness of a Hart lyric reminds us that life is not always a song. Along with the rest of the Songbook series, this is popular vocal music at its best and sets standards never previously attained.

● TRACKS: *Have You Met Miss Jones?; You Took Advantage Of Me; Ship Without A Sail; To Keep My Love Alive; Dancing On The Ceiling; The Lady Is A Tramp; With A Song In My Heart; Manhattan; Johnny One Note; I Wish I Were In Love Again; Spring Is Here; It Never Entered My Mind; This Can't Be Love; Thou Swell; My Romance; Where Or When; Little Girl Blue; Give It Back To The Indians; Ten Cents A Dance; There's A Small Hotel; I Don't Know What Time It Was; Everything I've Got; I Could Write A Book; Blue Room; My Funny Valentine; Bewitched; Mountain Greenery; Wait Till You See Her; Lover; Isn't It Romantic?; Here In My Arms; Blue Moon; My Heart Stood Still; I've Got Five Dollars.*

● FIRST RELEASED 1957
● UK PEAK CHART POSITION: did not chart
● USA PEAK CHART POSITION: 11

 978 SINGS SOUL BALLADS (785) ▼ OTIS REDDING

Otis Redding epitomized 60s soul, proving equally adept at up-tempo styles and reflective ballads. By devoting an entire album to the latter mode, the singer created a measured, inspirational collection. Burning versions of songs from R&B's past are adapted and infused with elegant intensity, in particular his hypnotic reading of O.V. Wright's 'That's How Strong My Love Is'. 'Mr. Pitiful', co-written with guitarist Steve Cropper, offers Redding a slightly faster perspective without breaking the mood of reflection. *Soul Ballads* is an emotional highpoint in the singer's sadly foreshortened career.

● TRACKS: *That's How Strong My Love Is; Chained And Bound; A Woman, A Lover, A Friend; Your One And Only Man; Nothing Can Change This Love; It's Too Late; For Your Precious Love; I Want To Thank You; Come To Me; Home In Your Heart; Keep Your Arms Around Me; Mr. Pitiful.*

● FIRST RELEASED 1965
● UK PEAK CHART POSITION: 30
● USA PEAK CHART POSITION: 147

 979 KIMONO MY HOUSE (-) ▲ SPARKS

Somewhere between art and glam rock, Sparks and Roxy Music were the doyens of whatever label this music is called. The familiar hit single 'This Town Ain't Big Enough For Both Of Us' is on this album, and worthy of owning simply to find out what on earth Russell Mael was singing about; for example, 'Zoo time is she and you time'. Without the lyric sheet, the lyrics are obliterated by the catchiness of the song. Meanwhile, on *Top Of The Pops*, the Adolph Hitler lookalike Brother, Ron Mael, merely stared and stood like Bill Wyman. Their finest album containing some wonderful arty pop.

● TRACKS: *This Town Ain't Big Enough For Both Of Us; Amateur Hour; Falling In Love With Myself Again; Here In Heaven; Thank God It's Not Christmas; Hasta Manana Monsieur; Talents Is An Asset; Complaints; In My Family; Equator; Barbecutie; Lost And Found.*

● FIRST RELEASED 1974
● UK PEAK CHART POSITION: 4
● USA PEAK CHART POSITION: 101

 980 HEAD HUNTERS (710) ▼ HERBIE HANCOCK

Head Hunters has spawned a thousand copies and copyists, but is only strengthened through comparison. One of the most enduring works of the 70s' jazz/funk legacy, and surely one of Herbie Hancock's most enjoyable and infectious recordings, the album was released in the deeply groovy days of 1973, and soon became the best-selling record in jazz history. Loping along on a glorious bed of springy wah-wah and synth bass, the group used all the new technology of the time, and Hancock himself seemed to revel (as he still does) in the latest keyboard sounds available to him. Jazz/funk has never again sounded so exciting and dangerous.

● TRACKS: *Chameleon; Watermelon Man; Sly; Vein Melter.*

● FIRST RELEASED 1974
● UK PEAK CHART POSITION: did not chart
● USA PEAK CHART POSITION: 13

981 **WISH** (806) ▼
THE CURE

U ndoubtedly more commercial than previous albums, *Wish* nevertheless represented the Cure doing what they do best, oblivious to prevailing musical trends. Once again, Robert Smith tore out his innards and offered them to the listener (the wrenching and chilling 'Apart'), spitting bile in 'Cut' and effectively evoking the feeling of wretched, helpless drunkenness in 'Open'. Amid the darkness, there is still time for a couple of classic pop songs, particularly the catchy 'Friday I'm In Love', and the customary obsessive love odes. Although frequently dismissed by hardcore Cure fans as too pop-orientated, *Wish* managed to strike a balance between the extremes of utter despair and intoxicating joy.

● TRACKS: *Open; High; Apart; From The Edge Of The Deep Green Sea; Wendy Time; Doing The Unstuck; Friday I'm In Love; Trust; Letter To Elise; Cut; To Wish Impossible Things; End.*

● FIRST RELEASED 1992
● UK PEAK POSITION: 1
● USA PEAK POSITION: 2

 982 **JOSEPH AND THE AMAZING TECHNICOLOR DREAMCOAT** (841) ▼

1991 LONDON CAST

S eventy three minutes of playing time from a show that originally ran for some 15 to 20 minutes, means that this album must be a recording of a contemporary production of Andrew Lloyd Webber and Tim Rice's biblical musical. In fact, it is from the highly successful 1991 London Palladium revival which starred Australian actor and pop star Jason Donovan as Joseph and Linzi Hateley as the Narrator. Donovan had a UK number 1 with 'Any Dream Will Do', and the album itself also topped the chart. Nine months after its release it was reported to have sold 500,000 copies.

● TRACKS: *Jacob And Sons; Joseph's Dreams; Poor, Poor Joseph; One More Angel In Heaven; Potiphar; Close Every Door; Go Go Go Joseph; Pharaoh Story; Poor Poor Pharaoh; Pharaoh's Dreams Explained; The Brothers Come To Egypt; Benjamin Calypso; Joseph All The Time; Jacob In Egypt; Stone The Crows; Those Canaan Days; Any Dream Will Do; Grovel Grovel; Song Of The King; Who's The Thief?*

● FIRST RELEASED 1991
● UK PEAK CHART POSITION: 1
● USA PEAK CHART POSITION: did not chart

 **983** **SHOW BOAT** (841) ▼
BROADWAY CAST

S ome acclaimed recordings were made of the 1932 Broadway production of Jerome Kern and Oscar Hammerstein II's masterpiece that reunited most of those who were in the 1927 original, with the important addition of Paul Robeson. However, this album features the cast of the 1946 revival, which, according to Hammerstein's sleeve note, was 'as fine a group as in the first company'. Kenneth Spencer plays the Robeson role and gives an inspired rendering of the classic 'Ol' Man River'. The principals include Carol Bruce, Charles Fredericks, and Jan Clayton who introduces a new song, the delightful 'Nobody Else But Me'. Felicitations to Sony Broadway for re-releasing the set on CD in 1993.

● TRACKS: *Overture; Cotton Blossom; Make Believe; Ol' Man River; Can't Help Lovin' Dat Man; Life Upon The Wicked Stage; You Are Love; Why Do I Love You?; Bill; Nobody Else But Me.*

● FIRST RELEASED 1946
● UK PEAK CHART POSITION: did not chart
● USA PEAK CHART POSITION: did not chart

 984 **RAGE AGAINST THE MACHINE** (–) ▲
RAGE AGAINST THE MACHINE

I t is easy to be sniffy about west coast rock's political pretensions, but Rage Against The Machine are nothing if not sincere (from cover artwork through to personal activism). Their 1992 debut album also demonstrated an awareness of the inherent contradictions of their existence, which few of their many critics have ever acknowledged. The music lifts elements from hip-hop and funk, but the spinal column is Tom Moreno's full-blooded chord work, which locates the group firmly within the metal pantheon. And if some of Zack de la Rocha's more cerebral moments are lost between the bluster, that's a trade-off with which RATM seem happy.

● TRACKS: *Bombtrack; Killing In The Name; Take The Power Back; Settle For Nothing; Bullet In The Head; Know Your Enemy; Wake Up; Fistful Of Steel; Township Rebellion; Freedom.*

● FIRST RELEASED 1993
● UK PEAK CHART POSITION: 17
● USA PEAK CHART POSITION: 45

985 **SPIRIT** (–) ▲
SPIRIT

H ow cool their own logo lettering looked, how the composite head cover stood out from the crowd of badly painted, dayglo, rubbish album sleeves. Spirit were just a bit more classy, not just because they were a bit jazzy and had a drummer who was in his 40s, but because they had some vision of how to fuse psych/jazz/rock. The use of strings and rock guitar is quite breathtaking; California was a precocious guitarist and Jay Ferguson's lead vocals are immaculate. The CD reissue has four bonus tracks. As the opening track, 'Fresh Garbage', states, you should 'look beneath your lid some morning'.

● TRACKS: *Fresh Garbage; Uncle Jack; Mechanical World; Taurus; Girl In Your Eye; Straight Arrow; Topanga Windows; Gramophone Man; Water Woman; The Great Canyon Fire In General; Elijah; Veruska; Free Spirit; If I Had A Woman; Elijah (alternate take).*

● FIRST RELEASED 1968
● UK PEAK CHART POSITION: did not chart
● USA PEAK CHART POSITION: 31

 986 **I STILL BELIEVE IN YOU** (836) ▼
VINCE GILL

V ince Gill wrote this album with eight song-writing partners, yet it still has a consistency and fluidity of its own. This is a truly great collection of love songs performed by a country singer with a beautiful tenor voice. Every track could make you weep but extra tissues are needed for 'One More Last Chance', I Still Believe In You' and 'Tryin' To Get Over You'. The care and attention lavished on this album is evident in every note, where nothing has been left to chance. The excellent musicians include Delbert McClinton, who played harmonica on Bruce Channel's 'Hey! Baby'.

● TRACKS: *Don't Let Our Love Start Slipping Away; No Future In The Past; Nothing Like A Woman; Tryin' To Get Over You; Say Hello; One More Last Chance; Under These Conditions; Pretty Words; Love Never Broke Anyone's Heart; I Still Believe In You.*

● FIRST RELEASED 1992
● UK PEAK CHART POSITION: did not chart
● USA PEAK CHART POSITION: 10

 **987** **FRIENDS** (–) ▲
THE BEACH BOYS

B efore *Pet Sounds* became so universally loved Brian Wilson always said that his favourite Beach Boys album was this one. This is the shortest album of their career, and very much a series of vignettes rather than songs. Nonetheless, it is a sheer delight, and one that the High Llamas tried to emulate with *Hawaii*. Dennis Wilson became noticed as a songwriter of note with 'Little Bird' and the beautiful 'Be Still'. Brian sang lead on 'Busy Doin' Nothin'', the most accurate song of his life in which he accurately directs you to his home. *Friends* passed a lot of people by, because it is so understated.

● TRACKS: *Meant For You; Friends; Wake The World; Be Here In The Morning; When A Man Needs A Woman; Passing By; Anna Lee, The Healer; Little Bird; Be Still; Busy Doin' Nothin'; Diamond Head; Transcendental Meditation.*

● FIRST RELEASED 1968
● UK PEAK CHART POSITION: 13
● USA PEAK CHART POSITION: 126

 988 **THE PAJAMA GAME** (956) ▼
ORIGINAL BROADWAY CAST

B roadway newcomers Richard Adler and Jerry Ross wrote the marvellous score for this show, which ran for well over 1,000 performances in New York. Few could have foreseen that the subject of a strike in a pyjama factory would produce great songs such as 'Hey, There', 'I'm Not At All In Love', 'Small Talk' and 'Hernando's Hideaway'. That fine singer John Raitt leads the cast, which also includes Janis Paige, Carol Haney and Eddie Foy Jnr. Every track, whether witty, romantic, or downright hilarious, is appealing on this enduring and memorable album from 1955.

● TRACKS: *Overture; The Pajama Game; Racing With The Clock; A New Town Is A Blue Town; I'm Not At All In Love; I'll Never Be Jealous Again; Hey, There; Her Is; Once A Year Day; Small Talk; There Once Was A Man; Steam Heat; Think Of The Time I Save; Hernando's Hideaway; Seven And A Half Cents; Finale.*

● FIRST RELEASED 1955
● UK PEAK CHART POSITION: did not chart
● USA PEAK CHART POSITION: did not chart

989 MADNESS (–) ▲
MADNESS

Only available on import in the UK, this was Madness's biggest album in the USA. With a track-listing that reads like a compilation, it is not difficult to see why it was so popular. Now firmly an 'establishment' band, it is easy to forget that the ska sound purveyed by Madness had its share of skinhead supporters and dubious lyrical concerns. Narrative opening lines such as 'Good morning miss/Can I help you son' ('House Of Fun') and 'Father wears his Sunday best' ('Our House') are guaranteed to make you sit back in anticipation. The cleverly barbed lyrics only add to the good-time value of these songs.

● TRACKS: *Our House; Tomorrow's Just Another Day; It Must Be Love; Primrose Hill; Shut Up; House Of Fun; Night Boat To Cairo; Rise And Fall; Blue Skinned Beast; Cardiac Arrest; Grey Day; Madness (Is All In The Mind).*

● FIRST RELEASED 1983
● UK PEAK CHART POSITION: did not chart
● USA PEAK CHART POSITION: 41

990 THE COMPLETE LIVE AT THE PLUGGED NICKEL 1965 (–) ▲   MILES DAVIS

With Wayne Shorter on sax, Herbie Hancock on piano, Ron Carter on bass and Tony Williams (just 20 years old) on drums, this is regarded as Davis's most creative line-up. *Plugged Nickel* covers seven sets over two days and is an important historical document, not least in demonstrating how the chemistry between five strong musical personalities changes between sessions. To those unable to see him live, Davis's contemporaneous studio albums created a relatively mainstream impression. It was only when this material started to emerge in 1975 that his groundbreaking work in applying chromatic techniques to classic compositions became widely appreciated.
● TRACKS: i) *If I Were A Bell; Stella By Starlight; Walkin'; I Fall In Love Too Easily; The Theme* ii) *My Funny Valentine; Four; When I Fall In Love* iii) *Agitation; 'Round About Midnight; Milestones; The Theme* iv) *All Of You; Oleo; I Fall In Love Too Easily; No Blues; I Thought About You; The Theme* v) *If I Were A Bell; Stella By Starlight; Walkin'; I Fall In Love Too Easily; The Theme* vi) *All Of You; Agitation; My Funny Valentine; On Green Dolphin Street; So What; The Theme* vii) *When I Fall In Love; Milestones; Autumn Leaves; I Fall In Love Too Easily; No Blues; The Theme* viii) *Stella By Starlight; All Blues; Yesterdays; The Theme.*
● FIRST RELEASED 1997
● UK PEAK CHART POSITION: did not chart
● USA PEAK CHART POSITION: chart

991 THICK AS A BRICK (–) ▲
JETHRO TULL

One other reason to bemoan the passing of vinyl (the other being the sound) is the flamboyant album sleeves. This one had a fold-out spoof replica of the St Cleve Chronicle, a typical local newspaper perfectly reproduced. Much reading and chortling could be had with this on one's lap. The suite of music is excellent, although the original production is muddied. It consists of one track and the CD does at least mean you do not have to get up and turn over to side two, as this really is one album that has to played right through. Make up your own mind what it's all about.

● TRACKS: *Thick As A Brick*

● FIRST RELEASED 1972
● UK PEAK CHART POSITION: 5
● USA PEAK CHART POSITION: 1

992 RUMOR AND SIGH (–) ▲
RICHARD THOMPSON

Thompson's albums with Mitchell Froom in the producer's chair tended to be hit-or-miss affairs, and at times on *Rumor And Sigh* the singer's distinctive English vocal inflections and biting guitarwork are lost in Froom's kitchen-sink approach to production. Part of Froom's problem must have been coping with Thompson's own wild stylistic approach, ranging from acoustic ballads ('1952 Vincent Black Lightning'), through radio-friendly rock ('Keep Your Distance', 'You Dream Too Much'), to demonic rock 'n' rollers ('I Feel So Good', 'Mother Knows Best'). *Rumor And Sigh* also showcases Thompson's lyrical extremes, from the intense ('I Misunderstood', 'Mystery Wind') to the throwaway ('Don't Sit On My Jimmy Shands', 'Psycho Street'), via the wonderful narrative approach of '1952 Vincent Black Lightning'.
● TRACKS: *Read About Love; I Feel So Good; I Misunderstood; Grey Walls; You Dream Too Much; Why Must I Plead; 1952 Vincent Black Lightning; Backlash Love Affair; Mystery Wind; Don't Sit On My Jimmy Shands; Keep Your Distance; Mother Knows Best; God Loves A Drunk; Psycho Street.*
● FIRST RELEASED 1991
● UK PEAK CHART POSITION: 32
● USA PEAK CHART POSITION: did not chart

993 OFFRAMP (565) ▼
PAT METHENY GROUP

Opening with some beautiful synclavier and Lyle Mays' exquisite soaring synths on 'Barcarole', this is an atmosphere album. It moves from delicacy to beauty and is arguably the most complete album of his incredible career. The delightful 'James' (a tribute to James Taylor, listen to the guitar inflections) is complemented by the awesome 'Au Lait'; and if that was not enough, this contains surely Metheny's finest moment, 'Are You Going With Me', a song that builds and builds over the most fabulous rhythm, and even after nearly nine minutes it leaves you begging for more. A stunning piece of music that is neither jazz nor rock.

● TRACKS: Barcarole; Are You Going With Me?; Au Lait; Eighteen; Offramp; James; The Bat Part II.

● FIRST RELEASED 1983
● UK PEAK CHART POSITION: did not chart
● USA PEAK CHART POSITION: 50

994 AOXOMOXOA (–) ▲
THE GRATEFUL DEAD

For a Dead album to contain so many of their regular stage numbers, it is surprising that it has sold so poorly over the years - magnificent classics such as 'St Stephen', where you can feast your ears on Phil Leshs' incredible bass playing, or the early Robert Hunter tales by listening to the story of 'Dupree's Diamond Blues'. 'High ho the carrion crow fol de roll de riddle', sings Garcia on 'Mountains Of The Moon' (hardly acid rockers) and you can feel the tremendous build-up as they start 'Cosmic Charlie', with Weir and Garcia meshing guitars. You can be forgiven for skipping 'What Becomes Of The Baby', however; most people do.

● TRACKS: St Stephen; Dupree's Diamond Blues; Rosemary; Doin' That Rag; Mountains Of The Moon; China Cat Sunflower; What's Becomes Of The Baby; Cosmic Charlie.

● FIRST RELEASED 1969
● UK PEAK CHART POSITION: did not chart
● USA PEAK CHART POSITION: 73

995 BILLIES'S BLUES (–) ▲
BILLIE HOLIDAY

An album that collects her work between 1935 and 1939. Fifteen tracks recorded with Teddy Wilson And His Orchestra, including historically important tracks such as 'The Way You Look Tonight' and 'A Sunbonnet Blue'. The remastering using 3-Dimensional Sound has removed the obligatory crackles and pops, which were standard issue in the 30s. The remaining 10 tracks are those recorded with her own orchestra, which features some excellent playing from band members such as Buck Clayton, Artie Shaw, Irving Fazola and Bunny Berigan. 'I Cried for You' and 'Night And Day' are particularly impressive. Vital stuff for any student of the magnificent Lady Day.

● TRACKS: A Sunbonnet Blue; What A Little Moonlight Can Do; Billie's Blues; Eeny Meeny Miny Mo; These 'N' That 'N' Those; One, Two, Button Your Shoe; The Way You Look Tonight; With Thee I Swing; The Man I Love; A Fine Romance; It's Like Reaching For The Moon; Let's Call A Heart A Heart; I Cried For You; No Regrets; Who Loves You?; That's Life, I Guess; On The Sentimental Side; What A Night, What A Moon, What A Boy!; I Must Have That Man; Spreadin' Rhythm Around; You Go To My Head; Yankee Doodle Never Went To Town; Night And Day; Easy To Love; Yesterdays.

● FIRST RELEASED 1935
● UK PEAK CHART POSITION: did not chart
● USA PEAK CHART POSITION: did not chart

996 IN-A-GADDA-DA-VIDA (984) ▼
IRON BUTTERFLY

For many years this late 60s heavyish extravaganza was the biggest-selling record in Atlantic's history. The reason was the title track, a meorable but ponderous 17-minute slice of self-indulgence. It is all here: drum solo (takka takka, ding ding, ba boom boom), guitar solo sounds like it's played with a tenon saw, and finally an overlong church organ solo, that needed the beef of a Hammond instead of a Vox Farfisa sound. The vocals are great, but in a strange sort of way so is the whole album. Often put down, but glorious stuff, especially the Rhino reissue with the extra tracks and the fluttering butterfly cover.

● TRACKS: Most Anything You Want; My Mirage; Termination; Are You Happy; In-A-Gadda-Da-Vida; Flowers And Beads; In-A-Gadda-Da-Vida (Live Version); In-A-Gadda-Da-Vida (Single Version).

● FIRST RELEASED 1968
● UK PEAK CHART POSITION: did not chart
● USA PEAK CHART POSITION: 4

997 LIKE SOMEONE IN LOVE (–) ▲
ELLA FITZGERALD

An album of sensitive arrangements by the underrated Frank DeVol, this collection was staple diet for 50s lounge romantics. Perched with a martini and a cherry in one of those triangular glasses, this is immaculate music. Fitzgerald stepped outside the pattern of recording the *Songbook* series and used some lesser-known writers. Both 'Hurry Home', by Meyer, Emmerick and Bernier, and 'Night Wind', by Rothberg and Pollock, are strong tracks. She later re-recorded 'How Long Has This Been Going On', while the title track is so perfect it could never be done again. The CD reissue has four bonus tracks to make this a collection by which to propose marriage.

● TRACKS: *There's A Lull In My Life; More Than You Know; What Will I Tell My Heart; I Never Had A Chance; Close Your Eyes; We'll Be Together Again; Then I'll Be Tired Of You; Like Someone In Love; Midnight Sun; I Thought About You; You're Blase; Night Wind; What's New; Hurry Home; How Long Has This Been Going On; I'll Never Be The Same; Lost In A Fog; Everything Happens To Me; So Rare.*

● FIRST RELEASED 1958
● UK PEAK CHART POSITION: did not chart
● USA PEAK CHART POSITION: did not chart

998 BAT OUT OF HELL II (–) ▲
MEAT LOAF

What a great idea: put Eddie and Jim Steinman back together again. Write some songs that sound like the 25-million-selling *Bat Out Of Hell* and call it . . . For once, whoever conceived this marketing plan was absolutely spot on. The time was right and the songs, while not up to the famous parent, were good. The lead single, 'I'd Do Anything For Love (But I Won't Do That)', featured an expensive video using a *Beauty And The Beast* theme. It helped to sell the album, but no other track on the album had quite the same power. They all sounded like Steinman/Meat Loaf songs.

● TRACKS:*I'll Do Anything For Love (But I Won't Do That); Life Is A Lemon And I Want My Money Back; Rock And Roll Dreams Come Through; It Just Won't Quit; Out Of The Frying Pan (And Into The Fire); Objects In The Rear View Mirror May Appear Closer Than They Are; Wasted Youth; Everything Louder Than Everything Else; Good Girls Go To Heaven (Bad Girls Go Everywhere); Back Into Hell; Lost Boys And Golden Girls.*

● FIRST RELEASED 1993
● UK PEAK CHART POSITION: 1
● USA PEAK CHART POSITION: 1

999 BUG (–) ▲
DINOSAUR JR

Bug opens with one of alternative rock's stellar moments, the incomparable 'Freak Scene'. Despite a teenage diet of Sham 69 and 999, frontman J. Mascis had nevertheless grown up into one hell of a tunesmith. 'Freak Scene' has it all - a devastating guitar break and simple but touching lyrics. Not only that, but Mascis and co appeared completely lethargic, to the point of indifference, about their role as saviours of the guitar in rock music. Amazing. The rest of *Bug* isn't half bad either, especially when Mascis drops some of his belligerence - 'Pond Song' is almost folksy at times. If you thought they were going soft, try closing track 'Don't' at top volume and see your speakers melt.

● TRACKS: *Freak Scene; No Bones; They Always Come; Yeah We Know; Let It Ride; Pond Song; Budge; The Post; Don't.*

● FIRST RELEASED 1988
● UK PEAK CHART POSITION: did not chart
● USA PEAK CHART POSITION: did not chart

1000 GOT MY MOJO WORKIN' (–) ▲
JIMMY SMITH

Nobody, but nobody, has ever made the Hammond organ work so hard as Smith. He is the undisputed king of jazz organ, and defined the sound of 'soul jazz' throughout the 60s. His work with arrangers such as *Oliver Nelson* represents the commercial peak of his long career. This album is one of many on the Verve label that it was cool to tuck under your arm and say that you owned. Smooth covers of 'C-Jam Blues', 'Satisfaction' and 'Hi Heel Sneakers' complement the originals as another entirely different way of playing them. The bargain CD reissue has the complete *Hoochie Coochie Man* as a fantastic bonus.

● TRACKS: *Hi-Heel Sneakers; (I Can't Get No) Satisfaction; 1-2-3; Mustard Greens; Got My Mojo Working; Johnny Come Lately; C-Jam Blues; Hobson's Hop; I'm Your Hoochie Coochie Man; One Mint Julip; Ain't That Just Like A Woman; Boom Boom; Blues And The Abstract Truth; TNT; (I Can't Get No) Satisfaction (alternate take).*

● FIRST RELEASED 1966
● UK PEAK CHART POSITION: 19 & did not chart
● USA PEAK CHART POSITION: 28 & 77

TOP 50 ARTISTS
OF ALL TIME

The Top 50 All Time Artists are listed on the right. Positions are calculated by the cumulative votes for each artist's albums that appear in the Top 1000 albums. The number of albums by each artist is shown on the far right.

The Beatles win by a mile; they are so far ahead that it is hard to imagine anybody ever being able to overtake them. Although Dylan's major albums have mostly taken a dive, his standing has increased because of the sheer number of albums in the list. *Blood On The Tracks,* however, is fast becoming *the* Dylan album.

Oasis and Radiohead have made the biggest leap; with just three albums each, theirs are the biggest successes. Further down is Miles Davis, with 13 albums, many quite lowly, but significant in their wide appeal. Frank Sinatra also has 13, although many have slipped in popularity. The poll had closed by the time he died; it would have been fascinating to see whether his death would have made a difference.

A happy surprise, for me, was Captain Beefheart having five albums in the list; maybe there is justice after all. Other pleasant shock horrors: the Pixies, Big Star and Nick Drake - for artists who could not get arrested when they were alive/current, this is a timely reminder of the power of cultism. It's a pity we took so damn long to realize their worth.

1	Beatles	14
2	Bob Dylan	12
3	Pink Floyd	10
4	Oasis	3
5	David Bowie	8
6	R.E.M.	9
7	U2	6
8	Radiohead	3
9	Rolling Stones	11
10	Nirvana	3
11	Led Zeppelin	6
12	The Beach Boys	8
13	Van Morrison	7
14	Jimi Hendrix	5
15	The Smiths	4
16	Miles Davis	13
17	Clash	4
18	Manic Street Preachers	4
19	Velvet Underground	4
20	Neil Young	9
21	Fleetwood Mac	5
22	Frank Sinatra	13
23	Marvin Gaye	6
24	Joni Mitchell	8
25	Bruce Springsteen	7
26	Byrds	6
27	Prince	4
28	Michael Jackson	5
29	Elvis Costello	9
30	Paul Simon	3
31	The Who	6
32	Captain Beefheart	5
33	The Band	4
34	Stevie Wonder	4
35	Bob Marley	6
36	Suede	3
37	Doors	5
38	Frank Zappa	8
39	Steely Dan	5
40	Smashing Pumpkins	3
41	Kate Bush	3
42	Lou Reed	4
43	Roxy Music	5
44	Elvis Presley	6
45	Grateful Dead	7
46	John Coltrane	7
47	Queen	5
48	Nick Drake	3
49	Big Star	3
50	Pixies	3

TOP 50 CHARTS BY GENRE

THE ALL TIME TOP 50 BLUES ALBUMS

1 King Of The Delta Blues Singers - Robert Johnson
2 Bluesbreakers With Eric Clapton - John Mayall And The Bluesbreakers
3 Texas Flood - Stevie Ray Vaughan
4 The Healer - John Lee Hooker
5 Peter Green's Fleetwood Mac - Fleetwood Mac
6 Live At The Regal - B.B. King
7 Damn Right I Got The Blues - Buddy Guy
8 Getting Ready - Freddie King
9 A Hard Road - John Mayall And The Bluesbreakers
10 The Sky Is Crying - Stevie Ray Vaughan
11 In Step - Stevie Ray Vaughan
12 Born Under A Bad Sign - Albert King
13 The Blues Of Lightnin' Hopkins - Lightnin' Hopkins
14 Couldn't Stand The Weather - Stevie Ray Vaughan
15 Muddy Waters At Newport - Muddy Waters
16 Bare Wires - John Mayall
17 Best Of - Muddy Waters
18 Moanin' In The Moonlight - Howlin' Wolf
19 Boss Of The Blues - Joe Turner
20 The Complete Recordings - Bessie Smith
21 Complete Library Of Congress Recordings - Lead Belly
22 The Late Fantastically Great - Elmore James
23 Just Jimmy Reed - Jimmy Reed
24 The Best Of Little Walter - Little Walter
25 Sings Down And Out Blues - Sonny Boy Williamson
26 My Kind Of Blues - B.B. King
27 The Complete Chess Folk Blues Sessions - John Lee Hooker
28 Big Maybelle - Big Maybelle
29 Muddy Waters Folk Singer - Muddy Waters
30 Getting Ready . . . - Freddie King
31 The London Howlin' Wolf Session - Howlin' Wolf
32 Gangster Of Love - Johnny 'Guitar' Watson
33 It's My Life, Baby! - Junior Wells
34 The Blues Of Otis Spann - Otis Spann
35 The Legend Of Sleepy John Estes - Sleepy John Estes
36 Second Winter - Johnny Winter
37 Hooker 'N' Heat - John Lee Hooker and Canned Heat
38 The Blues Alone - John Mayall
39 Ice Pickin' - Albert Collins
40 The Boss Man Of The Blues - Jimmy Reed
41 Blues From The Gutter - Champion Jack Dupree
42 Strong Persuader - Robert Cray
43 Showdown! - Albert Collins, Robert Cray, Johnny Copeland
44 Taj Mahal - Taj Mahal
45 Iceman - Albert Collins
46 Mr Lucky - John Lee Hooker
47 The Legendary Son House: Father Of Folk Blues - Son House
48 The Truth - T-Bone Walker
49 The Turning Point - John Mayall
50 Live At San Quentin - B.B. King

THE ALL TIME TOP 50 COUNTRY ALBUMS

1 Grievous Angel - Gram Parsons
2 The Gilded Palace Of Sin - Flying Burrito Brothers
3 Sweetheart Of The Rodeo - Byrds
4 Copperhead Road - Steve Earle
5 Red Headed Stranger - Willie Nelson
6 Guitar Town - Steve Earle
7 Johnny Cash At Folsom Prison - Johnny Cash
8 Shotgun Willie - Willie Nelson
9 Patsy Cline Showcase - Patsy Cline
10 Old No. 1 - Guy Clark
11 Johnny Cash At San Quentin - Johnny Cash
12 Blue - LeAnn Rimes
13 Moanin' The Blues - Hank Williams
14 Modern Sounds In Country And Western - Ray Charles
15 I Still Believe In You - Vince Gill
16 Come On Come On - Mary-Chapin Carpenter
17 Country Music Hall Of Fame - Jimmie Rodgers
18 Slim Whitman Favorites - Slim Whitman
19 Ramblin' Man - Hank Williams
20 Memorial Album - Hank Williams
21 Waylon & Willie - Waylon Jennings And Willie Nelson
22 Ol' Waylon - Waylon Jennings
23 Gunfighter Ballads And Trail Songs - Marty Robbins
24 Always On My Mind - Willie Nelson
25 Hank Williams Sings - Hank Williams
26 Okie From Muskogee - Merle Haggard
27 City Of New Orleans - Willie Nelson
28 Songs Our Daddy Taught Us - Everly Brothers
29 No Fences - Garth Brooks
30 Ropin' The Wind - Garth Brooks
31 Moonlight And Roses - Jim Reeves
32 Quarter Moon In A Ten Cent Town - Emmylou Harris
33 Guitars Cadillacs Etc Etc - Dwight Yoakam
34 When Tragedy Struck - Hank Snow
35 Killin' Time - Clint Black
36 If There Was A Way - Dwight Yoakam
37 Always And Forever - Randy Travis
38 My World - Eddy Arnold
39 Storms Of Life - Randy Travis
40 Trio - Dolly Parton, Linda Ronstadt, Emmylou Harris
41 Highways And Heartaches - Ricky Skaggs
42 Songs Of Tragedy - Hank Snow
43 The Sensational Charley Pride - Charley Pride
44 Same Train A Different Time - Merle Haggard
45 Salutes Hank Williams And Bob Wills - George Jones
46 Chill Of An Early Fall - George Strait
47 Changes In Latitudes, Changes In Attitudes - Jimmy Buffet
48 Joe Ely - Joe Ely
49 Garth Brooks - Garth Brooks
50 Will The Circle Be Unbroken - Nitty Gritty Dirt Band

THE ALL TIME TOP 50 FOLK ALBUMS

1 Liege And Lief - Fairport Convention
2 The Freewheelin' Bob Dylan - Bob Dylan
3 The Times They Are A Changin' - Bob Dylan
4 Kate & Anna McGarrigle - Kate & Anna McGarrigle
5 What We Did On Our Holidays - Fairport Convention
6 Unhalfbricking - Fairport Convention
7 Legend Of American Folk Blues - Woody Guthrie
8 Bob Dylan - Bob Dylan
9 The Kingston Trio At Large - Kingston Trio
10 Joan Baez In Concert - Joan Baez
11 Jack Orion - Bert Jansch
12 Miss America - Mary Margaret O'Hara
13 Here We Go Again! - Kingston Trio
14 Handful Of Earth - Dick Gaughan
15 Bert Jansch - Bert Jansch
16 Please To See The King - Steeleye Span
17 Below The Salt - Steeleye Span
18 Full House - Fairport Convention
19 The Big Wheel - Runrig
20 John Prine - John Prine
21 Ramblin' Boy - Tom Paxton
22 Joan Baez/5 - Joan Baez
23 Hard Station - Paul Brady
24 Battle Of The Field - Albion Country Band
25 Second Album - Martin Carthy
26 Chords Of Fame - Phil Ochs
27 Give A Damn - Johnstons
28 Sweet Revenge - John Prine
29 Penguin Eggs - Nic Jones
30 English Rock 'N' Roll The Early Years 1800-1850 - Oysterband
31 Norma Waterson - Norma Waterson
32 Basket Of Light - Pentangle
33 Alright Jack - Home Service
34 Joan Baez - Joan Baez
35 The Cutter And The Clan - Runrig
36 Who Knows Where The Time Goes - Judy Collins
37 Aqaba - June Tabor
38 Rise Up Like The Sun - Albion Band
39 The Things I Notice Now - Tom Paxton
40 For Pence And Spicy Ale - Watersons
41 The 5000 Spirits Or The Layers Of The Onion - Incredible String Band
42 The Book Of Invasions - Horslips
43 Deserters - Oysterband
44 Step Outside - Oysterband
45 Shifting Gravel - Four Men And A Dog
46 Last Of The True Believers - Nanci Griffith
47 Grave New World - Strawbs
48 Common Tongue - Waterson Carthy
49 Flesh And Blood - Maddy Prior
50 John Barleycorn - John Renbourn Group

THE ALL TIME TOP 50 HEAVY METAL ALBUMS

1 Led Zeppelin IV - Led Zeppelin
2 Physical Graffiti - Led Zeppelin
3 Led Zeppelin II - Led Zeppelin
4 Appetite For Destruction - Guns N'Roses
5 Metallica - Metallica
6 Led Zeppelin - Led Zeppelin
7 Master Of Puppets - Metallica
8 Back In Black - AC/DC
9 Van Halen - Van Halen
10 Houses Of The Holy - Led Zeppelin
11 Slippery When Wet - Bon Jovi
12 Blizzard Of Oz - Ozzy Osborne
13 Hysteria - Def Leppard
14 Highway To Hell - AC/DC
15 Led Zeppelin III - Led Zeppelin
16 The Number Of The Beast - Iron Maiden
17 Nothing's Shocking - Jane's Addiction
18 Paranoid - Black Sabbath
19 In Rock - Deep Purple
20 Moving Pictures - Rush
21 Machine Head - Deep Purple
22 Toys In The Attic - Aerosmith
23 Piece Of Mind - Iron Maiden
24 Ace Of Spades - Motörhead
25 Permanent Waves - Rush
26 1984 - Van Halen
27 Big Ones - Aerosmith
28 Cross Road - Bon Jovi
29 Pyromania - Def Leppard
30 Unleashed In The East - Judas Priest
31 Dressed To Kill - Kiss
32 Superunknown - Soundgarden
33 Get A Grip - Aerosmith
34 These Days - Bon Jovi
35 Permanent Vacation - Aerosmith
36 Black Sabbath - Black Sabbath
37 Space Ritual - Hawkwind
38 Rocks - Aerosmith
39 Dirt - Alice In Chains
40 For Those About To Rock We Salute You - AC/DC
41 Nine Lives - Aerosmith
42 Bad Company - Bad Company
43 Shout At The Devil - Mötley Crue
44 Misplaced Childhood - Marillion
45 Van Halen II - Van Halen
46 Burn - Deep Purple
47 Agents Of Fortune - Blue Oyster Cult
48 No Sleep Till Hammersmith - Motörhead
49 British Steel - Judas Priest
50 Use Your Illusion - Guns N'Roses

THE ALL TIME TOP 50 INDIE/PUNK ALBUMS

1 What's The Story (Morning Glory)? - Oasis
2 The Bends - Radiohead
3 Never Mind The Bollocks Here's The Sex Pistols - Sex Pistols
4 The Stone Roses - Stone Roses
5 OK Computer - Radiohead
6 The Queen Is Dead - Smiths
7 Definitely Maybe - Oasis
8 London Calling - Clash
9 Parklife - Blur
10 Dummy - Portishead
11 Be Here Now - Oasis
12 Screamadelica - Primal Scream
13 Everything Must Go - Manic Street Preachers
14 Different Class - Pulp
15 Urban Hymns - The Verve
16 Odelay - Beck
17 K - Kula Shaker
18 The Holy Bible - Manic Street Preachers
19 Blur - Blur
20 Moseley Shoals - Ocean Colour Scene
21 Dog Man Star - Suede
22 Closer - Joy Division
23 Mellon Collie And The Infinite Sadness - Smashing Pumpkins
24 The Clash - Clash
25 A Northern Soul - The Verve
26 Debut - Björk
27 Horses - Patti Smith
28 Doolittle - Pixies
29 Suede - Suede
30 Siamese Dream - Smashing Pumpkins
31 Pablo Honey - Radiohead
32 Marquee Moon - Television
33 In It For The Money - Supergrass
34 All Mod Cons - Jam
35 His'n'Hers - Pulp
36 Unknown Pleasures - Joy Division
37 BloodSugarSexMagic - Red Hot Chili Peppers
38 The Smiths - Smiths
39 Hatful Of Hollow - Smiths
40 It's Great When You're Straight . . .Yeah! - Black Grape
41 Maxinquaye - Tricky
42 The Second Coming - Stone Roses
43 The Ramones - Ramones
44 Placebo - Placebo
45 Tellin' Stories - Charlatans
46 Coming Up - Suede
47 Garbage - Garbage
48 Surfer Rosa - Pixies
49 Generation Terrorists - Manic Street Preachers
50 The New York Dolls - New York Dolls

THE ALL TIME TOP 50 JAZZ ALBUMS

1 Kind Of Blue - Miles Davis
2 A Love Supreme - John Coltrane
3 In A Silent Way - Miles Davis
4 The Blanton-Webster Years - Duke Ellington
5 Birth Of The Cool - Miles Davis
6 Sketches Of Spain - Miles Davis
7 Bitches Brew - Miles Davis
8 Charlie Parker On Dial Vols 1-6 - Charlie Parker
9 Blues And The Abstract Truth - Oliver Nelson
10 Blue Train - John Coltrane
11 Genius Of Modern Music Vols 1 & 2 - Thelonious Monk
12 Atomic Mr Basie - Count Basie
13 Lady In Autumn - Billie Holiday
14 The Complete Savoy Sessions - Charlie Parker
15 Giant Steps - John Coltrane
16 Hot Fives And Sevens 1-7 - Louis Armstrong
17 Miles Smiles - Miles Davis
18 Saxophone Colossus - Sonny Rollins
19 The Black Saint And The Sinner Lady - Charles Mingus
20 Maiden Voyage - Herbie Hancock
21 Milestones - Miles Davis
22 Complete Benny Goodman Vol 1-7 - Benny Goodman
23 Body And Soul - Coleman Hawkins
24 Gerry Mulligan Meets Ben Webster - Gerry Mulligan And Ben Webster
25 Lady In Satin - Billie Holiday
26 Mingus, Mingus, Mingus, Mingus, Mingus - Charles Mingus
27 Ella Fitzgerald Sings The Cole Porter Song Book - Ella Fitzgerald
28 The Sidewinder - Lee Morgan
29 The Koln Concert - Keith Jarrett
30 Song For My Father - Horace Silver Quintet
31 Money Jungle - Duke Ellington
32 April In Paris - Count Basie
33 Ellington Indigos - Duke Ellington
34 Hottest New Group In Jazz - Lambert, Hendricks And Ross
35 Waltz For Debby - Bill Evans
36 At Newport - Duke Ellington
37 The Revolution Will Not Be Televised - Gil Scott-Heron
38 Spirit Of Django - Martin Taylor
39 Mingus Ah Um - Charles Mingus
40 The George And Ira Gershwin Songbook - Ella Fitzgerald
41 Breezin' - George Benson
42 Facing You - Keith Jarrett
43 My Funny Valentine - Miles Davis
44 Heavy Weather - Weather Report
45 The Audience With Betty Carter - Betty Carter
46 Our Man In Paris - Dexter Gordon
47 Out To Lunch - Eric Dolphy
48 Concert By The Sea - Erroll Garner
49 Organ Grinder Swing - Jimmy Smith
50 Cookin' - Miles Davis

THE ALL TIME TOP 50 RAP ALBUMS

1 It Takes A Nation Of Millions To Hold Us Back - Public Enemy
2 Fear Of A Black Planet - Public Enemy
3 Paul's Boutique - Beastie Boys
4 3 Feet High And Rising - De La Soul
5 Follow The Leader - Eric B & Rakim
6 The Chronic - Dr. Dre
7 Paid In Full - Eric B & Rakim
8 By All Means Necessary - Boogie Down Productions
9 Ready To Die - Notorious B.I.G.
10 Enter The 36 Chambers - Wu-Tang Clan
11 Straight Outta Compton - NWA
12 Hypocrisy Is The Greatest Luxury - Disposable Heroes Of Hiphoprisy
13 The Score - Fugees
14 One For All - Brand Nubian
15 Life After Death - Notorious B.I.G.
16 The Low End Theory - A Tribe Called Quest
17 E-1999 Eternal - Bone Thugs-N-Harmony
18 Licensed To Ill - Beastie Boys
19 The Message - Grandmaster Flash & The Furious Five
20 Raising Hell - Run DMC
21 Apocalypse 91 . . . The Enemy Strikes Black - Public Enemy
22 Of The Heart, Of The Soul And Of The Cross: The Utopian Experience - PM Dawn
23 Straight Out Of The Jungle - Jungle Brothers
24 Strictly Business - EPMD
25 3 Years, 5 Months, And 2 Days In The Life Of - Arrested Development
26 Ghetto Music: The Blueprint Of Hip Hop - Boogie Down Productions
27 People's Instinctive Travels And The Paths Of Rhythm - A Tribe Called Quest
28 All Hail The Queen - Queen Latifah
29 Yo! Bum Rush The Show - Public Enemy
30 Mama Said Knock You Out - L.L. Cool J
31 OG (Original Gangster) - Ice-T
32 Cypress Hill - Cypress Hill
33 Bigger And Deffer - L.L. Cool J
34 Wanted: Dead Or Alive - Kool G Rap & DJ Polo
35 AmeriKKKa's Most Wanted - Ice Cube
36 Sleeping With The Enemy - Paris
37 I Wish My Brother George Was Here - Del Tha Funkee Homosapien
38 Return Of The Boom Bap - KRS-1
39 Blacks' Magic - Salt-N-Pepa
40 Sex Packets - Digital Underground
41 Criminal Minded - Boogie Down Productions
42 Nature Of A Sista' - Queen Latifah
43 Gangster Chronicle - London Posse
44 Midnight Marauders - A Tribe Called Quest
45 And Now The Legacy Begins - Dream Warriors
46 Step In The Arena - Gang Starr
47 Innercity Griots - Freestyle Fellowship
48 X Versus The World - Overlord X
49 Intelligent Hoodlum - Intelligent Hoodlum
50 Jazzmatazz Volume 1 - Guru

The All Time Top 50 Reggae Albums

1 Legend - Bob Marley And The Wailers
2 Catch A Fire - The Wailers
3 Natty Dread - Bob Marley And The Wailers
4 Live! - Bob Marley And The Wailers
5 Burnin' - The Wailers
6 Exodus - Bob Marley And The Wailers
7 Marcus Garvey - Burning Spear
8 Dreadlocks Dread - Big Youth
9 Dread Inna Babylon - U-Roy
10 Rastaman Vibration - Bob Marley
11 Kaya - Bob Marley And The Wailers
12 African Herbsman - Bob Marley
13 Social Living - Burning Spear
14 Equal Rights - Peter Tosh
15 Operation Radication - Yellowman
16 Mr. Mention - Buju Banton
17 Labour Of Love - UB40
18 A Dub Experience: Reggae Greats - Sly And Robbie
19 Reggae Greats - Toots And The Maytals
20 Reggae Greats - Black Uhuru
21 Right Time - Mighty Diamonds
22 Gussie Presenting - I-Roy
23 King Tubby Meets Rockers Uptown - Augustus Pablo
24 Wolf & Leopards - Dennis Brown
25 Satta Massa Gana - Abyssinians
26 The Wailing Wailers - The Wailers
27 Screaming Target - Big Youth
28 Soon Forward - Gregory Isaacs
29 Funky Kingston - Toots And The Maytals
30 Version Galore - U-Roy
31 Tease Me - Chaka Demus & Pliers
32 Flesh Of My Skin, Blood Of My Blood - Keith Hudson
33 Blackheart Man - Bunny Wailer
34 In The Dark/Roots Reggae - Toots And The Maytals
35 Heart Of The Congos - Congos
36 Love Me Forever - Carlton And His Shoes
37 Skylarking - Horace Andy
38 On Top - Heptones
39 As Raw As Ever - Shabba Ranks
40 Uprising - Bob Marley And The Wailers
41 Blackboard Jungle Dub - Upsetters
42 Version Galore, Sound Of Now - U-Roy
43 Black Woman And Child - Sizzla
44 Survival - Bob Marley And The Wailers
45 Cool Ruler - Gregory Isaacs
46 This is - Augustus Pablo
47 Choice Of Version - Prince Jazzbo
48 Natty Cultural Dread - Big Youth
49 Presenting I-Roy - I-Roy
50 Fabulous Greatest Hits - Prince Buster

THE ALL TIME TOP 50 SOUL/R&B ALBUMS

1 What's Going On - Marvin Gaye
2 Thriller - Michael Jackson
3 Songs In The Key Of Life - Stevie Wonder
4 Otis Blue - Otis Redding
5 Bad - Michael Jackson
6 Innervisions - Stevie Wonder
7 Live At The Apollo Vol. 1 - James Brown
8 Stand - Sly And The Family Stone
9 Off The Wall - Michael Jackson
10 Talking Book - Stevie Wonder
11 Secrets - Toni Braxton
12 Aretha: Lady Soul - Aretha Franklin
13 There's A Riot Going On - Sly And The Family Stone
14 Dusty In Memphis - Dusty Springfield
15 Let's Get It On - Marvin Gaye
16 HIStory Past, Present & Future, Book 1 - Michael Jackson
17 Can't Slow Down - Lionel Richie
18 I Never Loved A Man The Way I Love You - Aretha Franklin
19 Let's Stay Together - Al Green
20 Genius + Soul = Jazz - Ray Charles
21 Superfly - Curtis Mayfield
22 The Genius Of Ray Charles - Ray Charles
23 The Poet - Bobby Womack
24 3+3 - Isley Brothers
25 Crazy Sexy Cool - TLC
26 I Feel For You - Chaka Khan
27 I Want You - Marvin Gaye
28 This Is Soul - Various
29 Can't Get Enough - Barry White And The Love Unlimited Orchestra
30 The Man And His Music - Sam Cooke
31 Club Classics Volume 1 - Soul II Soul
32 Backstabbers - O'Jays
33 Complete & Unbelievable . . . The Dictionary Of Soul - Otis Redding
34 The Genius Hits The Road - Ray Charles
35 The Dock Of The Bay - Otis Redding
36 Rapture - Anita Baker
37 Fulfillingness' First Finale - Stevie Wonder
38 Trouble Man - Marvin Gaye
39 We Are One - Maze (Featuring Frankie Beverly)
40 Tell Mama - Etta James
41 Here My Dear - Marvin Gaye
42 Dangerous - Michael Jackson
43 When A Man Loves A Woman - Percy Sledge
44 What's The 411? - Mary J. Blige
45 Janet - Janet Jackson
46 Midnight Love - Marvin Gaye
47 Hot Buttered Soul - Isaac Hayes
48 You Got My Mind Messed Up - James Carr
49 The Soul Album - Otis Redding
50 Aretha Now - Aretha Franklin

ALL TIME FAVOURITE GENRES

We divided the albums into 13 categories, as they appeared in the list. It is interesting to see how the percentages worked out.

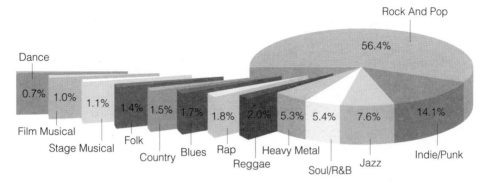

Rock And Pop 56.4%

Dance 0.7%

Film Musical 1.0%

Stage Musical 1.1%

Folk 1.4%

Country 1.5%

Blues 1.7%

Rap 1.8%

Reggae 2.0%

Heavy Metal 5.3%

Soul/R&B 5.4%

Jazz 7.6%

Indie/Punk 14.1%

ALL TIME FAVOURITE DECADES

Believe it or not, it was not the 60s.

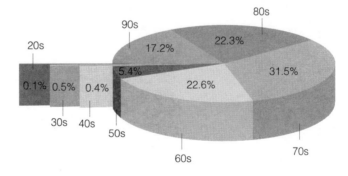

80s 22.3%

90s 17.2%

20s 0.1%

30s 0.5%

40s 0.4%

50s 5.4%

60s 22.6%

70s 31.5%

ALL TIME TOP 5 ALBUMS
BY 100 KEY ARTISTS

The recommendations for 100 key artists are purely subjective. I have approached it responsibly, and I have selected the best five albums by these artists. As for the choice of the 100 key artists, well they were also selected by the author. Complaints, as usual, to . . .

AEROSMITH
Toys In The Attic
Big Ones
Get A Grip
Permanent Vacation
Rocks

BAEZ, JOAN
Joan Baez In Concert
Joan Baez Vol 5
Farewell Angelina
Joan Baez Vol 2
Joan Baez

THE BAND
The Band
Music From Big Pink
Stage Fright
Rock Of Ages
Northern Lights-Southern Cross

BASIE, COUNT
Atomic Mr Basie
April In Paris
The Original American Decca Recordings
On My Way And Shouting Again
At Newport

THE BEACH BOYS
Pet Sounds
Surf's Up
Smiley Smile
Holland
Beach Boys Today

THE BEATLES
Revolver
Sgt. Pepper's Lonely Hearts Club Band
The Beatles (White Album)
Abbey Road
Rubber Soul

BOWIE, DAVID
The Rise And Fall Of Ziggy Stardust
Hunky Dory
Low
Station To Station
Aladdin Sane

BROWN, JAMES
Live At The Apollo Vol. 1
Pure Dynamite! Live At The Royal
Live At The Garden
I Got You (I Feel Good)
Papa's Got A Brand New Bag

BROWNE, JACKSON
Late For The Sky
For Everyman
I'm Alive
The Pretender
Jackson Browne aka Saturate Before Using

BUCKLEY, TIM
Starsailor
Goodbye & Hello
Dream Letter (Live In London, 1968)
Happy Sad
Blue Afternoon

BUSH, KATE
Hounds Of Love
The Dreaming
The Kick Inside
The Sensual World
Never For Ever

THE BYRDS
The Notorious Byrd Brothers
Younger Than Yesterday
Mr Tambourine Man
Turn! Turn! Turn!
Fifth Dimension

CAN
Future Days
Ege Bamyasi
Soon Over Babaluma
Tago Mago
Monster Movie

CAPTAIN BEEFHEART
Trout Mask Replica
Clear Spot
Safe As Milk
Strictly Personal
Lick My Decals Off Baby

CASH, JOHNNY
Johnny Cash At Folsom Prison
Johnny Cash At San Quentin
Orange Blossom Special
Ride This Train
American Recordings

CHARLES, RAY
Genius + Soul = Jazz
The Genius Of Ray Charles
The Genius Hits The Road
Modern Sounds In Country And Western
My World

CLAPTON, ERIC
461 Ocean Boulevard
MTV Unplugged
From The Cradle
Pilgrim
Slowhand

COLTRANE, JOHN
A Love Supreme
Blue Train
Giant Steps
My Favorite Things
Coltrane Jazz

COSTELLO, ELVIS
Imperial Bedroom
This Year's Model
My Aim Is True
Get Happy!!
Armed Forces

CSN FAMILY
Crosby, Stills And Nash - Crosby, Stills
    And Nash
Stephen Stills 1 - Stephen Stills
Deja Vu - Crosby, Stills, Nash And Young
If I Could Only Remember My Name -
    David Crosby
Wind On The Water - David Crosby And
    Graham Nash

THE CURE
Pornography
Kiss Me Kiss Me Kiss Me
Disintegration
Wish
Faith

DAVIS, MILES
Kind Of Blue
In A Silent Way
Birth Of The Cool
Sketches Of Spain
Bitches Brew

THE DOORS
The Doors
L.A. Woman
Morrison Hotel
Strange Days
Waiting For The Sun

DYLAN, BOB
Blonde On Blonde
Blood On The Tracks
Highway 61 Revisited
Bringing It All Back Home
The Freewheelin' Bob Dylan

ELLINGTON, DUKE
The Blanton-Webster Years
Money Jungle
Ellington Indigos
Ellington At Newport '56
Newport '58

FAIRPORT CONVENTION
Liege And Lief
What We Did On Our Holidays
Unhalfbricking
Full House
Jewel In The Crown

THE FALL
This Nation's Saving Grace
Shift Work
Dragnet
The Wonderful And Frightening World Of
Hex Enduction Hour

FITZGERALD, ELLA
Ella Fitzgerald Sings The Cole Porter
    Songbook
Ella Fitzgerald Sings The George
    And Ira Gershwin Songbook
Ella And Louis
Ella Fitzgerald Sings The Rodgers
    And Hart Songbook
Like Someone In Love

FLEETWOOD MAC
Rumours
Peter Green's Fleetwood Mac
Tango In The Night
Fleetwood Mac
Future Games

FRANKLIN, ARETHA
Aretha: Lady Soul
I Never Loved A Man The Way I Love You
Aretha Now
Soul '69
Amazing Grace

GAYE, MARVIN
What's Going On
Let's Get It On
I Want You
Trouble Man
Here My Dear

GENESIS
Selling England By The Pound
Duke
Genesis
The Lamb Lies Down On Broadway
Abacab

THE GRATEFUL DEAD
American Beauty
Workingman's Dead
Anthem Of The Sun
Live Dead
From The Mars Hotel

HARRIS, EMMYLOU
Pieces Of The Sky
Luxury Liner
Wrecking Ball
Roses In The Snow
Quarter Moon In A Ten Cent Town

HENDRIX, JIMI
Electric Ladyland
Are You Experienced
Axis: Bold As Love
Band Of Gypsies
Live At Monterey

HOOKER, JOHN LEE
The Healer
The Folk Blues Of John Lee Hooker
Mr Lucky
Don't Look Back
I'm John Lee Hooker

IRON MAIDEN
The Number Of The Beast
Piece Of Mind
Seventh Son Of A Seventh Son
Iron Maiden
No Prayer For The Dying

JACKSON, MICHAEL
Thriller
Bad
Off The Wall
HIStory Past, Present & Future, Book 1
Dangerous

JANSCH, BERT
Jack Orion
Bert Jansch
When The Circus Comes To Town
It Don't Bother Me
Nicola

JARRETT, KEITH
The Köln Concert
Facing You
Belonging
Standards Volume 1
Solo Concerts: Bremen And Lausanne

THE JEFFERSON AIRPLANE
Surrealistic Pillow
After Bathing At Baxter's
Volunteers
Crown Of Creation
Bless Its Pointed Little Head

JETHRO TULL
Stand Up
This Was
Songs From The Wood
Thick As A Brick
Aqualung

JOHN, ELTON
Goodbye Yellow Brick Road
Tumbleweed Connection
Elton John
Don't Shoot Me I'm Only The Piano Player
Captain Fantastic And The Brown Dirt
    Cowboy

KING, B.B.
Live At The Regal
Deuces Wild
Live At San Quentin
There's Always One More Time
Lucille

THE KINKS
The Kinks Are The Village Green
    Preservation Society
Face To Face
Something Else
Misfits
To The Bone

KISS
Dressed To Kill
Destroyer
Alive
Kiss
Love Gun

LED ZEPPELIN
Led Zeppelin IV
Physical Graffiti
Led Zeppelin II
Led Zeppelin
Houses Of The Holy

LITTLE FEAT
Feats Don't Fail Me Now
The Last Record Album
Sailin' Shoes
Dixie Chicken
Little Feat

MARLEY, BOB
Legend
Catch A Fire
Natty Dread
Live
Burnin'

MADONNA
Like A Prayer
Like A Virgin
Erotica
Madonna
Bedtime Stories

MARTYN, JOHN
Solid Air
Grace And Danger
Bless The Weather
Well Kept Secret
Glorious Fool

MAYALL, JOHN
Bluesbreakers With Eric Clapton
A Hard Road
Bare Wires
Turning Point
Wake Up Call

METALLICA
Metallica
Master Of Puppets
Kill 'Em All
Load
... And Justice For All

METHENY, PAT
Travels
Offramp
American Garage
As Falls Wichita, So Fall Wichita Falls
Letter From Home

MILLER, STEVE, BAND
Sailor
Fly Like An Eagle
Brave New World
Children Of The Future
Number 5

MINGUS, CHARLES
The Black Saint And The Sinner Lady
Mingus, Mingus, Mingus, Mingus,
  Mingus
Mingus Ah Um
Oh Yeah!
Jazz Composers Workshop

MITCHELL, JONI
Blue
Hejira
Court And Spark
The Hissing Of Summer Lawns
Ladies Of The Canyon

MONK, THELONIOUS
Genius Of Modern Music Volumes 1 & 2
Mysterioso
Thelonious Alone In San Francisco
Pure Monk
Monk's Music

MORRISON, VAN
Astral Weeks
Moondance
It's Too Late To Stop Now
Saint Dominic's Preview
Veedon Fleece

MULLIGAN, GERRY
Gerry Mulligan Meets Ben Webster
Jeru
What Is There To Say?
Two Of A Kind
Mulligan Plays Mulligan

NELSON, WILLIE
Red Headed Stranger
Shotgun Willie
Across The Borderline
Honeysuckle Rose
Slow Down Old World

NEWMAN, RANDY
Good Old Boys
Lonely At The Top
12 Songs
Little Criminals
Randy Newman

PETTY, TOM
Damn The Torpedoes
Full Moon Fever
Into The Great Wide Open
Southern Accents
Wildflowers

PINK FLOYD
Dark Side Of The Moon
Wish You Were Here
The Wall
The Piper At The Gates Of Dawn
Meddle

PRESLEY, ELVIS
Sun Collection
Elvis Presley
King Creole
Loving You
Elvis

PRINCE
Sign O' The Times
Purple Rain
Parade
Dirty Mind
1999

QUEEN
A Night At The Opera
Sheer Heart Attack
A Kind Of Magic
A Day At The Races
Queen 2

R.E.M.
Automatic For The People
Out Of Time
New Adventures In Hi-Fi
Green
Murmur

REDDING, OTIS
Otis Blue
Complete & Unbelievable . . .
  The Dictionary Of Soul
The Dock Of The Bay
The Soul Album
The Great Otis Redding Sings Soul Ballads

REED, LOU
Transformer
New York
Berlin
Rock N Roll Animal
Sally Can't Dance

THE ROLLING STONES
Exile On Main Street
Let It Bleed
Beggars Banquet
Sticky Fingers
Aftermath

ROXY MUSIC
For Your Pleasure
Avalon
Roxy Music
Stranded
Country Life

SANTANA
Abraxas
Santana
Caravanserai
Santana III
Shango

SIMON, PAUL
Graceland
There Goes Rhymin' Simon
The Paul Simon Songbook
Still Crazy After All These Years
Paul Simon

SINATRA, FRANK
Songs For Swingin' Lovers!
In The Wee Small Hours
Frank Sinatra Sings For Only The Lonely
Swing Easy!
A Swingin' Affair!

SMITH, JIMMY
Organ Grinder Swing
Got My Mojo Workin'
The Sermon
House Party
The Cat

THE SMITHS
The Queen Is Dead
The Smiths
Hatful Of Hollow
Meat Is Murder
Strangeways, Here We Come

SPIRIT
The Twelve Dreams Of Dr Sardonicus
Future Games
The Family That Plays Together
Spirit
Spirit Of '76

SPRINGFIELD, DUSTY
Dusty In Memphis
Everything's Coming Up Dusty
A Brand New Me
Where Am I Going?
Dusty Definitely

SPRINGSTEEN, BRUCE
Born To Run
Tunnel Of Love
Darkness At The Edge Of Town
Born In The USA
The River

SQUEEZE
East Side Story
Argybargy
Cosi Fan Tutti Frutti
Ridiculous
Cool For Cats

STEELY DAN
Countdown To Ecstasy
Can't Buy A Thrill
Pretzel Logic
Aja
Gaucho

STEWART, ROD
Every Picture Tells A Story
An Old Raincoat Will Never Let You Down
Gasoline Alley
Never A Dull Moment
Unplugged And Seated

THE STRANGLERS
Rattus Norvegicus
No More Heroes
The Raven
La Folie
Black And White

STREISAND, BARBRA
People
My Name Is Barbra
The Second Barbra Streisand Album
My Name Is Barbra, Two
Stoney End

TALKING HEADS
Remain In Light
Fear Of Music
Talking Heads '77
Stop Making Sense
More Songs About Buildings And Food

TAYLOR, JAMES
Sweet Baby James
Mud Slide Slim
J.T.
That's Why I'm Here
One Man Dog

THE TEMPTATIONS
Cloud Nine
Wish It Would Rain
Temptin' Temptations
Gettin' Ready
With A Lot O' Soul

THOMPSON, RICHARD
I Want To See The Bright Lights Tonight
  (with Linda)
Shoot Out The Lights (with Linda)
Pour Down Like Silver (with Linda)
Hand Of Kindness
Hokey And Pokey (with Linda)

TRAFFIC
The Low Spark Of High Heeled Boys
Traffic
John Barleycorn Must Die
Dear Mr Fantasy
When The Eagle Flies

UB40
Labour Of Love
Signing Off
Present Arms
Present Arms In Dub
UB44

U2
The Joshua Tree
Achtung Baby
The Unforgettable Fire
Zooropa
War

VAUGHAN, STEVIE RAY
Texas Flood
The Sky Is Crying
In Step
Couldn't Stand The Weather
Soul To Soul

WAITS, TOM
Rain Dogs
Swordfishtrombones
Blue Valentine
Small Change
Bone Machine

THE WHO
The Who Sell Out
Who's Next
Quadrophenia
Tommy
Sings My Generation

WONDER, STEVIE
Songs In The Key Of Life
Innervisions
Talking Book
Fulfillingness' First Finale
Music Of My Mind

XTC
Oranges & Lemons
Mummer
Skylarking
Nonsuch
Black Sea

YOUNG, NEIL
After The Goldrush
Harvest
Everybody Knows This Is Nowhere
Rust Never Sleeps
Tonight's The Night

ZAPPA, FRANK
Hot Rats
We're Only In It For The Money
Freak Out
Joe's Garage
One Size Fits All

ZZ TOP
Tres Hombres
Eliminator
Afterburner
Recycler
Deguello

★ *And finally . . .*

THE ALL TIME FIVE WORST ALBUMS EVER MADE

There is always at least one per collection. You know, the one you like to bring out and play to your friends. The one that is truly wretched, but you actually paid money for it!

I shelled out many times for absolute dogs. What about David Peel's *Have A Marijuana* or *Iron Butterfly Live* or Love's *False Start*? None of these were so terrible; there was a glimmer of hope or merit in them.

Sadly, I cannot say the same for the five below. The first four are absolutely diabolical. The fifth was chosen by my research editor Nic Oliver. I hope it's as bad as he says it is.

1 Lord Sutch And His Heavy Friends - Screaming Lord Sutch
2 Metal Machine Music - Lou Reed
3 Having Fun With Elvis On Stage - Elvis Presley
4 The Transformed Man - William Shatner
5 Initiation - Todd Rundgren

THE ALL TIME FIVE MOST CONSISTENTLY OVERRATED ALBUMS

Does it get up your nose as much as it does mine, that albums like the ones below sell billions of copies, and yet other excellent albums by the same artists get overlooked, and often ignored?

1 Brothers In Arms - Dire Straits
2 Rumours - Fleetwood Mac
3 Hotel California - Eagles
4 Bat Out Of Hell - Meat Loaf
5 Bridge Over Troubled Water - Simon & Garfunkel

● For *Brothers In Arms* read the debut, *Dire Straits*
● For *Rumours* read *Fleetwood Mac*, or better still, *Then Play On*.
● For *Hotel Bloody California* read *Desperado*.
● For *Bat Out Of Hell* read . . . well there isn't one actually.
● For *Bridge Over Troubled Water* read *Bookends*.

★ *Your suggestions for the last two categories please.*

TOP 1000 CHECK LIST

1 Revolver - The Beatles
2 Sgt. Pepper's Lonely Hearts Club Band - The Beatles
3 The Beatles (White Album) - The Beatles
4 Nevermind - Nirvana
5 Abbey Road - The Beatles
6 Pet Sounds - The Beach Boys
7 Automatic For The People - R.E.M.
8 The Dark Side Of The Moon - Pink Floyd
9 (What's The Story) Morning Glory? - Oasis
10 The Bends - Radiohead
11 The Rise And Fall Of Ziggy Stardust And The Spiders From Mars - David Bowie
12 Electric Ladyland - The Jimi Hendrix Experience
13 Never Mind The Bollocks Here's The Sex Pistols - Sex Pistols
14 The Stone Roses - Stone Roses
15 Astral Weeks - Van Morrison
16 Hunky Dory - David Bowie
17 Blonde On Blonde - Bob Dylan
18 The Joshua Tree - U2
19 Rumours - Fleetwood Mac
20 Rubber Soul - The Beatles
21 OK Computer - Radiohead
22 Velvet Underground & Nico - The Velvet Underground
23 The Queen Is Dead - The Smiths
24 Blood On The Tracks - Bob Dylan
25 Definitely Maybe - Oasis
26 Highway 61 Revisited - Bob Dylan
27 Exile On Main Street - The Rolling Stones
28 Achtung Baby - U2
29 London Calling - The Clash
30 Parklife - Blur
31 Wish You Were Here - Pink Floyd
32 What's Going On - Marvin Gaye
33 The Fat Of The Land - Prodigy
34 Dummy - Portishead
35 Jagged Little Pill - Alanis Morissette
36 Be Here Now - Oasis
37 Screamadelica - Primal Scream
38 Graceland - Paul Simon
39 Led Zeppelin IV - Led Zeppelin
40 Forever Changes - Love
41 Everything Must Go - Manic Street Preachers
42 Different Class - Pulp
43 Blue Lines - Massive Attack
44 Let It Bleed - The Rolling Stones
45 Urban Hymns - The Verve
46 The Wall - Pink Floyd
47 Sign 'O' The Times - Prince
48 Kind Of Blue - Miles Davis
49 The Band - The Band
50 Physical Graffiti - Led Zeppelin
51 Out Of Time - R.E.M.
52 Bridge Over Troubled Water - Simon And Garfunkel
53 Blue - Joni Mitchell

54 Odelay - Beck
55 K - Kula Shaker
56 The Holy Bible - Manic Street Preachers
57 Blur - Blur
58 Thriller - Michael Jackson
59 Hounds Of Love - Kate Bush
60 Moseley Shoals - Ocean Colour Scene
61 Trout Mask Replica - Captain Beefheart And The Magic Band
62 Dog Man Star - Suede
63 Born To Run - Bruce Springsteen
64 Music For the Jilted Generation - Prodigy
65 Songs In The Key Of Life - Stevie Wonder
66 Stanley Road - Paul Weller
67 The Doors - The Doors
68 Closer - Joy Division
69 Transformer - Lou Reed
70 Are You Experienced - The Jimi Hendrix Experience
71 Mellon Collie And The Infinite Sadness - Smashing Pumpkins
72 Woodface - Crowded House
73 After The Goldrush - Neil Young
74 The Clash - The Clash
75 The Notorious Byrd Brothers - The Byrds
76 Tubular Bells - Mike Oldfield
77 Bat Out Of Hell - Meat Loaf
78 Leftism - Leftfield
79 Purple Rain - Prince And The Revolution
80 Legend - Bob Marley
81 A Northern Soul - The Verve
82 Grace - Jeff Buckley
83 Ten - Pearl Jam
84 In Utero - Nirvana
85 Debut - Björk
86 Dig Your Own Hole - Chemical Brothers
87 A Night At The Opera - Queen
88 Horses - Patti Smith
89 Brothers In Arms - Dire Straits
90 Doolittle - Pixies
91 Bringing It All Back Home - Bob Dylan
92 Harvest - Neil Young
93 New Adventures In Hi-Fi - R.E.M.
94 Older - George Michael
95 Younger Than Yesterday - The Byrds
96 Suede - Suede
97 Songs For Swinging Lovers - Frank Sinatra
98 Little Earthquakes - Tori Amos
99 Siamese Dream - Smashing Pumpkins
100 Pablo Honey - Radiohead
101 Spice - Spice Girls
102 Tapestry - Carole King
103 Marquee Moon - Television
104 Imagine - John Lennon
105 Led Zeppelin II - Led Zeppelin
106 Beggars Banquet - The Rolling Stones
107 Sticky Fingers - The Rolling Stones
108 In It For The Money - Supergrass
109 All Mod Cons - The Jam

110 His 'N' Hers - Pulp
111 Unknown Pleasures - Joy Division
112 Appetite For Destruction - Guns N'Roses
113 Moondance - Van Morrison
114 BloodSugarSexMagik - Red Hot Chili Peppers
115 The Smiths - The Smiths
116 Otis Blue - Otis Redding
117 Bad - Michael Jackson
118 Bryter Layter - Nick Drake
119 MTV Unplugged In New York - Nirvana
120 Low - David Bowie
121 The Who Sell Out - The Who
122 A Love Supreme - John Coltrane
123 So - Peter Gabriel
124 Innervisions - Stevie Wonder
125 Hatful Of Hollow - The Smiths
126 Crosby Stills & Nash - Crosby, Stills And Nash
127 It's Great When You're Straight, Yeah! - Black Grape
128 Fun House - The Stooges
129 Maxinquaye - Tricky
130 The Velvet Underground - The Velvet Underground
131 It Takes A Nation Of Millions To Hold Us Back - Public Enemy
132 Live At The Apollo Vol. 1 - James Brown
133 Who's Next - The Who
134 Moby Grape - Moby Grape
135 Countdown To Ecstasy - Steely Dan
136 No Other - Gene Clark
137 The Second Coming - Stone Roses
138 The Piper At The Gates Of Dawn - Pink Floyd
139 Ramones - The Ramones
140 The Lexicon Of Love - ABC
141 Grievous Angel - Gram Parsons
142 A Hard Day's Night - The Beatles
143 If Only I Could Remember My Name - David Crosby
144 White On Blonde - Texas
145 Tunnel Of Love - Bruce Springsteen
146 Plastic Ono Band - John Lennon
147 Imperial Bedroom - Elvis Costello
148 August And Everything After - Counting Crows
149 Liege And Lief - Fairport Convention
150 I Want To See The Bright Lights Tonight - Richard And Linda Thompson
151 Everybody Knows This Is Nowhere - Neil Young
152 Can't Buy A Thrill - Steely Dan
153 Sun Collection - Elvis Presley
154 Placebo - Placebo
155 Stand - Sly And The Family Stone
156 Disraeli Gears - Cream
157 Third/Sister Lovers - Big Star
158 Off The Wall - Michael Jackson
159 Talking Book - Stevie Wonder

327 Some Girls - The Rolling Stones
328 Setting Sons - Jam
329 Blue Train - John Coltrane
330 In My Tribe - 10,000 Maniacs
331 The Orb's Adventures Beyond The Ultraworld - The Orb
332 Rum, Sodomy & The Lash - The Pogues
333 Please Please Me - The Beatles
334 Bandwagonesque - Teenage Fanclub
335 Let's Stay Together - Al Green
336 Synchronicity - The Police
337 Making Movies - Dire Straits
338 The Low Spark Of High Heeled Boys - Traffic
339 Genius + Soul = Jazz - Ray Charles
340 Anthem Of The Sun - The Grateful Dead
341 Unhalfbricking - Fairport Convention
342 1967-70 - The Beatles
343 Highway To Hell - AC/DC
344 The Stranger - Billy Joel
345 Endtroducing... - DJ Shadow
346 III - Led Zeppelin
347 Face Value - Phil Collins
348 Lifes Rich Pageant - R.E.M.
349 Daydream Nation - Sonic Youth
350 Nice 'n' Easy - Frank Sinatra
351 Freak Out - Frank Zappa/ Mothers Of Invention
352 After Bathing At Baxter's - Jefferson Airplane
353 Grand Prix - Teenage Fanclub
354 Future Days - Can
355 Saturday Night Fever - Various
356 The Yes Album - Yes
357 The Buddy Holly Story - Buddy Holly
358 Genius Of Modern Music Vols. 1 & 2 - Thelonious Monk
359 Superfly - Curtis Mayfield
360 Come Dance With Me - Frank Sinatra
361 On The Beach - Neil Young
362 A Salty Dog - Procol Harum
363 The Number Of The Beast - Iron Maiden
364 Bluesbreakers With Eric Clapton - John Mayall
365 Happy Trails - Quicksilver Messenger Service
366 Late For The Sky - Jackson Browne
367 Aladdin Sane - David Bowie
368 L.A.M.F. - The Heartbreakers
369 Nothing's Shocking - Jane's Addiction
370 New York - Lou Reed
371 The Genius Of Ray Charles - Ray Charles
372 Atomic Basie - Count Basie
373 September Of My Years - Frank Sinatra
374 Lady In Autumn - Billie Holiday
375 Paranoid - Black Sabbath
376 Faith - George Michael
377 Parade - Prince And The Revolution
378 Once Upon A Time - Simple Minds
379 Copperhead Road - Steve Earle
380 Oklahoma! - Various
381 Odessey & Oracle - The Zombies
382 Everclear - American Music Club
383 The Poet - Bobby Womack
384 Too-Rye-Ay - Dexy's Midnight Runners

385 3+3 - The Isley Brothers
386 Dry - PJ Harvey
387 Good Old Boys - Randy Newman
388 Texas Flood - Stevie Ray Vaughan And Double Trouble
389 Bookends - Simon And Garfunkel
390 All Things Must Pass - George Harrison
391 Exodus - Bob Marley
392 Reggatta De Blanc - The Police
393 Tracy Chapman - Tracy Chapman
394 Ege Bamyasi - Can
395 Paul's Boutique - The Beastie Boys
396 Smiley Smile - The Beach Boys
397 Dare - The Human League
398 Zuma - Neil Young
399 Stranded - Roxy Music
400 Ten Summoners Tales - Sting
401 King Of America - Elvis Costello
402 Hats - Blue Nile
403 Ommadawn - Mike Oldfield
404 With A Little Help From My Friends - Joe Cocker
405 Low-Life - New Order
406 Live At Fillmore East/The Fillmore Concerts - The Allman Brothers Band
407 I Against I - Bad Brains
408 The Hangman's Beautiful Daughter - Incredible String Band
409 Freedom - Neil Young
410 Fear Of Music - Talking Heads
411 The Complete Savoy Sessions - Charlie Parker
412 Giant Steps - John Coltrane
413 Stand Up - Jethro Tull
414 The Hot Fives And Sevens 1-7 - Louis Armstrong
415 Crazy Sexy Cool - TLC
416 Sweet Baby James - James Taylor
417 Holland - The Beach Boys
418 Gish - Smashing Pumpkins
419 Marcus Garvey - Burning Spear
420 West Side Story - Original Broadway Cast
421 The Undertones - The Undertones
422 In Rock - Deep Purple
423 Suicide - Suicide
424 Singles Going Steady - Buzzcocks
425 Selling England By The Pound - Genesis
426 Manassas - Stephen Stills Manassas
427 The Rolling Stones - The Rolling Stones
428 Something Else By The Kinks - The Kinks
429 Begin - The Millennium
430 Oranges & Lemons - XTC
431 Greatest Hits - Abba
432 A Walk Across The Rooftops - The Blue Nile
433 3 Feet High And Rising - De La Soul
434 Out Of The Blue - Electric Light Orchestra
435 Live Dead - Grateful Dead
436 Calypso - Harry Belafonte
437 Miles Smiles - Miles Davis
438 Outlandos D'Amour - The Police
439 Pretenders II - The Pretenders
440 Moving Pictures - Rush
441 Saxophone Colossus - Sonny Rollins
442 Spirit Of Eden - Talk Talk

443 Red Headed Stranger - Willie Nelson
444 Desperado - The Eagles
445 I Feel For You - Chaka Khan
446 Risqué - Chic
447 Rio - Duran Duran
448 Spring Hill Fair - The Go-Betweens
449 Volunteers - Jefferson Airplane
450 You Can't Hide Your Love Forever - Orange Juice
451 There Goes Rhymin' Simon - Paul Simon
452 Shoot Out The Lights - Richard And Linda Thompson
453 Alf - Alison Moyet
454 Machine Head - Deep Purple
455 Tumbleweed Connection - Elton John
456 Spike - Elvis Costello
457 Joe's Garage - Frank Zappa
458 I Want You - Marvin Gaye
459 Jordan: The Comeback - Prefab Sprout
460 Today - The Beach Boys
461 Oar - Alexander 'Skip' Spence
462 Future Games - Spirit
463 Sailor - Steve Miller Band
464 Heroes - David Bowie
465 Elton John - Elton John
466 Shake Some Action - Flamin' Groovies
467 Roadmaster - Gene Clark
468 Live Through This - Hole
469 Sound Affects - The Jam
470 Pearl - Janis Joplin
471 Like A Virgin - Madonna
472 Loveless - My Bloody Valentine
473 Seal - Seal
474 The Healer - John Lee Hooker
475 Veedon Fleece - Van Morrison
476 The Basement Tapes - Bob Dylan And The Band
477 Be Yourself Tonight - Eurythmics
478 Legend Of American Folk Blues - Woody Guthrie
479 Toys In The Attic - Aerosmith
480 Nebraska - Bruce Springsteen
481 King Creole - Elvis Presley
482 Follow The Leader - Eric B & Rakim
483 Music For A New Society - John Cale
484 Ladies Of The Canyon - Joni Mitchell
485 The La's - The La's
486 Dreadlocks Dread - Big Youth
487 Fly Like An Eagle - Steve Miller Band
488 The Singles 1969-1973 - Carpenters
489 The Black Saint And the Sinner Lady - Charles Mingus
490 461 Ocean Boulevard - Eric Clapton
491 Maiden Voyage - Herbie Hancock
492 World Machine - Level 42
493 Here's Little Richard - Little Richard
494 Love Is The Thing - Nat 'King' Cole
495 The Division Bell - Pink Floyd
496 Scott 3 - Scott Walker
497 Spiderland - Slint
498 Guitar Town - Steve Earle
499 This Is Soul - Various
500 Band On The Run - Wings
501 Traffic - Traffic
502 The "Chirping" Crickets - The Crickets

503 The Chronic - Dr Dre
504 Touch - Eurythmics
505 Stutter - James
506 Milestones - Miles Davis
507 Jesus Of Cool - Nick Lowe
508 Animals - Pink Floyd
509 Lonely At The Top - Randy Newman
510 Pawn Hearts - Van Der Graaf Generator
511 Five Live Yardbirds - The Yardbirds
512 John Barleycorn Must Die - Traffic
513 12 Songs - Randy Newman
514 Big Hits High Tide And Green Grass - The Rolling Stones
515 Nuggets Original Artyfacts From The First Psychedelic Era - Various Artists
516 Diva - Annie Lennox
517 Can't Get Enough - Barry White
518 Complete Benny Goodman Vols. 1-7 - Benny Goodman
519 Stranger In Town - Bob Seger
520 Body And Soul - Coleman Hawkins
521 Young Americans - David Bowie
522 Dire Straits - Dire Straits
523 New Miserable Experience - Gin Blossoms
524 Ingénue - k.d. lang
525 Metal Box - PiL
526 No More Heroes - The Stranglers
527 Tim Hardin 2 - Tim Hardin
528 Damn The Torpedoes - Tom Petty And The Heartbreakers
529 Woodstock - Various
530 Tres Hombres - ZZ Top
531 Endless Summer - The Beach Boys
532 Stage Fright - The Band
533 Peter Green's Fleetwood Mac - Fleetwood Mac
534 Don't Shoot Me I'm Only The Piano Player - Elton John
535 Johnny Cash At Folsom Prison - Johnny Cash
536 Fabulous - Little Richard
537 Country Life - Roxy Music
538 The Man And His Music - Sam Cooke
539 Kings Of The Wild Frontier - Adam And The Ants
540 Heaven Up Here - Echo And The Bunnymen
541 Piece Of Mind - Iron Maiden
542 The Dreaming - Kate Bush
543 Dizzy Heights - Lightning Seeds
544 Erotica - Madonna
545 Kick Out The Jams - The MC5
546 Ace Of Spades - Motörhead
547 Weld - Neil Young And Crazy Horse
548 Let It Be - Replacements
549 Permanent Waves - Rush
550 Club Classics Vol. One - Soul II Soul
551 Spiders - Space
552 The Dream Of The Blue Turtles - Sting
553 Breakfast In America - Supertramp
554 1984 - Van Halen
555 Gerry Mulligan Meets Ben Webster - Gerry Mulligan and Ben Webster
556 Band Of Gypsies - Jimi Hendrix
557 Back Stabbers - The O'Jays

558 Complete & Unbelievable . . . The Dictionary Of Soul - Otis Redding
559 Avalon Sunset - Van Morrison
560 The Harder They Come - Various
561 Let It Be - The Beatles
562 Lady In Satin - Billie Holiday
563 The Cars - The Cars
564 Mingus Mingus Mingus Mingus - Charles Mingus
565 Pornography - The Cure
566 The Captain And Me - The Doobie Brothers
567 Ella Fitzgerald Sings The Cole Porter Songbook - Ella Fitzgerald
568 Trust - Elvis Costello
569 This Nation's Saving Grace - The Fall
570 The Sidewinder - Lee Morgan
571 Days Of Future Passed - Moody Blues
572 The Genius Hits The Road - Ray Charles
573 Dread Inna Babylon - U-Roy
574 Big Ones - Aerosmith
575 Selected Ambient Works 1985-1992 - Aphex Twin
576 Positive Vibration - Bob Marley And The Wailers
577 Cross Road - Bon Jovi
578 Pyromania - Def Leppard
579 Paid In Full - Eric B. & Rakim
580 Revenge - Eurythmics
581 Tango In The Night - Fleetwood Mac
582 For Everyman - Jackson Browne
583 Unleashed In The East - Judas Priest
584 Dressed To Kill - Kiss
585 Throwing Copper - Live
586 Altered Beast - Matthew Sweet
587 Vengeance - New Model Army
588 Pretty Hate Machine - Nine Inch Nails
589 Peter Gabriel 3 - Peter Gabriel
590 Pour Down Like Silver - Richard And Linda Thompson
591 Shotgun Willie - Willie Nelson
592 The Köln Concert - Keith Jarrett
593 Live At The Regal - B.B. King
594 Sunflower - Beach Boys
595 Oh Mercy - Bob Dylan
596 Strictly Personal - Captain Beefheart And His Magic Band
597 Waiting For The Sun - The Doors
598 Bandstand - Family
599 Fleetwood Mac - Fleetwood Mac
600 Song For My Father - Horace Silver Quintet
601 The Dock Of The Bay - Otis Redding
602 Sheer Heart Attack - Queen
603 Superunknown - Soundgarden
604 Phil Spector's Christmas Album - Various
605 Get A Grip - Aerosmith
606 Rapture - Anita Baker
607 William Bloke - Billy Bragg
608 Kaya - Bob Marley & The Wailers
609 These Days - Bon Jovi
610 By All Means Necessary - Boogie Down Productions
611 Boston - Boston
612 Give 'Em Enough Rope - The Clash
613 Everybody Else Is Doing It, So Why Can't We - The Cranberries

614 American Dream - Crosby Stills Nash And Young
615 Kiss Me Kiss Me Kiss Me - The Cure
616 Money Jungle - Duke Ellington
617 Loving You - Elvis Presley
618 Idlewild - Everything But The Girl
619 Middle Of Nowhere - Hanson
620 I'm Your Man - Leonard Cohen
621 Berlin - Lou Reed
622 Pronounced Leh-Nerd-Skin-Nerd - Lynyrd Skynyrd
623 Seventh Sojourn - Moody Blues
624 Republic - New Order
625 Ready To Die - Notorious B.I.G.
626 Dirty Mind - Prince
627 Fulfillingness' First Finale - Stevie Wonder
628 Don't Stand Me Down - Dexy's Midnight Runners
629 Permanent Vacation - Aerosmith
630 Fontanelle - Babes In Toyland
631 Worker's Playtime - Billy Bragg
632 Prayers On Fire - Birthday Party
633 Black Sabbath - Black Sabbath
634 The Blasters - Blasters
635 Another Side Of Bob Dylan - Bob Dylan
636 April In Paris - Count Basie
637 She's So Unusual - Cyndi Lauper
638 Ellington Indigos - Duke Ellington
639 Sweet Dreams - Eurythmics
640 Heaven Or Las Vegas - Cocteau Twins
641 Future Games - Fleetwood Mac
642 Sinatra At The Sands - Frank Sinatra
643 Space Ritual Alive - Hawkwind
644 Life - Inspiral Carpets
645 I'm Alive - Jackson Browne
646 Night And Day - Joe Jackson
647 Joni Mitchell - Joni Mitchell
648 Judy At Carnegie Hall - Judy Garland
649 Hottest New Group In Jazz - Lambert, Hendricks And Ross
650 The Last Record Album - Little Feat
651 Trouble Man - Marvin Gaye
652 We Are One - Maze (Featuring Frankie Beverly)
653 Tigerlily - Natalie Merchant
654 Ram - Paul And Linda McCartney
655 A Kind Of Magic - Queen
656 Black And Blue - Rolling Stones
657 Third - Soft Machine
658 Talking Heads '77 - Talking Heads
659 Everything's Different Now - 'Til Tuesday
660 Enter The Wu-Tang (36 Chambers) - Wu-Tang Clan
661 How Dare You! - 10CC
662 Rocks - Aerosmith
663 Dirt - Alice In Chains
664 Waltz For Debby - Bill Evans
665 Bob Dylan - Bob Dylan
666 Reckless - Bryan Adams
667 Last Time Around - Buffalo Springfield
668 Lick My Decals Off, Baby - Captain Beefheart And The Magic Band
669 Cosmo's Factory - Creedence Clearwater Revival
670 Repercussion - The dB's

671 Sunshine Superman - Donovan
672 At Newport - Duke Ellington
673 One Size Fits All - Frank Zappa/ Mothers Of Invention
674 The Revolution Will Not Be Televised - Gil Scott-Heron
675 The Kick Inside - Kate Bush
676 Songs Of Love And Hate - Leonard Cohen
677 Daydream - The Lovin' Spoonful
678 Spirit Of Django - Martin Taylor
679 Modern Lovers - Modern Lovers
680 Message From The Country - The Move
681 Substance - New Order
682 Straight Outta Compton - NWA
683 My Fair Lady - Original Broadway Cast
684 The Patsy Cline Showcase - Patsy Cline
685 Heavy Soul - Paul Weller
686 Bossanova - Pixies
687 A Day At The Races - Queen
688 Hand Of Kindness - Richard Thompson
689 Crime Of The Century - Supertramp
690 Tanx - T. Rex
691 Flood - They Might Be Giants
692 South Pacific - Various
693 Sound Of Music - Original Broadway Cast
694 African Herbsman - Bob Marley And The Wailers
695 C'mon Kids - The Boo Radleys
696 Damn Right, I've Got The Blues - Buddy Guy
697 Teaser And The Firecat - Cat Stevens
698 Mingus Ah Um - Charles Mingus
699 Chicago Transit Authority - Chicago
700 Crocodiles - Echo And The Bunnymen
701 Tell Mama - Etta James
702 Shift Work - The Fall
703 Rock And Rollin' With - Fats Domino
704 Lumpy Gravy - Frank Zappa
705 Getting Ready... - Freddie King
706 Bluejean Bop! - Gene Vincent
707 The Sound Of 65 - The Graham Bond Organization
708 Dookie - Green Day
709 The Idiot - Iggy Pop
710 Between The Lines - Janis Ian
711 Crown Of Creation - Jefferson Airplane
712 Joe Cocker! - Joe Cocker
713 Joy Of A Toy - Kevin Ayers
714 The Kingston Trio At Large - The Kingston Trio
715 The Man-Machine - Kraftwerk
716 New York Tendaberry - Laura Nyro
717 Songs From A Room - Leonard Cohen
718 Sailin' Shoes - Little Feat
719 Vivid - Living Colour
720 Here My Dear - Marvin Gaye
721 Dangerous - Michael Jackson
722 In Search Of The Lost Chord - Moody Blues
723 Viva Hate - Morrissey
724 Mott The Hoople - Mott The Hoople
725 Vs - Pearl Jam
726 When A Man Loves A Woman - Percy Sledge
727 Hello, I Must Be Going - Phil Collins

728 Reckoning - R.E.M.
729 Little Criminals - Randy Newman
730 Arc Of A Diver - Steve Winwood
731 Rattle And Hum - U2
732 Hymns To The Silence - Van Morrison
733 Easy Rider - Various
734 Violent Femmes - Violent Femmes
735 Pink Flag - Wire
736 Fragile - Yes
737 Elephant Mountain - The Youngbloods
738 For Those About To Rock AC/DC
739 Nine Lives - Aerosmith
740 Bad Company - Bad Company
741 Star - Belly
742 Nick Of Time - Bonnie Raitt
743 Social Living - Burning Spear
744 Tea For The Tillerman - Cat Stevens
745 I Feel Like I'm Fixin' To Die - Country Joe And The Fish
746 Disintegration - The Cure
747 Damned Damned Damned - The Damned
748 Hypocrisy Is The Greatest Luxury - Disposable Heroes Of Hiphoprisy
749 The George And Ira Gershwin Songbook - Ella Fitzgerald
750 Blood And Chocolate - Elvis Costello
751 Brain Salad Surgery - Emerson, Lake And Palmer
752 Eden - Everything But The Girl
753 Music In A Doll's House - Family
754 The Score - Fugees
755 Breezin' - George Benson
756 From The Mars Hotel - Grateful Dead
757 Old No. 1 - Guy Clark
758 Pills 'N' Thrills And Bellyaches - Happy Mondays
759 Tuesday Night Music Club - Sheryl Crow
760 The Pretender - Jackson Browne
761 Joan Baez In Concert - Joan Baez
762 A Hard Road - John Mayall And The Bluesbreakers
763 Facing You - Keith Jarrett
764 Autobahn - Kraftwerk
765 Rock 'N' Roll Animal - Lou Reed
766 What's The 411? - Mary J. Blige
767 100% Fun - Matthew Sweet
768 My Funny Valentine - Miles Davis
769 Shout At The Devil - Mötley Crüe
770 Texas Fever - Orange Juice
771 The Paul Simon Songbook - Paul Simon
772 Equal Rights - Peter Tosh
773 Randy Newman - Randy Newman
774 Gaucho - Steely Dan
775 Dream Letter (Live In London 1968) - Tim Buckley
776 Oliver! - Various
777 Heavy Weather - Weather Report
778 Goodbye Jumbo - World Party
779 Misplaced Childhood - Marillion
780 Janet - Janet Jackson
781 The Sky Is Crying - Stevie Ray Vaughan And Double Trouble
782 Operation Radication - Yellowman
783 Escape - Journey

784 Midnight Love - Marvin Gaye
785 Heart - Heart
786 Going For The One - Yes
787 Bring The Family - John Hiatt
788 I Just Can't Stop It - The Beat
789 Beatles For Sale - The Beatles
790 The Audience With Betty Carter - Betty Carter
791 One For All - Brand Nubian
792 Mr. Mention - Buju Banton
793 One Dozen Berrys - Chuck Berry
794 Green River - Creedence Clearwater Revival
795 David Ackles - David Ackles
796 Let's Dance - David Bowie
797 Music for The Masses - Depeche Mode
798 Our Man In Paris - Dexter Gordon
799 Captain Fantastic And The Brown Dirt Cowboy - Elton John
800 Elvis - Elvis Presley
801 Pieces Of The Sky - Emmylou Harris
802 Out To Lunch! - Eric Dolphy
803 Concert By The Sea - Erroll Garner
804 Dragnet - The Fall
805 This Is Fats Domino - Fats Domino
806 Weasels Ripped My Flesh - Frank Zappa/ Mothers Of Invention
807 Gene Clark With The Gosdin Brothers - Gene Clark
808 Split - The Groundhogs
809 Hot Buttered Soul - Isaac Hayes
810 You Got My Mind Messed Up - James Carr
811 Blows Against The Empire - Jefferson Starship
812 Organ Grinder Swing - Jimmy Smith
813 For The Roses - Joni Mitchell
814 Cookin' - Miles Davis
815 The Marble Index - Nico
816 Life After Death - The Notorious B.I.G.
817 The Sound Of Music - Original Broadway Cast
818 The Soul Album - Otis Redding
819 Queen 2 - Queen
820 Buena Vista Social Club - Ry Cooder & The Buena Vista Social Club
821 Pocket Full Of Kryptonite - Spin Doctors
822 It's My Life - Talk Talk
823 Stop Making Sense - Talking Heads
824 Tim Hardin 1 - Tim Hardin
825 Into The Great Wide Open - Tom Petty And The Heartbreakers
826 Labour Of Love - UB40
828 Aretha Now - Aretha Franklin
829 Jack Orion - Bert Jansch
830 Cheap Thrills - Big Brother And The Holding Company
831 Don't Try This At Home - Billy Bragg
832 The Serpent's Egg - Dead Can Dance
833 From Elvis In Memphis - Elvis Presley
834 Unplugged - Eric Clapton
835 Baduizm - Erykah Badu
836 The Wonderful And Frightening World Of - The Fall
837 Foo Fighters - Foo Fighters

838 Uncle Meat - Frank Zappa/ Mothers Of Invention

839 City To City - Gerry Rafferty

840 In The Dark - Grateful Dead

841 My Favorite Things - John Coltrane

842 Shadows And Light - Joni Mitchell

843 Big Science - Laurie Anderson

844 Dixie Chicken - Little Feat

845 Miss America - Mary Margaret O'Hara

846 Round About Midnight - Miles Davis

847 Oliver! - Original London Cast

848 Travels - Pat Metheny

849 The Final Cut - Pink Floyd

850 Hokey Pokey - Richard and Linda Thompson

851 Steel Wheels - Rolling Stones

852 Born Under A Bad Sign - Albert King

853 A Dub Experience Reggae Greats - Sly & Robbie

854 Sonny Rollins Vol. 2 - Sonny Rollins

855 East Side Story - Squeeze

856 The Slider - T.Rex

857 More Songs About Buildings And Food - Talking Heads

858 Full Moon Fever - Tom Petty

859 Reggae Greats - Toots And The Maytals

860 Mr Fantasy - Trafffic

861 Van Halen II - Van Halen

862 Grease - Various

863 Whitney Houston - Whitney Houston

864 Germfree Adolescents - X Ray Spex

865 Eliminator - Z.Z. Top

866 The Original American Decca Recordings - Count Basie

867 One Of These Nights - The Eagles

868 Savage - Eurythmics

869 Great Balls Of Fire! - Jerry Lee Lewis

870 Duke - Genesis

871 Madonna - Madonna

872 Gris Gris - Dr. John

873 Johnny Cash At San Quentin - Johnny Cash

874 One Step Beyond - Madness

875 Burn - Deep Purple

876 Mystery Girl - Roy Orbison

877 Bless The Weather - John Martyn

878 This Was - Jethro Tull

879 Out Of The Cool - Gil Evans

880 Fearless - Family

881 Sinatra And Swingin' Brass - Frank Sinatra

882 Fire And Water - Free

883 The Wild, The Innocent & The E Street Shuffle - Bruce Springsteen

884 Agents Of Fortune - Blue Oyster Cult

885 Blind Faith - Blind Faith

886 Nashville Skyline - Bob Dylan

887 Saucerful Of Secrets - Pink Floyd

888 Free Peace Sweet - Dodgy

889 Eagles - The Eagles

890 Hex Enduction Hour - The Fall

891 Pieces Of You - Jewel

892 Coltrane Jazz - John Coltrane

893 Here We Go Again! - The Kingston Trio

894 Bedtime Stories - Madonna

895 No Sleep 'Til Hammersmith - Motörhead

896 The Shape Of Jazz To Come - Ornette Coleman

897 Slanted And Enchanted - Pavement

898 Into The Purple Valley - Ry Cooder

899 Scott 2 - Scott Walker

900 Chairs Missing - Wire

901 Blues Brothers - Various

902 Shazam - The Move

903 California Bloodlines - John Stewart

904 Janet Jackson's Rhythm Nation 1814 - Janet Jackson

905 Night Owl - Gerry Rafferty

906 The Beast Inside - Inspiral Carpets

907 Handful Of Earth - Dick Gaughan

908 Violator - Depeche Mode

909 Made In Japan - Deep Purple

910 Time Out - Dave Brubeck

911 Talking With The Taxman About Poetry - Billy Bragg

912 The Low-End Theory - A Tribe Called Quest

913 Jailbreak - Thin Lizzy

914 The Raven - Stranglers

915 E.1999 Eternal - Bone Thugs-N-Harmony

916 Sail Away - Randy Newman

917 End Of The Century - Ramones

918 Monster - R.E.M.

919 Gold Against The Soul - Manic Street Preachers

920 The Scream - Siouxsie And The Banshees

921 Boys For Pele - Tori Amos

922 Your Arsenal - Morrissey

923 On The Threshold Of A Dream - Moody Blues

924 Impressions - John Coltrane

925 Monterey International Pop Festival - Jimi Hendrix/ Otis Redding

926 Magical Mystery Tour - The Beatles

927 Back From Rio - Roger McGuinn

928 Blue - LeAnn Rimes

929 Its A Shame About Ray - Lemonheads

930 The Blues Of Lightnin' Hopkins - Lightnin' Hopkins

931 The Louis Armstrong Story 1-7 - Louis Armstrong

932 Diesel And Dust - Midnight Oil

933 The Monkees - The Monkees

934 Brewing Up With - Billy Bragg

935 The Southern Harmony And Musical Companion - The Black Crowes

936 Piano Man - Billy Joel

937 Brave New World - The Steve Miller Band

938 Ring A Ding Ding! - Frank Sinatra

939 Promenade - The Divine Comedy

940 The B-52's - The B-52's

941 Akoustic Band - Chick Corea

942 Love Chronicles - Al Stewart

943 Songs From The Wood - Jethro Tull

944 The Papas And The Mamas - Mamas And Papas

945 Smash - Offspring

946 Moanin' The Blues - Hank Williams

947 Can I Have My Money Back - Gerry Rafferty

948 Licensed To III - The Beastie Boys

949 Sinatra Swings - Frank Sinatra

950 More Of The Monkees - The Monkees

951 The Family That Plays Together - Spirit

952 Couldn't Stand The Weather - Stevie Ray Vaughan And Double Trouble

953 How Will The Wolf Survive - Los Lobos

954 No Jacket Required - Phil Collins

955 Modern Sounds In Country And Western Music - Ray Charles

956 Bert Jansch - Bert Jansch

957 Bedsitter Images - Al Stewart

958 Muddy Waters At Newport - Muddy Waters

959 Bellybutton - Jellyfish

960 Belonging - Keith Jarrett

961 Reggae Greats - Black Uhuru

962 The King And I - Various

963 Jazz Samba - Stan Getz

964 Rid Of Me - PJ Harvey

965 Stop The World I Want To Get Off - Original London Cast

966 Someday My Prince Will Come - Miles Davis

967 Kill 'Em All - Metallica

968 ESP - Miles Davis

969 Standards Vol 1 - Keith Jarrett

970 Hair - Original Broadway Cast

971 Ella And Louis - Ella Fitzgerald & Louis Armstrong

972 Bare Wires - John Mayall

973 Through The Past, Darkly - The Rolling Stones

974 Hello, Dolly! - Original Broadway Cast

975 Midnight Blue - Kenny Burrell

976 Burgers - Hot Tuna

977 Ella Fitzgerald Sings The Rodgers And Hart Songbook - Ella Fitzgerald

978 Sings Soul Ballads - Otis Redding

979 Kimono My House - Sparks

980 Head Hunters - Herbie Hancock

981 Wish - The Cure

982 Joseph And The Amazing Technicolor Dreamcoat - 1991 London Cast

983 Show Boat - Broadway Cast

984 Rage Against The Machine - Rage Against The Machine

985 Spirit - Spirit

986 I Still Believe In You - Vince Gill

987 Friends - The Beach Boys

988 The Pajama Game - Original Broadway Cast

989 Madness - Madness

990 The Complete Live At The Plugged Nickel 1965 - Miles Davis

991 Thick As A Brick - Jethro Tull

992 Rumor And Sigh - Richard Thompson

993 Offramp - Pat Metheny Group

994 Aoxomoxoa - The Grateful Dead

995 Billies's Blues - Billie Holiday

996 In-A-Gadda-Da-Vida - Iron Butterfly

997 Like Someone In Love - Ella Fitzgerald

998 Bat Out Of Hell II - Meat Loaf

999 Bug - Dinosaur Jr

1000 Got My Mojo Workin' - Jimmy Smith

INDEX